Handbook of Violence F

The *Handbook of Violence Risk Assessment, Second Edition,* builds on the first edition's comprehensive discussion of violence risk assessment instruments with an update of research on established tools and the addition of new chapters devoted to recently developed risk assessment tools.

Featuring chapters written by the instrument developers themselves, this handbook reviews the most frequently used violence risk assessment instruments—both actuarial and structured professional judgment—that professionals use to inform and structure their judgments about violence risk. Also included are broader chapters that address matters such as the consideration of psychopathy and how the law shapes violence risk assessment.

Already the primary reference for practitioners, researchers, and legal professionals in this area, this second edition's easy-to-access, comprehensive, and current information will make it an indispensable reference for those in the field.

Kevin S. Douglas, LLB, PhD, is Professor of Clinical-Forensic Psychology at Simon Fraser University; Researcher at Helse Bergen HF Competence Centre in Forensic Psychiatry; and Senior Research Advisor at the Oslo University Hospital Competence Centre in Forensic Psychiatry.

Randy K. Otto, PhD, ABPP, has been a faculty member at the University of South Florida since 1989. His primary appointment is in the Department of Mental Health Law and Policy, and he has adjunct appointments in the Departments of Psychology and Criminology.

International Perspectives on Forensic Mental Health

A Routledge Book Series

Edited by Patricia Zapf
Palo Alto University

The goal of this series is to improve the quality of health care services in forensic and correctional settings by providing a forum for discussing issues and disseminating resources related to policy, administration, clinical practice, and research. The series addresses topics such as mental health law; the organization and administration of forensic and/or correctional services for persons with mental disorders; the development, implementation and evaluation of treatment programs and interventions for individuals in civil and criminal justice settings; the assessment and management of violence risk, including risk for sexual violence and family violence; and staff selection, training, and development in forensic and/or correctional systems. The book series will consider proposals for both monographs and edited works on these and related topics, with special consideration given to proposals that promote evidence-based best practices and that are relevant to international audiences. Workbooks and manuals targeted toward practitioners and reflecting evidence-based practice and intervention will also be considered.

Published Titles:

Handbook of Violence Risk Assessment, Second Edition
Edited by Kevin S. Douglas and Randy K. Otto

Sexual Predators: Society, Risk and the Law
Robert A. Prentky, Howard E. Barbaree & Eric S. Janus

Learning Forensic Assessment, Second Edition
Edited by Rebecca Jackson and Ronald Roesch

Evaluating Juvenile Transfer and Disposition Law, Science, and Practice
Kirk Heilbrun, David DeMatteo, Christopher King, Sarah Filone

Handbook of Forensic Mental Health Services
Ronald Roesch, Alana N. Cook

A Treatment Manual for Justice Involved Persons with Mental Illness Changing Lives and Changing Outcomes
Robert D. Morgan, Daryl Kroner, Jeremy F. Mills

Forthcoming Titles:

Safeguarding Forensic Violence Risk Assessment A Review Across Western Nations
Michiel van der Wolf

Handbook of Violence
Risk Assessment

Second Edition

Edited by Kevin S. Douglas
and Randy K. Otto

Routledge
Taylor & Francis Group

NEW YORK AND LONDON

Second edition published 2021
by Routledge
52 Vanderbilt Avenue, New York, NY 10017

and by Routledge
2 Park Square, Milton Park, Abingdon, Oxon, OX14 4RN

Routledge is an imprint of the Taylor & Francis Group, an informa business

© 2021 Taylor & Francis

First edition published by Routledge 2015

Library of Congress Cataloging-in-Publication Data
Names: Douglas, Kevin S., editor. | Otto, Randy K., editor.
Title: Handbook of violence risk assessment / edited by Kevin S. Douglas and Randy K. Otto.
Description: Second edition. | New York, NY : Routledge, 2021. | Series: International perspectives on forensic mental health | Includes bibliographical references and index.
Identifiers: LCCN 2020035958 (print) | LCCN 2020035959 (ebook) | ISBN 9781138698703 (hbk) | ISBN 9781138698697 (pbk) | ISBN 9781315518374 (ebk)
Subjects: LCSH: Violence. | Violence—Forecasting. | Risk assessment. | Forensic psychiatry.
Classification: LCC HM1116 .H363 2021 (print) | LCC HM1116 (ebook) | DDC 303.6—dc23
LC record available at https://lccn.loc.gov/2020035958
LC ebook record available at https://lccn.loc.gov/2020035959

ISBN: 978-1-138-69870-3 (hbk)
ISBN: 978-1-138-69869-7 (pbk)
ISBN: 978-1-315-51837-4 (ebk)

Typeset in Baskerville
by Apex CoVantage, LLC

Contents

Contributors

Madison Almond, BA (Hons)
Department of Psychology
Simon Fraser University
Burnaby, BC, Canada

Dana Anderson, PhD
Simcoe Psychology
Barrie, Ontario, Canada

Leena K. Augimeri, PhD
SNAP International Headquarters
Child Development Institute
Toronto, Canada

Patrick A. Bartel, PhD
Youth Forensic Psychiatric Services
Vancouver, British Columbia, Canada

Andrea Blackman, BA
SNAP International Headquarters
Child Development Institute
Toronto, Ontario, Canada

Douglas P. Boer, PhD
Centre for Applied Psychology
University of Canberra
Canberra, Australia

James Bonta, PhD
Consultant, Corrections and Criminal Behaviour
Ottawa, Ontario, Canada

Randy Borum, PsyD
School of Information
University of South Florida
Tampa, Florida, USA

David DeMatteo, JD, PhD
Department of Psychology & Thomas R. Kline School of Law
Drexel University
Philadelphia, Pennsylvania, USA

Kevin S. Douglas, LLB, PhD
Department of Psychology
Simon Fraser University
Burnaby, British Columbia, Canada
&
Competence Centre in Forensic Psychiatry
Helse Bergen HF
Bergen, Norway
&
Competence Centre in Forensic Psychiatry
Oslo University Hospital
University of Oslo
Oslo, Norway

John F. Edens, PhD
Department of Psychological & Brain Sciences
Texas A&M University
College Station, Texas, USA

Pia Enebrink, PhD
Department of Clinical Neuroscience
Karolinska Institute
Stockholm, Sweden

Adelle E. Forth, PhD
Department of Psychology
Carleton University
Ottawa, Ontario, Canada

Erin K. Fuller, MA
Department of Psychology
Simon Fraser University
Burnaby, British Columbia, Canada

Cameron Geddes, BSc
Psychiatry, University of British Columbia
BC Mental Health & Substance Use Services
Vancouver, British Columbia, Canada

Andrea Gibas, PhD
Ontario Shores Centre for Mental Health Sciences
Whitby, Ontario, Canada

Laura S. Guy, PhD
Department of Psychology
Simon Fraser University
Burnaby, British Columbia, Canada

Emily Haney-Caron, JD, PhD
John Jay College of Criminal Justice and the Graduate Center
City University of New York
New York, New York, USA

R. Karl Hanson, PhD
Carleton University
Ottawa, Ontario, Canada

Grant T. Harris, PhD
Department of Psychology
Queen's University
Kingston, Ontario, Canada
&
Department of Psychiatry
University of Toronto
Toronto, Ontario, Canada

Stephen D. Hart, PhD
Department of Psychology
Simon Fraser University
Burnaby, British Columbia, Canada
&
Faculty of Psychology
University of Bergen
Bergen, Norway

Kirk Heilbrun, PhD
Department of Psychology
Drexel University
Philadelphia, Pennsylvania, USA

N. Zoe Hilton, PhD
Department of Psychiatry,
University of Toronto
Toronto, Ontario, Canada
&
Waypoint Research Institute
Penetanguishene, Ontario, Canada

Robert D. Hoge, PhD, C.Psych
Department of Psychology
Carleton University
Ottawa, Ontario, Canada

Depeng Jiang, PhD
Department of Community Health Sciences
University of Manitoba
Winnipeg, Manitoba, Canada

Brian Judd, PhD
Private Practice
Olympia, Washington, USA

P. Randall Kropp, PhD
British Columbia Forensic Psychiatric Services Commission
Vancouver, British Columbia, Canada
&

Department of Psychology
Simon Fraser University
Burnaby, British Columbia, Canada

Benjamin Locklair, JD, PhD
Philadelphia Department of Behavioral Health and Intellectual disAbility Services
Philadelphia, Pennsylvania, USA

Henny P. B. Lodewijks, PhD
Lodewijks Advies
Zutphen, The Netherlands

John Monahan, PhD
School of Law
University of Virginia
Charlottesville, Virginia, USA

Elyse Mowle, PhD
ICF, Inc.
Washington, District of Columbia, USA
&
Department of Psychological & Brain Sciences
Texas A&M University
College Station, Texas, USA

Tonia L. Nicholls, PhD
Psychiatry, University of British Columbia
BC Mental Health & Substance Use Services
Vancouver, British Columbia, Canada

Mark E. Olver, PhD
Department of Psychology
University of Saskatchewan
Saskatoon, Saskatchewan, Canada

Randy K. Otto, PhD
Department of Mental Health Law & Policy
University of South Florida
Tampa, Florida, USA

Karen Petersen, PhD
Psychiatry, University of British Columbia
Vancouver, British Columbia, Canada

Robert A. Prentky, PhD
Department of Psychology
Farleigh Dickinson University
Teaneck, New Jersey, USA

Vernon L. Quinsey, PhD
Departments of Psychology, Biology, and Psychiatry,
Queen's University
Kingston, Ontario, Canada

Marnie E. Rice, Ph.D.
Department of Psychiatry and Behavioural Neurosciences
McMaster University
Hamilton, Ontario, Canada
&
Department of Psychology
Queen's University
Kingston, Ontario, Canada
&
Department of Psychiatry
University of Toronto
Toronto, Ontario, Canada

Sue Righthand, PhD
Department of Psychology
University of Maine
Orono, Maine, USA

Catherine S. Shaffer, PhD
Department of Psychology
Simon Fraser University
Burnaby, British Columbia, Canada

Sanjay Shah, JD, PhD
Atlas Psychological Services
Atlanta, Georgia, USA

Christopher Slobogin, JD, LLM
College of Law
Vanderbilt University
Nashville, Tennessee, USA

Areti Smaragdi, PhD
SNAP International Headquarters
Child Development Institute
Toronto, Ontario, Canada

Agnes Veldhuizen, MSc
Center for Forensic Outpatient Treatment
The Forensic Care Specialists
Utrecht, The Netherlands

Vivienne de Vogel, PhD
Center for Social Innovation
HU University of Applied Sciences
Utrecht, The Netherlands
&
Department of Research
The Forensic Care Specialists
Utrecht, The Netherlands

Michiel de Vries Robbé, PhD
Department of Child and Adolescent Psychiatry

Amsterdam UMC, VU University Medical Center
Amsterdam, The Netherlands
&
Department of Psychiatry and Behavioural Neurosciences
McMaster University
Hamilton, Ontario, Canada

Margaret Walsh, BA
SNAP International Headquarters
Child Development Institute
Toronto, Ontario, Canada

Christopher D. Webster, PhD
Department of Psychiatry
University of Toronto
Toronto, Ontario, Canada
&
Department of Psychology
Simon Fraser University
Burnaby, British Columbia, Canada
&
Department of Child and Youth Care
University of Victoria
Victoria, British Columbia, Canada
&
Child Development Institute
Toronto, Ontario, Canada

Stephen C. P. Wong, PhD
Department of Psychology
University of Saskatchewan
Saskatoon, Saskatchewan, Canada
&
Centre for Forensic Behavioural Science
Swinburne University of Technology
Melbourne, Australia

J. Stephen Wormith, PhD
Department of Psychology
University of Saskatchewan
Saskatoon, Saskatchewan, Canada

Kento Yasuhara, PhD
Psychology Department
University of New Haven
New Haven, CT, USA

Foreword

Christopher D. Webster

As a member of the Ontario Review Board and the British Columbia Review Board, I read, each year, dozens of formal reports from mental health professionals in the various disciplines. Insofar as it is the Boards which make the actual decisions as to whether to detain, to release into the community under conditions, or to grant absolute discharge, we, as members, are heavily reliant on the risk assessments provided by our colleagues on the other side of the table. Oftentimes, these reports are first rate and we do not have to torture the clinicians too greatly during questioning. At other times the reports are sub-standard by any reasonable criterion. Even if the clinicians claim to have followed some recognized and published scheme, it seems as if they are not using the scheme to full advantage. For sure, too, at times, we are left wondering if the framework adopted is even the right one (e.g., an HCR-20 V3 [see Chapter 12] might have been used in the assessment of a 19-year-old when a START:AV [see Chapter 15] would have been more fitting and appropriate; a VRAG-R [see Chapter 7] score is used as the sole basis to underpin a recommendation on behalf of an Indigenous person). As well, while sitting on a Board—one held at a well-resourced hospital or community service—it is impossible not to wonder why no attempts have been made to find out if the various assessment schemes are "working" in the particular context. It sometimes seems as though these devices are "plucked off the shelf" and that users are content to assume the guides in question have been validated elsewhere. There can be an absence of realization that follow-along studies are required to find out how these devices are performing in the specific circumstances in which they are being employed. This is in spite of the fact that our colleagues in the Netherlands have long demonstrated the value of attaching, whenever possible, a researcher to each clinical team (de Vogel, van den Broek, & de Vries Robbé, 2014; de Vries Robbé, personal communication, August 3, 2020).

Our colleagues on the "front lines" deserve sympathy. Caseloads tend to be high. Beds are filled as soon as they are vacated. Every day our colleagues are hounded for reports by Courts and Boards. As well, patients have to be interviewed and treated. Yet in all of this, risk assessment and risk management stand out as key issues. It is not a matter of "packing in" the requisite information during a residency or internship in the vain expectation that this pool of knowledge will last for a career. This is very much an evolving field. We have learned a great deal over the course of the 43 years I have been involved. At that early time we had, aside from the work of Häfner and Böker (1973, 1982) in Germany, not much beyond the inspired findings of "Operation Baxstrom" (Steadman & Halfon, 1971; Steadman & Keveles, 1972). This "opportunistic" study taught us that as clinicians we are apt to over-predict violence on a statistical basis. We also had at that time little besides the thoughtful commentaries from the front lines by Saleem Shah (1975) and Peter Scott (1977). Then we got the 1981 book by John Monahan. This was an organizational masterpiece; he told us, in effect, that we needed to "smarten up" in terms of defining prediction and outcome measures. So there were two main emerging threads in the late 1970s/early 1980s—Clinical and Organizational. The third thread—devices—began to evolve in the late 1980s/early 1990s. Since then we have seen remarkable developments in the third aspect—actuarial/statistical and Structured Professional Judgment schemes—which is, of course, the focus of this book.

In this way we have a three-component model: (1) a large array of assessment schemes which have been subject to varying degrees of scientific test; (2) a pool of internationally connected clinicians, many of whom are highly able educators; and (3) organizational support—specialized journals, commendable publishers, worldwide distributors, professional organizations, and even, thanks to the late Dr. Derek Eaves, the International Association of Forensic Mental Health Services. This third arm is key. When we started out with the HCR-20 V1 in 1995 (Webster, Eaves, Douglas, & Wintrup, 1995), we had no way to get it into the hands of would-be users. All we had was a part-time student in a basement room struggling to keep up with inquiries and orders. It took time to set up a distribution service and to arrange for the delivery of educational events.

The area of risk evaluation is in constant flux. How could it be otherwise? It is not as if these days we are assessing on the basis of the kinds of crimes most commonly carried out in 1975. We'd not even heard of the sorts of offences now committed via the internet. Drug abuse back then was not as prevalent as it is today. Diagnostic frameworks have been amended. As well, new realizations arise about how particular sub-populations have been discriminated against. Women are more apt than before to express dissatisfactions concerning their roles and opportunities in Western society. Attitudes toward law enforcement shift. One senior colleague remarked to me that any risk evaluation scheme that has been in existence and unmodified for more than ten years or so needs to be approached with suspicion.

Our editors have served, and will continue to serve, in all three aspects of the "triad." This book, like its forerunner, fits into the organizational/administrative/policy slot. Bearing in mind the rate at which papers and even books on risk assessment and management appear, it is *essential* there be periodic *consolidations*. Busy administrators/policy wonks, clinicians, and researchers need to be able to reach for a single source, one which integrates information and points, as does Professor Heilbrun (see Chapter 1), to where we should now be headed. The field needs a text of this style every decade. Just as a submarine needs to surface periodically, so, too, does our field need to come up for air and a good look around.

By this stage I hope readers are clear that in referring to the "triad" I'm not harking back to fire-setting, cruelty to animals, and bed-wetting (cf. the still much-cited Hellman & Blackman, 1966). Recently I saw the movie *Ford versus Ferrari*. The movie, starring Matt Damon, centers on the idea that to win the Le Mans, three things are needed: (1) the right car loaded with the latest engineering advances (cf., the properly chosen assessment device or devices); (2) a driver who not only knows how to turn the wheel and apply the brakes, but who comprehends the internal workings, capabilities, and limits of the machine (cf., a clinician or team of professionals possessing much-needed acumen); and (3) an organization to back the enterprise (i.e., to finance it, to get the research done, to arrange publicity, and so on). Our area is no different. No matter how "wonderful" the scheme might be, it is of little use if clinicians do not take the trouble to learn how to "drive" it as the originators intended. As well, to prove itself, the car and driver must be subject to the actualities of the "race" (i.e., submit themselves to the rigors of trials as set by journal editors, audiences at scientific and professional meetings, etc.).

Let me end with a couple of comments on the structure of the book. I counted the number of contributors to the various chapters. I discovered I know approximately half of them. What encourages me is that I don't know the other half. That's good. It means we have plenty of upcoming researchers, clinicians, and policy-inclined folks entering the fray. My second comment is based on my "research." As noted previously, Douglas/Otto books are needed every ten years or so. On a whim, I took the first three chapters to pop up on my screen. I then counted all references cited as being published in 2010 or earlier and all those published in 2011 or later. The scores were 52/52, 83/40, and 18/16 (i.e., 153/108). To me, this is evidence that the contributors did what the editors asked them to do: namely, bring the book up to date. It also helps reinforce my point that this field is continually "on the march."

I wish the editors, the contributors, and the publisher all due success for the new edition. It is not a book that needs to be shelved; it needs to be read. My hope, too, is that that some evaluees, and perhaps their counsel, will benefit from gaining a close understanding of how the many formats are designed to work and how the ensuing results should be interpreted. The work we do has far-reaching implications for making decisions on behalf of civilly detained patients, forensic psychiatric patients, and persons held in prisons while suffering from mental and personality disorders. The book is a "call to arms."

References

de Vogel, V., van den Broek, E., & de Vries Robbé, M. (2014). The use of the HCR-20V3 in Dutch forensic psychiatric practice. *International Journal of Forensic Mental Health, 13*, 109–121.

Häfner, H., & Böker, W. (1973). Mentally disordered violent offenders. *Social Psychiatry, 8*, 220–229.

Häfner, H., & Böker, W. (1982). *Crimes of violence by mentally disordered offenders* (H. Marshall, trans.). Cambridge: Cambridge University Press (Original work published 1973).

Hellman, D. S., & Blackman, N. (1966). Enuresis, firesetting, and cruelty to animals: A triad predictive of adult crime. *American Journal of Psychiatry, 122*, 1431–1435.

Monahan, J. (1981). *Predicting violent behavior: An assessment of clinical techniques.* Beverly Hills, CA: Sage.

Scott, P. D. (1977). Assessing dangerousness in criminals. *British Journal of Psychiatry, 131*, 127–142.

Shah, S. A. (1975). Dangerousness and civil commitment of the mentally ill: Some public policy considerations. *American Journal of Psychiatry, 132*, 501–505.

Steadman, H. J., & Halfon, A. (1971). The Baxstrom patients: Backgrounds and outcomes. *Seminars in Psychiatry, 3*, 376–386.

Steadman, H. J., & Keveles, G. (1972). The community adjustment and criminal activity of the Baxstrom patients: 1966–1970. *American Journal of Psychiatry, 129*, 80–86.

Webster, C. D., Eaves, D., Douglas, K. S., & Wintrup, A. (1995). *The HCR-20 scheme: The assessment of dangerousness and risk.* Burnaby, BC: Mental Health, Law, and Policy Institute, and Forensic Psychiatric Services Commission of British Columbia.

Introduction and Overview

Kevin S. Douglas and Randy K. Otto

In the Introduction and Overview to the first edition of this book, we wrote that,

> [because risk] for violence directed towards others was relevant to a variety of legal (e.g., civil commitment, criminal sentencing, parole decisions, disposition in delinquency proceedings) and clinical matters (e.g., case management of and decision making regarding clients who pose a risk of harm to others), its accurate assessment is of concern to legal, correctional, and mental health professionals.

This remains true today.

In the 11 years since publication of the first edition of this book, how has the field changed? How has it remained the same? There have been important developments in the law that have shaped risk assessment (for instance, whether the entire risk assessment enterprise is fair to certain subgroups), and important conceptual developments in violence risk assessment (for instance, greater emphasis on risk formulation; scenario planning; integration with risk reduction, treatment, and management; and examinees' strengths and protective factors). New measures are available, as well. Other measures—long in use and well-established at the time of the 2010 edition—have either been revised substantially or have been subjected to much greater evaluation. Much more is known about the "actuarial versus structured professional judgment" (SPJ) debate, and on the performance and role of complementary instruments often used within violence risk assessment (for instance, measures of psychopathy).

Hence, a second edition of the *Handbook of Violence Risk Assessment* was warranted. As with the first edition, we sought—where possible—to have instrument authors describe their tools and the research examining their utility. Where this was not possible, we invited scholars who had a great deal of knowledge and experience using and evaluating the instruments to author these chapters. We have continued the focus on the most commonly used and researched violence risk assessment instruments.

The second edition does include some new additions. We expanded Part I with two new chapters, in addition to revisions of the original two chapters. As with the first edition, this second edition includes a critical overview of key themes, findings, and developments in the risk assessment field, including an evaluation of the empirical support for both actuarial and SPJ measures (Heilbrun, Yasuhara, Shah, & Locklair). It also contains a chapter on the appropriate use, and limitations, of measures of psychopathy within risk assessment (DeMatteo, Haney-Caron, Mowle, & Edens).

As previously mentioned, there are two new chapters in Part I—one of these reviews what we have called "brief and emerging measures" (Shaffer, Fuller, & Guy). This chapter includes a review of ten measures that are either intended as screening or triaging devices, with some empirical evaluation, or more comprehensive measures that, while showing promise, do not yet have substantial empirical evaluation. The second addition, authored by Christopher Slobogin, addresses key legal issues and developments with respect to violence risk assessment.

As with the first edition, the remainder of the second edition focuses on risk assessment instruments. As we did in the first edition, we asked authors to follow a template: (a) an overview of the instrument(s); (b) a description of instrument development, and populations with which it can be used; (c) a discussion of the research regarding its reliability and validity; (d) a review of limitations and future directions; and (e) a case example that provides guidance to instrument users around issues of report-writing and risk communication.

The careful reader will realize that we changed the organizational structure for the second edition. Rather than grouping instruments according to the population with which they are used, we organized them based on the approach they employ. We grouped instruments according to whether they are actuarial or SPJ in nature, and further divided actuarial instruments into whether they used "empirical" item selection (that is, derived from one or more specific samples), or "rational" item selection (that is, derived from a broad canvassing of the empirical and professional literatures). Because all SPJ instruments use rational item selection, no such distinction was necessary. Instruments are otherwise presented in alphabetical order.

Part II, Empirical-Actuarial Measures, includes the following instruments: Classification of Violence Risk (COVR; Monahan); the Static-99 Revised and related measures such as the STABLE-2007 (Hanson & Anderson); and the Violence Risk Appraisal Guide (VRAG) and related instruments (its revision, the VRAG-Revised; the Sex Offender Risk Appraisal Guide, or SORAG; the Ontario Domestic Assault Risk Assessment, or ODARA; and the Domestic Violence Risk Appraisal Guide, or DVRAG), by Hilton, Rice, Harris, Judd, and Quinsey.

Part III, Rational-Actuarial Measures, includes the following instruments: the Level of Service (LS) instruments for adults (Wormith & Bonta) and youth (Hoge; the Youth Level of Service/Case Management Inventory, or YLS/CMI); and the Violence Risk Scale, or VRS, and its Sex Offender Version, VRS-SO (Olver & Wong).

In Part IV, the following SPJ instruments are reviewed: the Early Assessment Risk List measures, for Boys (EARL-20B) or Girls (EARL-21G), by Augimeri, Walsh, Enebrink, Jiang, Blackman, and Smaragdi; the Historical-Clinical-Risk Management-20 Version 3, with brief review of its predecessor, Version 2 (Douglas & Shaffer); the Juvenile Sex Offender Assessment Protocol-II, or J-SOAP-II (Prentky & Righthand);[1] the Sexual Violence Risk-20 (SVR-20) Versions 1 and 2 and Risk for Sexual Violence Protocol (RSVP), by Hart and Boer; the Short-Term Assessment of Risk and Treatability, or START (Nicholls, Petersen, Almond, & Geddes); the Spousal Assault Risk Assessment Guide, or SARA (Versions 1–3), by Kropp & Gibas; the Structured Assessment of Protective Factors, or SAPROF, and its derivatives (de Vries Robbé, de Vogel, & Veldhuizen); and the Structured Assessment of Violence Risk in Youth, or SAVRY (Borum, Lodewijks, Bartel, & Forth).

As such, 14 chapters focus on a single instrument or group of related instruments. Together, more than 25 instruments are covered in these chapters. Adding the chapter on measures of psychopathy and the chapter on brief and emerging measures, over 35 of the most commonly used and researched instruments for violence risk assessment are described and reviewed in this second edition.

Authors were free to represent their opinions on the appropriate uses and the degree of validation of their measures. Of course, as readers may surmise, some authors likely disagree with others on the relative support for the various measures. We invite readers to read the chapters critically and, with guidance from the chapter authored by Heilbrun and his colleagues, which considers the degree of support for various approaches to risk assessment, decide for themselves.

We are very grateful for the time, effort, and expertise put into all of the chapters by their respective authors and hope that our readers will be similarly appreciative.

Note

1. The Juvenile Sex Offender Assessment Protocol-II, or J-SOAP-II, is best described as neither actuarial nor SPJ, because it does not offer estimates about risk, either categorically or numerically. It does quantify the proportion of total possible risk factors present on its various scales, which is intended to guide treatment efforts, and ultimately inform a clinician's assessment of risk. In principle, methods could be developed to use this instrument in either an actuarial or SPJ format, but that would be inconsistent with its developers' intentions. We have categorized this instrument, for purposes of organization, along with the SPJ instruments.

Part I

Core Themes and Critical Analysis of the Field

Chapter 1

Approaches to Violence Risk Assessment
Overview, Critical Analysis, and Future Directions

Kirk Heilbrun, Kento Yasuhara, Sanjay Shah, and Benjamin Locklair

The problems presented by violence in contemporary society have been an important consideration for many decades. As the law has turned to the behavioral and medical sciences to improve the prospects for accurately appraising and managing the risk of violent behavior, the past thirty years have witnessed the development and validation of specialized tools for the prediction and management of certain kinds of serious violence and criminal offending. The second edition of this book offers a description of some of these tools, developed for specific purposes in legal contexts, and the relevant research associated with them.

Risk Assessment Considerations

This chapter provides a context in which the specific tools described in subsequent chapters can be considered. There are six important considerations applicable to risk assessment tools that will be addressed in the first section: context, purpose, population, parameters, approach, and applicability. Subsequent sections of the chapter focus on approaches to risk assessment, the major features of each approach, the strengths and weaknesses of each approach, and their respective states of validation. The present chapter does not provide an in-depth review of the validation data relevant to specific tools. That is addressed in the subsequent chapters describing the various risk assessment tools.

Context

The first consideration in conducting a violence risk assessment involves the broad context in which this appraisal is being conducted. Such context influences the nature of the decision to be made, who is responsible for this decision, and the consequences that can result from differing appraisals. There are four important (and different) contexts in which a risk assessment is likely to be conducted: legal, clinical, school/workplace, and threats to protectees. *Legal contexts* are those in which a legal (or quasi-legal) decision-maker must render a decision in the course of litigation or administrative tribunal. Such contexts may be in the domain of criminal or civil proceedings (see, e.g., Melton et al., 2018). Decisions in this context may involve initial civil commitment or criminal sentencing, release from incarceration or secure hospitalization, or steps that may be associated with a planned release (such as community notification or post-sentence civil commitment for sexual offenders).

Clinical contexts involve circumstances under which interventions are delivered to reduce the risk of violence or offending in the broader context of a treatment relationship. This context is sufficiently broad to include interventions in secure settings (e.g., jails, prisons, forensic hospitals) as well as those delivered using some leverage (e.g., to individuals on parole, probation, diversion from prosecution, or juvenile home-based placement) and others using no leverage at all (e.g., mental health treatment delivered on a voluntary basis to individuals in the community, in jurisdictions in which there is a settled *Tarasoff*-type obligation to warn or protect).

School/workplace contexts encompass threats of harm to others that are typically not yet a part of formal legal proceedings, in which both the seriousness of the threat and the nature of the indicated risk-reduction strategies are important parts of the overall appraisal. Assessment in these settings is typically conducted in response to the concerns raised by the actions of specific individuals such as students or employees, rather than in a broader process involving all individuals in the setting.

Finally, *threats to protectees* also involve the dual issues of threat seriousness and risk management. However, they differ because they are directed toward specific individuals (those under the protection of the Secret Service or federal marshals, for example), or the kind of broader targets involved in domestic or international terrorism. Included as well in this category are threats involving potential harm to a domestic partner, where there is typically a specified victim and the initial appraisal is made by police who are called to the scene.

Most of the chapters in this book are devoted to different specialized risk assessment tools that are almost entirely applicable in legal contexts. Accordingly, that will also be the focus of discussion in this chapter. It should be noted that a number of specialized measures referenced in this chapter and described further in this book would be appropriate for use in *clinical* and *threats to protectees* contexts, as these have just been described.

Purpose

One of the important influences on contemporary conceptions of risk assessment is the Risk-Need-Responsivity (RNR) model described by Canadian researchers (see Chapter 8, this volume; Andrews, Bonta, & Hoge, 1990; Andrews, Bonta, & Wormith, 2006; Bonta & Andrews, 2017). This involves the appraisal of three related domains. *Risk* refers to the probability that the examinee will engage in a certain kind of behavior in the future, typically either violence/violent offending, or criminal offending of any kind, with higher-risk individuals receiving more intensive intervention and management services under the risk principle. This kind of risk classification has most frequently been measured by using static risk factors, which do not change through planned intervention, although some tools (e.g., the LS measures; see Andrews & Bonta, 2001; Andrews, Bonta, & Wormith, 2004; Chapters 8 and 9; and all structured professional judgment tools, for example, Douglas, Hart, Webster, & Belfrage, 2013; Kropp & Hart, 2015; see also Hart, Douglas, & Guy, 2017; Chapters 11-18 in this volume) use both static risk factors and risk-relevant needs. *Needs* are variables describing deficits which are related to the probability of such targeted outcomes; they are composed of dynamic risk factors (called *criminogenic* needs in the RNR model) or protective factors that have the potential to change through such planned intervention. Targeting interventions to address criminogenic needs is the goal described by the need principle. *Responsivity* refers to the extent to which an individual is likely to respond to intervention(s) enacted to reduce the probability of the targeted outcome behavior.

A comparable distinction involving risk assessment in legal contexts has been made between prediction and risk management (Heilbrun, 1997), in which it was observed that some legal decisions are best informed by a prediction of whether the individual will reoffend or otherwise behave violently. Perhaps the most frequent example of such a decision involves civil commitment, in which the legal decision-maker must decide whether the likelihood that the individual will harm others (or self) is sufficient to justify involuntary hospitalization. There is a limited risk management component to this decision, although future decisions regarding such individuals (such as release from hospitalization) must consider risk management to a much greater extent. If the risk is sufficiently high, the court will presumably grant the petition for civil commitment. If not, the petition is likely to be denied (or granted on grounds other than risk to harm others). But under neither circumstance would the court be particularly concerned with a specific approach to lowering the violence risk. In contrast to civil commitment, when the court *does* maintain jurisdiction over the individual following the decision—for example, when the defendant is diverted to mental health court or committed as Not Guilty by Reason of Insanity—then both level of risk and the nature of the risk-relevant needs can help inform the court's decision.[1]

Specialized risk assessment tools are designed to provide information that either is particular to the question of prediction or that addresses both risk and needs (with associated implications for intervention). This will be discussed in greater detail subsequently in this chapter. To our knowledge, there are no specialized tools that focus *only* on risk reduction (although a number of tools include risk reduction intervention-planning as a primary goal). However, there is a technique (anamnestic assessment) derived from applied behavior analysis that promotes the informed selection of risk-relevant needs based on the individual's history. Such an approach can also be used with risk-need tools, in a manner to be discussed later in this chapter.

Populations

One of the important considerations in risk assessment involves the population to which the individual being assessed actually belongs. There are important differences in base rates of violence, risk factors and protective factors,[2] and risk-relevant interventions for differing populations. In addition, specialized tools are typically derived and validated to apply to a single population (e.g., juvenile offenders) or related populations (adult offenders or insanity acquittees, sex offenders), but not across widely discrepant populations.

There are four considerations in delineating a population for risk assessment purposes. These are age, gender, behavioral health status, and location. *Age* typically refers to three distinct groups: preadolescent children, adolescents, and adults (and possibly older adults). *Gender* is important because a specialized tool may not be validated for females or may use different norms. The *behavioral health status* of a population refers to whether it is selected through assessment, intervention, or legal action as having a number of individuals with behavioral health problems. Since justice-involved and behavioral health are among the populations to which risk assessment is most often applied, it is particularly important to distinguish behavioral health populations without formal justice involvement at the relevant time (e.g., those who are civilly committed) from general offender populations in which behavioral health problems are not part of the selection criteria. This can become more complex when considering populations such as criminal defendants who have been adjudicated Not Guilty by Reason of Insanity which, by definition, include both behavioral health and offending among the selection criteria.

Finally, the variable of *location* refers to the setting from which the population is drawn. Offending populations can be drawn from the community (e.g., those on probation or parole) or from an institutional setting. School and work are examples of settings with populations that are typically not offenders. There can again be increased complexity when the risk appraisal involves assessment of individuals in one setting but considers their risk for violence or offending in another—such as when convicted persons or insanity acquittees are appraised for their risk of violence in the community following release from prison or the hospital, respectively. The consideration of these four variables—age, gender, behavioral health status, and setting—allows the identification of a population with sufficient specificity to determine whether a given risk assessment tool should be used. This choice is straightforward when the examinee is part of a specific population for which a particular tool was developed (e.g., use of a sexual violence risk tool with an individual convicted of a sex offense).

Parameters

The next important consideration in risk assessment involves what is being predicted, with what frequency of outcome, at what probability or category of risk, in what setting, over what period of time, and the nature of the risk factors and protective factors involved in the appraisal. It is important to specify, in the beginning, what outcome(s) are of concern. The broader the class of outcomes, the higher the base rate will be. The impact of base rates is discussed elsewhere in this chapter. It is also necessary to consider how this outcome will be measured. Both researchers and practitioners have employed approaches to appraising violent behavior or violent offending that include (1) self-report, (2) the report of collateral observers, and (3) official records (e.g., rearrest, rehospitalization). In the context of non-criminal community violence in the United States, the most sensitive of these measures is self-report, with collateral observation second and official records a distant third (Monahan et al., 2001; Steadman et al., 1998). But this may vary widely across jurisdictions, countries, and contexts, depending on whether the individual has a strong incentive to deny or minimize self-reported impairments or intentions, whether s/he is seen regularly by a collateral observer, and the extent to which official records are likely to reflect the occurrence of such behavior.

Next, we consider the specific parameters of the behavior itself. Are we targeting serious violence only, or is more minor aggression considered as well—or only a specific type of violence (e.g., sexual reoffending)? Are verbal threats included? What about behavior (such as arson) that may be directed at property but has the potential to harm other persons? This is a crucial question for researchers, but it is also important for practitioners to be as specific as possible. It is also important to indicate whether the appraisal would consider a single act of the behavior as a "yes," or whether the specified outcome encompasses possible multiple acts of the behavior (e.g., as part of stalking or child abuse). In addition, the appraisal must designate an outcome period of time. For some risk assessment, the relevant outcome period might be quite short—perhaps no longer than 24 to 48 hours, for instance, when an individual is being considered for involuntary hospitalization. Intermediate outcome periods often used in community and correctional outcome research in the last decade tend to range from 6 to 12 months. Much longer periods, up to 5 to 10 years, have been used in the development of some specialized tools and were more typical of violence research in the 1980s and 1990s. These research-employed outcome periods may be quite applicable to a given case in practice—or poorly applicable. This should be clarified whenever possible.

In both research and practice, location is a particularly important aspect of context in risk assessment. There is a substantial difference between the appraisal of violence risk in an institutional setting such as a juvenile placement, prison, or hospital versus risk in the community if and when the examinee is living in the community. The degree of structure associated with the former means greater monitoring by staff, clearer expectations and less tolerance for deviation from these expectations, lack of access to drugs and alcohol (presumably), and the provision in some instances of interventions to lower violence risk. There is also a much higher probability of detection and imposition of consequences in response to violent behavior that is displayed in institutional settings. In the community, in contrast, there is a wider range of circumstances encountered in daily living. An individual may be at work or in school, which itself may be the specific context in which violence risk is assessed. The individual may be living in a setting with others who may be targets for violence, particularly when domestic tensions are exacerbated by substance use and weapons are readily accessible. But location is a very important parameter in risk assessment; while it contributes to the situational influences on violent behavior, it has been investigated less extensively than have personal variables (Silver, 2001; Steadman, 1982). Fortunately, that is changing. Some investigators have pursued the measurement of situational influences on violence in hospitals (Ogloff & Dafferns, 2006; Welsh, Bader, & Evans, 2013) and prisons (Abbiati, Palix, Gasser, & Moulin, 2019; Cooke, Wozniak, & Johnstone, 2008) through the development and review of specialized tools that may prove useful when validated and may influence the development of comparable tools for measuring community violence risk.

The next parameter involves the manner in which risk level is to be communicated. As discussed in more detail later in this chapter, there are currently differences in the structure of specialized tools that center on whether a risk assessment should provide a quantitative estimate of the probability of violence, or a categorical appraisal that seeks to distinguish lower- from higher-risk individuals without using a specific number. However, it is fair to say that one of the shared purposes of contemporary risk assessment tools involves providing some appraisal of relative risk. By contrast, a process can also be employed in risk appraisal that seeks only to identify risk factors and protective factors applicable to the individual being assessed. This process, sometimes termed "anamnestic" assessment (meaning recollection or account of one's history; Melton et al., 2018; Otto, 2000), will also be discussed in this chapter. Risk communication is a particularly important consideration in practice, as the entire risk assessment process may be misunderstood or discounted if risk communication is ineffective.

Finally, the important parameters in risk assessment include the identification of risk factors (associated with increased risk of violent outcome), promotive factors (associated with increased likelihood of a favorable outcome, such as responsible behavior), and protective factors (associated in a decrease in risk when risk factors are present). Specialized risk assessment tools have selected the risk and protective factors that are most relevant and empirically related to outcome for their populations of use. They vary in how they select these factors; some do so from a specific dataset or meta-analysis, while others review the broader empirical literature to identify important, recurring influences. This has been an area addressed by researchers on a group level—but it must be considered by practitioners seeking to include individualized considerations into their risk assessment in every evaluation they conduct.

Approach

For the purposes of this chapter, three approaches to risk assessment are described: actuarial,[3] structured professional judgment (SPJ), and anamnestic. Actuarial assessment is "a formal method" that "uses an equation, a formula, a graph, or an actuarial table to arrive at a probability, or expected value, of some outcome" (Grove & Meehl, 1996, p. 294). It uses predictor variables that can be quantified, either through classification (e.g., gender) or rating with a high degree of reliability. The predictors, and the weights assigned to them (if applicable), are validated against the outcome that is being predicted through research. Both the risk factors and, if applicable, their weights, are typically derived empirically as well (although neither empirical item selection nor weighting is a required element of the actuarial approach), from a single dataset or larger meta-analysis. So it is the quantified, mechanistic, reproducible combination of predictive factors, validated through empirical research against known outcomes and yielding a total score, that is the *sine qua non* of actuarial assessment.

SPJ involves the presentation of specified risk (and protective) factors, which are usually derived from a broad review of the literature rather than from analysis of a specific dataset. Risk factors are well-operationalized so, as with the actuarial approach, their applicability can be coded reliably (usually as no, possibly, or yes). Evaluators complete an SPJ tool by rating all the specified factors after examining the subject of the assessment, perhaps interviewing collateral informants, and reviewing records and other relevant data sources. Then, when rating overall risk, evaluators consider the presence and individual relevance of the identified risk (and protective) factors, develop a formulation of risk (why the individual acted in a violent manner), specify future scenarios of concern (what the individual will do again that worries the evaluator), and the anticipated nature and intensity of management, treatment, or supervision needs in reaching an overall conclusion about risk. This is accomplished by having the evaluator draw this conclusion, however, rather than having the rated risk factors combined in a predetermined fashion using an established formula, as is done in actuarial assessment. This procedure makes it more feasible to use risk factors that are dynamic (potentially changeable through planned intervention) as contrasted with the static (unchanging through planned intervention), largely historical risk factors that constitute the large majority of the risk factors that make up actuarial instruments.

Actuarial and SPJ risk assessment approaches are similar in several respects. Both employ variables that have been selected for their demonstrated relationship to the outcome of violence (although actuarial measures typically rely upon variables drawn from a single dataset, while SPJ approaches have tended to use variables for which there appears to be broad empirical support in the literature). Both specify the variables to be considered, and both require that these variables be sufficiently well-operationalized so they can be coded or rated reliably.

These approaches differ in some important respects as well. Actuarial approaches combine their risk factors into a score, which should be cross-validated against known outcomes in the validation phase of developing an actuarial risk assessment tool. SPJ approaches do not combine risk factors numerically in a predetermined or mechanistic fashion, instead providing structured guidance to allow the user to make the judgment as to whether the individual is (for example) high, moderate, or low risk. The respective accuracy of both approaches is discussed later in this chapter.

The third risk assessment approach might better be characterized as a process than a specialized tool.[4] Anamnestic assessment (Melton et al., 2018) uses applied behavior analytic strategies to gather detailed information about the individual's history of violence. For each prior violent event, the individual is questioned in detail concerning the preceding and subsequent thoughts, feelings, and behaviors; the act itself; those involved; and other relevant details (e.g., whether drugs or alcohol were ingested, by whom, and at what level; whether weapons were involved, and their source; how victim[s] were targeted; where and when the event occurred). The goal of this process is not to derive an estimate of violence risk. Rather, the evaluator can use this procedure to identify risk factors and protective factors that recur across violent acts. Such information can help make more accurate ratings on such factors if a formal risk assessment tool is used. It can also facilitate identification of risk-relevant intervention targets—dynamic risk factors that are present during different violent acts that may, if improved through targeted intervention, reduce that individual's risk of future violence.

The use of unstructured clinical judgment will not be discussed for several reasons. First, more than 50 years of research has compared the accuracy of unstructured clinical judgment with actuarial approaches, with a consistent, modest advantage in predictive accuracy observed for the latter (see meta-analyses conducted by Ægisdóttir et al., 2006; Fazel, Singh, Doll, & Grann, 2012; Grove, Zald, Lebow, Snitz, & Nelson, 2000). Several meta-analyses are relevant. In the area of violence prediction, Mossman's (1994) meta-analysis indicated that clinical predictions were more accurate than chance (AUC = .67) but less accurate than the mean AUC for all studies (.78), for cross-validated discriminant function predictions (.71), or for behavior-based predictions (.78). Second, it seems clear that much of the progress that has been made during the last two decades in developing risk assessment approaches that are more accurate and scientifically supported has resulted in increasing their structure, both in the selection of risk factors and the way in which they are rated and combined. Unstructured clinical judgment by itself is no longer a useful or necessary approach to appraising violence risk. (When there are no applicable structured measures available, evaluators should at least "structure" their risk appraisals by focusing on known risk factors for the target outcome, derived from the scientific literature, the individual's history, or both.) However, in the context of a risk assessment conducted as part of broader forensic assessment, clinical judgment does facilitate important aspects of data gathering such as interviewing of the individual and third parties, identifying and reviewing relevant records, interpreting all data, and reasoning toward conclusions (Heilbrun, 2009).

Another meta-analysis (Campbell, French, & Gendreau, 2009) incorporated 88 studies conducted between 1980 and 2006, focusing on prediction of violence (mostly nonsexual) in adults. The mean effect sizes of actuarial and SPJ measures were comparable. Newer instruments, as well as those developed using criminological-related theories or research, showed larger effects than did measures developed using less-relevant theory.

More recently, Fazel et al. (2012) performed a systematic review and meta-analysis using tools commonly used to predict or structure judgments about violence, sexual offending, and general offending. They used 73 samples (24,847 participants from 13 countries, with a reoffending rate of 23.7% over a mean of 49.6 months). Risk assessment tools produced low to moderate positive predictive values (median 41%) when predicting violent offending, but had higher negative predictive values (ranging from 81% to 95%). Instruments designed to predict or structure judgments about violent offending performed better than those used in the context of sexual or general offending. Their conclusion was that such specialized measures were very accurate in identifying low-risk individuals, but substantially less accurate in identifying high-risk individuals.

Applicability

The value of a specialized risk assessment tool depends upon its applicability. This section has outlined several important considerations in judging the potential utility of a particular tool. To what extent are the nature of the evaluation and the attributes of the specialized tool congruent? Such congruence should be judged according to context, purpose, populations, and parameters. The information needed to make this decision should be included in the manual of the specialized tool—one reason why it is important to have such a manual when using a specialized tool in practice (American Education Research Association, American Psychological Association, & National Council on Measurement in Education, 2014; Heilbrun, Rogers, & Otto, 2002). As this book offers chapters describing specialized tools focusing on children, adolescents, and adults in juvenile, criminal, and civil contexts, it will be clear that these respective tools are congruent with the kind of risk assessment described in those chapters.

Approaches to Risk Assessment

In this section, we offer a more detailed discussion of the functions of each of the major approaches to risk assessment described previously—actuarial, structured professional judgment, and anamnestic. It is useful to distinguish two major goals in risk assessment: prediction/classification, and risk reduction (Heilbrun, 1997). Some legal decisions call for expert evaluations that are strongly focused on the question of prediction. Examples include civil commitment, end of sentence sexual offender commitment, and criminal sentencing.

In the case of civil commitment and end of sentence sexual offender commitment, the legal decision-maker is concerned with whether the risk of violent behavior or future sexual offending is sufficiently high to justify a decision restricting individual liberty on public safety grounds—but the court will not retain jurisdiction and make subsequent decisions based on whether this risk has been decreased. By contrast, a legal decision to involuntarily hospitalize a defendant found Not Guilty by Reason of Insanity may indeed involve the retention of such jurisdiction—so the court might be informed by accurate information concerning both risk level and risk reduction potential. Regarding criminal sentencing, many states apply risk assessment in order to make individualized decisions regarding supervision and services. Some states (e.g., Virginia, Utah) apply risk assessment as a front-end approach in determining appropriate sentences. For instance, higher-risk offenders may receive longer sentences and lower-risk offenders shorter sentences when there is discretion on the part of the court (e.g., Monahan & Skeem, 2016).

Table 1.1 summarizes three important questions in risk assessment and the extent to which each of these questions is typically addressed by actuarial, SPJ, and anamnestic assessment. The strength of actuarial assessment, presuming that the tool is appropriately derived and cross-validated, is in facilitating a quantitative estimate of risk level. However, this is a double-edged sword. Because of the inextricably quantitative nature of actuarial risk assessment, actuarial tools lend themselves to research that calculates accuracy using statistical measures such as sensitivity, specificity, and Area Under the Curve (in ROC analysis), as well as 95% confidence intervals of the risk categories. This is important in promoting empirically supported practice. However, actuarial tools that are not sound—derived on relatively small samples (to which most statistical procedures are highly vulnerable), not well-validated, and/or having wide confidence intervals that make it difficult to meaningfully distinguish between risk categories—may advertise more than they can deliver. Developers of actuarial tools differ on their stance of whether to solely use actuarial methods to derive risk estimates, or to use actuarial tools as one component of a broader assessment approach (e.g., compare the approaches recommended by Monahan in still Chapter 5 and Hilton et al. in still Chapter 7).

SPJ tools typically have one section that functions much like an actuarial measure of risk, providing several risk factors which can be scored and summed to yield an overall risk measure for research purposes. In practice, evaluators are encouraged to consider all risk factors, including the total number of risk factors, but are not required to link their judgments directly and proportionately to linear numerical indices, as most actuarial measures require. The juxtaposition of these two practices raises a philosophical question ("How much accuracy is sufficient?") and a practical question ("How much accuracy is feasible?") regarding the prediction of violence. In the next section, the evidence regarding the relative accuracy of each approach is discussed. But it should also be noted that the third approach, anamnestic assessment, is not well-suited at all for drawing a quantitative conclusion about the risk for future violence.

When an individual's risk is being considered over a period of time, this often reflects an interest in how that risk might have changed. Skeem and her colleagues (2006) have distinguished between risk status (relatively unchanging aspects of violence risk) and risk state (aspects of risk that do change, even over short periods of time). If there are interventions being delivered with the goal of decreasing the person's likelihood of violent behavior, it is important to appraise the impact of such interventions through considering how overall risk may have changed. Some actuarial tools (e.g., the Level of Service/Case Management Inventory—Chapter 8 of this volume—and the Violence Risk Scale—still Chapter 10) do this, as they incorporate dynamic risk factors and hence provide a different overall "risk score" as the dynamic variables change. Other actuarial tools (e.g., the Classification of Violence Risk—still Chapter 5—and the

Table 1.1 Approaches and Important Questions in Risk Assessment

Approach \ Question	Prediction/Classification	Reflects Change in Risk Status	Provides Information for Risk Reduction Intervention Planning
Actuarial	Yes	Variable	Limited
Structured professional judgment	Yes	Yes	Yes
Anamnestic	No	Limited	Yes

Violence Risk Appraisal Guide-revised—still Chapter 7) do not; they are designed to provide a stable estimate of the individual's risk that focuses on risk status.

SPJ tools are designed to appraise risk needs as well as risk status, so they offer a way of estimating change in risk state. They do so in the same manner that they provide the risk estimate: the evaluator considers the applicable risk factors, including the dynamic factors, and whether there is a perceived change in the necessary intensity of intervention or management, or the level or configuration of risk factors to be addressed. The evaluator then judges whether the overall risk has changed as a result. Further, it is important for evaluators to appraise and convey whether risk factors, and the relevance of such risk factors, have changed. Research has demonstrated that changes (increases or decreases) in SPJ-tool risk factors, and their relevance, are predictive of changes (increases or decreases) in subsequent inpatient and community violent behavior (Hogan & Olver, 2016, 2019).

Rather than assuming that a single risk estimate remains valid over time, it is important to provide periodic reassessments of risk factors (Douglas & Skeem, 2005). However, the question of how accurately any risk tools gauge the *change* in overall violence risk has seldom been researched (Heilbrun, Douglas, & Yasuhara, 2009). In one study, 30 male forensic psychiatric inpatients were administered the HCR-20, Version 2 (Webster, Douglas, Eaves, & Hart, 1997) and the Short-Term Assessment of Risk and Treatability (START; Webster, Martin, Brink, Nicholls, & Desmarais, 2009; still Chapter 15) every three months for a year (Wilson, Desmarais, Nicholls, Hart, & Brink, 2013). The investigators reported that changes in dynamic risk factors significantly predicted institutional violence even after controlling for static factors. Dynamic risk factors were better predictors than historical risk factors of short-term institutional violence for periods of up to six months. The researchers suggested that changes in dynamic risk factors over time "are associated with future aggression beyond what can be predicted with historical variables alone" (Wilson et al., 2013, p. 385). In a study of short- (1 year) and long-term (11 years) risk level, improvements in dynamic risk and protective factors on the HCR-20[V3] (still Chapter 12) and the Structured Assessment of Protective Factors for violence risk (SAPROF; de Vogel, de Ruiter, Bouman, & de Vries Robbé, 2009, 2012) during treatment were associated with lower violent recidivism rates (de Vries Robbé, de Vogel, Douglas, & Nijman, 2015). Findings indicated that non-recidivists made greater improvements during treatment than recidivists.

Several other studies have considered the relationship between changes in dynamic risk factors and violence risk. Following individuals released from civil and forensic hospitalization, investigators (Michel et al., 2013) reported that 6 of the 10 C and R items on the HCR-20 changed over time—and that this change was positively associated with changes in observed violence. This positive relationship (an increase in C and R item-defined risk associated with an increase in observed violence) has been reported by other investigators as well (Hogan & Olver, 2016; Penney, Marshall, & Simpson, 2016).

Anamnestic approaches can descriptively convey previous and current changes in risk-relevant needs through linkage with an intervention plan designed to address the specific risk factors identified in the initial assessment. When individualized risk factors are reduced in number and intensity through treatment, it is reasonable to assume that risk has been reduced. But how much? Over what period of time? These and related questions have not yet been answered through research.

Actuarial measures that accurately estimate risk do provide some information relevant to intervention planning by distinguishing between higher- and lower-risk individuals, applying the RNR risk principle that higher risk individuals are appropriate for more intensive interventions over a longer period of time (Andrews & Bonta, 2006). Unless dynamic factors are assessed, actuarial measures do not offer specific treatment targets and cannot measure changes in risk after interventions are implemented. However, static risk factors can inform other aspects of risk-relevant intervention decision. For instance, Olver and Wong (2011) reported that Static-99 (Chapter 6 of this volume) predicted sexual recidivism well among offenders with a smaller treatment change versus those with greater treatment change. Static measures may also be used to design interventions based on both risk and needs, assuming risk-relevant needs can be measured in another way (see, e.g., Quinsey, Harris, Rice & Cormier, 1998; 2005). For example, assessing risk using an actuarial measure and risk-relevant needs using a separate measure, or by using anamnestic assessment, could identify at least four categories of risk needs (high risk/high needs, high risk/low need, low risk/high needs, and low risk/low needs) with associated needs for intervention and monitoring that differ considerably across categories.

Validation of Actuarial, Structured Professional Judgment, and Anamnestic Approaches to Risk Assessment

In this section, we highlight important trends in the empirical literature relevant to actuarial and structured professional judgment approaches to risk assessment. In addition, we discuss studies that offer an empirical comparison of the performance of tools of each type. There are no empirical studies on anamnestic risk assessment to be reviewed, but we offer brief comments on the validation status of this approach.

Actuarial Approaches to Violence Risk Assessment

The empirical literature in this area features a number of meta-analyses conducted since the development of the first specialized actuarial violence risk assessment instruments. These are in addition to the meta-analytic studies noted earlier citing a consistent, modest advantage in accuracy for actuarial relative to unstructured clinical prediction over 50 years of research (Ægosdóttir et al., 2006; Grove et al., 2000). The Mossman (1994) meta-analysis indicates that clinical predictions were more accurate than chance (AUC = .67) but modestly less accurate than cross-validated discriminant function predictions (AUC = .71)—a difference that was statistically significant (p = .004).

An important meta-analysis conducted more than two decades ago (Bonta, Law, & Hanson, 1998) considered studies of mentally disordered offenders and used outcomes of any kind of criminal recidivism (general offending) and crimes against persons (violent offending). As demonstrated in Table 1.2, there are a number of indications for support of predictors that could be incorporated into actuarial or SPJ prediction, including historical variables (criminal history, juvenile delinquency, hospital admissions, violence, escape), personality variables (antisocial personality), and substance abuse. The positive predictor with the largest recidivism effect size for violent recidivism was objective risk assessment (a measure that can be reliably scored, as contrasted with clinical judgment).

Two meta-analyses described earlier (Campbell et al., 2009; Fazel et al., 2012) included actuarial measures as well as SPJ measures. The mean effects of actuarial measures were comparable to SPJ measures (Campbell et al, 2009), while the positive predictive values (median = .41) of all measures were considerably lower than the negative predictive values. This means that actuarial (and other) risk assessment measures are quite accurate in identifying low-risk individuals, but less accurate in specifying who is high risk.

Consistent with the observed predictive strength of both historical variables and antisocial personality disorder, psychopathy is moderately associated with violent offending in the community. In one meta-analysis (Gendreau, Goggin & Smith, 2002), investigators compared the Psychopathy Checklist-Revised (PCL-R; Hare, 1991, 2003) with the Level of Service Inventory-Revised

Table 1.2 Predictors of General and Violent Recidivism Among Mentally Disordered Offenders

	General		Violent	
	Recidivism Effect Size	N	Recidivism Effect Size	N
Positive Predictors				
Objective risk assessment	.39	1,295	.30	2,186
Adult criminal history	.23	4,312	.14	2,163
Juvenile delinquency	.22	4,312	.20	985
Antisocial personality	.18	1,736	.18	1,634
Nonviolent criminal history	.18	2,910	.13	1,108
Institutional adjustment	.13	627	.14	711
Hospital admissions	.12	1,874	.17	948
Poor living arrangements	.12	39	NR	
Gender (male)	.11	1,936	NR	
Substance abuse (any)	.11	234	.08	2,013
Family problems	.10	730	.19	1,481
Escape history	.10	646	NR	
Violent history	.10	2,240	.16	2,878
Drug abuse	.09	1,050	NR	
Marital status (single)	.07	987	.13	1,068
Negative Predictors				
Mentally disordered offender	−.19	3,009	−.10	2,866
Homicide index offense	−.17	1,147	NR	
Age	−.15	3,170	−.18	1,519
Violent index	−.14	905	−.04	2,241
Violent index (broadly defined)	−.10	3,240	.08	1,950
Sex offense	−.08	2,371	.04	1,636
Not guilty by reason of insanity	−.07	1,761	−.07	1,208
Psychosis	−.05	2,733	−.04	1,208
Mood disorder	−.04	1,856	.01	1,520
Treatment history	−.03	3,747	NR	
Offense seriousness	−.01	1,368	.06	1,879

Source: From Bonta et al. (1998)

(Andrews & Bonta, 1995; still Chapter 8) in their respective associations with both general and violent recidivism. Using over 50 studies, they found a slight difference in favor of the LSI-R for strength of association with violent recidivism.[5] Both specialized tools performed well, but this comparison is consistent with the tendency to use the PCL-R as a benchmark against which other tools are compared.[6]

Other meta-analyses have been conducted addressing the predictive validity of the PCL-R (Hare, 1991) for violent criminal recidivism. Walters (2003) described the capacities of the PCL-R and the Lifestyle Criminality Screening Form[7] (Walters, White, & Denney, 1991) to predict both general and violent criminal recidivism among offenders. The tools were equally effective in predicting criminal recidivism (AUC values were .67 for the PCL-R and .67 for the LCSF).

Another meta-analysis (Leistico, Salekin, DeCosta, & Rogers, 2008) considered the relationship between the PCL measures and antisocial conduct, including criminal recidivism. Using 95 published studies providing a merged dataset with over 15,000 participants, they observed a significant relationship between both Factor 1 (mean weighted $d = .40$) and Factor 2 (mean weighted $d = .57$) scores and the outcome of interest (violent offense recidivism risk). Factor 2 effect sizes were significantly larger than those for Factor 1. Effect sizes were also moderated by participant characteristics, including gender, race, and setting (correctional versus hospital settings). This potentially limits the utility of the PCL-R in some settings, and for some people.

A meta-analysis addressing the incremental validity to various specialized measures relative to the PCL-R (Yang, Wong, & Coid, 2010) concluded that most specialized risk measures had comparable predictive validity, with few differences across measures. Factor 1 of the PCL (interpersonal and affective features) was less effective in risk assessment than Factor 2 (antisocial behavior history), with only two instruments—the HCR-20 and the OGRS—adding incremental validity to the PCL-R. This is consistent with the meta-analytic findings (Guy, Douglas, & Hendry, 2010) that the HCR-20 and the PCL-R performed comparably with respect to predictive accuracy (both had AUC values of .69).

Instruments designed more specifically to predict violence, and with a particular age cohort, may have superior performance to those designed to predict general offending (e.g., the Level of Service family of measures) or not designed as a risk assessment measure (e.g., the PCL-R). One relevant meta-analysis (Singh, Grann, & Fazel, 2011) observed that the SAVRY (an SPJ tool) produced the largest effect, with the LS and PCL-R having the smallest. Consistent with this, another meta-analysis (Fazel, Singh, Doll, & Grann, 2012) identified the VRAG (an actuarial measure) as well as a number of SPJ measures as having higher predictive validity than the LS and PCL-R, designed for more general outcomes (odds ratios of 6.1 versus 2.84).

The current view about the PCL-R as a risk assessment measure reflects the reality that it was developed as a measure of a personality disorder rather than as a specialized risk measure; once other such specialized risk measures have appeared and received research support, it is more appropriate to use them for the purpose of risk assessment. We note that the PCL-R has been among the actuarial measures of violence risk considered by researchers over nearly three decades. Typically, however, larger reviews (e.g., meta-analyses, meta-reviews) have included a number of actuarial measures of risk. For example, one meta-analysis focusing on risk assessment with sex offenders (Hanson & Morton-Bourgon, 2009) concluded that actuarial measures were more accurate than unstructured clinical judgment for three outcomes: any offending, violent offending, and sexual offending. SPJ measures had intermediate effect sizes. Actuarial measures were particularly effective with sexual recidivism outcomes, although there were only six SPJ studies included—and three of them used summary risk ratings as opposed to summation of scores.[8]

Other meta-analyses have reported comparable predictive effectiveness of actuarial and SPJ measures (see Olver, Stockdale, & Wormith, 2009; Viljoen, Mordell, & Beneteau, 2012). Smith, Cullen, and Latessa (2009) addressed the question of whether the Level of Service Inventory Revised (LSI-R; Andrews & Bonta, 2001) performed acceptably with a sample of female offenders. Smith et al. reviewed 25 published and unpublished datasets to evaluate the effect size of the relationship between LSI-R total score and recidivism for female offenders. The researchers found that the effect sizes in these studies were basically equivalent to the effect sizes found in samples of male offenders, indicating that the LSI-R worked comparably well with female offenders. Nevertheless, they suggested that a specialized risk assessment measure specific to females might perform even better (see also Manchak, Skeem, Douglas, & Siranosian, 2009).

These meta-analyses provided considerable evidence for the utility of the actuarial prediction of violent behavior, including criminal recidivism. Additional evidence comes from the MacArthur Risk Assessment Study (Monahan et al., 2001; Steadman et al., 1998), the largest and best-designed study to date of violent behavior in the community committed by those who had been discharged from inpatient mental health treatment facilities. The original MacArthur data were combined with additional validation data (Monahan, Steadman, Robbins et al., 2005) to yield an actuarial tool (the Classification of Violence Risk, or COVR; Monahan, Steadman, Appelbaum et al., 2005; see still Chapter 5) that is effective in predicting serious acts of violence in the community committed by individuals with mental disorder. There was some shrinkage in the accuracy rates from derivation sample (AUC = .88) to the cross-validation sample (AUC = .63–.70, depending on the definition and measurement of outcomes), which is typical upon cross-validation.

Moving from meta-analysis to single cases, there have been recent developments in the debate concerning the applicability of actuarial measures to prediction in single cases. Some (see, e.g., Hart, Michie, & Cooke, 2007; Cooke & Michie, 2010; Hart & Cooke, 2013) have argued that the application of an actuarial prediction to a single case creates such serious statistical problems that those results are nearly meaningless when so applied. These arguments have not met with universal agreement within the field (see, e.g., Harris & Rice, 2007, 2015; Mossman, 2007, 2015), but the statistical issues involved were sufficiently complex that for several years the debate remained active. Some have concluded that the statistical arguments against the accuracy of actuarial instruments in the individual case are not persuasive (Imrey & Dawid, 2015; although cf. Hart & Cooke, 2013). It *is* important that an actuarial tool be derived and validated on large samples, both to increase its generalizability and to ensure that the confidence intervals are narrow and the risk categories do not overlap. An earlier discussion of this debate may be found elsewhere (Heilbrun et al., 2009).

One of the active debates in the field over the years has involved the way in which actuarial weighting and scoring can miss certain influences that may apply in the individual case. Relatively few studies of the impact of "clinical overrides" of actuarial risk levels—the "adjusted actuarial" procedure—have been published. Apparently the first such study (Gore, 2008) considered the accuracy of the actuarial versus "adjusted actuarial" conclusions in 383 cases in which there had been a clinical override of the Minnesota Sex Offender Screening Tool-Revised (MnSOST-R; Epperson et al., 2003) risk level. The clinical adjustment did not yield increased accuracy, but it also did not lower the overall accuracy substantially. MnSOST-R actuarial levels were more accurate than the adjusted levels, but the difference was not statistically significant. In addition, the direction of the adjustment was not related to measured predictive accuracy. Upon conducting their meta-analysis, Hanson and Morton-Bourgon (2009) concluded that clinical adjustment to actuarial prediction tended to decrease overall predictive accuracy. Wormith and colleagues (this volume) discuss research with the LS system that fails to show support for adjustment of actuarial predictions in terms of enhancing predictive accuracy, and they recommend that they be used only sparingly, under extraordinary circumstances. Scurich and Krauss (2013) found that clinical adjustment significantly increased mock juror willingness to commit an offender under a sexually violent predator (SVP) statute, but only when the adjustment was upward (i.e., indicating higher risk). Downward adjustment had no effect on the mock jurors.

In addition, the process of weighting predictors in the course of actuarial assessment has been considered in another study. Using 10 well-established risk factors for violent criminal recidivism from the HCR-20, the investigators (Grann & Långström, 2007) considered the impact of four different weighting schemes in applying these predictors to 404 forensic psychiatric patients who had been released to their communities in Sweden. These weighting approaches included Nuffield's method, bivariate and multivariate logistic regression, and an artificial neural network procedure. Upon cross-validation, they reported that simpler weighting techniques did not increase predictive accuracy over an unweighted approach. In addition, more complex weighting procedures were associated with significant shrinkage.

The findings of these two studies (Gore, 2008; Grann & Långström, 2007) may suggest that the use of empirically validated risk factors in prediction yields an increase in accuracy over unstructured judgment, but there may be limits to the increases in accuracy that can be achieved through the specific weighting and combination of predictors that are typically present in actuarial prediction (a point made roughly 40 years ago by Dawes, 1979). Accordingly, some commentators have opposed the practice of weighting the risk factors in risk assessment instruments, when simple unit weighting (equal weights for all risk factors) is more accurate (see Harris & Rice, 2015; Grann & Långström, 2007).

On this point, Kroner, Mills, and Reddon (2005) compared the predictive accuracy of three widely recognized actuarial tools (the PCL-R, LSI-R, and VRAG), another approach using "General Statistical Information on Recidivism," and four additional instruments that had been constructed through randomly selecting items from the total pool of original items. Intriguingly, none of the three actuarial tools or the fourth using general statistical information on recidivism was more accurate in predicting post-release failure than the four randomly generated instruments. The investigators argued that the development of better risk theory, yielding the capacity to test hypotheses and explain behavior, is necessary to advance the process of risk assessment in the criminal justice and mental health fields. A related explanation—that there is a ceiling on the predictive accuracy that can be obtained using any approach that incorporates empirically supported risk factors, regardless of how these factors are weighted or combined—is discussed in more detail later in this chapter.

Structured Professional Judgment Approaches to Violence Risk Assessment

Structured professional judgment is an approach to risk assessment that began to be used in the 1990s and has continued to evolve (see Douglas, 2019). It is more recent than actuarial risk assessment, and also less oriented toward quantifying conclusions. Rather than yielding a final numerical score, SPJ tools typically call for a risk judgment of low, moderate, or high. Assuming that an SPJ tool uses risk factors whose rating can be quantified, it is possible to study that tool by using these risk factors in an actuarial sense—by obtaining a "total score" and relating that score to observed outcome. However, it is important to test SPJ tools in the way it is recommended they be used. Rather than relying on specific weights for predictors that would be derived using an actuarial approach, the SPJ approach uses risk factors that have support in the broad empirical literature; it also makes the general assumption that the presence of a greater number of risk factors is typically associated with higher risk (Douglas & Kropp, 2002). Research on the relationship between final risk judgments and outcomes is most meaningful in testing this approach. That is what we will describe in this section.

There have been 45 published studies and at least one dissertation (McGowan, 2007) addressing the relationship between final SPJ risk judgments and violence (Douglas, 2019). Of these 45 studies, 39 have yielded findings to the effect that SPJ judgments are significantly predictive of violent recidivism.[9] In addition, 18 of these studies assessed whether the SPJ "final judgment" adds incremental predictive accuracy to the use of the tool elements combined in an actuarial fashion (Douglas, 2019). In 16 of these 18 studies, such incremental validity was observed.

Taken together, these studies provide very strong evidence that structured professional judgment is an efficacious approach to risk assessment. But how does it compare to actuarial assessment? In certain respects this is not a meaningful question, as actuarial and structured professional judgment share several important features. Both use risk factors that are specified *a priori* and can be rated reliably. In both *data selection* and *data coding*, therefore, these approaches are quite similar. It is in *data combination* that they diverge. Actuarial approaches combine data according to an established formula derived and validated on specific datasets; SPJ approaches call for the combination of data into a professional judgment that is "structured" through provision of risk factors (obtained from the broader literature but typically not from any specific dataset) and guided formulation (or integration of risk factors) that can be rated reliably.

Accordingly, we might attribute observed differences between actuarial and SPJ approaches to their divergence in data combination, as they are similar in data selection and data coding. With that in mind, we now review studies that have compared these approaches.

Actuarial vs. Structured Professional Judgment Approaches to Violence Risk Assessment

Over the last two decades, a number of meta-analyses and reviews have compared the performance of actuarial versus SPJ measures. We regard such aggregate analyses and reviews as the most stable form of evidence on this question. We will summarize the relevant findings of such studies (discussed earlier, particularly in the Validation of Actuarial Approaches section) first, and then discuss the most relevant of these in greater detail. Generally, the evidence seems to identify little meaningful difference between actuarial and SPJ approaches to predictive accuracy—even when some of the studies reviewed use summed item scores rather than summary judgments for SPJ measures. Further, to the extent that a measure is developed for a more specific purpose (e.g., predicting violence rather than general offending), or for use with a more specific population (e.g., adolescents, adults), that seems to enhance its effectiveness.

Douglas and his colleagues (2005) compared the respective predictive validities of an SPJ measure (the HCR-20) and several actuarial measures (the Violence Risk Appraisal Guide and the Hare Psychopathy Checklist-Revised and Psychopathy Checklist: Screening Version), among others. Several indices were related to violent recidivism with large effect sizes. These included HCR-20 structured risk judgments, VRAG scores, and behavioral scales of psychopathy measures (PCL-R Factor 2, Cooke and Michie's (2001) Factor 3, and PCL-SV Part 2). These findings are consistent with strong predictive performance by actuarial measures, but not with a noteworthy advantage to such measures. The HCR-20 structured risk judgments were also strongly related to violent outcomes.

A similar comparison between the HCR-20 and two actuarial measures (the Level of Service Inventory-Revised edition and the Psychopathy Checklist-Revised) was conducted on offenders in Germany (Dahle, 2006). The investigator noted only minor differences in predictive accuracy among these measures. As with the study by Douglas and his colleagues (2005), all measures performed reasonably well, but without noteworthy advantage to any particular measure. It is worth noting that in the latter study, direct entry of variables by the investigator into the regression equation resulted in significance of both the VRAG score and HCR summary risk rating, while stepwise entry (using automatic entry of the most strongly predictive variables in succession, after the variance accounted for by previously entered variables is no longer considered) yielded significance for only the HCR summary risk ratings.

In another comparison of an actuarial measure (the Static-99) with an SPJ measure (the SVR-20), de Vogel, de Ruiter, van Beek, and Mead (2004) observed significantly better predictive performance of the latter. They scored these tools using file information from 122 sex offenders who had been admitted to a Dutch forensic psychiatric hospital between 1974 and 1996 and had been released to and residing in the community for almost 12 years. Base rates of reconvictions over this period were 39% (sexual offenses), 46% (nonsexual violent offenses), and 74% (any offenses). Predictive validity for the SVR-20 was good for both the total score (AUC = .80) and the final risk judgment (AUC = .83), and reasonably good but significantly lower for the Static-99 total score (AUC = .71) and risk categories (AUC = .66).

A study with adolescents (Catchpole & Gretton, 2003) compared two actuarial approaches—the Youth Level of Service/Case Management Inventory (YLS/CMI; Hoge & Andrews, 2002; still Chapter 9) and the Psychopathy Checklist: Youth Version (PCL:YV; Forth, Kosson, & Hare, 2003)—with the Structured Assessment of Violence Risk in Youth (SAVRY; Borum, Bartel, & Forth, 2002; still Chapter 18). A total of 133 participants were obtained from consecutive referrals from youth court judges. The YLS/CMI ratings were completed by probation officers; the PCL:YV and the SAVRY were coded using file data. Follow-up periods ranged between 7 and 61 months, with a mean of 35.8 months. Violent recidivism was among the outcomes measured. For such violent recidivism, the SAVRY (AUC = .81) was most accurate predictively, followed by the PCL:SV (AUC = .73) and the YLS/CMI (AUC = .64).

The relationship between the PCL-R and the HCR-20 (Version 2) was considered in samples (k = 34) containing both (Guy, Douglas, & Hendry, 2010). The two instruments had equivalent AUC values (.69). The investigators were able to determine (through using raw data sets) that the HCR-20 added unique incremental validity to the PCL-R, but the PCL-R did not add such validity to the HCR-20—and removing the psychopathy item from the HCR-20 did not decrease its predictive accuracy.

Hanson and Morton-Bourgon (2009) conducted a meta-analysis of 118 sex offender studies and reported that actuarial measures produced the largest effect sizes, with unstructured clinical judgment having the smallest. SPJ measures (with the exception of the SVR-20, which had the largest effect size) were intermediate in the effect sizes reported, although the small number of SPJ studies meant that a meaningful comparison between actuarial and SPJ effectiveness was not possible. In another meta-analysis focusing on risk assessment of youth, the measure with the strongest effect size was the SAVRY (an SPJ tool) (.30 to .38), while lower effect sizes were observed for the YLS/CMI (an actuarial measure; .26 to .32). No meaningful differences between actuarial and SPJ measures were reported in another meta-analysis of adolescent sexual offender assessment (Viljoen, Mordell, & Beneteau, 2012). This is very consistent with findings from a different meta-analysis (Singh, Grann, & Fazel, 2011) reporting the strongest effect sizes for the SAVRY and the weakest for the LS measures.

Nine risk assessment tools in another meta-analysis (including the HCR-20 and VRAG) predicted violence at approximately a moderate level. These measures included both actuarial and SPJ approaches and considered whether any of the included risk assessment measures could improve on the accuracy associated with the PCL-R. There were few differences between measures, with only the HCR-20 (based on 16 samples) and the Offender Group Reconviction Scale (Copas & Marshall, 1998; based on two samples) adding the predictive accuracy of the PCL-R. It is noteworthy that the meta-analysis did not use the summary risk ratings (provided by the evaluators) from the SPJ measures (Yang et al., 2010).

There are a growing number of studies on which to base a conclusion about the relative predictive accuracy of actuarial measures versus SPJ approaches using a "final judgment" as the risk classification. But the available evidence at present, much of it gathered since the first version of this chapter was written a decade ago, strongly suggests that actuarial and SPJ approaches are at least comparable in predictive accuracy for violent outcomes. This is an important observation, as this book details the structure and functions of both SPJ and actuarial risk assessment tools.

Anamnestic Approaches to Violence Risk Assessment

The anamnestic approach to risk assessment does not lend itself easily to research on predictive accuracy. Indeed, the identification of risk factors, particularly those that are subject to change and hence targets for intervention, by using the individual's own history of violence is much better suited to risk management. But focusing part of the risk assessment on the individual's history of violence will remain an important step when informing a broader legal decision. Three considerations are worth noting in this respect. First, the assumption of some relationship between the number of risk factors present and the overall risk level has some support from SPJ studies that allow the evaluator to make a final judgment in light of the number and intensity of observed risk factors. Final predictions made in this context seem about as accurate as actuarial predictions. Second the process of "individualizing" the evaluation of forensic mental health assessment (FMHA) is quite important as a broad principle in forensic assessment, including risk assessment done in forensic contexts (Heilbrun, 2009). Third, there are occasionally exceptions that involve a substantial difference in the individual's personal attributes or situation that distinguish their present from most of their history. One of the best ways to learn about such exceptions is through obtaining detailed information about a person's history of violent behavior and the circumstances surrounding each event.[10]

Although it would be difficult, it is certainly feasible to investigate the extent to which anamnestic assessments accurately identify level of risk and relevant treatment targets and lead to intervention planning that is more effective in reducing risk. Such research would be similar to a "clinical trial" in which one approach (using anamnestic risk assessment) was compared with others (e.g., a standard risk assessment tool, "usual practice" by a treatment team, and perhaps some combinations). The added demand to deliver interventions makes this a more challenging study than the typical "administer tool à observe outcome" design of a prediction study. But this is true for any investigation of risk reduction, and it would be important to use the anamnestic approach for what it should do best (identify treatment targets to reduce risk) as well as what it may do (help inform an accurate conclusion about risk level).

Future Directions

The development of specialized assessment tools continues to provide one of the best avenues to promoting empirically informed practice. The various chapters in this book provide descriptions of risk assessment tools that have been developed and validated for some of the various purposes and populations described in the present chapter. Promising directions for risk assessment include increased application of risk assessment to risk reduction planning and delivery, combining data gathered by use of risk assessment measures with data from other measures that may provide moderating influences (e.g., clinical functioning, situational variables), and the incorporation of the influences of trauma and adverse experience into risk assessment and risk reduction. Practitioners might observe a modest advantage accruing from the development of a specialized measure with a specific population, such as adolescence, or for a specific purpose, such as assessing the risk of violent offending rather than general offending. Researchers might consider the accumulating evidence that specialized measures, whatever their numerous advantages, may be hitting a ceiling in their observed accuracy defined by AUC values around .80. This might suggest that modifications in our approach to developing and using specialized risk assessment measures are needed. Both practitioners and researchers might consider the chapters that follow in light of these conclusions.

Notes

1. There are occasional exceptions in which a court does maintain jurisdiction over an individual following civil commitment, such as in cases involving individuals committed as sexually violent predators.
2. The term "protective factor" has been used imprecisely in much of the literature in this area. A recent useful clarification has been provided by Monahan and Skeem (2016), who described "risk factors" as influences directly associated with adverse outcomes, "promotive factors" as influences directly associated with favorable outcomes, and "protective factors" as those reducing the influence of risk factors (in effect, moderating the influence of risk factors).
3. The "adjusted actuarial" debate addresses whether the results of actuarial risk assessment should be modified in light of other considerations. As noted elsewhere (Heilbrun, 2009), this can involve either "adjusting" the score or the final risk level yielded by the actuarial tool at the scoring stage, or adjusting their meaning at the interpretation stage. Changing a score or risk level at the scoring stage is extremely problematic. Actuarial tools were designed and validated to be used with an established algorithm. Changing this (for whatever reason) would raise questions about the meaning of the adjusted score. It would substitute clinical judgment for the actuarial algorithm, reducing accuracy over multiple cases. If the evaluator is not clear about doing this, the result may appear actuarial when it is something different. For these reasons, adjusting actuarial results at the scoring stage should not be done. At the interpretation

stage, however, the actuarial tool may be one of multiple sources of information contributing to the final conclusion. In forensic mental health assessment, no single source of information is considered definitive and final opinions result from integration across sources (Heilbrun, 2001). But actuarial measures provide valuable data concerning violence risk, so deviation from their conclusions should involve (1) noting the actuarial results, (2) describing the deviation, (3) noting the information contributing to the different opinion, and (4) describing the logic underlying the evaluator's reasoning.

4. Anamnestic assessment is described here as a distinct kind of risk assessment. However, it is a useful complement to other aspects of risk appraisal in any evaluation. In fact, it is similar to the formulation aspect of SPJ, which attempts to answer *why* a person has been violent, and acknowledged as such by SPJ developers (Douglas, Hart, Webster, & Belfrage, 2013). In effect, it provides a way of individualizing the risk assessment that increases both accuracy and associated credibility—both important considerations in forensic mental health assessment.

5. They reported effect sizes of .26 for the LSI-R and .21 for the PCL-R, a difference the authors suggest is significant using fail-safe calculations. Fail-safe analyses indicated that there would need to be 37 additional PCL-R studies with the maximum observed effect size, or 22 LSI-R effect sizes of 0, in order for their predictive performance to be equal.

6. It might also be noted that there is some judgment required in rating certain items on each of these tools, but the items are combined through numerical scores, and the total score is considered to be the indicator of risk—so each qualifies as an "actuarial" tool in this respect. It is also somewhat ironic that the PCL-R has come to be considered by some as a benchmark for the performance of risk assessment tools; it was not developed as a risk assessment measure, but as a way of assessing a specific personality disorder.

7. The LCSF is a procedure that uses only information from the file to rate an individual's irresponsibility, self-indulgence, interpersonal intrusiveness, and social rule-breaking.

8. This is a common methodological problem in aggregate reviews of the effectiveness of SPJ measures. Such measures are designed to use professional judgment ("summary judgment") after considering item content rather than sum item scores. To the extent that summary judgment enhances SPJ effectiveness (discussed elsewhere in this chapter), using summed item scores rather than summary judgments artificially truncates the effectiveness of SPJ measures.

9. These studies include Arbach-Lucioni, Andres-Pueyo, Pomarol-Clotet, & Gomar-Sones, 2011; Belfrage, Strand, Ekman, & Hasselborg, 2012; Braithwaite, Charette, Crocker, & Reyes, 2010; Catchpole & Gretton, 2003; de Vogel & de Ruiter, 2005, 2006; de Vogel, de Ruiter, Hildebrand, Bos, & van de Ven, 2004; de Vogel, de Ruiter, van Beek, & Mead, 2004; de Vries Robbé, de Vogel, & de Spa, 2011; de Vries Robbé, de Vogel, Koster, & Bogaerts, 2014; de Vries Robbé, de Vogel, Douglas, & Nijman, 2015; de Vries Robbé, de Vogel, Wever, Douglas, & Nijman, 2016; Desmarais, Nicholls, Wilson, & Brink, 2012; Dolan & Rennie, 2008; Douglas, Ogloff, & Hart, 2003; Douglas, Yeomans, & Boer, 2005; Enebrink, Långström, & Gumpert, 2006; Folino, 2015; Gammelgård, Koivisto, Eronen, & Kaltiala-Heino, 2008; Ho et al., 2015; Hogan & Olver, 2016; Jovanović, Toševski, Ivković, Damjanović, & Gašić, 2009; Kropp & Hart, 2000; Langton, Hogue, Daffern, Mannion, & Howells, 2009; Lodewijks, de Ruiter, & Doreleijers, 2008; Lodewijks, Doreleijers, & de Ruiter, 2008; Lodewijks, Doreleijers, de Ruiter, & Borum, 2008; Meyers & Schmidt, 2008; Neal, Miller, & Shealy, 2015; Neves, Goncalves, & Palma-Oliveira, 2011; O'Shea, Picchioni, Mason, Sugarman, & Dickens, 2014; O'Shea et al., 2016; Nonstad et al., 2010; Pedersen, Rasmussen, & Elsass, 2010; Penney, Lee, & Moretti, 2010; Rajlic & Gretton, 2010; Sada et al., 2016; Schaap, Lammers, & de Vogel, 2009; Schmidt, Campbell, & Houlding, 2011; Sjöstedt & Långström, 2002; Strub, Douglas, & Nicholls, 2014; van den Brink, Hooijschuur, van Os, Savenije, & Wiersma, 2010; Verbrugge, Goodman-Delahunty, & Frize, 2011; Viljoen et al., 2008, 2016; Vincent, Chapman, & Cook, 2011.

10. The presence of an exceptional circumstance or substantial change in personal characteristics might suffice to cause the evaluator to avoid using a risk assessment measure that does not allow the incorporation of such a difference into the formal evaluation.

References

Abbiati, M., Palix, J., Gasser, J., & Moulin, V. (2019). Predicting physically violent misconduct in prison: A comparison of four risk assessment instruments. *Behavioral Sciences and the Law, 37*, 61–77.

Ægosdóttir, S., White, M. J., Spengler, P. M., Maugherman, L. A., Cook, R. S., Nichols, C. N., . . . Rush, J. D. (2006). The meta-analysis of clinical judgment project: Fifty-six years of accumulated research on clinical versus statistical prediction. *The Counseling Psychologist, 34*, 341–382.

American Educational Research Association, American Psychological Association, & The National Council on Measurement in Education. (2014). *Standards for educational and psychological testing*. Washington, DC: American Educational Research Association.

Andrews, D. A., & Bonta, J. (1995). *The level of service inventory-revised*. Toronto, ON: Multi-Health Systems.

Andrews, D. A, & Bonta, J. (2001). *Level of service inventory-revised (LSI-R): User's manual*. Toronto, ON: Multi-Health Systems.

Andrews, D. A., & Bonta, J. (2006). *The psychology of criminal conduct* (4th ed.). Newark, NJ: LexisNexis.

Andrews, D. A, Bonta, J., & Hoge, R. (1990). Classification for effective rehabilitation: Rediscovering psychology. *Criminal Justice and Behavior*, *17*, 19–52.

Andrews, D. A., Bonta, J., & Wormith, J. S. (2004). *Level of service/case management inventory (LS/CMI): An offender assessment system user's manual*. North Tonawanda, NY: Multi-Health Systems.

Andrews, D. A., Bonta, J., & Wormith, S. (2006). Recent past and near future of risk/need assessment. *Crime and Delinquency*, *52*, 7–27.

Arbach-Lucioni, K., Andres-Pueyo, A., Pomarol-Clotet, E., & Gomar-Sones, J. (2011). Predicting violence in psychiatric inpatients: A prospective study with the HCR-20 violence risk assessment scheme. *Journal of Forensic Psychiatry & Psychology*, *22*, 203–222.

Belfrage, H., Strand, S., Ekman, L., & Hasselborg, A. (2012). Assessing risk of patriarchal violence with honour as a motive: Six years experience using the PATRIARCH checklist. *International Journal of Police Science & Management*, *14*, 20–29.

Bonta, J., & Andrews, D. (2017). *The psychology of criminal conduct* (6th ed.). New York: Routledge.

Bonta, J., Law, M., & Hanson, K. (1998). The prediction of criminal and violent recidivism among mentally disordered offenders: A meta-analysis. *Psychological Bulletin*, *124*, 123–142.

Borum, R., Bartel, P., & Forth, A. (2002). *Manual for the structured assessment of violence risk in youth: Consultation version*. Tampa: University of South Florida, Florida Mental Health Institute.

Braithwaite, E., Charette, Y., Crocker, A. G., & Reyes, A. (2010). The predictive validity of clinical ratings of the short-term assessment of risk and treatability (START). *International Journal of Forensic Mental Health*, *9*, 271–281.

Campbell, M. A., French, S., & Gendreau, P. (2009). The prediction of violence in adult offenders: A meta-analytic comparison of instruments and methods of assessment. *Criminal Justice and Behavior*, *36*, 567–590.

Catchpole, R. E. H., & Gretton, H. M. (2003). The predictive validity of risk assessment with violent young offenders: A 1-year examination of criminal outcome. *Criminal Justice and Behavior*, *30*, 688–708.

Childs, K., Frick, P., Ryals, J., Lingonblad, A., & Villio, M. (2014). A comparison of empirically based and structured professional judgment estimation of risk using the structured assessment of violence risk in youth. *Youth Violence and Juvenile Justice*, *12*, 40–57.

Cooke, D. J., & Michie, C. (2001). Refining the construct of psychopathy: Towards a hierarchical model. *Psychological Assessment*, *13*, 171–188.

Cooke, D. J., & Michie, C. (2010). Limitations of diagnostic precision and predictive utility in the individual case: A challenge for forensic practice. *Law and Human Behavior*, *34*, 269–274.

Cooke, D. J., Wozniak, E., & Johnstone, L. (2008). Casting light on prison violence in Scotland: Evaluating the impact of situational risk factors. *Criminal Justice and Behavior*, *35*, 1065–1078.

Copas, J., & Marshall, P. (1998). The offender group reconviction scale: The statistical reconviction score for use by probation officers. *Journal of the Royal Statistical Society*, *47C*, 159–171.

Daffern, M., & Howells, K. (2007). The prediction of imminent aggression and self-harm in personality disordered patients of a high security hospital using the HCR-20 clinical scale and the dynamic appraisal of situational aggression. *International Journal of Forensic Mental Health*, *6*, 137–143.

Dahle, K. P. (2006). Strengths and limitations of actuarial prediction of criminal reoffence in a German prison sample: A comparative study of LSI-R, HCR-20 and PCL-R. *International Journal of Law and Psychiatry*, *29*, 341–442.

Dawes, R. (1979). The robust beauty of improper linear models. *American Psychologist*, *34*, 571–582.

Desmarais, S. L., Nicholls, T., Wilson, C. M., & Brink, J. (2012). Reliability and validity of the short-term assessment of risk and treatability (START) in assessing risk for inpatient aggression. *Psychological Assessment*, *24*, 685–700.

de Vogel, V., & de Ruiter, C. (2005). The HCR-20 in personality disordered female offenders: A comparison with a matched sample of males. *Clinical Psychology & Psychotherapy*, *12*, 226–240.

de Vogel, V., & de Ruiter, C. (2006). Structured professional judgment of violence risk in forensic clinical practice: A prospective study into the predictive validity of the Dutch HCR-20. *Psychology, Crime & Law, 12*, 321–336.

de Vogel, V., de Ruiter, C., Bouman, Y., & de Vries Robbé, M. (2009). *SAPROF: Guidelines for the assessment of protective factors for violence risk* (English version). Utrecht, The Netherlands: Forum Educatief.

de Vogel, V., de Ruiter, C., Bouman, Y., & de Vries Robbé, M. (2012). *SAPROF: Guidelines for the assessment of protective factors for violence risk* (2nd ed.). Utrecht, The Netherlands: Vander Hoeven Stichting.

de Vogel, V., de Ruiter, C., Hildebrand, M., Bos, B., & van de Ven, P. (2004). Type of discharge and risk of recidivism measured by the HCR-20: A retrospective study in a Dutch sample of treated forensic psychiatric patients. *International Journal of Forensic Mental Health, 3*, 149–165.

de Vogel, V., de Ruiter, C., van Beek, D., & Mead, G. (2004). Predictive validity of the SVR-20 and static 99 in a Dutch sample of treated sex offenders. *Law and Human Behavior, 28*, 235–251.

de Vries Robbé, M., de Vogel, V., & de Spa, E. (2011). Protective factors for violence risk in forensic psychiatric patients: A retrospective validation study of the SAPROF. *International Journal of Forensic Mental Health, 10*, 178–186.

de Vries Robbé, M., de Vogel, V., & Douglas, K. (2013). Risk factors and protective factors: A two-sided dynamic approach to violence risk assessment. *Journal of Forensic Psychiatry & Psychology, 24*, 440–457.

de Vries Robbé, M., de Vogel, V., Douglas, K. S., & Nijman, H. L. I. (2015). Changes in dynamic risk and protective factors for violence during inpatient forensic psychiatric treatment: Predicting reductions in postdischarge community recidivism. *Law and Human Behavior, 39*, 53–61. doi:10.1037/lhb0000089.

de Vries Robbé, M., de Vogel, V., Koster, K., & Bogaerts, S. (2014). Assessing protective factors for sexually violent offending with the SAPROF. *Sexual Abuse: A Journal of Research and Treatment, 27*, 51–70.

de Vries Robbé, M., de Vogel, V., Wever, E. C., Douglas, K. S., & Nijman, H. L. I. (2016). Risk and protective factors for inpatient aggression. *Criminal Justice and Behavior, 43*, 1364–1385.

Dolan, M. C., & Rennie, C. E. (2008). The "structured assessment of violence risk in youth" as a predictor of recidivism in a United Kingdom cohort of adolescent offenders with conduct disorder. *Psychological Assessment, 20*, 35–46.

Douglas, K. S. (2019). Evaluating and managing risk for violence using structured professional judgment. In A. Day, C. Hollin, & D. Polaschek (Eds.), *Wiley international handbook of correctional psychology* (pp. 429–445). Hoboken, NJ: Wiley & Sons.

Douglas, K. S., Hart, S. D., Groscup, J. L., & Litwack, T. R. (2014). Assessing violence risk. In I. Weiner & R. K. Otto (Eds.), *The handbook of forensic psychology* (4th ed., pp. 385–441). Hoboken, NJ: Wiley & Sons.

Douglas, K. S., Hart, S. D., Webster, C. D., & Belfrage, H. (2013). *HCR-20 (version 3): Assessing risk for violence, user guide*. Burnaby, BC: Mental Health, Law, and Policy Institute, Simon Fraser University.

Douglas, K. S., & Kropp, P. R. (2002). A prevention-based paradigm for violence risk assessment: Clinical and research applications. *Criminal Justice and Behavior, 29*, 617–658.

Douglas, K., & Ogloff, J. R. P. (2003). The impact of confidence on the accuracy of structured professional and actuarial violence risk judgments in a sample of forensic psychiatric patients. *Law and Human Behavior, 27*, 573–587.

Douglas, K. S., Ogloff, J. R. P., & Hart, S. D. (2003). Evaluation of a model of violence risk assessment among forensic psychiatric patients. *Psychiatric Services, 54*, 1372–1379.

Douglas, K. S., & Skeem, J. (2005). Violence risk assessment: Getting specific about being dynamic. *Psychology, Public Policy, and Law, 11*, 347–383.

Douglas, K. S., Yeomans, M., & Boer, D. P. (2005). Comparative validity analysis of multiple measures of violence risk in a sample of criminal offenders. *Criminal Justice and Behavior, 32*, 479–510.

Enebrink, P., Långström, N., & Gumpert, C. H. (2006). Predicting aggressive and disruptive behavior in referred 6- to 12-year-old boys: Predictive validation of the EARL-20B risk/needs checklist. *Assessment, 13*, 356–367.

Epperson, D., Kaul, J., Huot, S., Goldman, R., & Alexander, W. (2003). *Minnesota sex offender screening tool-revised (MnSOST-R) technical paper: Development, validation, and recommended risk level cut scores*. Currently unpublished manuscript. Retrieved April 9, 2008, from www.psychology.iastate.edu/~dle/TechUpdatePaper12-03.pdf

Fazel, S., Singh J. P., Doll, H., & Grann, M. (2012). Use of risk assessment instruments to predict violence and antisocial behaviour in 73 samples involving 24 827 people: Systematic review and meta-analysis. *British Medical Journal, 345*, e4692. doi:10.1136/bmj.e4692

Folino, J. (2015). Predictive efficacy of violence risk assessment instruments in Latin-America: Predictive efficacy of violence risk assessment instruments in Latin-America. *The European Journal of Psychology Applied to Legal Context, 7*, 51–58.

Forth, A., Kosson, D., & Hare, R. (2003). *The psychopathy checklist: Youth version.* Toronto, ON: Multi-Health Systems.

Gammelgård, M., Koivisto, A., Eronen, M., & Kaltiala-Heino, R. (2008). The predictive validity of the structured assessment of violence risk in youth (SAVRY) among institutionalised adolescents. *Journal of Forensic Psychiatry & Psychology, 19*, 352–370.

Garcia-Mansilla, A., Rosenfeld, B., & Cruise, K. (2011). Violence risk assessment and women: Predictive accuracy of the HCR-20 in a civil psychiatric sample. *Behavioral Sciences and the Law, 29*, 623–633.

Gendreau, P., Goggin, C., & Smith, P. (2002). Is the PCL-R really the "unparalleled" measure of offender risk? A lesson in knowledge cumulation. *Criminal Justice and Behavior, 29*, 397–426.

Gore, K. (2008). Adjusted actuarial assessment of sex offenders: The impact of clinical overrides on predictive accuracy. *Dissertation Abstracts International: Section B: The Sciences and Engineering, 68*(7B), 4824.

Grann, M., Belfrage, H., & Tengstrom, A. (2000). Actuarial assessment of risk for violence: Predictive validity of the VRAG and the historical part of the HCR-20. *Criminal Justice and Behavior, 27*, 97–114.

Grann, M., & Långström, N. (2007). Actuarial assessment of violence risk: To weigh or not to weigh? *Criminal Justice and Behavior, 34*, 22–36. http://dx.doi.org/10.1177/0093854806290250

Grann, M., & Wedin, I. (2002). Risk factors for recidivism among spousal assault and spousal homicide offenders. *Psychology, Crime & Law, 8*, 5–23.

Gray, N., Taylor, J., & Snowden, R. (2011). Predicting violence using structured professional judgment inpatients with different mental and behavioral disorders. *Psychiatry Research, 187*, 248–253.

Grove, W., & Meehl, P. (1996). Comparative efficiency of informal (subjective, impressionistic) and formal (mechanical, algorithmic) prediction procedures: The clinical-statistical controversy. *Psychology, Public Policy, & Law, 2*, 293–323.

Grove, W., Zald, D., Lebow, B., Snitz, B., & Nelson, C. (2000). Clinical versus mechanical prediction: A meta-analysis. *Psychological Assessment, 12*, 19–30.

Guy, L., Douglas, K. S., & Hendry, M. (2010). The role of psychopathic personality disorder in violence risk assessments using the HCR-20. *Journal of Personality Disorders, 24*, 551–580.

Hanson, R. K., & Morton-Bourgon, K. E. (2009). The accuracy of recidivism risk assessment for sexual offenders: A meta-analysis of 118 prediction studies. *Psychological Assessment, 21*, 1–21.

Hanson, R. K., Morton-Bourgon, K. E., & Harris, A. (2003). Sexual offender recidivism risk: What we know and what we need to know. *Annals of the New York Academy of Sciences, 989*, 154–166.

Hare, R. (1991). *The Hare Psychopathy Checklist-revised.* Toronto, ON: Multi-Health Systems.

Hare, R. (2003). *The Hare Psychopathy Checklist-revised* (2nd ed.). Toronto, ON: Multi-Health Systems.

Harris, G. T., & Rice, M. E. (2007). Characterizing the value of actuarial violence risk assessments. *Criminal Justice and Behavior, 34*, 1638–1658.

Harris, G. T., & Rice, M. E. (2013). Bayes and base rates: What is an informative prior for actuarial violence risk assessment? *Behavioral Sciences and the Law, 31*, 103–124.

Harris, G. T., & Rice, M. E. (2015). Progress in violence risk assessment and communication: Hypothesis versus evidence. *Behavioral Sciences and the Law, 33*, 128–145.

Harris, G. T., Rice, M., & Cormier, C. (2002). Prospective replication of the "violence risk appraisal guide" in predicting violent recidivism among forensic patients. *Law and Human Behavior, 26*, 377–394.

Harris, P. (2006). What community supervision officers need to know about actuarial risk assessment and clinical judgment. *Federal Probation, 70*, 8–14.

Hart, S. (2009). Evidence-based assessment of risk for sexual violence. *Chapman Journal of Criminal Justice, 1*, 143–165.

Hart, S. D., & Cooke, D. (2013). Another look at the (im-)precision of individual risk estimates made using actuarial risk assessment instruments. *Behavioral Sciences and the Law, 31*, 81–102.

Hart, S. D., Douglas, K. S., & Guy, L. S. (2017). The structured professional judgment approach to violence risk assessment: Origins, nature, and advances. In M. Rettenberger & L. Craig (Series Eds.) & D. Boer (Vol. Ed.), *The Wiley-Blackwell handbook on the assessment, treatment and theories of sexual offending: Volume 1. Assessment* (pp. 643–666). Oxford: Wiley-Blackwell.

Hart, S. D., Michie, C., & Cooke, D. (2007). Precision of actuarial risk assessment instruments: Evaluating the "margins of error" of group versus individual predictions of violence. *British Journal of Psychiatry, 190*(Suppl. 49), s60–s65.

Heilbrun, K. (1997). Prediction versus management models relevant to risk assessment: The importance of legal context. *Law and Human Behavior, 21,* 347–359.

Heilbrun, K. (2001). *Principles of forensic mental health assessment.* New York: Kluwer Academic, Plenum Press.

Heilbrun, K. (2009). *Evaluation for risk of violence in adults.* New York: Oxford University Press.

Heilbrun, K., Douglas, K., & Yasuhara, K. (2009). Violence risk assessment: Core controversies. In J. Skeem, K. Douglas, & S. Lilienfeld (Eds.), *Psychological science in the courtroom: Controversies and consensus* (pp. 333–357). New York: Guilford Press.

Heilbrun, K., Rogers, R., & Otto, R. (2002). Forensic assessment: Current status and future directions. In J. Ogloff (Ed.), *Psychology and law: Reviewing the discipline* (pp. 120–147). New York: Kluwer Academic, Plenum Press.

Ho, R. M., Cheung, H. H., Lai, T. T., Tam, V. F., Yan, C. K., Chan, W. L., & Yuen, K. K. (2015). Use of the historical, clinical, risk management-20 to assess the risk of violence by discharged psychiatric patients. *Hong Kong Medical Journal, 21,* 45–47.

Hogan, N. R., & Olver, M. E. (2016). Assessing risk for aggression in forensic psychiatric inpatients: An examination of five measures. *Law and Human Behavior, 40,* 233–243.

Hogan, N. R., & Olver, M. E. (2019). Static and dynamic assessment of violence risk among discharged forensic patients. *Criminal Justice and Behavior, 46,* 923–928.

Hoge, R., & Andrews, D. (2002). *The youth level of service/case management inventory manual and scoring key.* Toronto, ON: Multi-Health Systems.

Imrey, P. B., & Dawid, A. P. (2015). A commentary on statistical assessment of violence recidivism risk. *Statistics and Public Policy, 2,* 1–18.

Jovanović, A. A., Toševski, D. L., Ivković, M., Damjanović, A., & Gašić, M. J. (2009). Predicting violence in veterans with posttraumatic stress disorder. *Vojnosanitetski Pregled: Military Medical & Pharmaceutical Journal of Serbia & Montenegro, 66,* 13–21.

Kroner, D., Mills, J., & Reddon, J. (2005). A coffee can, factor analysis, and prediction of antisocial behavior: The structure of criminal risk. *International Journal of Law and Psychiatry, 28,* 360–374.

Kropp, P. R., & Hart, S. D. (2000). The spousal assault risk assessment (SARA) guide: Reliability and validity in adult male offenders. *Law and Human Behavior, 24,* 101–118.

Kropp, P. R., & Hart, S. D. (2015). *Spousal assault risk assessment guide user's manual* (3rd ed.). Vancouver, BC: Protect International Risk and Safety Services, Inc.

Kropp, P., Hart, S., & Lyon, D. (2002). Risk assessment of stalkers: Some problems and possible solutions. *Criminal Justice and Behavior, 29,* 590–616.

Langton, C. M., Hogue, T. E., Daffern, M., Mannion, A., & Howells, K. (2009). Prediction of institutional aggression among personality disordered forensic patients using actuarial and structured clinical risk assessment tools: Prospective evaluation of the HCR-20, VRS, static-99, and risk matrix 2000. *Psychology, Crime & Law, 15,* 635–659.

Leistico, A., Salekin, R., DeCosta, J., & Rogers, R. (2008). A large-scale meta-analysis relating the Hare measures of psychopathy to antisocial conduct. *Law and Human Behavior, 32,* 28–45.

Lodewijks, H. P. B., de Ruiter, C., & Doreleijers, T. A. H. (2008). Gender differences in violent outcome and risk assessment in adolescent offenders after residential treatment. *International Journal of Forensic Mental Health, 7,* 133–146.

Lodewijks, H. P. B., Doreleijers, T. A. H., & de Ruiter, C. (2008). SAVRY risk assessment in relation to sentencing and subsequent recidivism in a Dutch sample of violent juvenile offenders. *Criminal Justice and Behavior, 35,* 696–709.

Lodewijks, H. P. B., Doreleijers, T. A. H., de Ruiter, C., & Borum, R. (2008). Predictive validity of the structured assessment of violence in youth (SAVRY) during residential treatment. *International Journal of Law and Psychiatry, 31,* 263–271.

Manchak, S. M., Skeem, J. L., Douglas, K. S., & Siranosian, M. (2009). Does gender moderate the predictive utility of the level of service inventory-revised (ISA-R) for serious violent offenders? *Criminal Justice and Behavior, 36,* 425–442.

Marczyk, G., Heilbrun, K., Lander, T., & DeMatteo, D. (2003). Predicting juvenile recidivism with the PCL: YV, MAYSI, and YLS/CMI. *International Journal of Forensic Mental Health, 2,* 7–18.

McGowan, M. (2007). The predictive validity of violence risk assessment within educational settings. *Dissertation Abstracts International: Section A: Humanities and Social Sciences, 68*(3A), 876.

Melton, G., Petrila, J., Poythress, N., Slobogin, C., Otto, R., Mossman, D., & Condie, L. (2018). *Psychological evaluations for the courts: A handbook for mental health professionals and lawyers* (4th ed.). New York: Guilford Press.

Meyers, J. R., & Schmidt, F. (2008). Predictive validity of the structured assessment for violence risk in youth (SAVRY) with juvenile offenders. *Criminal Justice and Behavior, 35*, 344–355.

Michel, S., Riaz, M., Webster, C., Hart, S., Levander, S., Muller-Isberner, R., . . . Hodgins, S. (2013). Using the HCR-20 to predict aggressive behavior among men with schizophrenia living in the community: Accuracy of prediction, general and forensic settings, and dynamic risk factors. *International Journal of Forensic Mental Health, 12*, 1–13. doi:10.1080/14999013.2012.760182

Monahan, J., & Skeem, J. (2016). Risk assessment in criminal sentencing. *Annual Review of Clinical Psychology, 12*, 489–513.

Monahan, J., Steadman, H., Appelbaum, P., Grisso, T., Mulvey, E., Roth, L., . . . Silver, E. (2005). *Classification of Violence Risk: Professional manual.* Lutz, FL: PAR.

Monahan, J., Steadman, H., Robbins, P. C., Appelbaum, P., Banks, S., Grisso, T., . . . Silver, E. (2005). Prospective validation of the multiple iterative classification tree model of violence risk assessment. *Psychiatric Services, 56*, 810–815.

Monahan, J., Steadman, H., Silver, E., Appelbaum, P., Robbins, P. C., Mulvey, E., . . . Banks, S. (2001). *Rethinking risk assessment: The MacArthur study of mental disorder and violence.* New York: Oxford University Press.

Mossman, D. (1994). Assessing predictions of violence: Being accurate about accuracy. *Journal of Consulting and Clinical Psychology, 62*, 783–792.

Mossman, D. (2007). Avoiding errors about "margins of error". *British Journal of Psychiatry, 191*, 561.

Mossman, D. (2015). From group data to useful probabilities: The relevance of actuarial risk assessment in individual instances. *Journal of the American Academy of Psychiatry and the Law, 43*, 93–102.

Neal, T. M., Miller, S. L., & Shealy, R. C. (2015). A field study of a comprehensive violence risk assessment battery. *Criminal Justice and Behavior, 42*, 952–968.

Neves, A. C., Goncalves, R. A., & Palma-Oliveira, J. M. (2011). Assessing risk for violent and general recidivism: A study of the HCR-20 and the PCL-R with a non-clinical sample of Portuguese offenders. *International Journal of Forensic Mental Health, 10*, 137–149.

Nonstad, K., Nesset, M. B., Kroppan, E., Pedersen, T. W., Nöttestad, J. A., Almvik, R., & Palmstierna, T. (2010). Predictive validity and other psychometric properties of the short-term assessment of risk and treatability (START) in a Norwegian high secure hospital. *International Journal of Forensic Mental Health, 9*, 294–299.

Ogloff, J., & Daffern, M. (2006). The dynamic appraisal of situational aggression: An instrument to assess risk for imminent aggression in psychiatric inpatients. *Behavioral Sciences and the Law, 24*, 799–813.

Olver, M. E., Stockdale, K. C., & Wormith, J. S. (2009). Risk assessment with young offenders: A meta-analysis of three assessment measures. *Criminal Justice and Behavior, 36*(4), 329–353.

Olver, M., & Wong, S. (2011). A comparison of static and dynamic assessment of sexual offender risk and need in a treatment context. *Criminal Justice and Behavior, 38*, 113–126.

O'Shea, L., Picchioni, M., Mason, F., Sugarman, P., & Dickens, G. (2014). Differential predictive validity of the Historical, Clinical and Risk Management Scales (HCR–20) for inpatient aggression. *Psychiatry Research, 220*, 669–678.

O'Shea, L. E., Thaker, D., Picchioni, M. M., Mason, F. L., Knight, C., & Dickens, G. L. (2016). Predictive validity of the HCR-20 for violent and non-violent sexual behaviour in a secure mental health service. *Criminal Behaviour and Mental Health, 26*, 366–379. doi:10.1002/cbm.1967

Otto, R. K. (2000). Assessing and managing violence risk in outpatient settings. *Journal of Clinical Psychology, 56*, 1239–1262.

Pedersen, L., Rasmussen, K., & Elsass, P. (2010). Risk assessment: The value of structured professional judgments. *International Journal of Forensic Mental Health, 9*, 74–81.

Penney, S. R., Lee, Z., & Moretti, M. M. (2010). Gender differences in risk factors for violence: An examination of the predictive validity of the structured assessment of violence risk in youth. *Aggressive Behavior, 36*, 390–404.

Penney, S. R., Marshall, L. A., & Simpson, A. I. F. (2016). The assessment of dynamic risk among forensic psychiatric patients transitioning to the community. *Law and Human Behavior, 40*, 374–386.

Quinsey, V., Harris, G., Rice, M., & Cormier, C. (1998). *Violent offenders: Appraising and managing risk*. Washington, DC: American Psychological Association.

Quinsey, V., Harris, G., Rice, M., & Cormier, C. (2005). *Violent offenders: Appraising and managing risk* (2nd ed.). Washington, DC: American Psychological Association.

Rajlic, G., & Gretton, H. (2010). An examination of two sexual recidivism risk measures in adolescent offenders. *Criminal Justice & Behavior, 37*, 1066–1085. doi:10.1177/0093854810376354

Sada, A., Robles-García, R., Martínez-López, N., Hernández-Ramírez, R., Tovilla-Zarate, C. A., López-Munguía, F., . . . Fresán, A. (2016). Assessing the reliability, predictive and construct validity of historical, clinical and risk management-20 (HCR-20) in Mexican psychiatric inpatients. *Nordic Journal of Psychiatry, 70*, 1–6.

Schaap, G., Lammers, S., & de Vogel, V. (2009). Risk assessment in female forensic psychiatric patients: A quasi-prospective study into the validity of the HCR-20 and PCL-R. *The Journal of Forensic Psychiatry & Psychology, 20*, 354–365.

Schmidt, F., Campbell, M., & Houlding, C. (2011). Comparative analyses of the YLS/CMI, SAVRY, and PCL-YV in adolescent offenders: A 10-year follow-up into adulthood. *Youth Violence and Juvenile Justice, 9*, 23–42.

Scurich, N., & Krauss, D. (2013). The effect of adjusted actuarial risk assessment on mock-jurors' decisions in a sexual predator commitment proceeding. *Jurimetrics, 53*, 395–413.

Silver, E. (2001). *Mental illness and violence: The importance of neighborhood context*. El Paso, TX: LFB Scholarly Publishing.

Singh, J. P., Grann, M., & Fazel, S. A. (2011). A comparative study of violence risk assessment tools: A systematic review and metaregression analysis of 68 studies involving 25,980 participants. *Clinical Psychology Review, 31*, 499–513.

Sjöstedt, G., & Långström, N. (2002). Assessment of risk for criminal recidivism among rapists: A comparison of four different measures. *Psychology, Crime and Law, 8*, 25–40.

Skeem, J., Schubert, C., Odgers, C., Mulvey, E., Gardner, W., & Lidz, W. (2006). Psychiatric symptoms and community violence among high-risk patients: A test of the relationship at the weekly level. *Journal of Consulting and Clinical Psychology, 74*, 967–979.

Smith, P. H., Cullen, E. T., & Latessa, E. J. (2009). Can 14,737 women be wrong? A meta-analysis of the LSI-R and recidivism for female offenders. *Criminology and Public Policy, 8*(1), 1601–1626.

Steadman, H. (1982). A situational approach to violence. *International Journal of Law and Psychiatry, 5*, 171–186.

Steadman, H., Mulvey, E., Monahan, J., Robbins, P. C., Appelbaum, P., Grisso, T., . . . Silver, E. (1998). Violence by people discharged from acute psychiatric facilities and by others in the same neighborhoods. *Archives of General Psychiatry, 55*, 393–401.

Strub, D. S., Douglas, K. S., & Nicholls, T. L. (2014). The validity of version 3 of the HCR-20 violence risk assessment scheme amongst offenders and civil psychiatric patients. *International Journal of Forensic Mental Health, 13*, 148–159.

van den Brink, R. H. S., Hooijschuur, A., van Os, T. W. D. P., Savenije, W., & Wiersma, D. (2010). Routine violence risk assessment in community forensic mental healthcare. *Behavioral Sciences & the Law, 28*, 396–410.

Verbrugge, H. M., Goodman-Delahunty, J., & Frize, M. C. J. (2011). Risk assessment in intellectually disabled offenders: Validation of the suggested ID supplement to the HCR-20. *International Journal of Forensic Mental Health, 10*, 83–91.

Viljoen, J., Mordell, S., & Beneteau, J. (2012). Prediction of adolescent sexual reoffending: A meta-analysis of the J-SOAP-II, ERASOR, J-SORRAT-II, and static-99. *Law and Human Behavior, 36*, 423–438.

Viljoen, S., Nicholls, T. L., Roesch, R., Gagnon, N., Douglas, K., & Brink, J. (2016). Exploring gender differences in the utility of strength-based risk assessment measures. *International Journal of Forensic Mental Health, 15*, 1–15.

Viljoen, J. L., Scalora, M., Cuadra, L., Bader, S., Chávez, V., Ullman, D., & Lawrence, L. (2008). Assessing risk for violence in adolescents who have sexually offended: A comparison of the J-SOAP-II, J-SORRAT-II, and SAVRY. *Criminal Justice and Behavior, 35*, 5–23.

Vincent, G. M., Chapman, J., & Cook, N. (2011). Predictive validity of the SAVRY, racial differences, and the contribution of needs factors. *Criminal Justice and Behavior, 38*, 42–62.

Vitacco, M., Gonsalves, V., Tomony, J., Smith, B., & Lishner, D. (2012). Can standardized measures of risk predict inpatient violence? Combining static and dynamic variables to improve accuracy. *Criminal Justice and Behavior, 39*, 589–606.

Walters, G. (2003). Predicting criminal justice outcomes with the psychopathy checklist and lifestyle criminality screening form: A meta-analytic comparison. *Behavioral Sciences & the Law, 21*, 89–102.

Walters, G., White, T., & Denney, D. (1991). The lifestyle criminality screening form: Preliminary data. *Criminal Justice and Behavior, 18*, 406–418.

Webster, C., Douglas, K., Eaves, D., & Hart, S. (1997). *HCR-20. Assessing risk for violence, version 2*. Burnaby, BC: Simon Fraser University and Forensic Psychiatric Services Commission of British Columbia.

Webster, C., Martin, M., Brink, J., Nicholls, T., & Desmarais, S. (2009). *Short-term assessment of risk and treatability (START): Clinical guide for evaluation risk and recovery* (Version 1.1). Hamilton, ON: St. Joseph's Healthcare.

Welsh, E., Bader, S., & Evans, S. E. (2013). Situational variables related to aggression in institutional settings. *Aggression and Violent Behavior, 18*, 792–796.

Welsh, J., Schmidt, F., McKinnon, L., Chattha, H., & Meyers, J. (2008). A comparative study of adolescent risk assessment instruments: Predictive and incremental validity. *Assessment, 15*, 104–115.

Wilson, C., Desmarais, S., Nicholls, T., Hart, S., & Brink, J. (2013). Predictive validity of dynamic factors: Assessing violence risk in forensic psychiatric inpatients. *Law and Human Behavior, 37*, 377–388. doi:10.1037/lhb0000025

Yang, M., Wong, S., & Coid, J. (2010). The efficacy of violence prediction: A meta-analytic comparison of nine risk assessment tools. *Psychological Bulletin, 136*, 740–767.

Chapter 2

The Use of Measures of Psychopathy in Violence Risk Assessment

David DeMatteo, Emily Haney-Caron, Elyse Mowle, and John F. Edens

Introduction and Description of the PCL Measures

Current conceptualizations of psychopathy stem largely from Cleckley's (1941) seminal work, *The Mask of Sanity*, and the work of others around that time, including Karpman's (1946, 1948) descriptions of idiopathic versus symptomatic subtypes of psychopathy. Changing conceptualizations of psychopathy are reflected in the various iterations of the American Psychiatric Association's (APA) *Diagnostic and Statistical Manual of Mental Disorders* (DSM). The first two DSMs largely reflect Cleckley's conceptualization of the disorder, termed "sociopathic personality disturbance" in the first DSM (APA, 1952) and "personality disturbance, antisocial type" in DSM-II (APA, 1968). In DSM-III (APA, 1980), the disorder was renamed "antisocial personality disorder" and moved away from the personality traits described by Cleckley and toward more behaviorally based characteristics. Later DSMs made relatively minor changes to the primarily behaviorally oriented diagnostic features and continued to focus most heavily on criminal activity and other forms of antisocial conduct as important features. The APD criteria in DSM-5 were identical to those used in DSM-IV, and DSM-5 indicates that the disorder includes features "commonly included in traditional conceptions of psychopathy" (APA, 2013, p. 660). Additionally, one major change in the diagnosis of Conduct Disorder (CD) in the DSM-5 was the inclusion of a new specifier labeled "Limited Prosocial Emotions." This specifier can be applied to children and adolescents with CD who also show psychopathic-like characteristics (i.e., lack of remorse or guilt, callousness, shallow affect, and/or lack of concern about performance) and in many respects conceptually overlaps with the item content of Factor 1 of the Psychopathy Checklist: Youth Version (PCL:YV; Forth, Kosson, & Hare, 2003; described later in this chapter).

Perhaps in part because of dissatisfaction with DSM conceptualizations of psychopathy since DSM-III, since the 1980s the construct of psychopathy has been operationalized in many research and clinical contexts using instruments developed by Robert Hare and colleagues. These instruments include the Psychopathy Checklist (PCL; Hare, 1980), Psychopathy Checklist-Revised (PCL-R; Hare, 1991, 2003), Psychopathy Checklist: Screening Version (PCL:SV; Hart, Cox, & Hare, 1995), and the Psychopathy Checklist: Youth Version (PCL:YV; Forth et al., 2003).

In contrast to recent DSM formulations of APD, the PCL measures place some emphasis on characteristics not overtly tied to antisocial conduct, such as interpersonal and affective features thought by many to be more representative of the disorder. There is substantial empirical evidence that the PCL-R operationalizes a construct important within the criminal justice system, but there are significant debates (e.g., Skeem & Cooke, 2010a) about the extent to which the PCL-R adequately operationalizes the core features of psychopathy. Due to space limitations, this chapter focuses primarily on PCL research relevant to violence risk assessment (for broader reviews, see Hare, 2003; Patrick, 2018; Richards et al., 2016; Skeem & Cooke, 2010a).

PCL-R and PCL:SV

The PCL-R is a 20-item construct rating scale used in research and clinical settings to assess psychopathy among adults. Standard administration involves a semi-structured interview and review of collateral data, although scoring the PCL-R without the interview is common in research settings. The PCL:SV is a 12-item tool derived from the PCL-R. PCL:SV Total scores correlate highly with PCL-R Total scores in offenders with and without intellectual disabilities (Pouls & Jeandarme, 2014), at least when used with forensic/correctional samples and scored based on the same information. Examiners rate each PCL item on a 3-point scale based on the degree to which the personality/behavior of the examinee matches the item description in the manual—0 (item does not apply to the individual), 1 (item applies to a certain extent), or 2 (item applies)—which results in scores ranging from 0 to 40 for the PCL-R (and 0 to 24 for the PCL:SV).

The PCL-R was normed on offender and forensic psychiatric samples but has been used with other populations, including community samples (e.g., DeMatteo, Heilbrun, & Marczyk, 2005, 2006; McGregor, Castle, & Dolan, 2012). Moreover, a large body of research suggests that the descriptive properties and correlates of the PCL-R are similar for male and female offenders (e.g., Gray & Snowden, 2016; see Hare, 2003, for a relevant review). Though some research found differences in item loadings and factor structure of the PCL-R for men and women (Dolan & Völlm, 2009), at least one study found adequate fit for both three- and four-factor models (Warren et al., 2003). However, psychopathic traits in women may be less predictive of violent recidivism (Weizmann-Henelius, Virkkunen, Gammelgård, Eronen, & Putkonen, 2015), though meta-analyses have produced somewhat inconsistent and conflicting results (Edens, Campbell, & Weir, 2007; Leistico, Salekin, DeCosta, & Rogers, 2008).

Research generally suggests PCL-R scores in the aggregate are not unduly influenced by the examinee's race or ethnicity (Skeem, Edens, Camp, & Colwell, 2004), with relatively similar descriptive properties and correlates of the PCL-R for Caucasian, African American, and Hispanic/Latino populations (Sullivan, Abramowitz, Lopez, & Kosson, 2006; Vachon, Lynam, Loeber, & Stouthamer-Loeber, 2012). That said, this research is limited (but growing), and at least one study found differences in the PCL-R's ability to predict violence among African American and Latino inmates relative to European American inmates (Walsh, 2013), and some have called for caution in using the PCL-R with diverse populations (e.g., Leistico et al., 2008). The predictive validity of PCL measures with various racial and ethnic groups is discussed in greater detail later in this chapter.

Early exploratory factor analyses of the PCL supported a two-factor solution, with Factor 1 primarily reflecting the interpersonal and affective characteristics of psychopathy and Factor 2 primarily reflecting antisocial and socially deviant characteristics (Harpur, Hare, & Hakstian, 1989). Later researchers proposed three-factor (e.g., Cooke & Michie, 2001; Hall, Benning, & Patrick, 2004) and four-factor models (e.g., Forth et al., 2003; Vitacco, Rogers, Neumann, Harrison, & Vincent, 2005). In early work, Cooke and Michie (2001) proposed a hierarchical three-factor model—reflecting interpersonal, affective, and lifestyle features—based on a confirmatory factor analysis of 13 PCL-R items. Studies replicated this three-factor model (e.g., Cooke, Michie, Hart, & Clark, 2004), but some researchers argue the superiority of a four-factor model that retains items explicitly tied to criminal history (e.g., Hare, 2003; Neumann, Hare, & Johansson, 2013). In recent years, the PCL-R has adopted the four-factor model that retains the antisocial factor (Hare, 2016). The first-order factors map onto a model consistent with the traditional two-factor model (Hare & Neumann, 2008); Factor 1 contains Interpersonal and Affective Factors and Factor 2 subsumes Lifestyle and Antisocial Factors.

Proponents of the three-factor model argue criminal behavior is "causally downstream" from the core features of the disorder and many factors other than psychopathy may cause such conduct, while advocates of the four-factor model assert antisocial behavior is part of the "core" of psychopathy (see Cooke et al., 2004). The relevance of a history of antisocial conduct to the core construct of psychopathy cannot be determined by cross-sectional factor-analytic methods, which examine patterns of relationships among variables rather than their causal relevance to the disorder itself (Edens, Skeem, & Kennealy, 2009; Skeem & Cooke, 2010a). Newer statistical techniques, such as network analysis, may inform this debate and suggest that nonspecific antisocial behavior may be less central than some have argued (Verschuere et al., 2018).

The legal system is primarily interested in psychopathy as a categorical construct—an offender is or is not a psychopath—due to the need to make discrete placement decisions, but there is no naturally occurring diagnostic cutoff for categorizing individuals as "psychopaths" given that almost all taxometric studies using appropriate statistical methods indicate that PCL scores represent an underlying dimensional construct rather than a latent dichotomy (e.g., Edens, Marcus, Lilienfeld, & Poythress, 2006; Guay, Ruscio, Hare, & Knight, 2007; Walters, 2014a; Walters, Marcus, Edens, Knight, & Sanford, 2011). However, PCL Total scores of 30 and above are often used somewhat arbitrarily to categorize examinees into "psychopath/non-psychopath" groups (DeMatteo et al., 2014b), and there is precedent for using lower cutoff scores in research settings (e.g., Serin, 1996), or in European countries (e.g., Cooke & Michie, 1999). Notably, a score of 30 or greater can be achieved through 14 million unique response combinations (Balsis, Busch, Wilfong, Newman, & Edens, 2017).

PCL:YV

The PCL:YV has the same administration procedures, scoring, and number of items as the PCL-R. The PCL:YV "is a downward extension of the PCL-R" to adolescents that assesses similar content domains (interpersonal, affective, antisocial, and behavioral features) (Forth et al., 2003, p. 2), but some PCL-R items (e.g., many short-term marital relationships) were modified on the PCL:YV to permit assessment of these characteristics among adolescents (Forth et al., 2003). The PCL:YV is used with adolescents aged 12 to 18 in applied and research contexts. Although early research suggested the four-factor model of psychopathy developed with the PCL-R is a good fit with the PCL:YV (Forth et al., 2003; Vitacco et al., 2005), later research found the three- and four-factor models provided a similar fit (Jones, Cauffman, Miller, & Mulvey, 2006), including with adolescent girls (Kosson et al., 2013). The PCL:YV is a dimensional measure of psychopathy, and the manual does not provide categorical cut scores.

The PCL:YV's reliability and predictive validity are consistent with adult PCL measures (Olver & Stockdale, 2010), but some research suggests the PCL:YV has lower concurrent and predictive validity with adolescent females (Schmidt, McKinnon, Chattha, & Brownlee, 2006; Vincent, Odgers, McCormick, & Corrado, 2008). Further, an item response theory study of the PCL:YV found that 4 of the 20 items function differently for boys and girls (Tsang et al., 2015). The PCL:YV demonstrates concurrent validity in Caucasian and Indigenous Canadian groups (Schmidt et al., 2006), but black youth have significantly (albeit only modestly) higher PCL:YV scores than white youth (McCoy & Edens, 2006).

Predicting Adverse Outcomes With the PCL Measures

The PCL measures assess for psychopathy, not violence risk, but there is great interest in psychopathy and the PCL measures because PCL Total scores are *prospectively* associated with various forms of antisocial conduct, including violent and nonviolent recidivism among released offenders (e.g., Edens et al., 2007; Leistico et al., 2008). The PCL measures are also used to inform clinical judgments of violence risk in U.S. and Canadian courts (DeMatteo & Edens, 2006; DeMatteo,

Murrie, Edens, & Lankford, 2019; DeMatteo et al., 2014b). For example, in U.S. capital cases, prosecution-retained experts have offered testimony about violence risk based, in part, on PCL-R scores (DeMatteo et al., 2014b; see DeMatteo et al., 2020). In Canada, the PCL measures are widely used to inform risk assessment in the federal penal system, and they may be used to help justify indeterminate commitment in some contexts (Gagnon, Douglas, & DeMatteo, 2007). Elevated PCL-R scores have been used alongside other indicators to classify high-risk offenders with "dangerous and severe personality" disorders in the United Kingdom (Howard, Khalifa, Duggan, & Lumsden, 2012).

The PCL-R has been incorporated into two actuarial risk assessment instruments—Violence Risk Appraisal Guide (VRAG; Quinsey, Harris, Rice, & Cormier, 2006) and Sex Offender Risk Appraisal Guide (SORAG; Quinsey et al., 2006)—and three structured professional judgment instruments—Historical-Clinical-Risk Management-20, Version 2 (HCR-20 V3; Webster, Douglas, Eaves, & Hart, 1997; in the most recent HCR-20 [Version 3, Douglas et al., 2014], use of the PCL-R/SV is optional), Sexual Violence Risk-20 (SVR-20; Boer, Hart, Kropp, & Webster, 1997), and Risk for Sexual Violence Protocol (RSVP; Hart et al., 2003). Some large-scale studies and meta-analyses suggest PCL measures *in isolation* function as well as or better than elaborate risk assessment tools such as the VRAG and HCR-20 (e.g., Campbell, French, & Gendreau, 2009; Yang, Wong, & Coid, 2010), but other research suggests these measures may improve on the predictive validity of the PCL measures alone (e.g., Gendreau, Coggin, & Smith, 2002) and other research indicates some structured professional judgment risk assessment tools perform as well without the PCL-R (e.g., Guy, Douglas, & Hendry, 2010).

These results are not surprising given that PCL conceptualizations of psychopathy are heavily weighted towards a history of social deviance and criminality (see Scott, 2014; Skeem & Cooke, 2010a, 2010b), which would be expected to be modestly to moderately predictive of criminal behavior. Although the PCL was informed by the personality criteria for psychopathy espoused by Cleckley and others (see Patrick, 2006, for an alternate perspective), it places considerable weight on socially deviant behaviors, as evidenced by ongoing debates concerning the theoretical and etiological significance of the Antisocial facet identified in some (e.g., Forth et al., 2003; Vitacco et al., 2005) but not all (e.g., Cooke & Michie, 2001) factor analyses of PCL measures. These debates focus on whether antisocial conduct is a core component of the disorder or whether it is simply "causally downstream" as a natural consequence of psychopathic traits. If the Antisocial facet is not part of the "core" of the *construct* of psychopathy, and if the predictive validity of the PCL *measures* is primarily the result of their operationalization of "generic" social deviance (i.e., propensities toward antisocial behavior not specific to psychopathy), then a strong argument could be made that it is not psychopathy per se that is important for violence risk assessment (Edens et al., 2009; Skeem & Cooke, 2010a). That Factor 1 traits in isolation are significantly less relevant to violence risk than Factor 2 traits and other risk assessment instrument scores (Yang et al., 2010) bolsters concerns that psychopathy may be less important to risk assessment than a well-validated assessment of criminogenic background variables.

In applied settings, examiners appear unconcerned with debates regarding the construct of psychopathy and instead focus on the utility of PCL measures. Of note, attributing psychopathic traits to offenders can profoundly impact perceptions of their dangerousness and views on appropriate legal dispositions (see Berryessa & Wohlstetter, 2019; Edens, Petrila, & Kelley, 2018; Kelley, Edens, Mowle, Penson, & Rulseh, 2019, for discussion of the stigmatizing effects of psychopathy). If these traits are less central to identifying higher-risk individuals, examiners should eschew focusing on them when interpreting risk assessment data.

A key question relating to use of PCL measures in the legal system is what qualifications, training, and experience are needed before an examiner is "qualified" to use these measures. As noted by Edens et al. (2018), the question of what constitutes "adequate" training on the PCL measures raises ethical issues regarding examiner competence and certification and legal questions regarding the recognition of expert witnesses. According to the APA's (2010) *Ethical Principles of Psychologists and Code of Conduct*, "competence" is based on relevant "education, training, supervised experience, consultation, study, or professional experience" (p. 4), but the ethics code does not provide guidelines regarding minimum thresholds in these areas.

The PCL-R manual suggests minimum qualifications to use the PCL in clinical contexts, including an advanced degree (social, medical, or behavioral sciences) and completion of graduate courses in psychometrics and psychopathology (Hare, 2003). Although Hare (2003) asserted he has "no professional or legal authority to determine who can and cannot use the PCL-R" (p. 16), Edens et al. (2018) noted that the suggested qualifications are given considerable weight when evaluating examiner competence to administer, score, and interpret the instrument.

Evaluator competence is significant because growing evidence suggests that some examiners provide highly suspect PCL ratings in judicial contexts (e.g., DeMatteo et al., 2014a, 2014b; Edens, 2006; Edens, Cox, Smith, DeMatteo, & Sörman, 2015; Edens & Vincent, 2008; Murrie et al., 2009; Sturup et al., 2014). Whether these PCL ratings reflect questionable competence or some other, more pernicious, influence (e.g., bias) is unclear—although a growing body of research (e.g., Murrie et al., 2009) raises the specter of allegiance effects (i.e., a tendency for an evaluator to draw conclusions favorable to the retaining party).

Method of and Rationale for Development of the PCL Measures

In the following sections, we review the evidence concerning the reliability and validity of the PCL measures, focusing mostly on the PCL-R and PCL:YV. Because latent variable research that statistically controls for various forms of measurement error in psychopathy scores ignores the real-world significance of such error on clinical and forensic decision-making, we focus primarily on research findings that examine the types of raw scores that would be used in real-world applications of these instruments.

Reliability

The manual for the second edition of the PCL-R presents classical test theory indices of reliability for large samples of criminal offenders and forensic psychiatric patients (Hare, 2003). PCL-R data from North American samples were obtained from 6,500+ male and female criminal offenders and 1,200+ male forensic psychiatric patients using the standard administration procedure, and from 2,500+ male criminal offenders and 400+ male forensic psychiatric patients using file-review-only administration. The PCL:SV manual reports reliability data from samples of female and male inmates ($N = 149$), male and female forensic psychiatric outpatients and inpatients ($N = 120$), male and female patients in civil psychiatric settings ($N = 217$), and male and female undergraduates ($N = 100$) (Hart et al., 1995). The normative data are discussed in following sections (see Book, Clark, Forth, & Hare, 2006, for a review of PCL measure psychometric properties).

Internal Consistency

The PCL-R manual (Hare, 2003) reports corrected item-total correlations (r) based on standard administration. The mean correlation was .45 for male criminal offenders (.45 for file-review-only administration), .38 for male forensic psychiatric patients (.51 for file-review-only administration), and .40 for female criminal offenders.

Other measures of internal consistency were generally high (Hare, 2003). For the pooled samples using the standard administration procedure, Cronbach's alphas were .85 for male criminal offenders, .81 for male forensic psychiatric patients, and .82 for female criminal offenders, yielding a mean of .84 across the pooled samples (.87 for file-review-only administration) (Hare, 2003). For the pooled samples using the standard administration procedure, mean inter-item correlation coefficients were .23 for male criminal offenders, .19 for male forensic psychiatric patients, and .19 for female criminal offenders, yielding a mean of .22 across the pooled samples (.25 for file-review-only administration) (Hare, 2003).

Although limited, research suggests the PCL:YV demonstrates many desirable psychometric properties. Forth et al. (2003) reported Cronbach's alphas of .85 for institutionalized samples, .87 for probation samples, and .94 for clinic/community samples, and mean inter-item correlations of .23 among institutionalized samples, .25 among probation samples, and .43 among clinic/community samples. Campbell, Pulos, Hogan, and Murry (2005) reported a mean Cronbach's alpha of .85 for the PCL:YV based on $k = 18$ (published and unpublished) reliability estimates. More recent research by Bauer, Whitman, and Kosson (2011) explored the reliability of the PCL:YV when used with girls, and reported internal consistency similar to the normative sample, including Cronbach's alpha of .82 and corrected item-to-total correlations for each item of .19 or above.

The PCL:SV manual reports corrected item-total correlations of the PCL:SV items (r) for 11 samples, with all item-total correlations in the acceptable range ($\geq .40$) (Hart et al., 1995). Cronbach's alphas across samples averaged .84 (range .69–.91) for total scores across samples, Part 1 Cronbach's alphas had a weighted mean of .81 (range .58–.89) across samples, and Part 2 Cronbach's alphas had a weighted mean of .75 (range .66–.84) across samples (Hart et al., 1995). Weighted mean inter-item correlations were .32 for Total score, .42 for Part 1, and .35 for Part 2. Across six samples ($N = 1,655$) from the United States and United Kingdom, the PCL:SV had Cronbach's alpha and mean inter-item correlations, respectively, of .73, .48 for Interpersonal; .81, .59 for Affective; .65, .38 for Impulsive Lifestyle; and .65, .38 for Antisocial Behavior (Walters et al., 2007).

Although the PCL measures demonstrate relatively high levels of internal consistency, growing research suggests considerable heterogeneity among high scorers on these measures (Edens et al., 2009). Several cluster analyses of PCL scores demonstrate the existence of variants or subtypes of psychopathy (see Poythress & Skeem, 2006). Although an extensive review of these data is not possible here, it is clear that all "psychopaths" are not alike. Unfortunately, the implications of these putative subtypes for risk assessment purposes is largely unstudied (for informed speculation, see Skeem, Poythress, Edens, Lilienfeld, & Cale, 2003).

Interrater Reliability

Many studies report high levels of rater agreement for PCL-R scores (see Hare, 2003). According to the manual for the second edition of the PCL-R, the pooled ICC for male criminal offenders was .86 for a single rating (ICC_1) and .92 for the average of two ratings (ICC_2) (Hare, 2003). Also, ICC_1 was .88 and ICC_2 was .93 for male forensic psychiatric patients, and ICC_1 was .94 and ICC_2 was .97 for female criminal offenders. More recently, a study of interrater reliability among 280 raters who completed formal PCL-R training and scored six practice cases found low reliability for several individual items ($ICC_{A,1}$ values of .14–.82), at best marginal reliability (see Edens & Boccaccini, 2017; Nunnally & Bernstein, 1994)[1] for total scores ($ICC_{A,1} = .75$) and Factor 2 scores ($ICC_{A,1} = .78$), and even lower reliability for Factor 1 scores ($ICC_{A,1} = .65$) (Blais, Forth, & Hare, 2017). Ratings of cases with higher psychopathy had somewhat better reliability than cases with low or moderate psychopathy.

Recent studies have examined interrater reliability among clinicians in legal contexts. In one of the first field reliability studies, Murrie et al. (2009) compared PCL-R scores in 35 sexually violent predator (SVP) civil commitment trials in which opposing clinicians (one for the prosecution and one for the defense) reported PCL-R Total scores for the same individual. Differences in PCL-R Total scores from opposing clinicians were typically in a direction that supported the retaining party. The ICC for the PCL-R Total score from a single rater was .42, well below values reported in previous research and the PCL-R manual. The authors noted that "[l]ess than half of the variance in the data set of PCL-R scores could be attributed to the offender's true level of psychopathy as measured by the PCL-R" (Murrie et al., 2009, p. 37). As a follow-up, Boccaccini, Murrie, Rufino, and Gardner (2014) examined PCL-R scores of 558 sex offenders by 14 state-contracted evaluators and found ICCs of .32 for Total score, .23 for Factor 1, .25 for Factor 2, .18 for Facet 1, .13 for Facet 2, .24 for Facet 3, and .19 for Facet 4. A similar study, which examined SVP evaluations of 331 individuals conducted by psychologists and psychiatrists retained by the Department of Children and Families, reported single-rater ICCs of .60 for Total score, .48 for Factor 1, and .72 for Factor 2, noting a particularly low ICC (.39) for Facet 1 (Miller et al., 2012). Only one field study, which included Canadian sex offenders in federal custody, reported ICCs similar to those reported in the PCL-R manual: .90 for Total score, .78 for Factor 1, .90 for Factor 2, and .76 for Facet 1 (Ismail & Looman, 2018).

Two case law reviews examined the reliability of PCL-R scores in legal contexts. The first, reporting on 29 U.S. SVP appellate cases, reported a single-rater ICC of .58, with scores by prosecutor-retained experts significantly higher than those by defense experts (DeMatteo et al., 2014a). The second examined a wide range of Canadian criminal cases ($N = 102$) and reported a single-rater ICC of .59 for all cases (.66 for cases involving a sexual offense and .46 for nonsexual offense cases; Edens et al., 2015). This suggests the poor reliability reported for the PCL-R in SVP contexts likely extends to other forensic contexts as well (see Jeandarme et al., 2017). It is important to note that cases in which there is considerable disagreement in PCL-R scores may be more likely to be appealed, so the appellate cases reviewed by DeMatteo et al. (2014b) may not be representative of trial court cases.

The initial interrater reliability estimates for the PCL:YV were established on relatively small samples (Forth et al., 2003). The ICCs for two independent raters were .95 for probation samples ($n = 63$) and .96 for institutionalized ($n = 103$) and clinic/community samples ($n = 25$). Campbell et al. (2005) calculated a mean estimate of interrater reliability based on their review of published and unpublished studies examining PCL scores among youth, reporting a mean ICC estimate (based on PCL ratings made by two or more independent raters) of .91.

The PCL:SV manual reports interrater reliability for college students, inmates, and civil and forensic psychiatric patients; weighted mean single-rater ICCs were .84 for Total scores, .77 for Part 1 scores, and .82 for Part 2 scores; ICCs for averaged ratings were .92 for Total scores, .88 for Part 1 scores, and .91 for Part 2 scores; the weighted mean kappa for the diagnosis of psychopathy was .48 (Hart et al., 1995). PCL:SV interrater reliability data for six samples resulted in ICCs from .67 to .91 (Walters et al., 2007). These statistics are for evaluators coding the same videotaped interview or file; ICC scores from a field study likely would be lower.

Contributors to low interrater reliability vary across studies but include level of PCL-R training, with smaller differences among those who complete PCL-R training (Boccaccini et al., 2014; cf. Blais et al., 2017); evaluator allegiance (Boccaccini, Turner, Murrie, & Rufino, 2012); regression to the mean (Sturup et al., 2014); poor item operationalization (Rufino, Boccaccini, & Guy, 2011); and evaluator personality traits (Miller, Rufino, Boccaccini, Jackson, & Murrie, 2011). When considered alongside research reporting mostly poor interrater reliability in forensic settings, this research suggests the need for considerable caution in using/interpreting PCL scores in these contexts—notably Factor 1 scores, which seem particularly unreliable in adversarial settings. We are not aware of research on PCL:YV allegiance effects, but anecdotal accounts of considerable discrepancies raise similar concerns regarding its use in adversarial contexts (Edens & Vincent, 2008).

Validity

A well-developed body of research suggests the PCL-R's construct validity is supported by convergent/divergent correlations with theoretically relevant variables (see Patrick, 2018, for an overview). Although space limitations preclude a full discussion of the PCL-R's validity, PCL-R scores are related to several clinical, self-report, and demographic variables (see Book et al., 2006, and Hare, 2003, for reviews). PCL-R scores are strongly related to DSM diagnoses of Antisocial Personality Disorder (APD; Hart & Hare, 1989), prototypicality ratings of APD (Hart & Hare, 1989), and APD symptom counts (Hildebrand & de Ruiter, 2004).

PCL-R scores are correlated to varying degrees with self-report personality measures. For example, early research demonstrated that PCL-R Total scores were positively correlated with Minnesota Multiphasic Personality Inventory (MMPI) and MMPI-2 Scales 9 (Hypomania) and 4 (Psychopathic Deviate) and negatively correlated with Scales 5 (Masculinity-Femininity) and 10 (Social Introversion) (Hare, 2003). More recently, generally similar results (Klein Haneveld, Kamphuis, Smid, & Forbey, 2017) have been reported for the MMPI-2 Restructured Form (Ben-Porath & Tellegen, 2008). The PCL-R also correlates in expected ways with the Personality Assessment Inventory (Morey, 2007) in terms of positive associations with the Antisocial Features and Aggression scales, as well as somewhat more modest correlations with Borderline Features and Drug Problems scales (Morey et al., in press). PCL-R scores are also correlated with self-report psychopathy measures, including the Psychopathic Personality Inventory (PPI) and Levenson's Self-Report Psychopathy Scale (Hare, 2003).

The PCL-R Total score is unrelated, or weakly and inconsistently related, to other variables, such as anxiety, depression, and suicide (Hare, 2003). The lack of association with anxiety runs counter to historical conceptualizations of psychopathy (e.g., Cleckley, 1941). These inconsistencies may be attributable to PCL Total scores including both the "old" Factors 1 and 2 items, given that these factors have shown preferential correlates with important constructs such as anxiety. They may also stem from the existence of etiologically distinct psychopathy subtypes among which the PCL-R *alone* is unable to differentiate (Poythress & Skeem, 2006). These findings may inform the debate regarding the relationship between the psychopathy construct and the PCL measures, supporting Skeem and Cooke's argument (2010a, 2010b) that PCL-R overreliance resulted in drift from the Cleckleyan construct of psychopathy (see Hare & Neumann, 2010, for a reply).

Total PCL:YV scores are positively correlated with various clinical constructs, including Conduct Disorder, Oppositional Defiant Disorder, and Adjustment Disorder, and substance use, anger, aggression, and interpersonal problems on the Adolescent Psychopathology Scale (Salekin et al., 2004). PCL:YV scores also correlate positively with the Aggressive, Delinquent, Externalizing, and Internalizing scales of the Child Behavior Checklist and the Youth Self-Report (YSR), and with the Depression subscale of the YSR (Schmidt et al., 2006). Notably, these correlations differ for female and male youth, providing some support for considering the construct validity of the PCL:YV separately for these populations (Schmidt et al., 2006).

Predictive Validity

The ability of the PCL measures to predict antisocial behavior takes precedence in any discussion of violence risk assessment. Many studies, including several large meta-analyses among several populations, have examined the predictive validity of the PCL measures, and researchers have begun to take a more sophisticated look at the ability of these measures to predict various outcomes. Although the PCL measures are not risk assessment measures per se, they are prospectively associated with several forms of antisocial and violent behavior. In addition to presenting key findings regarding the predictive validity of the PCL measures, we examine the role of moderator variables (e.g., sex, race, ethnicity).

COMMUNITY RECIDIVISM

Several meta-analyses have examined the ability of PCL measures to predict criminal recidivism in the community (see Douglas, Vincent, & Edens, 2018, for a review). A few caveats are worth noting. Although some studies distinguish between types of recidivism (e.g., general vs. violent vs. sexual), other studies combine these categories to include *any* recidivism. Further, the metric used to quantify recidivism varies, with some studies using dichotomous statistical measures (e.g., chi-square, Phi) and others using more sophisticated statistical techniques that incorporate time at risk prior to reoffending (e.g., survival or Cox regression). Finally, although the studies discussed in this subsection focus primarily on recidivism in the community, they often included findings on institutional recidivism, which makes it difficult to neatly categorize some studies.

Some meta-analyses have examined the relationship between PCL-R-measured psychopathy and criminal recidivism. Gendreau et al. (2002) reported a weighted effect size (Phi coefficient) for the PCL-R of .23 for general recidivism ($k = 30$) and .21 for violent recidivism ($k = 26$). Walters (2003b) relied on 50 effect size estimates from 42 studies that prospectively assessed the relationship between PCL and PCL-R Factor scores and community recidivism. Factor 2 was moderately predictive of community recidivism ($r = .29$; $k = 34$), whereas Factor 1 was less robustly associated with recidivism ($r = .18$; $k = 34$).

Leistico et al. (2008) examined the relationship between PCL measures and antisocial conduct (recidivism and institutional infractions) in 95 studies ($N = 15,826$). They found that PCL Total, Factor 1, and Factor 2 scores were moderately associated with increased antisocial conduct, with mean weighted effect sizes (Hedges' d) of .55, .38, and .60, respectively. Consistent with prior meta-analyses, Factor 2 had a stronger relationship with antisocial conduct than Factor 1. They found that effect sizes were significantly moderated by several variables and concluded that predictions of antisocial conduct based on PCL measures should be "interpreted more cautiously for members of minority ethnic groups, males, and prisoners than for Caucasians, females, and psychiatric patients" (p. 40). A comprehensive review of violence risk assessments concluded that the PCL-R demonstrated low predictive validity for general and violent offending compared to the VRAG, Static-99, and HCR-20 (Singh, Grann, & Fazel, 2011).

Most recent research on community recidivism and PCL measures focuses on more specific questions, including interactions of PCL-R facets with several variables (e.g., age, ethnicity, treatment). In a study on the relationship between age and recidivism, PCL-R Total, Lifestyle, and Antisocial facet scores moderately predicted general recidivism at an average of 24 years post-release, and predicted violent recidivism within shorter follow-up periods, but increased age at release was associated with lower rates of recidivism for both high- and low-PCL-R-rated offenders (Olver & Wong, 2015). A meta-analysis examining the interaction of the Interpersonal-Affective and Social Deviance factors of the PCL-R reported that the Social Deviance factor is more uniquely predictive of violence than Interpersonal-Affective traits, and that the factors did not interact to predict violence (Kennealy, Skeem, Walters, & Camp, 2010).

Other studies have examined the predictive ability of the PCL measures in subtypes of offenders. The PCL:SV adequately predicted reconviction for general and violent offenses among offenders with intellectual disabilities (Gray, Fitzgerald, Taylor, MacCulloch, & Snowden, 2007). In a sample of high-risk psychopathic offenders, positive therapeutic change was significantly associated with a reduction in risk of violent recidivism after controlling for psychopathy scores (Olver, Lewis, & Wong, 2013). However, in contrast to previous studies, Factor 1 was a stronger predictor of future violence than Factor 2.

The ability of PCL measures to predict criminal recidivism among females has received less research attention. Among female forensic psychiatric patients, the PCL-R did not post-dict (Schaap, Lammers, & de Vogel, 2009) or predict (Weizmann-Henelius et al., 2015) recidivism, although some international research with female offenders (e.g., Eisenbarth, Osterheider, Nedopil, & Stadtland, 2012) stands in contrast to these findings. The PCL-R's predictive ability for recidivism among females may depend on the population (e.g., psychiatric hospital vs. pre-sentencing) and type of recidivism.

Only a few studies have examined racial/ethnic differences in the PCL-R's predictive ability. Olver, Neumann, Wong, and Hare (2013) found that the PCL-R predicted general and violent recidivism in Aboriginal and non-Aboriginal Canadian men, with Factor 2 but not Factor 1 significantly predicting recidivism. However, Walsh (2013) found that psychopathy was more strongly predictive of criminal violence for European Americans than African Americans, and the PCL-R was not significantly related to future violence for Latin American offenders. More recently, a study of 1,163 Canadian offenders reported that Indigenous men scored higher on the PCL-R—and had higher rates of recidivism—than non-Indigenous men, but the PCL-R had moderate to high predictive accuracy for predicting violent and general recidivism in both Indigenous and non-Indigenous groups (Olver et al., 2018). Additionally, a recent study of 1,742 Caucasian, African American, and Hispanic offenders in the United States concluded the PCL-R lacked predictive power for predicting recidivism among Hispanic offenders and noted that Facet 4 scores predicted fewer violent arrests among Hispanic offenders but greater violent arrests among African American offenders (Gatner et al., 2018).

A growing body of research has examined the ability of PCL measures to predict criminal recidivism in youthful offenders. In a meta-analysis of PCL measures across 21 non-overlapping samples of male and female juvenile offenders, psychopathy was significantly associated with general and violent recidivism, with weighted mean correlation coefficients of .24 ($n = 2,787$) and .25 ($n = 2,067$), respectively (Edens et al., 2007). Despite positive effect sizes, the effects for violent recidivism were too heterogeneous to aggregate meaningfully, suggesting the relationship between PCL scores and violence across studies was too diverse to be explained simply by chance variability. Moderator analyses revealed that a large proportion of the variability among effect sizes was attributable to the percentage of Caucasian participants in each sample; studies with higher proportions of non-Caucasian participants reported lower effect sizes than the more racially homogeneous (primarily Caucasian) samples. In another study of the PCL:YV, race/ethnicity (Caucasian, African American, Hispanic) did not directly predict recidivism or moderate the relationship between PCL:YV scores and recidivism (Edens & Cahill, 2007). Two other meta-analyses reported that PCL measure scores significantly predicted general and violent recidivism (Olver, Stockdale, & Wormith, 2009; Asscher et al., 2011). Moderator analyses found that associations between violent recidivism and psychopathy were stronger for samples with both males and females compared to samples of solely males *or* females (Asscher et al., 2011).

Several studies published after the Asscher et al. (2011) meta-analysis support the predictive use of PCL measures. Most of these studies consider the effects of sex, age, and/or race/ethnicity on the relationship between psychopathy and recidivism in youth. In a sample of high-risk male adolescents, PCL:YV facets were more strongly related to future criminality for African Americans than for European Americans (Vitacco, Neumann, & Caldwell, 2010). A still-developing literature supports the comparable predictive validity (and reliability) of the PCL:YV among Indigenous youth and White youth (.e.g., McCuish, Mathesius, Lussier, & Corrado, 2018). A study of youth and adult recidivism outcomes found that the PCL:YV was a stronger predictor of youth recidivism than adult recidivism (Stockdale, Olver, & Wong, 2010). Walters (2014b) reported that Factor 2 contributed the majority of the predictive variance of the PCL:YV in males and females. In contrast, Caldwell (2011) reported high Interpersonal facet scores predicted violent offending among youth who were placed in most facilities, but was not predictive of offending for youth placed in a program designed to use a Cognitive Behavioral Therapy approach to treat aggression and other behavior problems. A more recent study by Chauhan et al. (2014) reported that the PCL:YV did not predict self-reported delinquent behavior or violent offending at 2-year or 4.5-year follow-up among female youth.

INSTITUTIONAL MISCONDUCT

The ability of PCL scores to predict general and violent recidivism in the community is well established, although the magnitude of this relationship is modest to moderate and the variability of the strength of this relationship across studies raises concern. The ability of PCL measures to predict institutional misconduct has been a greater source of controversy. Importantly, from a methodological standpoint, many early studies provided postdictive or concurrent evidence rather than predictive evidence regarding the relationship between the PCL-R and institutional misconduct, which raises questions about the true relationship between the PCL-R and institutional misbehavior. Fortunately, the ability of PCL measures to *predict* institutional misconduct among correctional populations has received increased attention (e.g., Edens, Buffington-Vollum, Keilen, Roskamp, & Anthony, 2005; Guy, Edens, Anthony, & Douglas, 2005; Walters, 2003a, 2003b). Most studies report non-significant or small-to-moderate correlations between the PCL measures and measures of institutional misconduct. Given the large body of research in this area, we focus on meta-analyses.

Walters (2003a, 2003b) conducted two seminal meta-analyses. In a meta-analysis of 14 studies, Walters (2003a) reported a moderate association ($r = .27$) between psychopathy as measured by PCL-R Total scores and several measures of institutional adjustment, but he did not report analyses related to violent institutional misconduct. In another meta-analysis, Walters (2003b) examined the ability of the PCL and PCL-R Factor scores to predict institutional adjustment (violent and nonviolent) and community recidivism (general, violent, and sexual) among forensic patients and prison inmates across 42 studies. PCL-R Factor 2 was moderately predictive of institutional adjustment ($r = .27$; $k = 16$) and community recidivism ($r = .29$; $k = 34$), whereas Factor 1 was less robustly associated with these outcome measures.

In a large meta-analysis of published and unpublished studies, Guy et al. (2005) coded 273 effect sizes to examine the relationship between the PCL, PCL-R, and PCL:SV and institutional misconduct in civil psychiatric, forensic psychiatric, and correctional facilities. Mean weighted effect sizes for PCL Total and Factor and 2 scores were highly heterogeneous and weakest for physically violent institutional misconduct ($r_w = .17$, $.15$, and $.14$, respectively). For PCL Total scores, the weighted average correlation coefficients were $.29$ ($k = 38$) for any institutional misconduct and $.21$ ($k = 12$) for non-aggressive institutional misconduct. Effect sizes for physically violent institutional misconduct were smaller in U.S. prison samples ($r_w = .11$) than non-U.S. prison samples ($r_w = .23$). Having a sample of mostly Caucasian participants was not a significant moderator, but results approached significance in several analyses. This raises concerns about using PCL measures to predict violence among U.S. prison samples.

Although some studies published since the Guy et al. (2005) meta-analysis found that PCL measures predict institutional misconduct (e.g., Huchzermeier, Bruss, Geiger, Andreas Kernbichler, & Aldenhoff, 2008), and most studies report similarly weak effects (e.g., Camp, Skeem, Barchard, Lilienfeld, & Poythress, 2013; McDermott, Edens, Quanbeck, Busse, & Scott, 2008; Walters & Mandell, 2007). For example, a study of 99 forensic inpatients found that PCL-R Total scores did not predict inpatient aggression, though Facet 4 and Factor 2 were significant predictors, albeit small in magnitude (Hogan & Olver, 2016). Similarly, a study of 73 forensic psychiatric patients with intellectual disabilities found that the HCR-20, but not the PCL-R, significantly predicted institutional aggression (Morrissey et al., 2007). Taken together, this research cautions against using PCL measures to predict institutional misconduct in adults.

Several studies have examined the ability of PCL measures to predict institutional misconduct among youth. Early narrative reviews supported the ability of PCL measures to predict outcomes such as youth adjustment to incarceration or detention (e.g., Vincent & Hart, 2002). Edens and Campbell (2007) conducted the first meta-analysis of the relationship between psychopathy and institutional misconduct among adolescents. They examined effect sizes for total misconduct, aggressive behavior, and physically violent behavior across 15 non-overlapping data sets from 13 studies ($N = 1,310$), and they reported weighted mean correlation coefficients of .24 ($k = 15$) for total misconduct, .25 ($k = 14$) for aggressive misconduct, and .28 ($k = 10$) for physically violent misconduct. Based on these results, including considerable heterogeneity among effect sizes for aggressive and physically violent misconduct, Edens and Campbell concluded that the relationship between psychopathy and measures of institutional misconduct among adolescents is "considerably less robust and somewhat weaker" than suggested by early narrative reviews (p. 23).

Since the Edens and Campbell (2007) meta-analysis, other studies have yielded a more nuanced understanding of the predictive validity of PCL measures for youth institutional misconduct. Caldwell (2011) found that PCL:YV Affective facet scores predicted institutional misconduct during the first 3 weeks in placement prior to treatment, but not during the last 3 weeks of placement. Kimonis, Skeem, Cauffman, and Dmitrieva (2011) reported that incarcerated youth with secondary psychopathy were significantly more likely to engage in institutional violence over a 2-year period than were youth with primary psychopathy.

Incremental Validity

Even though PCL measures are not risk assessment instruments per se, research suggests they are prospectively associated with various forms of antisocial conduct, such as general and violent recidivism among released offenders. As such, a logical next question is whether the PCL measures add appreciably to what clinicians and researchers can obtain from empirically established risk factors or from other measures often used in violence risk assessment evaluations. Several researchers have addressed the question of whether there is anything unique about the predictive utility of psychopathy once other risk factors and risk assessment measures are taken into account (see Douglas et al., 2018, for a brief review).

PSYCHOPATHY VS. OTHER RISK FACTORS

Skeem and Mulvey (2001) examined the incremental validity of psychopathy using data from the MacArthur Violence Risk Assessment Study (Monahan et al., 2001), which examined 134 risk factors among 1,136 patients admitted to civil psychiatric inpatient facilities. The PCL:SV was administered to roughly 750 participants during the first or second follow-up interview, which were 10 and 20 weeks post-discharge. Using hierarchical logistic regression, Skeem and Mulvey (2001) found that the PCL:SV added to the model fit produced by 15 covariates alone. Based on propensity score analyses that held constant the non-specific psychopathy-related variance, the correlation between the PCL:SV and violence was reduced from .26 to .12. They concluded that the .14 reduction in the correlation coefficient represented the "unique" variance of psychopathy in terms of predicting violence. Of note, violence was dichotomized as any act of violence over a 1-year follow-up period, which included the 10- or 20-week period before the PCL:SV was completed, meaning that at least some violent outcomes may have pre-dated the collection of PCL:SV data.

Walters, Knight, Grann, and Dahle (2008) examined the incremental validity of the four facet scores of the PCL-R and PCL:SV to predict general and violent recidivism among six forensic/correctional samples with follow-up time periods ranging from 20 weeks to 10 years. Results revealed that Facet 4 (Antisocial) demonstrated incremental validity relative to Facets 1 (Interpersonal), 2 (Affective), and 3 (Lifestyle), whereas Facets 1, 2, and 3 demonstrated minimal incremental validity relative to Facet 4. In all 11 analyses, Facet 4 contributed unique variance to predictions of recidivism above and beyond Facets 1, 2, and 3; Facets 1, 2, and 3 added unique variance to recidivism predictions above and beyond Facet 4 in only 2 of 11 analyses. They concluded that the antisocial component of the PCL measures is a robust predictor of recidivism, and that the interpersonal, affective, and lifestyle components add little.

A more recent study examined the PCL-R's incremental validity compared to age and criminal history among adult male inmates in Canada ($n = 198$) and the United States ($n = 122$) (Walters, 2012). The PCL-R did not add predictive power to the model when added after age and criminal history for general or violent recidivism, including when analyses were re-run with only White inmates. The PCL-R Total score was incrementally valid over age and criminal history only in predicting general recidivism for the U.S. sample. Walters (2012) concluded, "[W]ithout Facet 4 (antisocial), the PCL-R may not be particularly effective in predicting . . . recidivism" (p. 409).

PSYCHOPATHY VS. RISK ASSESSMENT MEASURES

Several researchers have compared the PCL measures to risk assessment tools to gauge the incremental predictive validity of psychopathy. In a metaregression of nine risk assessment tools across 68 studies ($N = 25,980$, including 2,645 with PCL-R data), Singh et al. (2011) reported that the PCL-R was the weakest predictor of offending, concluding that the results "argue against the view of some experts that the PCL-R is unparalleled in its ability to predict future offending" (p. 509). Perhaps unsurprisingly, a meta-analysis of studies including both a risk assessment measure and a self-report measure found that self-report measures developed specifically for criminal offender and antisocial populations with items devoted to criminal offending and antisocial behavior perform similarly to risk assessment measures (including the PCL) in predicting recidivism (Walters, 2006).

In a meta-analysis of 28 studies, Yang et al. (2010) compared between two and nine risk assessment tools and their subscales in predicting violent recidivism: VRAG, HCR-20, PCL-R, PCL:SV, Risk Matrix 2000 for Violence (RM2000V; Thornton, 2007), General Statistical Information for Recidivism (GSIR; Bonta, Harman, Hann, & Cormier, 1996), LSI/LSI-R, Offender Group Reconviction Scale (OGRS; Copas & Marshall, 1998), and VRS. The PCL-R was included in 16 of 28 studies ($N = 3,854$ participants); Factors 1 and 2 in 13 studies (Ns = 3,895 and 3,995, respectively); and the PCL:SV in 8 studies ($N = 2,506$). The AUCs for the instruments and their subscales ranged from .56 to .71, with most falling between .65 and .68. The AUC of the PCL-R was .65 and the AUC of the PCL:SV was .68; Factor 1 had the lowest AUC (.56) and was the only instrument or subscale whose confidence interval included .5; Factor 2 had an AUC of .67. The OGRS and HCR-20 predicted violent recidivism significantly better than the PCL-R. Yang et al. (2010) concluded that the PCL measures are generally comparable to other risk assessment tools, but noted that the lack of predictive efficacy of Factor 1 suggests that the ability of the PCL measures to predict violence is driven by past criminal/antisocial behavior captured by Factor 2—as reflected in earlier research (e.g., Guy et al., 2010).

Not all studies support the incremental validity of the PCL in predicting violence. A study of the incremental validity of the PCL-R and PPI in predicting violence reported that the PPI adds incremental validity over the PCL-R due to the inclusion of impulsive antisociality variables, but the PCL-R adds no incremental validity to the PPI (Camp et al., 2013). Coid et al. (2011) examined the predictive ability of each item on the PCL-R, VRAG, and HCR-20, and then compared the measures using only the independently predictive items. For the PCL-R, 13 of the 20 items were independently predictive of violent reconviction. The PCL-R had an AUC of .63 (correct prediction of violent offending 73.5% of the time; correct prediction of nonviolent offending 60.4% of the time), and the subscale created from the most predictive items (P3, P10, and P20) had an AUC of .68 (correct prediction of violent offending 75.6% of the time; correct prediction of nonviolent offending 59.5% of the time). The PCL-R did not outperform the VRAG or HCR-20. Combining the significantly independently predictive items from all three measures into a new index resulted in a modest increase in predictive ability, with an AUC of .72 (correctly predicting violent reoffending 71.6% of the time and nonviolent reoffending 63.0% of the time). More recently, Hogan and Olver (2016) examined the incremental validity of the PCL-R, HCR-20, START, VRS, and VRAG-Revised in a sample of 92 Canadian adult forensic psychiatric inpatients in a maximum-security unit. PCL-R Total scores produced no significant AUCs; Facet 4 and Factor 2 both had small but significant AUCs (.66 and .65, respectively). In contrast, total scores for the HCR-20, START, and VRS were predictive of inpatient aggression.

One meta-analysis compared the predictive utility of the PCL:YV to the Youth Level of Service/Case Management Inventory (YLS/CMI; Hoge & Andrews, 2002) (Edens et al., 2007). The analysis was based on five studies comparing the PCL:YV to the YLS/CMI using either general recidivism (combined $n = 799$) or violent recidivism (combined $n = 727$) as outcomes. The measures performed comparably. For general recidivism, the weighted mean effect size was .27 for the PCL:YV Total scores and .25 for the YLS/CMI. For violent recidivism, the weighted mean effect size was .24 for the PCL:YV Total scores and .21 for the YLS/CMI. Unfortunately, based on the reported analyses, Edens et al. (2007) were not able to directly address whether either measure demonstrated any incremental validity over the other in terms of predicting recidivism. However, based on the high average intercorrelation ($r_w = .77$) in the three studies that reported associations between the measures, Edens et al. (2007) concluded that it "seems unlikely that the measures were accounting for much if any unique variance in these outcomes" (p. 68).

Since the Edens et al. (2007) meta-analysis, several studies examined the PCL:YV's incremental validity. Dolan and Rennie (2008) examined the predictive and incremental validity of the Structured Assessment of Violence Risk in Youth (SAVRY) and PCL:YV in 99 male adolescents assessed while in custody and followed for 12 months post release. The SAVRY was a modest but better predictor of recidivism than the PCL:YV. Douglas, Epstein, and Poythress (2008) examined the incremental validity of the PCL:YV, Antisocial Process Screening Device (APSD; Frick & Hare, 2001), and Childhood Psychopathy Scale (CPS; Lynam, 1997) in predicting reoffending in a sample of 83 delinquent youth. The predictive validity of the self-report measures (APSD, CPS) was better than the PCL:YV's predictive validity, and all of the predictive effects for the measures of psychopathic features disappeared when relevant covariates (e.g., substance use, conduct disorder, young age) were entered into multivariate predictive models. The PCL:YV did not make it into the incremental stage of analyses.

Welsh, Schmidt, McKinnon, Chattha, and Meyers (2008) examined the incremental validity of the PCL:YV, YLS/CMI, and SAVRY among 133 Canadian youth referred by youth court judges for mental health assessment. For general and violent recidivism, the PCL:YV was a significant predictor when entered first into the model until the SAVRY was entered, and it was significant when entered second after the YLS/CMI but not after the SAVRY; it was not significant when entered third. Similarly, Hilterman, Nicholls, and van Nieuwenhuizen (2014) reported that the PCL:YV was not a significant predictor of self-reported violent or general offending one year post-assessment when entered into the model after the YLS/CMI or SAVRY.

One other study deserves comment. In a 2005 investigation using the MacArthur data, Skeem, Miller, Mulvey, Tiemann, and Monahan compared the incremental utility of the Five Factor Model of personality, measured by the Neuroticism Extraversion Openness-Five Factor Inventory (NEO-FFI; Costa & McCrae, 1992), and the PCL:SV for modeling the relationship with violence among 769 civil psychiatric patients. Skeem et al. (2005) found that after controlling for previous misbehavior, the NEO-FFI and PCL:SV shared much of their violence postdictive variance. After controlling for previous misbehavior and NEO-FFI scores, the PCL:SV modestly increased the amount of variance explained for violent behaviors. They noted that the overlap in variance was attributable to the violence-related constructs tapped by antagonism on the PCL:SV Factor 2 and the NEO-FFI. Moreover, they noted each measure supplied some unique postdictive variance; the PCL:SV contributed some Factor 1 features, most notably conning-manipulative traits.

Summary and Concluding Comments

In recent years, use of the PCL-R by forensic mental health professionals in U.S., Canadian, and European courts to assess risk of future violence has increased considerably (DeMatteo et al., 2014b; Edens et al., 2015). Because the appropriateness of any measure used in a forensic context is primarily dependent on the extent to which the measure meaningfully addresses the referral question, the validity of PCL measures in violence risk assessments depends on the extent to which inferences drawn from the measures are empirically defensible.

Since the first edition of this chapter was published, researchers have continued to examine the ability of the PCL measures to predict future violence, leading to a more detailed understanding of the abilities and limits of using the PCL measures for risk assessment purposes. This chapter reviewed the most recent literature regarding the utility of the PCL measures in violence risk assessments. As this chapter demonstrates, the predictive validity of the PCL measures depends on several factors, including the behavior predicted (e.g., general vs. violent vs. sexual recidivism), the context in which the offender is or will be located (e.g., correctional facility vs. community), the prediction timeframe, and demographic variables such as age, sex, and race. As such, a referral question relating to future violence should be sufficiently specific (see DeMatteo et al., 2014b, 2019; Edens, 2006).

The research reviewed in this chapter leads to four conclusions regarding the relationship between the PCL measures and recidivism/violence risk. First, the interrater reliability of the PCL-R in real-world adversarial contexts that call for recidivism/violence risk assessments is troublingly poor. A large body of research has suggested ICC values around .6 or even .5—and so much of the variance in PCL scores when used in the field is accounted for by something *other* than psychopathy (Murrie et al., 2009). Moreover, comprehensive reviews of (mostly) appellate cases in the United States and Canada revealed poor PCL-R interrater reliability, both for cases involving sexual offenses and nonsexual offenses (DeMatteo et al., 2014a, 2014b; Edens et al., 2015). Of note, the poor interrater reliability does not appear to be entirely random error because there is evidence of an allegiance effect in which PCL-R scores by prosecution-retained experts are higher than PCL-R scores by defense-retained experts (Murrie et al., 2009). These studies raise serious concerns about using the PCL-R to predict violence risk in adversarial contexts.

Second, the PCL's predictive validity depends on the outcome being predicted and the characteristics of the sample. Taken together, the available research suggests the following conclusions:

a. The PCL has a modest to at best moderate relationship with future community violence, with most of the explanatory variance attributable to Factor 2 and Facet 4. Further, the PCL measures in isolation are relatively weak predictors of offending compared to risk assessment measures (Singh et al., 2011; Yang et al., 2010). The relationship between the PCL and community violence is less clear when it comes to racial/ethnic minority, female, and juvenile offenders. Most meta-analyses reviewed in this chapter evidenced considerable heterogeneity among effect sizes, so any discussion of "average" effect sizes may be misleading. As such, even if the research is considered in the most favorable light, experts should not blindly rely on these meta-analyses as establishing that the PCL is a reliable and valid predictor of future violence.

b. The PCL has a limited ability to predict institutional misconduct. Most studies report non-significant or small-to-moderate correlations between PCL measures and various types of institutional misconduct, with somewhat better results for predicting nonviolent infractions. The relationship between psychopathy and institutional misconduct among adolescents is unclear, although some research (e.g., Caldwell, 2011) has yielded more promising results.

c. Although not discussed in this chapter due to space limitations, there is mixed evidence regarding the PCL's ability to predict sexual reoffending. Some studies have found that PCL-R scores do not predict sexual reoffending (Murrie, Boccaccini, Caperton, & Rufino, 2012), whereas others have concluded that PCL scores are relevant to recidivism risk (Hawes, Boccaccini, & Murrie, 2013). Moreover, a large meta-analysis found the predictive effects were stronger for scores calculated for research rather than for clinical use (Hawes et al., 2013).

Third, there is mixed evidence regarding the incremental validity of the PCL measures in predicting violence. Although some studies have found the PCL provides unique explanatory variance above and beyond other risk factors in predicting violence (e.g., Skeem & Mulvey, 2001; Tengström, Hodgins, Grann, Langström, & Kullgren, 2004), more recent research suggests that much of the PCL-R's predictive power is attributable to Facet 4 (Antisocial) (Walters, 2012; Walters et al., 2008), which suggests that the PCL does not add considerably to the prediction of violence once criminal history is accounted for.

Fourth, violence risk assessments should not rely solely on the results of the PCL. If the PCL is used, it should be part of a more comprehensive risk assessment battery, which could mean using an actuarial measure (e.g., VRAG, SORAG) or structured professional judgment instrument (HCR-20, SVR-20, RSVP) that incorporates the PCL-R, or using the PCL-R along with other measures that provide risk-relevant data. As with almost any type of forensic mental health assessment, an evaluator's conclusions in the context of a risk assessment are more defensible when they are based on multiple sources of data, including multiple testing procedures (see Conroy & Murrie, 2007; Heilbrun, DeMatteo, Brooks Holliday, & LaDuke, 2014).

Our review of the existing research also revealed some shortcomings in what is known about the relationship between the PCL and future violence. When we wrote the first edition of this chapter, we noted that research using more ethnically and racially diverse samples would make a considerable contribution to the field, as would more research with girls and women. Researchers have taken some strides to improve our understanding of these understudied groups, but more research is needed to parse out the complex relationship among race, ethnicity, sex, psychopathy, and violence. We also need longer-term follow-up studies with juveniles, which would be helpful in examining the ability of the PCL to make long-term violence predictions.

In the first edition of this chapter, we recommended that clinicians look past the rhetoric and ask pragmatic questions about the utility of the PCL in specific contexts. We stand by that recommendation, which we believe has become more critical in light of recent research. The PCL-R is often referred to as the "gold standard" of psychopathy measures, but recent research raises questions about the interrater reliability of the PCL-R in real-world contexts, the predictive validity of the PCL-R in some contexts, and clinicians' ability to avoid being biased by the side that retains them in adversarial contexts. As such, simply concluding that the PCL-R is valid ignores that validity is not a static property of a measure; rather, it is a question of the accuracy of the inferences that may be drawn from a measure in specific contexts (Messick, 1995).

The research reviewed in this chapter can provide guidance to evaluators who use the PCL measures clinically. The decision to use the PCL warrants close scrutiny. Evaluators should be able to defend its application, relevance, and implications in each context in which it is used (see Hare, 2003). The PCL should be considered only in contexts in which inferences drawn from the results are empirically defensible. This highlights the importance of having a well-defined and circumscribed referral question. For example, using the PCL-R with an incarcerated adult male offender to inform an assessment of community violence risk permits an evaluator to draw meaningful and empirically defensible inferences relevant to the referral question. By contrast, using the PCL-R to predict institutional violence places one on shakier ground in light of the weak-to-modest relationship between the PCL and future institutional violence.

Only using the PCL in contexts in which it has demonstrated probative value is consistent with best practice (see DeMatteo, Hodges, & Fairfax-Columbo, 2016) and several provisions of APA's *Ethical Principles of Psychologists and Code of Conduct* (APA, 2010) and *Specialty Guidelines for Forensic Psychology* (APA, 2013). For example, Standard 9.02(a) of the *Ethics Code* states: "Psychologists administer, adapt, score, interpret, or use assessment techniques, interviews, tests, or instruments in a manner and for purposes that are appropriate in light of the research on or evidence of the usefulness and proper application of the techniques" (p. 12). Standard 9.02(b) of the *Ethics Code* further states: "Psychologists use assessment instruments whose validity and reliability have been established for use with members of the population tested" (p. 12). Similarly, Guideline 10.02 of the *Specialty Guidelines* states: "Forensic practitioners use assessment procedures in the manner and for the purposes that are appropriate in light of the research on or evidence of their usefulness and proper application" and that "Forensic practitioners use assessment instruments whose validity and reliability have been established for use with members of the population assessed" (p. 15). Using the PCL with these Standards and Guidelines in mind, and being aware of the most current relevant research, is an effective way to promote best practices.

Note

1. Although some have argued that interrater reliability estimates as low as ICC = .60 may represent "good" reliability, Nunnally and Bernstein (1994) clearly demonstrate that as values drop below .90, using such instruments in practice for individual case decision-making becomes increasingly problematic because the confidence intervals surrounding the obtained scores become exceedingly large (see p. 265 for a concrete example).

References

American Psychiatric Association. (1952). *Diagnostic and statistical manual of mental disorders*. Washington, DC: Author.

American Psychiatric Association. (1968). *Diagnostic and statistical manual of mental disorders* (2nd ed.). Washington, DC: Author.

American Psychiatric Association. (1980). *Diagnostic and statistical manual of mental disorders* (3rd ed.). Washington, DC: Author.

American Psychological Association. (2010). *Ethical principles of psychologists and code of conduct*. Washington, DC: Author.

American Psychological Association. (2013). Specialty guidelines for forensic psychology. *American Psychologist, 68*, 7–19.

Asscher, J. J., van Vugt, E. S., Stams, G. J. J., Deković, M., Eichelsheim, V. I., & Yousfi, S. (2011). The relationship between juvenile psychopathic traits, delinquency and (violent) recidivism: A meta-analysis. *Journal of Child Psychology and Psychiatry, 52*, 1134–1143.

Balsis, S., Busch, A. J., Wilfong, K. M., Newman, J. W., & Edens, J. F. (2017). A statistical consideration regarding the threshold of the psychopathy checklist—revised. *Journal of Personality Assessment, 99*, 494–502.

Bauer, D. L., Whitman, L. A., & Kosson, D. S. (2011). Reliability and construct validity of psychopathy checklist youth version scores among incarcerated adolescent girls. *Criminal Justice and Behavior, 38*, 965–987.

Ben-Porath, Y. S., & Tellegen, A. (2008). *MMPI—2—RF (Minnesota multi-phasic personality inventory—2—restructured form): Manual for administration and scoring.* Minneapolis: University of Minnesota Press.

Berryessa, C. M., & Wohlstetter, B. (2019). The psychopathic "label" and effects on punishment outcomes: A meta-analysis. *Law and Human Behavior, 43,* 9–25.

Blais, J., Forth, A. E., & Hare, R. D. (2017). Examining the interrater reliability of the Hare psychopathy checklist-revised across a large sample of trained raters. *Psychological Assessment, 29,* 762–775.

Boccaccini, M. T., Murrie, D. C., Rufino, K. A., & Gardner, B. O. (2014). Evaluator differences in psychopathy checklist-revised factor and facet scores. *Law and Human Behavior, 38,* 337–345.

Boccaccini, M. T., Turner, D. B., Murrie, D. C., & Rufino, K. A. (2012). Do PCL-R scores from state or defense experts best predict future misconduct among civilly committed sex offenders? *Law and Human Behavior, 36,* 159–169.

Boer, D. P., Hart, S. D., Kropp, P. R., & Webster, C. D. (1997). *Manual for the sexual violence risk-20: Professional guidelines for assessing risk of sexual violence.* Vancouver, BC: British Columbia Institute on Family Violence and Mental Health, Law, & Policy Institute, Simon Fraser University.

Bonta, J., Harman, W. G., Hann, R. G., & Cormier, R. B. (1996). The prediction of recidivism among federally sentenced offenders: A re-validation of the SIR scale. *Canadian Journal of Criminology, 38,* 61–79.

Book, A. S., Clark, H. J., Forth, A. E., & Hare, R. D. (2006). The PCL-R and PCL: YV: Forensic applications and limitations. In R. P. Archer (Ed.), *Forensic uses of clinical assessment instruments* (pp. 147–179). Mahwah, NJ: Erlbaum.

Caldwell, M. F. (2011). Treatment-related changes in behavioral outcomes of psychopathy facets in adolescent offenders. *Law and Human Behavior, 35,* 275–287.

Camp, J. P., Skeem, J. L., Barchard, K., Lilienfeld, S. O., & Poythress, N. G. (2013). Psychopathic predators? Getting specific about the relation between psychopathy and violence. *Journal of Consulting and Clinical Psychology, 81,* 467–480.

Campbell, J. S., Pulos, S., Hogan, M., & Murry, F. (2005). Reliability generalization of the psychopathy checklist applied in youthful samples. *Educational and Psychological Measurement, 65,* 639–656.

Campbell, M. A., French, S., & Gendreau, P. (2009). The prediction of violence in adult offenders: A meta-analytic comparison of instruments and methods of assessment. *Criminal Justice and Behavior, 36,* 567–590.

Chauhan, P., Ragbeer, S. N., Burnette, M. L., Oudekerk, B., Reppucci, N. D., & Moretti, M. M. (2014). Comparing the youth psychopathic traits inventory (YPI) and the psychopathy checklist—youth version (PCL-YV) among offending girls. *Assessment, 21,* 181–194.

Cleckley, H. (1941). *The mask of sanity.* St. Louis, MO: Mosby.

Coid, J. W., Yang, M., Ullrich, S., Zhang, T., Sizmur, S., Farrington, D., & Rogers, R. (2011). Most items in structured risk assessment instruments do not predict violence. *Journal of Forensic Psychiatry and Psychology, 22,* 3–21.

Conroy, M. A., & Murrie, D. C. (2007). *Forensic assessment of violence risk: A guide for risk assessment and risk management.* Hoboken, NJ: John Wiley & Sons, Inc.

Cooke, D. J., & Michie, C. (1999). Psychopathy across cultures: North America and Scotland compared. *Journal of Abnormal Psychology, 108,* 58–68.

Cooke, D. J., & Michie, C. (2001). Refining the construct of psychopathy: Towards a hierarchical model. *Psychological Assessment, 13,* 171–188.

Cooke, D. J., Michie, C., Hart, S. D., & Clark, D. (2004). Reconstructing psychopathy: Clarifying the significance of antisocial and socially deviant behavior in the diagnosis of psychopathic personality disorder. *Journal of Personality Disorders, 18,* 337–357.

Copas, J., & Marshall, P. (1998). The offender group reconviction scale: The statistical reconviction score for use by probation officers. *Journal of the Royal Statistical Society, 47*C, 159–171.

Costa, P. T., & McCrae, R. R. (1992). *Revised NEO personality inventory (NEO-PI-R) and NEO five-factor inventory (NEO-FFI) professional manual.* Odessa, FL: Psychological Assessment Resources.

DeMatteo, D., & Edens, J. F. (2006). The role and relevance of the psychopathy checklist-revised in court: A case law survey of U.S. courts (1991–2004). *Psychology, Public Policy, and Law, 12,* 214–241.

DeMatteo, D., Edens, J. F., Galloway, M., Cox, J., Smith, S. T., & Formon, D. (2014a). The role and reliability of the Psychopathy Checklist-Revised in U.S. sexually violent predator evaluations: A case law survey. *Law and Human Behavior, 38,* 248–255.

DeMatteo, D., Edens, J. F., Galloway, M., Cox, J., Smith, S. T., Koller, J. P., & Bersoff, B. (2014b). Investigating the role of the psychopathy checklist-revised in United States case law. *Psychology, Public Policy, and Law, 20*, 96–107.

DeMatteo, D., Hart, S. D., Heilbrun, K., Boccaccini, M. T., Cunningham, M. D., Douglas, K. S., . . . Reidy, T. J. (2020). Statement of concerned experts on the use of the Hare Psychopathy Checklist-Revised in capital sentencing to assess risk for institutional violence. *Psychology, Public Policy, and Law, 26*(2), 133–144.

DeMatteo, D., Heilbrun, K., & Marczyk, G. (2005). Psychopathy, risk of violence, and protective factors in a noninstitutionalized and noncriminal sample. *International Journal of Forensic Mental Health, 4*, 147–157.

DeMatteo, D., Heilbrun, K., & Marczyk, G. (2006). An empirical investigation of psychopathy in a noninstitutionalized and noncriminal sample. *Behavioral Sciences and the Law, 24*, 133–146.

DeMatteo, D., Hodges, H., & Fairfax-Columbo, J. (2016). An examination of whether psychopathy checklist-revised (PCL-R) evidence satisfies the relevance/prejudice admissibility standard. In B. H. Bornstein & M. K. Miller (Eds.), *Advances in psychology and law* (Vol. 2, pp. 205–239). New York: Springer Publishing Co.

DeMatteo, D., Murrie, D. C., Edens, J. F., & Lankford, C. (2019). Psychopathy in the courts. In M. DeLisi (Ed.), *Routledge international handbook of psychopathy and crime* (pp. 645–664). New York: Routledge, Taylor & Francis Group.

Dolan, M. C., & Rennie, C. E. (2008). The structured assessment of violence risk in youth as a predictor of recidivism in a United Kingdom cohort of adolescent offenders with conduct disorder. *Psychological Assessment, 20*, 35–46.

Dolan, M. C., & Völlm, B. (2009). Antisocial personality disorder and psychopathy in women: A literature review on the reliability and validity of assessment instruments. *International Journal of Law and Psychiatry, 32*, 2–9.

Douglas, K. S., Epstein, M. E., & Poythress, N. G. (2008). Criminal recidivism among juvenile offenders: Testing the incremental and predictive validity of three measures of psychopathic features. *Law and Human Behavior, 32*(5), 423-438.

Douglas, K. S., Hart, S. D., Webster, C. D., Belfrage, H., Guy, L. S., & Wilson, C. M. (2014). Historical-clinical-risk management-20, version 3 (HCR-20V3): Development and overview. *The International Journal of Forensic Mental Health, 13*(2), 93–108.

Douglas, K. S., Vincent, G. M., & Edens, J. F. (2018). Risk for criminal recidivism: The role of psychopathy. In C. J. Patrick (Ed.), *Handbook of psychopathy* (2nd ed., pp. 682–709). New York: Guilford Press.

Edens, J. F. (2006). Unresolved controversies concerning psychopathy: Implications for clinical and forensic decision-making. *Professional Psychology: Research and Practice, 37*, 59–65.

Edens, J. F., & Boccaccini, M. T. (2017). Taking forensic mental health assessment "out of the lab" and into "the real world": Introduction to the special issue on the field utility of forensic assessment instruments and procedures. *Psychological Assessment, 29*, 599–610.

Edens, J. F., Buffington-Vollum, J. K., Keilen, A., Roskamp, P., & Anthony, C. (2005). Predictions of future dangerousness in capital murder trials: Is it time to "disinvent the wheel?" *Law and Human Behavior, 29*, 55–86.

Edens, J. F., & Cahill, M. A. (2007). Psychopathy in adolescence and criminal recidivism in young adulthood: Longitudinal results from a multi-ethnic sample of youthful offenders. *Assessment, 14*, 57–64.

Edens, J. F., & Campbell, J. S. (2007). Identifying youths at risk for institutional misconduct: A meta-analytic investigation of the psychopathy checklist measures. *Psychological Services, 4*, 13–27.

Edens, J. F., Campbell, J. S., & Weir, J. M. (2007). Youth psychopathy and criminal recidivism: A meta-analysis of the psychopathy checklist measures. *Law and Human Behavior, 31*, 53–75.

Edens, J. F., Cox, J., Smith, S. T., DeMatteo, D., & Sörman, K. (2015). How reliable are psychopathy checklist—revised scores in Canadian criminal trials? A case law review. *Psychological Assessment, 27*, 447–456.

Edens, J. F., Marcus, D. K., Lilienfeld, S. O., & Poythress, N. G. (2006). Psychopathic, not psychopath: Taxometric evidence for the dimensional structure of psychopathy. *Journal of Abnormal Psychology, 115*, 131–144.

Edens, J. F., Petrila, J., & Kelley, S. E. (2018). Legal and ethical issues in the assessment and treatment of psychopathy. In C. J. Patrick (Ed.), *Handbook of psychopathy* (2nd ed., pp. 732–751). New York: Guilford Press.

Edens, J. F., Skeem, J. L., & Kennealy, P. J. (2009). The psychopathy checklist in the courtroom: Consensus and controversies. In J. L. Skeem & S. O. Lilienfeld (Eds.), *Psychological science in the courtroom: Consensus and controversy* (pp. 175–201). New York: Guilford Press.

Edens, J. F., & Vincent, G. M. (2008). Juvenile psychopathy: A clinical construct in need of restraint? *Journal of Forensic Psychology Practice, 8*, 186–197.

Eisenbarth, H., Osterheider, M., Nedopil, N., & Stadtland, C. (2012). Recidivism in female offenders: PCL-R Lifestyle Factor and VRAG show predictive validity in a German sample. *Behavioral Sciences and the Law, 30*(5), 575–584.

Forth, A. E., Kosson, D. S., & Hare, R. D. (2003). *The psychopathy checklist: Youth version.* Toronto, ON: Multi-Health Systems.

Frick, P. J., & Hare, R. D. (2001). *The antisocial process screening device.* Toronto, ON: Multi-Health Systems.

Gagnon, N., Douglas, K., & DeMatteo, D. (2007, June). *The introduction of the psychopathy checklist-revised in Canadian courts: Uses and misuses.* Paper presented at the 7th Annual Conference of the International Association of Forensic Mental Health Services, Montreal, Quebec.

Gatner, D. T., Blanchard, A. J. E., Douglas, K. S., Lilienfeld, S. O., & Edens, J. F. (2018). Psychopathy in a multiethnic world: Investigating multiple measures of psychopathy in Hispanic, African American, and Caucasian offenders. *Assessment, 25*, 206–221.

Gendreau, P., Coggin, C., & Smith, P. (2002). Is the PCL-R really the "unparalleled" measure of offender risk? A lesson in knowledge cumulation. *Criminal Justice and Behavior, 29*, 397–426.

Gray, N. S., Fitzgerald, S., Taylor, J., MacCulloch, M. J., & Snowden, R. J. (2007). Predicting future reconviction in offenders with intellectual disabilities: The predictive efficacy of VRAG, PCL-SV, and the HCR-20. *Psychological Assessment, 19*, 474–479.

Gray, N. S., & Snowden, R. J. (2016). Psychopathy in women: Prediction of criminality and violence in UK and USA psychiatric patients resident in the community. *Psychiatry Research, 237*, 339–343. Advanced online publication.

Guay, J., Ruscio, J., Hare, R., & Knight, R. A. (2007). A taxometric analysis of the latent structure of psychopathy: Evidence for dimensionality. *Journal of Abnormal Psychology, 116*, 701–716.

Guy, L. S., Douglas, K. S., & Hendry, M. C. (2010). The role of psychopathic personality disorder in violence risk assessments using the HCR-20. *Journal of Personality Disorders, 24*, 551–580.

Guy, L. S., Edens, J. F., Anthony, C., & Douglas, K. S. (2005). Does psychopathy predict institutional misconduct among adults? A meta-analytic investigation. *Journal of Consulting and Clinical Psychology, 73*, 1056–1064.

Hall, J. R., Benning, S. D., & Patrick, C. J. (2004). Criterion-related validity of the three-factor model of psychopathy: Personality, behavior, and adaptive functioning. *Assessment, 11*, 4–16.

Hare, R. D. (1980). A research scale for the assessment of psychopathy in criminal populations. *Personality and Individual Differences, 1*, 111–119.

Hare, R. D. (1991). *The Hare psychopathy checklist-revised manual.* North Tonawanda, NY: Multi-Health Systems.

Hare, R. D. (2003). *The Hare psychopathy checklist-revised manual* (2nd ed.). North Tonawanda, NY: Multi-Health Systems.

Hare, R. D. (2016). Psychopathy, the PCL-R, and criminal justice: Some new findings and current issues. *Canadian Psychology, 57*, 21–34.

Hare, R. D., & Neumann, C. S. (2008). Psychopathy as a clinical and empirical construct. *Annual Review of Clinical Psychology, 4*, 217–246.

Hare, R. D., & Neumann, C. S. (2010). The role of antisociality in the psychopathy construct: Comment on Skeem and Cooke (2010). *Psychological Assessment, 22*, 446–454.

Harpur, T. J., Hare, R. D., & Hakstian, A. R. (1989). Two-factor conceptualization of psychopathy: Construct validity and assessment implications. *Psychological Assessment: A Journal of Consulting and Clinical Psychology, 1*, 6–17.

Hart, S. D., Cox, D. N., & Hare, R. D. (1995). *The Hare PCL: Screening version.* North Tonawanda, NY: Multi-Health Systems.

Hart, S. D., & Hare, R. D. (1989). Discriminant validity of the psychopathy checklist in a forensic psychiatric population. *Psychological Assessment: A Journal of Consulting and Clinical Psychology, 1*, 211–218.

Hart, S. D., Kropp, P. R., Laws, D. R., Klaver, J., Logan, C., & Watt, K. A. (2003). *The risk for sexual violence protocol (RSVP): Structured professional guidelines for assessing risk of sexual violence.* Burnaby, BC: Mental Health, Law, and Policy Institute, Simon Fraser University, Pacific Psychological Assessment Corporation and the British Columbia Institute Against Family Violence.

Hawes, S. W., Boccaccini, M. T., & Murrie, D. C. (2013). Psychopathy and the combination of psychopathy and sexual deviance as predictors of sexual recidivism: Meta-analytic findings using the psychopathy checklist—revised. *Psychological Assessment, 25*, 233–243.

Heilbrun, K., DeMatteo, D., Brooks Holliday, S., & LaDuke, C. (Eds.). (2014). *Forensic mental health assessment: A casebook* (2nd ed.). New York: Oxford University Press.

Hildebrand, M., & de Ruiter, C. (2004). PCL-R psychopathy and its relation to DSM-IV axis I and axis II disorders in a sample of male forensic psychiatric patients in the Netherlands. *International Journal of Law and Psychiatry, 27*, 233–248.

Hilterman, E. L. B., Nicholls, T. L., & van Nieuwenhuizen, C. (2014). Predictive validity of risk assessments in juvenile offenders: Comparing the SAVRY, PCL:YV, and YLS/CMI with unstructured clinical assessments. *Assessment, 21*, 324–339.

Hogan, N. R., & Olver, M. E. (2016). Assessing risk for aggression in forensic psychiatric inpatients: An examination of five measures. *Law and Human Behavior, 40*, 233–243.

Hoge, R., & Andrews, D. (2002). *Youth level of service/case management inventory*. Toronto, ON: Multi-Health Systems.

Howard, R., Khalifa, N., Duggan, C., & Lumsden, J. (2012). Are patients deemed "dangerous and severely personality disordered" different from other personality disordered patients detained in forensic settings? *Criminal Behaviour and Mental Health, 22*, 65–78.

Huchzermeier, C., Bruss, E., Geiger, F., Andreas Kernbichler, M. A., & Aldenhoff, J. (2008). Predictive validity of the psychopathy checklist: Screening version for intramural behaviour in violent offenders-a prospective study at a secure psychiatric hospital in Germany. *Canadian Journal of Psychiatry, 53*, 384–391.

Ismail, G., & Looman, J. (2018). Field inter-rater reliability of the psychopathy checklist—revised. *International Journal of Offender Therapy and Comparative Criminology, 62*, 468–481.

Jeandarme, I., Edens, J. F., Habets, P., Bruckers, L., Oei, K., & Bogaerts, S. (2017). PCL-R field validity in prison and hospital settings. *Law and Human Behavior, 41*, 29–43.

Jones, S., Cauffman, E., Miller, J. D., & Mulvey, E. (2006). Investigating different factor structures of the psychopathy checklist: Youth version: Confirmatory factor analytic findings. *Psychological Assessment, 18*, 33–48.

Karpman, B. (1946). A yardstick for measuring psychopathy. *Federal Probation, 10*, 26–31.

Karpman, B. (1948). The myth of the psychopathic personality. *American Journal of Psychiatry, 104*, 523–534.

Kelley, S. E., Edens, J. F., Mowle, E. N., Penson, B. N., & Rulseh, A. (2019). Dangerous, depraved, and deathworthy: A meta-analysis of the correlates of perceived psychopathy in jury simulation studies. *Journal of Clinical Psychology, 75*, 627–643.

Kennealy, P. J., Skeem, J. L., Walters, G. D., & Camp, J. (2010). Do core interpersonal and affective traits of PCL-R psychopathy interact with antisocial behavior and disinhibition to predict violence? *Psychological Assessment, 22*, 569–580.

Kimonis, E. R., Skeem, J. L., Cauffman, E., & Dmitrieva, J. (2011). Are secondary variants of juvenile psychopathy more reactively violent and less psychosocially mature than primary variants? *Law and Human Behavior, 35*(5), 381–391.

Kosson, D. S., Neumann, C. S., Forth, A. E., Salekin, R. T., Hare, R. D., Krischer, M. K., & Sevecke, K. (2013). Factor structure of the Hare psychopathy checklist-youth version (PCL: YV) in adolescent females. *Psychological Assessment, 25*, 71–83.

Klein Haneveld, E., Kamphuis, J. H., Smid, W., & Forbey, J. D. (2017). Using MMPI—2—RF correlates to elucidate the PCL—R and its four facets in a sample of male forensic psychiatric patients. *Journal of Personality Assessment, 99*, 398–407. doi:10.1080/00223891.2016.1228655

Leistico, A. M., Salekin, R. T., DeCosta, J., & Rogers, R. (2008). A large-scale meta-analysis relating the Hare measures of psychopathy to antisocial conduct. *Law and Human Behavior, 32*, 28–45.

Lynam, D. R. (1997). Pursuing the psychopath: Capturing the fledgling psychopath in a nomological net. *Journal of Abnormal Psychology, 106*, 425–438.

McCoy, W. K., & Edens, J. F. (2006). Do Black and White youths differ in levels of psychopathic traits? A meta-analysis of the psychopathy checklist measures. *Journal of Consulting and Clinical Psychology, 74*, 386–392.

McCuish, E. C., Mathesius, J. R., Lussier, P., & Corrado, R. R. (2018). The cross-cultural generalizability of the psychopathy checklist: Youth version for adjudicated indigenous youth. *Psychological Assessment, 30*, 192–203.

McDermott, B. E., Edens, J. F., Quanbeck, C. E., Busse, D., & Scott, C. L. (2008). Examining the role of static and dynamic risk factors in the prediction of inpatient violence: Variable- and person-focused analyses. *Law and Human Behavior, 32,* 325–338.

McGregor, K., Castle, D., & Dolan, M. (2012). Schizophrenia spectrum disorders, substance misuse, and the four-facet model of psychopathy: The relationship to violence. *Schizophrenia Research, 136,* 116–121.

Messick, S. (1995). Validity of psychological assessment: Validation of inferences from persons' responses and performances as scientific inquiry into score meaning. *American Psychologist, 50,* 741–749.

Miller, A. K., Rufino, K. A., Boccaccini, M. T., Jackson, R. L., & Murrie, D. C. (2011). On individual differences in person perception: Raters' personality traits relate to their psychopathy checklist-revised scoring tendencies. *Assessment, 18,* 253–260.

Miller, C. S., Kimonis, E. R., Otto, R. K., Kline, S. M., & Wasserman, A. L. (2012). Reliability of risk assessment measures used in sexually violent predator proceedings. *Psychological Assessment, 24,* 944–953.

Monahan, J., Steadman, H. J., Silver, E., Appelbaum, P. S., Robbins, P. C., Mulvey, E. P., . . . Banks, S. (2001). *Rethinking risk assessment: The MacArthur study of mental disorder and violence.* New York: Oxford University Press.

Morey, L. C. (2007). *Personality assessment inventory professional manual* (2nd ed.). Odessa, FL: Psychological Assessment Resources.

Morey, L. C., Paulino, M. F., Penson, B. N., Simoes, M., Marques, P. B., & Alho, L. (in press). Assessment of psychopathy and antisocial behavior. In P. B. Marques, M. Paulino, & L. Alho (Eds.), *Psychopathy and criminal behavior.* New York: Elsevier.

Morrissey, C., Hogue, T., Mooney, P., Allen, C., Johnston, S., Hollin, C., . . . Taylor, J. L. (2007). Predictive validity of the PCL-R in offenders with intellectual disability in a high secure hospital setting: Institutional aggression. *The Journal of Forensic Psychiatry and Psychology, 18,* 1–15.

Murrie, D. C., Boccaccini, M. T., Caperton, J., & Rufino, K. (2012). Field validity of the psychopathy checklist-revised in sex offender risk assessment. *Psychological Assessment, 24,* 524–529.

Murrie, D. C., Boccaccini, M. T., Turner, D. B., Meeks, M., Woods, C., & Tussey, C. (2009). Rater (dis)agreement on risk assessment measures in sexually violent predator proceedings: Evidence of adversarial allegiance in forensic evaluation? *Psychology, Public Policy, and Law, 15,* 19–53.

Neumann, C. S., Hare, R. D., & Johansson, P. T. (2013). The psychopathy checklist-revised (PCL—R), low anxiety, and fearlessness: A structural equation modeling analysis. *Personality Disorders: Theory, Research, and Treatment, 4,* 129–137.

Nunnally, J., & Bernstein, I. (1994). *Psychometric theory* (3rd ed.). New York: McGraw-Hill.

Olver, M. E., Lewis, K., & Wong, S. C. (2013). Risk reduction treatment of high-risk psychopathic offenders: The relationship of psychopathy and treatment change to violent recidivism. *Personality Disorders: Theory, Research, and Treatment, 4,* 160–167.

Olver, M. E., Neumann, C. S., Sewall, L. A., Lewis, K., Hare, R. D., & Wong, S. C. (2018). A comprehensive examination of the psychometric properties of the Hare psychopathy checklist-revised in a Canadian multisite sample of indigenous and non-indigenous offenders. *Psychological Assessment, 30,* 779–792.

Olver, M. E., Neumann, C. S., Wong, S. P., & Hare, R. D. (2013). The structural and predictive properties of the psychopathy checklist—revised in Canadian aboriginal and non-aboriginal offenders. *Psychological Assessment, 25,* 167–179.

Olver, M. E., & Stockdale, K. C. (2010). Psychopathy and youth violence: Research, controversies and clinical utility. *British Journal of Forensic Practice, 12,* 3–13.

Olver, M. E., Stockdale, K. C., & Wormith, J. S. (2009). Risk assessment with young offenders a meta-analysis of three assessment measures. *Criminal Justice and Behavior, 36,* 329–353.

Olver, M. E., & Wong, S. P. (2015). Short- and long-term recidivism prediction of the PCL-R and the effects of age: A 24-year follow-up. *Personality Disorders: Theory, Research, and Treatment, 6,* 97–105.

Patrick, C. J. (2006). Back to the future: Cleckley as a guide to the next generation of psychopathy research. In C. J. Patrick (Ed.), *Handbook of psychopathy* (pp. 605–618). New York: Guilford Press.

Patrick, C. J. (Ed.). (2018). *Handbook of psychopathy* (2nd ed.). New York: Guilford Press.

Pouls, C., & Jeandarme, I. (2014). Psychopathy in offenders with intellectual disabilities: A comparison of the PCL-R and PCL:SV. *International Journal of Forensic Mental Health, 13,* 207–216.

Poythress, N., & Skeem, J. L. (2006). Disaggregating psychopathy: Where and how to look for variants. In C. J. Patrick (Ed.), *Handbook of psychopathy* (pp. 172–192). New York: Guilford Press.

Quinsey, V. L., Harris, G. T., Rice, M. E., & Cormier, C. A. (2006). *Violent offenders: Appraising and managing risk* (2nd ed.). Washington, DC: American Psychological Association.

Richards, H. J., Gacono, C. B., Cunliffe, T. B., Kivisto, A. J., Smith, J. M., & Bodholdt, R. (2016). Assessing psychopathy in adults: The Hare psychopathy checklist-revised and psychopathy checklist screening version. In C. B. Gacono (Ed.), *The clinical and forensic assessment of psychopathy: A practitioner's guide* (2nd ed., pp. 137–166). New York: Routledge, Taylor & Francis Group.

Rufino, K. A., Boccaccini, M. T., & Guy, L. S. (2011). Scoring subjectivity and item performance on measures used to assess violence risk: The PCL-R and HCR-20 as exemplars. *Assessment, 18*, 453–463.

Salekin, R. T., Leistico, A. M. R., Neumann, C. S., DiCicco, T. M., & Duros, R. L. (2004). Psychopathy and comorbidity in a young offender sample: Taking a closer look at psychopathy's potential importance over disruptive behavior disorders. *Journal of Abnormal Psychology, 113*, 416–427.

Schaap, G., Lammers, S., & de Vogel, V. (2009). Risk assessment in female forensic psychiatric patients: A quasi-prospective study into the validity of the HCR-20 and PCL-R. *Journal of Forensic Psychiatry & Psychology, 20*(3), 354–365.

Schmidt, F., McKinnon, L., Chattha, H. K., & Brownlee, K. (2006). Concurrent and predictive validity of the psychopathy checklist: Youth version across gender and ethnicity. *Psychological Assessment, 18*, 393–401.

Scott, R. (2014). Psychopathy—an evolving and controversial construct. *Psychiatry, Psychology and Law, 21*, 687–715.

Serin, R. C. (1996). Violent recidivism in criminal psychopaths. *Law and Human Behavior, 20*, 207–217.

Singh, J. P., Grann, M., & Fazel, S. (2011). A comparative study of violence risk assessment tools: A systematic review and metaregression analysis of 68 studies involving 25,980 participants. *Clinical Psychology Review, 31*, 499–513.

Skeem, J. L., & Cooke, D. J. (2010a). Is criminal behavior a central component of psychopathy? Conceptual directions for resolving the debate. *Psychological Assessment, 22*, 433–445.

Skeem, J. L., & Cooke, D. J. (2010b). One measure does not a construct make: Directions toward reinvigorating psychopathy research-reply to Hare and Neumann (2010). *Psychological Assessment, 22*, 455–459.

Skeem, J. L., Edens, J. F., Camp, J., & Colwell, L. H. (2004). Are there racial differences in levels of psychopathy? A meta-analysis. *Law and Human Behavior, 28*, 505–527.

Skeem, J. L., Miller, J. D., Mulvey, E. P., Tiemann, J., & Monahan, J. (2005). Using a five-factor lens to explore the relationship between personality traits and violence in psychiatric patients. *Journal of Consulting and Clinical Psychology, 73*, 454–465.

Skeem, J. L., & Mulvey, E. P. (2001). Psychopathy and community violence among civil psychiatric patients: Results from the MacArthur violence risk assessment study. *Journal of Consulting and Clinical Psychology, 69*, 358–374.

Skeem, J. L., Poythress, N. G., Edens, J. F., Lilienfeld, S. O., & Cale, E. (2003). Psychopathic personality or personalities? Exploring potential variants of psychopathy and their implications for risk assessment. *Aggression and Violent Behavior, 8*, 513–546.

Stockdale, K. C., Olver, M. E., & Wong, S. C. (2010). The psychopathy checklist: Youth version and adolescent and adult recidivism: Considerations with respect to gender, ethnicity, and age. *Psychological Assessment, 22*, 768–781.

Sturup, J., Edens, J. F., Sörman, K., Karlberg, D., Fredriksson, B., & Kristiansson, M. (2014). Field reliability of the psychopathy checklist-revised among life sentenced prisoners in Sweden. *Law and Human Behavior, 38*, 315–324.

Sullivan, E. A., Abramowitz, C. S., Lopez, M., & Kosson, D. S. (2006). Reliability and construct validity of the psychopathy checklist-revised for Latino, European American, and African American male inmates. *Psychological Assessment, 18*(4), 382–392.

Tengström, A., Hodgins, S., Grann, M., Langström, N., & Kullgren, G. (2004). Schizophrenia and criminal offending: The role of psychopathy and substance use disorders. *Criminal Justice and Behavior, 31*, 367–391.

Thornton, D. (2007). *Scoring guide for risk matrix 2000.9/SVC.* Retrieved from www.birmingham.ac.uk/Documents/college-les/psych/RM2000scoringinstructions.pdf

Tsang, S., Schmidt, K. M., Vincent, G. M., Salekin, R. T., Moretti, M. M., & Odgers, C. L. (2015). Assessing psychopathy among justice involved adolescents with the PCL: YV: An item response theory examination across gender. *Personality Disorders: Theory, Research, and Treatment, 6*, 22–31.

Vachon, D. D., Lynam, D. R., Loeber, R., & Stouthamer-Loeber, M. (2012). Generalizing the nomological network of psychopathy across populations differing on race and conviction status. *Journal of Abnormal Psychology, 121*, 263–269.

Verschuere, B., van Ghesel Grothe, S., Waldorp, L., Watts, A. L., Lilienfeld, S. O., Edens, J. F., ... Noordhof, A. (2018). What features of psychopathy might be central? A network analysis of the psychopathy checklist-revised (PCL-R) in three large samples. *Journal of Abnormal Psychology, 127*, 51–65.

Vincent, G. M., & Hart, S. D. (2002). Psychopathy in childhood and adolescence: Implications for the assessment and management of multi-problem youths. In R. R. Corrado, R. Roesch, S. D. Hart, & J. K. Gierowski (Eds.), *Multi-problem violent youth: A foundation for comparative research on needs, interventions, and outcomes* (pp. 150–163). Washington, DC: IOS Press.

Vincent, G. M., Odgers, C. L., McCormick, A. V., & Corrado, R. R. (2008). The PCL: YV and recidivism in male and female juveniles: A follow-up into young adulthood. *International Journal of Law and Psychiatry, 31*, 287–296.

Vitacco, M. J., Neumann, C. S., & Caldwell, M. F. (2010). Predicting antisocial behavior in high-risk male adolescents: Contributions of psychopathy and instrumental violence. *Criminal Justice and Behavior, 37*, 833–846.

Vitacco, M. J., Rogers, R., Neumann, C. S., Harrison, K., & Vincent, G. (2005). A comparison of factor models on the PCL-R with mentally disordered offenders: The development of a four-factor model. *Criminal Justice and Behavior, 32*, 526–545.

Walsh, Z. (2013). Psychopathy and criminal violence: The moderating effect of ethnicity. *Law and Human Behavior, 37*, 303–311.

Walters, G. D. (2003a). Predicting criminal justice outcomes with the psychopathy checklist and lifestyle criminality screening form: A meta-analytic comparison. *Behavioral Sciences and the Law, 21*, 89–102.

Walters, G. D. (2003b). Predicting institutional adjustment and recidivism with the psychopathy checklist factor scores: A meta-analysis. *Law and Human Behavior, 27*, 541–558.

Walters, G. D. (2006). Risk-appraisal versus self-report in the prediction of criminal justice outcomes. *Criminal Justice and Behavior, 33*, 279–304.

Walters, G. D. (2012). Psychopathy and crime: Testing the incremental validity of PCL-R-measured psychopathy as a predictor of general and violent recidivism. *Law and Human Behavior, 36*, 404–412.

Walters, G. D. (2014a). The latent structure of psychopathy in male adjudicated delinquents: A cross-domain taxometric analysis. *Personality Disorders: Theory, Research, and Treatment, 5*, 348–355.

Walters, G. D. (2014b). Predicting self-reported total, aggressive, and income offending with the youth version of the psychopathy checklist: Gender- and factor-level interactions. *Psychological Assessment, 26*, 288–296.

Walters, G. D., Gray, N. S., Jackson, R. L., Sewell, K. W., Rogers, R., Taylor, J., & Snowden, R. J. (2007). A taxometric analysis of the psychopathy checklist: Screening version: Further evidence of dimensionality. *Psychological Assessment, 19*, 330–339.

Walters, G. D., Knight, R. A., Grann, M., & Dahle, K. (2008). Incremental validity of the psychopathy checklist facet scores: Predicting release outcome in six samples. *Journal of Abnormal Psychology, 117*, 396–405.

Walters, G. D., & Mandell, W. (2007). Incremental validity of the psychological inventory of criminal thinking styles and psychopathy checklist: Screening version in predicting disciplinary outcome. *Law and Human Behavior, 31*, 141–157.

Walters, G. D., Marcus, D. K., Edens, J. F., Knight, R., & Sanford, G. (2011). In search of the psychopathic sexuality taxon: Indicator size does matter. *Behavioral Sciences and the Law, 29*, 23–39.

Warren, J. I., Burnette, M. L., South, S. C., Preeti, C., Bale, R., Friend, R., & Van Patten, I. (2003). Psychopathy in women: Structural modeling and comorbidity. *International Journal of Law and Psychiatry, 26*, 223–242.

Webster, C. D., Douglas, K. S., Eaves, D., & Hart, S. D. (1997). *HCR-20: Assessing risk for violence* (Version 2). Burnaby, BC: Mental Health, Law, and Policy Institute, Simon Fraser University.

Weizmann-Henelius, G., Virkkunen, M., Gammelgård, M., Eronen, M., & Putkonen, H. (2015). The PCL-R and violent recidivism in a prospective follow-up of a nationwide sample of female offenders. *Journal of Forensic Psychiatry and Psychology, 26*, 667–685.

Welsh, J. L., Schmidt, F., McKinnon, L., Chattha, H. K., & Meyers, J. R. (2008). A comparative study of adolescent risk assessment instruments predictive and incremental validity. *Assessment, 15*, 104–115.

Yang, M., Wong, S. C. P., & Coid, J. (2010). The efficacy of violence prediction: A meta-analytic comparison of nine risk assessment tools. *Psychological Bulletin, 136*, 740–767.

Chapter 3

Brief and Emerging Violence Risk Assessment Measures

Catherine S. Shaffer, Erin K. Fuller, and Laura S. Guy

Meta-analytic reviews have identified at least 400 structured violence risk assessment measures used by professionals working in health, justice, and general community settings (Singh et al., 2014). These include well-researched and widely used measures, measures that have received relatively less empirical or clinical attention but nevertheless show considerable promise to assist in the evaluation of risk, and locally developed or "homegrown" measures that have limited, if any, research support.

In this chapter, we discuss structured measures with some research and professional uptake, but which do not yet have an established research base or usership. Some of these measures were developed to screen for violence risk or guide immediate action rather than facilitate a comprehensive risk assessment. We were interested in evaluating measures that show considerable clinical promise in the screening or assessment of risk for different types of violence. We excluded from consideration measures that: (1) do not have evaluations of psychometric properties published in peer-reviewed scholarly journals; (2) were developed for use by a single institution or jurisdiction; (3) were not developed explicitly for the purpose of risk assessment (e.g., behavioural checklists, personality assessments); (4) are not administered by clinicians (e.g., victim judgment tools, self-report appraisals of risk); and (5) were not published in or translated into English. The tools on which we chose to focus use different assessments methods (i.e., structured professional judgment [SPJ] and actuarial) and address diverse outcomes (i.e., general and specific forms of violence) among adults or youth.

Space limitations allowed us to focus on ten measures: Dynamic Appraisal of Situational Aggression—Inpatient Version (Ogloff & Daffern, 2006), Dynamic Appraisal of Situational Aggression—Youth Version (Daffern & Ogloff, 2014), Dynamic Appraisal of Situational Aggression: Women's Version (Riordan et al., 2019), Violence-Risk Screening-10 (Hartvig et al., 2007), Domestic Violence Screening Instrument (Williams & Houghton, 2004; Williams & Grant, 2006), Dynamic Risk Assessment for Offender Re-Entry (Serin, 2007; Serin, Mailloux, & Wilson, 2012), Juvenile Sexual Offense Recidivism Risk Assessment Tool—II (Epperson, Ralston, Fowers, DeWitt, & Gore, 2006), Guidelines for Stalking Assessment and Management (Kropp, Hart, & Lyon, 2008), Stalking Risk Profile (MacKenzie et al., 2009), and Assessment of Risk for Honour-Based Violence (Kropp, Belfrage, & Hart, 2013).

We first review screening tools, then turn our attention to more comprehensive risk assessment measures. *Screening* tools are brief and meant to be completed relatively quickly. They typically are developed to identify individuals in need of a more comprehensive evaluation ("screening in"), or to identify individuals presumed to pose relatively lower levels of risk ("screening out") who would not be subjected to more resource-heavy assessments. They also may assist in determining whether immediate intervention is required. By virtue of their brevity, screening tools are not intended to facilitate long-term risk management. In contrast, risk *assessment* tools are intended to provide a comprehensive evaluation of risk posed and, in some cases, to facilitate development of an individually tailored risk management plan. For a more in- depth discussion of these issues, see Vincent, Terry, and Maney (2009).

For each measure reviewed, we provide a brief description (including the model of risk assessment, the criterion it is designed to assess, target populations, intended applications, and content), a summary of its psychometric properties (with a focus on interrater reliability and predictive validity), and an analysis of its professional uptake (including countries of use and user feedback regarding the acceptability and feasibility of administering the tool in practice). Given that the SPJ tools described in this chapter were developed through similar means and share similar features, we briefly review universal features of these instruments at the onset to avoid repetition in the text. As is the case for all SPJ tools, the four described in this chapter: (1) were developed through a systematic review of the relevant scientific and professional literatures, including analysis of standards of practice, ethical codes, and relevant legal principles; (2) are intended for use with males and females by trained professionals working in diverse settings (e.g., mental health, law enforcement, human resources, security); (3) should be completed after considering multiple sources of information (e.g., interview with the examinee and collateral sources, and review of diverse types of files, such as mental health, legal, school, employment, and social media); (4) comprise items assessed on a 3-level scale (*not present, possibly or partially present, present*); (5) allow for consideration of case-specific factors not included on the tool; (6) require evaluators to exercise professional judgment in reaching a final conclusory opinion or summary risk rating (SRR) of low, moderate, or high risk (however, total numerical scores may be generated for research purposes); and (7) allow for reassessments of risk. As with all actuarial tools, a defining hallmark of the four reviewed in this chapter is that *a priori* algorithmic rules for combining the data are applied to yield a total numerical score. See the chapter by Heilbrun et al. (Chapter 1 in this volume), for a detailed description of the actuarial and SPJ methods of violence risk assessment. In the final section of this chapter, we discuss directions for future research.

Screening Tools

General Violence

Dynamic Appraisal of Situational Aggression—Inpatient Version (DASA-IV)

DESCRIPTION

The DASA-IV (Ogloff & Daffern, 2006) is an actuarial measure designed to assess risk for imminent inpatient violence (i.e., within the next 24 hours) and identify targets for staff intervention. The DASA-IV is to be used by a qualified health care professional, such as a psychiatric nurse, with men and women aged 18 years and older who are residing in inpatient forensic or civil psychiatric settings.

The DASA-IV was developed by empirically testing the association between inpatient aggression and all items on the Brøset Violence Checklist (BVC; Almvik, Woods, & Rasmussen, 2000), six items on the Historical-Clinical-Risk Management-20, Version 2 (HCR-20; Webster, Douglas, Eaves, & Hart 1997), and other empirically derived risk factors (Ogloff & Daffern, 2006) over a 6-month period among a sample of forensic psychiatric patients in Australia. The DASA-IV comprises seven items that together yielded the highest Area Under the Curve (AUC) value in the development sample: two from the HCR-20 (negative attitudes, impulsivity), two from the BVC (irritability, verbal threats), and three additional risk factors (sensitive to perceived provocation, easily angered when requests are denied, and unwillingness to follow direction). Each item is coded as *absent* (0) or *present* (1) over the previous 24-hour period. A total score is derived from summing each item score, with a score of 0 indicating low risk for violence over the upcoming 24-hour period, 1 to 3 indicating moderate risk, 4 or higher indicating high risk, and 6 to 7 indicating imminent risk. Generally, re-evaluations of risk using the DASA-IV should occur every 24 hours.

A youth and a women's version of the DASA were also developed. The DASA-Youth Version (DASA-YV; Daffern & Ogloff, 2014) is comprised of all seven items on the DASA-IV and four additional items (anxious or fearful, low empathy/remorse, significant peer rejection, and outside stressors), which were adapted or developed from a measure of general violence, the Structured Assessment of Violence Risk in Youth (SAVRY; Borum, Bartel, & Forth, 2006), and from the DASA-YV validation study (Daffern & Ogloff, 2014). The DASA: Women's Version (DASA:WV; Riordan et al., 2019) is comprised of all DASA-IV items, as well as two items from the HCR-20 Female Additional Manual (covert/manipulative behaviour and low self-esteem; de Vogel, de Vries Robbé, van Kalmthout, & Place, 2011), and a rating of ward atmosphere (disturbing/unsettling and/or aggressive tension/threats of violence).

PSYCHOMETRIC PROPERTIES

At least three peer-reviewed studies have examined the reliability of the DASA-IV or DASA-YV. These studies have reported excellent interrater reliability (IRR; see Cicchetti & Sparrow, 1981) of the DASA-IV total score among psychiatric nurses working at an adult forensic psychiatric hospital (Krippendorff's alpha = .92; Chan & Chow, 2014) and supervision staff working at a juvenile psychiatric facility (single measures intraclass correlation coefficient [ICC_1] = .91; Chu, Hoo, Daffern, & Tan, 2012) and good IRR of the DASA-YV total score among a youth inpatient psychiatric sample (Kappa [κ] = .79) (Dutch & Patil, 2018). Although violence risk assessment measures are not intended to measure a single underlying psychological construct, Chan and Chow (2014) found high internal consistency (see Nunnally & Bernstein, 1978), as indicated by Cronbach's alpha (α) for the DASA-IV total score (α = .86). IRR for DASA-IV risk bins and individual items has not been published. To date, no peer-reviewed studies have examined the reliability of the DASA-WV.

With respect to concurrent validity, the DASA-IV total score has been found to have a large association with the BVC total score (r = .67; Chu, Thomas, Daffern, & Ogloff, 2013, Spearman rank-order coefficient [r_s] = .96; Chan & Chow, 2014) and the HCR-20 Clinical scale "score" (r = .73; Chu, Thomas et al., 2013). With respect to incremental validity (here, the extent to which one tool increases the predictive validity beyond that of other tools or factors), several peer-reviewed studies have found the DASA-IV total score outperformed the HCR-20 Clinical "score" (e.g., Chu et al., 2013; Ogloff & Daffern, 2006), as well as structured and unstructured clinical judgment (Griffith et al., 2013). In Chu, Thomas et al. (2013) comparison of DASA-IV risk bins and total score, the former did not add incrementally to the latter in the prediction of imminent physical aggression towards others. To our knowledge, no peer-reviewed studies have examined the concurrent validity of the DASA-YV or DASA-WV.

At least 15 peer-reviewed studies have examined predictive validity of the DASA-IV (Barry-Walsh, Daffern, Duncan, & Ogloff, 2009; Chan & Chow, 2014; Chu, Daffern, & Ogloff, 2013; Chu et al., 2012; Chu, Thomas et al., 2013; Daffern & Howells, 2007; Daffern et al., 2009; Dumais, Larue, Michaud, & Goulet, 2012; Griffith, Daffern, & Godber, 2013; Kasinathan et al., 2015; Lantta, Kontio, Daffern, Adams, & Valimaki, 2016; Maguire, Daffern, Bowe, & McKenna, 2017; Nqwaku et al., 2018; Riordan et al., 2019; Vojt, Marshall, & Thomson, 2010). Studies with civil and forensic psychiatric samples have indicated moderate to large predictive accuracy of DASA-IV total scores for any imminent inpatient aggression (r = .33 to .37; AUC = .55 to .97), verbal aggression (r = .30 to .40; AUC = .57 to .86), physical aggression towards objects (AUC = .66 to .82), physical aggression towards other patients (r = .33 to .40; AUC = .55 to .92) and staff (AUC = .48 to .80), and self-harm (AUC = .65 to .92).

Predictive validity of the DASA-YV has been evaluated in at least two peer-reviewed studies (Dutch & Patil, 2018; Kasinathan et al., 2015). These studies have indicated moderate to large predictive accuracy of DASA-YV total scores for any aggression (AUC = .75 to .90), verbal aggression (AUC = .74 to .92), physical aggression towards others (AUC = .72 to .84). and physical aggression against objects (AUC = .75 to .88). Incrementally utility of the DASA-IV or DASA-YV have not yet been examined.

At least one peer-reviewed study has examined the predictive validity of the DASA-WV. Riordan and colleagues (2019) reported moderate to large predictive accuracy of DASA-WV total scores for any aggression (AUC = .63 to .76), verbal aggression (AUC = .64 to .76), physical aggression towards others (AUC = .65 to .82), physical aggression towards objects (AUC = .63 and .82), and self-harm (AUC = .66 to .92) in a female forensic psychiatric inpatient sample. However, the DASA-WV did not improve predictive accuracy above the DASA-IV, so the authors did not recommended its use.

PROFESSIONAL UPTAKE

The DASA-IV has been translated into Finnish (Lantta, Daffern, Kontio, & Valimaki, 2015) and French (Dumais et al., 2012) and currently is used in inpatient settings in at least eight countries across four continents (Barry-Walsh et al., 2009; Chan & Chow, 2014; Chu et al., 2012; Chu Thomas et al., 2013; Daffern et al., 2009; Dumais et al., 2012; Griffith et al., 2013; Kasinathan et al., 2015; Lantta et al., 2015; Maguire et al., 2017; Vojt et al., 2010). Studies examining the perceived clinical utility of the DASA-IV have reported mixed results. Dumais and colleagues (2012) surveyed attitudes of psychiatric nurses towards the DASA-IV following its implementation at a civil psychiatric hospital in Canada. Most nurses (75.0% to 81.3%) had a positive view of the measure and perceived it as clinically relevant and helpful in preventing violence in the hospital. In contrast, Daffern and colleagues (2009) found that 12 of 16 psychiatric nurses who responded to the survey reported that administering the DASA-IV among a Dangerous and Severe Personality Disorder (DSPD) forensic psychiatric sample in England was not helpful. The main concern expressed was that the DASA-IV was unable to monitor rapid changes (i.e., over seconds, minutes, or hours) in affect and behaviour specific to DSPD patients. However, the authors noted that these findings may reflect a lack of full integration of the DASA-IV into clinical practice and insufficient training with some staff. Finally, Lantta and colleagues (2015) surveyed attitudes following implementation of the DASA-IV in mental health units in Finland. Nurses described the DASA-IV as easy and quick to administer and helpful in treatment monitoring and facilitating communication between staff, but difficult to complete.

Dutch and Patil (2018) surveyed attitudes of youth psychiatric nurses following the use of the DASA-YV. Most nurses (80%) reported that the DASA-YV was quick, easy to use, and applicable to all patients. They also reported that the DASA-YV helped them better observe patient behaviour, and that it predicted aggressive incidents better than intuition alone. All nurses felt that the tool helped them record instances of aggression and that it was useful as a daily tool.

Violence-Risk Screening-10 (V-RISK-10)

DESCRIPTION

The V-RISK-10 (Hartvig et al., 2007) is a SPJ measure developed to assist in the evaluation of risk for inpatient and outpatient violence among adult civil psychiatric patients. It was designed to screen patients for referral for a more comprehensive risk assessment (e.g., with the HCR-20) and identify individuals in need of immediate risk management efforts. It is intended for use by psychologists, psychiatrists, or general practitioners.

The V-RISK-10 was developed by empirically testing the association between violence and a 33-item measure, the Preliminary Scheme (Hartvig, Alfarnes, Ostberg, Skjonberg, & Moger, 2006) over a 1-year period among a sample of civil psychiatric patients in Norway. The Preliminary Scheme comprises 19 items from the HCR-20, Version 2 (Webster et al., 1997), six items from the BVC (Almvik et al., 2000), and eight risk factors derived from the empirical and professional literatures (Hartvig et al., 2006). Based on findings of this research (Hartvig et al., 2006), the V-RISK-10 was developed by identifying the 10 items with the best predictive validity (Hartvig et al., 2011). Of these 10 items, four capture both past and present functioning (e.g., previous and/or current substance use), four tap present functioning only (e.g., lack of empathy), and two address anticipated future functioning (e.g., exposure to and coping with future stressors). In the final administration step, evaluators select one of three options regarding next steps: no further detailed violence risk assessment, more detailed violence risk assessment, or implementation of preventive measures.

PSYCHOMETRIC PROPERTIES

To date, at least three peer-reviewed studies have examined the IRR of the V-RISK-10 when used by psychologists or physicians in their clinical-forensic practice. All found fair to good support, with ICC_1 values ranging from .35 to .87 and average measures intraclass correlation coefficient (ICC_2) values ranging from .77 to .89 for the total score (Bjørkly, Hartvig, Heggen, Brauer, & Moger, 2009; Roaldset, Hartvig, & Bjørkly, 2011; Yao, Li, Arthur, Hu, & Cheng, 2012). Adequate rater reliability also has been reported for the SRR, with an ICC_1 of .72 and ICC_2 of .85 (Bjørkly et al., 2009). A wider range of reliability coefficients has been reported at the item level (ICC_1 = .06 to .80 and ICC_2 = .29 to .96; Bjørkly et al., 2009; Yao et al., 2012).

To our knowledge, no peer-reviewed studies have examined the concurrent or incremental validity of the V-RISK-10. High levels of predictive validity of the V-RISK-10 have been demonstrated in at least eight peer-reviewed studies, with no differences in predictive accuracy as a function of gender (Eriksen et al., 2016; Eriksen, Færden, Lockertsen, Bjørkly, & Roaldset, 2018). With respect to inpatient violence, moderate to large effect sizes have been observed for any violence (AUC = .79 to .85), violent threats (AUC = .81), and physical violence (AUC = .89). Similarly, moderate to large effects for violence have been reported for patients discharged to the community (AUC = .69 to .80; Eriksen et al., 2016, 2018; Hartvig, Roaldset, Moger, Østberg, & Bjørkly, 2011; Roaldset et al., 2011; Roaldset, Hartvig, Linaker, & Bjørkly, 2012; Yao et al., 2012; Yao, Li, Arthur, Hu, & Cheng, 2014).

PROFESSIONAL UPTAKE

The V-RISK-10 has been translated into at least three languages (English, Danish, and Mandarin; Nielsen et al., 2015; Singh et al., 2014; Yao et al., 2012) and is used internationally on five continents (Singh et al., 2014), including at least seven countries. Results from an international survey of psychology, psychiatry, and nursing professionals indicated that V-RISK-10 users perceive it as helpful to monitor risk, conduct risk assessments, and develop case management plans (Singh et al., 2014).

Intimate Partner Violence

Domestic Violence Screening Instrument (DVSI)

DESCRIPTION

The DVSI (Williams & Houghton, 2004; Williams & Grant, 2006) is an actuarial measure designed to screen for risk of intimate partner violence (IPV) to indicate whether a more comprehensive risk assessment (e.g., the Spousal Assault Risk Assessment [SARA]; Kropp & Hart, 2015) should be conducted or whether immediate risk management plans should be put in place (Williams & Houghton, 2004). The development of the DVSI was prompted by the need to increase the speed with which IPV cases were processed. As such, the information required to complete the DVSI can be drawn from official (e.g., court and probation) records and offender management databases (Williams & Houghton, 2004).

The initial version of the DVSI (Williams & Houghton, 2004) was developed through analysis of local data to identify common variables associated with IPV, review of the empirical literature, and consultation with police and other professionals (e.g., judges, lawyers, victim service workers). The resulting 12 items were subsequently found to be statistically associated with IPV recidivism in a validation sample of 1,465 male offenders arrested for IPV offences committed against female partners. DVSI items pertain to the criminal history (e.g., history of IPV and non-IPV offenses) and social history (e.g., employment status, recent separation) of the offender, and whether weapons or children were present during the index IPV offense. Each item is scored from 0 to 2 or 0 to 3, depending on the presence and severity of the item. Total scores are calculated by summing item scores, with higher total scores indicating "the higher the risk for reoffending, noncompliance with court, and probation orders, and thus, the higher the risk to victims" (Williams & Houghton, 2004, p. 441). Moreover, a higher score is interpreted as an indication of the need for a more thorough IPV assessment.

In 2006, an 11-item version, the DSVI-Revised (DVSI-R; Williams & Grant, 2006), was developed by re-wording or removing redundant items. In addition, in response to users' feedback about wanting the option to exercise professional discretion, two SRRs were introduced for users to judge imminent risk (i.e., within the next 6 months) of violence toward (1) the victim and (2) other persons known to the victim or perpetrator.

PSYCHOMETRIC PROPERTIES

Reliability of the DVSI has been evaluated in at least four peer-reviewed studies. These studies reported acceptable internal consistency for the total score for the DVSI ($\alpha = .71$; Williams & Houghton, 2004) and DVSI-R ($\alpha = .73$ to .75; Stansfield & Williams, 2014; Williams, 2012; Williams & Stansfield, 2017) as well as acceptable item-total scale correlations ($r = .24$ to .72; Williams, 2012). IRR of the DVSI or DVSI-R has not been reported.

Support for the concurrent validity of the DVSI total score has been demonstrated through moderate to large associations with other measures of IPV risk, such as the SARA total "score" ($r = .53$ to .54; Hilton, Harris, Rice, Houghton, & Eke, 2008; Williams & Houghton, 2004) and SRR ($r = .57$; Williams & Houghton); the Domestic Violence Risk Appraisal Guide ($r = .50$; Hilton et al., 2008); and the Ontario Domestic Assault Risk Assessment ($r = .52$; Hilton et al., 2008). Its association with measures of risk for general violence and psychopathy is somewhat smaller: Level of Service Inventory-Revised (Andrews & Bonta, 1995) total score ($r = .17$; Williams & Houghton, 2004); VRAG (Quinsey, Harris, Rice, & Cormier, 2006) score ($r = .31$; Hilton et al., 2008); and Psychopathy Checklist-Revised (Hare, 2003) total score ($r = .34$; Hilton et al., 2008).

Predictive validity of the DVSI or DVSI-R has been examined in at least eight peer-reviewed studies. The initial version of the DVSI showed small to moderate predictive utility for the presence of any IPV or family violence rearrests (AUC = .61 to .65) and the total number of such rearrests ($r = .18$ to .21; Williams & Houghton, 2004). When IPV was identified using victim self-report data, the DVSI had small to moderate effect sizes for severe IPV (AUC = .60 to .68), and low to no predictive accuracy for any IPV (AUC = .50 to .60) and less severe IPV (AUC = .49 to .56; Campbell et al., 2005; Williams & Houghton, 2004).

The DVSI-R total score also has been found to have small to moderate utility in predicting the occurrence of IPV or family violence offenses (AUC = .61 to .65) and the total number of such offenses (r = .17 to .24), violations of protective or court orders (AUC = .67 to .72), offense severity (r = .18), and degree of victim injury (r = .19) (Gerstenberger & Williams, 2012; Hilton et al., 2008; Stansfield & Williams, 2014; Williams & Grant, 2006; Williams, 2012). Predictive accuracy was improved when the DVSI-R total score was combined with additional perpetrator, victim, and clinical variables (AUC = .84; Williams & Grant, 2006). In the three peer-reviewed studies that examined the predictive accuracy of DVSI-R SRRs, DVSI-R SRRs were predictive of any IPV recidivism (Odds Ratio = 1.69), imminent risk of violence towards the victim (AUC = .64 to .66), and imminent risk to others (AUC = .61 to .66) (Williams, 2012; Williams & Grant, 2006; Williams & Stansfield, 2017).

Although the DVSI-R total score has been found to add incrementally to the prediction of IPV above and beyond perpetrator demographic and offence characteristics (Gerstenberger & Williams, 2012; Williams & Grant, 2006), findings with respect to the incremental utility of DVSI-R SRRs are mixed. One peer-reviewed study found that the DVSI-R SRR for imminent risk to other persons known to the victim or perpetrator, but not the SRR for imminent risk towards victims, added incrementally to perpetrator characteristics in the prediction of IPV (Williams & Grant, 2006). In another study, neither imminent risk towards victims nor imminent risk to others was incrementally predictive beyond DVSI-R total scores (Williams, 2012).

PROFESSIONAL UPTAKE

The DVSI/DVSI-R is used in several U.S. jurisdictions to determine the suitable pretrial and disposition options for IPV offenders (Williams, 2012). Given its inclusion of SRRs, the DVSI-R has yielded more positive user feedback among field staff than the original DVSI (Williams & Grant, 2006).

Comprehensive Assessment Tools

General Violence

Dynamic Risk Assessment for Offender Re-Entry (DRAOR)

DESCRIPTION

The DRAOR (Serin, 2007; Serin et al., 2012) is a clinical rating scale designed to assist in the assessment and management of general and violent recidivism among male and female offenders aged 18 years or older under community supervision. It was developed based on two well-validated models of offender management: the Personal, Interpersonal, Community-Reinforcement perspective and the Risk-Need-Responsivity framework (Andrews & Bonta, 2010). The DRAOR is intended for use by probation and parole officers.

The DRAOR comprises 19 items divided into three subscales pertaining to dynamic risk factors that can change gradually (*Stable*, e.g., attitudes towards authority), dynamic risk factors that can change rapidly (*Acute*, e.g., opportunity for crime), and factors that have the potential to mitigate reoffence risk (*Protective*, e.g., social support). Items were selected following a review of the scientific literature on recidivism (Serin, 2007). Each Stable and Acute item is rated as *no problem*, *slight problem*, or *definite problem*, whereas each Protective item is rated as *not protective*, *slight/possible asset*, or *definite asset* using information obtained from interviews with the offender and collateral contacts (e.g., family, treatment providers) or other external sources (e.g., police intelligence activity). Evaluators identify risk scenarios and indicate their level of concern for imminent reoffending or violation of supervision conditions on a 6-point Likert-type scale from *Not Concerned* (1) to *Very Concerned* (6). Evaluators also indicate whether they intend to modify the frequency of supervision (increase, maintain, or decrease) based on the aforementioned level of concern. For research purposes, a total score may be calculated by summing scores of the Acute and Stable scales and subtracting the Protective scale score (Serin et al., 2016). It is recommended that DRAOR reassessments occur at each supervision contact (i.e., at least once a month) to ensure that any changes in the offender's circumstances are captured (Serin et al., 2012).

PSYCHOMETRIC PROPERTIES

IRR and internal consistency of the DRAOR have not been reported in peer-reviewed research. With respect to convergent validity, Yesberg and Polaschek (2015) reported the DRAOR total score had a moderate association (r = .30) with a measure of offenders' preparedness for release, the Release Proposal Feasibility Assessment Revised (Wilson, 2002), and small associations with a measure of criminal recidivism risk, the Violence Risk Scale (Wong & Gordon, 2002; r = .16 and .25 with Violence Risk Scale Static and Dynamic subscale scores, respectively).

Predictive utility of the DRAOR when used by probation officers has been examined in at least four peer-reviewed studies. Among low- to moderate- (Serin, Chadwick, & Lloyd, 2016) and high-risk (Yesberg & Polaschek, 2015) offenders, the DRAOR total score was a small to moderate predictor of general (AUC = .62 to .70) and violent (AUC = .60) recidivism, a small to large predictor of supervision violations (AUC = .55 to .72), and a small predictor of reimprisonment (AUC = .62). Similar results also have been obtained for Stable (AUC = .58 to .67), Acute (AUC = .55 to .70), and Protective (AUC = .60 to .70) subscale scores. Although some studies have provided weak support of the predictive utility of the DRAOR, modest AUC values may reflect improved case management of high-risk offenders, rather than a limitation of the predictive utility of the tool (Yesberg & Polaschek, 2015).

Consistent with claims that the DRAOR is a "gender-neutral" and dynamic risk assessment measure, it has been found to be predictive of recidivism irrespective of examinee gender (Yesberg, Scanlan, Hanby, Serin, & Polaschek, 2015; Scanlan, Yesberg, Fortune, & Polaschek, 2020) and sensitive to fluctuations in risk (Polaschek, Yesberg, & Chauhan, 2018; Serin, Chadwick et al., 2016). For instance, Serin, Gobeil et al. (2016) reported that over an average follow-up period of 65.6 days, the DRAOR scores of 85% of the study participants meaningfully changed.

With respect to incremental utility of the DRAOR, findings have been mixed. Yesberg and colleagues (2015) found that the DRAOR incrementally predicted reconvictions among men above an actuarial measure of risk, the Risk of Re-Conviction × Risk of Re-Imprisonment Model ([RoC*RoI], Bakker, Riley, & O'Malley, 1999). In contrast, Yesberg and Polaschek (2015) found that the DRAOR added incrementally to the RoC*RoI for women, but not for men.

PROFESSIONAL UPTAKE

The DRAOR has been implemented in New Zealand (Yesberg & Polaschek, 2015) and in some U.S. jurisdictions (Serin, Chadwick et al., 2016). In pilot testing in New Zealand, probation officers described the DRAOR as useful, user-friendly, easy to administer, and helpful in structuring their interactions with offenders (Yesberg & Polaschek, 2015).

Sexual Violence

Juvenile Sexual Offense Recidivism Risk Assessment Tool—II (JSORRAT-II)

DESCRIPTION

The JSORRAT-II (Epperson et al., 2006) is an actuarial measure designed to assist in the evaluation of risk of sexual violence among male juvenile offenders aged 12 to 17 years old who have been committed a sexual offence. It is the only known actuarial risk assessment measure designed specifically for adolescent sexual offenders and is intended for use by mental health and criminal justice professionals.

The JSORRAT-II comprises 12 items scored following review of file information pertaining to the youth's sexual and nonsexual offence history (e.g., number of adjudications for sexual offences), treatment history (i.e., completion of sex offender treatment), school history (e.g., school discipline problems), and victimization history (e.g., number of sexual abuse incidents in which the juvenile was a victim). Items were selected by identifying significant predictors of sexual reoffending among a sample of male youth adjudicated for a sex offence (Epperson et al., 2006). Five J-SORRAT-II items are scored as 0 or 1 and the remaining items are scored from 0 to 2 or 0 to 3 to indicate different levels of severity for the particular item. An item is scored as 0 if there is insufficient information to rate it. Total scores between 0 and 2 classify a youth as low risk to sexually reoffend, 3 and 4 as moderately low risk, 5 and 7 as moderate risk, 8 and 11 as moderately high risk, and 12 and above as high risk. JSORRAT-II assessments expire when the evaluee turns 18 years old.

PSYCHOMETRIC PROPERTIES

At least five peer-reviewed studies have found support for the IRR of JSORRAT-II total scores and individual items in research settings (i.e., when rated by research assistants). ICC_1 values for total scores have ranged from .89 to .97 (Epperson & Ralston, 2015; Ralston, Sarkar, Philipp, & Epperson, 2015, 2018; Ralston, Epperson, & Edwards, 2014; Viljoen et al., 2008), whereas individual items have displayed greater variability, with ICC_1 values ranging from .67 to 1.00 (Ralston et al., 2014). In addition, the JSORRAT-II has demonstrated excellent internal consistency (α = .97 to .99; Ralston et al., 2015, 2018).

With respect to convergent validity, the JSORATT-II total score has demonstrated a moderate correlation with the total score of the Juvenile-Sex Offender Assessment Protocol-II (Prentky & Righthand, 2003; r = .28, Viljoen et al. 2008) and a small correlation with the total score on the SAVRY (Borum, Bartel, & Forth, 2006; r = .19).

Predictive validity of the JSORRAT-II has been evaluated in at least eight peer-reviewed studies. In their 2012 meta-analytic review of seven JSORRAT-II studies (including four unpublished studies and the JSORRAT-II development sample), Viljoen, Mordell, and Beneteau (2012) reported small weighted effect sizes for sexual reoffending (r_w = .12; AUCw of .64 and .61 when the initial development sample was and was not included in the analysis, respectively). Subsequent to this meta-analysis, several peer-reviewed studies have provided further evidence for the predictive utility of the JSORRAT-II for sexual reoffending (AUC = .65 to .70; Epperson & Ralston, 2015; Ralston et al., 2014, 2015, 2018; but see also Rasmussen, 2018). To date, no peer-reviewed studies have examined the incremental validity of the JSORRATT-II.

PROFESSIONAL UPTAKE

The JSORRAT-II authors recommend that its use be limited to jurisdictions in which it has been validated (Epperson et al., 2006; i.e., California, Georgia, Iowa, Utah). As such, the JSORRAT-II currently is used in only a small number of states. To our knowledge no studies have examined user satisfaction for the JSORRAT-II.

Stalking

Guidelines for Stalking Assessment and Management (SAM)

DESCRIPTION

The SAM (Kropp, Hart, & Lyon, 2008) is a SPJ risk assessment measure developed to assess the risk of stalking or criminal harassment among individuals with a known or suspected history of stalking. The SAM defines stalking as any "unwanted and repeated communication, contact, or other conduct that deliberately or recklessly causes people to experience reasonable fear or concern for their safety or the safety of others known to them" (Kropp et al., 2008, p. 1).

The SAM comprises 30 risk factors across three domains pertaining to (1) the pattern and seriousness of the stalking behaviour (*Nature of Stalking*, e.g., intimidates victims, stalking is persistent); (2) the psychosocial adjustment and background of the perpetrator (*Perpetrator*, e.g., angry, intimate relationship problems); and (3) the ability of the victim to engage in self-protective behaviours (*Victim Vulnerability*, e.g., inconsistent behaviour toward perpetrator, employment and financial problems). Each risk factor is coded with respect to the perpetrator's (1) current or most recent pattern of stalking behaviour and (2) previous pattern of stalking, if applicable. Based on the presence and relevance of each item, evaluators provide several SRRs: (1) case prioritization; (2) risk for continued stalking; (3) risk for serious physical harm; (4) reasonableness of victim's fear; and (5) immediate action required (Kropp et al., 2008).

PSYCHOMETRIC PROPERTIES

At least six peer-reviewed studies have examined the reliability of the SAM. Good to excellent interrater reliability for the SAM total "score" (ICC_1 = .82, ICC_2 = .77 to .90), SRRs (ICC_1 = .39 to .77 and ICC_2 = .44 to .57 for case prioritization, ICC_1 = .66 to .71 and ICC_2 = .83 for future stalking, ICC_1 = .44 to .50 and ICC_2 = .61 and for serious physical harm), and domain "scores" (ICC_1 = .77 to .91 and ICC_2 = .64 to .87 for Nature of Stalking, ICC_1 = .68 to .92 and ICC_2 = .81 to .87 for Perpetrator, and ICC_1 = .44 to .72 and ICC_2 = .61 to .77 for Victim Vulnerability) have been reported among trained research assistants (Foellmi, Rosenfeld, & Galietta, 2016; Gerbrandij, Rosenfeld, Nijdam-Jones, & Galietta, 2018; Kropp, Hart, Lyon, & Storey, 2011; Shea, McEwan, Strand, & Ogloff, 2018; Storey & Hart, 2011; Storey, Hart, Meloy, & Reavis, 2009). At least one peer-reviewed study has examined the internal consistency of the SAM. Foellmi and colleagues (2016) reported good internal consistency for the SAM total "score" (α = .75) and "scores" on the Nature of Stalking (α = .60) and Perpetrator (α = .70) domains (there was insufficient information to rate the Victim Vulnerability domain).

With respect to concurrent validity, SAM total and subscale "scores" and SRRs have been found to have moderate to strong associations with the Brief Spousal Assault Form for the Evaluation of Risk (B-SAFER; Kropp, Hart, & Belfrage, 2005; r = .74 for total "scores", r = .36 to .64 for SRRs; Gerbrandij et al., 2018), Psychopathy Checklist: Screening Version (PCL:SV; Hart, Cox, & Hare, 1995; r = .20 to .51), and the Violence Risk Appraisal Guide (VRAG; r = .21 to .25; Kropp et al., 2011; Storey et al., 2009).

The predictive utility of the SAM has been evaluated in at least three peer-reviewed studies. Using Cox Proportional Hazard analyses (which examines the association between a tool and the imminence or rate of reoffending), Foellmi and colleagues (2016) found that SAM total "scores" were significantly associated with the imminence of stalking recidivism among offenders receiving community treatment (Hazard Ratio [HR] = 1.11, $p < .01$). Neither SRRs nor the Nature of Stalking and Perpetrator domains "scores" were significantly predictive. In a mixed sample of male intimate partner violence and stalking offenders, Gerbrandij and colleagues (2018) found that SAM total "scores" had weak predictive accuracy for stalking and violent recidivism (AUC = .40 to .60). However, Shea and colleagues (2018) found moderate to large predictive accuracy of total "scores" for stalking recidivism (AUC = .76) and case prioritization (AUC = .69) in a sample of female and male offenders with stalking-related charges who were participating in court-ordered assessment and/or treatment.

With respect to incremental validity, Gerbrandij and colleagues (2018) found that the SAM did not add incremental utility above and beyond the B-SAFER in the prediction of stalking or violent recidivism. In addition, the SAM did not add incremental utility above the PCL:SV in the prediction of violent recidivism. However, the SAM did improve the prediction of stalking recidivism above and beyond the PCL:SV.

PROFESSIONAL UPTAKE

The SAM has been translated into at least two languages (Swedish and Norwegian) and is used in at least four countries (Canada, Sweden, England, and Wales; Belfrage & Strand, 2009; Storey & Hart, 2011). In addition, professionals have been trained to use the SAM in Norway, Denmark, Holland, and Switzerland. Studies conducted in mental health and law enforcement settings have reported that the SAM has good perceived clinical or operational utility (Belfrage, & Strand, 2009; Kropp et al., 2011; Storey et al., 2009). Moreover, police officers have reported that the SAM was easy to code and helpful in initiating protective action (Belfrage & Strand, 2009).

Stalking Risk Profile (SRP)

DESCRIPTION

The SRP (MacKenzie et al., 2009) is a SPJ measure developed to assist in evaluation and management of different domains of risk related to stalking: stalking-related violence, stalking persistence, stalking recurrence, and psychosocial injury to the stalker (i.e., likelihood that persons engaging in stalking will experience significant psychological or social harm due to their behaviour). It is intended for use with individuals with a known or suspected history of stalking, defined as a "pattern of targeted, repeated, and unwanted intrusive acts that can be reasonably expected to cause apprehension, distress, or fear in the victim" (McEwan et al., 2018, p. 1). Due to the technical expertise required for SRP administration (e.g., use of standardized tests of cognitive functioning, personality traits, or interpersonal attachment style), it is meant to be used by mental health professionals or law enforcement professionals in collaboration with a qualified mental health professional.

The SRP incorporates the motivational typology of stalking developed by Mullen and colleagues (Mullen, Pathe, & Purcell, 2009; Mullen, Pathe, Purcell, & Stuart, 1999). Through use of a decision tree (see Mullen et al., 2006), the evaluator classifies the examinee into one of five types intended to indicate the apparent function of the stalker's behaviour (i.e., rejected, resentful, intimacy-seeking, incompetent suitor, or predatory) based on the nature of the examinee's relationship with the victim, the examinee's motivation for seeking unwanted contact with the victim, and the presence of specific psychopathology. There are 81 dynamic items on the SRP; however, only a subset is coded for each stalker type (McEwan et al., 2018). In other words, although each domain of risk includes "general" risk factors that are assessed for all stalker types, the SRP also recognizes that relevant risk factors and corresponding case management strategies vary by stalker motivation. Except for two items that are rated dichotomously, items are rated on a 3-level scale.

PSYCHOMETRIC PROPERTIES

At least one peer-reviewed study has reported psychometric properties of the SRP. Using data from 241 men and women who were charged with stalking or stalking-related offences, and underwent evaluation using the SRP, McEwan and colleagues (2018) found good to excellent IRR for SRRs (ICC_1 = .70 to .90), moderate to excellent IRR for domain scores (ICC_1 = .65 to .98), and excellent classification of stalker types (kappa [κ] = .98) between clinical/forensic psychologists and one of the first two authors of the SRP. With the exception of two items related to the examinee, Refusal to conform to legal directives (ICC_1 = .09) and Sense of entitlement (ICC_1 = .26), there was fair to substantial IRR for individual SRP items (ICC_1 > .61; exact ICC_1 values not reported). Internal consistency also was reported (r = .51 to .82 between domain scores and SRRs).

McEwan and colleagues (2018) reported moderate to large predictive accuracy for long-term (i.e., average 4-year) stalking persistence (AUC = .68), stalking recurrence involving the same (AUC = .68) or different (AUC = .66) victims, and any persistence or recurrence of stalking towards the same victim (AUC = .73). In contrast, predictive accuracy was weak to moderate for short-term (i.e., 6 month) stalking persistence (AUC = .53), stalking recurrence involving the same (AUC = .63) or different (AUC = .75) victims, and any persistence or recurrence of stalking towards the same victim (AUC = .63); however, these findings may reflect that the majority of participants were incarcerated during the 6-month period following their SRP assessment. Due to low base rates, predictive utility of the SRP for stalking-related physical violence or psychosocial injury to the stalker was not examined in the study. To our knowledge, no peer-reviewed studies have examined the concurrent or incremental validity of the SRP.

PROFESSIONAL UPTAKE

The SRP has been implemented in forensic psychiatric settings in at least three countries (Australia, England, and Wales; MacKenzie & James, 2011). Although user satisfaction for the SRP has not been evaluated empirically, editorial commentary has described it as being helpful for tailoring case management and treatment plans to specific stalker types (Schwartz-Watts, 2006).

Honour-Based Violence

Assessment of Risk for Honour-Based Violence (PATRIARCH)

DESCRIPTION

The PATRIARCH (Kropp, Belfrage, & Hart, 2013) is an SPJ measure designed to assist in assessment and management of risk for "any actual, attempted, or threatened physical harm, including forced marriages, with honor as the motive" (Belfrage, Strand, Ekman, & Hasselborg, 2011, p. 21). The PATRIARCH comprises 15 items across three domains: (1) nature of the examinee's history of honour-based violence, or HBV (e.g., attitudes that support HBV); (2) examinee risk factors (e.g., problems with cultural integration); and (3) victim vulnerability factors (e.g., extreme fear) that were taken from the B-SAFER. Items are rated for two time periods: current and in the past. Evaluators provide SRRs regarding case prioritization, risk of life-threatening violence, and risk of imminent violence.

Internal consistency of the PATRIARCH has been examined in at least two peer-reviewed studies. Belfrage and colleagues (2011) found that four Perpetrator (i.e., escalation, attitudes that support honour violence, high degree of insult, and personal problems) and two Victim Vulnerability (i.e., inconsistent behaviour and unsafe living situation) items correlated significantly with SRRs (r values not reported). Strand (2015) reported a large correlation between acute risk and risk for serious or fatal violence (Kendall's tau-b [τb] = 0.67). To our knowledge there are no peer-reviewed studies examining the IRR or validity of the PATRIARCH.

PROFESSIONAL UPTAKE

Professionals have been trained to use the PATRIARCH in Belgium, Canada, Norway, Sweden, and Switzerland. In research conducted in Sweden, criminal justice professionals perceived the PATRIARCH as easy to administer, and their use of the tool was associated with increased use of preventative measures for victims (e.g., initiation of no contact orders, protected living) and more comprehensive criminal investigations (Strand, 2015).

Summary and Directions for Future Research

With literally hundreds of tools developed to screen or assess risk for violence, evaluators must be informed consumers. In addition to ensuring the tool(s) selected have the requisite properties to address the referral question or assessment purpose (e.g., screening people in for further assessment, sorting people into groups of putatively lower and higher risk, rank-ordering people in terms of their relative risk for violence, identifying immediate risk management strategies, engaging in case management and reassessment over time, etc.), evaluators also should be guided by the quality and quantity of empirical support for the tool. In this chapter, we reviewed several tools that have clinical promise by virtue that there exists some research and professional uptake in support of their use, but for which a well-established empirical foundation has not yet accrued.

Each of the brief and emerging measures reviewed in this chapter has been evaluated in at least one peer-reviewed publication; however, measures vary in terms of the quantity and type of research support they have. Whereas some measures, such as the DASA-IV, DVSI/DVSI-R, JSORRATT-II, and V-RISK-10, have achieved moderate predictive accuracy in at least two studies, others, such as the DRAOR, PATRIARCH, SAM, and SRP, have limited or no evidence on their predictive utility, or findings are mixed (e.g., some studies have reported only modest predictive accuracy). Similarly, while some measures (e.g., the DVSI/DVSI-R, JSORRATT-II, V-RISK-10) have evidence to support their interrater reliability (and internal consistency) and concurrent incremental validity, others (e.g., the SRP) have limited or no evidence on these features available. Finally, some measures have research reporting their perceived user satisfaction (e.g., DASA-IV, DRAOR, SAM, PATRIARCH), whereas others do not (e.g., JSORATT-II). Future research efforts should be dedicated towards further investigating the psychometric properties and applicability of these measures.

We recommend that more work be conducted in terms of investigating whether the psychometric properties of these tools vary as a function of demographic characteristics (e.g., gender, race/ethnicity), level of risk, rater type, purpose of the evaluation (e.g., research assistants completing the tool for basic research paradigms versus professionals using the tool to make real-world case decisions in field settings), and geographic region (e.g., in the country where the tool was developed versus elsewhere). Researchers should also examine the degree to which clinical overrides or SRRs add incrementally to numerical scores, as well as the perceived clinical utility of these competing approaches to combining data; whether change on arguably dynamic measures is associated with increases or decreases in subsequent violence outcomes; and the degree to which measures whose primary purpose is to guide case management and intervention assist in case planning or treatment matching. Additionally, in several studies reviewed in this chapter, the author(s) of the risk assessment measure was also an author(s) on a study investigating the psychometric properties of that measure. Research by independent investigators is needed, as empirical evidence of a researcher allegiance effect has been reported (e.g., Singh, Grann, & Fazel, 2013; cf. Guy, 2008). Last, given that these measures show considerable promise to assist in the evaluation of risk, additional efforts, particularly with measures that are currently in use in a single country or a small number of U.S. states, should be made to validate and implement these measures in different jurisdictions.

References

Almvik, R., Woods, P., & Rasmussen, K. (2000). The broset violence checklist: Sensitivity, specificity, and interrater reliability. *Journal of Interpersonal Violence, 15*, 1284–1296. doi:10.1177/088626000015012003

Andrews, D. A., & Bonta, J. (1995). *LSI-R: The level of service inventory-revised.* Toronto, ON: Multi-Health Systems.

Andrews, D. A., & Bonta, J. (2010). *The psychology of criminal conduct* (5th ed.). Cincinnati, OH: Anderson Publishing Corporation.

Bakker, L., Riley, D., & O'Malley, J. (1999). *Risk of reconviction: Statistical models predicting four types of re-offending.* Wellington, NZ: Department of Corrections Psychological Service.

Barry-Walsh, J., Daffern, M., Duncan, S., & Ogloff, J. (2009). The prediction of imminent aggression in patients with mental illness and/or intellectual disability using the dynamic appraisal of situational aggression instrument. *Australasian Psychiatry, 17*, 493–496. doi:10.1080/10398560903289975

Belfrage, H., & Ekman, L. (2014). Threat assessment of targeted honor-based violence. In J. R. Meloy & J. Hoffmann (Eds.), *International handbook of threat assessment* (pp. 260–271). Oxford: Oxford University Press.

Belfrage, H., & Strand, S. (2009). Validation of the stalking assessment and management checklist (SAM) in law enforcement: A prospective study of 153 cases of stalking in two Swedish police counties. *International Journal of Police Science & Management, 11*, 67–76. http://dx.doi.org/10.1350/ijps.2009.11.1.110

Belfrage, H., Strand, S., Ekman, L., & Hasselborg, A. (2011). Assessing risk of patriarchal violence with honour as a motive: Six years experience using the PATRIACH checklist. *International Journal of Police Science & Management, 14*, 20–29. doi:10.1350/ijps.2012.14.1.250

Bjørkly, S., Hartvig, P., Heggen, F. A., Brauer, H., & Moger, T. A. (2009). Development of a brief screen for violence risk (V-RISK-10) in acute and general psychiatry: An introduction with emphasis on findings from a naturalistic test of interrater reliability. *European Psychiatry, 24*, 388–394. doi:10.1016/j.eurpsy.2009.07.004

Borum, R., Bartel, P., & Forth, A. (2006). *Manual for the structured assessment of violence risk in youth (SAVRY).* Odessa, FL: Psychological Assessment Resources.

Campbell, J. C., O'Sullivan, C., Roehl, J., & Webster, D. (2005). Intimate partner violence risk assessment validation study, final report. Washington, DC: National Institute of Justice.

Chan, O., & Chow, K. K. (2014). Assessment and determinants of aggression in a forensic psychiatric institution in Hong Kong, China. *Psychiatry Research, 220*, 623–630. doi:10.1016/j.psychres.2014.08.008

Chu, C. M., Daffern, M., & Ogloff, J. (2013). Predicting aggression in acute inpatient psychiatric setting using BVC, DASA, and HCR-20 clinical scale. *The Journal of Forensic Psychiatry and Psychology, 24*, 269–285. doi:10.1080/14789949.2013.773456

Chu, C. M., Hoo, E., Daffern, M., & Tan, J. (2012). Assessing the risk of imminent aggression in institutionalized youth offenders using the dynamic appraisal of situational aggression. *The Journal of Forensic Psychiatry and Psychology, 23*, 168–183. doi:10.1080/14789949.2012.668207

Chu, C. M., Thomas, S. D. M., Daffern, M., & Ogloff, J. R. P. (2013). Should clinicians use average or peak scores on a dynamic risk-assessment measure to most accurately predict inpatient aggression? *International Journal of Mental Health Nursing, 22*, 493–499. doi:10.1111/j.1447-0349.2012.00846.x

Cicchetti, D. V., & Sparrow, S. A. (1981). Developing criteria for establishing interrater reliability of specific items: Applications to assessment of adaptive behavior. *American Journal of Mental Deficiency, 86*, 127–137. Retrieved from http://psycnet.apa.org/psycinfo/1982-00095-001

Cohen, J. (1992). A power primer. *Psychological Bulletin, 112*, 155–159. doi:10.1037/0033-2909.112.1.155

Daffern, M., & Howells, K. (2007). The prediction of imminent aggression and self-harm in personality disordered patients of a high security hospital using the HCR-20 clinical scale and the dynamic appraisal of situational aggression. *International Journal of Forensic Mental Health, 6,* 137–143. doi:10.1080/14999013.2007.10471258

Daffern, M., Howells, K., Hamilton, L., Mannion, A., Howard, R., & Lilly, M. (2009). The impact of structured risk assessment followed by management recommendations on aggression in patients with personality disorder. *The Journal of Forensic Psychiatry and Psychology, 20,* 661–679. doi:10.1080/14789940903173990

Daffern, M., & Ogloff, J. R. P. (2014). *The dynamic appraisal of situational aggression: Youth version (DASA: YV).* Melbourne: Centre for Forensic Behavioral Science, School of Psychology, Psychiatry and Psychological Medicine, Monash University.

de Vogel, V., de Vries Robbé, M., van Kalmthout, W., & Place, C. (2011). *FAM-female additional manual: Additional guidelines to the HCR-20 for assessing risk for violence in women.* Utrecht: Forum Educatief.

Dumais, A., Larue, C., Michaud, C., & Goulet, M. (2012). Predictive validity and psychiatric nursing staff's perception of the clinical usefulness of the French version of the dynamic appraisal of situational aggression. *Issues in Mental Health Nursing, 33,* 670–675. doi:10.3109/01612840.2012.697254

Dutch, S. G., & Patil, N. (2018). Validating a measurement tool to predict aggressive behavior in hospitalized youth. *Journal of the American Psychiatric Nurses Association,* 1–9. Advance online publication. doi:1078390318809411

Epperson, D. L., & Ralston, C. A. (2015). Development and validation of the juvenile sexual offense recidivism risk assessment tool—II. *Sexual Abuse: A Journal of Research and Treatment, 27,* 529–558. doi:1079063213514452

Epperson, D. L., Ralston, C. A., Fowers, D., DeWitt, J., & Gore, K. S. (2006). Actuarial risk assessment with juveniles who sexually offend: Development of the Juvenile sexual offense recidivism risk assessment tool-II (JSORRAT-II). In D. S. Prescott (Ed.), *Risk assessment of youth who have sexually abused* (pp. 118–169). Oklahoma City: Wood 'N' Barnes.

Eriksen, B. M. S., Bjørkly, S., Færden, A., Friestad, C., Hartvig, P., & Roaldset, J. O. (2016). Gender differences in the predictive validity of a violence risk screening tool: A prospective study in an acute psychiatric ward. *International Journal of Forensic Mental Health,* 1–12. doi:10.1080/14999013.2016.1170740

Eriksen, B. M. S., Færden, A., Lockertsen, Ø., Bjørkly, S., & Roaldset, J. O. (2018). Predictive validity and gender differences in a biopsychosocial model of violence risk assessment in acute psychiatry. *Psychiatry Research, 264,* 270–280. doi:10.1016/j.psychres.2018.04.021

Foellmi, M. C., Rosenfeld, B., & Galietta, M. (2016). Assessing risk for recidivism in individuals convicted of stalking offenses: Predictive validity of the guidelines for stalking assessment and management. *Criminal Justice and Behavior, 43,* 600–616. doi:10.1177/0093854815610612

Gerbrandij, J., Rosenfeld, B., Nijdam-Jones, A., & Galietta, M. (2018). Evaluating risk assessment instruments for intimate partner stalking and intimate partner violence. *Journal of Threat Assessment and Management, 5,* 102–118. doi:10.1037/tam0000101

Gerstenberger, C. B., & Williams, K. R. (2012). Gender and intimate partner violence: Does dual arrest reveal gender symmetry or asymmetry? *Journal of Interpersonal Violence, 28,* 1561–1578. doi:10.1177/0886260512468325

Griffith, J. J., Daffern, M., & Godber, T. (2013). Examination of the predictive validity of the dynamic appraisal of situational aggression in two mental health units. *International Journal of Mental Health Nursing, 22,* 485–492. doi:10.1111/inm.12011

Guy, L. S. (2008). *Performance indicators of the structured professional judgement approach for assessing risk for violence to others: A meta-analytic survey* (Unpublished doctoral dissertation). Simon Fraser University, Burnaby, BC.

Hare, R. D. (2003). *Hare psychopathy checklist-revised* (2nd ed.). Toronto, ON: Multi-Health Systems.

Hart, S., Cox, D., & Hare, R. D. (1995). *Manual for the psychopathy checklist: Screening version (PCL: SV).* Toronto, ON: Multi Health Systems.

Hartvig, P., Alfarnes, S., Ostberg, B., Skjonberg, M., & Moger, T. A. (2006). Brief checklists for assessing violence risk among patients discharged from acute psychiatric facilities: A preliminary study. *Nordic Journal of Psychiatry, 60,* 243–248. doi:10.1080/08039480600780532

Hartvig, P., Østberg, B., Alfarnes, S., Moger, T. A., Skjønberg, M., & Bjørkly, S. (2007). *Violence risk screening—10 (V-RISK-10).* Oslo, Norway: Centre for Research and Education in Forensic Psychiatry.

Hartvig, P., Roaldset, J. O., Moger, T. A., Østberg, B., & Bjørkly, S. (2011). The first step in the validation of a new screen for violence risk in acute psychiatry: The inpatient context. *European Psychiatry, 26,* 92–99. doi:10.1016/j.eurpsy.2010.01.003

Hilton, N. Z., Harris, G. T., Rice, M. E., Houghton, R. E., & Eke, A. W. (2008). An indepth actuarial assessment for wife assault recidivism: The domestic violence risk appraisal guide. *Law and Human Behavior, 32*, 150–163. doi:10.1007/s10979-007-9088-6

Kasinathan, J., Marsland, C., Batterham, P., Gaskin, C., Adams, J., & Daffern, M. (2015). Assessing the risk of imminent aggression in mentally ill youth offenders. *Australasian Psychiatry, 23*, 44–48. doi:10.1177/1039856214563845

Kropp, P. R., Belfrage, H., & Hart, S. D. (2013). *Assessment of risk for honour based violence (PATRIACH)*. Vancouver, BC: ProActive Resolutions, Inc.

Kropp, P. R., & Hart, S. D. (2015). *SARA-V3: User guide for the third edition of the spousal assault risk assessment guide*. Vancouver, BC: ProActive Resolutions, Inc.

Kropp, P. R., Hart, S. D., & Belfrage, H. (2005). *Brief spousal assault form for the evaluation of risk (B-SAFER): User manual*. Vancouver, BC: ProActive ReSolutions, Inc.

Kropp, P. R., Hart, S. D., & Lyon, D. (2008). *Guidelines for stalking assessment and management (SAM): User manual*. Vancouver, BC: ProActive ReSolutions, Inc.

Kropp, P. R., Hart, S. D., Lyon, D. R., & Storey, J. E. (2011). The development and validation of the guidelines for stalking assessment and management. *Behavioral Sciences and the Law, 29*, 302–316. doi:10.1002/bsl.978

Lantta, T., Daffern, M., Kontio, R., & Valimaki, M. (2015). Implementing the dynamic appraisal of situational aggression in mental health units. *Clinical Nurse Specialist, 29*, 230–243. doi:10.1097/NUR.0000000000000140

Lantta, T., Kontio, R., Daffern, M., Adams, C. E., & Valimaki, M. (2016). Using the dynamic appraisal of situational aggression with mental health inpatients: A feasibility study. *Patient Preference and Adherence, 10*, 691–701. doi:10.2147/ppa.s103840

MacKenzie, R. D., & James, D. V. (2011). Management and treatment of stalkers: Problems, options, and solutions. *Behavioral Sciences & the Law, 29*, 220–239. doi:10.1002/bsl.980

MacKenzie, R. D., McEwan, T. E., Pathé, M., James, D. V., Ogloff, J. R. P., & Mullen, P. E. (2009). *Stalking risk profile: Guidelines for the assessment and management of stalkers*. Melbourne: Centre for Forensic Behavioural Science.

Maguire, T., Daffern, M., Bowe, S. J., & McKenna, B. (2017). Predicting aggressive behaviour in acute forensic mental health units: A re-examination of the dynamic appraisal of situational aggression's predictive validity. *International Journal of Mental Health Nursing, 26*, 472–481. doi:10.1111/inm.12377

McEwan, T. E., Shea, D. E., Daffern, M., MacKenzie, R. D., Ogloff, J. R., & Mullen, P. E. (2018). The reliability and predictive validity of the stalking risk profile. *Assessment, 25*, 259–276. doi:1073191116653470.

Mullen, P. E., Mackenzie, R., Ogloff, J. R., Pathé, M., McEwan, T., & Purcell, R. (2006). Assessing and managing the risks in the stalking situation. *Journal of the American Academy of Psychiatry and the Law Online, 34*, 439–450. Retrieved from www.jaapl.org/content/34/4/439.short

Mullen, P. E., Pathe, M., & Purcell, R. (2009). *Stalkers and their victims* (2nd ed.). New York: Cambridge University Press.

Mullen, P. E., Pathe, M., Purcell, R., & Stuart, G. W. (1999). Study of stalkers. *American Journal of Psychiatry, 156*, 1244–1249. Retrieved from http://ajp.psychiatryonline.org/doi/10.1176/ajp.156.8.1244

Nielsen, L. H., Mastrigt, S. van, Otto, R. K., Seewald, K., Ruiter, C. de, Rettenberger, M., Reeves, K. A., Rebocho, M. F., Pham, T. H., Mei Yee Ho, R., Grann, M., Godoy-Cervera, V., Folino, J. O., Doyle, M., Desmarais, S. L., Condemarin, C., Arbach-Lucioni, K., & Singh, J. P. (2015). Violence Risk Assessment Practices in Denmark: A Multidisciplinary National Survey. Scandinavian Journal of Forensic Science, 21(2), 103–110.https://doi.org/10.1515/sjfs-2015-000

Nquwaku, M., Draycott, S., Aldridge-Waddon, L., Bush, E. L., Tsirimokou, A., Jones, D., & Puzzo, I. (2018). Predictive power of the DASA-IV: Variations in rating method and timescales. *International Journal of Mental Health Nursing, 27*, 1661–1672. doi:10.1111/inm.12464

Nunnally, J. C., & Bernstein, I. H. (1978). *Psychometric theory*. New York: McGraw-Hill.

Ogloff, J. R. P., & Daffern, M. (2006). The dynamic appraisal of situational aggression: An instrument to assess risk for imminent aggression in psychiatric inpatients. *Behavioral Sciences and the Law, 24*, 799–813. doi:10.1002/bsl.741

Polaschek, D. L., Yesberg, J. A., & Chauhan, P. (2018). A year without a conviction: An integrated examination of potential mechanisms for successful re-entry in high-risk violent prisoners. *Criminal Justice and Behavior, 45*, 425–446. doi:10.1177/0093854817752757

Prentky, R., & Righthand, S. (2003). *Juvenile sex offender assessment protocol II (J-SOAP-II) manual*. Washington, DC: U.S. Department of Justice, Office of Justice Programs, Office of Juvenile Justice and Delinquency Prevention. Retrieved from www.ncjrs.gov/pdffiles1/ojjdp/202316.pdf

Quinsey, V. L., Harris, G. T., Rice, M. E., & Cormier, C. A. (1998). *Violent offenders: Appraising and managing risk*. Washington, DC: American Psychological Association.

Quinsey, V. L., Harris, G. T., Rice, M. E., & Cormier, C. A. (2006). *Violent offenders: Appraising and managing risk* (2nd ed.). Washington, DC: American Psychological Association.

Ralston, C. A., Epperson, D. L., & Edwards, S. R. (2014). Cross-validation of the JSORRAT-II in Iowa. *Sexual Abuse: A Journal of Research and Treatment, 28*, 534–554. doi:10.1177/1079063214548074

Ralston, C. A., Sarkar, A., Philipp, G. T., & Epperson, D. L. (2015). The impact of using documented but uncharged offense data on JSORRAT-II predictive validity. *Sexual Abuse: A Journal of Research and Treatment*, 1–17. Advance online publication. doi:10.1177/1079063215582011

Ralston, C. A., Sarkar, A., Philipp, G. T., & Epperson, D. L. (2017). The impact of using documented but uncharged offense data on JSORRAT-II predictive validity. *Sexual Abuse, 29*(2). doi:10.1177/1079063215582011

Ralston, C. A., Sarkar, A., Philipp, G. T., & Epperson, D. L. (2018). The impact of using documented but uncharged offense data on JSORRAT-II predictive validity. *Sexual Abuse, 29*, 186–202. doi:10.1177/1079063215582011

Rasmussen, L. A. L. (2018). Comparing predictive validity of JSORRAT-II and MEGA♪ with sexually abusive youth in long-term residential custody. *International Journal of Offender Therapy and Comparative Criminology, 62*, 2937–2953. doi:10.1177/0306624X17726550

Rice, M. E., & Harris, G. T. (2005). Comparing effect sizes in follow-up studies: ROC area, Cohen's d, and r. *Law and Human Behavior, 29*, 615–620. doi:10.1007/s10979-005-6832-7

Riordan, D., Browne, C., Korobanova, D., Kariuki, M., Daffern, M., & Dean, K. (2019). Imminent aggression in female forensic inpatients: A study assessing the predictive validity of the dynamic appraisal of situational aggression: Women's version (DASA: WV). *International Journal of Forensic Mental Health*. Online first. doi:10.1080/14999013.2019.1577315

Roaldset, J. O., Hartvig, P., & Bjørkly, S. (2011). V-RISK-10: Validation of a screen for risk of violence after discharge from acute psychiatry. *European Psychiatry, 26*, 85–91. doi:10.1016/j.eurpsy.2010.04.002

Roaldset, J. O., Hartvig, P., Linaker, O. M., & Bjørkly, S. (2012). A multifaceted model for risk assessment of violent behaviour in acutely admitted psychiatric patients. *Psychiatry Research, 200*, 773–778. doi:10.1016/j.psychres.2012.04.038

Scanlan, J. M., Yesberg, J. A., Fortune, C. A., & Polaschek, D. L. (2020). Predicting women's recidivism using the dynamic risk assessment for offender re-entry: Preliminary evidence of predictive validity with community-sentenced women using a "gender-neutral" risk measure. *Criminal Justice and Behavior*, 251–270. Advance online publication. doi:10.1177/0093854819896387

Schwartz-Watts, D. M. (2006). Commentary: Stalking risk profile. *Journal of the American Academy of Psychiatry and the Law Online, 34*, 455–457. Retrieved from www.jaapl.org/content/34/4/455.short

Serin, R. C. (2007). *The dynamic risk assessment for offender re-entry (DRAOR)*. Unpublished user manual.

Serin, R. C., Chadwick, N., & Lloyd, C. D. (2016). Dynamic risk and protective factors. *Psychology, Crime & Law, 22*, 151–170. doi:10.1080/1068316x.2015.1112013

Serin, R. C., Gobeil, R., Lloyd, C. D., Chadwick, N., Wardrop, K., & Hanby, L. (2016). Using dynamic risk to enhance conditional release decisions in prisoners to improve their outcomes. *Behavioral Sciences & the Law, 34*, 321–336. doi:10.1002/bsl.2213

Serin, R. C., Mailloux, D. L., & Wilson, N. J. (2012). *The dynamic risk assessment of offender re-entry (DRAOR)*. Unpublished user manual.

Shea, D. E., McEwan, T. E., Strand, S. J. M., & Ogloff, J. R. P. (2018). The reliability and predictive validity of the guidelines for stalking assessment and management (SAM). *Psychological Assessment, 30*, 1409–1240. doi:10.1037/pas0000589

Singh, J. P., Desmarais, S. L., Hurducas, C., Arbach-Lucioni, K., Condemarin, C., Dean, K., . . . Otto, R. K. (2014). International perspectives on the practical application of violence risk assessment: A global survey of 44 countries. *International Journal of Forensic Mental Health, 13*, 193–206. doi:10.1080/14999013.2014.922141

Singh, J. P., Grann, M., & Fazel, S. (2013). Authorship bias in violence risk assessment? A Systematic review and meta-analysis. *PLoS One, 8*, e72484. doi:10.1371/journal.pone.0072484

Stansfield, R., & Williams, K. R. (2014). Predicting family violence recidivism using the DVSI-R integrating survival analysis and perpetrator characteristics. *Criminal Justice and Behavior*, *41*, 163–180. doi:10.1177/0093854813500776

Storey, J. E., & Hart, S. D. (2011). How do police respond to stalking? An examination of the risk management strategies and tactics used in a specialized anti-stalking law enforcement unit. *Journal of Police and Criminal Psychology*, *26*, 128–142. doi:10.1007/s11896-010-9081-8

Storey, J. E., Hart, S. D., Meloy, J. R., & Reavis, J. A. (2009). Psychopathy and stalking. *Law and Human Behaviour*, *33*, 237–246. doi:10.1007/s10979-008-9149-5

Strand, S. (2015). Risk assessment and risk management: How the police work together with researchers to protect victims in cases of intimate partner violence, stalking, and honor-based violence. In P. C. Kratcoski & M. Edelbacher (Eds.), *Collaborative policing: Police, academics, professionals, and communities working together for education, training, and program implementation* (pp. 27–49). New York, NY: CRC Press.

Viljoen, J. L., Mordell, S., & Beneteau, J. L. (2012). Prediction of adolescent sexual reoffending: A meta-analysis of the J-SOAP-II, ERASOR, J-SORRAT-II, and static-99. *Law and Human Behavior*, *36*, 423–438. doi:10.1037/h0093938

Viljoen, J. L., Scalora, M., Cuadra, L., Bader, S., Chávez, V., Ullman, D., & Lawrence, L. (2008). Assessing risk for violence in adolescents who have sexually offended: A comparison of the J-SOAP-II, J-SORRAT-II, and SAVRY. *Criminal Justice and Behavior*, *35*, 5–23. doi:10.1177/0093854807307521

Vincent, G. M., Terry, A., & Maney, S. (2009). Risk/needs tools for antisocial behavior and violence among youthful populations. In J. T. Andrade (Ed.), *Handbook of violence risk assessment and treatment: New approaches for mental health professionals* (p. 377–423). New York, NY: Springer.

Vojt, G., Marshall, L. A., & Thomson, L. D. G. (2010). The assessment of imminent inpatient aggression: A validation study of the DASA-IV in Scotland. *The Journal of Forensic Psychiatry and Psychology*, *21*, 789–800. doi:10.1080/14789949.2010.489952

Webster, C. D., Douglas, K. S., Eaves, D., & Hart, S. D. (1997). *HCR-20: Assessing risk for violence (Version 2)*. Burnaby, Canada: Mental Health, Law, & Policy Institute, Simon Fraser University.

Williams, K. R. (2012). Family violence risk assessment: A predictive cross-validation study of the domestic violence screening instrument-revised (DVSI-R). *Law and Human Behavior*, *36*, 120–129. doi:10.1007/s10979-011-9272-6

Williams, K. R., & Grant, S. R. (2006). Empirically examining the risk of intimate partner violence: The revised domestic violence screening instrument (DVSI-R). *Public Health Reports*, *121*, 400–408. doi:10.1007/s10979-011-9272-6

Williams, K. R., & Houghton, A. B. (2004). Assessing the risk of domestic violence reoffending: A validation study. *Law and Human Behavior*, *28*, 437–455. doi:10.1023/b:lahu.0000039334.59297.f0

Williams, K. R., & Stansfield, R. (2017). Disentangling the risk assessment and intimate partner violence relation: Estimating mediating and moderating effects. *Law and Human Behavior*, *41*, 344–353. doi:10.1037/lhb0000249

Wilson, N. J. (2002). *Release-proposal feasibility assessment.* Unpublished manuscript.

Wong, S. C. P., & Gordon, A. (2000). *Violence risk scale.* Unpublished manuscript.

Wong, S. C. P., & Gordon, A. (2002). *Violence Risk Scale.* Saskatoon, Saskatchewan, Canada: Author.

Yao, X., Li, Z., Arthur, D., Hu, L., & Cheng, G. (2012). The application of a violence risk assessment tool among Chinese psychiatric service users: A preliminary study. *Journal of Psychiatric and Mental Health Nursing*, *19*, 438–445. doi:10.1111/j.1365-2850.2011.01821.x

Yao, X., Li, Z., Arthur, D., Hu, L., & Cheng, G. (2014). Validation of the violence risk screening-10 instrument among clients discharged from a psychiatric hospital in Beijing. *International Journal of Mental Health Nursing*, *23*, 79–87. doi:10.1111/j.1447-0349.2012.00890.x

Yesberg, J. A., & Polaschek, D. L. (2015). Assessing dynamic risk and protective factors in the community: Examining the validity of the dynamic risk assessment for offender re-entry. *Psychology, Crime & Law*, *21*, 80–99. doi:10.1080/1068316x.2014.935775

Yesberg, J. A., Scanlan, J. M., Hanby, L. J., Serin, R. C., & Polaschek, D. L. (2015). Predicting women's recidivism: Validating a dynamic community-based "gender-neutral" tool. *Probation Journal*, *62*, 33–48. doi:10.1177/0264550514562851

Chapter 4

Constitutional and Evidentiary Issues Concerning Risk Assessment

Christopher Slobogin

Introduction

The legal system routinely relies on clinical and actuarial evaluations of "risk," the term this chapter will use to refer to an individual's potential for committing a criminal offense or other unlawful act. For instance, opinions about risk offered by mental health professionals are almost always proffered in civil commitment hearings, commitment proceedings that follow insanity verdicts and determinations of incompetency to stand trial, and hearings pursuant to "sexual predator" laws authorizing post-sentence confinement or post-release community notification. Mental health professionals and correctional officials also frequently provide information about risk at pre-trial detention hearings, sentencing, parole and probation hearings, and prisoner re-entry proceedings, in both the adult and juvenile systems.

Despite the divergent settings in which expertise about risk is offered, the legal system treats it in a monolithic fashion. Many courts, including the U.S. Supreme Court, have recognized that assessing a person's potential for offending is a challenging enterprise (see *Heller v. Doe by Doe*, 1993, p. 324; *Barefoot v. Estelle*, 1983, pp. 900–901; *Addington v. Texas*, 1979, p. 429). Yet, with only a few isolated exceptions, the courts take a lenient approach toward expert testimony about "dangerousness," the term they often use to describe risk.

There are several possible reasons for this judicial nonchalance, all explored in more detail here. First, and most obviously, testimony about risk is usually proffered in proceedings that are not associated with stringent evidentiary requirements; commitment, pretrial detention, and sentencing hearings are generally considered more informal than criminal and civil trials and thus courts are less demanding of expert testimony in these proceedings, despite the high stakes that are often involved. Second, most courts are willing to put up with speculative testimony about risk because they do not see any alternative method of answering a question legislatures have required them to answer.

Finally, the courts' lax attitude toward testimony about risk may stem from a judicial unwillingness or inability to delve into the difficulties associated with risk assessment and management. The possibility of objectively ascertaining the accuracy of predictions from records or self-reports makes prediction testimony more susceptible to assessments of validity than many other types of psychological phenomena, such as insanity or diminished responsibility. Yet courts appear to be uncomfortable conducting in-depth analysis of prediction and risk assessment testimony. For instance, most courts pay little attention to the scientific basis of actuarial or other structured judgments about predictions, despite the plethora of research about risk assessment instruments. A few courts even reject actuarial-based testimony in favor of relatively unscientific "clinical" testimony, on the dubious assumptions that clinical predictions are "individualized" and that group-based actuarial instruments do not help address individual propensities.

This chapter begins with a discussion of how courts analyze the admissibility of risk testimony under the Constitution. It then examines the admissibility of expert opinion about risk under the rules of evidence and the interplay between these rules and standards of proof. Finally, it discusses a number of other legal and policy issues—involving the right to jury trial, discrimination on racial and other grounds, and fairness and justice claims—that do not directly raise admissibility questions but nonetheless might lead to concerns about legal reliance on risk assessments.

Admissibility Under the Constitution

Predictions of violence have been subject to constitutional challenge in a variety of legal contexts, usually on the ground that they are too suspect to form the basis for a deprivation of liberty. Initially, such claims sometimes prevailed. For instance, in *People v. Murtishaw* (1981), the California Supreme Court held that "evidence which is barely reliable enough to justify a civil judgment or a limited commitment is not reliable enough to utilize in determining whether a man should be executed." (p. 448). These challenges largely ended, however, when the Supreme Court held, in *Barefoot v. Estelle* (1983), that such predictions are constitutional when introduced at the sentencing stage of capital trials. If expert predictions about violence are a constitutionally permissible means of establishing a person's eligibility for execution, they presumably are constitutionally permissible for all purposes.

The prediction testimony in *Barefoot* came from Dr. James Grigson, who testified, based on a hypothetical question, that there was a "one hundred and absolute" chance that Barefoot would commit acts of violence that would constitute "a continuing threat to society" (an aggravating circumstance under Texas's death penalty statute) (p. 919). The specific argument the petitioner made in *Barefoot* was that mental health professionals like Grigson "are incompetent to predict with an acceptable degree of reliability that a particular criminal will commit other crimes in the future and so represent a danger to the community" (p. 896). The Supreme Court rejected this claim, holding that admission of expert testimony about the likelihood of future criminal acts in a capital sentencing hearing does not violate the Eighth Amendment's prohibition on cruel and unusual punishment or any other provision of the Constitution. The six-member majority gave, in effect, three reasons for its decision.

The Court began by disputing the contention that expert predictions of dangerousness are inevitably inaccurate. Noting that it had previously concluded, in *Jurek v. Texas* (1976), that lay persons have the ability to assess dangerousness, the Court reasoned "it makes little sense, if any, to submit that psychiatrists, out of the entire universe of persons who might have an opinion on the issue, would know so little about the subject that they should not be permitted to testify" (*Barefoot v. Estelle*, 1983, p. 897). Of course, this assertion assumes that *Jurek* was correct in concluding that laypeople have some ability to predict violence. It also ignores the possibility that, even if both laypeople and mental health professionals can address that issue, experts like Dr. Grigson might have little to add to what the jury could deduce for itself, yet at the same time exert outsized influence on the jury's decision because their "expert" label misleadingly suggests otherwise. As Justice Blackmun pointed out in his dissent, under most evidence codes, expert testimony must "assist" jurors in their deliberations and may not be unduly prejudicial (see Federal Rules of Evidence, 2016, §§ 401, 403).

Thus, the majority's conclusion appears to flow less from a belief that predictions by either juries or experts are usually accurate than from its conclusion that such predictions are an integral and necessary part of many legal contexts. In support of this second rationale, the *Barefoot* Court quoted the following language from Justice Stevens's opinion in *Jurek*:

> It is, of course, not easy to predict future behavior. The fact that such a determination is difficult, however, does not mean that it cannot be made. Indeed, prediction of future criminal conduct is an essential element in many of the decisions rendered throughout our criminal justice system. . . . The task that a Texas jury must perform in answering the statutory

question in issue is thus basically no different from the task performed countless times each day throughout the American system of justice.

(p. 897)

That the legal system regularly bases its decisions on the prediction of behavior says nothing, of course, about the accuracy of those predictions or about whether experts should be involved in making them. Justice Blackmun's dissent contended that, because of its suspect yet influential nature, expert prediction testimony should not be countenanced, at least in death penalty proceedings where the Court has insisted on heightened reliability. He also pointed out that this position did not have to mean that the prosecution would be unable to make its case. Blackmun asserted that

[l]ay testimony, frankly based on statistical factors with demonstrated correlations to violent behavior, would not raise this substantial threat of unreliable and capricious sentencing decisions, inimical to the constitutional standards established in our cases; and such predictions are as accurate as any a psychiatrist could make.

(p. 938)

But the Court was satisfied with the prevalent method of answering prediction questions, reflected in Dr. Grigson's testimony. As Justice White's majority opinion put it, "[t]he suggestion that no psychiatrist's testimony may be presented with respect to a defendant's future dangerousness is somewhat like asking us to disinvent the wheel" (p. 896).

The third reason the Court gave for permitting expert prediction testimony—in addition to the assertion that such testimony is not "entirely inaccurate" and that it is crucial to resolving a question the legal system wants answered—was that any inaccuracy that existed could be discerned by the jury. Aided by the adversarial process, the Court opined, laypeople can "separate the wheat from the chaff" when hearing expert prediction testimony (p. 900 n. 7). The Court continued: "[w]e are unconvinced . . . that the adversary process cannot be trusted to sort out the reliable from the unreliable evidence and opinion about future dangerousness, particularly when the convicted felon has the opportunity to present his own side of the case" (p. 901). Commentators have vehemently criticized this assumption, and research suggests that, contrary to the majority's assertion, the adversarial process does little to dent testimony about dangerousness, at least when it is clinical rather than actuarial in nature (*see* Diamond et al., 1996; Krauss & Sales, 2003; Krauss et al., 2004; Hilton et al., 2005).

Although these dissenting arguments have not prevailed, the Court's confidence in the adversarial process and expert prediction testimony does imply that criminal defendants should be entitled to expert assistance on the dangerousness issue, at least in capital sentencing proceedings. That position was subsequently affirmed in *Ake v. Oklahoma* (1985) and later cases (see *U.S. v. Troya*, 2013, summarizing Supreme Court case law on the issue). Some jurisdictions have relied on the same type of reasoning in requiring the state to provide the defense with expert assistance in commitment proceedings (see, e.g., *In re Barnard*, 1993; *In re Gannon*, 1973; Fl. Stat. § 394.4655(6(a)2), although, following *Ake*, in most jurisdictions the defendant is entitled to only one state-paid expert, the expert may be an employee of the state, and the expert need not testify for the defense if he or she does not agree with the defense theory of the case.

In the final part of its opinion, the *Barefoot* Court also concluded that expert testimony predicting violence did not have to be based on personal observation or an interview of the defendant, a finding that is particularly important in light of the increased use of actuarial risk assessment instruments that do not require face-to-face contact with the subject. In *Barefoot* itself, the Court allowed testimony by two experts who had not evaluated the defendant, based exclusively on the facts of a hypothetical question. In explanation, the Court noted that "[e]xpert testimony, whether in the form of an opinion based on hypothetical questions or otherwise, is commonly admitted as evidence where it might help the factfinder do its assigned job" (p. 903). The Court also asserted that cross-examination could expose hypothetical questions that relied on controverted facts or asked for ultimate conclusions as to dangerousness.

Although much has changed in the world of risk assessment since *Barefoot* was decided, the Court has not altered its views. In *Schall v. Martin* (1984), involving pretrial detention based on risk, the Court adhered to its position on prediction assessments, stating "there is nothing inherently unattainable about a prediction of future criminal conduct" (p. 278). The Court repeated that statement verbatim in *Kansas v. Hendricks* (1997), involving prediction in sexually violent predator (SVP) proceedings (p. 358), even though, in contrast to the sentencing context at issue in *Barefoot*, SVP commitment is based *solely* on determinations of dangerousness and, in contrast to pretrial detention settings, the deprivation of liberty can be prolonged (see Lave, 2011a, pp. 252–255).

All of these cases were decided before much of the most sophisticated research on prediction accuracy was conducted. Nonetheless, lower courts have avoided questioning *Barefoot*. For instance, in *United States v. Coonce* (2014), the defendant argued that predictions of violence should not be allowed as an aggravating factor in a death penalty proceeding, an argument based on numerous post-*Jurek* studies that demonstrated the suspect reliability of such testimony. The district court demurred, however:

> To the extent that studies may show that determinations of future dangerousness are so unreliable as to be per se improper, such a ruling would need to come from the United States Supreme Court. . . . This Court is not prepared to overrule the Supreme Court's reasoned decision on this matter.
>
> (pp. *4–5)

Similarly, in *Holiday v. Stephens* (2013), the court refused to choose between different means of assessing "future threat to society" even if they varied in accuracy, noting the Supreme Court's silence on the matter and stating that a lower court's role "is not to constitutionalize one method of psychological inquiry" (p. *28).

Admissibility Under the Rules of Evidence

Barefoot establishes a constitutional floor—a very low floor—that at most protects against expert prediction testimony that is not subject to the adversarial process. Evidentiary rules can, of course, be more restrictive. In fact, in every jurisdiction, expert testimony is subject to admissibility limits beyond the requirement of relevance that all evidence must meet. First, as indicated earlier, a witness cannot offer an expert opinion unless he or she possesses specialized knowledge that can "assist" the trier of fact—that is, add to what the court or jury can discern for itself (see, e.g., Fed.R.Evid. 702). This initial consideration usually boils down to an inquiry into the witness's qualifications.

Second, in most states, expert opinion evidence must clear an additional hurdle, which generally takes one of three forms. Depending upon the jurisdiction, the testimony must be based on methods, principles, and theories that: (1) "permit a reasonable opinion to be asserted" (see, e.g., *Dyas v. United States*, 1977); (2) are "generally accepted" in the relevant scientific community (*Frye v. United States*, 1923); or (3) have been subject to a verification process (*Daubert v. Merrell Dow Pharmaceuticals*, 1993). In general, the *Daubert* test, which applies in federal court and over half the states, is more demanding than the *Frye* test, which applies in most of the rest of the country, because it states that courts should usually look beyond general acceptance, to whether the subject matter of the testimony has been vetted using scientific or other testing methods that have produced error rates (see Saks & Faigman, 2005). Less demanding than either the *Daubert* formulation or *Frye* is the *Dyas* test, which merely requires a demonstration that the relevant scientific field exists. However framed (using *Daubert*, *Frye*, or *Dyas*), the focus of this second step in evidentiary analysis is the validity of the testimony's basis.

A third inquiry, one that has received particular attention since *Daubert*, concerns the "fit" of the expert testimony. Expert evidence must not only be valid in the abstract, but valid for the particular purpose the law considers pertinent. Further, even if the evidence fits the case in the abstract, ultimate admissibility requires balancing the generalizability of the relevant science to the matter in dispute against the possibility that the factfinder will misapprehend or misapply the evidence in a way that will reduce its usefulness in the actual case at hand.

Each of these issues—qualifications, validity, and fit—is considered here as they apply to opinions about risk. As a general matter, the courts do not engage in a close analysis of any of these issues in the prediction context.

Qualifications

For reasons that will become clear, in many prediction settings the only questions courts ask when considering admissibility have to do with the witness's qualifications. Ideally, courts would inquire into the witness's education about, training on, and experience with risk assessment, as well as the evaluation methodology the witness used to form opinions in the case at hand. However, in the absence of statutes requiring otherwise (see, e.g., *Masschusetts General Laws Annotated* (2020), 123A §1), courts rarely engage in detailed analysis of these matters, choosing instead to rely on generalizations about expertise.

For instance, most courts assume that all psychiatrists and psychologists are qualified to assess dangerousness. In *Addington v. Texas* (1979), dealing with civil commitment proceedings, the Supreme Court stated, "Whether the individual is mentally ill and dangerous to either himself or others and is in need of confined therapy turns on the meaning of the facts which must be interpreted by expert psychiatrists and psychologists" (p. 429). Consistent with this language, courts that address the issue ordinarily do not require psychiatrists or psychologists to demonstrate particular expertise in predicting violent behavior (see *In re Melton*, 1991; *Chambers v. State*, 1978). Instead, they assume that triers of fact will be able to determine the weight to attribute to a particular expert's testimony.

Courts also sometimes permit mental health professionals other than psychiatrists and psychologists to offer expert opinions about violence risk (see *Bean v. Department Health and Mental Hygiene*, 2008; *People ex rel. Strodtman*, 2011; *Schmidt v. Goddin*, 1982). If the professional has the requisite background, such decisions are not necessarily wrong. In *In re Commitment of Dodson* (2010), for instance, the court permitted a person with a bachelor's degree in science, a master's degree in counseling and psychotherapy, and a doctorate in family sciences to testify about whether Dodson had a "behavioral abnormality" that predisposed him "to engage in a predatory act of sexual violence." Crucial to the decision was that the expert had 12 years of experience treating sex offenders, had gone through training in the administration and interpretation of actuarial risk assessment tools, and had participated in 12 to 15 similar assessments.

In contrast, in *Johnson v. State* (2001) the state, in seeking to commit the respondent as a sexually violent predator (SVP), relied solely on the diagnostic opinion of a Department of Corrections employee who had a master's degree in counseling and described himself as an "associate psychologist." The initial decision by the trial court found his five years of experience in the Department of Corrections, including his involvement in preparing approximately 30 reports in SVP proceedings, sufficient to qualify him as an expert (p. 497). The Missouri Supreme Court nonetheless reversed, pointing out that the witness was not yet licensed and thus had to be supervised, but did not appear to have been supervised in this case. Moreover, the court found that, whereas psychiatrists, psychologists, and social workers are defined by state law as engaging in the practice of diagnosis, professional counselors are not permitted to assign diagnoses to individuals. The court held that

> [w]hile his experience treating sex offenders conceivably would qualify him to testify as an expert on many issues, diagnoses of mental disorders is not even arguably within his area of expertise, and his testimony on that point should have been excluded.
>
> (p. 499)

Validity

With respect to many types of expert testimony, qualifications are not enough. The basis of the testimony must also meet the *Dyas*, *Frye*, or *Daubert* tests described earlier. Although on their face the differences between these legal standards appear to be significant, as applied in the prediction setting they are largely hypothetical.

To begin with, in some settings many jurisdictions simply exempt qualified prediction testimony from the usual rules governing expert testimony. For instance, a number of states provide by statute that these rules do not apply in civil commitment proceedings; rather, all "relevant" evidence from qualified experts is admissible (Cal. Welf. Inst. Code, 2016, §5256.4; Iowa Code, 2015, §229.12; Tex Crim. Proc Code Ann. § 37.071). In other settings, the courts themselves have adopted the same rule. For example, in *Doe v. Poritz* (1995), the New Jersey Supreme Court held that, in reviewing claims under a community notification law for sex offenders, "[t]he rules of evidence shall not apply and the court may rely on documentary presentations, including expert opinions, on all issues" (p. 383). In another notification case, the Kentucky Supreme Court flatly stated that "the trial judge has the authority to accept the results of the risk assessment evaluation without qualifying the tests pursuant to *Daubert*" (*Hyatt v. Comm.*, 2002; see also *United States v. Fields*, 2007 (sentencing); *State v. Mahone*, 1985 (civil commitment)).

The reasoning behind these decisions may differ slightly depending on whether the jurisdiction follows *Dyas*, *Frye*, or *Daubert*. *In re Melton* (1991), a case involving civil commitment of a patient who had trouble adhering to his medication regimen, illustrates one court's reasoning in a *Dyas* jurisdiction. Echoing *Barefoot*, the court implied that virtually any type of prediction testimony ought to be admissible, because governing law could not be implemented without it. In the court's words,

> The legislature has effectively decided that "the state of the pertinent art or scientific knowledge [permits] a reasonable opinion to be asserted . . . by an expert," and we would be impermissibly intruding upon a legislative prerogative if we were to challenge that judgment.
>
> (p. 900)

Many courts have followed the *Melton* court's logic (see, e.g., *Commonwealth v. Bradway*, 2004; *People v. Stevens*, 1988).

In *Frye* jurisdictions, courts are more likely to point to the fact that testimony about risk is not "novel" and therefore is not subject to an inquiry into whether it is generally accepted. Judges also sometimes assert that prediction testimony does not have the "aura of infallibility" associated with other types of scientific evidence. On that assumption, they reason, the factfinder is equipped to analyze its foibles without judicial interference or onerous admissibility rules (see, e.g., *In re Commitment of R.S.*, 2002; *State v. Fields*, 2001).

Even in jurisdictions that follow *Daubert*, which is more explicitly focused on validity concerns, many courts treat prediction testimony differently from other types of expert testimony. Most dramatically, the Texas Court of Appeals, although willing to adhere to *Daubert* in other contexts (*Kelly v. State*, 1992), has refused to do so in cases involving prediction evidence. In *Nenno v. State* (1998), the expert offered no research in support of his opinion and admitted that he did not follow any "particular methodology for determining future dangerousness"; rather, his analysis was based on his "experience studying [thousands of] cases" (p. 562). The court, ignoring the voluminous research on the topic, held that predictions of violence are inherently a product of soft social science that may not be amenable to "hard science methods of validation, such as assessing the potential rate of error or subjecting a theory to peer review" (p. 561). For prediction testimony, the court concluded, the correct analysis should approximate the *Dyas* test:

> [t]he appropriate questions are (1) whether the field or expertise is a legitimate one, (2) whether the subject matter of the expert's testimony is within the scope of that field, and (3) whether the expert's testimony properly relies upon and/or utilizes the principles involved in the field.
>
> (p. 562; see also *Espada v. State*, 2008)

Four years later, the Fifth Circuit Court of Appeals, the federal circuit in which Texas is located, found this position rejecting the need for "hard science" validation of prediction testimony so clearly supported by state precedent that it characterized as "frivolous" any objection to such testimony (*Johnson v. Cockrell*, 2002, p. 254).

Even jurisdictions that do, in theory, impose special restrictions on expert prediction testimony seldom apply them rigorously. Typical is the decision in *In re Detention of Thorell* (2003), in which the Washington Supreme Court held that "the *Frye* standard has been satisfied by both clinical and actuarial determinations of future dangerousness" (p. 756). The petitioner in *Thorell* argued that actuarial, as opposed to clinical, risk assessment was a novel discipline that is suspect under *Frye*, but the court disagreed, finding testimony based on statistical analysis to be sufficiently accepted in the field. Most other courts are in agreement, whether *Frye*, *Daubert*, or *Dyas* is the applicable rule, and whether clinical or actuarial testimony is at issue (*see In re Girard*, 2013; *In re Commitment of Simons*, 2004; Janus & Prentky, 2003, pp. 1471, 1497).

There are scattered decisions to the contrary. For instance, a lower Florida court excluded actuarial prediction testimony under *Frye* because it found that the only professionals using the instruments in question were the approximately 150 psychologists performing sex offender evaluations (*In re Valdez*, 2000). A lower court in Washington held that, despite the Washington Supreme Court's holding in *Thorell*, risk assessments based on instruments that rely on dynamic variables should be subject to a *Frye* hearing, given their novelty (*Detention of Ritter v. State*, 2013). Even the normally compliant Texas Court of Appeals has held that testimony based on an un-validated and "idiosyncratic" methodology not used by other mental health professionals, proffered by a witness who acknowledged he was unaware of the literature on risk, was insufficient to meet the state's burden of proof (*Coble v. State*, 2010).

A few judges have gone further. For instance, in *United States v. Sampson* (2004), a federal district court judge stated:

> Developments in the law and more recent scientific research suggest that expert testimony on future dangerousness would be inadmissible under the Federal Rules of Evidence and is also too unreliable to be admitted in the penalty phase of a capital case . . . [I]t may be timely

for the Supreme Court to reconsider whether jurors can ascertain future dangerousness in a particular case with sufficient certainty.

Along the same lines is Judge Garza's concurrence in *Flores v. Johnson* (2000), which argued that expert prediction testimony "fails" *Daubert*. Specifically, he contended that "testing of these theories [about prediction] have never truly been done," that peer review of predictive science has been "negative," that "the rate of error, at a minimum, is fifty percent," and that "standards controlling the operation of the technique are non-existent" (pp. 464–465). Although some of Judge Garza's claims are exaggerated (at least with respect to actuarial and structured professional judgment techniques that have been subject to both testing and peer review), they signal that some jurists are willing to take a hard look at expert opinion about risk.

"Fit"

In theory, courts should not only inquire into a putative expert's qualifications and the validity of his or her methodology and conclusions, but they should also ensure that the proffered opinion addresses the precise issue before the court—an analysis of what many courts today call "fit." In *Daubert* the Supreme Court explained that Federal Rule of Evidence 702 "requires a valid scientific connection to the pertinent inquiry as a precondition to admissibility" (pp. 591–592). This language mandates that the scope of the expert's testimony be probative with respect to one or more facts in dispute. At least four fit issues could arise in connection with prediction testimony.

One of the more challenging such issues is one that can arise in any scientific context: When is information about groups relevant to resolving an individual case? (see generally, Faigman, Monahan, & Slobogin, 2014). In *Porter v. Commonwealth* (2008), for example, the Virginia Supreme Court upheld the trial court's exclusion of expert testimony, proffered by the defendant, that was based on a "statistical projection [of] future violent acts of an inmate who may be similarly situated to [the defendant]" (p. 440). The court stated that this sort of "statistical speculation" was inadmissible without a showing that it fit the defendant's particular case, explaining that "[n]othing in Porter's motion is a proffer of an 'individualized' or 'particularized' analysis of Porter's 'prior criminal record,' 'prior history,' his prior or current incarceration, or the circumstances of the crime for which he had been convicted" (p. 440). Thus, the court appeared to reject actuarial prediction testimony and to permit only subjective clinical judgment regarding future violence, despite the likely lower accuracy of the latter type of judgment.

Although most courts do not follow this holding (probably because, if they did, much prediction testimony presented by the prosecution would be inadmissible as well), a few other courts appear to agree. For instance, in *United States v. Taylor* (2008), the court demanded an "individualized inquiry" from the expert in a capital sentencing case, on the ground that "testimony regarding generalities of prison invites the jury to make decisions based upon group characteristics and assumptions" (pp. 941–942; see generally Mossman, Schwartz, & Elam, 2012). In *Rhodes v. State* (2008), the court reached the same conclusion even when a judge is making the sentencing decision. According to the court (p. 1195):

> The use of a standardized scoring model, such as the LSI-R [Level of Service Inventory-Revised], undercuts the trial court's responsibility to craft an appropriate, individualized sentence. Relying upon a sum of numbers purportedly derived from objective data cannot serve as a substitute for an independent and thoughtful evaluation of the evidence presented for consideration. As our Supreme Court recently noted in discussing the appellate review of sentences, "[a]ny effort to force a sentence to result from some algorithm based on the

number and definition of crimes and various consequences removes the ability of the trial judge to ameliorate the inevitable unfairness a mindless formula sometimes produces" (citing *Cardwell v. State* (2008, p. 1224). Therefore, it is an abuse of discretion to rely on scoring models to determine a sentence.

However, the Indiana Supreme Court subsequently made clear that its decision in *Cardwell*, cited in this quote from *Rhodes*, was not meant to eliminate algorithmic assessments from sentencing. In *Malenchik v. State* (2010), that court rejected the reasoning in *Rhodes*, noting that "evidence-based assessment instruments can be significant sources of valuable information for judicial consideration in deciding whether to suspend all or part of a sentence, how to design a probation program for the offender, whether to assign an offender to alternative treatment facilities or programs, and other such corollary sentencing matters" (p. 573). It went on to state:

> Having been determined to be statistically valid, reliable, and effective in forecasting recidivism, the assessment tool scores may, and if possible should, be considered to supplement and enhance a judge's evaluation, weighing, and application of the other sentencing evidence in the formulation of an individualized sentencing program appropriate for each defendant.
>
> (*Malenchik v. State*, 2010, p. 573)

It is also worth noting in this regard that, contrary to the apparent assumption of the courts in *Porter*, *Taylor*, and *Rhodes*, "individualized" clinical opinion is also based, in effect, on assumptions about groups made by the evaluator (e.g., "this young, white male with two prior crimes is like many others I have seen"). The difference, one that should argue *against* the admissibility of clinical prediction testimony, is that these stereotypes are both less likely to be related to available data on prediction and less transparent to the factfinder than when the evaluator relies on an instrument that explicitly sets out its criteria (as is the case with most actuarial and structured professional judgement instruments). Some courts appear to recognize this fact (see, e.g., *State v. Loomis*, 2016, p. 758, in which the Wisconsin Supreme Court favorably contrasted "evidence-based sentencing" with "ad hoc decision making").

A closely related fit issue, but one that more properly might lead to exclusion of actuarial prediction testimony, is the extent to which the sample upon which a risk assessment is based varies from the case at hand. For instance, a risk assessment instrument derived from a study conducted in Canada involving White prisoners charged with sex offenses is of limited empirical fit in a case involving an African American charged with homicide in the United States. This type of analysis can become even more fine-grained, as one commentator demonstrated with the following illustrative questions:

> Does a [risk assessment instrument] derived from a study comprised of a cohort that included convicted rapists generalize to those offenders diagnosed with pedophilia? Is an instrument that excluded from its construction sample noncoercive incest offenders useful in evaluating risk in offenders with a history of noncoercive incest?
>
> (Bechman, 2001, p. 29)

These types of questions arise most obviously in connection with actuarial prediction, although it should be a concern in structured and unstructured clinical prediction as well, given the earlier observation about clinical stereotyping.

A few courts have held that a failure to validate a risk assessment tool on the pertinent demographic group or local population renders it irrelevant (*Ewert v. Canada*, 2018; *State v. Gordon*, 2018).

Others have cautioned that, while validation sample issues should not necessarily prevent using risk assessment instruments as the basis for expert testimony, judges should be aware that a given instrument may not have been normed on local populations and "must be constantly monitored and re-normed for accuracy due to changing populations and subpopulations" (*State v. Loomis*, 2016, p. 764). Most courts have been less sensitive to the issue. In *In re Commitment of Thomas* (2016) the petitioner argued that one state expert improperly used "outdated" 2000 norms for the Static-99, and that a second expert proffered by the state should have used the Static-99R rather than the Static-99. Consistent with earlier discussion noting that courts often tend to focus on qualifications, the court dismissed the challenges on the ground that both experts had "extensive and specialized experience" in using actuarial instruments and had adequately explained their evaluation methodology.

A third issue of fit concerns whether the expert has taken into account the likely dispositional outcome for the person who is being evaluated. Consider, for instance, expert testimony about risk in a capital sentencing proceeding. Prison is a highly regulated and tightly controlled environment, and research indicates that the assault rate by those in the life-without-parole population is considerably lower than it is in the general prison population (Cunningham, 2006). Arguably, this type of information should inform a conclusion about the risk level of a person who is subject to a death penalty proceeding, where the decision is between execution and life without parole. However, in *Estrada v. State* (2011), the Texas Court of Criminal Appeals rejected this position, concluding that under Texas law the question is "whether a defendant would constitute a continuing threat 'whether in or out of prison' without regard to how long the defendant would actually spend in prison if sentenced to life" (p. 281).

Another version of the dispositional fit issue has arisen in cases challenging use of risk assessment instruments to enhance or set a prison sentence, or to determine whether a convicted offender should be sent to prison in the first instance. Representative is the statement from the court in *Malenchik v. State* (2010): "[N]either the LSI-R nor the SASSI are intended nor recommended to substitute for the judicial function of determining the length of sentence appropriate for each offender" (p. 573) and thus they should not be used to "provide evidence constituting an aggravating or mitigating circumstance nor to determine the gross length of sentence" (p. 575). However, as indicated previously, *Malenchik* also stated that the results of these instruments may be used to create "individualized sentencing programs." Thus, it may be that the court in *Malenchik* was merely emphasizing that, as *State v. Loomis* (2016) put it, "[r]isk scores may not be used as the *determinative* factor in deciding whether the offender can be supervised safely and effectively in the community" (p. 757); the results of an actuarial instrument are relevant but cannot be dispositive on the incarceration issue, given the many other factors besides an offender's risk that are relevant to punishment. Consistent with that view, in *Morrell v. State* (2019), the court construed *Malenchik* to mean only that "the court is prohibited from labeling and finding [a high risk score] to be a separate aggravating circumstance"; it "is not prohibited from considering a defendant's assessment scores when fashioning an individualized sentence" (p. 798).

A final fit issue, probably the most important, concerns whether the law and the expert are using the same outcome measure. Depending on the context and the jurisdiction, the law might define dangerousness as: (1) "a probability that the individual will commit criminal acts of violence that constitute a continuing threat to society" (the definition under the Texas death penalty statute, Tex. Code § 37.071, Sec. 2(b)(2)), (2) whether the person is "likely to engage in a predatory act of sexual violence" (the definition under the Texas sexual predator statute, Tex Code § 841.003)), (3) whether the person is "likely to harm others" (the definition under the Texas civil commitment statute, Tex. Code § 574.034)) or (4) whether "in the near future" there is "a substantial likelihood [the person] will inflict serious bodily harm on . . . another person, as evidenced by recent behavior causing, attempting, or threatening such harm" (the definition under Florida's civil commitment statute, Fla. Stat., 2020, § 394.467(a)2b)).

Given these definitions, a conclusion that a person might commit one or two assaults within the next seven years, the type of prediction produced by some types of actuarial or structured professional judgment instruments, might not be relevant either in a Texas death penalty proceeding (because of the minor nature of the predicted harm) or in a Florida civil commitment proceeding (because the predicted harm is not necessarily imminent). And of course, unless the predicted harm is sexual in nature, such testimony would not be a good fit in a Texas sexual predator proceeding. At the same time, the fact that the predicted harm is not imminent, which would disqualify the testimony under civil commitment statutes like Florida's, does not matter in the capital sentencing or sex offender commitment contexts, which focus on harm in the "foreseeable future," and may not matter under the *Texas* civil commitment statute, which allows involuntary hospitalization on much broader grounds than Florida (see *Purify v. Watters*, 2010; *In re Detention of Hosier*, 2010). The fit issue requires that both courts and experts pay close attention to the relevant statutory framework.

Standards of Proof and the Definition of Dangerousness

Often confused with the rules governing expert testimony is the threshold of proof that must be met to show that a person is "dangerous." Success at admitting expert testimony is only half the battle; the party with the burden of proof (which, in virtually all the settings at issue here, will be the government) must still meet the relevant standard of proof. Litigants have often argued that, given the difficulty of predicting violence, this burden is impossible to meet (see, e.g., *United States v. Hager*, 2013). Assessing this argument requires an analysis of how the definition of dangerousness interacts with the relevant standard of proof, which, in descending order of rigor, will usually be either proof beyond a reasonable doubt, proof by clear and convincing evidence, or proof by a preponderance of evidence.

While the Supreme Court has strongly suggested that the standard of proof regarding dangerousness at capital sentencing is proof beyond a reasonable doubt (*Gregg v. Georgia*, 1976), it has explicitly held that the standard of proof need be no higher than clear and convincing evidence in civil commitment proceedings (*Addington v. Texas*, 1979), and no higher than a preponderance of the evidence in commitment proceedings following an insanity acquittal (*Jones v. United States*, 1983). Furthermore, most sexual predator statutes require only clear and convincing proof (*cf. United States v. Comstock, 2010*), and lower courts have held that the state need meet only the preponderance standard for the commitment of prisoners (*United States v. Muhammad*, 1999), and the even lower "some evidence" standard in parole cases (*In re Shaputis*, 2011). Finally, at least one lower court has held that, in determining whether an insanity acquittee who has initially been committed may be released at a periodic review proceeding, the burden of proof may be switched to the acquittee to show by clear and convincing evidence that he or she is not dangerous (*United States v. Weed*, 2004).

These decisions are based on a number of considerations, including whether the person is already experiencing a deprivation of liberty (in the prisoner commitment and parole settings), whether the consequences of the disposition involve treatment or similarly less "punitive" conditions (as in the civil commitment setting), and whether dangerousness can be presumed given previous proceedings (as in the insanity acquittee context). Of most relevance here is a fourth rationale: the uncertainty of predictions. In *Addington v. Texas* (1979), the case holding that civil commitment criteria need be proven only be clear and convincing evidence, the Supreme Court observed, "[g]iven the lack of certainty and the fallibility of psychiatric diagnosis, there is a serious question as to whether a state could ever prove beyond a reasonable doubt that an individual is both mentally ill and likely to be violent" (p. 430). Such a demanding standard, the Court cautioned, might well harm the respondent:

> If a trained psychiatrist has difficulty with the categorical "beyond a reasonable doubt" standard, the untrained lay juror—or indeed even a trained judge—who is required to rely upon expert opinion could be forced by the criminal law standard of proof to reject commitment for many patients desperately in need of institutionalized psychiatric care. Such "freedom" for a mentally ill person would be purchased at a high price.
>
> (p. 430)

Lower courts have followed *Addington's* lead in evaluating standard of proof questions (see, e.g., *United States v. Weed*, 2004; *Commonwealth v. Helms*, 1986; *Taylor v. Commissioner of Mental Health and Mental Retardation*, 1984; *In re Stephenson*, 1977).

Even applying the lower clear and convincing standard, one could argue that, outside of the most obvious cases, the government should lose. If quantified, proof beyond a reasonable doubt might be equated with a 95% level of certainty, the clear and convincing evidence standard with a 75% probability, and the preponderance standard at 51%. Most actuarial and structured professional judgment instruments have difficulty identifying a group of individuals with even a 50% chance of reoffending, much less a 75% or 95% chance (and, as noted in connection with the fit issue, even an instrument that can identify a person with a high likelihood of "recidivism" may not be measuring the outcome variable of interest).

One response to this dilemma might be to require only that the underlying facts (e.g., prior offenses, failure at treatment) be proven by the requisite standard of proof. Another is to define the term "dangerousness" in a way that facilitates the state's burden. Recall from previous discussion that the typical statute—whether in the capital sentencing context or the civil commitment setting—contains a description of how likely reoffending must be ("likely," "a probability," "substantial probability", etc.) in order for a person to be found dangerous. The interaction of this definition with the standard of proof could mean that even if the standard is beyond a reasonable doubt, the state's *ultimate* burden is much lower.

For instance, if dangerousness is defined in terms of likelihood of reoffending (i.e., 51%), then proving dangerousness beyond a reasonable doubt (i.e. 95%) does not require the same degree of certainty that would be required in a criminal trial, but rather something much lower, on the order of a 50% probability that violence will occur in the future (Monahan & Wexler, 1978). If instead dangerousness is defined in terms of a probability or a substantial probability, the ultimate level of risk that must be proven is probably lower still. In *Coble v. State* (2010), for instance, the Texas Court of Criminal Appeals found that "the Legislature declined to specify a particular level of risk or probability of violence" in capital cases (pp. 267–68). Thus, although dangerousness must be proven beyond a reasonable doubt under the Texas death penalty scheme, the definition of "dangerousness" remains unclear and could in fact be equated with a low probability of reoffending.

This inattention to the interaction of the standard of proof and the definition of dangerousness is unfortunate, since it is up to the courts and legislatures to decide the threshold of risk that justifies a deprivation of liberty or execution. As the New Jersey Supreme Court explained:

> It should be emphasized that while courts in determining dangerousness should take full advantage of expert testimony presented by the state and by defendant, the decision is not one that can be left wholly to the technical expertise of the psychiatrists and psychologists. The determination of dangerousness involves a delicate balancing of society's interest in

protection from harmful conduct against the individual's interest in personal liberty and autonomy. This decision, while requiring the court to make use of the assistance which medical testimony may provide, is ultimately a legal one, not a medical one.

(*State v. Krol*, 1975, p. 302)

Procedural and Fairness Concerns About Risk Assessment

Admissibility issues are the central concern of courts grappling with opinion testimony about risk. But there are also structural and fairness issues that arise in connection with such testimony, some of which may have constitutional dimensions. Addressed here are the implications for risk assessment of the Sixth Amendment's right to jury trial, the Fourteenth Amendment's Equal Protection Clause, the Eighth Amendment's prohibition on cruel and unusual punishment, and constitutional and subconstitutional concerns about equality, fairness, and justice.

The Right to Jury

The Sixth Amendment right to jury trial could have a significant impact on risk assessment in criminal cases, depending on how a jurisdiction's sentencing regime is structured. Traditionally sentencing has been the prerogative of judges, not juries. However, in a line of cases driven by *Apprendi v. New Jersey* (2000), the Supreme Court has established that, unless the right to jury is waived, a jury must find, beyond a reasonable doubt, any facts other than prior convictions that cause a sentence to be enhanced beyond either the statutory maximum for the crime charged or the maximum provided by what is usually called a "mandatory sentencing guideline" (which indicates where within the statutory range a sentence should fall for particular types of offenders) (see *Blakely v. Washington*, 2004; *United States v. Booker*, 2005). Applying *Apprendi*, the Supreme Court has also held that, in capital sentencing proceedings, a jury must find any facts that lead to a death sentence, because that sentence is more punitive than the maximum sentence (life) that can be imposed based simply on a capital murder conviction (*Ring v. Arizona*, 2002).

These cases are likely to affect the process for determining risk in at least some situations. For instance, *Ring* would seem to require that dangerousness be found by a jury in capital sentencing proceedings. *Apprendi* and its progeny might also lead courts to decide that a jury must make the dangerousness determination in *non*-capital cases, if that determination leads to a sentence enhancement beyond the statutory or guidelines maximum. By analogy to the requirement that each element of a crime be proven to the jury, *Apprendi* might even require a jury finding beyond a reasonable doubt with respect to each *individual* risk factor (other than prior convictions)—whether it be prior arrests, employment status, or "negative attitude"—that contributes to a sentence above the maximum. Although at least one lower court has questioned whether *Apprendi* applies to non-capital sentence enhancements based on risk (*Vandergriff v. State*, 2005), the issue is far from clear.

Even if this interpretation of *Apprendi* is accepted, however, its impact on most risk-based sentencing is likely to be minimal. Most non-capital sentences based on risk stay within both statutory ranges and guideline ranges, and thus do not trigger *Apprendi*. Further, if a jurisdiction's sentencing guidelines are "voluntary" (meaning that the judge has discretion not to follow them), the Sixth Amendment is not violated even if an offender's perceived risk extends the sentence beyond the guideline range (cf. *Luttrell v. Commonwealth*, 2004). In such jurisdictions, only if the offender's sentence were raised above the *statutory* maximum would *Apprendi* be implicated in such a jurisdiction. This is so even if one or more of the factors upon which the sentencing court relies is an arrest that is not prosecuted (a risk factor found in many assessment instruments) or that results in *acquittal* by a jury (Johnson, 2016, pp. 2–3).

Sexual predator statutes and other laws that permit post-sentence commitment also avoid running afoul of the Sixth Amendment because, according to the Supreme Court, the confinement that results in these settings is focused entirely on incapacitation and rehabilitation rather than retribution and deterrence and thus is a "civil" measure rather than "criminal punishment" (*Kansas v. Hendricks,* 1997). As the Sixth Amendment's plain language states, the right to jury applies only in "criminal prosecutions." For the same reason, the Sixth Amendment has no impact on other types of commitment proceedings.

The Equal Protection Clause

A second constitutional provision possibly implicated by risk assessment, in either the criminal *or* civil context, is the Equal Protection Clause of the Fourteenth Amendment, which could form the basis for a challenge that certain risk factors illegitimately discriminate between offenders. Under the Clause, discrimination claims are usually categorized under one of three "tiers." In most cases, the government may discriminate between groups or individuals as long as it can demonstrate any "rational" reason for doing so. But if the state action discriminates on the basis of certain "protected" categories, such as women, something more than a superficially rational justification is needed, and if the protected category is race or ethnicity, then a *"compelling"* justification is required (*United States v. Virginia,* 1996, pp. 530–534). Thus, while use of prior arrests, diagnosis, family life, and most other variables to differentiate between risk levels need only have a rational basis, use of factors such as gender, age, and alienage to determine risk could trigger "intermediate" scrutiny of the government's justification, and reliance on race, ethnicity, and religious beliefs as risk factors might require a compelling justification.

The government's goal of protecting the public through assessments of risk is undoubtedly strong. But because race, ethnicity, and religious beliefs are considered highly suspect classifications, traditional Fourteenth Amendment analysis would also require the government to show that their use as risk factors is crucial to achieving that objective. Such a showing is unlikely, given the less-than-robust correlation between these characteristics and risk, as well as the large number of other risk factors available to the government. In any event, the matter is now moot. In *Buck v. Davis* (2017), the Supreme Court bluntly stated, "It would be patently unconstitutional for a state to argue that a defendant is liable to be a future danger because of his race" (p. 764, see also *United States v. Taveras,* 2008, p. 336; *Gonzalez v. Quarterman,* 2006, p. 389; *Matter of Detention of Blogi,* 2008, applying *Buck* to use of Native American heritage as a risk factor).

In contrast, age and gender play a significant, if not crucial, role in many risk assessments, and under the Equal Protection Clause the government justification for using these quasi-suspect classifications need not be as strong. Thus, reliance on these characteristics as risk factors is less open to constitutional challenge (Monahan, 2006; *Brooks v. Commonwealth,* 2004). It might also be noted that, if risk assessment instruments exclude factors like age and gender, older people and women might be classified as higher risks than they actually are, which would be another form of discrimination (see *State v. Loomis,* 2016, p. 268). Nonetheless, given the fact that gender discrimination is entitled to intermediate scrutiny, it is far from clear that a risk assessment tool that explicitly relied on sex as a risk factor is constitutional (see Hellman, 2020).

An even more complicated question is whether risk assessment tools or approaches may include factors that might serve as proxies for suspect classifications such as race and gender. For instance, neighborhood or employment status could be statistical stand-ins for race; research on this issue is, at best, equivocal (compare Larson et al., 2016 to Skeem & Lowenkamp, 2016; Flores et al., 2016). Under current equal protection law, however, unless the intent behind using these types of factors is clearly race-motivated, an equal protection proxy claim is likely to fail (cf. *Washington v. Davis,* 1976; *San Antonio v. Rodriguez,* 1973, pp. 24–29; *McCleskey v. Kemp,* 1987). For this and other reasons, the argument made by Starr (2014) that using risk factors related to poverty violates the Equal Protection Clause is also unlikely to prevail (see Hamilton, 2015). Additionally, it should be noted that the one category of risk factors that most opponents of modern risk assessment would allow evaluators to consider—criminal history—is also closely associated with socioeconomic status and race (Taylor-Thompson, 1996, p. 2468). Short of abandoning risk assessment entirely, the constitutional issues, if they exist, are unavoidable.

Even if a particular risk assessment technique does not violate the Constitution, concerns about fairness arise, especially in connection with race. For instance, the claim has been made that, even if a risk assessment instrument is accurate in the sense that blacks and whites who pose the same risk receive the same scores or are assigned the same risk category, the instrument is unfair if, as research suggests is sometimes the case, it produces more black false positives than white false positives (Angwin et al., 2016). Other commentators have pointed out that, if blacks commit more crime than whites, the latter result is inevitable (Corbett-Davies et al., 2016), while still others suggest that blacks do not commit more crime than whites but are merely arrested and convicted more often than whites, especially with respect to drug crimes (Spohn, 2015). To date, courts have avoided this debate (see generally, Mayson, 2019). Thus, one court, while acknowledging the issue, merely cautioned judges to be aware that risk assessment instruments may "disproportionately classify minority offenders as having a higher risk of recidivism" (*State v. Loomis*, 2016, pp. 763–764).

The well-founded concern about the generalizations upon which risk assessment relies can and should be alleviated by two aspects of well-run risk management programs. First, individuals should always be able to present evidence of protective factors that were not considered in validating the risk assessment protocol. Furthermore, as required by the Supreme Court in the commitment context (*Kansas v. Hendricks*, 1997, pp. 363–364; *Parham v. J.R.*, 1979, p. 613), assessment of risk should be continuous, taking into account participation in rehabilitation efforts and the like. If this requirement is taken seriously, any given risk assessment can only increase a deprivation of liberty for a limited period of time.

The Eighth Amendment and Substantive and Procedural Justice

A closely related concern about risk assessment, albeit one that may apply only in the criminal sentencing context, is that it is fundamentally at odds with the purposes of punishment. Enhancing the sentence of an offender because of gender, age, or any other immutable characteristic strikes some as grossly unfair: men do not "deserve" more time in prison than women; youthful, single offenders are not necessarily more culpable than older, married ones (indeed, youth is often seen as a mitigator, cf. *Roper v. Simmons*, 2005); a person whose father leaves home (a risk factor on the Violence Risk Appraisal Guide-Revised) is not more blameworthy than a person with an intact family (Goodman, 1987; Netter, 2007). Others have expanded this criticism to include sentences based on any trait or characteristic, such as diagnosis or employment status, that is not directly related to commission of a criminal act (Monahan, 2006). It is argued that only risk factors to which moral blame can be attributed, such as prior crimes, are legitimately considered in a system of punishment. The Supreme Court itself appeared to adopt this stance when it stated in *Buck v. Davis* (2017) that a "basic premise" of the criminal justice system is that the "law punishes people for what they do, not who they are" (p. 778).

In constitutional terms, this argument is probably best framed as an Eighth Amendment claim, because that amendment's prohibition on cruel and unusual punishment has been interpreted to require some degree of proportionality between the harm an offender causes and the punishment that is imposed (Stinneford, 2011). However, despite its language in *Buck*, the Supreme Court does not appear ready to accept the argument that risk assessment based on factors unrelated to guilt is antithetical to criminal justice. It has even approved, over an Eighth Amendment objection, sentences of death that are based on dangerousness determinations linked to diagnosis and other non-criminal factors (*Jurek v. Texas*, 1976, pp. 275–276; *Barefoot v. Estelle*, 1983; see also *Pennsylvania ex rel. Sullivan v. Ashe*, 1937). One might also rebut an Eighth Amendment claim with the argument that risk-based sentences are, in fact, ultimately based on a prediction of what a person will do, not what he or she is; immutable risk factors are merely *evidence* of likely future conduct, in the same way that various pieces of circumstantial evidence that are not blameworthy in themselves (e.g., presence near the scene of the crime; possession of a weapon) can lead to a finding of guilt. Furthermore, as the Indiana Supreme Court stated in *Malenchik v. State*, 2010, p. 574), sentencing statutes typically *require* that presentence reports include and judges consider factors such as "the convicted person's history of delinquency or criminality, social history, employment history, family situation, economic status, education, and personal habits."

Even if risk assessment can be defended as a matter of theory, however, its increasing influence could alter the nature of criminal justice in undesirable ways (Feeley & Simon, 1992; Garland, 2001). Hollywood's images of regimes in which prisoners are selected according to genetic makeup or brain chemistry are discomfiting to many (Erickson, 2010). The difference between bio-prediction of this sort and an actuarial score, which often relies largely on static or congenital factors, is one of degree, not kind.

Linked with this existential concern are the negative consequences of unfair stigmatization that risk assessment might generate. For instance, under a risk assessment measure currently used in Virginia, a young male offender who has any other aggravating factor (e.g., a prior crime) is ineligible for diversion from prison (although judges may override that recommendation) (National Center for State Courts, 2002, p. 48). While young males may, all else being equal, be more likely to reoffend, official use of these characteristics in computing sentences may disproportionately taint this group in the eyes of parole officers who make risk assessments, police officers who make arrests, and the public at large. It may even contribute to more crime, if offenders convince themselves that the stereotype is accurate and act accordingly, or if those who do not fit the stereotype think they have a free ride or are ignored by law enforcement authorities pursuing those who fit the profile (Harcourt, 2007). Further, the procedural justice literature suggests that individuals lose respect for the law and become less compliant with it when they believe that the legal system is unfair (Tyler, 1990; Paternoster, Bachman, Brame, & Sherman, 1997), a belief that could easily develop among those who are deprived of liberty based on factors over which they have little or no control.

Heavy reliance on static risk factors that never change—including prior arrests and convictions—may also mean that meeting the relevant release criteria is impossible (unless, perhaps, the state is forced to meet increasingly higher levels of proof to continue confinement, see Slobogin, 2006, p. 144). This structural aspect of risk assessment may explain why so few offenders confined under post-sentence sex offender commitment statutes have been released (Morris, 2002, p. 561; Janus, 1996, p. 206; Lave, 2011b, pp. 426–427). To avoid both perceptions of injustice and legal paralysis, the optimal risk assessment might need to include a needs assessment and a risk management plan focused on dynamic risk factors, like many structured professional judgment instruments do.

At least one court has implicitly reached that conclusion. In holding Minnesota's sex offender commitment statute unconstitutional, the court in *Karsjens v. Jesson I* (2015) stressed that none of the over 700 individuals committed under that program since its modern inception in the 1990s had been released without conditions, and that very few had been released even with conditions. The court required that the state mental health department conduct an individualized risk assessment of all committed individuals, designed to determine whether they were treatable and, if so, whether treatment could take place in a community setting (*Karsjens v. Jesson II*, 2015, p. 950).

It must also be noted, however, that *Karsjens* was subsequently reversed by the Eighth Circuit Court of Appeals (*Karsjens v. Piper*, 2017).

The Right to Confrontation

A final constitutional issue is procedural rather than substantive. In order to evaluate both the accuracy of a risk assessment instrument and the legitimacy of the risk factors upon which it relies, researchers, lawyers, and courts need to know both the specific definition of the risk factors in the instrument and the weight assigned to them. Only in this way can tools be cross-validated and the issues raised by *Buck v. Davis* and the Eighth Amendment be addressed (see Stevenson & Slobogin, 2018). Unfortunately, many risk assessments instruments are not transparent in this regard, especially those that are developed by private companies or that are the product of sophisticated machine learning techniques. Some courts have held that test opaqueness does not violate due process so long as the petitioner has access to validation studies and the types of questions that are asked during the risk assessment (*Matter of Cone*, 2019, pp. 50–51; *State v. Loomis*, 2016, p. 761). But because they deny the individual access to the underlying algorithm, such holdings undermine a defendant's confrontation rights, which apply at sentencing as well as at trial. In *Gardner v. Florida* (1977), the Supreme Court stated:

> Our belief that debate between adversaries is often essential to the truth-seeking function of trials requires us also to recognize the importance of giving counsel an opportunity to comment on facts which may influence the sentencing decision in capital cases.
>
> (p. 360)

Although *Gardner* was a capital case, its reasoning arguably should apply to any information, including algorithmic information, that can enhance a person's sentence or commitment.

Conclusion

Risk assessment is a difficult enterprise, not only in the obvious sense that accurately assessing an individual's risk is challenging but because efforts to enhance accuracy may tend to increase explicit reliance on risk factors that are suspect for constitutional or fairness reasons. To date, the legal system has paid little attention to either issue. If it were to do so, courts might analyze opinions about risk relying on four metrics (see Slobogin, 2018).

One metric is qualifications. Courts should not accept an opinion simply because it comes from a licensed mental health professional or correctional official. Putative experts should have to demonstrate familiarity with the literature on risk, both generally and with respect to the specific methodology used. Judges should assess not only educational credentials but experience at carrying out risk assessments. An evaluation need not involve a face-to-face interview, at least as a legal matter (*Barefoot v. Estelle*, 1983; cf. American Psychological Association, 2010, ethics std. 9.01). However, in the absence of such an interview, the witness should, at most, offer an opinion about the subject's risk, not a recommendation as to a risk management plan.

A second metric is validity. At a minimum, the expert should be able to demonstrate that the evaluation procedure used is one that is generally accepted among experts in the field of risk assessment. Experts should also be able to report statistics that describe the validity and accuracy of any assessment techniques they employ and to demonstrate that the methodology provides risk estimates above chance levels. If that is not possible, the expert should only describe the subject's risk and protective factors, without venturing a conclusion as to whether the individual poses a "high," "moderate," or "low" risk; in the absence of empirical backing making clear what these terms mean, the latter language is merely guesswork which, at least in *Daubert* jurisdictions, should not be countenanced (see Scurich, 2018).

A third metric is fit. The assertion has been made that it is "impossible" to estimate a particular person's level of risk based on group data (Hart, 2009; Cooke & Michie, 2010). Even if that assertion is incorrect (see Imrey & Dawid, 2015; Hanson & Howard, 2010), a qualified expert using an approved methodology is of little use to the legal system unless the expert's probability estimates are based on research about a population that is similar to the subject's, take into account the likely available dispositions, and address the precise definition of dangerousness or risk relevant to the proceeding. If the testimony meets those requisites, the factfinder then has the tools to determine whether the relevant standard of proof is met.

A fourth metric that evaluators, if not the courts, should consider is the extent to which the risk and protective factors included in the assessment are sufficiently dynamic in nature. While explicit reliance on race as a risk factor is legally impermissible, to date it remains permissible to rely on factors that might be proxies for race, or that are static in nature or unrelated to guilt. Nonetheless, both substantive and procedural justice concerns counsel in favor of using an assessment methodology that depends as much as possible on mutable, dynamic factors over which the individual has control and that are transparent to the decision-maker.

References

Addington v. Texas, 441 U.S. 418 (1979).

Ake v. Oklahoma, 407 U.S. 68 (1985).

American Psychological Association. (2010). *Ethical principles of psychologists and code of conduct*. Retrieved from http//www.apa.org/ethics/code/principles.pdf

Angwin, J., Larson, J., Mattu, S., & Kirchner, L. (2016). Machine bias. *ProPublica*. Retrieved from www.pro publica.org/article/machine-bias-risk-assessments-in-criminal-sentencing

Apprendi v. New Jersey, 530 U.S. 446 (2000).

Barefoot v. Estelle, 463 U.S. 880 (1983).

Bean v. Department of Health and Mental Hygiene, 959 A.2d 778 (MD. 2008).

Bechman, D. C. (2001). Sex offender civil commitments: Scientists or psychics? *Criminal Justice, 16(2)*, 24–30.

Blakely v. Washington, 542 U.S. 296 (2004).

Brooks v. Commonwealth of Virginia, Record No. 2540-02-3 (VA. CT. App. 2004, January 28).

Buck v. Davis, 137 S.Ct. 759 (2017).

Cal. Welf. Inst. Code (West 2016).

Cardwell v. State, 895 N.E.2d 1219 (IN. 2008).

Chambers v. State, 568 S.W.2d 313, 324 (Tex. Crim. App. 1978).

Coble v. State, 330 S.W.3d 253 (Tex. Crim. App. 2010), cert. denied, 131 S. Ct. 3030 (2011).

Cooke, D. J., & Michie, C. (2010). Limitations of diagnostic precision and predictive utility in the individual case: A challenge for forensic practice. *Law & Human Behavior, 34*, 259–274.

Commonwealth v. Bradway, 816 N.E.2d 152 (MA. 2004).

Commonwealth v. Helms, 506 A.2d 1384, 1389 (PA. 1986).

Corbett-Davies, S., Pierson, E., Feller, A., & Goel, S. (2016). What makes an algorithm fair? *Medium*. Retrieved from https://medium.com/soal-food/what-makes-an-algorithm-fair-6ad64d75dd0c

Cunningham, M. D. (2006). Dangerousness and death: A nexus in search of science and reason. *American Psychologist, 61*(8), 828–839.

Daubert v. Merrell Dow Pharmaceuticals, Inc., 509 U.S. 579 (1993).

Detention of Ritter v. State, 312 P. 3d 723 (Wash. 2013).

Diamond, S. S., Casper, J. D., Heiert, C. L., & Marshall, A. (1996). Juror reactions to attorneys at trial. *Journal of Criminal Law & Criminology, 87*, 17–47.

Doe v. Poritz, 662 A.2d 367 (NJ. 1995).

Dyas v. U. S., 376 A.2d 827 (DC. 1977).

Erickson, S. K. (2010). Blaming the brain. *Minnesota Journal of Law, Science & Technology, 11*, 27–77.

Espada v. State, 2008 WL 4809235 (Tex. Crim. App. 2008).

Estrada v. State, 313 S.W.3d 274 (Tex. Crim. App. 2010), cert. denied, 131 S. Ct. 905 (2011).

Ewert v. Canada, 2 S.C.R. 165 (Can. 2018).

Faigman, D., Monahan, J., & Slobogin, C. (2014). Group to individual (G2i) inference in scientific expert testimony. *University of Chicago Law Review, 81*, 417–480.

Federal Rules of Evidence. (2016). Retrieved from www.rulesofevidence.org/

Feeley, M., & Simon, J. (1992). The new penology: Notes on the emerging strategy of corrections and its implications. *Criminology, 30*, 449–480.

Flores, A., Lowencamp, C., & Bechtel, K. (2016). False positives, false negatives and false analyses: A rejoinder to "machine bias": There's software used across the country to predict future criminals, and it's biased against blacks. *Federal Probation, 80*, 1–35.

Flores v. Johnson, 210 F.3d 456 (5th Cir. 2000).

Fla. Stat. (West 2020).

Frye v. United States, 293 F. 1013 (DC. 1923).

Gardner v. Florida, 430 U.S. 349.351 (1977).

Garland, D. (2001). *The culture of control: Crime and social order in contemporary society.* Oxford: Oxford University Press.

Gonzalez v. Quarterman, 458 F.3d 384 (5th Cir. 2006).

Goodman, D. S. (1987). Demographic evidence in capital sentencing. *Stanford Law Review, 39*, 499–543.

Gregg v. Georgia, 428 U.S. 153 (1976).

Hamilton, M. (2015). Risk-needs assessment: Constitutional and ethical challenges. *American Criminal Law Review, 52*, 231–286.

Hanson, R. K., & Howard, P. D. (2010). Individual confidence intervals do not inform decision-makers about the accuracy of risk assessment evaluations. *Law & Human Behavior, 34*, 275–281.

Harcourt, B. (2007). *Against prediction: Profiling, policing and punishing in an actuarial age.* Chicago: University of Chicago Press.

Hart, S. (2009). Evidence-based assessment of risk for sexual violence. *Chapman Journal of Criminal Justice, 1*, 143–165.

Heller v. Doe by Doe, 509 U.S. 312 (1993).

Hellman, D. (2020). Sex, causation and algorithms: Equal protection in the age of machine learning. *Washington University Law Review, 98.*

Hilton, N. Z., Harris, G. T., Rawson, K., & Beach, C. A. (2005). Communicating violence risk information to forensic decision makers. *Criminal Justice and Behaviour, 32*, 97–116.

Holiday v. Stephens, 2013 WL 3480384 (S.D. Tex. 2013).

Hyatt v. Commonwealth, 72 S.W.3d 566 (2002).

Imrey, P., & Dawid, A. P. (2015). A commentary on statistical assessment of violence recidivism risk. *Statistics & Public Policy, 2*, 1–28.

In re Barnard, 616 N.E.2d 714 (1993).

In re Commitment of Dodson, 311 S.W.3d 194 (Ct. Appeals, Tex. 2010).

In re Commitment of R.S., 801 A.2d 219 (NJ. 2002).

In re Commitment of Simons, 821 N.E.2d 1184 (2004).

In re Commitment of Thomas, 2016 WL 2905153 (Wash. 2016).

In re Detention of Hosier, 2010 WL 5209371 (Wash. App. Div. 1 2010).

In re Detention of Thorell, 72 P. 3d 708 (Wash. 2003).

In re Gannon, 301 A.2d 493 (1973).

In re Girard, 294 P. 3d 236 (Kan. 2013).

In re Melton, 597 A.2d 892 (DC. 1991).

In re Shaputis, 265 P. 3d 253 (Cal. 2011).

In re Stephenson, 67 Ill. 2d 544, 10 Ill. Dec. 507, 367 N.E.2d 1273, 1277 (1977).

In re Valdez, No. 99-000045CI (Fla. 2000).

Iowa Code (West 2015).

Janus, E. (1996). Preventing sexual violence: Setting principled constitutional boundaries on sex offender commitments. *Indiana Law Journal, 72*, 157–213.

Janus, E., & Prentky, R. A. (2003). Forensic use of actuarial risk assessment with sex offenders: Accuracy, admissibility and accountability. *American Criminal Law Review, 40*, 1443–1499.

Johnson, B. L. (2016). The puzzling persistence of acquitted conduct in federal sentencing and what can be done about it. *Suffolk University Law Review, 49*, 1–45.

Johnson v. Cockrell, 306 F.3d 249, 254 (5th Cir. 2002).

Johnson v. State, 58 S.W.3d 496 (Mo. 2001).

Jones v. United States, 463 U.S. 354 (1983).

Jurek v. Texas, 428 U.S. 262 (1976).

Kansas v. Hendricks, 521 U.S. 346 (1997).

Karsjens v. Jesson I, 109 F.Supp.3d 1139 (2015, June).

Karsjens v. Jesson II, 146 F.Supp.3d 916 (2015, October).

Karsjens v. Piper, 845 F.3d 392 (8th Cir. 2017).

Kelly v. State, 824 S.W.2d 568 (Tex. Crim. App. 1992).

Krauss, D. A., Lieberman, J. D., & Olson, J. (2004). The effects of rational and experiential information processing of expert testimony in death penalty cases. *Behavioral Science & Law, 22*, 801–322.

Krauss, D., & Sales, B. D. (2003). The effects of clinical and scientific expert testimony on juror decision making in capital cases. *Psychology, Public Policy & Law, 7*, 267–310.

Larson, J., Mattu, S., Kirchner, L., & Angwin, J. (2016). *How we analyzed the COMPAS recidivism algorithm.* Retrieved from www.propublica.org/article/how-we-analyzed-the-compas-recidivism-algorithm

Lave, T. R. (2011a). Controlling sexually violent predators: Continued incarceration at what cost? *New Criminal Law Review, 14*, 212–270.

Lave, T. R. (2011b). Throwing away the key: Has the Adam Wash act lowered the threshold for sexually violent predator commitments too far? *University of Pennsylvania Journal of Constitutional Law, 14*, 391–428.

Luttrell v. Commonwealth, Record No. 2092–02–4 (Va. Ct. App. 2004, February 17).

Malenchik v. State, 928 N.E.2d 564 (Ind. 2010).

Matter of Cone, 435 P. 3d 45 (Kan. 2019).

Matter of Detention of Blogi, 3 Wash.App. 1006 (2008).

Mayson, S. (2019). Bias in, bias out. *Yale Law Journal, 128*, 2218–2299.

McKlesky v. Kemp, 481 U.S. 279 (1987).

Masschusetts General Laws Annotated (2020).

Monahan, J. (2006). A jurisprudence of risk: Forecasting harm among prisoners, predators and patients. *Virginia Law Review, 92*, 391–435.

Monahan, J., & Wexler, D. (1978). A definite maybe: Proof and probability in civil commitment. *Law & Human Behavior, 2*, 37–46.

Morrell v. State, 118 N.E.3d 793 (IN. CT. App. 2019).

Morris, G. (2002). Punishing the unpunishable—the abuse of psychiatry to confine those we love to hate. *Journal of American Academy of Psychiatry & Law, 30*, 556–562.

Mossman, D., Schwartz, A. H., & Elam, E. (2012). Risky business versus overt acts: What relevance do "actuarial," probabilistic risk assessments have for judicial decision on involuntary psychiatric hospitalization? *Houston Journal of Health Law & Policy, 11*, 365–453.

National Center for State Courts. (2002). *Offender risk assessment in Virginia: A three stage evaluation.* Retrieved from www.vcsc.state.va.us/risk_off_rpt.pdf

Nenno v. State, 970 S.W.2d 549 (Tex. Crim. App. 1998) (overruled on other grounds by, State v. Terrazas, 4 S.W.3d 720 (Tex. Crim. App. 1999)).

Netter, B. (2007). Using group statistics to sentence individual criminals: An ethical and statistical critique of the Virginia risk program. *Journal of Criminal Law & Criminology, 97*, 699–729.

Parham v. J.R., 442 U.S. 584 (1979).

Paternoster, R., Bachman, R., Brame, R., & Sherman, L. (1997). Do fair procedures matter? The effect of procedural justice on spouse assault. *Law & Society Review, 31*, 1630–1647.

Pennsylvania ex rel. Sullivan v. Ashe, 302 U.S. 51 (1937).

People ex rel. Strodtman, 2011 WL 5084951 (CO. App. 2011).

People v. Murtishaw, 631 P. 2d 446 (1981).

People v. Stevens, 761 P. 2d 768, 771 (CO. 1988).

Porter v. Commonwealth, 661 S.E.2d 415 (VA. 2008), cert. denied, 129 S. Ct. 1999 (2009).

Purify v. Watters, 2010 WL 4105504 (E.D. WI. 2010).

Rhodes v. State, 896 N.E.2d 1193 (IN. CT. App. 2008).

Ring v. Arizona, 536 U.S. 584 (2002).

Roper v. Simmons, 543 U.S. 551 (2005).

Saks, M. J., & Faigman, D. L. (2005). Expert evidence after Daubert. *Annual Review of Law & Social Science*, *1*, 105–138.

San Antonio v. Rodriguez, 411 U.S. 1 (1973).

Schall v. Martin, 467 U.S. 253 (1984).

Schmidt v. Goddin, 297 S.E.2d 701 (VA. 1982).

Scurich, N. (2018). The case against categorical risk assessments. *Behavioral Sciences & the Law, 36*, 554–564.

Skeem, J., & Lowenkamp, C. (2016). Risk, race, and recidivism: predictive bias and disparate impact. *Criminology, 54*, 680–712.

Slobogin, C. (2006). *Minding justice: Laws that deprive people with mental disability of life and liberty*. Cambridge, MA: Harvard University Press.

Slobogin, C. (2018). Principles of risk assessment. *Behavioral Sciences & the Law, 36*, 507–516.

Spohn, C. (2015). Race, crime and punishment in the twentieth and twenty-first centuries. *Crime and Justice, 44*, 49–92.

Starr, S. B. (2014). Evidence-based sentencing and the scientific rationalization of discrimination. *Stanford Law Review, 66*, 803–872.

State v. Fields, 35 P. 3d 82 (AR. 2001).

State v. Gordon, 919 N.W.2d 635 (Iowa. CT. App. 2018).

State v. Krol, 344 A.2d 289 (NJ. 1975).

State v. Loomis, 881 N.W.2d 749 (WI. 2016).

State v. Mahone, 379 N.W.2d 878 (WI. CT. App. 1985).

Stevenson, M., & Slobogin, C. (2018). Algorithmic risk assessment and the double-edged sword of youth. *Washington University Law Review, 96*, 1–26.

Stinneford, J. F. (2011). Rethinking proportionality under the cruel and unusual punishments clause. *Virginia Law Review, 97*, 899–977.

Taylor v. Commissioner of Mental Health and Mental Retardation, 481 A.2d 139 (ME. 1984).

Taylor-Thompson, K. (1996). Individual actor v. institutional player: Alternating visions of the public defender. *Georgetown Law Journal, 84*, 2419–2471.

Tex. Code (Vernon 2015).

Tyler, T. R. (1990). *Why people obey the law*. Princeton, NJ: Princeton University Press.

United States v. Booker, 543 U.S. 220 (2005).

United States v. Comstock, 627 F.3d 513, 515–16 (4th Cir. 2010).

United States v. Coonce, 2014 WL 1018081 (W.D. Mo. 2014).

United States v. Fields, 483 F.3d 313 (5th Cir. 2007).

United States v. Hager, 721 F.3d 167 (4th Cir. 2013).

United States v. Muhammad, 165 F.3d 327 (5th Cir. 1999).

United States v. Sampson, 335 F. Supp. 2d 166 (D. Mass. 2004).

United States v. Taveras. 585 F.Supp. 327 (2008).

United States v. Taylor, 583 F. Supp. 2d 923 (E.D. Tenn. 2008).

United States v. Troya, 733 F.3d 1125 (11th Cir. 2013).

United States v. Virginia, 518 U.S. 515 (1996).

United States v. Weed, 389 F.3d 1060, 1068 (10th Cir. 2004).

Vandergriff v. State, 125 P. 3d 360 (Alas. 2005).

Washington v. Davis, 426 U.S. 229 (1976).

Part II

Empirical-Actuarial Measures

Chapter 5

The Classification of Violence Risk (COVR)

John Monahan

The Classification of Violence Risk (COVR) was developed with the goal of offering clinicians a structured tool to assist in their estimation of the risk of violence to others posed by an individual with a mental disorder. COVR is an interactive software program designed to estimate violence risk over the first several months after discharge from a mental health facility.

Description of the Measure

Using a laptop or desktop computer, COVR guides the evaluator through a brief chart review and a 5- to 10-minute interview with the examinee. After the requested information has been entered, COVR generates a report that contains an empirically derived estimate of the examinee's violence risk, including the confidence interval for that estimate and a list of the risk factors that COVR took into account to produce the estimate. Detailed descriptions of the research constructing and validating the software and the statistical model on which it rests can be found in Monahan et al. (2001), and Monahan, Steadman, Robbins, et al. (2005).

COVR in Context

It may be useful to begin by situating COVR within the larger context of structured violence risk assessment (see Guy, Douglas, & Hart, 2015; Skeem & Monahan, 2016). This activity might usefully be seen as having three stages (Monahan, 2006). In the first stage—*selecting and measuring risk factors*—the mental health professional performing the assessment decides which risk factors to measure and how these risk factors should be measured. In unstructured (or clinical) risk assessment, risk factors are selected and measured based on the mental health professional's theoretical orientation and clinical experience, and may vary from case to case as theory and experience dictate. In contrast, in all forms of structured risk assessment, decisions about which risk factors to assess and how to measure them are made largely in advance, before the actual risk assessment process begins. Explicit rules specify a risk factor's operational definition and quantification. In structured risk assessment, the mental health professional performing the assessment has little discretion regarding the selection or measurement of risk factors: these decisions are for the most part "structured" for him or her in advance by the appearance of specified variables, with instructions on how these variables are to be scored, on a formal risk assessment instrument.

The second stage of violence risk assessment—*combining risk factors*—involves taking the person's individually measured risk factors (i.e., his or her "scores" or "ratings" on each of the risk factors) and assembling them into a single composite estimate of violence risk. In unstructured risk assessment, risk factors are assembled in an intuitive or holistic manner to generate a clinical opinion about violence risk. In some forms of structured risk assessment, risk factors are assembled into a composite estimate of risk by means of a mathematical process specified in advance. That process is sometimes as simple as adding the unweighted or weighted scores of the individual risk factors together to yield a total score, but it can involve more complex tree-based statistical procedures as well (see the section "Method of and Rationale for Development" later in this chapter).

In the last component of violence risk assessment—generating *a final risk estimate*—the mental health professional responsible for the risk estimate reviews the likelihood of violence produced by the first two components of the risk assessment process. In unstructured risk assessment, because the risk factors are already combined in an intuitive or holistic manner to generate a clinical opinion about violence risk, there is nothing to "review." The mental health professional's clinical opinion is his or her final estimate of violence risk. In some forms of structured risk assessment, however, the final risk estimate offered by the clinician may differ from the risk estimate produced by the first two (structured) components of the assessment process, based on additional (unstructured) information the clinician has gathered from interviews with the examinee or significant others, and/or review of collateral documents—information not included on the structured risk assessment instrument.

All forms of structured risk assessment specify in advance *at least* which risk factors are to be assessed and how those risk factors are to be measured (that is, the first component of the violence risk assessment process). Some tools (for example, the Historical-Clinical-Risk Management 20, Version 3—HCR-20 V3; see Chapter 12 in this volume) specify *only* the choice and measurement of risk factors.[1] COVR goes on to *also* specify the manner in which the risk factors are combined to yield an estimate of risk (that is, the second component of the violence risk assessment process). But COVR allows the clinician to review this estimate, in the context of other available information, before issuing his or her final risk estimate. Still other tools (for example, the Violence Risk Appraisal Guide, VRAG; see Chapter 7 in this volume) *completely structure* the violence risk assessment process. No clinical review is allowed: the structured risk estimate that is produced when the risk factors are combined is the final product of the risk assessment process. It is this final form of structured violence risk assessment that is properly termed "actuarial" (Meehl, 1954).

It is important to note that, in contrasting COVR with other structured violence risk assessment instruments (e.g., VRAG and HCR-20 V3) in the previous paragraph, I mean to contrast the instruments *used as their authors recommend they be used*. It is, of course, possible for a clinician to take any one of the three contrasted instruments and use it in a manner not envisioned by its developers. For example, one could administer the COVR and accept as final the risk estimate that it generates, without subjecting that estimate to the recommended clinical review. Or one could administer VRAG and use the obtained estimate to anchor what essentially becomes a clinical judgment, contrary to the admonition of its authors. Finally, despite the developers' explicit recommendations to the contrary, HCR-20 V3 could be used clinically in the same manner that it is often used in research. That is, it is possible "to treat the HCR-20 as an actuarial scale and simply sum the numeric item codes to yield . . . total scores, ranging from 0 to 40" (Webster, Douglas, Eaves, & Hart, 1997, p. 21). There is nothing preventing a clinician from using one of these instruments in an "off-label" manner. But the clinician who did so would be ethically obligated to inform the recipient of any resulting risk communication that the estimate of violence risk it provided was generated by nonstandard procedures.

The MacArthur Violence Risk Assessment Study

The COVR software was constructed from data generated in the MacArthur Violence Risk Assessment Study (Steadman et al., 2000). In this research, 1,136 patients in acute psychiatric facilities in three states were assessed in the hospital on 106 potential risk factors for violent behavior. The inclusion criteria were: (1) civil admissions; (2) between the ages of 18 and 40 years; (3) English speaking; (4) of Caucasian, African American, or Hispanic ethnicity; and (5) a medical record diagnosis of schizophrenia, schizophreniform disorder, schizoaffective disorder, depression, dysthymia, mania, brief reactive psychosis, delusional disorder, alcohol or other drug abuse or dependence, or a personality disorder (Monahan & Appelbaum, 2000; Monahan, Vesselinov, Robbins, & Appelbaum, 2016).

Examinees were followed for 20 weeks in the community after discharge from the hospital. Triangulated measures of violence to others included official police and hospital records, examinee self-report, and the report of a collateral informant (most often, a family member) who knew the examinee best in the community. The criterion measure of violence to others consisted of four acts: (1) any battery with physical injury, (2) the use of a weapon, (3) threats made with a weapon in hand, and (4) sexual assault.[2] (For a discussion of legal and ethical aspects of conducting this research, see Monahan, Appelbaum, Mulvey, Robbins, & Lidz, 1993.)

The COVR Software

COVR is capable of assessing those 40 risk factors for violence (see Table 5.1) that emerged as most predictive of violence in the MacArthur Violence Risk Assessment Study. However, in any given administration COVR assesses only the number of risk factors necessary to classify an examinee's violence risk, which may be considerably less than 40. Since COVR relies on a tree-based rather than a main-effects analytic strategy (see the section "Method of and Rationale for Development" later in this chapter), the same risk factors are not assessed for every examinee. Among the risk factors assessed most frequently by the COVR, however, are the seriousness and frequency of prior arrests, young age, male gender, being unemployed, the seriousness and frequency of having been abused as a child, a diagnosis of antisocial personality disorder, the *lack of* a diagnosis of schizophrenia, whether the individual's father used drugs or left the home before the individual was 15 years old, substance abuse, impaired anger control, and violent fantasies (for the implications of these risk factors for reducing violence risk, and not merely assessing it, see Monahan & Appelbaum, 2000).

Table 5.1 The 40 Risk Factors Included in COVR

Legal status	Motor impulsiveness
Major mental diagnosis and substance abuse	Parents fight with each other
Prior arrests—frequency	Valid attempt to kill self
Child abuse—seriousness	Sexual abuse before age 20
Diagnosis of schizophrenia, schizophreniform, schizoaffective	Marital status
	Threat/control override
Neurological screening—loss of consciousness	Prior hospitalization
Age	Thoughts of harming self
Anger reaction	Present at admission-suicide threat
Prior arrests—seriousness	Father's arrests
Employed full/part time	SIV—not frequent, not escalating, not while with
Schedule of imagined violence (SIV)	Target
Father's drug use	Age at first hospitalization
Lived with father until age 15	Present at admission—depression
Alcohol abuse diagnosis	Years of education
Drug abuse diagnosis	Hallucinations
Gender	Functioning score
Child abuse—frequency	Primary diagnosis
Diagnosis of antisocial personality disorder	Present at admission—decompensation
Perceived coercion	Present at admission—substance abuse
Prior violence	Present at admission—personal problems

The COVR is designed to be administered by professionals in any of the mental health disciplines. To date, it has been validated for clinical use only on acute psychiatric patients (see later in this chapter). If COVR is used with other populations, "caution rather than confidence is appropriate, at least until additional [validation] research has been conducted" (Monahan et al., 2001, p. 132).

METHOD OF AND RATIONALE FOR DEVELOPMENT

The empirical development of COVR took place in seven stages over an 18-year period (Monahan, 2018).

Stage One: Identifying Gaps in Methodology

When the MacArthur Violence Risk Assessment Study began in the mid-1980s, almost all existing studies of violence risk assessment suffered from one or more methodological problems. The studies (1) considered a constricted range of risk factors, often a few demographic variables or scores on a psychological test; (2) employed weak criterion measures of violence, usually relying solely on arrest; (3) studied a narrow segment of the patient population, typically males with a history of violence; and (4) were conducted at a single site. Based upon this critical examination of existing work, the authors designed the MacArthur Violence Risk Assessment Study with the aim of overcoming the identified methodological obstacles. To overcome the methodological problems found in existing studies, the MacArthur researchers (1) studied a large and diverse array of risk factors; (2) triangulated their outcome measurement of violence, adding patient self-report and the report of a collateral informant to data from official police and hospital records; (3) studied both men and women, regardless of whether they had a history of violence; and (4) conducted the study at three sites rather than at a single site.

Stage Two: Selecting Promising Risk Factors

Studies have suggested that a number of variables might be robust risk factors for violence among people with a mental disorder. The MacArthur research chose to assess risk factors in four domains: personal factors (e.g., demographic and personality variables), historical factors (e.g., past violence, mental disorder), contextual factors (e.g., social support, social networks), and clinical factors (e.g., diagnosis, specific symptoms). Next, the researchers chose what they believed to be the best of the existing measures of these variables, and they commissioned the development of a necessary measure where no adequate measure to assess a variable was available (e.g., the Novaco Anger Scale; Novaco, 1994).

Stage Three: Using Tree-Based Methods

The MacArthur researchers developed violence risk assessment models based on a "classification tree" method rather than on the usual linear regression method (Gardner, Lidz, Mulvey, & Shaw, 1996). A classification tree approach prioritizes an interactive and contingent model of violence— one that allows many different combinations of risk factors to classify an individual at a given level of risk (Breiman, Friedman, Olshen, & Stone, 1984). The particular questions to be asked in any assessment grounded in this approach depend on the answers given to prior questions. Factors that are relevant to the risk assessment of one individual may not be relevant to the risk assessment of another individual. This approach contrasts with a main-effects regression approach, in which a common set of questions is asked of everyone being assessed and every answer is weighted and summed to produce a score that can be used for predictive purposes.

Stage Four: Creating Different Cutoffs for High and Low Risk

Rather than relying on the standard single threshold for distinguishing among participants, the MacArthur researchers decided to employ two thresholds—one for identifying high-risk individuals and one for identifying low-risk individuals. The degree of risk presented by the intermediate "average-risk" group—those at neither high nor low risk—could not be statistically distinguished from the base rate of the sample as a whole.

Stage Five: Repeating the Classification Tree

To increase the predictive accuracy of the classification tree, data from those individuals designated as "average risk" were reanalyzed. That is, all of the participants who were not classified into groups designated as either "high" or "low" risk in the standard classification tree model were pooled together and reanalyzed. The reason for reanalyzing these data was to determine if the individuals who were not classified in the first iteration of the analysis might be different in some significant ways from the individuals who were so classified. This resulting classification tree model was referred to as an "iterative classification tree" (ICT) (Steadman et al., 2000). Using an iterative classification tree allowed the MacArthur researchers to classify many more examinees as "high" or "low" risk than did using a main-effects regression approach (Monahan et al., 2001, p. 104).

Stage Six: Combining Multiple Risk Estimates

An important characteristic of the classification tree methodology is that variables entered initially into the tree carry more weight in determining the risk group to which an individual is assigned. Therefore, as a final step, the authors estimated several different risk assessment models in an attempt to obtain multiple risk assessments for each individual. That is, different risk factors were chosen to be the lead variable upon which a classification tree was constructed. This was done by choosing, from among the variables that statistically qualified for "lead variable" status, those that were not simply different indices of the same underlying variable, such as, for example, "alcohol use" and "alcohol diagnosis" would have been. The basic idea motivating the combination of multiple risk estimates was that individuals who scored in the high-risk category on many classification trees were more likely to be violent than individuals who scored in the high-risk category on fewer classification trees. Analogously, individuals who scored in the low-risk category on many classification trees were less likely to be violent than individuals who scored in the low-risk category on fewer classification trees (Banks et al., 2004). The result of this "multiple iterative classification tree" procedure was to place each examinee into one of five categories whose rates of engaging in violence to others—as operationalized earlier—over the first several months after hospital discharge was 1%, 8%, 26%, 56%, or 76% (for discussions of how best to communicate violence risk estimates—as probabilities, as relative frequencies, or as categories [COVR allows users to choose any of these formats]—see Monahan et al., 2002; Monahan & Steadman, 1996; Slovic, Monahan, & MacGregor, 2000; Scurich, Monahan, & John, 2012).

Stage Seven: Developing the COVR Software

The multiple iterative classification tree models that were constructed had an impressive capacity to identify individuals with differing levels of violence risk. However, these models were also very computationally intensive and not suited to paper-and-pencil administration. As a result, the MacArthur researchers developed user-friendly software that could be employed to classify patients' violence risk.

Reliability

Reliability was addressed in the MacArthur Violence Risk Assessment Study by having each interviewer videotape five administrations of the risk assessment instrument and having those tapes blindly rescored by the other interviewers. This data set of 385 interviews yielded excellent kappa coefficients (alpha > .80) for all risk factors that appear in COVR (see Monahan et al., 2001, p. 149).

Validity

Of course, the successful construction of a structured risk assessment instrument does not answer the question of how well the instrument will perform when applied to new samples of individuals. As a rule, models constructed using procedures that rely on associations between variables in a particular sample are apt to lose predictive power when applied to new samples. This "shrinkage" is due to capitalization on chance associations in the original construction sample. Thus, it is essential to prospectively validate models on new samples to ensure that they maintain adequate levels of predictive power. Therefore, a prospective validation of the model of violence risk assessment was conducted (Monahan, Steadman, Robbins et al., 2005). In this research, supported by the National Institute of Mental Health, COVR software incorporating the multiple ICT procedure was administered to independent samples of acute inpatients ($n = 157$) and prospectively followed subsamples of discharged patients classified as at high or low violence risk.

Specifically, the COVR software was used to evaluate patients at two sites: Worcester, Massachusetts (a site in the construction study), and Philadelphia, Pennsylvania (not a site in the construction study). The selection criteria for this validation study were slightly broader than those used in the MacArthur development study: (1) between ages 18 and 60 years; (2) of any race/ethnic background (that is, not limited to Caucasian, African American, and Hispanic); and (3) with any psychiatric diagnosis. Expanding the eligible sample in this fashion allowed us both to compare the validation results with the original sample on which the software had been developed and to test the validity of the software in assessing violence risk for a broader group of examinees.

Laptop computers loaded with the COVR software were available at each facility. After informed consent had been obtained, chart and demographic data were entered, followed by examinee assessment with the software. Examinee self-report was relied upon for information not obtained from the chart, and probe questions were asked to clarify inconsistent answers. The software was administered by research interviewers (most often psychology graduate students). The average length of time to administer COVR was less than 10 minutes.

Based on the original MacArthur analysis results, examinees were assigned to (1) a high-risk category (equivalent to risk classes 4 and 5, the highest two risk classes in Banks et al., 2004), with an expected rate of violence of 63.6%; (2) a low-risk category (equivalent to risk class 1, the lowest risk class in Banks et al., 2004), with an expected rate of violence of 1.2%; or (3) an average-risk category (equivalent to risk classes 2 and 3, the intermediate risk classes in Banks et al., 2004), with an expected rate of violence of 15.6%. The examinees' treatment providers in the hospital were blind to the risk classification.

All of the high-risk individuals and a random sample of the low-risk individuals were selected for follow-up. Given limitations on resources, the need to maintain an adequate sample size in the groups that were followed, and because the primary aim of the study was to validate the high- and low-risk designations, examinees assessed as neither high nor low risk of violence (that is, examinees classified as being at average risk) were not followed up in the community. Examinees who had been selected for follow-up were recontacted in the community and interviewed at 10 weeks and 20 weeks from the date of discharge.

Using the strict operational definition of violence from the original study, results indicated that 9% of the individuals classified by COVR at hospital baseline as at low risk of violence were violent in the community within 20 weeks after discharge, compared to 35% of the individuals classified as at high risk of violence. When all individuals were blindly reclassified using the slightly more inclusive operational definition of violence (for example, including violence by an examinee shortly after he or she was readmitted to a hospital), the rate of violence observed in the low-risk group remained at 9%, but the rate of violence observed in the high-risk group rose to 49%.

Based on the findings of the original MacArthur study from which the COVR software has been developed, the rate of violence expected was 1.2% in the low-risk group and 63.6% in the high-risk group. The observed rates of violence that were obtained in this prospective sample of 9% and 49% for the low- and (recoded) high-risk groups, respectively, may reflect the shrinkage that can be expected whenever an actuarial instrument moves from construction to validation samples. It also could reflect a change in the base rate of violence from the previous samples to the new samples. Recent re-analyses of the dataset from the MacArthur Violence Risk Assessment Study include Skeem, Kennealy, Monahan, Peterson, and Appelbaum (2016), and Steadman, Monahan, Pinals, Vesselinov, and Robbins (2015).

Independent Validations

A number of independent investigators have validated the COVR. McDermott, Dualan, and Scott (2011), for example, used the instrument to the assess risk of physical aggression among patients in a forensic psychiatric hospital in California. Over a 20-week follow-up, COVR scores correlated .33 with physical aggression in the hospital, yielding an Area Under the Curve (AUC) of .73. Similarly, Snowden, Gray, Taylor, and Fitzgerald (2009) administered the COVR to forensic psychiatric patients in the United Kingdom. Over a 6-month follow-up, COVR scores correlated .45 with physical aggression in the hospital, yielding the same AUC of .73.

The most detailed independent validation of the COVR, and the one with a non-forensic patient sample most similar to the original MacArthur Study (Monahan et al., 2001), was conducted by Sturup, Kristiansson, and Lindqvist (2011). These investigators administered the COVR to civil psychiatric patients in Sweden. They examined COVR categorical scores as predictors of violence over the 20 weeks following discharge into the community. Sturup et al. reported community violence rates for each COVR risk category as follows, with the categorical community violence rates from the original MacArthur Study in parentheses: very low risk, 2% (1%); low risk, 4% (8%); average risk, 19% (26%); high risk, 29% (56%); and very high risk 50% (76%). The AUC was .77. While the ordinal relationship between COVR risk categories and community violence was the same as in the original MacArthur Study, the absolute rates of community violence were much lower in the Sturup et al. research than in the original MacArthur Study, which is not surprising given the relative prevalence of violence in Sweden and the United States: the base rate of patient violence reported by Sturup et al. was only one third that reported in the original MacArthur Study (6% vs. 19%).

Limitations and Necessary Future Research

Research on at least two issues is crucial if COVR is to become a commonly used tool for violence risk assessment. First, can one assume that examinees are accurate in their reports? Second, is clinical review of the COVR-generated risk estimate useful?

Can Examinee Self-Report Be Believed?

In both the original research in which COVR's multiple iterative classification tree methodology was developed and in the subsequent research in which that methodology was validated, the MacArthur researchers operated under the protection of a Federal Confidentiality Certificate, and the examinees studied were made aware of this protection (Monahan et al., 1993). The Certificate meant that most disclosures that the examinees made to the examiners were not discoverable in court and did not have to be reported to the police. In addition, in both the construction study and the validation study, the examinees were instructed that information from their police and hospital records was being collected, as well as information from interviewing a collateral informant who knew them well, to verify the information given by the examinee. Both of these components—the guarantee of confidentiality and the reliance on multiple information sources—may have encouraged examinees to be more candid in their self-reports than they otherwise would have.

When COVR is used in the real world of clinical practice, of course, Federal Confidentiality Certificates will not be obtainable. However, police records will sometimes, and collateral informants will often, be available in clinical practice. The important question remains: will examinees be as forthcoming and honest in answering questions when COVR is used as a tool to make actual decisions on the nature, or length, or venue of their care as they were when COVR was being constructed or validated and the answers had no personal impact? What is the clinician to do when he or she has reason to doubt the truthfulness of an examinee's response to a COVR question?

Many examinees' reports, of course, cannot be "verified," because they relate to events in their subjective experience (e.g., Does the examinee really daydream often about harming someone?). Other answers, in principle, can be verified, but perhaps only with great difficulty in usual clinical situations (e.g., Was the examinee's father actually arrested when the examinee was a child?). Still other answers may be verifiable, to a greater or lesser degree, by recourse to data in the examinee's existing hospital chart or outpatients record. What is the clinician to do when an examinee's answer to a question posed by COVR is inconsistent with other sources of data? Consider the following examples.

- When asked about abusing alcohol, Examinee A answers in the negative, yet the chart indicates that, when he was admitted to the hospital on the previous evening, he had a blood alcohol level of .30.
- When asked about past arrests, Examinee B denies ever having been arrested, yet the file contains previous evaluations for competence to stand trial on numerous charges.
- When asked whether she was abused as a child, Examinee C answers "Never," but there is a notation in the chart that the examinee's sister reported that the mother's boyfriend repeatedly sexually assaulted the examinee when she was a child.

Four courses of action are possible in situations involving conflicting information. First, the clinician could simply enter into the COVR the examinee's answers as the examinee reported them, even if the clinician were convinced that the examinee was being untruthful.

Second, the clinician could enter into the COVR his or her best judgment as to the factually correct answer to the question asked. For example, the clinician could choose to credit the toxicology report, indicating recent alcohol abuse over the examinee's self-reported denial of drinking, and enter "yes" to the appropriate alcohol abuse question.

Third, the clinician could confront the examinee when apparent discrepancies arise between his or her self-report and other data sources. For example, the clinician could say to the examinee who denied ever having been arrested, "I have a problem. You say you've never been arrested, but in your hospital record there's a competence report that says you were arrested for assault twice last year and once the year before. What about this?"

Finally, the clinician, on being convinced from information available in the record that the examinee was being untruthful in his or her answers, could simply terminate the administration of COVR and arrive at a risk estimate without the aid of this structured tool. For example, the clinician could base his or her clinical risk estimate entirely on information available in the chart or from other data sources that do not rely on the examinee's problematic self-reports.

Which of these options is recommended? It is important to emphasize that COVR was constructed and validated using a variant of the third option described earlier. Although information obtained from a collateral informant was never revealed to the examinee, the examinee would be confronted on any apparent inconsistencies between his or her answers and information contained in the hospital chart.

The first option of simply entering into the program the examinee's answers as given, even if the clinician is convinced that the examinee is being untruthful, is clinically and ethically inappropriate. If the clinician does *not* clearly note the examinee's apparent untruthfulness in the report that accompanies the COVR, the clinician would knowingly be basing a risk estimate on information that, in his or her best judgment, is invalid, without warning potential users of the estimate of its uncertain foundation. And if the clinician *does* clearly note the examinee's apparent untruthfulness in the accompanying report, the clinician would, in effect, be telling the decision-maker to disregard the risk estimate that the clinician had just offered.

The second option of the clinician entering into the COVR his or her best judgment as to the factually correct answer to the question asked, rather than the answer that the examinee provided, is problematic for two reasons. First, it makes no attempt to determine if there is an explanation for the apparent discrepancy that would indicate that the examinee's account is actually correct (for example, someone else's toxicology laboratory slip was mistakenly placed in the examinee's chart). Second, it varies from the procedures used to construct and validate the COVR, hence threatening the validity of the resulting estimate of risk. In the latter regard, to use clinician-generated answers rather than examinee-generated answers raises the question of whether a clinician can accurately detect an examinee's deception, when it occurs, without at the same time erroneously considering many true responses to be deceptive.

The recommendation of the COVR's authors is the third option—the examiner familiar with the contents of the chart should confront the examinee when apparent discrepancies arise between the chart information and the examinee's answers (Monahan, Steadman, Appelbaum et al., 2005, pp. 6–9). If the discrepancy is satisfactorily resolved, the clinician would then enter into the COVR the answer that the examinee provides. If the discrepancy is not satisfactorily resolved (for example, if, after confrontation, the clinician still credits a recent toxicology report indicating alcohol abuse over the examinee's denial), then the clinician would enter "missing" for that piece of data, rather than entering *either* the examinee's self-report *or* the clinician's own judgment about the accurate scoring of this item, being sure to note this action in an accompanying report. The rationale of the MacArthur researchers for this recommendation is that COVR contains 10 classification tree models but can produce a reliable estimate of risk using only 5 models (Banks et al., 2004). As long as at least 5 models contain no missing data due to the clinician disbelieving an examinee's answer (or due to any other reason), COVR will operate as designed. If more than 5 models contain missing data, COVR will not produce an estimate of risk, and the clinician will have to arrive at a risk estimate without the aid of this structured tool (that is, choose the fourth option, outlined earlier).

Is Clinical Review of COVR Risk Estimates Useful?

In the view of its authors, the COVR software is useful in informing, but not replacing, clinical decision-making regarding risk assessment. The authors recommended a two-phased violence risk assessment procedure in which an examinee is first administered the COVR, and then the preliminary risk estimate generated by the COVR is reviewed by the clinician ultimately responsible for making the risk assessment in the context of additional information believed to be relevant and gathered from clinical interviews, significant others, and/or available records. This clinical review would not quantitatively "revise" or "adjust" or "override" the actuarial risk score produced by the COVR (Monahan, Steadman, Appelbaum et al., 2005, p. 11)—e.g., it would not take the form of "10% higher than" or "20% lower than" the COVR estimate—but would be of a more qualitative nature (e.g., "higher than," or "much lower than" the COVR estimate). The authors of the COVR believed it essential to allow for such a review, for two reasons (Monahan et al., 2001, pp. 130–135). The first reason had to do with possible limits on the generalizability of the validity of the software. For example, is the predictive validity of COVR generalizable to forensic examinees, or to people outside the United States, or to people who are younger than 18 years old, or to the emergency room assessments of persons who have not recently been hospitalized? The predictive validity of this instrument may well generalize. Yet there comes a point at which the sample to which a structured risk assessment instrument is applied differs so much from the sample on which the instrument was constructed and validated that one would be hard pressed to castigate the evaluator who took the structured risk estimate as advisory rather than conclusive. (For discussion of the more general issue of the appropriateness of making inferences about individual people from group-based data such as that used in the MacArthur Violence Risk Assessment Study, see Faigman, Monahan, & Slobogin, 2014; Faigman, Slobogin, & Monahan, 2016; Guy et al., 2015; Hart & Cooke, 2013; Imrey & Dawid, 2015; Monahan & Skeem, 2016).

The second rationale for allowing a clinician the option to review a risk estimate produced by a structured tool is that the clinician may note the presence of rare risk or protective factors in a given case, and that these factors—precisely because they are rare—will not have been taken into account in the construction of the structured tool. In the context of structured tools for assessing violence risk, the most frequently mentioned rare risk factor is a direct threat, that is, an apparently serious statement of intention to do violence to a named victim.

A careful study of (1) *how often*, when they review the violence risk estimates generated by COVR, clinicians feel it necessary to revise those estimates; (2) *why* clinicians feel it necessary to revise the violence risk estimates provided by COVR, for example, what rare risk or protective factor is believed to be important in assessing violence risk in a given case, but (because it is rare) is not measured by COVR; and (3) *how much* clinicians want to revise COVR risk estimates, would be invaluable in this regard. Given the finding of Storey, Watt, Jackson, and Hart (2012, p. 296) on a different structured risk assessment instrument (the Static-99; see Chapter 6) that "overrides predicted recidivism in the wrong direction—that is, clinical overrides of increased risk were actually associated with lower recidivism rates and vice versa," clinicians should approach the option of revising COVR risk estimates with great caution.

Case Examples

The COVR Professional Manual (Monahan, Steadman, Appelbaum et al., 2005) gives three case examples of the use of the COVR in clinical practice:

Case Example #1: High Risk

Mr. Smith is a 27-year-old male salesman who has been hospitalized for the eighth time with a diagnosis of bipolar disorder. After 5 days in the hospital, he is being considered for discharge. Since an aggressive act toward Mr. Smith's wife while manic and intoxicated had precipitated his hospitalization, the clinician responsible for the discharge decision requests that COVR be administered. The next day, a COVR report is given to the responsible clinician that concludes: "The likelihood that Mr. Smith will commit a violent act toward another person in the next several months is estimated to be between 65% and 86%, with a best estimate of 76%." The report also lists the risk factors that were used to produce this estimate.

The clinician, after reviewing the COVR report and all the information in Mr. Smith's hospital chart, interviews Mr. Smith. The interview fails to uncover any unusual protective factors that would call into question the estimate of violence risk that COVR had produced. Moreover, it is clear that Mr. Smith's manic state has not fully resolved. The clinician decides not to discharge Mr. Smith, but rather, to continue a course of medication and anger management groups designed to lower his violence risk, and to recommend that Mr. Smith continue with anger management training and intensive substance abuse treatment in the community when he is discharged. With the examinee's consent, his wife is counseled about her risk should his symptoms recur and he start drinking again.

Case Example #2: Low Risk

Ms. Jones is a 42-year-old accountant who has been hospitalized for the first time for several days with a diagnosis of major depression. She is being considered for discharge. Since an ambiguous threat about a coworker had been noted by a nurse in her hospital chart, the clinician responsible for the discharge decision requests that COVR be administered. The next day, a COVR report, which is provided to the responsible clinician, concludes: "The likelihood that Ms. Jones will commit a violent act toward another person in the next several months is estimated to be between zero and 2%, with a best estimate of 1%." The report also lists the risk factors that were used to produce this estimate.

The clinician, after reviewing the COVR report and all the information in Ms. Jones's hospital chart, interviews Ms. Jones. The clinician fails to uncover any unusual risk factors that would call into question the estimate of violence risk that COVR had produced, and Ms. Jones explains the ambiguous comment, which turns out not actually to have been a threat, to the clinician's satisfaction. As she seems less depressed and is not suicidal, the clinician decides to discharge Ms. Jones and follow up with routine care in the community.

Case Example #3: Moderate Risk

Mr. Brown is a 21-year-old male security guard who has been hospitalized for several days with a diagnosis of borderline personality disorder with comorbid substance dependence, after getting into a shouting match with his girlfriend and cutting his arms. He is being considered for discharge. Since the chart indicates that Mr. Brown had been involuntarily hospitalized on two prior occasions as "dangerous to others," the clinician responsible for the discharge decision requests that COVR be administered. The next day, a COVR report is given to the responsible clinician that concludes: "The likelihood that Mr. Brown will commit a violent act toward another person in the next several months is estimated to be between 20% and 32%, with a best estimate of 26%." The report also lists the risk factors that were used to produce this estimate.

The clinician, after reviewing the COVR report and all the information in Mr. Brown's hospital chart, interviews Mr. Brown. During the interview, Mr. Brown states his apparently serious intention to "teach a lesson she'll never forget" to his girlfriend, who has told him that he can't come back to live with her. He also responds affirmatively to a question about whether he has a firearm in the house. The clinician believes that this clinical information is indicative of a high risk of imminent violence. The clinician decides not to discharge Mr. Brown at the current time, but rather to continue a course of medication and psychotherapy designed to lower his violence risk. The clinician also decides to inform Mr. Brown's former girlfriend of the threat.

Conclusion

The three forms of structured risk assessment described in this chapter all specify in advance *at least* which risk factors are to be addressed and how those risk factors are to be measured. Some forms of structured violence risk assessment (e.g., the HCR-20 V3; see Chapter 12 in this volume) structure *only* the choice and measurement of risk factors. Other forms of violence risk assessment, including the COVR, go on to *also* structure the manner in which the risk factors are combined to yield an estimate of risk. But COVR allows the clinician to review this estimate, in the context of other (unstructured) available information, before issuing his or her final risk estimate. Still other forms of violence risk assessment (e.g., VRAG, see Chapter 7 in this volume) are *completely structured* (i.e., actuarial) tools. No clinical review is allowed; the structured risk estimate that is produced when the risk factors are combined is the final product of the risk assessment process.

Notes

1. While, unlike the COVR, the HCR-20 does not mathematically structure the way that risk factors are combined, it provides structured conceptual guidance to clinicians on how to use case formulation to combine risk factors and derive a summary risk estimate (see Douglas et al., 2013, pp. 53–56).
2. The complete data set for the MacArthur Violence Risk Assessment Study is available for reanalysis at: http://macarthur.virginia.edu.

References

Banks, S., Robbins, P. C., Silver, E., Vesselinov, R., Steadman, H. J., Monahan, J., . . . Roth, L. H. (2004). A multiple-models approach to violence risk assessment among people with mental disorder. *Criminal Justice and Behavior, 31*, 324–340.

Breiman, L., Friedman, J., Olshen, R., & Stone, C. (1984). *Classification and regression trees.* Boca Raton, FL: CRC Press.

Douglas, K. S., Hart, S. D., Webster, C. D., & Belfrage, H. (2013). *HCR-20 (Version 3): Assessing risk for violence, user guide.* Burnaby, BC: Mental Health, Law, and Policy Institute, Simon Fraser University.

Faigman, D., Monahan, J., & Slobogin, C. (2014). Group to individual (G2i) inference in scientific expert testimony. *University of Chicago Law Review, 81*, 417–480.

Faigman, D., Slobogin, C., & Monahan, J. (2016). Gatekeeping science: Using the structure of scientific research to distinguish between admissibility and weight in expert testimony. *Northwestern University Law Review, 110*, 859–904.

Gardner, W., Lidz, C. W., Mulvey, E. P., & Shaw, E. C. (1996). A comparison of actuarial methods for identifying repetitively violent patients with mental illnesses. *Law and Human Behavior, 20*, 35–48.

Guy, L., Douglas, K., & Hart, S. (2015). Risk assessment and communication. In B. Cutler & P. Zapf (Eds.), *APA handbook of forensic psychology: Vol. 1. Individual and situational influences in criminal and civil contexts* (pp. 35–86). Washington, DC: American Psychological Association.

Hart, S., & Cooke, D. (2013). Another look at the (im-)precision of individual risk estimates made using actuarial risk assessment instruments. *Behavioral Sciences & the Law, 31*, 81–102.

Imrey, P., & Dawid, A. P. (2015). A commentary on statistical assessment of violence recidivism risk. *Statistics and Public Policy, 2*, 1–18.

McDermott, B., Dualan, I., & Scott, C. (2011). The predictive ability of the classification on violence risk (COVR) in a forensic psychiatric hospital. *Psychiatric Services, 62*, 430–433.

Meehl, P. (1954). *Clinical versus statistical prediction.* Minneapolis: University of Minnesota Press.

Monahan, J. (2006). "Tarasoff" at thirty: How developments in science and policy shape the common law. *University of Cincinnati Law Review, 75*, 497–521.

Monahan, J. (2018). Predictions of violence. In T. Grisso & S. Brodsky (Eds.), *The roots of modern psychology and law: A narrative history* (pp. 143–157). New York: Oxford University Press.

Monahan, J., & Appelbaum, P. S. (2000). Reducing violence risk: Diagnostically based clues from the MacArthur violence risk assessment study. In S. Hodgins (Ed.), *Effective prevention of crime and violence among the mentally ill* (pp. 19–34). Dordrecht, The Netherlands: Kluwer Academic.

Monahan, J., Appelbaum, P. S., Mulvey, E., Robbins, P., & Lidz, C. (1993). Ethical and legal duties in conducting research on violence: Lessons from the MacArthur risk assessment study. *Violence and Victims, 8,* 387–396.

Monahan, J., Heilbrun, K., Silver, E., Nabors, E., Bone, J., & Slovic, P. (2002). Communicating violence risk: Frequency formats, vivid outcomes, and forensic settings. *International Journal of Forensic Mental Health, 1,* 121–126.

Monahan, J., & Skeem, J. (2016). Risk assessment in criminal sentencing. *Annual Review of Clinical Psychology, 12,* 489–513.

Monahan, J., & Steadman, H. J. (1996). Violent storms and violent people: How meteorology can inform risk communication in mental health law. *American Psychologist, 51,* 931–938.

Monahan, J., Steadman, H. J., Appelbaum, P., Grisso, T., Mulvey, E., Roth, L., . . . Silver, E. (2005). *The Classification of Violence Risk.* Lutz, FL: Psychological Assessment Resources.

Monahan, J., Steadman, H. J., Robbins, P., Appelbaum, P., Banks, S., Grisso, T., Heilbrun, K., . . . Silver, E. (2005). An actuarial model of violence risk assessment for persons with mental disorders. *Psychiatric Services, 56,* 810–815.

Monahan, J., Steadman, H. J., Silver, E., Appelbaum, P. S., Robbins, P. C., Mulvey, E. P., . . . Banks, S. (2001). *Rethinking risk assessment: The MacArthur study of mental disorder and violence.* New York: Oxford University Press.

Monahan, J., Vesselinov, R., Robbins, P. C., & Appelbaum, P. S. (2016). Violence to others, violent self-victimization, and violent victimization by others among persons with a mental illness. *Psychiatric Services, 68,* 516–519.

Novaco, R. (1994). Anger as a risk factor for violence among the mentally disordered. In J. Monahan & H. Steadman (Eds.), *Violence and mental disorder: developments in risk assessment* (pp. 21–59). Chicago: University of Chicago Press.

Scurich, N., Monahan, J., & John, R. (2012). Innumeracy and unpacking: Bridging the nomothetic/idiographic divide in violence risk assessment. *Law and Human Behavior, 36,* 548–554.

Skeem, J., Kennealy, P., Monahan, J., Peterson, J., & Appelbaum, P. (2016). Psychosis uncommonly and inconsistently precedes violence among high-risk individuals. *Clinical Psychological Sciences, 4,* 40–49.

Skeem, J., & Monahan, J. (2016). Violence risk assessment: The state of the science. In R. Rosner & C. Scott (Eds.), *Principles and practice of forensic psychiatry* (3rd ed.). Abingdon: Taylor & Francis.

Snowden, R., Gray, N., Taylor, J., & Fitzgerald, S. (2009). Assessing risk of future violence among forensic psychiatric inpatients with the Classification of Violence Risk (COVR). *Psychiatric Services, 60,* 1522–1526.

Slovic, P., Monahan, J., & MacGregor, D. G. (2000). Violence risk assessment and risk communication: The effects of using actual cases, providing instruction, and employing probability versus frequency formats. *Law and Human Behavior, 24,* 271–296.

Steadman, H., Monahan, J., Pinals, D., Vesselinov, R., & Robbins (2015). Gun violence and stranger victims in the MacArthur violence risk assessment study. *Psychiatric Services, 66,* 1237–1241.

Steadman, H., Silver, E., Monahan, J., Appelbaum, P. S., Robbins, P. C., Mulvey, E. P., . . . Banks, S. (2000). A classification tree approach to the development of actuarial violence risk assessment tools. *Law and Human Behavior, 24,* 83–100.

Storey, J., Watt, K., Jackson, K., & Hart, S. (2012). Utilization and implications of the static-99 in practice. *Sexual Abuse: A Journal of Research and Treatment, 24,* 289–302.

Sturup, J., Kristiansson, M., & Lindqvist, P. (2011). Violent behavior by general psychiatric patients in Sweden: Validation of Classification of Violence Risk (COVR) software. *Psychiatry Research, 188,* 161–165.

Webster, C., Douglas, K., Eaves. D., & Hart, S. (1997). *HCR-20: Assessing risk for violence* (Version 2). Vancouver, BC: Simon Fraser University.

Chapter 6

Static-99R

An Empirical-Actuarial Risk Tool for Adult Males With a History of Sexual Offending

R. Karl Hanson and Dana Anderson

Introduction

Many people believe that individuals with a history of sexual offending are at high risk to reoffend, despite decades of research indicating overall low rates of sexual reoffending (recidivism). Research has also shown that not all individuals with a history of sexual offences are equally likely to reoffend. For some, the risk is substantial, whereas for others it is very low. Consequently, the assessment of risk for sexual violence is of paramount concern to public safety.

The field of assessment for sexual offence recidivism is growing. The decisions based on these risk assessments affect the individuals being evaluated and the community at large. Typically, assessments of sexual offence recidivism are used to make decisions regarding sentencing, treatment planning, and supervision intensity. Risk assessments are also used in high-stakes decisions that can have lifetime consequences, such as civil commitment in the United States, dangerous offender applications in Canada, and long-term community supervision orders.

One tool designed to evaluate the potential for sexual offence recidivism is the Static-99 Revised (Static-99R). This is an actuarial assessment tool for use with adult male sex offenders (age 18 years or older at the time of release from their most recent sexually motivated offence). The tool was developed from a program of research that examined historical variables that predict recidivism. Based on commonly available demographic and criminal history information, the Static-99R is designed to rank order sex offenders in terms of risk to sexually reoffend (i.e., relative risk levels) and provide expected sexual recidivism rates.

Static-99 (Hanson & Thornton, 1999, 2000) was originally developed by R. Karl Hanson and David Thornton. As a product of an empirical program of research, the Static-99 has periodically undergone changes and revisions. With applied use, the scoring criteria were refined and new rules were applied to special cases that had not been considered in the development samples (e.g., sexual offences against roadkill). Hanson and Thornton also created an alternate tool, Static-2002R, with the goal of increasing conceptual clarity and predictive accuracy (Hanson & Thornton, 2003; Hanson, Helmus, & Thornton, 2010). Static-2002 (now Static-2002R) did not replace Static-99R; instead, it had similar predictive accuracy and, in fact, incremental validity (Babchishin, Hanson, & Helmus, 2012). Consequently, we recommend that evaluators use the Static-99R, the Static-2002R, or both.

The popularity and use of the Static-99, however, has not waned. In 2009 a revised version of Static-99, called Static-99R, was released for use (Helmus, 2009; Helmus, Thornton, Hanson, & Babchishin, 2012). This revision stemmed from ongoing research pointing to a need to better account for the relationship between advanced age and reduced risk of recidivism, and to provide updated norms for comparison groups derived from more contemporary samples. When the Static-99 was revised, so was the Static-2002 (to the Static-2002R) for the same reasons.

The focus of this chapter will be on the development and use of the Static-99R, with passing reference to related measures by the same research team (RRASOR, Static-99, Static-2002R).

As well, an augmenting measure, the STABLE-2007, will be briefly discussed to illustrate how the inclusion of dynamic risk variables assists us with our assessment of risk and treatment and supervision decisions.

Description of Static-99R

The Static-99R consists of ten items, all empirically derived from multiple samples of sexual offenders (see recent meta-analysis of the items by Helmus & Thornton, 2015). Most of the ten items are scored dichotomously (i.e., 0 or 1), where the assignment of a point to the item indicates increased risk of sexual recidivism. Two items are given weights greater than one: Item 1 (Age at Release from Index Sexual Offence), which reflects the reduced potential of older offenders for recidivism; and Item 5 (Prior Sexual Offences), which indicates persistence of sexual offending, after being detected previously (see Figure 6.1, Static-99R Tally Sheet, for all items).

Static-99R total scores are interpreted based on quantitative tables (percentile ranks, risk ratios, sexual recidivism rates) as well as according to standardized risk levels (see Hanson, Babchishin, Helmus, Thornton, & Phenix, 2017). Percentile ranks describe the unusualness of the scores compared to other individuals in routine/complete samples of sexual offenders. Risk ratios express relative risk compared to individuals in the middle of the risk distribution. As well, tables are provided that link scores to sexual absolute recidivism rates over a fixed period of time (5 years and 10 years). The Static-99R results are best considered a baseline estimate of sexual recidivism risk, and may be utilized for the decision-making process for which it was intended (e.g., treatment intensity recommendations, supervision and risk management strategies, etc.).

Although the Static-99R has demonstrated utility for assessment of risk among adult male sexual offenders, it is not considered a comprehensive assessment, as it does not account for all variables known to have relevance to recidivism (Hanson, Helmus, & Harris, 2015; Olver, Wong, Nicholaichuk, & Gordon, 2007; Thornton & Knight, 2015). As well, most replications indicate it demonstrates only moderate predictive accuracy (AUC = .69 to .70; Helmus, Hanson, Thornton, Babchishin, & Harris, 2012), and estimating absolute recidivism rates from the individual scores has proven complex, given the variability of recidivism base rates across different samples (Helmus, Hanson et al., 2012).

The Static-99R measures demographic and historical variables, and does not directly assess dynamic risk factors linked to current psychological functioning and community adjustment. Static-99R also does not capture other issues that may prevent an offender from reoffending, such as severely deteriorated health or disability. Although such factors should obviously be considered in an overall evaluation of risk, such factors do not "over-ride" a Static-99R score. Changing a Static-99R score based on external factors distances the measure from its empirical base and reduces its predictive accuracy (Hanson & Morton-Bourgon, 2009).

It is, nonetheless, possible to change an overall assessment based on additional information. In many situations, we recommend supplementing Static-99R with measures of dynamic risk factors. In particular, our research group has promoted the use of STABLE-2007 (Hanson, Harris, Scott, & Helmus, 2007; Hanson et al., 2015) in combination with Static-99R. The research supporting STABLE-2007 began with a retrospective examination of dynamic risk variables that differentiated community-supervised sex offenders who reoffended from the community-supervised sex offenders who did not reoffend (Hanson & Harris, 1998, 2000). This research identified both stable and acute dynamic risk factors. Stable dynamic risk factors are ongoing, enduring patterns of behavior (e.g., lack of concern for others, chronic use of sex as a coping mechanism) whereas acute factors are short-term deteriorations in functioning (e.g., emotional collapse, victim access, substance use). Hanson and Harris (2000) combined

Static-99R—TALLY SHEET

Assessment date: _____ **Date of release from index sexual offence:** _____

Item #	Risk Factor	Codes		Score
1	Age at release	Aged 18 to 34.9		1
		Aged 35 to 39.9		0
		Aged 40 to 59.9		−1
		Aged 60 or older		−3
2	Ever Lived With	Ever lived with lover for at least two years?		
		Yes		0
		No		1
3	Index nonsexual violence— Any Convictions	No		0
		Yes		1
4	Prior nonsexual violence— Any Convictions	No		0
		Yes		1
5	Prior Sex Offences	Charges	Convictions	
		0	0	0
		1, 2	1	1
		3–5	2, 3	2
		6+	4+	3
6	Prior sentencing dates (excluding index)	3 or less		0
		4 or more		1
7	Any convictions for non-contact sex offences	No		0
		Yes		1
8	Any Unrelated Victims	No		0
		Yes		1
9	Any Stranger Victims	No		0
		Yes		1
10	Any Male Victims	No		0
		Yes		1
	Total Score	**Add up scores from individual risk factors**		

Nominal Risk Categories (2016 version)	Total	Risk Category
	−3, −2,	I—Very Low Risk
	−1, 0,	II—Below Average Risk
	1, 2, 3	III—Average Risk
	4, 5	IVa—Above Average Risk
	6 and higher	IVb—Well Above Average Risk

There [was, was not] sufficient information available to complete the Static-99R score following the coding manual (2016 version). I believe that this score [fairly represents, does not fairly represent] the risk presented by Mr. XXXX at this time. Comments/ Explanation: _____

_____   _____   _____

(Evaluator name)   **(Evaluator signature)**   **(Date)**

Figure 6.1 Static-99R Tally Sheet

stable and acute factors into a measure called the Sex Offender Needs Assessment Rating (SONAR), which was subsequently revised to produce the STABLE -2000 and ACUTE -2000 instruments. These two instruments were then validated in a prospective study comprised of over 1100 community-supervised offenders in the Dynamic Supervision Project (Hanson et al., 2007, 2015). Based on the research findings, the measures and scoring methods were slightly revised, resulting in the STABLE-2007 and ACUTE-2007. Subsequent research has demonstrated the utility of the STABLE-2007 in assessing sexual recidivism risk, and that the STABLE-2007 adds incrementally to measures of static risk factors, such as the Static-99R (Brankley, Babchishin, & Hanson, 2019).

Although the Static-99R scoring guide is publicly available (see www.static99.org), we recommend training in the use of Static-99R before attempting risk assessments that will inform decisions that will ultimately affect an individual's life. Researchers utilizing the instrument for research purposes are less likely to require the level of training that is required from the other individuals who provide assessments to courts or tribunals, to correctional services, to mental health facilities, to child protection agencies, or to any other party that will be linking the assessment to some action that will directly affect people (e.g., parole and probation officers, psychologists, sex offender treatment providers, and law enforcement involved in threat and risk assessment activities). Furthermore, individuals who have been trained in Static-99 or Static-99R prior to the release of the 2016 version of the coding manual are strongly recommended to obtain training on the updates to the coding manual, as there are many non-trivial changes (some of which may be missed if not pointed out by a trainer).

Target Population

As previously indicated, the Static-99R is an actuarial risk assessment instrument designed to assess risk of sexual recidivism for adult males who have already been charged with or convicted of at least one sexual offence against a child or non-consenting adult. The Static-99R may be used with offenders who are under some type of mental health commitment such as those found unfit to stand trial or not guilty by reason of insanity. Static-99R may also be used with first-time sex offenders. It is not recommended for females or young offenders (i.e., those who are younger than 18 years of age at time of release) or for the offenders whose only sexually motivated offences are prostitution-related offences, pimping, sex in a public location with consenting adults, or possession of child pornography or other possession of indecent materials (other forms of pornography offences, however, could be considered sufficient to use the Static-99R, as indicated in the 2016 version of the coding manual). As well, it is not for use with people who have been convicted of sexual relations with a similar age peer, where both are close in age but the peer is still under the age of consent (sometimes called Statutory Rape in the United States; see the coding manual for specific guidelines). The Static-99R is designed specifically for sexual recidivism risk and is not appropriate to use with those who have never committed a sexually motivated offence. It is also not to be used to make determinations of guilt/innocence for people accused of committing a sexual offence. The Static-99R can be used with people who have been charged with sexually motivated offences, even if the offender has not been convicted, as these types of offenders were included in the original samples to create the instrument.

In making decisions about the most appropriate tools to be utilized during the course of a risk assessment, the evaluator must consider not only the question(s) to be addressed in the risk assessment but also the extent to which the individual being evaluated is representative of the samples on which the tools have been normed and validated. To this end, professional judgement is still required for the process of risk assessment. Determining whether or not the Static-99R may be used requires an understanding of the populations for which normative information exists as well as understanding the characteristics of the individual and whether the individual falls outside the sampling frame.

Method and Rationale for Development

It would be naïve to think that the problems plaguing mankind today can be solved with means or methods which were applied or seemed to work in the past.

Mikhail Gorbachev

In a chapter provided in an earlier edition, we detailed the development of the original Static-99 (the predecessor to the Static-99R), which will be only briefly reviewed here. The Static-99 was created from two separate measures of static risk variables: the Rapid Risk Assessment for Sexual Offense Recidivism (RRASOR; Hanson, 1997), and the Structured Anchored Clinical Judgment scale—minimum (SACJ-Min), created by David Thornton (Grubin, 1998).

The four items comprising the RRASOR were derived from a meta-analytic study of variables related to sexual offence recidivism. Three of the four factors were scored as a 0 or 1 and the remaining factor (prior sex offenses) was scored on a scale of 0 to 3. After cross-validation on another sample, Hanson concluded he RRASOR was a reasonable screening tool, while noting that certain other factors well-established in the research as related to sexual offence recidivism were not included in the scale (e.g., psychopathy and phallometrically assessed atypical sexual interests).

The SACJ-Min employed a stepwise approach to assess risk of sexual and violent recidivism. The first step was based on the number of points scored on four historical variables and represented the risk level. The second step assessed the presence of aggravating factors, which would raise the risk level by a category if two or more aggravating factors were present, and the third stage examined current behavior and treatment completion. The items in the first two steps were subject to cross-validation and thus represented the minimum version of the scale, the SACJ-Min, which was combined with the RRASOR to form the Static-99 (based on the non-redundant items of the two scales). Neither the RRASOR nor the SACJ-Min is currently recommended for applied use. The SACJ-Min has been replaced by the Risk Matrix-2000 (see Lehmann, Thornton, Helmus, & Hanson, 2016) and the RRASOR has been replaced by the Static-99R and Static-2002R.

It is important to note that these items were selected based on their empirical association with sexual recidivism and not conceptual clarity. Nevertheless, it appears some underlying constructs are tapped to some degree by the individual items (e.g., sexual deviance may be associated with a history of offending against male victims, and general antisociality may be indicated by the total number of sentencing occasions; Brouillette-Alarie, Proulx, & Hanson, 2018). We will return to the construct validity of Static-99R later in this chapter.

Three Canadian samples were used to develop Static-99, mostly individuals released to the community in the 1970s and 1980s. Most of the follow-up data were collected in this period into the early 1990s, primarily from records from the federal police service (Royal Canadian Mounted Police; RCMP). A fourth sample from the United Kingdom (UK) was used for validation. This sample comprised 531 offenders from Her Majesty's Prison Service in England and Wales. Approximately 61% of the 531 offenders in this sample were child molesters. The offenders in the UK sample were released in 1979 and followed for 16 years (fixed follow-up). Within the follow-up period, 25% reoffended with a new sexual crime and 37% reoffended with any violent (including sexual) crime, where recidivism for these development samples was defined as a reconviction.

Since its development, subsequent research found that the Static-99 tool did not adequately account for the effect of advanced age on reduced potential for sexual recidivism, and that the previous norms associated with the Static-99 did not consider declining base rates of sexual offences since the mid-1990s. Consequently, Static-99 was revised. These revisions were based on 24 samples comprising over 8,000 sexual offenders (Helmus, Thornton et al., 2012). Eleven of these samples were from Canada, 6 from the United States, 2 from the UK, and the remainder came from Denmark, Sweden, Austria, Germany, and New Zealand. Over 80% of these offenders were released in 1990 or later. There were 14 samples that gave information regarding treatment, and of the offenders within these 14 samples, over 75% would have been considered "treated" (i.e., completed sex offender treatment), five samples of offenders were considered mixed, and one sample was untreated.

The authors examined estimated sexual and violent recidivism rates for different age groups across the different Static-99 risk categories and found that in general, within each category defined by Static-99 score, the recidivism rates were lower for older offenders (minor fluctuations noted). They also examined the incremental predictive validity of age at release for Static-99. After controlling for Static-99 scores, they noted that age had a significant negative relationship with recidivism. The authors did not find that the age relationship differed for the different categories of risk. The authors concluded that adjusted age weights were necessary in order to account for the finding that older offenders are less likely to reoffend, and to account for the findings that this negative relationship is nonlinear.

The authors derived the age weights using offenders in the Static-99 sample with less than 10 years of follow-up information, and they validated the age weights using offenders with follow-up periods of greater than 10. The new age weights were based on the data for sexual offence recidivism rather than overall violent recidivism. Different statistical analyses were used to guide the selection of the weights and ultimately similar (albeit not identical) results were obtained. Two methods were obtained based on the analyses, and the weights that were chosen were superior on 6 out of 7 statistical indicators. Therefore, the coding of the age item (age at release to the community following their most recent sexually motivated offence) changed from the Static-99 coding of offenders under the age of 25: 1 point; over 25 years of age: 0 points to the following coding on the Static-99R: offenders under age 35: 1 point; offenders 35 years of age up to (but not including) 40 years: 0 points; offenders 40 years of age up to (but not including) 60 years of age: -1 point; offenders age 60 years or older: -3 points.

The authors noted that in comparing the Static-99 and Static-99R using the validation sample, there was a slight increase in relative predictive accuracy (discriminating higher-risk from lower-risk offenders) for the Static-99R in risk for sexual offence recidivism (measured by the Area Under the Curve [AUC] values for fixed follow-up periods). However, the Static-99R was superior to the Static-99 in estimating absolute recidivism rates in that the Static-99R was less likely to over-estimate recidivism in offenders who are over 50 years of age at the time of release.

In addition to the new age weights, the authors revised the recidivism rate tables. The original Static-99 linked scores to one, and only one, sexual recidivism rate table. When the Static-99 was re-normed on larger, more contemporary samples, the sexual recidivism rates were notably lower across all risk categories (Harris, Helmus, Hanson, & Thornton, 2008). A more challenging finding was that the recidivism rates varied across settings and samples for reasons that were not fully understood (Helmus, Hanson et al., 2012). Subsequent analyses indicated that much of this variation could be attributed to the density of risk factors not assessed by the Static-99R (Hanson, Thornton, Helmus, & Babchishin, 2016). Using data from 8,805 sexual offenders from 21 samples, Hanson, Thornton et al. (2016) found that samples pre-selected as high risk reoffended at higher rates than did individuals from routine/complete samples. As well, the relationship between Static-99R scores and sexual recidivism rates was different for high risk/high need samples than for routine complete samples. Consequently, there are separate Static-99R recidivism rate tables for high risk/high need samples and routine/complete samples (see Phenix, Helmus, & Hanson, 2016).

The most recent development was assigning new risk category labels (Hanson, Babchishin et al., 2017). The updated recidivism rate information raised the question of whether the original cut-offs for risk levels were still valid. This question turned out to be more complicated than we initially imagined, and led to fundamental questions about the meaning and necessity of risk category labels. We concluded that the field of offender risk assessment could benefit from standardized risk/need levels applicable to all risk scales (Hanson, Babchishin et al., 2017), and that the names for Static-99R should align with these standardized risk levels (Hanson, Babchishin et al., 2017). Further comments regarding the development of a common language for risk communication is described later in this chapter.

Reliability

Given that Static-99R differs from Static-99 on only one of ten items, the extensive research on the rater reliably of Static-99 remains broadly applicable to Static-99R (for a summary, see Phenix & Epperson, 2015). Most studies have shown excellent levels of reliability for Static-99 scores in both research and applied settings (Hanson & Morton-Bourgon, 2009). Across 11 studies reporting interrater reliability, Helmus (2009) found consistently high reliability, with correlations ranging from .86 to .92 and intraclass correlations (ICCs) ranging from .84 to .95.

A number of interrater reliability studies have been conducted in the field for Sexually Violent Predator (SVP) evaluators. An early unpublished study by Hanson (2001) examined 55 cases scored on Static-99 from SVP evaluations in California and found an ICC of .87. Levenson (2004) conducted a larger field reliability study in Florida and also found strong rater agreement (ICC = .85) in Static-99 total scores for 281 offenders evaluated for SVP commitment in Florida. Murrie et al. (2009) examined interrater agreement for Texas SVP evaluators. Reliability of Static-99 scores was high when comparing scores of experts on the same side of a case (ICC = .84 for petitioners' experts and ICC = .95 for respondents' experts). However, when comparing scores from two competing sides (petitioners' experts with respondents' experts), the ICCs dropped into the .60 range, suggesting that biases resulting from adversarial allegiance may affect raters' scoring.

Field studies on interrater reliability have also been conducted in community supervision and treatment settings. In a Canadian study (the Dynamic Supervision Project), Static-99 scores across 88 cases produced an ICC of .91 (Hanson et al., 2015). Storey, Watt, Jackson, and Hart (2012) compared the ratings of clinicians in the field to those of researchers for 100 adult males who completed an outpatient sex offender treatment program and found excellent agreement for total scores on Static-99 (ICC = .92), and for most of the individual items (range ICC_1 = .56 to .89; median ICC_1 = .77).

Quesada, Calkins, and Jeglic (2014) examined the consistency of clinicians' item and total scores with those from researchers using a sample of 1,973 case files. Total scores showed a high degree of consistency, as reflected by an ICC = .92 for the combined sample of researchers and clinicians. There was exact agreement in total scores on 1,255 (63.6%) of the cases, though a small number of cases (n = 90) achieved the same score despite some disagreements at the item level. An additional 557 (28.2%) cases yielded total scores that were within 1 point of each other. Overall, then, total Static-99 scores calculated by the clinicians and researchers were identical or within one point of each other in 1,812 (91.8%) of the cases. Item-level agreement was also strong. Two of ten items produced outstanding agreement (K = 0.81 to 1.00 range), and the remaining eight items yielded substantial agreement (K = 0.61 to 0.80).

In a large study of field reliability with Static-99, Boccaccini et al. (2012) reviewed Static-99 scores generated by correctional officers in Texas for 600 sexual offenders in Texas and by doctoral-level evaluators for 135 sexual offenders in New Jersey. Texas evaluators produced an ICC of .79 and New Jersey evaluators produced an ICC of .88. In both samples, about 55% of cases had identical scores from raters, and an additional 33% had scores within 1 point of each other. So, 88% of the scores were the same or within one point of each other, consistent with other studies of interrater agreement on Static-99 scores.

For the Static-99R, McGrath, Lasher, and Cumming (2012) reported very high reliability (ICC = .89) when scored by researchers. Similarly, Thornton and Knight (2015) reported Static-99R interrater ICC of .89 for a single rater and .94 for the average of two raters. In a recent study, Jung (2016) examined the reliability of coding Static-99R data from police information using a sample of men who were charged with, but not convicted of, a sex offence. She examined the interrater reliability on 30 randomly selected cases and reported percentage agreement on Static-99R scores ranging from 73% to 100% (ICC = .95).

Noting the importance of assessing reliability of scores calculated in the field, Hanson, Lunetta, Phenix, Neeley, and Epperson (2014) assessed the reliability of Static-99R scores calculated by 55 corrections and probation officers in California who rated a common set of 14 cases. Overall rater reliability was acceptable (ICC = .78), and there was a substantial difference in the reliability of scores of more experienced (ICC = .85) and less experienced scorers (ICC = .71), pointing to the importance of practice. Experienced scorers were those who had scored 26 or more sexual offenders on Static-99R in the previous 12 months.

Validity

The validity of a measure refers to the credibility of the inferences made about individuals from test results (Joint Committee on Standards for Educational and Psychological Testing of the American Educational Research Association, the American Psychological Association, & The National Council on Measurement in Education, 2014). There is no single indicator of validity; instead, there are only more or less credible inferences. Whereas the original interpretative materials for Static-99 focused on expected recidivism rates for sexual reoffending and violent (including sexual) reoffending, the STATIC Development Team now presents more nuanced inferences that can be supported by the STATIC risk tools (Phenix, Fernandez et al., 2017; Hanson, Babchishin et al., 2017; Phenix, Helmus et al., 2016). Our views evolved in response to empirical findings on these risk tools, as well as to more general advances in the understanding of individuals with a history of sexual offending. The most recent user guidance for Static-99R addresses three quantitative indicators of risk (percentile ranks, expected recidivism rates, and risk ratios), as well as placement into one of five standardized risk levels. Based on research on the construct validity of the Static-99R items (Brouillette-Alarie, Babchishin, Hanson, & Helmus, 2016), we no longer support violent recidivism rate tables for Static-99R; instead, we recommend that evaluators interested in violent and general recidivism use the Brief Assessment of Recidivism Risk-2002R (BARR-2002R; Babchishin, Hanson, & Blais, 2016), which is comprised of a subset of Static-2002R items, or another risk tool specifically designed to assess risk for nonsexual reoffending.

Percentile Ranks

In psychology, the most commonly used metrics for reporting individuals' test results are based on percentile ranks, such as Z-Scores, T-Scores, and IQ scores. Percentile ranks measure the unusualness of particular characteristics (Crawford & Garthwaite, 2009). For example, individuals with Static-99R scores of 5 can be described as being in the top 15% in terms of their risk of sexual recidivism (Hanson, Lloyd, Helmus, & Thornton, 2012; Phenix, Helmus et al., 2016). Percentile ranks are easily understood and may be sufficient for certain resource allocation decisions (e.g., when treatment is provided only to the riskiest 15%). A limitation of percentile ranks for Static-99R is that they have no intrinsic relationship to the likelihood of the outcome. It is still quite possible for individuals to have a high percentile rank on Static-99R but still fall below a decision threshold based on the likelihood of the outcome (e.g., virtually certain to reoffend). Consequently, other quantitative indicators are useful to include when communicating the "riskiness" of the case at hand (Babchishin & Hanson, 2009). The percentile ranks for Static-99R in the Evaluators' Workbook (Phenix, Helmus et al., 2016) were based on a representative sample of 2,011 Canadian sexual offenders (Hanson, Lloyd et al., 2012). This distribution of scores has since been replicated in a representative sample of 1,626 sexual offenders from California (Lee, Restrepo, Satariano, & Hanson, 2016).

Absolute Risk

The most commonly reported quantitative risk information for the STATIC risk tools are absolute recidivism rates (Chevalier, Boccaccini, Murrie, & Varela, 2015). Recidivism rate tables are an intrinsic feature of actuarial risk tools (Dawes, Faust, & Meehl, 1989) and are central to decisions based on the absolute (not relative) likelihood of an outcome (e.g., is this offender more likely than not to sexually reoffend?).

Research on the Static-99R has found that the recidivism rates estimates are less stable than originally believed. Whereas there was little meaningful variation in the sexual recidivism rates across the three samples used to norm Static-99 (Hanson & Thornton, 2000), subsequent research on a much larger collection of studies (20+ samples) found substantial variation in recidivism rates across settings and samples (Helmus, 2009; Helmus, Hanson et al., 2012). The reasons for the variation are not fully understood; however, some variability is related to the degree to which samples are pre-selected on risk-relevant characteristics (Hanson, Thornton et al., 2016). For average or lower Static-99R scores, the observed recidivism rates are higher in high risk/high need samples (e.g., civil commitment, high-intensity treatment programs) than in routine, complete samples of sexual offenders. Consequently, evaluators interested in absolute recidivism rates frequently need to decide which reference group is most appropriate for the case at hand. For the individuals who obtain high Static-99R scores, however, selection of the reference group has little practical importance because the sexual recidivism rates are similar for the highest scores in both the high risk/high need samples and routine/complete samples.

The 2016 Evaluators' Workbook includes three sets of Static-99R sexual recidivism rates: for routine samples at 5 years (based on 4,325 individuals from 10 samples); for high risk/high need samples at 5 years (860 individuals from 5 samples), and for high risk/high need samples at 10 years (350 individuals from 2 samples; Hanson, Thornton et al., 2016, Table 7). Sexual recidivism rates for 15 years are no longer supported because of the instability of estimates based on small sample sizes (< 100 recidivists). Evaluators interested in using 5- or 10-year recidivism rates to project forward to longer follow-up times (e.g., lifetime) are encouraged to consult the extrapolation tables presented by Thornton, Hanson, Kelley, and Mundt (2019). The predicted values associated with specific Static-99R scores are logistic regression estimates based on fixed follow-up times. For most of these estimates, the 95% confidence intervals are quite narrow (±5%). It is important to remember, however, that confidence intervals are mainly determined by sample size (not predictive accuracy). Furthermore, logistic regression confidence intervals assume that Static-99R measures all risk-relevant characteristics, which is not the case (Hanson et al., 2015; Olver et al., 2016). Not only are there psychological risk factors that contribute incrementally to Static-99R scores (e.g., STABLE-2007 scores), there is greater variability across the routine samples than would be expected by chance. Consequently, evaluators are encouraged to consider the recidivism rate estimates as reasonable approximations while cautioning the readers of their reports that the actual likelihood for a particular individual could be higher or lower based on factors not measured by Static-99R.

Risk Ratios

In contrast to the variability observed in absolute recidivism rates, risk ratios for adjacent Static-99R scores are surprisingly stable across samples, settings, outcome criteria, and follow-up times (Hanson, Babchishin, Helmus, & Thornton, 2013; Helmus, Hanson et al., 2012). Risk ratios compare the recidivism rate of offenders with a particular score to the recidivism rate of a reference group (e.g., sexual offenders with a Static-99R score of 5 are 2.7 times more likely to sexually reoffend than those in the middle of the risk distribution [score of 2]). For Static-99R, risk ratios are calculated as hazard ratios from Cox regression survival analysis, with the reference group being individuals in the middle of the risk distribution (i.e., median score of 2). Risk ratios provide useful information, and we encourage evaluators to include such information in their reports. However, we also recommend that risk ratios always be presented with base rate information (because the base rates for sexual recidivism are low, it is easy to overestimate absolute recidivism rates from large risk ratios).

Similar to risk ratios, another indicator of validity is the ability of a prediction tool to discriminate between recidivists and non-recidivists. The most common metric for quantifying discrimination of risk prediction tools is the area under the receiver operating characteristic curve (AUC; Harris & Rice, 2007). The AUC can be interpreted as the probability that a randomly selected recidivist has a higher score than a randomly selected non-recidivist. A 2012 meta-analysis of 22 Static-99R studies involving 8,055 individuals found an average AUC value of .69 (Helmus, Hanson et al., 2012). Subsequent studies have found similar AUC values for Static-99R predicting sexual recidivism (Lee et al., 2016; McGrath et al., 2012; Olver et al., 2018; Smid, Kamphuis, Wever, & Van Beek, 2014). Although AUCs cannot be used to communicate the risk of particular individuals, evaluators may report them as a global indicator of Static 99R's predictive accuracy (i.e., discrimination; Helmus & Babchishin, 2017).

Violent and General Recidivism

Whereas the original Static-99 included recidivism rate tables for violent (including sexual) offences, Static-99R does not. This change was based on improved understanding of the predictors of violent and general recidivism among sexual offenders. Research on the construct validity of the STATIC risk scales indicated that at least three constructs are represented by the items: general criminality (e.g., any prior offences, history of nonsexual violence), persistence/paraphilia (prior sexual offences, noncontact sexual offences, male victims), and a third dimension related to young age and violent assaults on strangers (called Youthful Stranger Aggression by the authors; Brouillette-Alarie et al., 2016; Brouillette-Alarie & Hanson, 2015; Brouillette-Alarie, Proulx, & Hanson, 2018). All three factors predict sexual recidivism; however, only general criminality and age/stranger aggression predict violent and general recidivism (Babchishin et al., 2012; Lehmann et al., 2013). Consequently, it is possible to improve the prediction of violent and general recidivism by removing the persistence/paraphilia items, and considering only age and general criminality (Babchishin et al., 2016).

Given that general criminality is better measured by Static-2002R than Static-99R, we created a new risk tool using Static-2002R items. This risk tool, entitled Brief Assessment of Recidivism Risk-2002R (BARR-2002R), contains age at release and the General Criminality subscale items from Static-2002R. The BARR-2002R User Guide contains percentiles, risk ratios, and estimated 5-year recidivism rates for violent (including sexual) and general (any criminal) recidivism (Babchishin, Hanson, & Blais, 2013). In the validation sample, the AUC values (.72 to .77) for the BARR-2002R were as good or better than those of other standard measures of general criminality, and it showed adequate calibration (match between observed and predicted values; Babchishin et al., 2016).

Although violent recidivism rate tables for Static-99R were produced by the STATIC Development Team in 2009 and were used by some evaluators, we recommend that they be used no longer. Instead, evaluators interested in violent and general recidivism for sexual offenders should switch to the BARR-2002R, or to any one of the measures specifically designed for violence or general recidivism reviewed elsewhere in this book.

Generalizability Across Groups

Static-99R with Non-Caucasian Sex Offenders

Although most Static-99R research has been with groups of primarily Caucasian offenders or with groups with diverse ethnicities, recent years have seen an increase of Static-99R research on specific non-Caucasian samples (see Table 6.1). Indigenous sex offenders in Canada and Australia typically obtain higher scores than Caucasian offenders in these countries. In the United States, African Americans score relatively high on Static-99R whereas sexual offenders of Latino heritage score relatively low. It is important to remember, however, that differences in average scores across ethnic groups do not necessarily imply that the predictive accuracy will be low for non-Caucasian individuals.

In terms of predictive accuracy, the overall pattern of results is that Static-99R significantly discriminates between recidivists and non-recidivists of sex crimes for all ethnic groups studied so far. Nevertheless, there is also a general trend that the predictive accuracy is lower for non-Caucasians than for Caucasians. For the studies of Caucasian groups presented in Table 6.1, the AUC values ranged from .59 to .85, with a median of .75 ($k = 10$). For the non-Caucasian groups, the AUC values ranged from .52 to .82, with a median of .66 ($k = 16$). The reasons for the comparatively lower predictive accuracy for non-Caucasian groups are not fully known and remain an active topic of research.

A recent study by Lee, Hanson, and Blais (2020) found different patterns of Static-99R/Static-2002R scores between their Indigenous and White offenders they studied. The Indigenous offenders had fewer indicators of persistence/paraphilia (e.g., prior sex offences, noncontact offences, male victim) and more indicators of youthful stranger aggression (age at release, index nonsexual violence) and general criminality (prior involvement in the criminal system, prior nonsexual violence) than did their White counterparts. All three underlying constructs were predictive of sexual recidivism for the White group, whereas only the general criminality construct was predictive of sexual recidivism among the Indigenous group. In another study comparing White offenders to Black offenders, Lee, Hanson, Calkins, and Jeglic (2019) found that while Blacks displayed more general criminality than did Whites, and Whites displayed more paraphilic indicators than did Blacks, both general criminality and sexual criminality predicted recidivism for both groups.

The general pattern is that the predictive accuracy of Static-99R is lower for non-Caucasian compared to Caucasian offenders, although this is not always the case (Lee et al., 2019). Consequently, evaluators should be sensitive to ethnic, racial, and cultural differences when interpreting Static-99R scores. The extent to which reports explicitly address potentially cultural differences will depend on the specific racial/ethnic group, the risk prediction research available for that

Table 6.1 The Ability of Static-99R to Discriminate Between Sexual Recidivists and Non-Recidivists (AUC) Among Different Racial and Ethnic Groups

Study	Group	Base rate (%, n/N)	Follow-up (Years)	Mean (SD)	AUC [95% C.I.]
Babchishin et al. (2012)	Non-Aboriginal	12.1 (154/1,269)	6.3	3.1 (2.7)	.74 [.70, .78]
	Aboriginal	16.0 (51/319)	6.4	4.0 (2.3)	.71 [.64, .79]
Smallbone and Rallings (2013)	Non-Aboriginal	4.1 (13/320)	2.4	2.2 (2.7)	.77 [.68, .91]
	Aboriginal	9.0 (6/67)	2.4	3.7 (2.3)	.61 [.45, .77]
Varela, Boccaccini, Murrie, Caperton, and Gonzalez (2013)	Black	2.7 (11/411)	4.9	3.3 (2.1)	.65 [.51, .78]
	Latino	3.1 (18/588)	4.6	2.1 (2.2)	.57 [.41, .73]
	White	2.4 (22/912)	4.9	2.2 (2.6)	.59 [.45, .72]
Hanson et al. (2014)	Overall	4.8 (23/475)	5.0	2.2 (2.2)	.82 [.72, .92]
	Black	7.1 (7/99)	5.0	2.7 (2.1)	.77 [.56, .97]
	Latino	2.5 (5/200)	5.0	1.8 (2.2)	.73 [.41, .99]
	White	7.1 (10/140)	5.0	2.3 (2.4)	.85 [.72, .98]
Leguizamo, Lee, Jeglic, and Clakins (2017)	Overall	1.9 (9/483)	6.1	1.6 (1.9)	.72 [.53, .91]
	US-born Latino/ Puerto Rican	2.2 (6/268)	6.1	1.8 (1.9)	.82 [.64, .99]
	Other Latino	1.4 (3/215)	6.1	1.4 (1.8)	.52 [.19, .86]
Olver et al. (2018)	Non-Aboriginal	16.8 (76/660)	10.0	3.5 (2.8)	.72 [.66, .77]
	Aboriginal	23.9 (64/384)	10.0	4.6 (2.4)	.66 [.59, .74]
Boccaccini, Rice, Helmus, Murrie, and Harris (2017)	Overall	3.6 (1,249/34,687)	5.2	2.2 (2.0)	.65 [.63, .66]
	Caucasian	4.9 (389/7,938)			.65 [.62, .68]
	African American	4.5 (438/9,725)			.64 [.61, .67]
	Latino	3.0 (268/8,939)			.63 [.60, .67]
Lee and Hanson (2017)	White	5.8 (46/789)	5.0	2.0 (2.4)	.82 [.76, .88]
	Black	6.4 (30/466)	5.0	3.1 (2.3)	.74 [.64, .84]
	Latino	3.1 (22/719)	5.0	2.0 (2.2)	.70 [.59, .81]
Lee, Hanson, and Blais (2019)	White	19.3 (164/848)	10.0		.72 [.68, .76]
	Indigenous	24.0 (90/375)	10.0		.66 [.60, .72]
Lee et al. (2018)	White	10.6 (14/132)	10.0	2.4 (2.4)	.85 [.74, .96]
	Black	10.8 (10/93)	10.0	2.9 (2.2)	.63 [.42, .84]
Lee et al. (2019)	White	3.9 (11/282)	5.0	2.2 (2.3)	.76 [.64, .88]
	Black	5.5 (16/291)	5.0	2.7 (2.1)	.78 [.66, .90]

group, and the context of the risk communication. For example, addressing potential limitations of Static-99R scores would be recommended in a high-stakes assessment (e.g., Dangerous Offender hearing) of an individual of Inuit heritage in Canada. In contrast, we do not recommend affirmative disclosures of potential limitations for most routine correctional assessments, regardless of the ethnicity of the individuals being assessed.

Static-99R and Offenders With Mental Health Issues

The Static-99R samples contained significant numbers of individual offenders with severe and persistent mental illness. It is appropriate to use Static-99R to assess individuals with mental disorders, including schizophrenia and mood disorders. A review of the literature has also generally found static risk scales to discriminate well among sex offenders with major mental illness (Kelley & Thornton, 2015). Although sex offenders with a history of psychiatric hospitalization are, on average, at higher risk for reoffending than are other sex offenders, a history of psychiatric hospitalization provides limited information for risk prediction once established risk factors are considered (Lee & Hanson, 2016). In a sample of sex offenders with a history of psychiatric hospitalizations (Lee & Hanson, 2016), Static-99R showed good discrimination for sexual recidivism (AUC = .76, 95% CI of .62 to .89, n = 108, with 17 recidivists). Pending further calibration studies, there is no reason to suspect that the Static-99R would not be applicable to this subgroup.

Similarly, we recommend the use of Static-99R with sex offenders who have a developmental delay of the cognitive type, assessed as intellectual disability. Hanson, Sheahan, and VanZuylen (2013) found it showed strong discrimination between sexual recidivists and non-recidivists (d = 1.04); however, the sample size in that study was sufficiently small that (n = 66, 2 samples) future research is needed before these findings can be interpreted with confidence. The extent to which these individuals had additional, non-cognitive disabilities was not recorded. The use of Static-99R for individuals with very low IQ (< 55) should be done with caution because such individuals are rarely processed by the criminal justice system and so are likely only a tiny proportion of the Static-99R development and validation sample. Even if an individual with very low IQ was formally charged (making him technically part of the Static-99R sampling frame), we recommend that evaluators not use Static-99R scores on their own; instead, they should supplement their assessments with factors more closely tailored to the risk and needs of individuals with severe cognitive deficits (e.g., nature of social supports).

Standardized Risk Levels

In the original Static-99, total scores translated into one of the following risk categories: low, moderate-low, moderate-high, and high. The authors of the scale have since concluded that a revision to this interpretation is necessary in an effort to move toward a less arbitrary method of communicating risk that has more universally understood meaning (Phenix, Helmus et al., 2016). We recommend that risk levels communicate a global picture of the offender, implying information about multiple risk-relevant domains (e.g., age, lifestyle, protective factors, history, prognosis, dosage, and expected response to supervision and treatment). In our work with the Council on State Government Justice Centre, we have proposed 5 standardized risk/need levels for general correctional populations (Hanson et al., 2017), which are briefly described as follows.

Individuals in Risk Level I have no substantial criminogenic needs, or if they do, they are likely to be transitory in nature. These individuals are expected to reoffend at levels indistinguishable from that of men without a history of sex offending. They would be expected to have good personal resources and require little supervision or intervention. Basically, if it were not for the offence committed, they would be living a life similar to other individuals in the general population.

Level II describes individuals with few needs and good resources who are less likely to reoffend than average. Brief intervention strategies may be helpful, and they should be easily managed in a typical case management setting.

Level III individuals are in the middle of the risk distribution and comprise the greatest proportion of criminal justice populations. These individuals have some criminogenic and non-criminogenic needs requiring attention and may require structured intervention over a period of months. These offenders would be expected to have the typical rate of recidivism, and most would transition to Level II with appropriate intervention.

Level IV describes individuals whose criminogenic needs are higher than average, many of which are chronic and severe. They require comprehensive services with follow-up and support in the community. Custody may be helpful for managing risk in the short term, and for helping these individuals begin treatment programs.

Level V is the highest risk group, and it identifies individuals virtually certain to reoffend (over 80%). Their needs are likely to be chronic, severe, and in multiple domains. They have few strengths. These people would require structured and comprehensive intervention while in custody. Long-term follow-up and supervision would likely be necessary to mitigate risk.

Although the 5 levels were developed for general offenders, they can be adapted to describe the risk and needs of sexual offenders. For Static-99R, Level I (Very Low Risk, for scores of −3 to −2) describes generally prosocial individuals whose risk for sexual reoffending is indistinguishable from that of men with a nonsexual offence (i.e., similar to the rate of spontaneous sexual offences for individuals with a criminal conviction but no current or prior sexual offences; see Kahn, Ambroziak, Hanson, & Thornton, 2017). Level II (Below Average Risk, for scores of −1 to 0) describe individuals who are meaningfully lower risk than average, but still higher than nonsexual offenders. Individuals placed in Level II are approximately half as likely as those in the middle group in the distribution to reoffend. Level III (scores of 1 to 3) applies to individuals in the middle of the risk distribution. Level IVa identifies individuals (Above Average Risk, scores of 4 or 5) who are higher risk than the median group and are likely to have multiple criminogenic needs. The highest Static-99R Level (scores of 6 or more) captures the top 10% of the sample (Hanson, Babchishin et al., 2016). This group is labelled IVb, not V, because the expected sexual recidivism rates (e.g., over 5 years, 20.5% to 53%) are well below the virtually certain to reoffend rates (85% or more) associated with the standardized risk/need levels for general offenders.

Babchishin et al. (2016) found that placement in the standardized risk levels supported inferences about other risk-relevant characteristics. In their study, individuals placed in Level I were older (over age 60), had offended against family members or acquaintances, and displayed low levels of criminogenic needs (e.g., they were not sexually preoccupied, they cooperated with supervision, and were not impulsive). Individuals placed in Level II were somewhat younger (average age 50) than those in Level I but still older than the average age of the sample. They rarely had had a prior sexual offence, rarely had stranger victims, and displayed generally low levels of criminogenic needs. The individuals in Level III ranged in age from 18 to 80 years (average age close to the average age for the complete sample—39 to 40 years). Most had some prior involvement in the criminal justice system, although few had a prior sexual offence. Their average STABLE-2007 score was 6.8, indicating some criminogenic needs in several different areas. Most (89%) of the individuals placed in Level IVa had criminal histories, about a third had a prior sexual offence, and approximately half of the individuals in this group had stranger victims. Criminogenic needs in multiple areas were common among those in Level IVa. Finally, virtually all (99.1%) individuals in Level IVb had criminal histories (typically extensive), most (59%) had a previous sexual offence, and most (72%) had offended against strangers. More than half of those placed in Level IVb had clinically significant problems with sexual preoccupation, lack of cooperation with supervision, and impulsivity. Very few (10%) individuals classified as Level IVb had a stable intimate relationship. The average STABLE-2007 score for this group was 13, indicating unusually high levels of criminogenic needs. It is also worth noting that there were relatively small differences across the risk levels in terms of psychiatric history or developmental delay.

Readers should take away two points from these descriptions. First, readers experienced with offenders should easily recognize the distinctions described by the standardized risk levels, for both general and sexual offenders. This gives us hope that once the descriptions are provided, diverse professionals can have clear reference points upon which to build a common language for risk communication. The second point is that considerable inferences can be made about individuals' psychological functioning and community adjustment based on the small number of simple indicators contained in the Static-99R risk tool.

Static-99R Scores Do Not Indicate Perpetual Risk

Static-99R is scored at the time of release and does not change. Individuals, however, do change—sometimes by a lot. Such changes should be considered in an overall assessment of risk. There is strong evidence that the longer individuals remain free of sexual offending in the community, the lower their subsequent risk for sexual recidivism (Hanson, Harris, Helmus & Thornton, 2014). On average, a sex offender's risk halved every 5 years he does not reoffend while in the community. For example, if an offender's expected sexual recidivism rate was 20% during the first 5 years in the community, it would be 10% during the next 5 years (years 6 to 10), 5% for years 11 to 15, and 2.5% for years 16 to 20. These "time free" effects apply across risk levels, age at release, and offender type (adult-victim versus child-victim; Hanson et al., 2014).

Translating desistance from sexual offending into the language of the standardized risk/needs framework, Hanson and colleagues (Hanson, Harris, Letourneau, Helmus, & Thornton, 2018) noted that sex offenders placed in Level I based on their Static-99R scores were no higher risk than the risk of spontaneous sexual offending among offenders who had no prior history of committing sex offences (based on 5-year rates of sexual offending). They examined the timeframes to cross that same desistance threshold for offenders placed in the higher risk levels who had remained completely offence-free while at risk in the community. Individuals in Level II crossed the threshold after 3 to 6 years; individuals in Level III crossed the threshold after 8 to 13 years; and individuals in Level IVa crossed the threshold within 16 to 18 years. Even individuals in the lower end of Level 1Vb (i.e., scores of 6 on the Static-99R) crossed the desistance threshold at year 21.

The strengths and consistency of the time free effects has led the STATIC Development Team to recommend that the interpretative materials for Static-99R scores (recidivism rates, risk ratios, standardized risk levels) are valid for only 2 years after release (Phenix, Fernandez et al., 2017). For individuals who have more than 2 years in the community, evaluators need to consider behavior during the past 2 years in their overall assessment of risk. For individuals who have remained offence-free, their risk would be lower than that inferred from the Static-99R norms. For individuals who have committed new nonsexual offences, their risk may be higher (Hanson et al., 2018). For detailed information on evaluating lifetime risk, see section "Estimating Lifetime and Residual Risk" on www.static99.org.

The individual's psychological functioning and community adjustment also contributes incrementally to the information provided by Static-99R. Individuals may be higher or lower risk based on the density of their risk factors external to Static-99R. Adjusting Static-99R recidivism risk estimates is generally not advisable, unless evaluators use a validated risk tool shown to be incremental to Static-99R. These risk tools include STABLE-2007 (Hanson et al., 2015), Violence Risk Scale—Sexual Offender version (VRS-SO; Olver et al., 2018, 2007), Structured Risk Assessment—Forensic Version (Thornton & Knight, 2015), and the Sex Offender Treatment Intervention and Progress Scale (McGrath et al., 2012). The list of incremental measures even includes Static-2002R (Babchishin et al., 2012; Lehmann et al., 2013), which is remarkable considering the overlap in the information used to score Static-99R and Static-2002R.

Given that using multiple instruments addressing different constructs related to risk increases predictive accuracy, evaluators are encouraged to use Static-99R as part of an overall assessment that includes other risk tools. The use of multiple instruments, however, raises the question of how best to combined diverse sources of information (Babchishin et al., 2012; Mills & Kroner, 2006; Seto, 2005; Vrieze & Grove, 2010). One option is to use the mechanical rules that have been empirically validated for combining Static-99R with the STABLE-2007, VRS-SO, Structured Risk Assessment—Forensic Version (SRA-FV) or Sex Offender Treatment Intervention and Progress Scale (SOTIPS). Unstructured adjustments of Static-99R risk estimates are discouraged because they are most likely to degrade predictive accuracy (Hanson et al., 2015; Storey et al., 2012). Other approaches to combining the information from diverse risk tools are being explored and may be validated for applied use in the years ahead (Brouillette-Alarie et al., 2018; Vrieze & Grove, 2010).

Evaluators interested in absolute recidivism rate estimates can also use measures of dynamic risk factors to determine which Static-99R reference group is most appropriate: routine/complete or high risk/high needs (Hanson, Thornton et al., 2017; Phenix, Helmus, & Hanson, 2016). We recommend that the routine/complete norms be used in most cases; however, we also support the application of the high risk/high needs norms to individuals who score well above average (in percentile terms, top 10%–15%) on measures of criminogenic needs. Evaluators should note, however, that this approach to determining STATIC recidivism rates incorporates professional judgement regarding the similarity of the individual to these particular samples. Further, use of the Static-99R has not been empirically validated. Evaluators wanting a mechanical method of combining Static-99R with a dynamic scale should use the empirically derived combination rules referenced earlier (Hanson et al., 2015; McGrath et al., 2012; Olver et al., 2018; Thornton & Knight, 2015).

Directions for Future Research

Readers familiar with the Static-99 chapter in the previous edition of this book (Anderson & Hanson, 2010) will notice that much has changed. Advanced age has been accorded increased weight, there are new recidivism rate tables and new risk labels, and an updated scoring manual is available (Phenix, Fernandez et al., 2017). More significantly, however, is the expansion of the inferences possible from Static-99R scores. Originally, Static-99 addressed only recidivism rates, as well as relative risk expressed as vaguely defined nominal risk categories (Low, Low-Moderate, Moderate-High, High). Currently, Static-99R scores are linked to three quantitative indicators of risk (risk ratios, percentile ranks, absolute recidivism rates) integrated into 5 standardized risk levels. As new inferences are added to the interpretation of STATIC scores, there is a corresponding need for ongoing research to justify these inferences.

STANDARDIZED RISK LEVELS

The standardized risk levels are intended to be broadly applicable descriptions of the psychological functioning and risk-relevant propensities of individuals, and to provide direction concerning the appropriate responses of the correctional and forensic mental health systems (e.g., Level I—do almost nothing; Level IV—intensive treatment and monitoring for years). Consequently, unlike the original Static-99 risk categories, the standardized Static-99R risk categories are linked to testable hypotheses. For example, Level III (average risk) is intended to represent the middle of the risk distribution of sexual offenders. It is currently centred on a Static-99R score of 2 because that is the median value in large, representative samples (Hanson, Lloyd et al., 2012). If, however, the scale is further revised, then the thresholds for Level III of the revised scale could be based on research evidence. The thresholds for new, improved versions should conserve the intended meaning of the standardized risk levels while, hopefully, increasing the scope and precision of possible inferences.

One of the most exciting research agendas would address the amount of treatment necessary to meaningfully change the recidivism risk of sexual offenders. Although the results of any specific study are likely to be inconclusive, researchers could identify reliable patterns through meta-analysis. Prior to the standardized risk categories, it was difficult to aggregate findings across studies because there was no common metric for quantifying risk. Dose-response studies would not only inform the meaning of the Static-99R risk tool, but, more importantly, advance our overall understanding of individuals with a history of sexual crime.

Research is also needed on the latent constructs responsible for sexual recidivism risk. Currently, there is consensus that the risk for sexual crime is multidimensional. Sexual recidivism is related to general criminality (e.g., negative attitudes toward authority, impulsivity), sex crime-specific criminality (e.g., deviant sexual interests, emotional congruence with children), as well as a third factor centred on young age and stranger aggression, which may or may not have a psychological interpretation (Barbaree, Langton, & Peacock, 2006; Brouillette-Alarie et al., 2016; Brouillette-Alarie & Hanson, 2015; Brouillette-Alarie et al., 2018; Roberts, Doren, & Thornton, 2002; Jung et al., 2017). The standardized risk levels were originally developed for only one of these dimensions, i.e., general criminality (Hanson, Bourgon et al., 2017), and were subsequently adapted to Static-99R, which is known to have a multidimensional structure (Hanson, Babchishin et al., 2017). Although this is a reasonable approximation, future studies should consider the potential benefits of adopting an explicitly multidimensional approach to assessment and risk communication (Babchishin et al., 2016; McGrath, Lasher, Cumming, Langton, & Hoke, 2014).

There is also a need for ongoing research on combining diverse information into an overall evaluation of risk. Evaluators typically use multiple instruments when assessing violence risk (Neal & Grisso, 2014). Although there are credible, mechanical methods of combining different risk tools (e.g., Hanson et al., 2015; Olver et al., 2018), these procedures essentially create a new risk tool, which then requires the same types of reliability and validity studies required of each of the original tools. Consequently, there would be tremendous value in evidence-based principles for combining risk tools that are not scale specific. For example, there is evidence that averaging hazard ratios of diverse tools increases predictive accuracy and calibration (match between expected and observed recidivism rates; Babchishin et al., 2012; Lehmann et al., 2013). Another promising direction for research would be to examine the potential incremental effects of using additional risk tools when the results of each risk tool are first expressed in the standardized risk levels. Combining risk tools using empirically validated combination rules based on the standardized risk levels would be a much easier approach than averaging hazard ratios.

It would also be valuable to examine the combined effects of Static-99R scores, external measures of psychologically meaningful risk factors (e.g., STABLE-2007, SOTIPS), and time offence free in the community. Although community adjustment predictably improves the longer individuals remain offense free (Lasher & McGrath, 2017), we do not know whether improvements in dynamic risk factors can fully account for the time free effects observed in other long-term follow-up studies.

Static-99R Case Example

Mr. Shysty is a 35-year-old male serving a sentence of 4 years for Sexual Assault Causing Bodily Harm. The current offence was committed against an adult female with whom he worked. They saw each other at a pub close to their place of employment, sat with each other, drank together, and went to the apartment of the victim. Once inside the apartment, Mr. Shysty quickly made sexual advances, and the victim told him to "slow down." Mr. Shysty continued and the victim's resistance increased. She told him to leave and he instead forced her onto the couch, punched her repeatedly, and forced intercourse. The victim said she passed out and was not sure if she lost consciousness because she was hit or because she was drunk (there was no indication of concussion upon examination), and when she awoke, he was gone. She notified police and Mr. Shysty was arrested the following day. He was granted bail but violated his conditions one week later by attending the same pub and consuming alcohol.

Mr. Shysty's first criminal conviction occurred at age 18 years when he was caught with a large quantity of marijuana, cash, and other drug paraphernalia resulting in a charge and conviction for Possession for the Purpose of Trafficking. Mr. Shysty indicated that after (barely) completing high school, he had already developed a network of friends who sold drugs, and so he continued in this activity. After serving his jail sentence and probation, he continued to sell marijuana but then met the mother of his first child. She became pregnant shortly after they began dating. They moved in together and she gave him an ultimatum to quit selling drugs or she would leave with their daughter. He indicated he "straightened out" for a while and worked as a heavy equipment operator. After their relationship ended due to his alcohol use and infidelity, he reported that he enjoyed "playing the field" and being single. He said she left for good just two days after his daughter had her second birthday. He stated he has not had any significant relationship with a woman since separating from the mother of his daughter, and that separation occurred when he was 27 years of age. He said he still sees his daughter every other weekend and he pays child support. He was able to discuss her daughter's interests and knew how she was doing in school. He resumed his use of marijuana but did not return to selling drugs.

Mr. Shysty's frequenting of pubs and bars has led to other criminal charges and convictions for assaults against other males (6 charges on 6 occasions, and 3 convictions on separate occasions). He stated these fights started "for any reason," such as Mr. Shysty's advances toward females, other males challenging him, and general drunken rude exchanges. Most of these charges were laid prior to Mr. Shysty quitting his dealing, with the last one being laid at age 28. Mr. Shysty has two convictions for Driving While Impaired, with the most recent conviction occurring 6 years prior to the current offence. His current offence is the first conviction for a sexual offence; however, 5 years ago he was charged with assaulting a girlfriend. The criminal history indicates there was a withdrawn charge for Sexual Assault on the same sentencing date. When asked about this, Mr. Shysty reported that his previous girlfriend was jealous because he was sleeping with someone else. When she came to his apartment one evening to confront him about the infidelity, they began to push each other. He said he tried to leave and she blocked the doorway, so he shoved her out of the way. She called the police and reported that he had sexually assaulted her and he indicated she lied but he agreed to plead to the lesser charge of Assault "to get it over with" and avoid a conviction for Sexual Assault. No police report was available for this charge.

Mr. Shysty stated that he has no desire to return to a live-in relationship, as he feels women are generally going to "get their way, one way or another" and that he would prefer to have casual relationships. He stated that he does not mind that women work in the system, although he says that none of them ever believe him with respect to the previous assault conviction against his girlfriend. He said he has friends at work and most of them talked about how the victim of his current offence sleeps around a lot, but none of them talked to him after his arrest. He lost his job upon his arrest. He stated he believes he will be able to find a job when he has finished his sentence and stated that there are often jobs available for heavy equipment operators. He said he would also be interested in working in the mining industry.

Mr. Shysty has support from family, although they live in different parts of the province. He said his brother lives in a town approximately three hours away, along with his wife and their daughter. He said his brother's wife does not like him and he is not allowed to stay at their home when he visits. He described his brother as being "whipped" but said they have been together for almost 10 years so he understands his brother has to abide by his wife's wishes. Mr. Shysty's mother lives in another town just between where Mr. Shysty and his brother live. She lives alone, as Mr. Shysty's father passed away from pancreatic cancer 5 years ago. Mr. Shysty said his father was 65 years old when he died and that he was a heavy drinker. He said his mother also used to drink heavily but not as much since his father died. Mr. Shysty communicates with his mother and brother by telephone but mostly through social media (Facebook).

Mr. Shysty stated he does not have problems with money, he pays his bills regularly, and he has good credit. He has been living in a rented one-bedroom apartment for 3 years, which is the length of time he had his current job. Prior to that, he lived in town in another apartment while he worked at a different job. He said he left the previous job for the current one to make more money. He said he does not quit working without having another job lined up. He has been fired once for failing to attend work. Mr. Shysty said this was around the time his father died and he was having a difficult time and drinking a lot. Some days he would wake up and could tell he was still a bit drunk so he did not want to go to work and operate equipment. He said the absences led to getting fired.

Mr. Shysty said he does not have any close friends at the moment. He said he has some friends on Facebook he met on prior jobs but said he hasn't spoken to any of them since his arrest. The Post Sentence Community Assessment was completed with his mother and brother as the contacts, and while both indicated they would be supportive of him upon his return to the community, neither would be able to offer him a place to live long term, and the brother indicated he would not be able to offer him a place to stay for a short period, either. Both contacts indicated they did not know much about the current offence but said it was likely he was drunk when he did it. His mother said she thinks all of his legal problems have happened while he was drunk, and she commented he is just like his father. She noted his father had a terrible temper while drunk and once she even had to take the boys to her sister's home when they were very young to escape their father. She does not think her son remembers this, as he was only about 4 years old at the time, but she is certain he remembers his father's drinking and angry outbursts.

Mr. Shysty was reluctant to discuss much of his childhood, noting only that his parents drank frequently and sometimes there was a lot of yelling. He said his childhood was just about like anyone else's and he does not care to dwell in the past. Mr. Shysty said he did not feel he had much to complain about with regard to his upbringing, but is annoyed that neither his mother nor his brother would offer him a place to live. He indicated his mother would likely put him up for a short while if he were unable to secure a place of his own prior to release.

Mr. Shysty stated he needed to be careful around women and the current offence was a situation that "got out of hand." He said he enjoyed dating and casual relationships, but he would try to make sure that future sexual partners were not leading him on. He said he has had many "hook-ups" through online sites, such as Facebook, Plenty of Fish, and Tinder, and indicated they never resulted in the kind of trouble he is in right now. He figures he will be better off in the future to avoid sexual relationships with people he sees in some other context, such as work. Mr. Shysty indicated he has paid for sex with prostitutes on a couple of occasions, has visited strip clubs with his friends, and occasionally (once or twice a week) views pornography on the internet. He feels his sexual drive is normal for a man, but notes that some women have commented that they have trouble keeping up with him. He said he has many more partners than probably most men his age, but notes that most men his age are married, and that is why they "are deprived." Mr. Shysty denied using sexual behaviour, fantasy, pornography, etc., to cope with negative emotional states. He indicated he prefers to drink or smoke marijuana if he needs to "mellow out," and reserves sexual activity for when he is feeling good. Mr. Shysty indicated he would be willing to take programs as required. He said he thought his worst days were behind him but recognized the gravity of the current situation. He said he will probably have to quit drinking altogether, as it seems to get the best of him on most occasions.

Communicating Static-99R Information for Mr. Shysty

Below are two examples of how Static-99R scores could be communicated in applied reports. This first example is intended for audiences who are already familiar with Static-99R and who are working in jurisdictions where there are clear policies concerning the treatment, services, and supervision provided to individuals at different Static-99R risk levels (e.g., those with scores of 4 or higher receive intensive supervision and treatment). In such situations, the recipients of the report will be primarily interested in the standardized risk level. Detail descriptions of Static-99R and the risk levels are unnecessary because such information would already be well known to the reader. This type of brief communication is common in corrections.

The second example provides more information about Static-99R and the inferences that can be made from Static-99R scores. It also presents wording for describing the evaluator's decision concerning the recidivism rate tables to use (routine/complete versus high risk/high need). This example is appropriate when readers may be not familiar with Static-99R, or where there is no pre-established link between Static-99R scores and treatment and management decisions.

Other examples for communicating the information contained in Static-99R scores can be found in the *Static-99R and Static-2002R Evaluators' Workbook* (Phenix, Helmus et al., 2016) available at www.static99.org.

Standardized Risk Levels, Familiar Audience (e.g., routine corrections)

Mr. Shysty was scored on Static-99R. Static-99R is intended to position offenders in terms of their relative degree of risk for sexual reoffending based on commonly available demographic and criminal history information that correlates with sexual reoffending in adult male sex offenders. Static-99R has moderate accuracy in ranking offenders according to their relative risk for sexual recidivism, and is widely accepted by the scientific community and by applied evaluators. For further information, see www.static99.org.

Mr. Shysty's Static-99R score was based on criminal history records provided by the Royal Canadian Mounted Police dated August 15, 2016, and files provided by the Correctional Service of Canada as of September 3, 2016. As well, Mr. Shysty was interviewed on September 10, 2016, in order to verify the accuracy of the information contained in the police and correctional files.

Mr. Shysty received a total score of 4, which places him in Risk Level IVa [Above Average Risk] for being charged or convicted of another sexual offence.

Absolute Recidivism Rates—Routine Sample as Considered Reference Group

[The first two paragraphs would be the same as in the first example.]

Mr. Shysty received a total score of 4, which places him in Risk Level IVa [Above Average Risk] for being charged or convicted of another sexual offence. His score places him in the 80th percentile, meaning that out of 100 sexual offenders, 80 would be expected to have a lower score and 20 would have a higher score.

In routine samples of sexual offenders, the average 5 year sexual recidivism rate is between 5% and 15%. This means that out of 100 sexual offenders of mixed risk levels, between 5 and 15 would be charged with or convicted of a new sexual offence after 5 years in the community. Conversely, between 85 and 95 would not be charged or convicted of a new sexual offence during that time period.

On average, offenders with a Static-99R score of 4 have a sexual recidivism rate that is about twice the rate of the middle of the risk distribution.

In order to use Static-99R to estimate recidivism rates, it is necessary to select the reference group that the offender most closely resembles. Recidivism rate norms are provided for routine samples and samples that have been preselected to be high risk and high needs. The routine samples are the appropriate reference group for most situations, but it is possible that the high risk and high needs samples may be appropriate in some circumstances. This determination is based on the density of external risk factors not measured by Static-99R.

The STABLE-2007[1] was used to assess risk factors external to Static-99R. Mr. Shysty's STABLE-2007 score was 11, which is in the high end of the moderate range. Although identifying a number of concerns relevant to treatment needs and supervision, this evaluation of dynamic risk factors was considered insufficient justification to use norms other than the routine correctional samples as the reference group for Mr. Shysty.

In routine samples, the average 5-year sexual recidivism rate for individuals with a score of 4 is 11%. The margin of error for this estimate is between 10% and 12.1%, 19 times out of 20. A recidivism rate of between 10% and 12% means that out of 100 sexual offenders with the same risk score, between 10 and 12 would be charged with or convicted of a new sexual offence after 5 years in the community. Conversely, between 88 and 90 would not be charged with or convicted of a new sexual offence during that time period.

The values stated are based on the table entitled "Static-99R Routine Sample: Estimated 5-year Sexual Recidivism Rates" in Phenix, Helmus and Hanson (October 19, 2016) Static-99R & Static-2002R Evaluators' Workbook. Available from www.static99.org.

Mr. Shysty's risk for recidivism may be higher or lower than the estimates provided based on risk factors not measured by the Static-99R.

Individuals classified as Standardized Risk Level IVa, Above Average Risk, are expected to have many criminogenic needs, many of which are chronic and severe. Access to prosocial resources and strengths is likely limited due to significant barriers. Given the complexity and chronic nature of the criminogenic needs of people in this level, intensive, lengthy (200+ hours), and comprehensive services are required. Successful rehabilitation of these individuals typically involves gradual life changes over a long period of time (i.e., 10+ years) with increasingly lower rates of recidivism as they age. Nonsexual reoffending is common, with the greatest risk during the first few years following release.

Note

1. Hanson, R. K., Harris, A. J. R., Scott, T., & Helmus, L. (2007). *Assessing the risk of sexual offenders on community supervision: The dynamic supervision project* (Corrections User Report No. 2007-05). Ottawa: Public Safety Canada. Retrieved from www.publicsafety.gc.ca

References

Anderson, D., & Hanson, R. K. (2010). Static-99: An actuarial tool to assess risk of sexual and violent recidivism among sexual offenders. In R. K. Otto & K. Douglas (Eds.), *Handbook of violence risk assessment* (pp. 251–267). Milton Park: Routledge.

Babchishin, K. M., Blais, J., & Helmus, L. (2012). Do static risk factors predict differently for Indigenous sex offenders? A multi-site comparison of the original and revised Static-99 and Static-2002 scales. *Canadian Journal of Criminology and Criminal Justice, 54*, 1–43. doi:10.3138/cjccj.2010.E.40

Babchishin, K. M., & Hanson, R. K. (2009). Improving our talk: Moving beyond the low, moderate, and high typology of risk communication. *Crime Scene, 16*(1), 11–14. Retrieved from www.cpa.ca/cpasite/userfiles/Documents/Criminal%20Justice/Crime%20Scene%202009-05(1).pdf

Babchishin, K. M., Hanson, R. K., & Blais, J. (2013). *User guide for the brief assessment for recidivism risk—2002R (BARR-2002R)*. Unpublished manual. Retrieved from www.static99.org.

Babchishin, K. M., Hanson, R. K., & Blais, J. (2016). Less is more: Using Static-2002R subscales to predict violent and general recidivism among sexual offenders. *Sexual Abuse: A Journal of Research and Treatment, 28*, 187–217. doi:10.1177/1079063215569544

Babchishin, K. M., Hanson, R. K., & Helmus, L. (2012). Even highly correlated measures can add incrementally to predicting recidivism among sex offenders. *Assessment, 19*, 442–461. doi:10.1177/1073191112458312

Barbaree, H. E., Langton, C. M., & Peacock, E. J. (2006). The factor structure of static actuarial items: Its relation to prediction. *Sexual Abuse: A Journal of Research and Treatment, 18*, 207–226. doi:10.s11194-006-9011-6

Boccaccini, M. T., Murrie, D. C., Mercado, C., Quesada, S., Hawes, S., Rice, A. K., & Jeglic, E. L. (2012). Implications of Static-99 field reliability findings for score use and reporting. *Criminal Justice and Behavior, 39*, 42–58. doi:10.1177/0093854811427131

Boccaccini, M. T., Rice, A. K., Helmus, L. M., Murrie, D. C., & Harris, P. B. (2017). Field validity of the Static-99/R scores in a statewide sample of 34,687 convicted sexual offenders. *Psychological Assessment, 29*, 611–623. doi:10.1037/pas0000377

Brankley, A. E., Babchishin, K. M., & Hanson, R. K. (2019, in press). STABLE-2007 demonstrates predictive and incremental validity in assessing risk-relevant propensities for sexual offending: A meta-analysis. *Sexual Abuse*.

Brouillette-Alarie, S., Babchishin, K. M., Hanson, R. K., & Helmus, L. (2016). Latent constructs of static risk scales for the prediction of sexual aggression: A 3-factor solution. *Assessment, 23*(1), 96–111. doi:10.1177/1073191114568114

Brouillette-Alarie, S., & Hanson, R. K. (2015). Comparaison de deux mesures d'évaluation du risque de récidive des délinquants sexuels [Comparison of two recidivism risk measures for sexual offenders]. *Canadian Journal of Behavioural Science/Revue Canadienne des sciences du comportement, 47*, 292–304. doi:10.1037/cbs0000019

Brouillette-Alarie, S., Proulx, J., & Hanson, R. K. (2018). Three central dimensions of sexual recidivism risk: Understanding the latent constructs of Static-99R and Static-2002R. *Sexual Abuse: A Journal of Research and Treatment, 30*, 676–704. doi:10.1177/1079063217691965

Chevalier, C., Boccaccini, M. T., Murrie, D. C., & Varela, J. G. (2015). Static-99R reporting practices in sexually violent predator cases: Does norm selection reflect adversarial allegiance? *Law and Human Behavior, 39*, 209–218. doi:10.1037/lhb0000114

Crawford, J. R., & Garthwaite, P. H. (2009). Percentiles please: The case for expressing neuropsychological test scores and accompanying confidence limits as percentile ranks. *The Clinical Neuropsychologist, 23*, 193–204. doi:10.1080/13854040801968450

Dawes, R. M., Faust, D., & Meehl, P. E. (1989). Clinical versus actuarial judgment. *Science, 243*, 1668–1674. doi:10.1126/science.2648573

Grubin, D. (1998). *Sex offending against children: Understanding the risk*. Police Research Series, Paper 99. London: Home Office.

Hanson, R. K. (1997). *The development of a brief actuarial risk scale for sexual offense recidivism* (User Report 97-04). Ottawa: Department of the Solicitor General of Canada.

Hanson, R. K. (2001). *Note on the reliability of Static-99 as used by the California department of mental health evaluators*. Unpublished report, California Department of Mental Health, Sacramento, CA.

Hanson, R. K., Babchishin, K. M., Helmus, L., & Thornton, D. (2013). Quantifying the relative risk of sex offenders: Risk ratios for Static-99R. *Sexual Abuse: A Journal of Research and Treatment, 25*, 482–515. doi:10.1177/1079063212469060

Hanson, R. K., Babchishin, K. M., Helmus, L. M., Thornton, D., & Phenix, A. (2017). Communicating the results of criterion referenced prediction measures: Risk categories for the Static-99R and Static-2002R sexual offender risk assessment tools. *Psychological Assessment, 29*, 582–597. doi:10.1037/pas0000371

Hanson, R. K., Bourgon, G., McGrath, R., Kroner, D., D'Amora, D. A., Thomas, S. S., & Tavarez, L. P. (2017). *A five-level risk and needs system: Maximizing assessment results in corrections through the development of a common language*. New York: The Council of State Governments Justice Center.

Hanson, R. K., & Harris, A. J. R. (1998). *Dynamic predictors of sexual recidivism* (User Report 1998-01). Ottawa: Department of the Solicitor General of Canada.

Hanson, R. K., & Harris, A. J. R. (2000). Where should we intervene? Dynamic predictors of sex offense recidivism. *Criminal Justice and Behavior, 27*, 6–35. doi:10.1177/0093854800027001002

Hanson, R. K., Harris, A. J. R., Helmus, L., & Thornton, D. (2014). High risk sex offenders may not be high risk forever. *Journal of Interpersonal Violence, 29*, 2792–2813. doi:10.1177/0886260514526062

Hanson, R. K., Harris, A. J. R., Letourneau, E., Helmus, L. M., & Thornton, D. (2018). Reductions in recidivism risk based on time offence free in the community: Once a sexual offender, not always a sexual offender. *Psychology, Public Police, and Law, 24*, 48–63. doi:10.1037/law0000135

Hanson, R. K., Harris, A. J. R., Scott, T., & Helmus, L. (2007). *Assessing the risk of sexual offenders on community supervision: The dynamic supervision project* (Corrections User Report No. 2007-05). Ottawa: Public Safety Canada.

Hanson, R. K., Helmus, L., & Harris, A. J. R. (2015). Assessing the risk and needs of supervised sexual offenders: A prospective study using STABLE-2007, Static-99R and Static-2002R. *Criminal Justice and Behavior, 42*, 1205–1224. doi:10.1177/0093854815602094

Hanson, R. K., Helmus, L., & Thornton, D. (2010). Predicting recidivism among sexual offenders: A multi-site study of Static-2002. *Law and Human Behavior, 34*, 198–211. doi:10.1007/s10979-009-9180-1

Hanson, R. K., Lloyd, C. D., Helmus, L., & Thornton, D. (2012). Developing non-arbitrary metrics for risk communication: Percentile ranks for the Static-99/R and Static-2002/R sexual offender risk scales. *International Journal of Forensic Mental Health, 11*, 9–23. doi:10.1080/14999013.2012.667511

Hanson, R. K., Lunetta, A., Phenix, A., Neeley, J., & Epperson, D. (2014). The field validity of Static-99/R sex offender risk assessment tool in California. *Journal of Threat Assessment and Management, 1*(2), 102–117. doi:10.1037/tam0000014

Hanson, R. K., & Morton-Bourgon, K. E. (2009). The accuracy of recidivism risk assessments for sexual offenders: A meta-analysis of 118 prediction studies. *Psychological Assessment, 21*, 1–21. doi:10.1037/a0014421

Hanson, R. K., Sheahan, C. L., & VanZuylen, H. (2013). Static-99 and RRASOR predict recidivism among developmentally delayed sexual offenders: A cumulative meta-analysis. *Sexual Offender Treatment, 8*, 1–14.

Hanson, R. K., & Thornton, D. (1999). *Static-99: Improving actuarial risk assessments for sex offenders* (User Report 99-02). Ottawa: Department of the Solicitor General of Canada.

Hanson, R. K., & Thornton, D. (2000). Improving risk assessments for sex offenders: A comparison of three actuarial scales. *Law and Human Behavior, 24*, 119–136. doi:10.1023/A:1005482921333

Hanson, R. K., & Thornton, D. (2003). *Notes on the development of Static-2002* (User Report 2003-01). Ottawa: Department of the Solicitor General of Canada.

Hanson, R. K., Thornton, D., Helmus, L., & Babchishin, K. M. (2016). What sexual recidivism rates are associated with Static-99R and Static-2002R scores? *Sexual Abuse: A Journal of Research and Treatment, 28*, 218–252. doi:10.1177/1079063215574710

Harris, A. J. R., Helmus, L., Hanson, R. K., & Thornton, D. (2008, October). *Are new norms needed for Static-99?* Presentation at the 27th Annual Research and Treatment Conference of the Association for the Treatment of Sexual Abusers, Atlanta, GA.

Harris, G. T., & Rice, M. E. (2007). Characterizing the value of actuarial violence risk assessments. *Criminal Justice and Behavior, 34*, 1638–1658. doi:10.1177/0093854807307029

Helmus, L. (2009). *Re-norming Static-99 recidivism estimates: Exploring base rate variability across sex offender samples* (UMI No. MR58443) (Master's thesis). ProQuest Dissertations and Theses database. Carleton University, Ottawa.

Helmus, L. M., & Babchishin, K. M. (2017). Primer on risk assessment and the statistics used to evaluate its accuracy. *Criminal Justice and Behavior, 44*, 8–25. doi:10.1177/0093854816678898

Helmus, L., Hanson, R. K., Thornton, D., Babchishin, K. M., & Harris, A. J. R. (2012). Absolute recidivism rates predicted by Static-99R and Static-2002R sex offender risk assessment tools vary across samples: A meta-analysis. *Criminal Justice and Behavior, 39*, 1148–1171. doi:10.1177/0093854812443648

Helmus, L., & Thornton, D. (2015). Stability and predictive and incremental accuracy of the individual items of Static-99R and Static-2002R in predicting sexual recidivism: A meta-analysis. *Criminal Justice and Behavior, 42*, 917–937. doi:10.1177/0093854814568891

Helmus, L., Thornton, D., Hanson, R. K., & Babchishin, K. M. (2012). Improving the predictive accuracy of Static-99 and Static-2002 with older sex offenders: Revised age weights. *Sexual Abuse: A Journal of Research and Treatment, 24*, 64–101. doi:10.1177/1079063211409951

Joint Committee on Standards for Educational and Psychological Testing of the American Educational Research Association, the American Psychological Association, & The National Council on Measurement in Education. (2014). *Standards for educational and psychological testing*. Washington, DC: Author.

Jung, S. (2016). Sexual violence risk prediction in a police context. *Sexual Abuse: A Journal of Research and Treatment*. Advance online publication. doi:10.1177/1079063216681563

Jung, S., Ennis, L., Hermann, C. A., Pham, A. T., Choy, A. L., Corabian, G., & Hook, T. (2017). An evaluation of the reliability, construct validity, and factor structure of the Static-2002R. *International Journal of Offender Therapy and Comparative Criminology*, *61*, 464–487. doi:10.1177/0306624X15595228

Kahn, R. E., Ambroziak, G., Hanson, R. K., & Thornton, D. (2017). Release from the sex offender label. *Archives of Sexual Behavior*, *46*, 861–864. doi:10.1007/x10508-017-0972-y

Kelley, S. M., & Thornton, D. (2015). Assessing risk of sex offenders with major mental illness: Integrating research into best practices. *Journal of Aggression, Conflict and Peace Research*, *7*, 258–274. doi:10.1108/JACPR-02-2015-0162

Lasher, M. P., & McGrath, R. J. (2017). Desistance from sexual and other violent offending among child sexual abusers: Observations using the sex offender treatment intervention and progress scale. *Criminal Justice and Behavior*, *44*, 416–431. doi:10.1177/0093854816670194

Lee, S. C., & Hanson, R. K. (2016). Recidivism risk factors are correlated with a history of psychiatric hospitalization among sex offenders. *Psychological Services*, *13*, 261–271. doi:10.1037/ser0000081

Lee, S. C., & Hanson, R. K. (2017). Similar predictive accuracy of the Static-99R risk tool for White, Black, and Hispanic sex offenders in California. *Criminal Justice and Behavior*, *44*, 1125–1140. doi:10.1177/0093854817711477

Lee, S. C., Hanson, R. K., & Blais, J. (2020). Predictive accuracy of the Static-99R and Static-2002R risk tools for identifying Indigenous and White individuals at high risk for sexual recidivism in Canada. *Canadian Psychology/Psychologie Canadienne*, *61*(1), 42–57. https://doi.org/10.1037/cap0000182.

Lee, S. C., Hanson, R. K., Calkins, C., & Jeglic, E. (2019). Paraphilia and antisociality: Motivations for sexual offending may differ for American Whites and Blacks. *Sexual Abuse*. Advance online publication. doi:10.1177/1079063219828779

Lee, S. C., Hanson, R. K., Fullmer, N., Neeley, J., & Ramos, K. (2018). *The predictive validity of Static-99R over 10 years for sexual offenders in California: 2018 update*. Sacramento, CA: SARATSO (State Authorized Risk Assessment Tool for Sex Offenders) Review Committee. Retrieved from www.saratso.org

Lee, S. C., Restrepo, A., Satariano, A., & Hanson, R. K. (2016). *The predictive validity of Static-99R for sexual offenders in California: 2016 update*. Sacramento, CA: SARATSO (State Authorized Risk Assessment Tool for Sex Offenders) Review Committee. Retrieved from www.saratso.org

Leguizamo, A., Lee, S. C., Jeglic, E. L., & Clakins, C. (2017). Utility of the Static-99 and Static-99R with Latino sex offenders. *Sexual Abuse: Journal of Research and Treatment*, *29*, 765–785. doi:10.1177/1079063215618377

Lehmann, R. J. B., Hanson, R. K., Babchishin, K., Gallasch-Nemitz, F., Biedermann, J., & Dahle, K. P. (2013). Interpreting multiple risk scales for sex offenders: Evidence for averaging. *Psychological Assessment*, *25*, 1019–1024. doi:10.1037/a0033098

Lehmann, R. J. B., Thornton, D., Helmus, L. M., & Hanson, R. K. (2016). Developing non-arbitrary metrics for risk communication: Norms for the risk matrix 2000. *Criminal Justice and Behavior*, *43*(12), 1661–1687. doi:10.1177/0093854816651656

Levenson, J. S. (2004). Reliability of sexual violent predator civil commitment criteria in Florida. *Law and Human Behavior*, *28*, 357–368. doi:10.1023/B:LAHU.0000039330.22347.ad

McGrath, R. J., Lasher, M. P., & Cumming, G. F. (2012). The sex offender treatment intervention and progress scale (SOTIPS): Psychometric properties and incremental predictive validity with Static-99R. *Sexual Abuse: A Journal of Research and Treatment*, *24*, 431–458. doi:10.1177/1079063211432475

McGrath, R. J., Lasher, M. P., Cumming, G. F., Langton, C. M., & Hoke, S. E. (2014). Development of Vermont assessment of sex offender risk-2 (VASOR-2) reoffense risk scale. *Sexual Abuse: A Journal of Research and Treatment*, *26*, 271–290. doi:10.1177/1079063213486936

Mills, J. F., & Kroner, D. G. (2006). The effect of discordance among violence and general risk estimates on predictive accuracy. *Criminal Behaviour and Mental Health*, *16*, 155–166. doi:10.1002/cbm.623

Murrie, D. C., Boccaccini, M. T., Turner, D, B., Meeks, M., Woods, C., & Tussey, C. (2009). Rater (dis)agreement on risk assessment measures in sexually violent predator proceedings. *Psychology, Public Policy, and the Law*, *15*, 19–53.

Neal, T. M. S., & Grisso, T. (2014). Assessment practices and expert judgment methods in forensic psychology and psychiatry: An international snapshot. *Criminal Justice and Behavior*, *41*, 1406–1421. doi:10.1177/0093854814548449

Olver, M. E., Sowden, J. N., Kingston, D. A., Nicholaichuk, T. P., Gordon, A., Christofferson, S. M. B., & Wong, S. C. (2018). Predictive accuracy of violence risk scale—sexual offender version risk and change scores in treated Canadian aboriginal and non-aboriginal sexual offenders. *Sexual Abuse: A Journal of Research and Treatment, 30,* 254–275. doi:1079063216649594

Olver, M. E., Wong, S. C., Nicholaichuk, T., & Gordon, A. (2007). The validity and reliability of the violence risk scale-sexual offender version: Assessing sex offender risk and evaluating therapeutic change. *Psychological Assessment, 19,* 318–329. doi:10.1037/1040-3590.19.3.318

Phenix, A., & Epperson, D. L. (2015). Overview of the development, reliability, validity, scoring, and uses of the Static-99, Static-99R, Static-2002, and Static-2002R. In A. Phenix & H. M. Hoberman (Eds.), *Sexual offending: Predisposing conditions, assessments, and management* (pp. 437–455). New York: Springer.

Phenix, A., Fernandez, Y., Harris, A. J. R., Helmus, M., Hanson, R. K., & Thornton, D. (2017). *Static-99R coding rules: Revised 2016.* Ottawa: Public Safety Canada. Retrieved from www.static99.org

Phenix, A., Helmus, L., & Hanson, R. K. (2016). *Static-99R and Static-2002R evaluators' workbook.* Unpublished manual. Retrieved from www.static99.org

Quesada, S. P., Calkins, C., & Jeglic, E. L. (2014). An examination of the interrater reliability between practitioners and researchers on the Static-99. *International Journal of Offender Therapy and Comparative Criminology, 58,* 1364–1375. doi:10.1177/0306624X13495504

Roberts, C. F., Doren, D. M., & Thornton, D. (2002). Dimensions associated with assessments of sex offender recidivism risk. *Criminal Justice and Behavior, 29,* 569–589. doi:10.1177/009385402236733

Seto, M. C. (2005). Is more better? Combining actuarial risk scales to predict recidivism among adult sex offenders. *Psychological Assessment, 17,* 156–167. doi:10.1037/1040-3590.17.2.156

Smallbone, S., & Rallings, M. (2013). Short-term predictive validity of the Static-99 and Static-99-R for indigenous and nonindigenous Australian sexual offenders. *Sexual Abuse: A Journal of Research and Treatment, 25,* 302–316. doi:10.1177/1079063212472937

Smid, W. J., Kamphuis, J. H., Wever, E. C., & Van Beek, D. J. (2014). A comparison of the predictive properties of nine sex offender risk assessment instruments. *Psychological Assessment, 26,* 691–703. doi:10.1037/a0036616

Storey, J. E., Watt, K. A., Jackson, K. J., & Hart, S. D. (2012). Utilization and implications of the Static-99 in practice. *Sexual Abuse: A Journal of Research and Treatment, 24,* 289–302. doi:10.1177/1079063211423943

Thornton, D., Hanson, R. K., Kelley, S., & Mundt, J. (2019, in press). Estimating lifetime and residual risk for individuals who remain sexual offense free in the community: Practical applications. *Sexual Abuse, 19.*

Thornton, D., & Knight, R. A. (2015). Construction and validation of SRA-FV need assessment. *Sexual Abuse: A Journal of Research and Treatment, 27,* 360–375. doi:10.1177/1079063213511120

Varela, J. G., Boccaccini, M. T., Murrie, D. C., Caperton, J. D., & Gonzalez, E. (2013). Do the Static-99 and Static-99R perform similarly for White, Black, and Latino sexual offenders? *International Journal of Forensic Mental Health, 12,* 231–243. doi:10.1080/14999013.2013.846950

Vrieze, S. L., & Grove, W. M. (2010). Multidimensional assessment of criminal recidivism: Problems, pitfalls, and proposed solutions. *Psychological Assessment, 22,* 382–395. doi:10.1037/a0019228

Author Note

Author note: The views expressed are those of the authors and not necessarily those of Public Safety Canada. The authors wish to thank Kelly Babchishin for her review and helpful comments on this chapter.

Chapter 7

Actuarial Guides for Appraising the Risk of Violent Reoffending Among General Offenders, Sex Offenders, and Domestic Assaulters

N. Zoe Hilton, Marnie E. Rice, Grant T. Harris, Brian Judd, and Vernon L. Quinsey

In this chapter we describe a family of violence risk assessment instruments developed using similar follow-up research designs and empirical selection of items, and interpreted with reference to actuarial data. We first describe characteristics of these tools that distinguish them from other, non-actuarial instruments. We then describe three actuarial instruments for the assessment of violent recidivism risk. The third of these, the Violence Risk Appraisal Guide-Revised (VRAG-R, Rice, Harris, & Lang, 2013) is a revision of the overall scheme that permits assessment of both sexual and nonsexual offenders, incorporating an essentially lifetime follow-up and simplifying some of the scoring requirements. We next present an actuarial system for the assessment of domestic assault recidivism risk which consists of a brief front-line tool, the Ontario Domestic Assault Risk Assessment (ODARA; Hilton et al., 2004) and an algorithm for combining that tool with use of more in-depth information where available, the Domestic Violence Risk Appraisal Guide (DVRAG; Hilton, Harris, Rice, Houghton, & Eke, 2008). For all these instruments, we describe the empirical support and scoring procedures and provide case examples of individuals charged with violent, sexual, and domestic offenses.

The risk assessment instruments described in this chapter contrast with most others in this book in at least one of three principal ways. First, the present tools are all actuarial inasmuch as the items were selected based on their observed relationships with outcome in specific development samples, and they are accompanied by tables of measured recidivism rates (experience tables) and percentiles, also based on large samples. Actuarial tools differ from certain others that might use formulaic methods to yield a total score but did not use measured relationships in specific development samples to arrive at the formula and do not provide experience tables and percentile norms, both of which are defining properties of actuarial measures. Among psychologists, the impetus for developing actuarial violence risk assessments began more than a half century ago with the recognition that actuarial methods are generally more accurate than clinical judgment, experience, and intuition (Meehl, 1954; see also Ægisdóttir et al., 2006; Grove & Meehl, 1996) especially for violence risk (Hanson & Morton-Bourgon, 2007; Hilton, Harris, & Rice, 2006).

Second, the present actuarial tools and many of the others are alike in relying on clinical skill to evaluate some items, but the present tools differ from most in advising no modification of the score based on clinical judgment. This supplementary clinical discretion has been recommended by developers of some instruments to lower practitioner resistance, incorporate rare or idiosyncratic risk factors, allow application to new samples, adjust for offender aging, give credit for putative progress in therapy, recalibrate for possible differences in base rates, accommodate fear of making an error, and accede to the idea that such review is a professional responsibility. Recommendations and claims aside, no evidence supports contentions that any alteration (based on clinical judgment) of actuarial scores, as defined earlier, results in more accurate decisions compared to actuarially derived scores alone (Harris & Rice, 2015). Indeed, there is good reason to believe such revision generally results in decreased accuracy (see Grove & Meehl, 1996;

Hanson & Morton-Bourgon, 2007; Harris & Rice, 2007a; Hilton & Simmons, 2001; Janus & Meehl, 1997; Harris, Rice, Quinsey, & Cormier, 2015).

Third, the present violence risk assessments do not include items labeled "dynamic." Unfortunately, this term lacks a clear consensual meaning, such that identical constructs are called static in some assessments (e.g., sexual deviance in the SORAG) but dynamic in others (e.g., sexual deviance in the VRS-SO; see Chapter 10 in this volume). The definition we prefer for a dynamic factor is one that can be shown to change, and that when changed, alters risk (Hanson & Harris, 2000; Harris et al., 2015; Rice, 2008; see also Douglas & Skeem, 2005's "causal" dynamic risk factor). Furthermore, dynamic factors are of two types. "Stable" dynamic factors are ones that act much like static factors inasmuch as, once changed, they alter long-term risk, whereas "acute" or "fluctuating" dynamic factors are ones that must be measured very frequently because they change (and affect risk) during follow-up (Hanson & Harris, 2000; Harris et al., 2015). Returning to the earlier example of sexual deviance, empirical evaluations indicate that while initial or one-time measures of sexual deviance predict recidivism among sex offenders, pre-release changed measures of sexual deviance do not (e.g., Rice, Quinsey, & Harris, 1991), and thus sexual deviance does not meet our definition of a dynamic risk factor. Recent research indicating that changes in risk factors add to initial measurements of risk in the prediction of violent and sexual recidivism (e.g., Olver et al., 2018) shows promise for the development of risk assessment using measures that are actually dynamic as defined here. Further, within-subject fluctuations in various states (e.g., attitudes, moods, intoxication) indicate the imminence of violence, especially among those whose static risk is high (Mulvey et al., 2006; Quinsey, Coleman, Jones, & Altrows, 1997; Quinsey, Jones, Book, & Barr, 2006; Skeem et al., 2006). Thus, there is some evidence that such acute or fluctuating dynamic variables aid in anticipating when a high-risk offender might violently recidivate, although work on incorporating these findings into formal assessment continues. Actuarial risk assessments incorporating fluctuating dynamic factors, when developed, will be useful for short-term, post-release community management.

The Violence Risk Appraisal Guide (VRAG)

Description

The VRAG is an actuarial instrument that assesses the risk of violent recidivism among men charged with criminal violence (Harris, Rice, & Quinsey, 1993; Harris et al., 2015). The 12 VRAG items and their range of scores are shown in Table 7.1. Scores are divided into nine categories, each bearing a known likelihood of violent recidivism (acts for which a perpetrator is or could be charged with assault or other violent charges) in seven years and increasing linearly from 0% in the lowest category to 100% in the highest. There are also norms for ten years of opportunity. Each VRAG score is associated with a particular percentile whereby the violence risk of an individual examinee is evaluated according to his standing relative to a large sample of violent offenders.

The VRAG was developed to assess mentally disordered and normal male offenders convicted of violent offenses and has been validated for such offenders (e.g., Harris, Rice, & Cormier, 2002; Pham, Ducro, Marghem, & Réveillère, 2005; Snowden, Gray, Taylor, & MacCulloch, 2007; Thomson, 2005; Urbaniok, Noll, Grunewald, Steinbach, & Endrass, 2006; Yessine & Bonta, 2006), including sex offenders (e.g., Dempster, 1998; Harris et al., 2003; Lindsay et al., 2008; Rettenberger & Eher, 2007) where it has predicted dichotomous violent recidivism, and its severity and rapidity, all with large effect sizes (Rice & Harris, 2005). It has also predicted reported violence (where criminal charges have not necessarily been filed) among both male and female civil psychiatric patients (e.g., Doyle, Carter, Shaw, & Dolan, 2012; Gray et al., 2007; Harris, Rice, &

Table 7.1 Violence Risk Appraisal Guide Items and Ranges Indicating Relative Weights

Item	Score Range
1. Lived with both parents to age 16	5
2. Elementary school maladjustment	6
3. Alcohol problems	3
4. Never married	3
5. Nonviolent criminal history	5
6. Failure on prior conditional release	3
7. Age at index offense[a]	7
8. Victim injury[a]	4
9. Any female victim in index offense[a]	2
10. DSM-III Personality disorder	5
11. DSM-III Schizophrenia[a]	4
12. Psychopathy Checklist (Hare, 2003) score	17

Note: [a] Inversely scored item. See Harris, Rice, et al. (2015) for VRAG definitions, instructions, norms, and practice materials. Whether intended for research or individual assessment, the recommended basis for scoring the VRAG is a comprehensive psychosocial history (see Harris et al., 2015). This history should address childhood conduct, family background, antisocial and criminal behavior, psychological problems, and details of all offenses. Adequate psychosocial histories include more than past and present psychiatric symptoms and should rely on collateral information (i.e., material gathered from friends, family, schools, correctional facilities, police, and the courts). Scoring the VRAG is not a typical clinical task because it does not require contact between the examiner and examinee. Nevertheless, compiling the required psychosocial history does require clinical expertise.

Camilleri, 2004). Although the rank ordering of examinees' likelihood of violence is replicable across populations, norms may be expected to vary depending on follow-up time (Harris & Rice, 2007a). Users should have training in scoring the PCL-R and should demonstrate that they can score the VRAG to acceptable levels of reliability.

Method of and Rationale for Development

Outcome Variable

The VRAG was based directly on follow-up research in which the outcome variable was any new criminal charge for a violent offense. The definition of violence included homicide, attempted homicide, kidnapping, forcible confinement, wounding, assault causing bodily harm, armed robbery and rape. The VRAG was developed in a jurisdiction where a charge of assault or attempted murder can be filed even without physical contact between offender and victim, but very rarely, so assault was counted as violent recidivism. Sexual assaults involving physical contact were counted as violent, but noncontact sex offenses such as exhibitionism and voyeurism were excluded.

Violent recidivism was operationalized as subsequent criminal charges even though not everyone charged was convicted. Certainly, both criminal charges and convictions are imperfect measures of actual violent conduct: In addition to wrongful arrest and conviction, not every violent crime is reported to the authorities; not all police investigations result in the identification of a perpetrator; not all identified perpetrators are apprehended and arrested; and some guilty perpetrators are not convicted. Our research indicated, however, that charges entailed less measurement error than convictions (Harris et al., 2015; e.g., plea bargaining reduces some violent charges to nonviolent convictions). A design feature of modern criminal justice systems is that false positive errors (e.g. erroneously charging or convicting an innocent person) are much less preferable than all others—maximum accuracy of the outcome is of less concern than is avoiding false positives. In the empirical search for valid predictors of violence, our priority was different—the most accurate dependent variable. Although criminal charges appear to be an optimal measure, studies have also shown that criminal convictions, institutional records of aggression, and self-reported violence are generally predicted by the same variables, and, especially in this context, by VRAG scores.

Because most men in the VRAG development samples had been institutionalized, it was important that subsequent violence in other institutions, for which the offender might well have been charged had it occurred in the community, be considered. Records of subsequent institutionalizations (both correctional and psychiatric) were examined and violent acts that would have resulted in criminal charges had the incident occurred outside an institution were also recorded; however, fewer than 10% of the violent reoffenses were based on this criterion. It was also important not to count those offenders who had no opportunity to be violent because they were held in secure custody or had died. Consequently, official records were examined to address those possibilities. Finally, for the purposes of VRAG construction, the outcome data were analyzed as dichotomous so that the dependent variable in development analyses was at least one instance of violent recidivism. Opportunity was defined as release to the community, a minimum-security psychiatric hospital, or a halfway house. Three offenders who committed violent acts even though they did not technically have the opportunity to do so (e.g., by escaping from a secure facility and attacking a member of the public) were included as violent recidivists. On average, the development sample had 81.5 (SD = 60.6) months of opportunity to recidivate, defined as the duration between each subject's first opportunity and the study end date, or until the date of his first new violent offense (whichever occurred first). Time spent institutionalized for nonviolent offenses (or other reasons) was subtracted in the calculation of opportunity.

Independent Variables

The follow-up studies that formed the development research examined approximately 50 potential predictor variables for which there existed empirical support in the prediction of crime. These variables were coded masked to the outcome measures (and vice versa). Because many of the men had also been forensic patients, variables related to psychiatric history, distress, and diagnosis were also tested. Some variables were evaluated because clinicians attached importance to them (e.g., expressions of remorse, volunteering for treatment, whether the offender was regarded by clinicians as having "insight," etc.). In VRAG development, the tested variables reflected these categories: childhood history (e.g., DSM-III conduct disorder items, elementary school maladjustment, education), adult adjustment (e.g., criminal history, psychiatric history, employment, marital status, social support, socioeconomic status), index offense characteristics (e.g., number and sex of victims, severity of victim injuries, alcohol involvement, etc.), and assessment results obtained or obtainable early in the first post-index offense admission (e.g., IQ score, MMPI score, Level of Supervision Inventory score, DSM-III diagnoses, PCL-R score) all coded (blind to outcome) to a high standard of interrater reliability from institutional records that included thorough psychosocial history information.

Construction Samples

The goal was an actuarial instrument for the prediction of violent recidivism among serious offenders for whom the courts, clinicians, and criminal justice officials were required to make predictive decisions; i.e., those who have already committed at least one serious antisocial act. Offenders with only minor offenses and citizens who had committed no offenses were not the population of interest. We compiled a heterogeneous sample of 684 serious offenders using data from two previous studies (Rice, Harris, Lang, & Bell, 1990; Rice, Harris, & Cormier, 1992). Of these men, 613 had an opportunity to recidivate, and there were few differences between them and the 71 without opportunity: those with opportunity had less serious index offenses (this variable was inversely related to violent recidivism), were less likely to have a female victim, and were more likely to have married. There was no reason to expect that the development subjects were less dangerous than the others or that they were unrepresentative. The only exception to this was that the released group included no mass murderers (men who had killed more than three people), although there were some in the unreleased group.

Analytic Strategy

Potential predictor variables without a significant bivariate relationship with violent recidivism were not considered further. A few variables were highly collinear (e.g., prior criminal charges and prior convictions for violent offenses); from such pairs, the variable with the lower correlation with violent recidivism was dropped. Then we used least-squares stepwise multiple regression to select variables that made independent and incremental contributions to the prediction of violent recidivism. Separate analyses were run for variables in each of the categories described earlier. In addition, the development sample was subdivided (e.g., randomly, treated vs. assessed only). Only variables selected by the regression analyses in a majority of such subsidiary analyses were eligible in a final regression analysis that considered all variables that had survived thus far. Variables selected by this step became the 12 VRAG items. Subsequent testing indicated that logistic and Cox proportional hazards regression would have selected substantially the same items as would the use of continuous measures of violent recidivism—the number, severity, and rapidity of violent reoffenses (Harris et al., 2015).

Although unitary item weights would have performed almost as well (Harris et al., 1993; see also Grove & Meehl, 1996), the small improvement afforded by differential weights was considered worthwhile. The weights were derived not from the regression coefficients but using a simpler method described by Nuffield (1982) in which the weight is computed actuarially based on the item's base rate relationship with the dependent variable in the development sample. This computation, described in detail elsewhere (Harris et al., 1993, 2015), and meant that a score of zero could be recommended for missing items because that entailed adding the score for the overall base rate. Prorating is now preferred over this very conservative strategy (Harris et al., 2015). Briefly, the examiner first determines, on the basis of all the items that can be scored according to the manual, whether the examinee's score is positive (or negative). Then, the examinee is given the same proportion of positive (negative) points for the unscored items as obtained for the items that can be scored. The appendices of Harris et al. (2015) provide an extensive manual for the VRAG, including detailed scoring instructions, norms, answers to frequently asked questions, instructions for the compilation of suitable psychosocial histories, and practice case material.

Reliability, Psychometric Properties, and Validity

As a direct consequence of the methods used to determine item weights, the mean VRAG score in the development sample was very close to zero (.91, $SD = 12.9$). The first evaluation of interrater reliability used the independent coding by two trained raters of 20 randomly selected subjects and yielded a Pearson correlation coefficient of .90. Reliability coefficients exceeding .90 have also been reported in several subsequent evaluations (e.g., Douglas, Yeomans, & Boer, 2005; Ducro & Pham, 2006; Harris et al., 2002, 2003), including between clinicians and researchers (Harris, Rice, & Cormier, 2013), but the latter is not guaranteed (e.g., Crocker et al., 2015). In the development sample, the standard error of measurement was 4.1, roughly half the size of one

VRAG category. The 95% confidence intervals for each category showed that confidence tended to decrease slightly as scores increased (Harris et al., 1993), but the standard error of measurement and the observed rates of violent recidivism (and confidence intervals) indicated that any single "true" score can be expected to differ from the obtained score by more than a single VRAG category with a probability of less than .05 (Harris et al., 1993).

The VRAG predicted violent recidivism (base rate = 31%) in the development sample with a high degree of accuracy: the area under curve of the relative operating characteristic (AUC) was .76. The original sample (plus additional subjects not previously released) was followed-up with 10 years' mean opportunity (Rice & Harris, 1995). The base rate of violent recidivism was 43% and the AUC .was .74 for the VRAG's prediction of violent recidivism. In 52 studies using the VRAG or SORAG, the weighted average AUC ranged from .70 to .72 depending on the researchers (original research group or independent replications) or the quality of adherence to the intended application (Harris, Rice, & Quinsey, 2010), which is broadly equivalent to a large effect size (Rice & Harris, 2005). Under optimal conditions (high reliability; not dropping, replacing, or modifying items; fixed and equal follow-up durations), the VRAG yields AUCs of approximately .85 in predicting violent recidivism (Harris & Rice, 2003). There is evidence of good calibration of the observed and expected rates of violent recidivism (Rice et al., 2013).

The VRAG has been shown to generalize (although sometimes with lower effect sizes) across violent outcomes (number of violent reoffenses, institutional violence, very serious violence, self-reported violence, general recidivism, overall severity of violent recidivism, rapidity of violent failure); follow-up times (12 weeks to 10 years); countries (eight in North America and Europe); offender populations (mentally disordered offenders, sex offenders, violent felons, developmentally delayed sex offenders, emergency psychiatric patients, domestic assaulters, and juvenile offenders; for extensive review, see Harris et al., 2015, and for more recent validation studies see e.g., Churcher, Mills, & Forth, 2016; Coid et al., 2015; Folino, 2015; Livingston, Chu, Milne, & Brink, 2015; van Heesch, Jeandarme, Pouls, & Vervaeke, 2016). Some data suggest the VRAG predicts violence among women (Coid et al., 2009; Eisenbarth, Osterheider, Nedopil, & Stadtland, 2012; Harris et al., 2004), though not self-reported offenses (Hastings, Krishnan, Tangney, & Stuewig, 2011) or in mixed-sex samples (Doyle & Dolan, 2006; Gray et al., 2007; McDermott, Quanbeck, Scott, Edens, & Busse, 2007; Thomson, 2005), but there are few studies on serious female offenders specifically. Replications of the VRAG have generally reported that obtained rates of violent recidivism matched the predicted rates for each category, if the average score of the sample is similar, the follow-up duration is approximately the same as for the norms, and the outcome is similar (Harris & Rice, 2007a).

In several evaluations, the VRAG has been more accurate than the final output of comparable structured professional judgment (SPJ) schemes (Barbaree, Seto, Langton, & Peacock, 2001; Campbell, French, & Gendreau, 2009; Grann & Wedin, 2002; Gray et al., 2007; Pham, 2004; Pham, Ducro, Marghem, & Réveillère, 2005; Sjöstedt & Langström, 2002; see also Singh, Grann, & Fazel, 2011 regarding categorized scores and Yang, Wong, & Coid, 2011 regarding combined outcomes), often statistically significantly. Some of these studies used the total raw score on the SPJ instrument (although that is not advised for individual decision-making) as output rather than the recommended categorical judgment, and some of the comparisons involved outcomes other than generally violent recidivism or instruments not produced for violent recidivism specifically. We know of no report in which clinical intuition (structured or unstructured) statistically significantly outperformed the VRAG in the prediction of violent recidivism on the same cases. We regard this as consistent with the position that optimal long-term, pre-release violence risk assessment can currently be achieved by relying on a comprehensive set of static predictors without adjustment based on clinical judgment (c.f., Harris & Rice, 2003; Harris et al., 2002).

The Sex Offender Risk Appraisal Guide (SORAG)

Description and Development

Sex offenders' observed rates of violent recidivism were higher than expected based on their VRAG scores (Harris & Rice, 2007a; Rice & Harris, 1997) suggesting that separate norms might be required for men institutionalized for contact sex offenses against minors and sexual assaults against women. Also, personal variables associated with recidivism among sex offenders were slightly different from those of violent offenders without histories of sex offenses (Quinsey, Rice, & Harris, 1995; Rice, Harris, & Quinsey, 1990; Rice et al., 1991). For example, phallometrically assessed sexual deviance has only been reported to predict recidivism among sex offenders; an index offense of homicide indicates lower-than-average risk only among violent non-sex offenders; and the relationship between recidivism and the age and sex of prior victims differs between sex offenders[1] and other violent offenders. Furthermore, among sex offenders, there is evidence that officially detected violent recidivism is a better index of officially detected sexually motivated violence than sexual recidivism in records of charges and convictions alone (Rice, Harris, Lang, & Cormier, 2006).

Consequently, the VRAG was modified to optimize assessment of sex offenders' risk for violent recidivism by dropping two items (female victim in the index offense and victim injury in the index offense, both scored inversely) that did not afford incremental value among sex offenders and adding four that did (in decreasing order of weight: history of violent offenses, prior convictions for sex offenses, having an adult female or male child victim, and phallometrically assessed sexual deviance). Weights were computed and norms derived, as in the VRAG, using a development sample of 288 sex offenders from previous samples (Rice et al., 1990, 1991) where the outcome variable was, as with the VRAG, at least one subsequent charge for a violent offense. Some schemes use an alternative approach, using only criminal charges whose name reflects sexual motivation (e.g., rape, sexual assault, sexual battery, etc.), but this ranks offenders quite differently from an approach based on officially detected violent recidivism overall (Barbaree, Langton, & Peacock, 2006; Harris et al., 2003) and underestimates the rate of recidivism involving sex offenders' most serious sexually violent offenses, especially homicide. Among sex offenders, there is evidence that officially detected violent recidivism is a better index of officially detected sexually motivated violence than sexual recidivism recorded on police rap sheets alone (Rice, Harris, Lang, & Cormier, 2006).

Weights for all items were derived using the same method employed in the development of the VRAG (Nuffield, 1982). The result was the 14-item *Sex Offender Risk Appraisal Guide* (SORAG). The items and their range of scores are shown in Table 7.2. SORAG scores are associated with one of nine risk categories, each with a known likelihood of violent recidivism in seven years and increasing linearly from 7% to 100%. There are also norms for 10 years of opportunity. As for the VRAG, each SORAG score is also associated with a percentile rank. The base rate of violent recidivism in the development sample was 42% in seven years. Harris et al. (2015) provided an extensive manual for the SORAG with detailed scoring and coding instructions, norms for individual scores and the nine standard SORAG categories, answers to frequently asked questions, instructions for the compilation of suitable psychosocial histories, and practice case material. As with the VRAG, the SORAG can be prorated as long as no more than four items are missing or scored by substitution.

Reliability, Psychometric Properties, and Validity

In construction, the interrater reliability of the SORAG was .90 (Quinsey et al., 2006) and similarly high reliability coefficients have been reported in subsequent replication studies (e.g., Ducro & Pham, 2006; Harris et al., 2003; Langton et al., 2007). In the development samples,

Table 7.2 Sex Offender Risk Appraisal Guide Items and Ranges Indicating Relative Weights

Item	Score Range
1. Lived with both parents to age 16	5
2. Elementary school maladjustment	6
3. Alcohol problems	3
4. Never married	3
5. Nonviolent criminal history	5
6. Violent criminal history	7
7. Convictions for prior sex offenses	6
8. History of sex offenses against girls onlya	4
9. Failure on prior conditional release	3
10. Age at index offense[a]	7
11. DSM-III Personality Disorder	5
12. DSM-III Schizophrenia[a]	4
13. Phallometric test results	2
14. Psychopathy Checklist (Hare, 2003) score	17

Note: [a] Inversely scored item. See Harris, Rice et al. (2015) for SORAG definitions, instructions, norms, and practice materials.

SORAG scores had a mean of 8.90 (*SD* = 11.33) and a standard error of measurement of 3.58, and a mean of 9.99 (*SD* = 10.8) and very low standard error of measurement (.012) in a subsequent independent replication (Harris et al., 2003). That replication also reported a very close correspondence between observed rates of violent recidivism for the SORAG categories and those expected on the basis of the norms.

In development, the SORAG yielded an AUC of .75 in predicting violent recidivism that was replicated (.73) in the subsequent independent evaluation in which SORAG scores also significantly predicted the rapidity and severity of recidivism (Harris et al., 2003). In 14 non-overlapping samples of released sex offenders from six countries, SORAG scores have yielded a mean AUC of .73 in predicting violent recidivism, .75 for general recidivism, and .68 for sexual recidivism charges (Harris et al., 2015; see also Smid, Kamphuis, Wever, & Van Beek, 2014). The SORAG also predicted sexual, violent, and any chargeable offense in a small sample of men with intellectual disabilities (Fedoroff, Richards, Ranger, & Curry, 2016). As with the VRAG, accuracy is enhanced by not dropping or replacing SORAG items, high reliability, and constant follow-up duration (Harris & Rice, 2003; Harris et al., 2003; Langton et al., 2007). The accuracy of SORAG scores in predicting violent recidivism has been reported to be improved neither by the addition of less accurate actuarial tools (Seto, 2005) nor by additional structured or unstructured clinical intuition (Barbaree et al., 2001; Johansen, 2007).

The Violence Risk Appraisal Guide-Revised (VRAG-R)

Rationale for Development

The VRAG-R was developed in order to provide a single tool that was easier to score and validated for use with violent or sexual offenders. Like the VRAG and SORAG, the VRAG-R was developed from follow-up research, this time involving a follow-up of up to 49 years (Rice et al., 2013). It does not require knowledge of clinical diagnostic criteria in order to be scored or rely on a diagnostic system that has been made obsolete since the development of the VRAG and SORAG. Also, it does not require scoring of the entire PCL-R, only Facet 4, Antisociality, which is comprised of five items mostly relating to criminal history and childhood behavior problems, thereby improving the interrater reliability of the instrument and this potential source of examiner disagreement (e.g., Edens, Penson, Ruchensky, Cox, & Smith, 2016; Sturup et al., 2014).

Description and Development

The VRAG-R was constructed on a sample of 961 male offenders randomly selected from a total of 1,261 coded for previous follow-up studies (Harris et al., 1993; Harris et al., 2003; Quinsey, Rice, & Harris, 1995), including a small number not previously reported because they were not previously at risk of reoffending. Offenders had been released prior to 1995 and were followed through 2003 or later, such that analyses of fixed opportunity periods from 6 months to 49 years were possible. Two VRAG items did not show predictive value in these tests and were dropped from consideration (female victim in the index offense, injury to victim in the index offense). Two items requiring diagnostic criteria for psychiatric disorders (schizophrenia and personality disorder) were dropped in order to simplify and update scoring. Statistical tests were conducted to examine whether the item pertaining to alcohol use could be broadened to include other drug use, based on feedback from VRAG users. Promising interactions between antisociality and either substance abuse or age were also empirically explored, but did not provide incremental predictive accuracy.

The result is a 12-item actuarial risk assessment instrument. The items and their range of scores are shown in Table 7.3, and Harris et al. (2015) provided an extensive scoring manual with norms and answers to frequently asked questions. A prorating system was created, as with the VRAG, allowing the VRAG-R to be used for offenders with four or fewer missing items.

Reliability, Psychometric Properties, and Validity

Independent scoring of the VRAG-R for 10 offenders by two experienced raters yielded ICC = .99. The mean score was 8.61 for recidivists and −8.29 for non-recidivists. In construction, the VRAG-R showed a large predictive effect for dichotomous violent recidivism, AUC = .76, non-significantly higher than the original VRAG. In a validation sample of the remaining 300 cases, the AUC was .75 over the entire follow-up with fairly stable values over the fixed follow-ups of 6 months to 49 years, showing a consistently large effect.

Table 7.3 Violence Risk Appraisal Guide-Revised Items and Ranges Indicating Relative Weights

Item	Score Range
1. Lived with both parents to age 16	4
2. Elementary school maladjustment	7
3. Alcohol or drug problems	6
4. Marital status	2
5. Nonviolent criminal history	8
6. Failure on prior conditional release	6
7. Age at index offense[a]	9
8. Violent criminal history	6
9. Prior admissions to correctional institutions	8
10. Conduct disorder	7
11. Sex offending	5
12. Antisociality	12

Note: [a] Inversely scored item. See Harris, Rice et al. (2015) for VRAG-R definitions, instructions, norms, and practice materials.

An initial test of the VRAG-R to predict institutional violence (for which it was not designed) among 76 forensic patients was unsuccessful (Hogan & Olver, 2016). However, among 120 adult male correctional offenders in Canada, followed for an average of nearly 18 years, the VRAG-R predicted general and violent recidivism with AUCs of .65 to .66 (Glover et al., 2017). In a similar sample of 296 correctional offenders with a history of sex offenses, the VRAG-R predicted violent recidivism against adults and children in 5- and 10-year follow-ups, with AUCs of .70 to .78, and sexual outcomes with AUCs of .60 to .67 (associations with child-specific sexual offenses did not achieve statistical significance; Olver & Seewall, 2018). Another validation of the VRAG-R's predictive accuracy for violent recidivism among 534 sexual offenders within an average 7.6 years after release from prison in Austria yielded AUCs of .75 to .78 for violent and general recidivism, respectively, and .61 to .63 for sexual outcomes (Gregório Hertz, Rettenberger, & Eher, 2019).

Use of the VRAG-R vs. VRAG and SORAG

Although the VRAG and SORAG are roughly equivalent to the VRAG-R in predictive accuracy, the latter offers considerable advantages for the assessment of both sexual and violent offenders. In particular, the VRAG-R is much easier to score than its predecessors and is likely to be scored more reliably in field settings because it does not require administration of the entire PCL-R.

The Ontario Domestic Assault Risk Assessment (ODARA)

Description

The ODARA is a 13-item actuarial instrument designed to assess the risk of violent recidivism against a female domestic partner among men with a police report of such violence (Hilton et al., 2004). Development, scoring, and validation of the ODARA have been described in detail elsewhere (Hilton, Harris, & Rice, 2010; Hilton, in press) including norms, scoring details, answers to frequently asked questions, and practice case material. The 13 equally weighted dichotomous ODARA items are presented in Table 7.4. An item is treated as missing when the available documentation indicates that it might be present but the information is incomplete or ambiguous. The ODARA score may be prorated for up to five missing items, with some loss of predictive accuracy (Hilton, Harris, Popham, & Lang, 2010). Similar to the VRAG tools, ODARA scores are associated with one of seven categories, each with a known probability of domestic assault recidivism in an average of 51 months and increasing linearly from 5% in the lowest category to 70% in the highest. Norms also indicate the percentile rank for each ODARA score category (Hilton, in press; Hilton, Harris, Popham et al., 2010).

The ODARA differs from the other assessments in this chapter in that it was designed not to require a comprehensive psychosocial history. Created in collaboration with the Ontario Provincial Police primarily for police officers to use at the scene of a domestic call or during routine subsequent investigation, the ODARA was designed for efficient scoring based on information available to front-line users. The ODARA is also suitable for use in a structured interview by nurses, shelter counselors, or other victim service workers (Hilton, Harris, & Holder, 2009); however, it has not been validated without criminal record data.

Method of and Rationale for Development

Outcome variable

The original outcome variable was a subsequent physical assault against a woman with whom the man was living or had lived with at any time. The assault had to be evident either in narrative police reports (regardless of whether criminal charges were filed), or in criminal justice archives of charges and convictions. This approach was taken because the ODARA was expected to inform front-line law enforcement officers and other professionals before (or in the absence of) the decision to arrest or charge. It was also expected to inform conditional release decisions by police and courts after charges were filed. In subsequent analyses, ODARA scores also predicted subsequent criminal charges and convictions for domestic assault recidivism (Hilton, Carter, Harris, & Sharpe, 2008).

The development sample was followed up for an average of 4.8 years. Time at risk was initially defined for each offender as the time between his index assault and the date police and criminal records were retrieved for follow-up, or until the date associated with his next instance of domestic assault in the official record, regardless of any nonviolent or nondomestic offenses (mean = 4.3 years). Because we did not know how long an offender had spent in pre-trial or sentenced custody for nondomestic offenses, we could not compute the duration of actual opportunity to recidivate, and all cases without such opportunity were necessarily counted as non-recidivists. In addition, offenders who committed even very serious violent reoffenses resulting in conviction were treated as non-recidivists if the victim was not a female partner. In subsequent cross-validation, this restriction substantially reduced the predictive accuracy reported compared to that obtained when such nondomestic violent recidivists were dropped from the sample (Hilton & Harris, 2009).

Independent variables

We examined all variables for which there was any existing empirical support in the prediction of violent or criminal recidivism; items from existing nonactuarial domestic violence risk assessments; and all information about the offender, victim, their relationship, and the index and prior domestic incidents that we could glean from the police records. We excluded from consideration, however, any variable that could not reasonably be obtained by front-line investigating police officers.

Construction Sample

The goal was an actuarial instrument that predicted violent recidivism against a female domestic partner. The construction sample comprised 589 cases extracted in reverse chronological order from a large police archive covering most areas of Ontario, a province inhabited by over a third of the population of Canada. All cases in which there was clear evidence that a man had committed a physical assault (or, rarely, threatened death with a weapon in hand) were included (Hilton et al., 2004). Because no cases meeting these criteria were excluded on the basis of location, age, ethnicity, or socioeconomic status, the resulting sample was thought to represent the population of men with a police record for domestic assault; subsequent cross-validation with cases selected from Ontario's largest urban region supported this claim (Hilton, Harris et al., 2008).

Analytic Strategy

Potential items not yielding statistically significant bivariate associations with the outcome variable were dropped from consideration at the first step. Then, logistic regression with dichotomous domestic assault recidivism as the dependent variable, and setwise, stepwise selection of incrementally and independently valid predictor variables, was used in bootstrapped analyses (Hilton et al., 2004). Potential items were analyzed in six categories: index assault details, domestic offense history, nondomestic offense history, sociodemographic characteristics, relationship details, and victim reports. A final regression analysis selected the incremental and independent predictors from each set (Hilton et al., 2004).

Reliability, Psychometric Properties, and Validity

Mean ODARA score on construction was 2.89 (SD = 2.14, standard error of measurement = .48), and interrater reliability was ICC ≥ .90 among research coders. Subsequent tests of reliability and scoring accuracy with police officers and other front-line users from several disciplines replicated very high interrater reliabilities as well (ICC > .90) and average scoring errors of less than a half point after one-day training or online training (Hilton et al., 2004; Hilton & Ham, 2015; Hilton, Harris, Rice, Eke, & Lowe-Wetmore, 2007). ODARA norms, 95% confidence intervals, and low standard error of measurement indicate that cases have a probability of less than .05 of misclassification by more than one ODARA category (Hilton et al., 2004).

The ODARA predicted domestic assault recidivism (base rate = 30%) with a large effect size (Rice & Harris, 2005): AUC was .77 on construction and .72 on cross-validation with 100 comparable cases (Hilton et al., 2004). In a different sample limited to 346 men with an in-depth correctional file, AUC was .65 (Hilton, Harris, et al., 2008) and, in a third independent cross-validation limited to 391 men without such a record, AUC was .67, but up to .80 (and .74 on average) when using equal samples of domestic assault recidivists and men with no violent reoffenses (Hilton & Harris, 2009). The latter two successful replications included new samples drawn from the same police archive as used for ODARA construction, but these were supplemented by several hundred drawn from similar archives (according to the same criteria) of metropolitan police services in Canada's largest city. ODARA scores were associated with dichotomous domestic assault recidivism, the number of recidivistic offenses during follow-up, their severity and seriousness, and an estimate of the rapidity of recidivism (Hilton et al., 2004; Hilton, Harris et al., 2008).

The ODARA has since been reported to predict violent recidivism against an intimate partner in samples drawn from either police reports or custodial populations, and following index assaults not limited to a current or prior cohabiting relationship (e.g., Gerth, Rossegger, Singh, & Endrass, 2015; Hilton & Eke, 2016; Hilton, Harris et al., 2010; Jung & Buro, 2017; Luaria, McEwan, Luebbers, Simmons, & Ogloff, 2017; Olver & Jung, 2017; Rettenberger & Eher, 2013; Seewald, Rossegger, Urbaniok, & Endrass, 2017). It has been associated with intimate partner violence recidivism among female offenders with an AUC of .72, although women appear to recidivate at a substantially lower rate than men (Hilton, Popham, Lang, & Harris, 2014). In further research using the ODARA, we have reported that users make more proficient risk-related decisions when they have use of the ODARA score in their investigation (Hilton, Harris, & Rice, 2007), and that intimate partner violence offenders commit a broad range of additional offense types, also predicted by the ODARA (Hilton & Eke, 2016).

We have often been asked about the validity of domestic assault risk assessment in same-sex relationships, but to date we have been unable to identify a sufficiently large sample of such cases in official reports. Although some ODARA items are potentially changeable, as of yet there have been no studies of the predictive accuracy of change scores on the ODARA, or of putatively dynamic variables in any domestic violence risk assessment.

The Domestic Violence Risk Appraisal Guide (DVRAG)

Description

The DVRAG is a 14-item actuarial instrument that assesses a domestic assaulter's risk of violent recidivism against his partner among men with a police record for such violence (Hilton, Harris et al., 2008). It is intended for use only when there is sufficient correctional or clinical information to conduct an in-depth assessment, similar to the VRAG tools. The DVRAG items (Table 7.4) are the 13 ODARA items (now weighted) and PCL-R score. Development, scoring,

Table 7.4 Ontario Domestic Assault Risk Assessment and Domestic Violence Risk Appraisal Guide Items with DVRAG Ranges Indicating Relative Weights

Item	DVRAG Range[a]
1. Prior domestic assaults in the police record	6
2. Prior nondomestic assaults in the police record	6
3. Prior incarceral sentence of at least 30 days	3
4. Failure on prior conditional release	3
5. Threat to harm or kill anyone else at the index incident	1
6. Confinement of partner at index incident	1
7. Victim concern about possible future domestic assaults	2
8. Number of children	2
9. Victim's biological children from a previous partner	3
10. Violence against nondomestic victims	8
11. Substance abuse score	4
12. Assault on victim when pregnant	5
13. Barriers to victim support	5
14. Psychopathy Checklist (Hare, 2003) score[b]	7

Note: [a] All ODARA items are dichotomous. [b] Not included in the ODARA. See Hilton (in press) for updated definitions, instructions, norms, and practice materials.

and validation of the DVRAG are described in detail elsewhere (Hilton, in press; Hilton, Harris, Popham et al., 2010) including norms, scoring details, answers to frequently asked questions, and practice case material. The DVRAG can be prorated when as many as five items are missing (Hilton, in press; Hilton, Harris, Popham et al., 2010). The DVRAG gives more discrimination at the higher end, and less at the lower end, than the ODARA, its front-line companion tool.

Each DVRAG score is associated with one of seven categories, each with a known likelihood of domestic assault recidivism based on an average 5.1-year follow up and increasing linearly from 14% in the lowest category to 100% in the highest. Each category is associated with a percentile range to evaluate individuals' risk in comparison to a large sample of domestic assault offenders with a correctional history. Users should demonstrate they can score the DVRAG to an acceptable level of interrater reliability and should have either training in scoring the PCL-R or access to a reliable PCL-R score for the offender.

Development and Validation

The DVRAG was developed and cross-validated on cases from the ODARA research that had a correctional risk-needs assessment and sufficient information for reliable scoring of several additional assessments whose incremental validity was compared. This sample exhibited more domestic assault recidivism (49%) than had the larger ODARA sample over a similar average follow-up.

Outcome Variables

Unlike the other instruments described in this chapter, the DVRAG's components were selected on the basis of their association with multiple outcome variables: dichotomous domestic assault recidivism, the number of such offenses, the number involving severe violence, the Cormier-Lang score (Harris et al., 2015) for the seriousness of subsequent criminal charges for domestic assault, and the total victim injury caused in recidivistic domestic assaults (Hilton, Harris et al., 2008).

Independent Variables

The method used to develop the DVRAG involved testing scores on existing assessment instruments: the ODARA (Hilton et al., 2004), *Spousal Assault Risk Assessment* (SARA; Kropp and Gibas, Chapter 16 in this volume), the *Danger Assessment*, (DA; Campbell, 2007, *Domestic Violence Screening Instrument* (DVSI; Williams & Houghton, 2004), PCL-R (Hare, 2003) and a nine-item modification of the VRAG (ever married, female victim, and DSM-III schizophrenia were nearly invariant). Subsidiary analyses evaluated the incremental value of variables pertaining to the perpetrator's history of childhood aggression and antisociality, and exposure to abuse, neglect, and witnessing domestic violence as a child.

Analytic Strategy

The primary empirical question addressed in developing the DVRAG was, "If users have already completed the ODARA, what additional formal assessment can provide incremental value in assessing risk of domestic assault recidivism?" We anticipated a coherent system of actuarial assessment in which front-line users would derive an optimal appraisal of risk given available resources using the ODARA, which would inform and be refined by in-depth information for the purposes of sentencing, parole decisions, intervention prioritization, and other decisions further in the criminal justice process when additional assessment resources were available. Thus, we first identified the best bivariate predictors of each of the five outcomes. Then we used multivariate methods to identify which formal clinical assessments afforded the strongest independent and incremental value to their prediction.

PCL-R score was the best bivariate predictor of all but one outcome and made the only statistically significant independent and incremental improvement to the ODARA in four of the five outcomes. The DVRAG was established as the 13 ODARA items and the PCL-R score. Subsidiary analyses with all five outcomes indicated that no improvement to DVRAG accuracy was achieved by adding items reflecting childhood history of antisociality, abuse, and neglect. Weights for all 14 DVRAG items were derived using the same method employed for the VRAG tools (Nuffield, 1982).

Reliability, Psychometric Properties, and Validity

Mean DVRAG score in the development sample was 2.9 (SD = 8.9). Interrater reliability on new correctional file cases was r = .92, and standard error of measurement = 2.2. An experienced forensic clinician achieved acceptable reliability (r = .83) without specific DVRAG training (Hilton, Harris et al., 2008). Available reliability data and 95% confidence intervals for DVRAG categories imply a probability of less than .05 of being misclassified by more than one DVRAG category.

The DVRAG predicted dichotomous domestic assault recidivism with an AUC = .71 in the development sample and .70 in a second sample (base rate = 41%) of 346 cases (the same sample as that reported earlier as the second ODARA cross-validation sample; Hilton, Harris et al., 2008). In this cross-validation, the DVRAG was more accurate than the ODARA and each of the other tools evaluated. DVRAG score also significantly predicted the number of new assaults, their severity and seriousness, and victim injury (Pearson r's = .29 to .44 in cross-validation) and almost always did so more accurately than the other tools. In the combined samples, the PCL-R and modified VRAG predicted all five domestic assault outcomes and performed better than the nonactuarial domestic assault risk assessment instruments. Testing the DVRAG in a sample of 94 offenders incarcerated in Ontario, Canada, Gray (2012) reported an AUC of .713 for intimate partner violence at follow-up. Rettenberger and Eher (2013) reported an AUC of .71 among 66 domestic sex offenders in Austria.

Limitations and Future Directions: The Challenge of Actuarial Violence Risk Assessment

Developing and validating an actuarial assessment with a large effect in the assessment of violence risk does not guarantee its universal acceptance. After two decades, we recognize several thorny issues that lie outside the comparatively straightforward matter of empirically measured AUCs in follow-up studies. A few of these problems are technical. For example, if true base rates are very low (or very high), it can be argued (e.g., Grove & Vrieze, 2008, but also see Mossman, 2008) that the most appropriate decision is to treat all cases the same (e.g., release everyone), especially if the costs associated with false positive and false negative errors are regarded as equivalent (Harris & Rice, 2007a; Rice & Harris, 1995). An actuarial tool sharpens the focus on what is unknown (e.g., the true cost of misses versus false alarms) in ways that reliance on clinical intuition evidently does not. For example, actuarial data can be plotted in terms of sensitivity as a function of false alarm to illustrate the relative costs of decision errors. Elsewhere we have addressed some of these technical and values issues (Harris & Rice, 2007a), for example, in showing there are more data upon which to estimate long-term base rates than some commentators have implied.

Other troubles pertain to a misunderstanding and miscommunication of the statistical premises of actuarial risk assessment. In this regard, we note that Hart, Michie, and Cooke (2007) claimed that actuarial instrument scores are so imprecise as to be "virtually meaningless" and inapplicable to the individual offender, a claim now resoundingly refuted (e.g., Harris, Lowenkamp, & Hilton, 2015; Harris, Rice, & Quinsey, 2008; Imrey & Dawid, 2015; Mossman, 2015). We share some commentators' personal disagreement with aspects of statutes mandating preventative detention and incapacitation. However, elsewhere we have disagreed with Hart and colleagues' confusion of "precision" with "accuracy" leading to inappropriate standards for accuracy (Harris et al., 2008).

More fundamentally, however, we have not always appreciated the profoundly counter-intuitive nature of actuarial assessment (Harris, 2003). The fact that actuarial assessment is more accurate than clinical judgment guarantees that optimal risk assessment frequently forces practitioners to make decisions contrary to everything their own instincts, feelings, and experiences tell them. No doubt this is made even more difficult by an evolutionary history that has left each of us with an implicit (but powerfully influential) "theory of mind" facilitating human social interaction by providing serviceable causes and predictions for the conduct of others (Platek, Keenan, & Shackelford, 2007). Those who develop actuarial systems for insurance or weather forecasting need not surmount inherent theories-of-mortality or theories-of-meteorology. But optimal implementation of actuarial assessment in the prediction of human behavior surely faces resistance due to a specialized universal certainty that we know why people act the way they do and can use that knowledge to anticipate their actions.

We now believe that the benefits of actuarial risk assessment are becoming more widely understood, and experience in one of our own institutions indicates that such tools are used in practice than 10 or 15 years ago. Previously, forensic patient release decisions by an independent mental health review board were unrelated to actuarial scores overall but were related to such invalid indicators as physical attractiveness and perceived insight (Hilton & Simmons, 2001). Subsequently, a small positive association between risk and clinicians' recommendations to the review board was observed (McKee, Harris, & Rice, 2007). Our most recent analysis indicated that higher-risk patients were more likely to be detained in the most secure facility (Hilton, Simpson, & Ham, 2016). We regard such evidence of the association between dispositional decisions and actuarial measures that have a demonstrable empirical relationship to the outcome of inter-est as consistent with offenders' liberty interests, with the protection of the community, and with cost-effective allocation of resources.

Appendix—Examples

Space limitations preclude exemplifying the comprehensive psychosocial evaluation that forms the basis for VRAG-R and DVRAG scoring. Full accounts of that process, guidelines, norms, and practice materials are presented elsewhere (Hilton, in press; Hilton, Harris, Popham et al., 2010; Harris et al., 2015). Here we present brief synopses, especially to illustrate recommended formats for reporting actuarial scores for individual cases. The details reflect true cases rendered anonymous.

Example 1: VRAG-R in Case With Nonsexual Offense Charges

Brief History

Jesse Flynn is a 32-year-old, never-married male who was recently evaluated by a forensic mental health team at the request of the court to assess his mental state at the time of the July 12, 2010, assault of the mother of his live-in girlfriend of 3 years, and his risk of violent recidivism. Police reports and Mr. Flynn's subsequent self-report indicate that he returned home following a long day of work, briefly ate dinner, and smoked marijuana. Mr. Flynn then assaulted his girlfriend's mother, who had recently moved in with them, striking and stabbing her several times. The mother incurred serious wounds, but Mr. Flynn's girlfriend was able to run to a nearby residence and notify the authorities. Mr. Flynn was subsequently arrested at his trailer without incident. He was charged with Assault in the 1st Degree.

When interviewed in police detention on July 12 and 13, 2010, Mr. Flynn was disorganized in his presentation. Speech was pressured, and content was bizarre and incomprehensible. He initially stated that his girlfriend's mother came at him with a knife, but later stated that she had engaged in "demon talk" and that he felt threatened in response. Family members reported to the mental health team that Mr. Flynn demonstrated a pattern of erratic behavior in the days preceding the offense, abruptly quitting a job with a company owned by his stepfather, and had made veiled complaints about visual and auditory hallucinations. Following his arrest and deten-tion, Mr. Flynn evidenced florid delusional beliefs marked by paranoid themes and command auditory hallucinations.

Mr. Flynn was born and raised in central Michigan, the youngest of three males. Records indi-cate that his biological parents divorced when he was approximately four years of age. Following his parents' divorce, Mr. Flynn had only intermittent and infrequent contact with his father and was predominantly raised by his mother. Mr. Flynn reported that he did establish a stable relation-ship with his stepfather after his mother remarried when Mr. Flynn was in his middle teen years.

Behavioral difficulties first became apparent when Mr. Flynn was in the first grade. He was noted to have difficulty sitting still and was described as impulsive. His behavioral problems worsened over the years such that by the fifth grade Mr. Flynn was described as assaultive and aggressive, pre-scribed Ritalin, and was placed in a self-contained classroom. Mr. Flynn was described as becoming particularly aggressive when being disciplined for defiant behavior and on at least one occasion "trashed the classroom." Behavioral difficulties continued throughout his middle school and high school years, with Mr. Flynn reporting continued special education placement due to learning dif-ficulties. When interviewed as part of the current evaluation, he reported that he was expelled in the ninth grade following four prior suspensions for fighting. Mr. Flynn demonstrated better behavioral control in the remainder of high school with no suspensions, but continued to have failing grades. Despite all the academic challenges, Mr. Flynn graduated from high school in 2001.

Mr. Flynn reported that he began to use marijuana at the age of 12, and began drinking alcohol at the age of 13. He reported getting into a brawl at age 16 at a party in which he had been smoking marijuana and drinking. Criminal and correctional records show that he was charged with Malicious Mischief and Assault in the 4th Degree, incarcerated for 1 week, and placed on probation. As a condition of his probation, Mr. Flynn was referred to inpatient substance abuse treatment which he successfully completed, although in the ensuing years he relapsed, resumed using alcohol and marijuana, and began use of heroin.

Records also show that, while on probation for the Assault in the 4th Degree, Mr. Flynn incurred a charge for Assault in the 2nd Degree for his involvement in a gang-related incident in which another teen was seriously injured. Following one week of incarceration, Mr. Flynn was again released on probation which he successfully completed.

As an adult, Mr. Flynn incurred a charge for Driving Under the Influence of Alcohol and was sentenced to 365 days confinement, 362 days suspended, a $5000 fine, and revocation of his license pending completion of in-patient substance abuse treatment. While under court supervision, Mr. Flynn was again arrested and charged with Driving with License Suspended or Revoked. Records were unclear as to how Mr. Flynn was sanctioned for this latter offense; however, it does not appear that Mr. Flynn was incarcerated.

Throughout his 20s, Mr. Flynn maintained intermittent employment, principally performing warehouse and construction work. Employment became more sporadic in the weeks preceding the index offense as Mr. Flynn's behavior became more erratic and began to evidence the early symptoms of psychosis.

Actuarial Assessment

Mr. Flynn's score on the Violence Risk Appraisal Guide-Revised (VRAG-R), computed using criminal records and interview material gathered shortly after his admission, placed his risk for violent recidivism (defined as receiving a subsequent criminal charge or equivalent for a violent offense) in a group of offenders that comprised the eighth (i.e., second highest) of nine VRAG-R categories. Among male violent offenders in the studies described earlier, 11% obtained higher VRAG-R scores and approximately 78% in this category met the research criteria for having reoffended violently within an average of 12 years of opportunity after release.

Follow-up

Mr. Flynn was ultimately adjudicated Not Guilty by Reason of Insanity for the assault and remanded to a state mental hospital where he is currently undergoing intense pharmacological and behavioral treatment. Mr. Flynn is reportedly doing well and anticipates completion of treatment program in the locked psychiatric unit within the next two years, at which time he will enter an open psychiatric ward and begin a gradual transition into the community.

Example 2: VRAG-R in Case With Sexual Offense Charges

Brief History

John Doe (Date of birth: January 1, 1958) was referred for a risk assessment for purposes of calibrating release conditions as he transitioned into the community at the conclusion of his incarceration. Mr. Doe was 54 years old at the time he committed the index offenses which were seven counts of sexual assault against male victims, all between the ages of 9 and 12, and possession of child pornography (videotapes of sexual acts he engaged in with teenage males). He had two prior criminal charges, an indecent assault against a 15-year-old male committed more than a decade ago, and public mischief after he vandalized an acquaintance's car by scratching it with a key along one entire side following a dispute. Convicted in both instances, he was sentenced only to terms of probation for which he fulfilled the requirements without incident.

When interviewed, Mr. Doe described a quiet, socially isolated upbringing, although he was involved in some extracurricular activities such as team sports. This history was confirmed in interviews with his parents, who additionally reported that Mr. Doe obtained good grades and exhibited no discipline or behavior problems at school. They described no behaviors indicative of conduct disorder and there was no history of arrests or contact with police as a juvenile. After graduating from high school, Mr. Doe obtained full-time employment as a public sector employee. He lived with both his biological parents until moving into his own residence in his mid-20s. Mr. Doe acknowledged that he had a series of "minor problems" and technical violations at work that eventually resulted in his dismissal after 20 years of employment. He received social assistance, eventually filed for bankruptcy, and had been unemployed for almost two years at the time of his arrest. Mr. Doe and his parents denied any problems or concerns relating to alcohol or drug use, there was no history of substance abuse in his family of origin, and, according to police reports, neither alcohol nor drugs were involved in any of his offenses.

Mr. Doe acknowledged that he was sexually attracted to adolescent males and "young-looking" adult males. Mr. Doe said that he became sexually active at the age of 15 with a similar-aged male friend. He reported having approximately 300 to 400 male partners in his lifetime, most of them casual and hired as prostitutes. He was never married or involved in a common-law relationship. Mr. Doe stated that he restricted his sexual behavior to adult males until after he was dismissed from his public sector job and became distressed by his financial and employment prospects.

Mr. Doe scored 9 out of 40 on the PCL-R, and 1 on the five Facet 4 items (poor behavioral controls, early behavior problems, juvenile delinquency, revocation of conditional release, criminal versatility).

Actuarial Assessment

Mr. Flynn's score on the Violence Risk Appraisal Guide-Revised (VRAG-R), based upon review of his criminal records and the interview material summarized in this report, placed his risk of violent recidivism (defined as a subsequent criminal charge or equivalent for a violent offense) in a group of offenders that comprised the second lowest of nine VRAG-R categories. Among male violent offenders in the studies described earlier, 22% obtained lower VRAG-R scores, and approximately 24% in this category met the research criteria for having reoffended violently within an average of 12 years of opportunity after release.

Follow-up

Based upon his score falling into the second lowest VRAG-R category, it was determined that Mr. Doe could be managed in the community without undue allocation of supervisory resources. In accordance with case management plans, Mr. Doe was therefore recommended for graduated release to the community with ongoing supervision and involvement in community-based sexual deviancy treatment.

Example 3: ODARA in a Case of Intimate Partner Violence Reported to Police

Police Occurrence Report #1184

Police were dispatched to 47 First Street, Nortown, at 8:15 PM on October 15, 2006, in response to a call from a neighbor complaining about noise. Dispatched officers encountered a female who appeared to have been crying. No one else was at the location. While Officer #6409 was interviewing the woman, her husband (the accused) returned. He has no previous record with police. Based on statements from both parties and witnesses, officers determined that, at approximately 8:00 PM, while playing checkers, the victim and the accused began to argue about household expenses. The argument became heated and had been going on for approximately 25 minutes when the accused became very agitated and attempted to leave the room. The victim claims she demanded that he stay to deal with the problem at which time he told her to "Just shut up," and slapped her with an open hand across the face. He then left the residence on foot. Upon his return, the accused stated that he had gone to a friend's house. There was an odor of alcohol on his breath. He was cooperative with the investigation and was arrested and taken to the station without incident.

The victim reported she and the accused have been married for 18 years and currently reside together at 47 First Street. She stated that they argue regularly but most of the time it does not become physical. When asked about prior occurrences, she stated that he has grabbed or pushed her but could not recall a specific occasion. She stated that he is not violent with others and will walk away rather than fight. However, the victim stated that she is now worried that he will hit her again. The victim claimed that the accused drinks socially and will have several beers on the weekend, does not have a major drinking problem, but does tend to be more easily angered when drinking. She stated that the accused drank three beers during the evening and she was drinking ginger ale. Their only child is the victim's 20-year-old daughter from a previous relationship.

Actuarial Assessment

Based on the police investigation, the accused received a score of 3 on the Ontario Domestic Assault Risk Assessment (ODARA). This score comprises the fourth, or middle, of seven ODARA categories. Among domestic assaulters in the studies described earlier, seven out of ten scored 3 or less on the ODARA, and approximately 30% of those in this category committed another assault on a female partner that came to the attention of the police within an average of five years.

Follow-up

Based on the ODARA score submitted by police, the accused was eligible for bail. On December 19, 2006, the accused attended court and pled guilty to domestic assault and received a sentence of three months' probation. The only subsequent police contact occurred nine months later when officers were called to investigate neighbors' complaints about a loud argument. The accused and his wife admitted they were having an argument but both denied there had been any assault or threats of physical violence. Officers' investigation revealed no evidence to the contrary. A warning was issued and no further police action was taken.

Note

1. Paranthetically, our research indicates that the offender's age at first offense or index offense more effectively subsumes any attenuation in risk than simple aging in custody (Harris & Rice, 2007b; Rice & Harris, 2014).

References

Ægisdóttir, S., White, M. J., Spengler, P. M., Maugherman, A. S., Anderson, L. A., Cook, R. S., . . . Rush, J. D. (2006). The meta-analysis of clinical judgment project: Fifty-six years of accumulated research on clinical versus statistical prediction. *The Counseling Psychologist, 34,* 341–382.

Barbaree, H. E., Langton, C. M., & Peacock, E. J. (2006). Different actuarial risk measures produce different risk rankings for sexual offenders. *Sexual Abuse: A Journal of Research and Treatment, 18,* 423–440.

Barbaree, H. E., Seto, M. C., Langton, C. M., & Peacock, E. J. (2001). Evaluating the predictive accuracy of six risk assessment instruments for adult sex offenders. *Criminal Justice and Behavior, 28,* 490–521.

Campbell, J. C. (2007). Prediction of homicide of and by battered women. In J. C. Campbell (Ed.), *Assessing dangerousness: Violence by sexual offenders, batterers, and child abusers.* (2nd ed., pp. 85–104). New York: Springer.

Campbell, M., French, S., & Gendreau, P. (2009). The prediction of violence in adult offenders: A meta-analytic comparison of instruments and methods of assessment. *Criminal Justice and Behavior, 36,* 567–590. doi:10.1177/0093854809333610

Churcher, F. P., Mills, J. F., & Forth, A. E. (2016). The predictive validity of the two-tiered violence risk estimates scale (TTV) in a long-term follow-up of violent offenders. *Psychological Services, 13,* 232–245. doi:10.1037/ser0000073

Coid, J. W., Yang, M., Ullrich, S., Zhang, T., Sizmur, S., Farrington, D. P . . . Rogers, R. D. (2015). Improving accuracy of risk prediction for violence: Does changing the outcome matter? *International Journal of Forensic Mental Health, 14,* 23–32. doi:10.1080/14999013.2014.974085

Coid, J., Yang, M., Ullrich, S., Zhang, T., Sizmur, S., Roberts, C., . . . Rogers, R. D. (2009). Gender differences in structured risk assessment: Comparing the accuracy of five instruments. *Journal of Consulting and Clinical Psychology, 77,* 337–348. doi:10.1037/a0015155

Crocker, A. G., Nicholls, T. L., Seto, M. C., Côté, G., Charette, Y., & Caulet, M. (2015). The national trajectory project of individuals found not criminally responsible on account of mental disorder in Canada. Part 1: Context and methods. *Canadian Journal of Psychiatry, 60,* 98–105.

Dempster, R. J. (1998). *Prediction of sexually violent recidivism: A comparison of risk assessment instruments* (Unpublished Master's thesis). Department of Psychology, Simon Fraser University, Burnaby, BC.

Douglas, K. S., & Skeem, J. L. (2005). Violence risk assessment: Getting specific about being dynamic. *Psychology, Public Policy, and Law, 11,* 347–383.

Douglas, K. S., Yeomans, M., & Boer, D. F. (2005). Comparative validity analysis of multiple measures of violence risk in a sample of criminal offenders. *Criminal Justice and Behavior, 32,* 479–510.

Doyle, M., Carter, S., Shaw, J., & Dolan, M. (2012). Predicting community violence from patients discharged from acute mental health units in England. *Social Psychiatry and Psychiatric Epidemiology, 47,* 627–637.

Doyle, M., & Dolan, M. (2006). Predicting community violence from patients discharged from community mental health services. *British Journal of Psychiatry, 189,* 520–526.

Ducro, C., & Pham, T. (2006). Evaluation of the SORAG and the static-99 on Belgian sex offenders committed to a forensic facility. *Sexual Abuse: A Journal of Research and Treatment, 18,* 15–25.

Edens, J. F., Penson, B. N., Ruchensky, J. R., Cox, J., & Smith, S. T. (2016). Interrater reliability of violence risk appraisal guide scores provided in Canadian criminal proceedings. *Psychological Assessment.* Advance online publication. doi:10.1037/pas0000278

Eisenbarth, H., Osterheider, M., Nedopil, N., & Stadtland, C. (2012). Recidivism in female offenders: PCL-R lifestyle factor and VRAG show predictive validity in a German sample. *Behavioral Sciences & the Law, 30,* 575–584. doi:10.1002/bsl.2013

Fedoroff, J. P., Richards, D., Ranger, R., & Curry, S. (2016). The predictive validity of common risk assessment tools in men with intellectual disabilities and problematic sexual behaviors. *Research in Developmental Disabilities, 57,* 29–38. doi:10.1016/j.ridd.2016.06.011

Folino, J. O. (2015). Predictive efficacy of violence risk assessment instruments in Latin-America. *European Journal of Psychology Applied to Legal Context, 7,* 51–58. doi:10.1016/j.ejpal.2014.11.006

Gerth, J., Rossegger, A., Singh, J. P., & Endrass, J. (2015). Assessing the risk of severe intimate partner violence: Validating the DyRiAS in Switzerland. *Archives of Forensic Psychology, 1*(2), 1–15.

Grann, M., & Wedin, I. (2002). Risk factors for recidivism among spousal assault and spousal homicide offenders. *Psychology, Crime and Law, 8,* 5–23.

Gray, A. L. (2012). *Assessing risk for intimate partner violence: A cross-validation of the ODARA and DVRAG within a sample of incarcerated offenders* (Unpublished Master's thesis). Carleton University, Ottawa.

Gray, N. S., Fitzgerald, S., Taylor, J., MacCulloch, M. J., & Snowden, R. J. (2007). Predicting future reconviction in offenders with intellectual disabilities: The predictive efficacy of VRAG, PCL-SV and the HCR-20. *Psychological Assessment, 19*, 474–479.

Grove, W. M., & Meehl, P. E. (1996). Comparative efficiency of informal (subjective, impressionistic) and formal (mechanical, algorithmic) prediction procedures: The clinical—statistical controversy. *Psychology, Public Policy, and Law, 2*, 293–323.

Grove, W. M., & Vrieze, S. I. (2008). Predicting sex offender recidivism. I. Correcting for item overselection and accuracy overestimation in scale development. II. Sampling error-induced attenuation of predictive validity over base rate information. *Law and Human Behavior, 32*, 266–278. doi:10.1007/s10979-007-9092-x

Hanson, R. K., & Harris, A. J. R. (2000). Where should we intervene? Dynamic predictors of sexual offense recidivism. *Criminal Justice and Behavior, 27*, 6–35.

Hanson, R. K., & Morton-Bourgon, K. E. (2007). *The accuracy of recidivism risk assessments for sexual offenders: A meta-analysis* (Report No. 2007-01). Ottawa: Public Safety and Emergency Preparedness.

Hare, R. D. (2003). *The revised psychopathy checklist*. Toronto, ON: Multi-Health Systems.

Harris, G. T. (2003). Men in his category have a 50% likelihood, but which half is he in? *Sexual Abuse: A Journal of Research and Treatment, 15*, 389–393.

Harris, G. T., Lowenkamp, C. T., & Hilton, N. Z. (2015). Evidence for risk estimate precision: Implications for individual risk communication. *Behavioral Sciences and the Law, 33*, 111–127. doi:10.1002/bsl.2158

Harris, G. T., & Rice, M. E. (2003). Actuarial assessment of risk among sex offenders. *Annals of the New York Academy of Sciences, 989*, 198–210.

Harris, G. T., & Rice, M. E. (2007a). Characterizing the value of actuarial violence risk assessment. *Criminal Justice and Behavior, 34*, 1638–1656.

Harris, G. T., & Rice, M. E. (2007b). Adjusting actuarial violence risk assessments based on aging and the passage of time. *Criminal Justice and Behavior, 34*, 297–313.

Harris, G. T., & Rice, M. E. (2015). Progress in violence risk assessment and communication: Hypothesis versus evidence. *Behavioral Science and the Law, 33*, 128–145. doi:10.1002/bsl.2157

Harris, G. T., Rice, M. E., & Camilleri, J. A. (2004). Applying a forensic actuarial assessment (the violence risk appraisal guide) to nonforensic patients. *Journal of Interpersonal Violence, 19*, 1063–1074.

Harris, G. T., Rice, M. E., & Cormier, C. A. (2002). Prospective replication of the violence risk appraisal guide in predicting violent recidivism among forensic patients. *Law and Human Behavior, 26*, 377–394.

Harris, G. T., Rice, M. E., & Cormier, C. A. (2013). Research and clinical scoring of the psychopathy checklist can show good agreement. *Criminal Justice and Behavior, 11*, 1349–1362. doi:10.1177/0093854813492959

Harris, G. T., Rice, M. E., & Quinsey, V. L. (1993). Violent recidivism of mentally disordered offenders: The development of a statistical prediction instrument. *Criminal Justice and Behavior, 20*, 315–335.

Harris, G. T., Rice, M. E., & Quinsey, V. L. (2008). Shall evidence-based risk assessment be abandoned? *British Journal of Psychiatry, 192*, 154.

Harris, G. T., Rice, M. E., & Quinsey, V. L. (2010). Allegiance or fidelity? A clarifying reply. *Clinical Psychology: Science and Practice, 17*, 82–89.

Harris, G. T., Rice, M. E., Quinsey, V. L., & Cormier, C. A. (2015). *Violent offenders: Appraising and managing risk* (3rd ed.). Washington, DC: American Psychological Association.

Harris, G. T., Rice, M. E., Quinsey, V. L., Lalumière, M. L., Boer, D., & Lang, C. (2003). A multi-site comparison of actuarial risk instruments for sex offenders. *Psychological Assessment, 15*, 413–425.

Hart, S. D., Michie, C., & Cooke, D. J. (2007). Precision of actuarial risk assessment instruments. *British Journal of Psychiatry, 190*(Suppl. 49), s60–s65.

Hastings, M. E., Krishnan, S., Tangney, J. P., & Stuewig, J. (2011). Predictive and incremental validity of the violence risk appraisal guide scores with male and female jail inmates. *Psychological Assessment, 23*, 174–183. doi:10.1037/a0021290

Glover, A. J. J., Churcher, F. P., Gray, A. L., Mills, J. F., & Nicholson, D. E. (2017). A cross-validation of the violence risk appraisal guide—revised (VRAG—R) within a correctional sample. *Law and Human Behavior, 41*, 507–518. doi:10.1037/lhb0000257

Gregório Hertz, P., Rettenberger, M., & Eher, R. (2019). Cross-validation of the revised version of the violence risk appraisal guide (VRAG-R) in a sample of individuals convicted of sexual offenses. *Sexual Abuse.* Advanced online publication. doi:10.1177/1079063219841901

Hilton, N. Z. (in press). *Domestic violence risk assessment: Tools for effective prediction and management* (2nd ed.). Washington, DC: American Psychological Association.

Hilton, N. Z., Carter, A. M., Harris, G. T., & Sharpe, A. J. B. (2008). Does using non-numerical terms to describe risk aid violence risk communication? Clinician agreement and decision-making. *Journal of Interpersonal Violence, 23,* 171–188.

Hilton, N. Z., & Eke, A. W. (2016). Nonspecialization of criminal careers among intimate partner violence offenders. *Criminal Justice and Behavior, 43,* 1347–1363. doi:10.1177/0093854816637886

Hilton, N. Z., & Ham, E. (2015). Cost-effectiveness of electronic training in domestic violence risk assessment: ODARA 101. *Journal of Interpersonal Violence, 30,* 1065–1073. doi:10.1177/0886260514539762

Hilton, N. Z., & Harris, G. T. (2009). How nonrecidivism affects predictive accuracy: Evidence from a cross-validation of the Ontario domestic assault risk assessment (ODARA). *Journal of Interpersonal Violence, 24,* 326–337. doi:10.1177/0886260508316478

Hilton, N. Z., Harris, G. T., & Holder, N. L. (2009). Actuarial violence risk assessment in hospital-based partner assault clinics. *Canadian Journal of Nursing Research, 40.*

Hilton, N. Z., Harris, G. T., Popham, S., & Lang, C. (2010). Risk assessment among male incarcerated domestic offenders. *Criminal Justice and Behavior, 37,* 815–832. doi:10.1177/ 0093854810368937

Hilton, N. Z., Harris, G. T., & Rice, M. E. (2006). Sixty-six years of research on the clinical versus actuarial prediction of violence. *The Counseling Psychologist, 34,* 400–409.

Hilton, N. Z., Harris, G. T., & Rice, M. E. (2007). The effect of arrest on wife assault recidivism, controlling for pre-arrest risk. *Criminal Justice and Behavior, 34,* 1334–1344.

Hilton, N. Z., Harris, G. T., & Rice, M. E. (2010). *Domestically violent men: Risk assessment for criminal justice, offender intervention, and victim services.* Washington, DC: American Psychological Association.

Hilton, N. Z., Harris, G. T., Rice, M. E., Eke, A. W., & Lowe-Wetmore, T. (2007). Training front-line users in the Ontario domestic assault risk assessment (ODARA), a tool for police domestic investigations. *Canadian Journal of Police and Security Services, 5,* 95–98.

Hilton, N. Z., Harris, G. T., Rice, M. E., Houghton, R. E., & Eke, A. W. (2008). An indepth actuarial assessment for wife assault recidivism: The domestic violence risk appraisal guide. *Law and Human Behavior, 32,* 150–163. doi:10.1007/s10979-007-9088-6

Hilton, N. Z., Harris, G. T., Rice, M. E., Lang, C., Cormier, C. A., & Lines, K. J. (2004). A brief actuarial assessment for the prediction of wife assault recidivism: The Ontario domestic assault risk assessment. *Psychological Assessment, 16,* 267–275.

Hilton, N. Z., Popham, S., Lang, C., & Harris G. T. (2014). Preliminary validation of the ODARA for female intimate partner violence offenders. *Partner Abuse, 5,* 189–203. doi: 10.1891/1946-6560.5.2.189

Hilton, N. Z., & Simmons, J. L. (2001). Actuarial and clinical risk assessment in decisions to release mentally disordered offenders from maximum security. *Law and Human Behavior, 25,* 393–408.

Hilton, N. Z., Simpson, A., & Ham, E. (2016). The increasing influence of risk assessment on forensic patient review board decisions. *Psychological Services, 13,* 223–231. doi:10.1037/ser0000068

Hogan, N. R., & Olver, M. E. (2016). Assessing risk for aggression in forensic psychiatric inpatients: An examination of five measures. *Law and Human Behavior, 40,* 233–243.

Imrey, P. B., & Dawid, P. (2015). A commentary on statistical assessment of violence recidivism risk. *Statistics and Public Policy, 2,* 1–18. doi:10.1080/2330443X.2015.1029338

Janus, E. S., & Meehl, P. E. (1997). Assessing the legal standard for predictions of dangerousness in sex offender commitment proceedings. *Psychology, Public Policy and Law, 3,* 33–64.

Johansen, S. H. (2007). Accuracy of predictions of sexual offense recidivism: A comparison of actuarial and clinical methods. *Dissertation Abstracts International: Section B. The Sciences and Engineering, 68*(3–13), 1929.

Jung, S., & Buro, K. (2017). Appraising risk for intimate partner violence in a police context. *Criminal Justice and Behavior, 44,* 240–260. doi:10.1177/0093854816667974

Langton, C. M., Barbaree, H. E., Seto, M. C., Peacock, E. J., Harkins, L., & Hansen, K. T. (2007). Actuarial assessment of risk for reoffense among adult sex offenders. *Criminal Justice and Behavior, 34,* 37–59.

Luaria, I., McEwan, T. E., Luebbers, S., Simmons, M., & Ogloff, J. R. P. (2017). Evaluating the Ontario domestic assault risk assessment in an Australian frontline police setting. *Criminal Justice and Behavior, 44,* 1545–1558. doi:10.1177/0093854817738280

Lindsay, W. R., Hogue, T., Taylor, J. L., Steptoe, L., Mooney, P., O'Brien, G., Johnston, S., & Smith, A. H. W. (2008). Risk assessment in offenders with intellectual disability: A comparison across three levels of security. *International Journal of Offender Therapy and Comparative Criminology, 52,* 90–111.

Livingston, J. D., Chu, K., Milne, T., & Brink, J. (2015). Probationers mandated to receive forensic mental health services in Canada: Risks/needs, service delivery, and intermediate outcomes. *Psychology, Public Policy, and Law, 21,* 72–84. doi:10.1037/law0000031

McDermott, B. E., Quanbeck, C. D., Scott, C. L., Edens, F., & Busse, D. (2007). Examining the role of static and dynamic risk factors in the prediction of in-patient violence. *Law and Human Behavior, 32,* 325–338.

McKee, S. A., Harris, G. T., & Rice, M. E. (2007). Improving forensic tribunal decisions: The role of the clinician. *Behavioral Sciences and the Law, 25,* 485–506.

Meehl, P. E. (1954). *Clinical vs. statistical prediction.* Minneapolis: University of Minnesota Press.

Mossman, D. (2008). Analyzing the performance of risk assessment instruments: A response to Vrieze and Grove (2007). *Law and Human Behavior, 32,* 279–291. doi:10.1007/s10979-007-9123-7.

Mossman, D. (2015). From group data to useful probabilities: The relevance of actuarial risk assessment in individual instances. *Journal of the American Academy of Psychiatry and the Law, 43,* 93–102.

Mulvey, E. P., Odgers, C., Skeem, J., Gardner, W., Schubert, C., & Lidz, C. (2006). Substance use and community violence: A test of the relation at the daily level. *Journal of Consulting and Clinical Psychology, 74,* 743–754.

Nuffield, J. (1982). *Parole decision-making in Canada: Research towards decision guidelines.* Ottawa: Supply and Services Canada.

Olver, M. E., & Jung, S. (2017). Incremental prediction of intimate partner violence: An examination of three risk measures. *Law and Human Behavior, 41,* 440–453. doi:10.1037/lhb0000251

Olver, M. E., Sowden, D., Kingston, D. A., Nicholaichuk, T. P., Gordon, A., Beggs Christofferson, S., & Wong, S. C. P. (2018). Predictive accuracy of VRS-SO risk and change scores in treated Canadian Aboriginal and non-Aboriginal sexual offenders. *Sexual Abuse, 30,* 254–275. doi:10.1177/1079063216649594

Pham, T. H. (2004). *Assessing risk for violence in a Belgian forensic population: Concurrent and predictive validity of the Hare psychopathy checklist, the violence risk assessment guide (VRAG) and the historical clinical risk-20 items (HCR-20).* Unpublished manuscript.

Pham, T. H., Ducro, C., Marghem, B., & Réveillère, J. (2005). Evaluation du risque de récidivie au sein d'une population de délinquants incarcéréré ou interné en Belgique francophone. *Annales Médico Psychologiques, 163,* 842–845.

Platek, S. M., Keenan, J. P., & Shackelford, T. K. (2007). *Evolutionary cognitive neuroscience.* Cambridge, MA: The MIT Press.

Quinsey, V. L., Coleman, G., Jones, B., & Altrows (1997). Proximal antecedents of eloping and reoffending among mentally disordered offenders. *Journal of Interpersonal Violence, 12,* 794–813.

Quinsey, V. L., Jones, G. B., Book, A. S., & Barr, K. N. (2006). The dynamic prediction of antisocial behavior among forensic psychiatric patients: A prospective field study. *Journal of Interpersonal Violence, 21,* 1–27.

Quinsey, V. L., Rice, M. E., & Harris, G. T. (1995). The actuarial prediction of sexual recidivism. *Journal of Interpersonal Violence, 10,* 85–105.

Rettenberger, M., & Eher, R. (2007). Predicting reoffence in sexual offender subtypes: A prospective validation study of the German version of the sex offender risk appraisal guide (SORAG). *Sexual Offender Treatment, 2,* 1–12.

Rettenberger, M., & Eher, R. (2013). Actuarial risk assessment in sexually motivated intimate-partner violence. *Law and Human Behavior, 37,* 75–86. doi:10.1037/b0000001

Rice, M. E. (2008). Current status of violence risk assessment: Is there a role for clinical judgment? In G. Bourgon, R. K. Hanson, J. D. Pozzulo, K. E. Morton Bourgon, & C. L. Tanasichuk (Eds.), *Proceedings of the North American correctional and criminal justice psychology conference* (pp. 20–23). Ottawa: Canadian Psychological Association. Retrieved from www.cpa.ca/cpasite/UserFiles/Documents/Criminal%20Justice/NACCJPC%20Proceedings_Eng_Feb2008.pdf

Rice, M. E., & Harris, G. T. (1995). Violent recidivism: Assessing predictive validity. *Journal of Consulting and Clinical Psychology, 63,* 737–748.

Rice, M. E., & Harris, G. T. (1997). Cross validation and extension of the violence risk appraisal guide for child molesters and rapists. *Law and Human Behavior, 21,* 231–241.

Rice, M. E., & Harris, G. T. (2005). Comparing effect sizes in follow-up studies: ROC, Cohen's d and r. *Law and Human Behavior, 29,* 615–620.

Rice, M. E., & Harris, G. T. (2014). What does it mean when age is related to sex offenders' recidivism? *Law and Human Behavior, 38,* 151–161. doi:10.1037/lhb0000052

Rice, M. E., Harris, G. T., & Cormier, C. A. (1992). Evaluation of a maximum security therapeutic community for psychopaths and other mentally disordered offenders. *Law and Human Behavior, 16,* 399–412.

Rice, M. E., Harris, G. T., & Lang, C. (2013). Validation of and revision to the VRAG and SORAG: The violence risk appraisal guide—revised (VRAG-R). *Psychological Assessment, 25,* 951–965. doi:10.1037/a0032878

Rice, M. E., Harris, G. T., Lang, C., & Bell, V. (1990). Recidivism among male insanity acquittees. *Journal of Psychiatry and Law, 18,* 379–403.

Rice, M. E., Harris, G. T., Lang, C., & Cormier, C. A. (2006). Violent sex offenses: How are they best measured from official records? *Law and Human Behavior, 30,* 525–541.

Rice, M. E., Harris, G. T., & Quinsey, V. L. (1990). A followup of rapists assessed in a maximum security psychiatric facility. *Journal of Interpersonal Violence, 5,* 435–448.

Rice, M. E., Quinsey, V. L., & Harris, G. T. (1991). Sexual recidivism among child molesters released from a maximum security psychiatric institution. *Journal of Consulting and Clinical Psychology, 59,* 381–386.

Seewald, K., Rossegger, A., Urbaniok F., & Endrass, J. (2017). Assessing the risk of intimate partner violence: Expert evaluations versus the Ontario domestic assault risk assessment. *Journal of Forensic Psychology Research and Practice, 17,* 217–231. doi:10.1080/24732850.2017.1326268

Seto, M. C. (2005). Is more better? Combining actuarial risk scales to predict recidivism among adult sex offenders. *Psychological Assessment, 17,* 156–167.

Singh, J. P., Grann, M., & Fazel, S. (2011). A comparative study of violence risk assessment tools: A systematic review and metaregression analysis of 68 studies involving 25,980 participants. *Clinical Psychology Review, 31,* 499–513.

Sjöstedt, G., & Langström, N. (2002). Assessment of risk for criminal recidivism among rapists: A comparison of four different measures. *Psychology, Crime and Law, 8,* 25–40.

Skeem, J. L., Schubert, C., Odgers, C., Mulvey, E. P., Gardner, W., & Lidz, C. (2006). Psychiatric symptoms and community violence among high-risk patients: A test of the relationship at the weekly level. *Journal of Consulting and Clinical Psychology, 74,* 967–979.

Smid, W. J., Kamphuis, J. H., Wever, E. C., & Van Beek, D. J. (2014). A comparison of the predictive properties of nine sex offender risk assessment instruments. *Psychological Assessment, 26,* 691–703. doi:10.1037/a0036616

Snowden, R. J., Gray, N., Taylor, J., & MacCulloch, M. J. (2007). Actuarial prediction of violent recidivism in mentally disordered offenders. *Psychological Medicine, 37,* 1539–1549. doi:10.1017/S0033291707000876

Sturup, J., Edens, J. F., Sörman, K., Karlberg, D., Fredriksson, B., & Kristiansson, M. (2014). Field reliability of the psychopathy checklist-revised among life sentenced prisoners in Sweden. *Law and Human Behavior, 38,* 315–324. doi:10.1037/lhb0000063

Thomson, L. (2005, June). *Risk assessment in patients with schizophrenia in a high security hospital.* Forensic Psychiatry Research Society. Edinburgh: University of Edinburgh.

Urbaniok, F., Noll, T., Grunewald, S., Steinbach, J., & Endrass, J. (2006). Prediction of violent and sexual offences: A replication study of the VRAG in Switzerland. *Journal of Forensic Psychiatry and Psychology, 17,* 23–31.

van Heesch, B., Jeandarme, I., Pouls, C., & Vervaekea, G. (2016). Validity and reliability of the VRAG in a forensic psychiatric medium security population in Flanders. *Psychology, Crime & Law.* Advance online publication. doi:10.1080/1068316X.2016.1168423

Williams, K. R., & Houghton, A. B. (2004). Assessing the risk of domestic violence reoffending: A validation study. *Law and Human Behavior, 28,* 437–455.

Yang, M., Wong, S. C. P., & Coid, J. (2011). The efficacy of violence prediction: A meta-analytic comparison of nine risk assessment tools. *Psychological Bulletin, 136*, 740–767. doi:10.1037/a0020473

Yessine, A. K., & Bonta, J. (2006). Tracking high-risk, violent offenders: An examination of the national flagging system. *Canadian Journal of Criminology and Criminal Justice, 48*, 573–607.

Author Note

Author Note: The first edition of this chapter, "The Violence Risk Appraisal Guide, Sex Offender Risk Appraisal Guide and Violence Risk Appraisal Guide-Revised for Violence Risk Assessment and the Ontario Domestic Assault Risk Assessment and Domestic Violence Risk Appraisal Guide for Domestic Assault Risk Assessment," was authored by Marnie E. Rice, Grant T. Harris, and N. Zoe Hilton. The late Drs. Rice and Harris did not view or approve this second edition. We are indebted to these colleagues for decades of collaboration.

Rational-Actuarial Measures

Chapter 8

Risk/Need Assessment for Adults and Older Adolescents

The Level of Service (LS) Instruments

J. Stephen Wormith and James Bonta

The Level of Service (LS) assessment instruments, from their beginning in the late 1970s (Andrews, 1982), sought to: (a) standardize and render transparent the information that guided the discretionary decisions of correctional professionals, (b) make that information a matter of record, (c) develop the capacity of professionals to assess risk of criminal recidivism, and (d) identify dynamic risk factors (or criminogenic needs). The standardization and transparency of these tools meets the ethical and legal standards required of decision-making in forensic contexts (American Psychological Association, 2013). Knowledge about level of risk assists in making decisions about amount of supervision and in planning treatment and intervention. Knowledge of dynamic risk factors assists in the selection of intermediate targets of change for purposes of reducing reoffending and preventing crime.

By the mid-1980s the risk-need model of correctional assessment and rehabilitation had become the Risk-Need-Responsivity model (RNR; Andrews, Bonta, & Hoge, 1990). From the start, general cognitive social learning strategies were seen as universally applicable (general responsivity) with an appreciation for specific responsivity (factors affecting individual responsiveness to intervention or programming) being developed in the 1980s and 1990s. By the late 1990s, the RNR model formally included principles having to do with systematic attention to staffing and management issues (Andrews, 2001; Bonta & Andrews, 2007). By the 2010s, RNR was arguably the preeminent model for effective intervention in corrections (Andrews, Bonta, & Wormith, 2011; Bonta & Andrews, 2017; Wormith & Zidenberg, 2018).

The development of LS instruments and the RNR model continue to interact. Three major sources of LS content are the opinions of correctional and forensic professionals, a broad and flexible theoretical perspective on human behavior (including criminal behavior), and the research literatures on the prediction of criminal behavior and crime prevention. The interactions among opinion, theory, research, and the RNR model will be evident throughout this overview of the instruments and their properties.

Today, the LS instruments are among the world's most widely used offender risk/need assessment tools (Singh et al., 2014). In America, 25 states use an LS instrument (Holwell, Undated; Interstate Commission for Adult Offender Supervision, 2007), 9 of 13 Canadian jurisdictions use either the LSI-R or LS/CMI (Wormith, Ferguson, & Bonta, 2013), and the use of LS instruments is evident in Australia, Bermuda, British Virgin Islands, Cayman Islands, China, Chile, Denmark, Germany, Hong Kong, Ireland, Israel, Netherlands, New Zealand, Pakistan, Portugal, Scotland, Singapore, Trinidad and Tobago, Sweden, and the United Kingdom. In addition, use of an LS instrument is increasing in popularity in forensic psychiatric settings (Neal & Grisso, 2014). In 2010 alone, there were more than one million administrations of LS from around the world and documented with the publisher, Multi-Health Systems (MHS; Wormith, 2011).

Description of the LS Instruments

The risk/need component of the LS instruments is actuarial-based. Although the items were (rationally) selected based on evidence of their association with recidivism (and subsequently cross-validated many times over), LS risk/need entails mechanical scoring with evidence-based contingency tables linking score categories with outcomes. The instruments were designed with reference to the prediction of general recidivism, although the underlying theory suggests wide-applicability across specific forms of rule violations, including violence.

Although the original LS instrument was designed for use with probationers and parolees (Andrews, 1982), it has proven useful with other community corrections samples and within prisons, jails and halfway houses, and forensic mental health clinics and hospitals. A youth version of this tool is available for adolescents who are 12 to 17 years of age; Hoge & Andrews, 2002; see Chapter 9 in this volume). The LS instruments were not designed to assist in setting the severity of the criminal penalty on the basis of seriousness of the offence. That is, the LS instruments are not comprehensive surveys of the aggravating and mitigating factors that may be relevant at time of sentencing. In so far as risk, need, and responsivity considerations are relevant at time of sentencing, however, use of the LS is appropriate (Andrews & Dowden, 2007).

Detailed scoring manuals allow professionals with specific LS training to use the instrument even if they have not had prior formal training in psychological assessment. The core instruments can be scored on the basis of interviews with the offender and collaterals (e.g., family member), reviews of files and official records, and, in some settings, psychological test data (e.g., paper-and-pencil assessments of antisocial thinking). Some research projects have relied on paper-and-pencil questionnaire versions, computerized self-report versions, and reviews of case files and official records. The publisher of the LS materials offers computerized data entry and scoring, web-based versions, and computerized record systems that amount to clinically relevant and psychologically informed management information systems.

The Level of Service Inventory-Revised (LSI-R)

LSI-R (Andrews & Bonta, 1995) is a 54-item survey of indicators of risk/need distributed across ten subcomponents. Each item is scored as risk indicator absent (0) or present (1), while a circled item number indicates insufficient information to score the item. Subcomponent scores are the simple sum of the number of items checked within that sub-component. The total LSI-R risk/need score is the sum of checked items.

Some of the dynamic items include a 4-item rating scale from "0" through "3" wherein "0" is a very unsatisfactory condition (very high risk) and "3" is a very satisfactory situation (very low risk). Zero and 1 ratings lead to a checked item, and ratings of 2 or 3 indicate that the item should not be checked. The descriptions for rating particular items greatly sharpen the construct that is being assessed. The ratings also facilitate more sensitive assessments of change than are possible with binary scoring. Description of the subcomponents and examples of the items are available in Andrews, Bonta, and Wormith (2010).

The Level of Service/Case Management Inventory (LS/CMI)

In addition to providing a general risk/need score, the LS/CMI (Andrews, Bonta, & Wormith, 2004) assists in structuring an RNR-based service plan and service delivery, and assessing case progress through to case closure (see Andrews et al., 2010; Bonta & Andrews, 2017). It was preceded by a well-researched pilot version, the Level of Service Inventory-Ontario Revision (LSI-OR; Andrews, Bonta, & Wormith, 1995), which is still in use today in the Canadian province of Ontario.

LS/CMI General Risk/Need is composed of eight subcomponents and a total of 43 items, most of which are based on the LSI-R. Antisocial Personality Pattern (APP), the eighth subcomponent, replaces LSI-R's Emotional/Personal and concentrates on the personality and behavioral elements of a propensity for antisocial conduct. It focuses on early and diverse patterns of misconduct, criminal thinking, generalized trouble, and indications that an assessment for psychopathy might be warranted. The LSI-R subtotals of Financial, Accommodation, and Emotional/Personal do not contribute to the general risk/need score but are represented elsewhere in the LS/CMI. A sample LS/CMI profile of the Central Eight risk/need factors may be found in the case study at the end of this chapter.

The concept of offender strengths is formally represented by the opportunity to rate each of the eight subcomponents as an area of strength. A strength rating indicates that the area is one in which positive circumstances may be built upon in a case plan. An example of this would involve a significant other (friend, family member, school or work associate, recreational partner) in a directly supportive role in service delivery. Strength factors may also function in a protective fashion, reducing the criminogenic effects of other risk factors. The inclusion of strength notations is consistent with ongoing research on the role of strength factors (Wanamaker, Jones, & Brown, 2018), but they were introduced primarily on the strong opinions of LS users who want the case plan to reflect the totality of the person and not just risk factors. Health, mental health, and social concerns are expanded in Section 4 of the LS/CMI, as are responsivity issues in Section 5. Additionally, there is a detailed review of personal problems with criminogenic potential and a detailed review of the variety of antisocial acts (Section 2.1).

The Level of Service/Risk-Need-Responsivity (LS/RNR)

Some potential users indicated that they did not require all of the sections in the LS/CMI and requested an intermediate version between LSI-R and LS/CMI. LS/RNR (Andrews, Bonta & Wormith, 2008) is composed of Sections 1, 2, and 5 of the LS/CMI and explicitly excludes the case management component, thus making it more appropriate for agencies that already have an existing case management system (CMS), particularly if their CMS is in sync with the Central Eight.

The Level of Service Inventory-Revised: Screening Version (LSI-R: SV)

The eight-item LSI-R: SV (Andrews & Bonta, 1998) was introduced as a preliminary screening instrument for agencies faced with extremely large numbers of cases. Cases falling in the moderate and/or high risk categories are subject to a full LS assessment for purposes of program planning. This version has been the focus of less research than the other LS instruments, and therefore it does not comprise a major focus of this chapter.

Development: Rationale and Methods

The original LS instrument, the Level of Supervision Inventory (LSI), was developed in close consultation with Ottawa, Ontario, probation and parole officers and managers, senior personnel, and groups of officers and managers from across the province of Ontario. The sixth pilot version (LSI-VI) was implemented province wide (Andrews, 1982), and then, with minor revisions, it became the Level of Service Inventory-Revised (LSI-R; Andrews & Bonta, 1995). The input from the probation and parole officers was significant. The goal was to produce an instrument that made sense to them and fit with their skill sets and their manner of working. The regular duties of all officers included the preparation of presentence reports for the courts and officers routinely produced a narrative social-legal history based on interviews with cases and collaterals and reviews of official records. Thus, the subcomponents of the LSI-R fit very neatly with the domains and procedures officers were used to working with.

A professional override (discretion) has always been part of the LSI risk/need approach, and during development a monitoring of the overrides was helpful in uncovering information judged very valuable by the officers. For example, the items sampling the indicators of alcohol and drug abuse were added because substance abuse on the part of the offender was a frequent rationale for increasing supervision level. Research on the use of the override with the LS/CMI is reviewed in the "Issues" section of this chapter.

The research literature on risk assessment (both published and unpublished government research reports) was reviewed. Items were included in the first draft of the LS instrument if their predictive power was indicated by the results of one or more of the studies. The specific wording was shaped by consistency with social learning theory and with "appropriateness" for the probation context. The final items in LSI-R additionally had empirical support from the first and second follow-up of the construction sample (Andrews, 1982; Andrews & Robinson, 1984).

The original three-level risk categorization for LSI-R reflected two considerations. First, discussions with probation officers and managers indicated a level of comfort with a 3- or 4-level designation of risk and with one that roughly divided the sample into equal numbers of cases. Second, cutoff scores were sought to fit the outcome data. A general rule was established wherein a new risk level was introduced when an increase of at least 5% in the recidivism rate from one score to the next was maintained for at least the next 4 score increments. That is, we wanted to be fairly certain if the cutoff was 6, then the recidivism rates for those scoring 7 and 8 would be distinctly higher than that found at score 6 and below. A finer distinction was desired with LS/CMI and a 5-level risk/need was introduced. Again, the specific cutoff scores were selected to reflect "real" dividing points in the outcome distribution. We also knew by the time of LS/CMI that approximately 50% of a probation sample would be Very Low Risk or Low Risk.

The route to LS/CMI was very similar to that followed with LSI-R, although the sophistication of the officers with regard to assessment was substantially greater than in the 1970s, the research and theoretical literature was much grander, the research had been subjected to considerable meta-analytic reviews, the movement toward some version of a general personality and cognitive social learning theory of crime was awash in criminology, and the RNR model had become more sophisticated. Consultations with teams of officers and managers from every geographic region of Ontario were arranged, and representatives of prisons were also involved. It was, we suppose, a series of focus groups aimed at improved assessment and treatment.

Yet, there was consensus in regard to several of the following issues: the validity of the LSI-R with female offenders, Indigenous offenders, violent offenders, sex offenders, and spouse abusers; the neglect of strengths; the neglect of noncriminogenic needs; and the ability of the LSI-R to predict violence. Some of our responses to these issues are evident in the additional subsections of LS/CMI. Others are evident in the studies reviewed in the validity section of this chapter with particular attention to validity with different types of offenders, females, ethnicity, mental status, and socioeconomic circumstances, and with different types of outcome measures.

In accord with the consultations and the research, Section 2.2 of the LS/CMI directly reflects a concern with a violent past and with the variety of prior offenses. These were added to enhance validity in the prediction of violence and serious crime. Section 2.1 items, in conjunction with Section 1, now provide a near exhaustive set of criminogenic need areas. Section 4 surveys the noncriminogenic areas that may be important in case planning for motivational and/or humanitarian purposes.

An additional element in our approach to instrument development was our stance on item selection through multiple regression. With the exception of LSI-R: SV (our screening version), we were never looking for the minimum number of items required to predict recidivism. We were looking for predictive items that suggested not only risk level but the appropriate intermediate targets of change for purposes of reduced reoffending. An efficient predictive formula is not necessarily the most useful formula, the most predictive, or the least expensive. Less efficient formulas may be as predictive and yet much more useful in program planning. For LS/CMI, however the Emotional/Personal, Financial, and Accommodation sections of LSI-R were dropped from the General Risk/Need score because they offered little in the way of incremental value and were not highly correlated with recidivism. Thus, those issues are now represented in the social, health, and mental health set along with major concerns in work with women and minorities. On the other hand, in keeping with the Central Eight, Antisocial Pattern was added to the LS/CMI's General Risk/Need score to reflect the empirically demonstrated phenomenon that having multiple risk/need domains is itself a risk factor (i.e., the total risk is greater than the sum of the risk domains when multiple risk/need domains exist.)

Factorial purity or multidimensionality was never a major concern in the development of the instrument. We are well aware that a single major factor underlies much of the predictive power of attitudes, associates, history, and problems in the domains of home, school, and work, but it was never our intention to produce a statistically pure measure. Once again, the multiple domains represent different potential targets of change, no matter that they may reflect the same underlying dimension of antisociality.

Reliability

The LS instruments have been submitted to reliability and related psychometric analyses in a variety of settings and jurisdictions. Types of analyses, including internal consistency, and interrater and test-retest reliability, were reported in detail by Andrews and colleagues (2010). Three other forms of reliability, item-total correlations, inter-subsection correlations, and subsection-total correlations, all of which are measures of internal consistency, and standard errors of measurement are provided in the LS manuals (Andrews & Bonta, 1995; Andrews et al., 2004). The following is a very brief summary of these earlier reviews of LS reliability including updates (i.e., Folsom & Atkinson, 2007; Guay, 2016; Hogg, 2011; Wormith & Hogg, 2011).

Internal Consistency

Internal consistency is typically measured by Cronbach's alpha, and the coefficient may be calculated for the complete instrument and its various subsections. Scales with fewer items will have lower alpha estimates, and this has commonly been found with the LS. Fourteen studies of the LSI-R found alphas for the total 54-item scale ranging from .64 to .94 with a mean coefficient of .84. Alphas' coefficients for the subsections also varied considerably as evidenced by the mean coefficients. Criminal History, Education/Employment, and Alcohol/Drugs produced mean alphas from .75 to .78, followed by Leisure/Recreation, Companions, Emotional/Personal, and Attitudes/Orientation, which were from .59 to .66. The remaining subsections, Finance, Family/Marital, and Accommodation, had alphas of .41 to .53.

Alpha coefficients for the LS/CMI are based on 12 data sets collected in Canada and one from the United States, consisting of data from nine different states. The alpha coefficients for the 43-item risk/need scale were consistently high, ranging from .86 to .92, with an average of .90 (95% CI: .87 to .91). Some of the subsections had relatively high internal consistency, specifically Criminal History with a mean alpha of .76, Education/Employment (.81), Companions (.68), and Alcohol/Drug Problem (.75). Others remained low, including Family/Marital (.45), Leisure/Recreation (.56), and Procriminal Attitude/Orientation (.64). As expected, the new subsection,

Antisocial Pattern, with an average alpha of .56, produced low coefficients because, by design, it included items from all other subsections of the LS/CMI.

Interrater, Test-Retest, and Parallel Forms Reliability

There have been very few studies of interrater reliability. The first, by Stewart (2011), examined the interrater reliability of both the LSI-R and LS/CMI on a sample of 101 federally incarcerated women in Canada. However, as this was an archival study, only file information was used to conduct the retrospective assessments. Intraclass correlations (ICCs) for the LSI-R and LS/CMI were .98 and .94, respectively, for the total score. The degree of rater agreement was quite varied across the various domains. Of the domains common to both versions, Criminal History, Education/Employment, and Alcohol/Drug Problem were greater than .90 on both instruments. They were followed by Family/Marital (ICC = .85 and .85, respectively), Associates (ICC = .77 and .60, respectively) and Leisure/Recreation (ICC = .70 and .48). Agreement was lowest for Procriminal Attitude/Orientation (ICC = .41 and .34, respectively).

The second study, which may simulate more closely a real-world setting was a small study conducted by Labrecque and his colleagues (Labrecque et al., 2018). Four university students were trained in the LS/CMI along with a group of probation officers in Oregon. The students listened to nine audio recordings of LS/CMI assessments administered by probation officers. The ICCs were satisfactory to good but lower than those reported by Stewart (2011). For example, the ICC for the total score was only .64, and the highest was .76 for the Family/Marital domain.

For a review of the simultaneous impact of two sources of variation (time and assessor) on reliability coefficients, see Andrews et al. (2010). Concerning parallel forms of LS, following Rowe (1996), who found a correlation of .96 between the LSI-R and LS/CMI on 340 male incarcerated offenders, Stewart's (2011) investigation reported a correlation of .88 between the LSI-R and LS/CMI.

Summary of Reliability

The internal consistency of the total score of both versions of the LS is high. However, the internal consistency of individual sections is quite variable, in part due to the very few items in some domains (i.e., two to four). Test-retest reliability is high over the short term, but these correlations deteriorate over time because of the dynamic nature of instrument. We are less concerned about internal consistency than interrater reliability, particularly at the domain level, where one domain may draw on multiple constructs, which may be related to each other only minimally but are related to future antisocial and criminal behavior. The quest for high interrater reliability has been instructive. Caution must be exercised by any agency that introduces the LS, particularly if a large number of examiners administer the instrument. To this end, staff training is crucial and is discussed in more detail in a later section.

Validity

Construct Validity of LSI

The general personality and cognitive social psychology model that underlies the LS instruments hypothesizes that there are individual differences in the propensity to engage in crime and that this propensity is partly determined by variations in risk/need factors as measured by the LS subcomponents. The validity of the general construct "propensity to engage in crime" and the subconstructs/facets as measured by the LS subcomponents can be tested in many different ways.

Two approaches commonly used involve factor analysis and testing the convergent/divergent validities of the construct.

Factor Analytic Evidence

As noted earlier, construct validity as assessed by factor analysis has never been a major concern in the development of the LS instruments. All of the factor analytic studies that have been conducted involved an exploratory technique closely associated with factor analysis (principal component analysis, using varimax rotation). Briefly, factor analytic studies of the LSI-R have yielded either one-factor (Palmer & Hollin, 2007), two-factor (Andrews, Bonta, Motiuk, & Robinson, 1984; Bonta & Motiuk, 1986a; Hollin, Palmer, & Clark, 2003; Loza & Simourd, 1994; Simourd & Malcolm, 1998), or three-factor solutions (Andrews et al., 1984; Bonta & Motiuk, 1986b, Stevenson & Wormith, 1987). For a detailed review of these and other studies, see Andrews et al. (2010). However, whether they produce one, two, or three factors, all have generated one factor that measures a propensity to engage in crime.

This propensity is now better reflected in LS/CMI General Risk/Need with the addition of Antisocial Pattern and the movement of Emotional/Personal, Financial, and Accommodation items to Section 4. Accordingly, in a large study of 3,682 offenders, Guay (2016) conducted an exploratory factor analysis of the eight subsections of the LS/CMI. Using a French translation of the LS/CMI with provincial offenders from Quebec, Canada, he obtained a single-factor solution that accounted for 48% of the variance. The factor solution generated a Keyser-Meyer-Olkin (KMO) index of .87, which is considered "meritorious" (Kaiser, 1974). The strongest factor loadings were on Antisocial Pattern (.84), Companions (.77), and Criminal History (.72).

In a smaller Australian study of 302 offenders, Gordon, Kelty, and Julian (2015) found a two-factor solution with a KMO index of .82. The two factors accounted for 42% of the variance. The strongest factor loadings were on Antisocial Pattern (.93) for the first factor and for the second factor, Leisure/Recreation (.77) had the highest factor loading.

Predictive Validity

When it comes to predictive validity, few offender assessment instruments have been the subject of as much research as the LS instruments. At least nine meta-analyses have been conducted on LS with adult offenders. Some of these studies examined LS exclusively (e.g., Smith, Cullen & Latessa, 2009; Olver, Stockdale, & Wormith, 2014; Wilson & Gutierrez, 2014), while others examined two or more instruments (Gendreau, Little, & Goggin, 1996; Gendreau, Goggin, & Smith, 2002; Campbell, French, & Gendreau, 2009; Singh, Grann, & Fazel, 2011; Walters, 2006; Yang, Wong, & Coid, 2010), although typically the instruments had been administered to different samples in different jurisdictions, which makes between-instrument comparisons difficult. Moreover, many of these validation studies examined instruments' relationships with various kinds of recidivism, particularly violent and sexual recidivism. It should also be noted that the LS was originally designed to predict antisocial behavior generally, and only recently did LS/CMI begin to focus more directly on violent behavior, with an added supplementary section.

The most definitive meta-analysis of LS to date was conducted by Olver et al. (2014). They identified 126 predictive validity studies of LS instruments with 151 independent samples comprising 137,931 offenders released between 1981 and 2012, primarily from Canada and the United States (84%). Most offenders were male (80.5%) and white (63%). Thirteen of these studies examined youth versions of the LS (YLS/CMI) and were not disaggregated in many of the analyses. Multiple kinds of outcome were analyzed, including general (weighted mean = 36.0%), nonviolent (35.2%), violent (13.7%), and sexual (6.5%) recidivism, as well as institutional miscon-duct. The mean follow-up time across studies was 36.4 months $(SD = 23.8)$.

Table 8.1 summarizes the principal findings. Weighted random effect sizes for both the total score and domain scores were strongest for general recidivism, followed by violent recidivism, and then sexual recidivism where a number of domains were no longer significant. Among the domains, Education/Employment and Antisocial Pattern were as highly correlated with both general and violent recidivism as the total LS score. In addition, examinations of institutional behavior as an outcome in relation to LS total score generated predictive validities of .24 $(k = 16)$ for any misconduct and .21 $(k = 15)$ for serious misconduct.

Many concerns have been expressed over the last two decades about the generalizability of the LS across gender, race, and nationality. These critiques and related studies, culminating in Olver et al.'s (2014) meta-analysis, are summarized next.

Gender Bias

Questions about the applicability and appropriateness of the Central Eight risk factors generally, and the LS specifically, have been expressed for both theoretical and empirical reasons (Brown & Motiuk, 2008; Hannah-Moffat, 2009; Morash, 2009; Taylor & Blanchette, 2009). Noteworthy is that the Central Eight risk factors that are reflected in the LS (especially the LS/CMI) have been found predictive of general and violent recidivism regardless of gender (Eisenberg et al., 2019). Basically, the debate revolves around the concepts of gender-neutral risk factors versus gender-specific pathways to crime. A sufficient number of studies have examined the predictive validity of LS by gender that comparisons have now been conducted meta-analytically.

A meta-analysis by Gendreau et al. (2002) was undertaken to compare the LSI-R to the PCL-R, but it also reported predictive validity by gender. Based on 10 female samples and 18 male samples from 1986 to 1999, they cited mean correlations of .45 for females and .33 for males. Holtfreter and Cupp (2007) conducted a systematic review of 11 LSI-R studies with women published between 1986 and 2006. They concluded that the LSI-R performs moderately well

Table 8.1 Predictive Validity Estimates of LS Total Score and Domains on General, Violent, and Sexual Recidivism

LS Scale	General Recidivism			Violent Recidivism			Sexual Recidivism		
	r	(95% CI)	k	r	(96% CI)	k	r	(95% CI)	k
Total score	.29	(.27–.31)	124	.23	(.19–.27)	39	.11	(.03–.18)	7
Criminal History	.28	(.25–.32)	55	.21	(.16–.27)	18	.11**	(.03–.20)	5
Education/Employment	.24	(.21–.27)	55	.20	(.15–.24)	19	.07c	(−.04–.18)	5
Family/Marital	.14	(.12–.16)	54	.11	(.09–.14)	19	.07c	(.01–.14)	5
Financiala	.12	(.09–.15)	29	.09	(.01–.18)	5	–		
Accommodationa	.14	(.11–.16)	30	.15	(.04–.25)	5	–		
Companions	.22	(.19–.25)	58	.17	(.11–.22)	19	.04c	(−.09–.16)	5
Leisure/Recreation	.16	(.13–.19)	53	.12	(.08–.16)	19	.12	(.08–.16)	5
Alcohol/Drug Problem	.20	(.16–.23)	54	.13	(.09–.18)	19	.00c	(−.11–.11)	5
Personal/Emotionala	.14	(.10–.18)	45	.17	(.09–.25)	12	−.02c	(−.21–.16)	4
Antisocial Patternb	.31	(.26–.35)	10	.23	(.22–.24)	7	–		
Procriminal Attitude	.19	(.16–.22)	55	.18	(.14–.21)	19	.09c	(.00–.18)	5

Note: All weighted random effect sizes (r) are significant at $p < .001$, unless otherwise stated. Dashes denote insufficient k (< 2) to compute effect sizes. Prediction of sexual recidivism is among sexual offenders only while the prediction of general and violent recidivism is across all offender groups. a = LSI and LSI-R only. b = LS/CMI only. c = Not significant; ** $p < .01$. CI = confidence interval.

Source: Adapted from Olver, Stockdale, and Wormith (2014), Tables 3 and 4.

for women who are economically motivated for crime and for the prediction of more serious reoffending, but its application to women whose lives are affected by "gendered circumstances" is problematic.

However, Smith, Cullen, and Latessa (2009) examined studies over a similar timeframe (1984 to 2007) and found quite different results. They reported a mean correlation of .34 with recidivism (random effects), of which 88% was for rearrest, reconviction, or reincarceration, across 27 samples. Length of follow-up was a significant moderator whereby follow-ups of less than 1 year generated a mean correlation of .43, while follow-ups of more than 2 years were associated with a mean correlation of .28. Importantly, the 16 studies that included both male and female offenders in their samples generated mean correlations of .24 for males and .28 for females.

These discrepant results led Andrews and colleagues to search for possible sources of variability in the predictive validity among the LS scales. They found adult male samples generated an unweighted mean correlation of .41 ($k = 7$) and adult female samples produced an unweighted mean correlation of .45 ($k = 7$; Andrews et al., 2011). A follow-up study examined gender differences more specifically in five LS/CMI data sets, four from Canada and one from the UK, and all of which included both male and female samples, in an effort to unearth their possible sources. The results were compelling for the overall gender neutrality of the LS/CMI, while also illustrating gender differences in more detailed analyses. The LS/CMI total score was highly correlated with recidivism among males (.39), but even more highly with females (.53). The gender difference was then traced to the enhanced predictive validity of the Substance Abuse section with women. Moreover, recidivism rates for low-risk women were lower than their low-risk male counterparts, which could have implications for test interpretation and application in the field (Andrews et al., 2012).

The previously mentioned and most complete meta-analysis of LS to date also examined its predictive validity by gender (Olver et al., 2014). As seen in Table 8.2, the predictive validity of

Table 8.2 Predictive Validity Estimates of Level of Service Total Score for General and Violent Recidivism by Gender, Ethnicity, and Jurisdiction

Demographic Characteristics	General Recidivism			Violent Recidivism		
	r	(95% CI)	k	r	(95% CI)	k
Gender (All studies)						
Male	.30	(.27–.34)	80	.24	(.20–.27)	30
Female	.31	(.26–.35)	45	.26	(.20–.32)	12
Gender (Within studies)						
Male	.29	(.24–.34)	31	.29	(.21–.35)	6
Female	.29	(.24–.35)	31	.25	(.22–.27)	6
Ethnicity (All studies)						
Ethnic minority	.27	(.22–.32)	36	.24	(.17–.31)	6
Nonminority	.29	(.23–.34)	24	.23	(.10–.35)	5
Ethnicity (within studies)						
Ethnic minority	.29	(.23–.34	29	.24	(.17–.31)	6
Nonminority	.28	(.23–.34)	23	.21	(.06–.34)	4
Jurisdiction (All studies)						
Canada	.38	(.35–.41)	51	.2	(.23–.29)	28
United States	.20	(.18–.23)	52	.12	(.11–.13)	7
Outside North America	.30	(.28–.33)	19	.20	(.14–.26)	4

Source: Adapted from Olver, Stockdale, and Wormith (2014), Tables 5, 7, 8, and 9.

Note: All weighted random effect sizes (r) are significant at $p < .001$. The k for ethnic minority is higher than for nonminority in within-study comparisons because k's were provided for more than one ethnic minority in some studies and individual effect sizes were computed for each minority group. CI = confidence interval.

the LS total score was comparable, and not significantly different as indicated by overlapping 95% confidence intervals, for male and female offenders on both general and violent recidivism. When compared only on studies that included both males and females from the same offender population, the similarities in predictive validity for general and violent reoffending were maintained although slightly higher for males in the prediction of violent recidivism (.29 and .25, respectively).

An examination of Table 6 from Olver et al. (2014) also revealed few differences in the predictive validity of individual domains between male and female offenders. Substance Abuse produced slightly higher predictive validity for females than males on general recidivism (.25 and .19, respectively), while Education/Employment (.24 and .17, respectively) and Antisocial Pattern (.22 and .17, respectively) produced slightly higher predictive validity for males than females on violent recidivism. However, and keeping in mind that there were relatively few studies, these pairs of correlations were not significantly different from each other.

Olver et al. (2014) also examined mean LS scores by gender. Comparisons between male and female mean scores found relatively small, but variable, differences ($d = .05$ to .38). Males scored significantly higher on LS total score, Prior Offenses (Criminal History), Companions, Leisure/ Recreation, Alcohol/Drug Problem, Antisocial Pattern, and Procriminal Attitude/Orientation. Females scored significantly higher on Education/Employment, Family/Marital, Financial, Accommodation, and Personal/Emotional. These findings are of interest for descriptive reasons, suggesting that there may be differences in the presence and degree of certain criminogenic needs by gender, but do not invalidate the predictive validity of the instrument for women.

Racial Bias

In 2014, then U.S. Attorney General Eric Holder ignited a debate over the potential of offender risk instruments to be racially biased (see also Chapter 4 by Slobogin focusing on legal issues in risk assessment, this volume). In a speech to a gathering of defense lawyers, he declared that these assessment instruments "may exacerbate unwarranted and unjust disparities" (Holder, 2014). Although race itself is a predictor of recidivism (Gendreau et al., 1996) the inclusion of race into risk scales would have very little public support (Scurich & Monahan, 2016). However, some scholars argue that factors common to these instruments such as employment and marital status are really proxies for race. They also reason that since race is beyond an individual's control and the law assigns great weight to personal responsibility, it would be unjust to use risk scales with minorities (Harcourt, 2015). The controversy appears to have peaked with a recent article published in *ProPublica*, a magazine specializing in investigative journalism in the public interest. Angwin, Larson, Mattu, and Kirchner (2016) analyzed risk scores from the Correctional Offender Management Profiling for Alternative Sanctions (COMPAS) instrument and found Blacks were more likely to score high risk than Whites. The authors then concluded that COMPAS, and perhaps other actuarial risk assessment instruments, were racially biased.

Although not everyone may agree with the *ProPublica* and conclusions, it did challenge researchers to ensure that risk/need instruments fairly assess minority groups. The critical question to ask is, do scores on the instrument predict recidivism equally for minorities and non-minorities? A number of studies have been examining the predictive validity of LS scores with diverse racial groups. Most of these studies were with Indigenous offenders in Canada (e.g., Bonta, 1989), not surprisingly given the Canadian origins of the LS instruments, followed by a few studies from Australia and the United States. Three meta-analyses are particularly instructive. The first, by Gutierrez, Wilson, Rugge, and Bonta (2013), examined the predictive validity of the Central Eight risk/need factors for Indigenous ($N = 57,315$) and non-Indigenous ($N = 204,977$) offenders. They found that all eight risk/need factors predicted general and violent recidivism for both samples. In other words, the factors specifically measured by the LS/CMI and LS/RNR are relevant to the assessment of risk and needs.

A second meta-analysis (Wilson & Gutierrez, 2014) was explicitly with the LS instruments. The review included 12 studies on the use of the LS with Indigenous offenders ($N = 21,807$). General recidivism was the only outcome criterion described, and they found an r of .31 (converted from Cohen's d reported in the article) for Indigenous offenders. The authors then selected studies that had both Indigenous and non-Indigenous samples (i.e., a within-study comparison) and calculated the effect size *difference* for both groups (absolute predictive validity estimates were not reported for the two groups). They found that the LS predicted equally well for the medium- and high-risk groups but under-classified the low-risk Indigenous offenders (an issue of calibration). However, the overall total LS score which was higher for Indigenous offenders did significantly predict recidivism for both groups, although not as well for Indigenous offenders as for the non-Indigenous group.

Wilson and Gutierrez (2014) suggested three possible reasons for the issue of calibration, that is, the finding that the higher risk/need score and lower predictive validity estimate for Indigenous offenders, particularly at the lower range of risk. First, there may be bias in the criminal justice system (e.g., over-policing and over-conviction) that introduces an external factor in the prediction process that compromises the dependent variable. Second, the LS instrument may not capture risk factors that are culturally specific to Indigenous offenders either from a sociological perspective (e.g., history of colonization) or a psychological perspective (e.g., the meaning of "family" in an Indigenous culture). Third, and we favor this explanation, the same risk factors apply to both groups, but Indigenous offenders simply have more risk factors (recall the Gutierrez et al. [2013] study of the Central Eight risk/need factors). That is, they are more likely to be unemployed, have less education, and have less access to appropriate, prosocial recreational opportunities. The greater number of risk factors may produce a ceiling effect or a restriction in range and lower predictive validity estimates for Indigenous offenders. Why this minority group has more of these risk factors than the majority group is a sociological question.

The third meta-analysis included an analysis of the LS with American minority offenders. In Olver et al.'s (2014) review of the predictive validity of the LS instruments, they provided summaries of effect sizes for ethnic minorities in the United States (Table 6 of Olver et al.). They also provided analyses of the U.S. general recidivism data that focused on African Americans and Hispanics. The mean random effect size for minorities ranged from $r = .18$ to .21 depending on the definition of "minority." These estimates were significantly lower than the r values for nonminority offenders ($r = .29$; Table 5 of Olver et al.). Olver and his colleagues also reported lower predictive validity estimates for Hispanics than for African Americans ($r = .22$ vs. $r = .32$; Table 6 of Olver et al., outlier removed for African American). However, the differences were not significant with overlapping confidence intervals for random effects.

Therefore, not only is the predictive accuracy of the LS dependent on the type of minority, but additional analyses, described next, found that country of study and type of LS instrument are also related to effect size. Mean random effect sizes for specific minority groups were as follows: Black (outlier removed), .32 ($k = 8$); Asian, .32 ($k = 4$); Indigenous, .30 ($k = 13$); and Hispanic, .22 ($k = 6$). It is also noted that ethnic minorities scored significantly higher than nonminorities in within-study comparisons on all domains except the personal/emotional domain (from the LSI-R) where nonminorities scored significantly higher. Most of these differences may be considered small ($d < .30$) with two, education/employment (.40) and antisocial pattern (.50), being moderate. As was the case for gender, one should not infer racial bias from mean differences in risk/need scores, but rather consider possible differences in the magnitude and extent of risk/needs in relation to racial background.

International Bias

We have been both curious and concerned about the variability in predictive validity of LS across international and even regional boundaries (Andrews et al., 2011, 2012; Olver et al., 2014). It is a complex issue illustrated by the fact that effect size variability in Olver et al.'s (2014) investigation was highest in the United States, where the mean effect size was lowest, indicating that predictive validities of the LS in the United States were both high and low (see Olver et al.'s Table 6). Although the search for a thorough and empirical explanation continues, various candidates have been suggested. Some of these explanations include the following: assessor training; supervision and quality assurance mechanisms; author allegiance or affiliation; heterogeneity of samples; differences in criminal justice systems including laws/criminal codes, policing practices, and court processing; and the operational definition of recidivism, including length of follow-up and type of outcome (Andrews et al., 2011, 2012; Olver et al., 2014; Yang et al., 2010).

We also thought that a detailed examination of the predictive validities of individual domains would shed some light on the matter. However, the pattern of differences was very consistent, with validities for the total LS score and all domains being highest in Canada, followed by other countries (primarily in Europe), and then the United States (Table 8.3). It may be noteworthy that this included the Prior Offenses (Criminal History) domain, which is a static risk segment of the LS and most likely the easiest domain to score because there are few issues of assessor judgment. This finding suggests that there is some extra-assessment factor or factors impacting the predictive validity of the LS across jurisdictions. This position is supported by a meta-analysis by Yang et al. (2010) that found a similar predictive validity pattern by country (Holland, followed by Canada, followed by Sweden, the United Kingdom, and Germany, followed by the United States), not only on LS, but, importantly, on eight other risk assessment instruments. On the other hand, the magnitude of the different predictive validities on the personal/emotional domain, one that is dynamic and need-based, suggest that there may be some sources of variability in validity that do emanate from the assessment process including the quality and thoroughness of both the assessor investigation and the data sources that are used to complete the investigation. We encourage researchers and agencies that use the LS to pursue this matter through further research in their own jurisdictions.

Table 8.3 Predictive Validity Estimates of LS Total Score and Domains on General Recidivism by Jurisdiction

LS Scale	Canada			United States			Outside North America		
	r	(95% CI)	k	r	(96% CI)	k	r	(95% CI)	k
Total score	.38	(.35–.41)	51	.20	(.18–.23)	52	.30	(.28–.33)	19
Criminal History	.36	(.33–.40)	27	.19	(.13–.24)	16	.27	(.22–.31)	12
Education/Employment	.30	(.27–.33)	27	.18	(.15–.21)	17	.21	(.18–.24)	11
Family/Marital	.18	(.16–.19)	27	.09	(.06–.12)	16	.15	(.11–.18)	11
Financial[a]	.19	(.14–.23)	10	.08	(.05–.10)	13	.15	(.10–.19)	6
Accommodation[a]	.22	(.16–.29)	12	.11	(.08–.14)	12	.13	(.09–.17)	6
Companions	.30	(.27–.32)	29	.15	(.11–.18)	18	.19	(.16–.23)	11
Leisure/Recreation	.25	(.24–.26)	25	.09	(.06–.12)	17	.14	(.10–.18)	11
Alcohol/Drug Problem	.25	(.21–.28)	26	.15	(.11–.18)	17	.18	(.14–.23)	11
Personal/Emotional[a]	.24	(.17–.31)	17	.04	(.02–.06)	16	.13	(.07–.19)	12
Antisocial Pattern[b]	—			—			—		
Procriminal Attitude	.27	(.24–.30)	27	.12	(.09–.16)	17	.16	(.13–.19)	11

Source: Adapted from Olver, Stockdale, and Wormith (2014), Tables 9 and 10.

Note: All weighted random effect sizes (r) are significant at p < .001. Dashes denote insufficient k (< 2) to compute effect sizes. a = LSI and LSI-R only. b = LS/CMI only. CI = confidence interval.

In summary, the relationship between the predictive validity of the LS instruments and recidivism is complex. Researchers have identified a number of potential moderators and possible explanations for the generally smaller effect size estimates for some minority offenders. That said, based upon the available meta-analytic evidence, the predictive validity of the LS instruments is certainly above chance and in many cases on par with Caucasian offenders. This does not mean that further research is unnecessary, but it does give confidence for the use of the LS with racially disparate groups.

Comparison of Instruments

Numerous meta-analyses and systematic reviews have compared the predictive validity of the LS to a wide array of popular assessment instruments (e.g., Campbell et al., 2009; Gendreau et al., 1996, 2002; Singh et al., 2011; Singh & Fazel, 2010; Walters, 2006; Yang et al., 2010). Comparatively, in some reviews the LS performed well (e.g. Campbell et al., 2009; Geraghty & Woodhams, 2015), in some it performed poorly (e.g. Singh et al., 2011), and in some the authors determined that there was no systematic difference between a collection of instruments including the LS (e.g., Yang et al., 2010). Moreover, drawing any conclusions from these studies is difficult because of the vastly different samples, jurisdictions, and outcome measures (e.g., most commonly violent recidivism, but also general and sexual recidivism) used to validate the different instruments, in spite of efforts to impose statistical controls.

Relatively few studies have compared the LS to other instruments on a common sample with an identical outcome measure. To date, these have been individual studies, typically conducted within a single jurisdiction or correctional agency. Five relatively small ($N = 61$ to 201) Canadian studies have compared the LS to the following instruments on more than one occasion: PCL-R (4 studies), SIR/GSIR (3 studies), VRAG (3 studies) (Kroner & Mills, 2001; Loza & Green, 2003; Mills & Kroner, 2006; Stewart, 2011; Wormith, Olver, Stevenson, & Girard, 2007). Weighted mean correlations for the common LS and PCL-R studies ($k = 4$) were .37 and .24 for general and violent recidivism, respectively, for the LSI-R, and .26 and .17, respectively, for the PCL-R. Weighted mean correlations for the common LS and VRAG studies ($k = 3$) were .39 and .24 for general and violent recidivism, respectively, for the LSI-R, and .34 and .20 for the VRAG. Weighted mean correlations for the common LS and SIR/GSIR studies ($k = 3$) were .42 and .26 for general and violent recidivism, respectively, for the LS-R, and .43 and .30, respectively, for the SIR/GSIR. For a review of LS convergent validity (i.e. the extent to which LS and its domains correlate with other measures of similar or related constructs, including personality characteristics), see Andrews, Bonta, and Wormith (2010).

Finally, we would like to comment on the predictive validity of the LS/CMI, a "fourth generation" assessment tool. Earlier, Bonta (1996) had described "generations" of offender assessment. First generation was clinical judgment, second-generation instruments were actuarial, static scales, and then we had third-generation risk/need tools (e.g., LSI-R). Today we have the integration of case management protocols with risk and need assessment to form the fourth-generation assessment instruments. Because the LS/CMI is relatively new, there are fewer but a growing number of direct tests of its predictive validity. Hence, Olver et al. (2014) examined it along with other versions of LS (Table 8.4). As anticipated by Andrews et al. (2010), there is mounting evidence that LS/CMI may be a stronger predictor than the LSI-R for general recidivism and at least as strong for violent recidivism. One study that applied both versions to a common group of federally incarcerated female offenders in Canada (Stewart, 2011) revealed the same kind of pattern for the LS/CMI and LSI-R, specifically .47 and .42, respectively, for general recidivism, and .30 and .29, respectively, for violent recidivism.

Table 8.4 Predictive Validity Estimates for Adult Versions of the Level of Service Instruments for General and Violent Recidivism

Level of Service Version	General Recidivism			Violent Recidivism		
	r	(95% CI)	k	r	(95% CI)	k
LSI/LSI-VI	.32	(.27–.37)	20	.21	(.15–.28)	2
LSI-R	.25	(.22–.28)	55	.23	(.16–.28)	14
LSI-SV	.27	(.20–.33)	4	–		
LS/CMI	.42	(.38–.47)	12	.27	(.22–.32)	11

Source: Adapted from Olver, Stockdale, and Wormith (2014), Table 12.

Note: All weighted random effect sizes (r) are significant at $p < .001$. Dashes denote insufficient k (< 2) to compute effect sizes. LSI/LSI-VI = Level of Supervision Inventory/Level of Supervision Inventory-VI; LS/CMI = Level of Service/Case Management Inventory (includes LSI-OR = Level of Service Inventory-Ontario Revision); LSI-SV = Level of Service Inventory-Screening Version; LSI-R = Level of Service Inventory-Revised. CI = confidence interval.

In summary, meta-analytic reviews indicate that the predictive validity of the LS is equal to that of any other offender risk instrument, with respect to the prediction of both general and violent recidivism. It is also noteworthy that LS scores predict institutional misconducts, making the instrument highly relevant to institutional classification decisions.

The Risk Principle and the LS Instruments

The risk principle directs that intensive levels of services are to be reserved for medium- to high-risk offenders while less intensive services are provided to low-risk offenders. The evidence for the risk principle now appears beyond question (Andrews & Dowden, 2006; Bonta & Andrews, 2007, 2017). Risk in most studies, however, has been assessed by relatively simple measures (e.g., a compilation of criminal history variables). There have been a few studies specifically testing the risk principle with the LSI-R as the measure of offender risk. Here, there is the expectation that use of the LSI-R to make decisions on assigning the appropriate level of service would result in lower rates of recidivism.

In the first test of the Risk Principle with the LSI-R, Andrews and Robinson (1984; Andrews et al., 1984) randomly assigned 190 probationers to either routine supervision or an augmented service (joint supervision by a professional probation officer coupled with a volunteer). High-risk offenders who received augmented services demonstrated lower recidivism rates than high-risk offenders receiving routine probation services (28% vs. 58% respectively). Low-risk offenders receiving augmented services showed an increase in recidivism compared to their counterparts who received routine supervision (7% to 14%), although the latter differences were not statistically significant. This interaction effect between LSI-R risk level and service level has been replicated by the authors of the LSI-R (Bonta & Motiuk, 1987, 1990; Bonta, Wallace-Capretta & Rooney, 2000; Motiuk & Bonta, 1991) and independent researchers (Bourgon & Armstrong, 2005). For a review of dynamic predictive validity of LS (i.e., the extent to which changes in LS scores over time, without systematic [experimental] intervention, correspond to changes in offender outcome; see Andrews et al., 2010).

What is notable about the Risk/Need-by-Service interaction is that not only do higher-risk offenders benefit from enhanced services, but lower-risk offenders are not subjected to unnecessary restrictions of liberty. In a number of studies, it was clearly demonstrated that application of the LSI-R would result in more appropriate levels of supervision than relying on routine classification procedures. For example, Bonta and Motiuk (1987, 1990) have shown that using the

LSI-R to identify lower-risk inmates for placement in a correctional halfway house resulted in more inmates being diverted to community-based residential facilities. In another study (Bonta & Motiuk, 1992), use of the LSI-R to inform custodial security placement decisions was estimated to reduce rates of over-classification by 38 percent.

Summary of Validity

The concurrent, divergent, and, most importantly, predictive validity of the LS instruments is well established. The evidence on predictive validity is substantial, and this research also expands on the many uses of the LS instruments (not the least of which is the prediction of violence including violent institutional misconduct). Validity with many different offender samples (e.g., women, mentally disordered, racial minorities) has also been demonstrated. The evidence of dynamic predictive validity opens the door to the use of the instruments for case planning and monitoring. More work is needed on the predictive validity of the subcomponents, the role of strengths and responsivity factors, predictive validity with specific offender groups (including violent, sexual, domestic violence, driving while impaired, and internet-based offenders), and the modernization of scoring and classification techniques. We are now seeing this research beginning to emerge, particularly with the more recent LS/CMI.

Issues, Limitations, and Need for Future Research in the Evolution of Risk/Needs Assessments and the LS

Risk/needs technology continues to develop with new offender assessment instruments being published at a dizzying pace. As new instruments emerge, researchers of existing instruments, the LS included, need to consider what new features and what value can be added to improve their own instruments. When research with extant instruments comes to light, the validity and utility of these assessments may also be questioned. Together, the forces of market competition and discovery guide an evolution in risk/needs assessment (a survival of the fittest, so to speak). Many factors contribute to this evolution, and we will discuss but a few, namely, training, the override principle, communicating risk, and scope of application, with particular reference to the LS.

Training and Quality Assurance

The reliability, and eventually the validity, of a risk/need assessment depend partly on the quality of training on the instrument. Training in the administration of a risk/need instrument usually is in the form of live group training, although online training is becoming popular (Global Institute of Forensic Research, 2016). *In vivo* trainings tend to be delivered by the authors and associates closely aligned to the test originators of the test instrument or trainers who go through a rigorous certification process. In the case of the LS instruments, which are among the most widely used offender risk/need instruments in the world, the demand for training far outstripped the ability of the authors to provide LS training. Thus, a process had to be developed to be able to train large numbers of correctional staff in the proper administration of the LS.

A process of certifying trainers began soon after the publication of the LSI-R. In 1996 the authors held a workshop for a select group of correctional practitioners from Canada and the United States. The workshop consisted of an educational component summarizing the LSI-R research and a number of mock interviews that provided supervised practice on the administration and scoring of the LSI-R. The invitees also completed a knowledge test of the LSI-R and RNR research with a minimum passing grade of 80%. After the workshop, the participants who met the passing grade returned to their respective agencies and delivered their own LSI-R training to staff based on a structured training agenda provided at the workshop. The staff at these trainings completed evaluation forms that were submitted to the authors for review. This three-step process (attending training by the test authors, passing the knowledge test, and obtaining acceptable training ratings) led to a certification of "LSI-R Expert Trainer."

As the LSI-R Expert Trainers from the 1996 workshop began to conduct their own training, some who were trained expressed an interest in becoming Expert Trainers. Thus, a new procedure was instituted. Applicants were required to have administered at least 50 LSI-Rs, submit a letter of support, and meet certain educational and experience requirements (e.g., a university degree in the social sciences). The next step was passing a knowledge test based upon the LSI-R and the Psychology of Criminal Conduct (once again an 80% mark or higher). The third step was to submit a video-recorded LSI-R interview of a client along with the scoring for review by one of the authors of the LSI-R. Lastly, the candidate delivered their own LSI-R training and submitted evaluations from participants.

Subsequent to the publication of the LS/CMI, a similar certification process was established. Certification as a "LS/CMI Master Trainer" was more complex as the LS/CMI is a more comprehensive assessment involving not only LSI-R type of risk and needs factors but also requiring the evaluation of other theoretically relevant indices of criminal behavior and formulation of case plans. A postgraduate degree and a minimum of 20 LS/CMI administrations formed some of the essential elements of the first step, and the knowledge test required a grade of 85% or higher. Finally, LS/CMI Master Trainer applicants submit a video of themselves delivering two modules of training. The LS/CMI Master Trainers also sign a contract with MHS to ensure that the training follows the curriculum developed by the authors.

Expert and Master Trainers can train users of the LS and other trainers, but only within the agency or organization. For example, an Expert or Master Trainer may hold a special training of trainers within a Department of Corrections, but the resultant trainers can train users only for that Department of Corrections. Only an Expert/Master Trainer can cross agency/organizational boundaries for training. Also, not all LSI-R Expert Trainers are LS/CMI Master Trainers, and the Expert Trainers must meet the LS/CMI certification requirements. However, LS/CMI Master Trainers have all the privileges of the Expert Trainers (i.e., a LSI-R Expert Trainer cannot conduct LS/CMI training with the Master Trainer status). This scrutiny has paid off as researchers have shown that LS validity estimates increase and adherence to RNR-based practices improves with LS-focused training and experience (Dyck, Campbell, & Wershler, 2018; Flores, Lowenkamp, Holsinger, & Latessa, 2006; Lowenkamp, Latessa, & Holsinger, 2004).

The Override Principle and Its Relation to Validity

The "override principle" is a lesser-known component of the popular RNR model, one that was not granted notation in the RNR acronym (Andrews et al., 1990). Also known as "professional discretion" (Andrews & Bonta, 2010), the concept harkens back to the work of Paul Meehl (1954), who first initiated the clinical versus statistical debate as to which approach is superior in the prediction of human behavior and then, ironically, attempted to reconcile it. To illustrate the need to align the two approaches, Meehl (1957) offered the "broken leg" metaphor, whereby a clinical piece of information (a broken leg) rendered the examinee's performance being inaccurately predicted when based solely on an objective test (e.g., normal blood test). Appreciating this notion, and perhaps buoyed by the success of the structured professional judgment (SPJ) movement, researchers and clinicians have attempted various kinds of integration of these methods now for at least 60 years with various instruments, but generally without a great deal of success (e.g., Abbott, 2011; Cohen, Pendergast, & VanBenschoten, 2016; Eher, Retternberger, Matthes, &

Schilling, 2010; Holt, 1958; Krauss, 2004; Storey, Watt, Jackson, & Hart, 2012; Wormith & Goldstone, 1984). Nonetheless, researchers and clinicians continue to discuss means of combining statistical prediction with clinical judgment to augment the predictive validity of various instruments including the LS/CMI.

The LSI-R set the stage for the override by offering cutoff scores for various risk levels and declared them as "guidelines" to be used in conjunction with "good sound judgment by experienced professionals" (Andrews & Bonta, 1995, p. 14). The manual also pointed out that there may be "circumstances requiring special attention." Research had demonstrated that less than 10% of LS assessments required a professional override. These cases were divided equally between increases and decreases in the risk/needs level (p. 12).

The fourth-generation LS/CMI was more explicit about modifying a score-based risk finding with additional information. It did so by building a specific "override" step into the administration protocol. For example, after all scoring is complete (this includes general and specific risk/need, strengths, prison experience, other client issues, and special responsivity considerations), the LS/CMI instructions require the assessor to declare whether use of a client-based, or clinical, override is in order to increase or decrease the score-derived risk level and, if so, to explain why, before proceeding to the case management plan. According to the manual (Andrews et al., 2004), clinical overrides of the risk/need score "should be supported by logical argument and reasonable evidence" (p. 28). The LS/CMI protocol also requires the assessor to explain what factors, situations, strengths, or extenuating circumstances justify an increase or decrease in the offender's risk level. Based on past experiences with LSI-R, the LS/CMI manual declared, "It is . . . expected that overrides will be used in fewer than 10% of the cases" (p. 4). Other instruments that have incorporated an override feature into their administration protocol. They include a general risk/need assessment, the Correctional Offender Management Profiling for Alternative Sanctions (COMPAS; Brennan & Oliver, 2000) on which an 8% to 15% override rate is expected, and a sex offender-specific assessment, the Minnesota Sex Offender Screening Tool-Revised (MnSOST-R; Epperson, Kaul, & Hesselton, 1998).

In order to accommodate internal policies of criminal justice agencies that use the LS/CMI, the protocol also permits the use of a policy override, which operates in the same manner as the clinical override. If an offender cannot be classified at the risk level that is commensurate with his or her risk/need score for some internal administrative or policy reason, an administrative override, with explanation, is applied. The U.S. Federal Probation's risk tool, the Post-Conviction Risk Assessment (PCRA; Johnson, Lowenkamp, VanBenschoten, & Robinson, 2011), also allows for a policy or administrative override. The creation of these two distinct kinds of overrides differentiates their underlying rationale and allows researchers to study their impact on the accuracy of the assessment separately.

The use of the override feature of the LS/CMI has been monitored in Ontario over numerous years and found to vary considerably. When first implemented in a pilot format in 1995 as the LSI-OR, the override was used sparingly at 2.7% (Girard & Wormith, 2004). This was quite likely because assessors were either becoming adjusted to changes from its predecessor, the LSI, or were learning to conduct a risk assessment in the first place. At this time, the ratio of increased-to-decreased risk was approximately equal (i.e. 47.4% and 52.6%, respectively). Consequently, the predictive validity of the LS/CMI before and after the use of the override was virtually the same.

By 2004, the picture had changed considerably. An examination of the LS/CMI of a large cohort of probationers and prisoners ($N = 26,450$) in Ontario revealed that correctional workers had used the override on 15.0% of the nonsex offenders and 35.1% of the sexual offenders (Wormith, Hogg, & Guzzo, 2012). Among the nonsexual offender population, considerably more changes were made to increase risk rather than decrease risk (13.5% and 1.6%, respectively). Yet the difference in rate was even more for sexual offenders (33.5% and 1.6%, respectively). More problematically, the correlation between risk level and general recidivism decreased from .42 to .37 for nonsexual offenders and from .45 to .26 for sexual offenders. In other words, the LS/CMI became significantly less predictive of general recidivism for sexual offenders than nonsexual offenders after the override provision was enacted. The same pattern was found for violent recidivism, but not sexual recidivism. In an effort to understand the source of deteriorating predictive validity with use of the override, follow-up analyses identified a number of variables that contributed to using the override but had no incremental predictive validity to the prediction of recidivism (personal problems, social, health, and mental health needs, and responsivity) and others that did have incremental predictive validity but were unrelated to use of the override (i.e., history of perpetration and age [being young]).

A subsequent study comparing Driving While Impaired (DWI) offenders to the remainder of the offender population in Ontario in 2010 and 2011 revealed that the use of the override remained high at 14% for non-DWI offenders and 7.8% for DWI offenders (Pilon, Jewell, & Wormith, 2015). Again, the predictive validity correlations between the risk level and general recidivism fell for the non-DWI offenders from .40 to .38 and minimally for the DWI offenders from .29 to .28. However, different rates of use have been found elsewhere in Canada. The override was invoked less frequently (6.5%) and more often to decrease risk level rather than increase it (60.2% vs. 39.8%) in the province of Quebec. However, use of the override still resulted in lower predictive validity for the instrument (Guay & Parent, 2016).

The pattern described in these studies is reminiscent of other research examining the use of the override with other risk assessment instruments, such as the PCRA (Johnson et al., 2011) and the MnSOST-R (Epperson et al., 1998). This includes the relatively high frequency of use (10% to 25%; Epperson & Gore, 2004; McCafferty, 2017), the marked tendency to use it to increase risk rather than decrease it (Cohen et al., 2016), and the negative impact of its use on predictive validity (Cohen et al., 2016; Duwe & Rocque, 2018). Therefore, although not banning the override principle, researchers and scale developers have begun to urge more caution and restraint in its use (Duwe & Rocque, 2018; Guay & Parent, 2016). In order to minimize the inappropriate use of overrides, organizations may wish to enhance managerial oversite and challenge staff belief in their own personal judgment (Schaefer & Williamson, 2018).

Effective Communication of LS Assessments

Communicating the results of an offender risk assessment has, justifiably, become the focus of considerable attention among scale developers, researchers, and clinicians and is in need of systematic research and dialogue (DeClue & Zavodny, 2014; Hanson & Bourgon, 2017; Hanson, Babchishin, Helmus, Thornton & Phenix, 2017). The American Psychological Association's (American Psychological Association, 2013) updated guidelines for forensic psychologists state:

> Forensic practitioners make reasonable efforts to ensure that the products of their services, as well as their own public statements and professional reports and testimony, are communicated in ways that promote understanding and avoid deception. When in their role as expert to the court or other tribunals, the role of forensic practitioners is to facilitate understanding of the evidence in dispute.
>
> (Guideline 11.01, Accuracy, Fairness, and Avoidance of Deception; p. 16)

Although the concept of communicating risk assessments in a manner that promotes understanding may seem straightforward to the clinician, the product may not be so straightforward to the consumer or decision-maker, who is about to make an important choice about the life of the offender.

The LS scale developers, researchers, and users have considered various means of communicating the results of an LS assessment. One consideration has been the number of risk levels to craft and their associated risk labels. Options included three and four levels of risk, both used by versions of the LSI and LSI-R, and five levels of risk, which was finally settled on for the LS/CMI. Originally, the traditional high, medium, and low categories were defined, but then the two extreme groups were essentially subdivided to generate very high and very low risk. This modification added increased specificity to the range of risk predicted in each category, while maintaining the categories' symmetrical structure.

It was introduced for two reasons. First, the LS/CMI, like its predecessors, was designed for, and is being applied to, offenders with dramatically different degrees of risk. This is easily seen in the distribution of scores for prisoners and probationers (Andrews et al., 2004). Secondly, the diversity of criminal justice decisions that are, in practice, informed by the LS/CMI is vast. They range from absolute discharge and termination of supervision to intensive supervision and indeterminate incarceration. A group of researchers is now working with the U.S. Council of State Government's Justice Center to develop a standardized and psychologically meaningful five-level risk scheme that could transcend individual instruments and jurisdictions (Hanson, Bourgon et al., 2017). However, at least one state agency, Nebraska Probation, has elected to use seven risk levels, subdividing medium risk into medium low, medium, and medium high, with considerable success as measured by significantly different recidivism rates by risk level (Wiener, Reed, Delgado, & Caldwell, 2014).

In order to adhere to APA guideline 11.01, LS assessors are encouraged to report additional information about a specific assessment beyond the determined risk level. This may include the precise score and the range of scores that the pertinent risk level covers. This allows the reader to determine precisely where an offender falls within a certain risk level. Reports may also cite the percentile at which an offender falls and the corresponding recidivism rate of one's score. For purposes of clarification, it is critical to explain the difference between percentile and percent recidivism and to describe the type(s) of recidivism (e.g., general, violent, sexual) that are being cited. It is also important to describe the norms on which these statistics are based. Although LS manuals offer aggregated norms across multiple studies, jurisdictions, and countries, the development and use of local norms is encouraged (Wormith, 2014). For clinicians and case managers, it is also important to describe the criminogenic needs that are identified from LS assessments. The LS/CMI includes a risk/need profile (Table 8.5), on which the Central Eight risk/need domains are plotted graphically by the five risk levels, and enables the assessor to group, order, and describe criminogenic needs in terms of their severity.

Extending the Use of the LS Beyond Corrections

During the past few years there has been growing attention to the use of risk instruments in areas of the criminal justice system outside of corrections. In Holder's 2014 address, his specific concern was the use of potentially biased instruments in the courts. Incarcerations rates are much higher for African Americans and Indigenous offenders than for Whites. One explanation for the over-incarceration of racial minorities is systemic bias in the criminal justice system beginning with differential police arrest practices all the way to harsher sentencing for minorities. Given that minorities score higher on risk assessment instruments, LS included, the use of structured risk assessment with minorities could potentially contribute to the over-incarceration of disadvantaged segments of society (Starr, 2014). Whether or not risk assessment does place minorities at a disproportionate risk for criminal justice intervention is an empirical question, but it is important to understand how the LS and similar risk/need instruments function in court settings.

Actuarial risk assessments have been used in sentencing for decades, but their use for the purpose of preventative detention has been limited to the most serious cases in countries such as

Table 8.5 A Risk/Need Profile (LS/CMI) of a High Risk/Needs Offender (Case Example of Michael Cooper)

Risk/Need	CH	E/E	F/M	L/R	Co	A/DP	PA/O	ASP	Total	R/NI	Override
Very High	8	**−9**	4	−	4	**−8**	4	4	**0+**	**Very High**	**Very High**
High	**−7**	−7	3	2	3	**−6**	3	3	0–29	High	High
Medium	−5	−5	2	1	2	−4	2	2	1–19	Medium	Medium
Low	−3	−3	1	−	1	−2	1	1	−10	Low	Low
Very Low	−1	−1	0	0	0	0	0	0	−4	Very Low	Very Low

Note: CH = Criminal History; E/E = Education/Employment; F/M = Family/Marital; L/R = Leisure/ Recreation; Co = Companions; A/DP = Alcohol/Drug Problem; PA/O = Procriminal Attitude/Orientation; ASP = Antisocial Pattern; R/NI = Score-Based Risk/Need Level; Override = Risk/Need Level if Override Used. Examinee scores and categories are presented in **bold**.

Australia, Canada, Germany, and the United States (Blais & Bonta, 2015). Recently, the use of risk assessment in sentencing has been considerably expanded, calling it "evidence-based sentencing" (Starr, 2014). In our view, there are three questions to consider. First, is the risk assessment predictive of criminal behavior? Second, does the introduction of risk assessment meet court standards for expert evidence? And third, are the reasons for using risk assessment beneficial to the court, the offender, and the community. As already described in this chapter, the LS instruments do predict criminal behavior across settings, gender, and race. The remaining two questions require further discussion.

Historically, education and professional training were sufficient to persuade the court that one's opinion and use of whatever assessments selected by the professional were accepted as scientific evidence (for a thorough discussion of legal principles of admissibility, and their application to different types of risk assessment, see Chapter 4, this volume). This is called the *Frye* guidelines (i.e., generally accepted by the profession). In 1993, the U.S. Supreme Court ruled in *Daubert v. Merrell Dow Pharmaceuticals* that a higher level of standards should be applied to what the court accepts as "scientific evidence." In addition to general professional acceptance, evidence must be grounded in the scientific method, specify error rates, and be peer reviewed (Glancy & Saini, 2009). The LS instruments appear to meet the Daubert standard. Their predictive validity has been established by researchers who are independent of the developers and in different countries. Furthermore, statistical reporting allows for estimates of false positives and false negatives, and this evidence has been published in peer-reviewed publications. Cases involving LS instruments have been accepted as evidence by the courts in Canada (Queen's Bench for Saskatchewan, 2006) and the United States (Indiana Supreme Court, 2010). Thus, the LS may be viewed as meeting some of the courts' highest standards for scientific evidence.

The third question pertains to the utilitarian function of risk assessment, and in particular the LS, to the criminal justice stakeholders. Monahan and Skeem (2016; Skeem & Monahan, 2011) have asked whether or not the courts need a risk assessment simply to predict recidivism or to do more, to inform the process of reducing recidivism. First, one is reminded that simple recidivism prediction is a double-edged sword. It can serve to identify low-risk offenders for diversion from prisons. This would avoid the criminogenic effect of association with higher-risk offenders and the costs of imprisoning offenders who have a low probability of reoffending. This purpose is consistent with the ethical and legal principle of the least restrictive alternative (Rubin, 1975). However, simple prediction is also useful to identify high-risk offenders requiring additional restrictions. Some offender assessment instruments, such as the Psychopathy Checklist-Revised (Hare, 2003), have been used extensively to justify harsh penal penalties for high-risk offenders (Blais, 2015; DeMatteo & Edens, 2006; Zinger & Forth, 1998). With respect to the LS, the manual explicitly states that the instrument is *not* to be used for this purpose (Andrews & Bonta, 1995; Andrews et al., 2004).

Second, rather than using the LS for assisting the courts in formulating a just penalty, its main value in sentencing is to create a disposition that reduces the offender's chances of reoffending. This is facilitated by providing the judge with information on the criminogenic needs of the accused and, in the case of the LS/CMI, a proposed plan to address these needs. Yes, the LS will identify high-risk offenders and with it will come increased supervision, but the supervision is in tandem with a treatment plan. The ultimate goal of the LS is to reduce recidivism, which benefits the offender and the community.

The application of the LS fits into a framework of "therapeutic jurisprudence" (Winick & Wexler, 1991). Within this model, the law has the potential to become a therapeutic agent that values personal well-being (Birgden, 2015; Birgden & Ward, 2003). Not everyone will agree with the term, but there is a noticeable shift in many courts towards rehabilitation and away from strictly punishment (James, 2015). Interest in risk assessment by the courts has been so great as to spur the National Center for State Courts (Casey et al., 2014) to publish a primer on risk/needs assessment. A major vehicle for providing LS information to the courts has been through presentence reports (Bonta, Bourgon, Jesseman, & Yessine, 2005; Jung, Brown, Ennis, & Ledi, 2015). For example, in 2013, the Supreme Court of West Virginia went so far as to institute a policy that the LS/CMI be administered to all felony offenders *prior* to sentencing (Riggs, 2013). The main argument for the policy is that judges should have as much information as possible to craft the sentence in a way that addresses the offender's criminogenic needs and promotes public safety.

The use of the LS and similar risk/need assessment instruments are not without controversy (Eckhouse, Lum, Conti-Cook, & Ciccolini, 2019). Specifically, concerns have been raised that risk could trump the principle of proportionality (Cole, 2007), that it is unethical and unjust to punish someone based on what they may do (James, 2015), that the instruments lack transparency since individual items and their scoring are often proprietary (Kaufmann, 2009), and that one cannot make decisions of risk for an individual based on an assessment developed from a group (Netter, 2007; Starr, 2014). These are serious issues, and researchers and practitioners need to give them serious consideration. However, we agree with Andrews and Dowden (2007) that there are good reasons why RNR-based instruments like the LS should be used in sentencing. Most judges want risk information (Bonta et al., 2005; Riggs, 2013), and providing it has a number of benefits. Judges, as part of their deliberations, already assess the risk of the accused and, without evidence-based guidance, are likely to misjudge an offender's risk (Krauss, 2004). Identifying the low-risk offender and diverting him/her to community-based sanctions spares the human and financial costs associated with imprisonment. Perhaps, most importantly, reduced recidivism is best achieved through RNR-based rehabilitation where the LS is the foundation, and for this task the courts can be a valuable partner in this effort.

Summary and Conclusions

The LSI-R and LS/CMI have yielded an impressive array of validity coefficients of considerable utility. In prediction of both general recidivism and violence, LS risk/need does as well as alternative assessment instruments. One of the strengths of the LS instruments is the extensive evidence of dynamic predictive criterion validity wherein changes in dynamic item scores are associated with shifts in reoffending rates. Also of note is the evidence of LSI-R Risk/Need-by-Service interaction. In brief, use of the LS renders decisions reliable, valid, and transparent. In the process, public protection is enhanced by assigning supervision and service according to risk/need, cost-effectiveness is enhanced by assigning low-risk cases to minimal supervision and service, as is implementation of the least restrictive and least costly interpretation of the penalty while respecting public protection.

Some limitations are specific to the LS products, while others are limitations of the field as a whole. Most notably, apart from LSI-R-SV, the LS instruments include many more items than are required to assess risk. Indeed, there is no need to conduct an LSI-R or LS/CMI assessment if all that is required is a one-time determination of level of risk. The need, responsivity, and other information are not required unless service planning is required. However, LSI-R-SV has been the focus of very little research, in particular in the prediction of violence (Daffern, Ogloff, Ferguson, & Thomson, 2005; Livingston, Chu, Milne, & Brink, 2015; Olver et al., 2014; Yessine & Bonta, 2006).

A specific hypothesis is that use of LS/CMI will enhance service planning and delivery that is in adherence with RNR and hence promote positive intermediate and ultimate outcomes. At this point, the extant research suggests that practitioners fail to fully take advantage of their assessments in developing risk intervention strategies (Viljoen, Cochrane, & Jonnson, 2018). Dyck and her colleagues (2018) found that probation officers, even though they administered the LS/CMI, still showed poor adherence to the RNR principles in their case plans. Nevertheless, continued research on the interplay between assessment and case management will contribute directly to understanding assessment issues but also to theories of criminal conduct and to the theory and practice of effective crime prevention. Inter-site and inter-agency studies with LS/CMI will promote understanding of the contributions of broader social and cultural contexts to service planning and delivery and to outcomes. We have had a long-term interest in the inter-connections among: (a) worker factors, (b) case factors, (c) service plans, (d) service delivery, (e) intermediate outcomes, and (f) ultimate outcome (Andrews & Kiessling, 1980; Hoge & Andrews, 1986). Agencies employing the LS/CMI have the opportunity to turn their service sites into field experiments. These data will provide quantitative estimates of the value of shifts in service and supervision.

According to available evidence, the predictive validity of LS risk/need is very robust across different types of people. However, some developmental and psychological criminologists and some feminist criminologists have suggested that age of onset and gender-specific pathways to crime are important moderators of the predictive validity of risk/need factors. Both deserve further exploration. We appreciate the importance of maximizing the applicability of risk/need assessments to all offenders, regardless of age, gender, ethnicity, and nationality, and strive to that end.

Case Example: An LS/CMI Assessment of a High-Risk/Need Offender

Michael Cooper is serving a sentence of three years for armed robbery, possession of a dangerous weapon, and escaping lawful custody. This is his fifth term of imprisonment. Mr. Cooper has reached his parole eligibility date and he is under review for possible parole release. An assessment was requested to advise the Parole Board on Mr. Cooper's likelihood of completing his period of parole supervision without reoffending or violating the terms of his release, and identify services and strategies that would maximize his chances of success.

Criminal History

Mr. Cooper has accumulated 24 prior convictions, including five previous assaults (all nonsexual), one of which occurred while in custody. His first arrest occurred at age 14 for shoplifting. Mr. Cooper has never been on probation or parole. His first offense as an adult was for assaulting a police officer, and he was sentenced to six months in jail. Police were called to a disturbance in a bar, and when they confronted a drunken Mr. Cooper, he swore at them and took a swing at one of the officers. Previous parole applications were always denied.

Mr. Cooper escaped from the minimum security camp to which he was transferred after serving half of his current prison term. He was working on a road gang and absconded when the supervising staff's attention was diverted. Mr. Cooper was apprehended a few hours later. Records indicate that Mr. Cooper has had 15 prior institutional misconducts ranging from possession of contraband (drugs) to assaulting staff. The assault on a staff member occurred when he was told to go to his cell following an argument with another inmate. Mr. Cooper pushed a correctional officer and warned that he knew where the officer lived, so he had better watch out. Following his escape and assault, Mr. Cooper was transferred to a maximum security facility where he is currently housed.

Repeated efforts were required to have Mr. Cooper attend an interview for his parole assessment. When he finally did attend an interview, he asked if the meeting would take long because he had to get to the gym for his workout. When asked to describe the present offenses, Mr. Cooper painted a picture of an innocent man who was wrongly convicted. He says that he and his friends were returning from a hunting trip when they were pulled over by the police. Apparently a local convenience store was robbed and the description of the robbers matched Mr. Cooper and his two friends. Arrest records and court transcripts are in conflict with this view. Both hidden camera and eyewitness evidence were used in the trial to confirm that Mr. Cooper and his friends were indeed the correct suspects. The witnesses testified that the perpetrators appeared to be under the influence of drugs, and that guns were used to threaten the clerk. Although the offenses were committed with two accomplices, there is no evidence that the crimes were part of gang activity or organized crime. The co-accused were friends of Mr. Cooper, one of whom he had met while in prison, and the other was a longtime criminal associate.

Education/Employment

Mr. Cooper reported that he had numerous difficulties in school as he was growing up. He repeated grade 3 and was placed into special education classes when he was 11 years old. Mr. Cooper remembered seeing the school psychologists for "tests" but could not elaborate any further. His difficulties in keeping up with the academic work and frustration over his poor reading skills ("I would get my 'b's' and 'd's' mixed up") led to numerous conflicts with other students who teased him and with teachers. Suspensions were frequent, and he finally left school when he was 16 years old and midway through grade 9.

After Mr. Cooper left school, which coincided with his leaving home, he lived either with friends or on the street. He supported himself by relying on the charity of others, committing crimes or receiving welfare assistance. Mr. Cooper never worked for more than a few weeks at a time and either quit or was fired. He was not working prior to this term of imprisonment, and he has no employment offer upon release. As indicated by Mr. Cooper's employment history, he has no legitimate means of financial support. He has never worked long enough to establish a credit rating or save money. All his income appears to derive from illegitimate activities or from social assistance programs. He owes money to others for drugs and worries about meeting up with these individuals in the community.

Family/Marital

At present, Mr. Cooper is single. He had a common-law partner prior to incarceration and she left him shortly after sentencing. His third assault conviction occurred during a domestic dispute about his drug use. Mr. Cooper claims that he pushed his girlfriend out of the way in order to leave the apartment and meet his friends at a local bar. She fell and sustained bruises but was not injured otherwise. In Mr. Cooper's view, he treated her well, like all of his other girlfriends, and he denied feeling upset over her departure and said that "there are other fish in the sea." He is in no hurry to find a new girlfriend and says that he wants to enjoy his bachelorhood when released.

Mr. Cooper receives weekly visits from his mother and sister. His older brother will visit about once a month, but he has not spoken with his younger brother for three months because of this brother's recent incarceration for theft charges. Mr. Cooper described his family as close-knit and that he is always welcomed at his mother's home. However, he does not wish to impose on her, saying that she has had a difficult life with his father. His father was a violent man who would often beat her and sometimes the children. Mr. Cooper denied any sexual abuse from the father, and his closeness to his mother made up for the father's aloofness. Eventually, Mr. Cooper ran away from home because of this situation. The father was subsequently arrested and imprisoned. The father died in prison from a drug overdose. Mr. Cooper reported that he could have returned home, but by then he had become used to living on his own. Although Mr. Cooper has not lived at home for many years, he still visits his mother and siblings regularly. They spend special occasions together and during these gatherings an uncle (on his mother's side) and someone who he greatly admires usually attends. Mr. Cooper describes these gatherings as happy events filled with laughter and emotional warmth.

Leisure/Recreation

It comes as little surprise that Mr. Cooper shows little interest in legitimate activities. Quite the opposite, he expressed disdain about people who would spend all day "doing the 9–5" in order to make enough money to give to charities so that people like himself can get "food for free." When asked if he had ever participated in an organized activity such as the Kiwanis organization or a church group, he went into a long diatribe of what a waste of time it is to do something for no money. When asked to describe a typical day on the street, Mr. Cooper responded that it was all "sex, drugs, and rock and roll." Most of his spare time is spent with friends in bars, which is where his fourth assault charge took place. When a stranger would not give up a pool table to other waiting patrons, Mr. Cooper struck the man with a pool cue. No injuries were sustained, but the police were called.

Companions

Mr. Cooper began stealing when he was 14 years old, and after leaving home and school, he quickly established himself within a criminal social network. Never having worked, he has also never established any relationships with non-criminal individuals. Mr. Cooper further volunteered that he enjoys his life on the street and the excitement of crime. His friends are described as loyal associates who look after each other and help each other when in trouble.

Alcohol/Drug Problem

After leaving home, Mr. Cooper soon took up drinking with the people he met. He reported that the drinking "got pretty bad," but that he left the drinking behind when he was introduced to cocaine. For Mr. Cooper, injecting cocaine is described as a wonderful sensation, and he was hooked right from the first time.

Much of Mr. Cooper's life appears to revolve around cocaine. He steals in order to buy the drug, which he uses on a daily basis when in the community. When imprisoned for the present offenses, Mr. Cooper had to be supervised in the prison hospital during de-toxification. He had been rushed to hospitals on numerous occasions as a result of unintentional drug overdoses and advised by doctors that his cocaine abuse was affecting his heart. Despite feelings of paranoia when taking large amounts of cocaine, Mr. Cooper said that he would continue taking the drug for the powerful rush it gives. He did admit that he cannot continue such a destructive path, but he felt he was still young and healthy enough to handle it and that he will quit when he is older. Although none of his offenses have been for drug possession or trafficking, his fifth assault charge occurred in the residence of a known drug dealer. Mr. Cooper insists that he had simply accompanied some friends to the residence when a dispute broke out over "business," and neighbors heard the fracas and called the police. The resident claimed that he had been assaulted without provocation.

Procriminal Attitude/Orientation

Throughout the interview Mr. Cooper expressed attitudes and values supportive of criminal behavior. He described his criminal friends in glowing terms, and stated that victims of some of his crimes "had it coming to them" and most of the laws "that I supposedly broke are stupid." Prosocial activities were devalued and ridiculed. A good illustration is Mr. Cooper's views on volunteer organizations. As noted earlier, Mr. Cooper states that he was wrongly arrested and convicted and his frequent institutional misconducts and reluctance to attend this pre-parole interview reflect a negative attitude towards following correctional rules. When asked how he would feel about reporting to a parole officer on a regular basis if paroled, Mr. Cooper answered that he saw no need to do this since he should not have been imprisoned in the first place.

Other Client (Examinee) Issues

Mr. Cooper has not had a stable residence since leaving his mother's home. Between his frequent incarcerations, Mr. Cooper has lived either with friends, at hostels, or, in good weather, on the street. During his last release, he had lived in five different places. His friends are all known offenders and the temporary shelters where he has lived are situated in neighborhoods with high levels of criminal activity.

Except for special education classes and the school psychologists, Mr. Cooper has never seen a mental health professional. Mr. Cooper described himself as an outgoing and energetic person who will not back down from a confrontation. He has no respect for people who try to exert their authority over him. He denied any feelings of nervousness, insomnia, or physical complaints. None of the drug overdoses were classified as suicide attempts, and he denies any hallucinations or delusions save when he injects too much cocaine.

In reviewing prison files and the results from the interview, it appears that Mr. Cooper has not formed any enduring emotional attachments to others. Despite what he reports about relationships with his mother and siblings, they appear transitory. He sees them only on special occasions or when he needs some money (his mother and younger sister have often loaned him money). He has had numerous relationships, but none have lasted more than a few months. When describing past assaults, Mr. Cooper showed no remorse over his actions and insists that either he was the "real" victim or the victim "deserved it." Further assessment into the possibility of a personality disorder may be warranted as it may have a bearing on how this examinee needs to be supervised and his responsiveness to treatment.

Summary and Recommendations

From all indications in Mr. Cooper's record and interview, there appears to be little motivation to change his criminal lifestyle. Mr. Cooper's score of 36 on the LS/CMI placed him in the "Very High" range for risk of reoffending (see Table 8.5). Sixty-one percent of offenders with similar scores were convicted for a new crime leading to a custodial sentence within one year of release (Andrews et al., 2004). Girard and Wormith (2004) reported that 83 percent of a sample of nonsexual offenders in the Very High risk category was convicted of a new offense within 2.5 years of their release from custody. Moreover, almost half (48%) of them were convicted of a new violent offense compared to 24% for all nonsexual offenders (the base rate). The assessment did not produce any information suggesting that his risk level should be overridden to a lower level (Table 8.5). Although there have not been any serious injuries as a result of Mr. Cooper's violent outbursts, he is considered to be at continued risk for both general and violent recidivism. The diversity of victims, locations, and circumstances of his violence suggest a generalized pattern of violent and property crime, most of which has been linked to his drug use and general antisocial lifestyle.

The results also indicate a number of areas that must be addressed if Mr. Cooper is to decrease his risk of both violent and nonviolent criminal behavior. He is severely addicted to cocaine, all his peers are criminal, he has no employment or academic skills, he has a low frustration tolerance, and he shows extremely supportive attitudes towards criminal behavior and negative attitudes toward prosocial behavior. Items that were flagged in the Specific Risk Need Factors section of the LS/CMI for further attention include the following: clear problems of compliance; threat from third party; problem solving/self-management skills deficits; anger management deficits; intimidating/controlling; poor social skills; physical assault, extra-familial (adult victim); physical assault, intra-familial (partner victim); assault on an authority figure; and weapon use. The only strength in Mr. Cooper's profile is his positive relationship with his mother. At least, in her home he abstains from drug use, although it is difficult to ascertain how long he would be able to avoid drugs and violence by simply residing in her home. Nevertheless, Mr. Cooper's relationship with his mother can serve as a possible strength on which to build a case management plan.

Until Mr. Cooper accepts a willingness to try to cease using cocaine and abandon his violent and criminal lifestyle, an early release would not be recommended. While imprisoned, continued efforts should be made to engage Mr. Cooper in working in the prison industry and seeking psychological counseling to focus on his anger, drug abuse, and procriminal attitudes. When Mr. Cooper is released to the community either on parole or post-release supervision, there are a number of suggestions for his community case management. Mr. Cooper should be required to reside at his mother's house. Apparently, this is one place where he does not do drugs. A referral to an intensive outpatient substance abuse program for offenders is strongly recommended. Participation in a weekly anger management program that targets aggressive behavior through social skills training and self-control is recommended. Intensive supervision commensurate with his degree of risk is also recommended.

References

Abbott, B. R. (2011). Throwing the baby out with the bath water: Is it time for clinical judgment to supplement actuarial risk assessment? *Journal of the American Academy of Psychiatry and Law, 39*, 222–230.

American Educational Research Association, American Psychological Association, & National Council on Measurement in Education. (1999). *The standards for educational and psychological testing.* Washington, DC: American Educational Research Association.

American Psychological Association. (2013). Specialty guidelines for forensic psychologists. *American Psychologist, 68*, 7–19.

Andrews, D. A. (1982). *The level of supervision inventory (LSI): The first follow-up.* Toronto, ON: Ontario Ministry of Correctional Services.

Andrews, D. A. (2001). Principles of effective correctional programs. In L. L. Motiuk & R. C. Serin (Eds.), *Compendium 2000 on effective correctional programming* (pp. 9–17). Ottawa: Correctional Services of Canada.

Andrews, D. A., & Bonta, J. (1995). *Level of service inventory-revised.* Toronto, ON: Multi-Health Systems.

Andrews, D. A., & Bonta, J. (1998). *Level of service inventory-revised: Screening version.* Toronto, ON: Multi-Health Systems.

Andrews, D. A., & Bonta, J. (2010). *The psychology of criminal conduct* (5th ed.). Newark, NJ: LexisNexis, Matthew Bender.

Andrews, D. A., Bonta, J., & Hoge, R. D. (1990). Classification for effective rehabilitation: Rediscovering psychology. *Criminal Justice and Behavior, 17,* 19–52.

Andrews, D. A., Bonta, J., Motiuk, L. L., & Robinson, D. (1984). *Some psychometrics of practical risk/needs assessment.* Paper presented at the Annual Meeting of the American Psychological Association, Toronto, ON.

Andrews, D. A., Bonta, J., & Wormith, J. S. (1995). *The level of service inventory-Ontario revision (LSI-OR): Interview and scoring guide.* Toronto, ON: Ministry of the Solicitor General and Correctional Services.

Andrews, D. A., Bonta, J., & Wormith, J. S. (2004). *The level of service/case management inventory (LS/CMI).* Toronto, ON: Multi-Health Systems.

Andrews, D. A., Bonta, J., & Wormith, J. S. (2008). *The level of service/risk-need-responsivity (LS/RNR).* Toronto, ON: Multi-Health Systems.

Andrews, D. A., Bonta, J., & Wormith, J. S. (2010). The level of service (ls) assessment of adults and older adolescents. In R. K. Otto & K. Douglas (Eds.), *Handbook of violent risk assessment tools* (1st ed.). New York: Routledge.

Andrews, D. A., Bonta, J., & Wormith, J. S. (2011). The risk-need-responsivity (RNR) model: Does adding the good lives model contribute to effective crime prevention? *Criminal Justice and Behavior, 38,* 735–755.

Andrews, D. A., Bonta, J., Wormith, S. J., Guzzo, L., Brews, A., Rettinger, J., & Rowe, R. (2011). Sources of variability in estimates of predictive validity: A specification with level of service risk and need. *Criminal Justice and Behavior, 38,* 413–432.

Andrews, D. A., & Dowden, C. (2006). Risk principle of case classification in correctional treatment. *International Journal of Offender Therapy and Comparative Criminology, 50,* 88–100.

Andrews, D. A., & Dowden, C. (2007). The risk-need-responsivity model of assessment and human service in prevention and corrections: Crime-prevention jurisprudence. *Canadian Journal of Criminology and Criminal Justice, 50,* 439–464.

Andrews, D. A., Guzzo, L., Raynor, P., Rowe, R. C., Rettinger, J., Brews, A, & Wormith, J. S. (2012). Are the major risk/need factors predictive of both female and male reoffending? A test with the eight domains of the level of service/case management inventory. *International Journal of Offender Therapy and Comparative Criminology, 56,* 113–133.

Andrews, D. A., & Kiessling, J. J. (1980). Program structure and effective correctional practices: A summary of the CaVIC research. In R. R. Ross & P. Gendreau (Eds.), *Effective correctional treatment* (pp. 439–463). Toronto, ON: Butterworth.

Andrews, D. A., & Robinson, D. (1984). *The level of supervision inventory: Second report.* Toronto, ON: Ontario Ministry of Correctional Services.

Angwin, J., Larson, J., Mattu, S., & Kirchner, L. (2016, May 23). Machine bias: There's software used across the country to predict future criminals. And it's biased against blacks. *ProPublica.* Retrieved from https://www.propublica.org/article/machine-bias-risk-assessments-in-criminal-sentencing

Birgden, A. (2015). Maximizing desistance: Adding therapeutic jurisprudence and human rights to the mix. *Criminal Justice and Behavior, 42,* 19–31.

Birgden, A., & Ward, T. (2003). Pragmatic psychology through the therapeutic jurisprudence lens: Psycholegal soft spots in the criminal justice system. *Psychology, Public Policy, and Law, 9,* 334–360.

Blais, J. (2015). Preventative detention decisions: Reliance on expert assessments and evidence of partisan allegiance within the Canadian context. *Behavioral Sciences and the Law, 33,* 74–91.

Blais, J., & Bonta, J. (2015). Tracking and managing high risk offenders: A Canadian initiative. *Law and Human Behavior, 39,* 253–265.

Bonta, J. (1989). Native inmates: Institutional response, risk, and needs. *Canadian Journal of Criminology, 31,* 49–62.

Bonta, J. (1996). Risk-needs assessment and treatment. In A. T. Harland (Ed.), *Choosing correctional options that work* (pp. 18–32). Thousand Oaks, CA: Sage.

Bonta, J., & Andrews, D. A. (2007). *Risk-need-responsivity model for offender assessment and treatment* (User Report No. 2007-06). Ottawa: Public Safety Canada.

Bonta, J., & Andrews, D. A. (2017). *The psychology of criminal conduct* (6th ed.). New York: Routledge.

Bonta, J., Bourgon, G., Jesseman, R., & Yessine, A. K. (2005). *Presentence reports in Canada* (User Report 2005-03). Ottawa: Public Safety Canada.

Bonta, J., & Motiuk, L. L. (1986a). *Use of the level of supervision inventory for assessing incarcerates.* Paper presented at the 94th Annual Convention of the American Psychological Association, Washington, DC.

Bonta, J., & Motiuk, L. L. (1986b). *The LSI in institutions: Toronto Jail, Hamilton-Wentworth detention centre, Ottawa-Carleton detention centre* (Report #1). Toronto, ON: Ontario Ministry of Correctional Services.

Bonta, J., & Motiuk, L. L. (1987). The diversion of incarcerated offenders to correctional halfway houses. *Journal of Research in Crime and Delinquency, 24,* 302–323.

Bonta, J., & Motiuk, L. L. (1990). Classification to halfway houses: A quasi-experimental evaluation. *Criminology, 28,* 497–506.

Bonta, J., & Motiuk, L. L. (1992). Inmate classification. *Journal of Criminal Justice, 20,* 343–353.

Bonta, J., Wallace-Capretta, S., & Rooney, J. (2000). A quasi-experimental evaluation of an intensive rehabilitation supervision program. *Criminal Justice and Behavior, 27,* 312–329.

Bourgon, G., & Armstrong, B. (2005). Transferring the principles of effective treatment into a "real world" prison setting. *Criminal Justice and Behavior, 32,* 3–25.

Brennan, T., & Oliver, W. L. (2000). *Evaluation of reliability and validity of COMPAS scales: National aggregate sample.* Traverse City, MI: Northpointe Institute for Public Management.

Brown, S., & Motiuk, L. (2008). Using dynamic risk factors to predict criminal recidivism in a sample of male and female offenders. *Canadian Psychology/Psychologie Canadienne, 49*(2A), 298.

Campbell, M. A., French, S., & Gendreau, P. (2009). The prediction of violence in adult offenders: A meta-analytic comparison of instruments and methods of assessment. *Criminal Justice and Behavior, 36,* 567–590.

Casey, P. M., Elek, J. K., Warren, R. K., Cheesmen, F., Kleiman, M., & Ostrom, B. (2014). *Offender risk & needs assessment: A primer for courts.* Washington, DC: National Center for State Courts.

Cohen, T. H., Pendergast, B., & VanBenschoten, S. W. (2016). Examining overrides of risk classifications for offenders on federal supervision. *Federal Probation, 80,* 12–21.

Cole, D. P. (2007). The umpires strike back: Canadian judicial experience with risk assessment. *Canadian Journal of Criminology and Criminal Justice, 49,* 493–517.

Daffern, M., Ogloff, J. R. P., Ferguson, M., & Thomson, L. (2005). Assessing risk for aggression in a forensic psychiatric hospital using the level of service inventory-revised: Screening version. *International Journal of Forensic Mental Health, 4,* 201–206.

DeClue, G., & Zavodny, D. L. (2014). Forensic use of the static-99R: Pt. 4. Risk communication. *Journal of Threat Assessment and Management, 1,* 145–161.

DeMatteo, D., & Edens, J. F. (2006). The role and relevance of the psychopathy checklist-revised in court. *Psychology, Public Policy, and Law, 12,* 214–241.

Duwe, G., & Rocque, M. (2018). The home-field advantage and the perils of professional judgment: Evaluating the performance of the Static-99R and the MnSOST-3 in predicting sexual recidivism. *Law and Human Behavior, 42,* 269–279.

Dyck, H. L., Campbell, M. A., & Wershler, J. L. (2018). Real-world use of the risk-need-responsivity model and the level of service/case management inventory with community-supervised offenders. *Law and Human Behavior, 42,* 258–268.

Eckhouse, L., Lum, K., Conti-Cook, C., & Ciccolini, J. (2019). Layers of bias: A unified approach for understanding problems with risk assessment. *Criminal Justice and Behavior, 46,* 185–209.

Eher, R., Retternberger, M., Matthes, A., & Schilling, F. (2010). Stable dynamic risk factors in child sexual abusers: The incremental predictive power of narcissistic personality traits beyond the STATIC-99/STABLE-2007 priority categories on sexual reoffense. *Sexual Offender Treatment, 5,* 1–12.

Eisenberg, M. J., Van Horn, J. E., Dekker, J., Assink, M., Van Der Put, C. E., Hendricks, J., & Stams, G. J. J. M. (2019). Static and dynamic predictors of general and violent recidivism in the forensic outpatient population: A meta-analysis. *Criminal Justice and Behavior, 46,* 732–750.

Epperson, D. L., & Gore, K. S. (2004). *Investigation of clinical overrides of the MnSOST-R and the resulting impact on predictive accuracy.* Paper presented at the 23rd research and treatment convention of the Association for the Treatment of Sexual Abusers, Albuquerque, NM.

Epperson, D. L., Kaul, J. D., & Hesselton, D. (1998). *Final report on the development of the Minnesota sex offender screening tool—revised.* Paper presented at the 17th Annual Conference of the Association and Treatment of Sexual Abusers, Vancouver, BC.

Flores, A. W., Lowenkamp, C. T., Holsinger, A. M., & Latessa, E. J. (2006). Predicting outcome with the level of service inventory-revised: The importance of implementation integrity. *Journal of Criminal Justice, 34*, 523–529.

Folsom, J., & Atkinson, J. L. (2007). The generalizability of the LSI and the CAT to the prediction of recidivism in female offenders. *Criminal Justice and Behavior, 34*, 1044–1056.

Geraghty, K. A., & Woodhams, J. (2015). The predictive validity of risk assessment tools for female offenders: A systematic review. *Aggression and Violent Behavior, 21*, 25–38.

Gendreau, P., Goggin, C., & Smith, P. (2002). Is the PCL-R really the "unparalleled" measure of offender risk? *Criminal Justice and Behavior, 29*, 397–426.

Gendreau, P., Little, T., & Goggin, C. (1996). A meta-analysis of the predictors of adult offender recidivism: What works! *Criminology, 34*, 575–607.

Girard, L., & Wormith, J. S. (2004). The predictive validity of the level of service inventory-Ontario revision on general and violent recidivism among various offender groups. *Criminal Justice and Behavior, 31*, 150–181.

Glancy, G. D., & Saini, M. (2009). The confluence of evidence-based practice and "Daubert" within the fields of forensic psychiatry and the law. *Journal of the American Academy of Psychiatry and the Law, 37*, 438–441.

Global Institute of Forensic Research. (2016). Retrieved from www.gifrinc.com

Gordon, H., Kelty, S. F., & Julian, R. (2015). Psychometric evaluation of the level of service/case management inventory among Australian offenders completing community-based sentences. *Criminal Justice and Behavior, 42*, 1089–1109.

Guay, J. P. (2016). L'évaluation du risque et des besoins criminogènes à la lumière des données probantes: Une étude de validation de la version française de l'Inventaire de niveau de service et de gestion des cas -LS/CMI [French validation of the level of service/case management inventory- LS/CMI]. *European Review of Applied Psychology/Revue Européenne de Psychologie Appliquée, 66*, 199–210.

Guay, J. P., & Parent, G. (2016). *Broken legs, clinical overrides and recidivism risk: An analysis of decisions to adjust risk levels with the LS/CMI.* Unpublished report, University of Montreal, Montreal, Quebec.

Gutierrez, L., Wilson, H. A., Rugge, T., & Bonta, J. (2013). The prediction of recidivism with aboriginal offenders: A theoretically informed meta-analysis. *Canadian Journal of Criminology and Criminal Justice, 55*, 55–99.

Hannah-Moffat, K. (2009). Gridlock or mutability: Reconsidering "gender" and risk assessment. *Criminology & Public Policy, 8*, 209–219.

Hanson, R. K., Babchishin, K. M., Helmus, L. K., Thornton, D., & Phenix, A. (2017). Communicating the risk of criterion references prediction measures: Risk categories for the Static-99R and the Static-2002R sexual offender risk assessment tools. *Psychological Assessment, 29*, 582–597.

Hanson, R. K., & Bourgon, G. (2017). Advancing sexual offender risk assessment: Standardized risk levels based on psychologically meaningful offender characteristics. In F. Taxman (Ed.), *Handbook on risk and need assessment: Theory and practice* (pp. 244–268). New York: Routledge.

Hanson, R. K., Bourgon, G., McGrath, R. J., Kroner, D., D'Amora, D. A., Thompson, S. S., & Tavarez, L. P. (2017). *A five-level risk and needs system: Maximizing assessment results in corrections through the development of a common language.* New York: The Council of State Governments Justice Center.

Harcourt, B. (2015). Risk as a proxy for race: The dangers of risk assessment. *Federal Sentencing Reporter, 27*, 237–243.

Hare, R. D. (2003). *The Hare psychopathy checklist-revised* (2nd ed.). Toronto, ON: Multi-Health Systems.

Hogg, S. M. (2011). *The level of service inventory (Ontario Revision) scale validation for gender and ethnicity: Addressing reliability and predictive validity* (Unpublished Master's thesis). Department of Psychology, University of Saskatchewan, Saskatoon.

Hoge, R. D., & Andrews, D. A. (1986). A model for conceptualizing interventions in social service. *Canadian Psychology, 27*, 332–341.

Hoge, R. D., & Andrews, D. A. (2002). *Youth Level of service/case management inventory: User's manual.* Toronto, ON: Multi-Health Systems.

Holder, E. (2014). *Attorney General Eric Holder speaks at the national association of criminal defense lawyers 57th annual meeting.* Retrieved from www.justice.gov/opa/speech/attorney-general-eric-holder-speaks-national association-criminal-defense-lawyers-57th

Holt, R. R. (1958). Clinical and statistical predictions: Reformation and some new data. *Journal of Abnormal and Social Psychology, 56*, 1–12.

Holtfreter, K., & Cupp, R. (2007). Gender and risk assessment: The empirical status of the LSI-R for women. *Journal of Contemporary Criminology, 23*, 363–382.

Holwell, T. (Undated). *LSI-R, LS/RNR and LS/CMI documentation.* Unpublished report, Public Safety Division, Multi-Health Systems, Toronto, ON. Retrieved from www.scstatehouse.gov/Archives/Citizens InterestPage/SentencingReformComm

Hollin, C. R., Palmer, E. J., & Clark, D. (2003). Level of service inventory-revised profile of English prisoners: A needs analysis. *Criminal Justice and Behavior, 30*, 422–440.

Indiana Supreme Court. (2010). J. S. vs. State of Indiana. No. 79So2-1006-CR-296.

Interstate Commission for Adult Offender Supervision. (2007). *SO assessment information survey 4–2007.* Retrieved from www.interstatecompact.org/resources/surveys/survey_results/SexOffender_Assessment_042007.pdf

James, N. (2015). *Risk and needs assessment in the criminal justice system.* Washington, DC: Congressional Research Service.

Johnson, J., Lowenkamp, C. T., VanBenschoten, S. W., & Robinson, C. (2011). The construction and validation of the federal post sentence risk assessment (PCRA). *Federal Probation, 75*, 16–29.

Jung, S., Brown, K., Ennis, L., & Ledi, D. (2015). The association between presentence risk evaluations and sentencing outcome. *Applied Psychology in Criminal Justice, 11*, 111–125.

Kaiser, H. F. (1974). An index of factorial simplicity. *Psychometrika, 39*, 31–36.

Kaufmann, P. M. (2009). Protecting raw data and psychological tests from wrongful disclosure: A primer on the law and other persuasive strategies. *The Clinical Neuropsychologist, 23*, 1130–1159.

Krauss, D. A. (2004). Adjusting risk of recidivism: Do judicial departures worsen or improve recidivism prediction under federal sentencing guidelines? *Behavioral Science and the Law, 22*, 731–750.

Kroner, D. G., & Mills, J. F. (2001). The accuracy of five risk appraisal instruments in predicting institutional misconduct and new convictions. *Criminal Justice and Behavior, 28*, 471–489.

Labrecque, R. M., Campbell, C. M., Elliott, J., Kinga, M., Christmann, M., Page, K., . . . Roller, K. (2018). An examination of the inter-rater reliability and rater accuracy of the level of service/case management inventory. *Corrections: Policy, Practice and Research, 3*, 105–118.

Livingston, J. D., Chu, K., Milne, T., & Brink, J. (2015). Probationers mandated to receive forensic mental health services in Canada: Risk/needs, service delivery, and intermediate outcomes. *Psychology, Public Policy, and Law, 21*, 72–84.

Lowenkamp, C. T., Latessa, E. J., & Holsinger, A. M. (2004). Empirical evidence on the importance of training and experience in using the level of service inventory-revised. *Topics in Community Corrections*, 49–53.

Loza, W., & Green, K. (2003). The self-appraisal questionnaire. *Journal of Interpersonal Violence, 18*, 781–797.

Loza, W., & Simourd, D. J. (1994). Psychometric evaluation of the level of supervision inventory (LSI) among male Canadian federal offenders. *Criminal Justice and Behavior, 21*, 468–480.

McCafferty, J. T. (2017). Professional discretion and the predictive validity of a juvenile risk assessment instrument: Exploring the overlooked principle of effective correctional classification. *Youth Violence and Juvenile Justice, 15*, 103–118.

Meehl, P. E. (1954). *Clinical versus statistical predictions: A theoretical analysis and a review of the evidence.* Minneapolis: University of Minnesota Press.

Meehl, P. E. (1957). When shall we use our heads instead of the formula? *Journal of Counseling Psychology, 4*, 268–273.

Mills, J. F., & Kroner, D. G. (2006). The effect of discordance among violence and general recidivism risk estimates on predictive accuracy. *Criminal Behaviour and Mental Health, 16*, 155–166.

Monahan, J., & Skeem, J. L. (2016). Risk assessment in criminal sentencing. *Annual Review of Clinical Psychology, 12*, 489–513.

Morash, M. (2009). A great debate over using the level of service inventory-revised (LSI-R) with women offenders. *Criminology & Public Policy, 8*, 172–181.

Motiuk, L. L., & Bonta, J. (1991). *Prediction and matching in corrections: An examination of the risk principle in case classification.* Paper presented at the Annual Convention of the Canadian Psychological Association, Calgary, Alberta.

Neal, T. M. S., & Grisso, T. (2014). Assessment practices and expert judgment methods in forensic psychology and psychiatry. *Criminal Justice and Behavior, 41*, 1406–1421.

Netter, B. (2007). Using group statistics to sentence individual criminals: An ethical and statistical critique of the Virginia risk assessment program. *Journal of Criminal Law & Criminology, 97*, 699–729.

Olver, M. E., Stockdale, K. C., & Wormith, J. S. (2014). Thirty years of research on the level of service scales: A meta-analytic examination of predictive accuracy and sources of variability. *Psychological Assessment, 26*, 156–176.

Palmer, E. J., & Hollin, C. R. (2007). The level of service inventory-revised with English women prisoners: A needs and reconviction analysis. *Criminal Justice & Behavior, 34*, 971–984.

Pilon, A. J. M., Jewell, K. M., & Wormith, J. S. (2015). *Impaired drivers and their risk of reoffending*. Report submitted to Public Safety Canada. Saskatoon, Saskatchewan: Centre for Forensic Behavioural Science & Justice Studies, University of Saskatchewan.

Queen's Bench for Saskatchewan. (2006). Attorney General for Saskatchewan v. Q. (K.). SKQB 516.

Riggs, L. (2013, February 6). Supreme court requires report before sentencing. *Wetzel Chronicle*. Retrieved from www.wetzelchronical.com/page/content.detail/id/512251.html

Rowe, R. C. (1996). *Parole decision making in Ontario*. Toronto, ON: Ontario Ministry of the Solicitor General and Correctional Services.

Rubin, S. (1975). Probation or prison—applying the principle of the least restrictive alternative. *Crime and Delinquency, 21*, 331–336.

Schaefer, L., & Williamson, H. (2018). Probation and parole officers' compliance with case management tools: Professional discretion and override. *International Journal of Offender Therapy and Comparative Criminology, 62*, 4565–4584.

Scurich, N., & Monahan, J. (2016). Evidence-based sentencing: Public openness and opposition to using gender, age, and race as risk factors for recidivism. *Law and Human Behavior, 40*, 36–41.

Simourd, D. J., & Malcolm, P. B. (1998). Reliability and validity of the level of service inventory-revised among federally incarcerated sex offenders. *Journal of Interpersonal Violence, 13*, 261–274.

Singh, J. P., Desmarais, S. L., Hurducas, C., Arbach-Lucioni, K., Condemarin, C., Dean, K., . . . Otto, R. K. (2014). International perspectives on the practical application of violence risk assessment: A global survey of 44 countries. *International Journal of Forensic Mental Health, 13*, 193–206.

Singh, J. P., & Fazel, S. (2010). Forensic risk assessment: A metareview. *Criminal Justice and Behavior, 37*, 965–988.

Singh, J. P., Grann, M., & Fazel, S. (2011). A comparative study of violence risk assessment tools: A systematic review and metaregression analysis of 68 studies involving 25,980 participants. *Clinical Psychology Review, 31*, 499–513.

Skeem, J. L., & Monahan, J. (2011). Current directions in violence risk assessment. *Current Directions in Psychological Science, 20*, 38–42.

Smith, P., Cullen, F. T., & Latessa, E. J. (2009). Can 14,373 women be wrong? A meta-analysis of the LSI-R and recidivism for female offenders. *Criminology & Public Policy, 8*, 183–208.

Starr, S. B. (2014). Evidence-based sentencing and the scientific rationalization of discrimination. *Stanford Law Review, 66*, 803–872.

Stevenson, H. E., & Wormith, J. S. (1987). *Psychopathy and the level of supervision inventory* (User Report No. 1987-25). Ottawa: Solicitor General Canada.

Stewart, C. A. (2011). *Risk assessment of federal female offenders* (Unpublished dissertation). University of Saskatchewan, Saskatoon.

Storey, J., Watt, K., Jackson, K., & Hart, S. (2012). Utilization and implications of the static-99 in practice. *Sexual Abuse: A Journal of Research and Treatment, 24*, 289–302.

Taylor, K. N., & Blanchette, K. (2009). The women are not wrong: It is the approach that is debatable. *Criminology & Public Policy, 8*, 221–229.

Viljoen, J. L., Cochrane, D. M., & Jonnson, M. R. (2018). Do risk assessment tools help manage and reduce risk of violence and reoffending? A systematic review. *Law and Human Behavior, 42*, 181–214.

Walters, G. (2006). Risk-appraisal versus self-report in the prediction of criminal justice outcomes: A meta-analysis. *Criminal Justice and Behavior, 33*, 279–304.

Wanamaker, K. A., Jones, N. J., & Brown, S. L. (2018). Strengths-based assessment for use with forensic populations: A critical review. *International Journal of Forensic Mental Health, 17*, 202–221.

Wiener, R. L., Reed, K., Delgado, H., & Caldwell, A. (2014). *Validation study of the LS/CMI assessment tool in Nebraska*. Report prepared for Nebraska State Probation Administration. Lincoln, NE: Law, Psychology

Program, University of Nebraska. Retrieved from https://supremecourt.nebraska.gov/sites/suprem ecourt.ne.gov/files/reports/courts/validation-study-ls-cmi-assessment-tool-ne.pdf

Wilson, H. A., & Gutierrez, L. (2014). Does one size fit all? A meta-analysis examining the predictive ability of the level of service inventory (LSI) with aboriginal offenders. *Criminal Justice and Behavior, 41*, 196–216.

Winick, B. J., & Wexler, D. B. (1991). *Essays in therapeutic jurisprudence*. Durham, NC: Carolina Academic Press.

Wormith, J. S. (2011). The legacy of D. A. Andrews in the field of criminal justice: How theory and research can change policy and practice. *International Journal of Forensic Mental Health, 10*, 78–92.

Wormith, J. S. (2014). The risks of communicating sexual offender risk. *Journal of Threat Assessment and Management, 1*, 162–178.

Wormith, J. S., Ferguson, M., & Bonta, J. (2013). Offender classification and case management and their application in Canadian corrections. In J. Winterdyk & M. Weinrath (Eds.), *Adult corrections in Canada* (pp. 171–198). Whitby, ON: de Sitter Publications.

Wormith, J. S., & Goldstone, C. S. (1984). The clinical and statistical prediction of recidivism. *Criminal Justice and Behavior, 11*, 3–34.

Wormith, J. S., & Hogg, S. M. (2011). *The predictive validity of sexual offender recidivism with a general risk/needs assessment inventory*. Report to the Ministry of Community Safety and Correctional Services of Ontario. Saskatoon: Centre for Forensic Behavioural Science and Justice Studies. Retrieved from www.usask.ca/cfbsjs/research/pdf/research_reports/LSI%20And%20sexual%20offenders%20FINAL.pdf

Wormith, J. S., Hogg, S., & Guzzo, L. (2012). The predictive validity of a general risk/need assessment inventory on sexual offender recidivism and an exploration of the professional override. *Criminal Justice and Behavior, 39*, 1511–1538.

Wormith, J. S., Olver, M. E., Stevenson, H. E., & Girard, L. (2007). The long-term prediction of recidivism using diagnostic, personality, and risk/need approaches to offender assessment. *Psychological Services, 4*, 287–305.

Wormith, J. S., & Zidenberg, A. M. (2018). The historical roots, current status, and future applications of the risk-need-responsivity model (RNR). In E. L. Jeglic & C. Calkins (Eds.), *New frontiers in offender treatment: The translation of evidence-based practices to correctional settings* (pp. 11–41). Chan, Switzerland: Springer Nature.

Yang, M., Wong, S. C. P., & Coid, J. (2010). The efficacy of violence prediction: A meta-analytic comparison of nine risk assessment instruments. *Psychological Bulletin, 136*, 740–767.

Yessine, A. K., & Bonta, J. (2006). Tracking high-risk, violent offenders: An examination of the national flagging system. *Canadian Journal of Criminology and Criminal Justice, 48*, 574–607.

Zinger, I., & Forth, A. E. (1998). Psychopathy and Canadian criminal proceedings: The potential for human rights abuse. *Canadian Journal of Criminology, 40*, 237–277.

Chapter 9

The Youth Level of Service/Case Management Inventory

Robert D. Hoge

Youth Level of Service/Case Management Inventory

The Youth Level of Service/Case Management Inventory 2.0 (YLS/CMI 2.0; Hoge & Andrews, 2011) is designed to assist the professional in evaluating risk and needs in youthful offenders (ages 12–18). The instrument is considered an actuarial risk/need assessment tool in that it is based on empirically derived content and yields quantitative estimates of risk and need levels. It may also be used as a structured professional judgment instrument—that is, without algorithmic decision-making or quantitative risk estimates—to help guide clinical judgments about risk and needs. The format of the instrument is consistent with the results of a considerable body of research noted in this chapter that demonstrates the superiority of these approaches to clinical assessments.

The measure is useful in evaluating risk for both general and violent offending, and these risk assessments may be relevant in a variety of contexts, including pre-trial diversion, detention, and disposition/sentencing. The measure is also designed to provide information about need areas, and this can be important in case planning and management. The YLS/CMI 2.0 is appropriate for use with a wide range of professionals, including psychologists, social workers, probation officers, and child care workers. Use of the instrument requires some background in child and adolescent psychology and specialized training in administering and interpreting the measure. A detailed description of the instrument is provided later.

The YLS/CMI 2.0 was originally developed from data collected from samples of Canadian juvenile offenders. However, the instrument has been successfully used with male and female youth from community and institutional settings, various ethnic groups (e.g., Canadian Aboriginal, African American), and in a variety of national contexts (e.g., United States, United Kingdom, Singapore, Croatia, Trinidad, Mexico). Psychometric research with the measure has also been conducted for a wide range of samples and contexts. As indicated in this chapter, the current version, YLS/CMI 2.0, retains the original risk/need items of YLS/CMI. Some modifications have been made in other sections of the measure.

Rationale for Development

The YLS/CMI 2.0 is based on recent theories of the causes of criminal activity in youth (see Guerra, Williams, Tolan, & Modecki, 2008; Thornberry et al., 2012) and on the considerable empirical research conducted on the causes and correlates of youth crime (see Heilbrun, Lee, & Cottle, 2005; Hoge, Guerra, Boxer, 2008; Lipsey & Derzon, 1998). This research has identified the factors in Table 9.1 as significant correlates of youthful delinquent activity.

The nature of the links between the criminogenic factors and antisocial behavior is complicated, and the relevance of the factors to different gender, ethnic, and cultural groups is not

Table 9.1 Major Risk/Need Factors

Proximal Factors

History of conduct disorder
Antisocial attitudes, values, and beliefs
Dysfunctional parenting
Dysfunctional behavior and personality traits
Poor school/vocational achievement
Antisocial peer associations
Substance abuse
Poor use of leisure time

Distal Factors

Criminal/psychiatric problems in family of origin
Family financial problems
Poor accommodations
Negative neighborhood environments

always well established. However, there is strong support for an association between these factors and delinquency.

A history of delinquent activity or conduct disorder, the first factor identified in Table 9.1, clearly constitutes a major predictor of future antisocial behavior. Those youth demonstrating an established pattern of defiance and conduct problems are at the highest risk of continuing antisocial actions.

The second factor, and perhaps the most significant one, reflects the young person's attitudes, values, and beliefs regarding antisocial actions. These function as both direct and indirect determinants of behavior. Where these attitudes and values are antisocial in nature, they are going to guide the individual to antisocial behaviors as well as serving as subsequent justifications for the actions.

Aspects of the family environment, particularly those relating to parent-child relations, constitute another set of contributors. These generally impact indirectly on delinquent activity through their influence on the youth's attitudinal, personality, and behavioral dispositions. In other cases, though, the parent may have a more direct impact, as, for example, where lax supervision provides the youth with increased opportunities to engage in criminal acts.

The fourth set of variables closely linked with youthful antisocial behavior reflects behavioral and personality attributes of the youth. Impulsivity, attentional problems, aggressivity, and addictive patterns of behavior are a few of these constructs. It is clear from research (and clinical experience) that a youth's engagement in a delinquent act in a particular situation reflects, to some extent, the more-or-less stable behavioral and personality attributes he or she brings to the situation.

Poor academic achievement, problems in school adjustment, and low educational aspirations have all been implicated in antisocial activities. The link between these variables and delinquent activity is complex, but it is clearly present.

Antisocial, procriminal associates constitutes another type of variable identified in research as closely linked with youthful delinquency. These associates may include peers of the youth, parents, siblings, or others in the youth's environment. Antisocial associates may impact on the delinquent activity by influencing the youth's reactions to the immediate situation or more indirectly by fostering the adoption of antisocial attitudes and modes of behaviors.

Substance abuse, whether involving alcohol or illicit drug use, is linked with delinquent activity. There may be direct links where, for example, a crime is committed to obtain the substance, or the effects may be more indirect where the use contributes to impulsive behaviors. Finally, poor use of leisure time constitutes one of the important proximal factors. In many cases the youth simply has too much free time and engages in the antisocial behavior as a response to boredom.

These eight factors are identified as the most immediate or proximal correlates of juvenile antisocial behavior. A second set of factors shown in Table 9.1 are considered more distal. They are important, but they tend to operate through their influence on the proximal factors, although the mechanisms of their influence is not always fully understood (Andrews & Bonta, 2010; Rutter, Giller, & Hagel, 1998). These include criminal or psychiatric problems in the family, financial or accommodation problems in the family, and negative neighborhood environments.

The Risk-Need-Responsivity model (Andrews & Bonta, 2010; Andrews, Bonta, & Hoge, 1990, Hoge, 2015) provides a theoretical link between these criminogenic factors and assessment and case planning (see also Wormith & Bonta, Chapter 8, this volume). The model also provides a framework for YLS/CMI 2.0. Three concepts are represented in the model. *Risk factors* refer to characteristics of the youth or his or her circumstances placing them at risk for antisocial behaviors. We can treat the criminogenic factors identified in Table 9.1 as the major risk factors.

Need factors refer to the subset of risk factors that can be changed through interventions, and, if changed, reduce the chances of future antisocial behaviors. These are sometimes referred to as dynamic risk factors. To illustrate, a history of conduct disorder constitutes a risk factor; youths exhibiting such a history are at higher risk for delinquent behavior than those who don't. However, this is an historical variable and cannot be changed (although the probability of future antisocial behaviors can, of course, be reduced through effective interventions). Antisocial peer associations is another risk factor, but this can be considered a dynamic risk or need factor. We can intervene to reduce these associations and, if we succeed, will reduce the youth's risk for reoffending.

Responsivity factor is the third relevant concept. Responsivity factors refer to characteristics of the youth or his or her circumstances that, while not directly related to his or her delinquent activity, should be taken into account in case planning. Examples include reading ability, motivation to change, and emotional maturity. We can also include here strength or protective factors, such as the availability of a cooperative parent or an interest in sport (see Andrews & Bonta, 2010; Hoge, 2015; Hoge & Andrews, 2011 for further discussions of these concepts).

The YLS/CMI 2.0 is based on this work identifying the major criminogenic risk and need factors and on four principles of best practice (Andrews & Bonta, 2010; Hoge, 2015). The *assessment principle* states that interventions with the offender should be based on standardized assessments of risk, need, and responsivity. These assessments have been shown superior to informal, clinical assessments in a variety of contexts (Bonta, 2002; Borum & Verhaagen, 2006; Douglas, Yeomans, & Boer, 2005; Grisso, 1998; Grove & Meehl, 1996).

The *risk principle of case classification* is based on the finding that effective programs provide intensive services for high-risk cases and less intensive services for lower-risk cases. For example, in the case of probation, close and intensive monitoring should be reserved for those at greatest risk for continuing antisocial behavior. Similarly, lengthy and expensive treatment programs should involve those with high levels of need. The principle is important for a number of reasons. First, we have limited resources and should not waste them on youth who do not really require the services. Second, over-involvement of lower risk youth in the system may have negative consequences (see Dishion, McCord, & Poulin, 1999; McAra & McVie, 2007). This is illustrated where low-risk youth incarcerated with high-risk youth begin to show increased levels of risk for future reoffending.

The *need principle of case classification* is based on the finding that effective programs target the specific needs of the youth; that is, they focus on eliminating or ameliorating those specific factors placing the youth at risk for antisocial behavior. If the youth's delinquency relates to inadequate parenting and associations with antisocial peers, then interventions should focus on those specific areas of need. Two considerations underlie this principle. First, by observing the principle, we make maximum use of our limited resources; we are going to target them where they are most needed. Second, research discussed in the reviews and meta-analyses cited earlier demonstrates that interventions have their greatest impact where they focus on the needs of the individual. Unfortunately, many juvenile justice systems are rigid in the programming and do not permit the needed levels of individualization. In other words, interventions should be individualized and tailored to the youth.

The *responsivity principle of case classification* states that the choice of interventions should reflect non-criminogenic factors that might also have a bearing on responses to interventions. For example, there is little point in placing a youth with limited reading skills in a cognitive behavior modification program requiring the reading of complicated material. Another illustration would involve a girl whose delinquent activities are clearly associated with her associations with an anti-social group of youth and drug abuse. However, she may also be suffering from depression and anxiety associated with past abuse, and those conditions would have to be taken into account in planning an intervention since they might interfere with the treatments provided for the peer group association and substance abuse risks.

We have also included strength or protective considerations as responsivity factors, and it is important to consider these in case planning. For example, if a cooperative parent is available, he or she should certainly be involved in the intervention. Similarly, a risk related to poor use of leisure time could be easily addressed where the youth has an interest in a particular sport.

Purposes of the Measure

The YLS/CMI 2.0 is designed to aid the professional in assessing the youth's risk, need, and responsivity factors with the goal of insuring that the risk, need, and responsivity principles are observed in case planning. The instrument is particularly useful in forensic or correctional decisions regarding appropriate levels of security and supervision and in planning intervention strategies within community and institutional settings. It may also prove useful in early prevention programs where it is important to provide an early identification of potential risk and need factors.

Development of the instrument reflected several goals. First, we wanted to ensure that the measure included the full range of risk, need, and responsivity factors associated with youth crime. Second, an effort was made to ensure a direct link between the risk/needs assessment and case planning to help insure that the risk, need, and responsivity principles are observed. For this reason, a case management component involving the identification of specific goals and means of achievement for the case is built directly into the instrument. A third goal was to incorporate a professional override feature. This was included to ensure that the final judgment about risk level and needs rests with the responsible professional and that exceptional circumstances can be recognized. Generating support for the reliability and validity of the measure was the fourth goal. As will be seen later in this chapter, considerable psychometric research has now been conducted with the measure. A fifth goal was to ensure that the instrument would be accepted as a useful and practical tool by the professional. To this end, considerable consultation with probation officers, psychologists, and social workers was carried out before the final form of the instrument was developed. Finally, because the items in Part I are based largely on dynamic risk items, the instrument is also designed to assist in reviewing changes in risk/need levels over time.

Description of the YLS/CMI 2.0

The YLS/CMI 2.0 User's Manual, Quick Score Forms, and supporting materials are available from Multi-Health Systems (Hoge & Andrews, 2011). The following is a description of the various sections of the measure.

Part I: Assessment of Risk and Needs. The 42 items in this section reflect the risk and need factors identified in the literature as most closely linked with general and violent youth crime. The eight domains of Part I are identified in Figure 9.1. Each domain is defined by a set of items established in research as correlates of juvenile offending.

The assessor indicates each item that is true of the youth. An opportunity is also provided for indicating if a strength or protective factor is represented in a domain in recognition of the critical role played by these factors (Guerra, Kim, & Boxer, 2008). These are made at the same time as the risk assessment and are designed to reflect the presence of a positive factor that could be utilized in case planning. For example, we might record that there is an individual in the family who can represent a resource in case planning, or that the youth shows a particular strength in an academic area. The 42 items in Part I are identical to those in the original version, and, hence, earlier reliability and validity research remains relevant.

Part II: Summary of Risks and Needs. This section provides an opportunity to calculate risk/needs subtotals for each of the eight domains as well as an overall risk/needs score. The YLS/CMI 2.0 form also provides score ranges for low, moderate, high, and very high risk levels. These are based on a large sample of offenders and are presented separately for male and female youth and custodial and community samples.

Part III: Assessment of Other Needs and Special Considerations. This section provides an opportunity to record information about issues that, while not directly related to the youth's delinquent activity, may have a bearing on the development of an intervention plan. These include the responsivity factors discussed earlier. Additional items have been added to the original listing in the YLS/CMI 2.0 revision.

Items are divided into two categories. The first includes circumstances relating to parenting and the family such as "drug/alcohol abuse," "financial/accommodation problems," and "cultural/ethnic" issues. The second includes characteristics and conditions of the youth such as "physical disability," "depressed," "witness to family violence," and "pregnancy issues."

Part IV: Your Assessment of the Juvenile's General Risk/Need Level. An opportunity for a professional override is provided in this section. The professional completing the inventory can record in this section whether they agree or disagree with the risk/need level indicated by the inventory. Where

Domains	Sample Items
1. Prior and Current Offenses	Three or more prior convictions Prior custody
2. Family Circumstances/Parenting	Inadequate supervision Poor relations (father-youth)
3. Education/Employment	Disruptive classroom behavior Truancy
4. Peer Relations	Some antisocial friends No/few positive friends
5. Substance Abuse	Chronic drug use Substance use linked to offenses
6. Leisure/Recreation	Limited organized activities No personal interests
7. Personality/Behavior	Physically aggressive Short attention span
8. Attitudes/Orientation	Antisocial/procriminal attitudes Callous, little concern for others

Figure 9.1 Domains and Sample Items for Part I of the Youth Level of Service/Case Management Inventory

they disagree, they are asked to describe the basis for the override. This section is included to ensure that special circumstances can be accommodated and that final decisions rest with the responsible professional. An example is the case where a youth scored at the moderate risk/ need level, but, because of the recent death of a grandfather who was a key to holding the family together, the probation officer felt that the level of risk should now be elevated to high. The provision in this section is designed to ensure that exceptional circumstances can be recognized.

Part V: Contact Level. This section provides an opportunity to indicate the level of supervision appropriate in the particular case. This will normally reflect the overall level of risk/need recorded for the case. The categories are Administrative/Paper, Minimum Supervision, Medium Supervision, and Maximum Supervision.

Part VI: Case Management Plan. The final section is used to assist in formulating a case plan. The professional is asked first to indicate a set of goals for the youth. These should reflect the specific needs identified in Part I. If, for example, chronic alcohol use is identified as a need, then one goal should be to address the pattern of alcohol use. Next, the means for achieving the goal is identified. The rule is that these should be stated in specific and concrete terms. For example, the means of achieving the reduction in alcohol use would be addressed by providing one-on-one counseling to the youth twice per week and ensuring that they attend regular AA meetings. The format of this section differs slightly from the earlier edition.

Scoring, Interpretation, and Implementation of the YLS/CMI 2.0

The YLS/CMI 2.0 is designed for use by front-line staff members in juvenile justice and correctional settings. This includes psychologists, social workers, probation officers, and other youth workers. It is also useful with some modifications in school and mental health settings where the criminal history domain may not be relevant and where separate norms would have to be developed. Although professional training in a mental health area is not required for use of the measure, specialized training in administering, scoring, and interpreting the measure is necessary.

Scoring of items on the YLS/CMI 2.0 should be based on as broad a range of information as possible. A comprehensive interview with the youth and an examination of available file information will be the primary bases for scoring. An interview guide associated with the instrument is available. Interviews with collaterals such as parents, teachers, probation officers, and others should be utilized where available. Reconciling contradictory information will depend on the judgment of the assessor.

Where a more intensive psychological assessment of the youth is indicated, the YLS/CMI 2.0 can be used to summarize the results from a battery of assessment instruments (Hoge, 2008; Hoge & Andrews, 1996). For example, the youth might be administered the WISC-R, Wide Range Achievement Test, and a standardized personality test such as the MMPI-A. The results of these tests along with the interview and file information would be used as a basis for identifying risk/need factors through the YLS/CMI 2.0. This procedure might be appropriate where serious psychological or developmental deficits are suspected.

Total and domain scores from the YLS/CMI 2.0 are designed to assist in case planning. Several guidelines can be offered for establishing the goals and means of achieving goals:

- The goals of the intervention should be directly relevant to the specific risks and needs of the youth as identified in Part I.
- The goals should be stated in concrete terms. For example, the goal might be to improve school performance and attendance over a 4-week period.
- The means of achievement should also be stated in concrete terms. To illustrate, if the goal is improvement in school performance, then specific interventions should be indicated (e.g.,

enroll in homework club, access tutorial help with reading, establish token economy reward program).

- Goals and means of achievement should be timely. Young people do not think in terms of long-term events; it is important to be able to evaluate progress in achieving goals within fairly limited timeframes.
- Goals should be realistic. Youth must make progress in meeting their needs, but there is no point in setting them up for failure.
- Progress on the goals should be re-evaluated at periodic intervals; a case review version of the YLS/CMI 2.0 is available.

Care should be taken in introducing an instrument such as the YLS/CMI 2.0 into a juvenile justice or probation system. The following are some important implementation guidelines:

- A commitment to the use of standardized assessments should be included in the mission statement of the agency.
- All professionals in the system should be provided with an introduction to the YLS/CMI 2.0, including judges, prosecuting attorneys, police, and other relevant personnel. This does not require intensive training in the application of the measure, but it would involve familiarizing them with the purpose of the measure.
- The instrument should be introduced into the system in a rational manner that takes account of existing procedures. Efforts should be made to reduce redundancy in the assessment process.
- Comprehensive training should be provided all professionals using the measure by a qualified trainer. The training should involve extensive practice with the measure and checks to insure that adequate levels of interrater agreement are being achieved.
- A resource person should be available to answer questions about use of the measure and to monitor quality control.
- Periodic retraining should be provided where needed.

Several cautions should be observed in using an instrument such as the YLS/CMI 2.0. First, the measure should be used only by individuals with training in scoring, interpreting, and applying the measure. Second, scores from the instrument should not be used in a rigid way in making decisions. For example, a total YLS/CMI 2.0 score should not be used as a cutoff for determining whether a youth receives a community or custodial sentence. Final decisions about the youth should rest with the responsible professional and not a single assessment tool. Third, the use of the instrument as a basis for "net widening" should be guarded against. This problem may arise where youth with high risk/need scores are assigned severe dispositions regardless of other considerations.

Psychometric Research With the YLS/CMI 2.0

The following section describes some of the psychometric research conducted with the YLS/CMI 2.0. A more complete summary of the psychometric properties of the measure is provided in the YLS/CMI 2.0 *User's Manual* (Hoge & Andrews, 2011).

Normative Data

Norms reported in the YLS/CMI 2.0 User's Manual are based on a large geographically representative sample from the United States. The sample included 12,798 youthful offenders between the ages of 12 and 18 years (72% male and 28% female). The sample included Caucasian, Latino, and other racial and cultural groups. It generally reflects the racial/ethnic distribution in the United States. Additional information about the sample is found in the User's Manual. Norms are reported separately for male and female and community and custodial samples. Norms for other national settings are also available.

Reliability

Several researchers have reported reliability data from research based on samples of adjudicated offenders. Rowe (2002) reported a coefficient alpha value of .91 for the total risk/need score and a mean coefficient alpha value of .72 for the eight subscales. Schmidt, Hoge, and Gomes (2005) obtained a mean coefficient alpha value of .69 for the subscales.

Poluchowicz, Jung, and Rawana (2000) reported an interrater agreement coefficient of .75 for the overall risk/need score based on 33 cases scored by two independent raters. These researchers also reported adequate interrater agreement for all subscales except Leisure/Recreation (*median r* = .70). Additional support for interrater agreement has been provided in research cited in the User's Manual.

Construct Validity

Construct validity is supported in several studies reporting relations between YLS/CMI 2.0 scores and alternative measures of externalizing disorders. Perfect agreement is not expected in these cases because the YLS/CMI 2.0 represents a broader construct than the alternative measures. However, the analyses do bear on the ability of YLS/CMI 2.0 scores to reflect a conduct disorder construct.

An example of this research is provided by Schmidt et al. (2005) who reported significant correlations between Total Risk/Need scores from the YLS/CMI 2.0 and parallel scores from the following parent and self-report measures of behavioral maladjustment: Child Behavior Checklist (Parent), Child Behavior Checklist (Youth), Jesness Asocial Index, Social Skills Rating System, and Personal Experience Screening Questionnaire. Table 9.2 summarizes these correlations. Similar results have been reported by Rowe (2002) and Viljoen, Elkovitch, Scalora, and Ullman (2009).

Concurrent Validity

Hoge and Andrews (1996) presented information about concurrent validity by comparing YLS/CMI 2.0 sub-scores across three disposition categories (probation, open custody, secure custody).

Table 9.2 Correlations of Total YLS/CMI 2.0 Scores With Selected Assessment Measures

	Total YLS/CMI 2.0 Score
Parent CBCL—Total Problem Score	.46 ***
Parent CBCL—Externalizing Score	.54 ***
Parent CBCL—Internalizing Score	.34 ***
Youth CBCL—Total Problem Score	.46 ***
Youth CBCL—Externalizing Score	.53 ***
Youth CBCL—Internalizing Score	.32 ***
Parent SSRS Standard Problem Behavior Score	.50 ***
Jesness Asocial Index	.47 ***
PESQ Total Problem Severity Score	.47 ***

Source: Schmidt et al. (2005).

Note: Ns range from 29 to 71,*** $p < .001$. CBCL = Child Behavior Checklist; SSRS = Social Skills Rating System; PESQ = Personal Experience Screening Questionnaire.

As expected, risk/need scores increased linearly and significantly across those three disposition categories.

Jung (1996) compared a group of adjudicated offenders with a sample of high school students who have had no involvement with the juvenile justice system. The delinquent group obtained significantly higher total and subscale scores than the non-delinquent group.

Predictive Validity

A number of researchers have analyzed relations between YLS/CMI 2.0 risk/need total and sub-scores and indices of general and violent reoffending based on prospective designs. (Recall that risk/need items are identical in the two versions of the instrument.) Table 9.3 provides a sampling of these correlation results.

Categorical analyses have been reported in several studies. For example, Jung (1996) and Jung and Rawana (1999) divided their sample into two groups: those who reoffended within six months following the conclusion of the disposition and those who had not reoffended. The total YLS/CMI 2.0 score was higher for the recidivists ($M = 15.74$, $SD = 8.01$) than for non-recidivists ($M = 9.22$, $SD = 7.46$). The differences were significant ($F(1, 249) = 38.55$, $p < .001$; Cohen's $d = .88$). The researchers also compared the two groups in terms of scores from the eight subscales and reported that the subscores were significantly higher in each case for the reoffending group. YLS/CMI 2.0 total and subscores were significantly predictive of reoffending for males and females and Aboriginal and non-Aboriginal samples. The researchers also calculated predictive accuracy analyses using a linear discriminant analysis based on the eight YLS/CMI 2.0 subscores to predict reoffending. The analysis yielded a 75.38% correct classification value (RIOC = 20.10).

The analyses just cited were based on official records and reflect general and violent recidivism. Separate analyses by gender have been reported and support the predictive validity of scores for both male and female youth (e.g., Jung & Rawana, 1999). Support for the predictive validity of the risk/need scores is also reported for a variety of racial and ethnic groups (e.g., Bechtel, Lowencamp, & Latessa, 2007; Chu et al., 2015). Summary reviews and meta-analyses of predictive validity results based on correlational and predictive accuracy analyses provide support for the predictive validity of YLS/CMI 2.0 risk/need scores for a variety of samples, outcome measures, and contexts (Hoge & Andrews, 2011; Olver, Stockdale, & Wormith, 2009; Schwalbe, 2007).

Table 9.3 Sample Correlations Between YLS/CMI 2.0 Total and Subscores and Indices of Reoffending

YLS/CMI 2.0 Subscore	Hoge and Andrews (1996)		Rowe (2002)		Schmidt et al. (2005)	
	r	N	r	N	r	N
Prior Convictions/ Dispositions			.25**	408	.05	110
Family/Parenting	.27**	331	.18**	408	.30**	110
Education/Employment	.22**	331	.36**	408	.22*	110
Peer Relations	.14*	331	.35**	408	.30**	110
Substance Abuse	.12*	331	.14*	408	.18	110
Leisure/Recreation	.13*	331	.27**	408	.31**	110
Personality/Behavior	.21**	331	.32**	408	.23*	110
Attitudes/Orientation	.29**	331	.32**	408	.31**	110
Total YLS/CMI 2.0	.30**	331	.41***	408	.32**	110

Dynamic Validity

Both Rowe (2002) and Vieira, Skilling, and Peterson-Badali (2009) provided support for dynamic validity by showing that changes in YLS/CMI 2.0 risk/need scorers were associated in the predicted direction with changes in reoffending rates. Increased YLS/CMI 2.0 scores were associated with increases in reoffending and decreased scores associated with lower reoffending.

Case Studies

Two case studies will be presented for illustrative purposes, one representing a moderate risk/need case and the other a high risk/need case. Both are adapted from cases presented in the YLS/CMI 2.0 User's Manual (Hoge & Andrews, 2011).

Moderate Risk Case

Jack is a 14-year-old male convicted of three counts of breaking and entering and theft. The YLS/CMI 2.0 was completed by the probation officer as part of the predisposition report prepared for the court. The instrument was completed on the basis of a comprehensive interview with Jack, an interview with his mother, telephone interviews with Jack's school principal and two teachers, an interview with Jack's earlier probation officer, and a review of file information. Jack was friendly and cooperative during the interview, although reluctant to reveal some information.

Risk/Needs Scores (Parts I and II): Jack has been convicted of three counts of breaking and entering and theft and has seven prior convictions for similar offenses. The value of the stolen items was generally not significant. He has served two periods of probation, with numerous infractions during those probation periods. He obtained a score of 3/5 on the *Prior and Current Offenses/ Disposition* domain, placing him in the high risk/need range for this category.

Jack is an only child living with his mother. There has been no contact with the biological father for some years. There is a positive bond between mother and youth, but the mother has a history of psychiatric and substance abuse problems. An abusive common-law partner lived in the home until about two years ago. The mother appears to care about Jack, but her parenting practices have been very poor. Jack received a score of 5/6 on the *Family Circumstances/ Parenting* domain, placing him in the high risk/need range for this category.

The youth has never presented a behavior problem in school and has generally related well to teachers and other youth. Although of apparently at least normal intelligence, his academic performance has generally been below average. Truancy has been a significant problem in the past. His score on the *Education/Employment* domain was 2/7, placing him in the moderate range.

Jack is generally described as a loner, with few friends. However, his most recent offenses were in association with an antisocial peer. He appears to have few positive acquaintances or friends. His score of 3/4 on the *Peer Relations* domain places him in the high risk/need range for this category.

There is no evidence of any form of substance abuse, and his score of 0 on the *Substance Abuse* domain places him in the low risk/need category.

Jack spends most of his time alone and doesn't seem to have any interest beyond playing video games. His score on the *Leisure/Recreation* items was 3/3, placing him in the high risk/need range.

None of the items on the *Personality/Behavior* domain (e.g., physically aggressive, poor frustration tolerance) was checked, indicating a low score on this domain. A Strength was checked in this case because the youth presented as a friendly and cooperative individual.

Two items indicating a lack of motivation for addressing his issues were checked on the *Attitudes/ Orientation* domain, indicating a moderate risk/need score for the subscale (2/5).

Jack's *Overall Total Risk/Need* score was 18, placing him in the moderate risk/need range. His standings on the individual domains were as follows:

- Current Offenses/Dispositions: 3/5 (moderate)
- Family Circumstances/Parenting: 5/6 (high)
- Education/Employment: 2/7 (moderate)
- Peer Relations: 3/4 (moderate)
- Prior and Substance Abuse: 0/5 (low)
- Leisure/Recreation: 3/3 (high)
- Personality/Behavior: 0/7 (low)
- Attitudes/Orientation: 2/5 (moderate)

A Strength was indicated for Personality/Behavior.

Assessment of Other Needs and Special Considerations (Part III): items checked under Family/Parents included marital conflict, financial problems, and significant family trauma (relating to the recent death of the maternal grandfather). Items checked under Youth included underachievement, victim of neglect, shy/withdrawn, and poor social skills.

Your Assessment of the Juvenile's General Risk/Need Level (Part IV): the probation officer agreed with the moderate overall risk/need score.

Contact Level (Part V): intensive probation supervision was recommended, along with consideration of out-of-home placement.

Case Management Plan (Part VI): three initial goals and means of achievement were recommended. The first goal was an increase in involvement in external activities, and the means of achievement was to encourage continued involvement in Boys and Girls Club activities and to follow up an interest in sea cadets. The second goal was to improve school performance, and the means was to enroll Jack in a special afterschool program for low-achieving students which also involved some recreational activities. The final goal was to improve the coping and parenting skills of the mother. The means of achievement in this case was to encourage the mother's continued contact with a community mental health worker.

High Risk Case

Michael is a 17-year-old male convicted of several counts of assault. The YLS/CMI 2.0 was completed by the probation officer as part of the predisposition report for the court. The instrument was completed on the basis of information from a file review (prior probation and police reports), an interview with Michael's mother, a telephone interview with a previous principal of Michael's, and a comprehensive interview with Michael. Michael was friendly and cooperative throughout the assessment process. His behavior while in detention was without problems.

Risk/Need Scores (Parts I and II): Michael has been convicted of two counts of felony and one count of misdemeanor assaults. The assaults relate to two incidents where a group of youth forced themselves into homes and assaulted residents. The accused and victims were known to one another. No serious injuries resulted from the assaults. Michael's criminal history includes convictions for robbery, burglary, disorderly conduct, and assaults. He has received one secure custody disposition and four probation dispositions. He has three violations for probation violations. Michael obtained a score of 5/5 on the *Prior and Current Offenses/Disposition* domain, placing him in the high risk/need range.

Michael lives with his mother and three siblings. The family has had no contact with the father for some years. The family is cohesive and the children and mother obviously care for one another. However, the mother has a history of substance abuse (although abstinent for some months) and a minor delinquent history. Although the mother is a caring person, her parenting practices have been dysfunctional, and the children are essentially out of control. Michael obtained a score of 5/6 on the *Family Circumstances/Parenting* domain placing him in the high risk/need range. A Strength was also indicated due to the mother's concern and commitment to addressing the family's problems.

Michael has recently been expelled from school for fighting with other students. His educational history reveals a pattern of low academic achievement and some behavior problems. Educational assessments indicate that he is at least of normal intelligence and there are no obvious learning disabilities. Michael is out of school and making no efforts to find a job. His score on the *Education/Employment* domain was 5/7, placing him in the high risk/need range.

The youth associates almost exclusively with a group of antisocial individuals, some of whom have minor involvement with the juvenile justice system. He has no prosocial associations. His score on the *Peer Relations* domain was 4/4, placing him in the high risk/need category.

There is some suspicion that Michael has been involved in a minor way in the drug trade, but no proof was available. He admits to occasional use of cannabis, but there is no evidence of other forms of substance abuse. His score on the *Substance Abuse* domain was 1/5, placing him in the moderate range.

Michael is not involved in any organized activities and doesn't participate in a positive way in any hobbies or sports. Mostly he just "hangs around" with his friends. He scored 3/3 on the *Leisure/Recreation* domain, placing him in the high risk/need category.

Michael has a history of verbal and physical assaults, and it is apparent that he has difficulty in controlling his emotions. He expresses little remorse for the victims of his assaults, feeling they deserved what they got. He obtained a score of 4/7 on the *Personality/Behavior* domain, placing him in the moderate risk/need category. On the other hand, the probation officer who dealt with him indicated that, in spite of all of his problems, Michael came across as a likeable youth and that adults who have dealt with him generally saw considerable potential for improvement. For this reason, a Strength was indicated.

Because of his antisocial attitudes, defiant behavior, and generally passive responses to prior helping efforts, Michael obtained a score of 3/5 on the *Attitudes/Orientation* domain, placing him in the moderate range.

Michael's total YLS/CMI 2.0 score was 31, placing him at the high end of the high risk/need range. His scores on the 8 domains may be summarized as follows:

- Current Offenses/Dispositions: 5/5 (high)
- Family Circumstances/Parenting: 5/6 (high)
- Education/Employment: 5/7 (high)
- Peer Relations: 4/4 (high)
- Prior and Substance Abuse: 1/5 (moderate)
- Leisure/Recreation: 3/3 (high)
- Personality/Behavior: 4/7 (moderate)
- Attitudes/Orientation: 3/5 (moderate)

Strengths were indicated for Family Circumstances/Parenting and Personality/Behavior.

Assessment of Other Needs and Special Considerations (Part III): four items were checked under the Family/Parent category: chronic history of offenses, drug/alcohol abuse, financial/accommodation problems, and cultural/ethnic issues. Two items were checked in the Youth category: underachievement, and peers outside age range.

Your Assessment of the Juvenile's General Risk/Need Level (Part IV): the probation officer in this case agreed with the high overall risk/need range.

Contact Level (Part V): maximum supervision was indicated as the appropriate contact level in this case.

Case Management Plan (Part VI): the disposition in this case involved a custody sentence that was suspended conditional on attendance at and successful completion of a day treatment program for high-risk youth and young adults accompanied by close probation supervision.

Three initial goals were identified. The first was to reduce Michael's anger level and help him improve anger management skills. The means of achievement involved receiving counseling in the day treatment program and attendance at an anger management program. The second goal was directed toward improvements in educational skills and attitudes. The means of achievement involved attendance at the special education classes available in the program and receipt of counseling. The third goal was to improve the family situation. This was to be achieved through encouraging the mother's continued attendance at a drug counseling program and the family's participation in a family counseling program available from Family Service Agency.

Final Comments

Valid and comprehensive intake assessments are critical to the delivery of effective services to the offender. The careful identification of risk and need factors is needed to guide decisions about appropriate levels of supervision and security and about the interventions required to reduce the youth's risk for engaging in future antisocial activities. Research and clinical experience also support the importance of basing these assessments on standardized instruments. The YLS/CMI 2.0 has been presented as an example of such an instrument.

The YLS/CMI 2.0 presents a number of strengths in addition to its value in assessing risk and need factors. For example, it can help to insure consistency in the assessment of the client since all professionals are basing their evaluation on the same factors. In the same sense the measure can facilitate communication among professionals, since all are using a similar terminology to describe the risk and need characteristics of the youth. Finally, an instrument of this type can help the professionals defend decisions. They can point out that the assessment of the client was based on research-based and validated measure.

There are also advantages for management in the use of the YLS/CMI 2.0. For example, it can assist in systematically collecting a broad range of information about agency clients and the kinds of interventions they are provided. This information may be important in audits of agency activities and in advocating for funding. Where reassessments of YLS/CMI 2.0 scores are conducted, information can be of value in evaluating the effectiveness of the agency's interventions. Finally, information collected with the instrument can assist in allocating resources within the agency. For example, workloads can be adjusted on the basis of the risk/need levels of the clients being dealt with by the worker.

There are, however, a number of areas in which further research is required. While some predictive validity studies using violent reoffending as the outcome variable have been reported, much of the research has focused on general indices of reoffending, and additional information about the prediction of violent offending is needed. As well, future research should focus on more specific indices of violent offending, taking into account the seriousness of the offense, the nature of the aggression, the circumstances of the action, and the type of victim.

While data are available regarding the validity of the YLS/CMI 2.0 for males and females and certain ethnic and minority groups, additional research is needed for groups and cultures. Research is now underway on the predictive validity of the scores for Hispanic American youth and young people in other cultures (e.g., Singapore, Russia, Taiwan), and these results should be available shortly.

References

Andrews, D. A., & Bonta, J. (2010). *The psychology of criminal conduct* (5th ed.). Florence, KY: Anderson.

Andrews, D. A., Bonta, J., & Hoge, R. D. (1990). Classification for effective rehabilitation: Rediscovering psychology. *Criminal Justice and Behavior, 17*, 19–52.

Bechtel, K., Lowencamp, C. T., & Latessa, E. (2007). Assessing the risk of re-offending for juvenile offenders using the youth level of service/case management inventory. *Journal of Offender Rehabilitation, 45*, 85–108.

Bonta, J. (2002). Offender risk assessment: Guidelines for selection and use. *Criminal Justice and Behavior, 29*, 355–379.

Borum, R., & Verhaagen, D. (2006). *Assessing and managing violence risk in youth.* New York: Guilford Press.

Chu, C. M., Lee, Y., Zeng, G., Yim, G., Yeh Tan, C., Ang, Y., . . . Ruby, K. (2015). Assessing youth offenders in a non-western context: The predictive validity of the YLS/CMI ratings. *Psychological Assessment, 27*, 1013–1021.

Dishion, T. J., McCord, J., & Poulin, F. (1999). When interventions harm: Peer groups and problem behavior. *American Psychologist, 54*, 755–764.

Douglas, K., Yeomans, M., & Boer, D. (2005). Comparative validity analysis of multiple measures of violence risk in a sample of criminal offenders. *Criminal Justice and Behavior, 32*, 479–510.

Grisso, T. (1998). *Forensic evaluation of juveniles.* Sarasota, FL: Professional Resource Press.

Grove, W. M., & Meehl, P. E. (1996). Comparative efficiency of informal (subjective, impressionistic) and formal (mechanical, algorithmic) prediction procedures: The clinical-statistical controversy. *Psychology, Public Policy, and the Law, 2*, 293–323.

Guerra, N. G., Kim, T. E., & Boxer, P. (2008). What works: Best practices with juvenile offenders. In R. D. Hoge, N. G. Guerra, & P. Boxer (Eds.), *Treating the juvenile offender* (pp. 79–102). New York: Guilford Press.

Guerra, N. G., Williams, K., Tolan, P., & Modecki, K. (2008). Theoretical and research advances in understanding the causes of juvenile offending. In R. D. Hoge, N. G. Guerra, & P. Boxer (Eds.), *Treating the juvenile offender* (pp. 33–53). New York: Guilford Press.

Heilbrun, K., Lee, R., & Cottle, C. (2005). Risk factors and intervention outcomes: Meta-analyses of juvenile offending. In K. Heilbrun, N. Goldstein, & R. Redding (Eds.), *Juvenile delinquency: Prevention, assessment, and intervention* (pp. 111–133). New York: Oxford University Press.

Hoge, R. D. (2015). Risk/need/responsivity in juveniles. In K. Heilbrun, D. DeMatteo, & N. Goldstein (Eds.), *APA handbook of psychology and juvenile justice* (pp. 179–196). Washington, DC: American Psychological Association.

Hoge, R. D., & Andrews, D. A. (1996). *Assessing the youthful offender: Issues and techniques.* New York: Plenum Press.

Hoge, R. D., & Andrews, D. A. (2011). *Youth level of service/case management inventory 2.0 users' manual.* North Tonawanda, NY: Multi-Health Systems.

Hoge, R. D., Guerra, N. G., & Boxer, P. (Eds.). (2008). *Treating the juvenile offender.* New York: Guilford Press.

Jung, S. (1996). *Critical evaluation of the validity of the risk/need assessment with aboriginal young offenders in Northwestern Ontario* (Unpublished M.A. thesis). Lakehead University, Thunder Bay.

Jung, S., & Rawana, E. P. (1999). Risk-need assessment of juvenile offenders. *Criminal Justice and Behavior, 26*, 69–89.

Lipsey, M. W., & Derzon, J. H. (1998). Predictors of violent or serious delinquency in adolescence and early adulthood: A synthesis of longitudinal research. In R. Loeber & D. Farrington (Eds.), *Serious and violent juvenile offenders: Risk factors and successful interventions* (pp. 86–105). Thousand Oaks, CA: Sage.

McAra, L., & McVie, S. (2007). The impact of system contact on patterns of desistance from offending. *European Society of Criminology, 4*, 315–345.

Olver, M. E., Stockdale, K. C., & Wormith, J. S. (2009). Risk assessment with young offenders: A meta-analysis of three assessment measures. *Criminal Justice and Behavior, 36*, 329–353.

Poluchowicz, S., Jung, S., & Rawana, E. P. (2000, June). *The interrater reliability of the ministry risk/need assessment form for juvenile offenders.* Presentation at the Annual Conference of the Canadian Psychological Association, Montreal, Quebec.

Rowe, R. (2002). *Predictors of criminal offending: Evaluating measures of risk/needs, psychopathy, and disruptive behavior disorders* (Unpublished doctoral dissertation). Department of Psychology, Carleton University, Ottawa.

Rutter, M., Giller, H., & Hagell, A. (1998). *Antisocial behavior by young people.* Cambridge: Cambridge University Press.

Schmidt, F., Hoge, R. D., & Gomes, L. (2005). Reliability and validity analyses of the youth level of service/case management inventory. *Criminal Justice and Behavior, 32*, 329–344.

Schwalbe, C. S. (2007). Risk assessment for juvenile justice: A meta-analysis. *Law and Human Behavior, 31*, 449–462.

Thornberry, T. P., Giordano, P. G., Uggen, M. M., Masten, A. A., Bulten, E., & Donker, A. G. (2012). Explanations for offending. In R. Loeber & D. P. Farrington (Eds.), *From juvenile delinquency to adult crime* (pp. 47–85). New York: Oxford University Press.

Vieira, T. A., Skilling, T. A., & Peterson-Badali, M. (2009). Matching court-ordered services with treatment needs: Predicting treatment success with youth offenders. *Criminal Justice and Behavior, 36*, 385–401.

Viljoen, J. L., Elkovitch, N., Scalora, M. J., & Ullman, D. (2009). Assessment of re-offense risk in adolescents who have committed sexual offenses: Predictive validity of the ERASOR, PCL:YV, YLS/CMI, and static 99. *Criminal Justice and Behavior, 36*, 981–1000.

Chapter 10

Two Treatment and Change-Oriented Risk Assessment Tools

The Violence Risk Scale (VRS) and Violence Risk Scale—Sexual Offense Version (VRS-SO)

Mark E. Olver and Stephen C. P. Wong

For persons with entrenched patterns of violence not caused specifically by a mental illness, the assessment, prediction, and treatment of the violent behaviors are the three major links essential to reduce their risk of violence and, consequently, societal violence. Assessments designed to identify the probable causes of violence that are dynamic or changeable, when integrated with treatment targeting these causes, can reduce future violence (see Wong, Gordon, & Gu, 2007). The now extensive so-called "what works" literature, that addresses the issues of effective recidivism reduction treatment, supports the efficacy of such treatment (see Bonta & Andrews, 2017). Violence risk assessment and prediction should be considered as the prerequisite of a general recidivism or violence reduction strategy and should be guided by the theoretical underpinnings of effective correctional treatment.

The "what works" literature and the theory of Psychology of Criminal Conduct (PPC) (Bonta & Andrews, 2017) have identified the Risk-Need-Responsivity (RNR) principles as useful guidelines for recidivism reduction treatment (see also Wormith & Bonta, Chapter 8, this volume). Treatment approaches that follow the RNR show higher efficacy in reducing reoffending than those that do not follow such principles (McGuire, 2008, p. 2591).

The Risk principle addresses the question of "who" to treat and directs that the intensity of treatment should match the person's risk level, i.e., higher-risk offenders should receive more intensive treatment. The Need principle addresses the question of "what" to treat and directs that the person's criminogenic needs (i.e., linked to violence or criminality), such as criminal attitudes, criminal associates, etc., must be identified as targets for treatment. Successful treatment of criminogenic needs should reduce recidivism, whereas treatment of some non-criminogenic needs, though beneficial, will not reduce recidivism. The Responsivity principle addresses the question of "how" to deliver treatment and directs that, to maximize treatment effectiveness, treatment delivery must accommodate the person's idiosyncratic characteristics including his or her cognitive and intellectual abilities, learning styles, level of motivation and readiness for treatment, and cultural background.

Rationale and Theoretical Underpinnings in the Development of the VRS and VRS-SO

Reducing violent recidivism, including sexual reoffending, is central to many forensic treatment programs. To provide treatment for conditions related to violence, one needs a tool to identify appropriate treatment targets and assess treatment change. The Violence Risk Scale (VRS; see Wong & Gordon, 2006) and the Violence Risk Scale-Sexual Offense version (VRS-SO; see Olver, Wong, Nicholaichuk, & Gordon, 2007) integrate the assessment and prediction of violence risk with risk-reduction treatment and measuring treatment change. The tools were developed guided by the RNR and theory of PCC (Bonta & Andrews, 2017). Assessments using the VRS/VRS-SO inform "who" to treat by identifying offenders' level of violence risk, "what" to treat by identifying dynamic risk predictors linked to violence as treatment targets, and "how" to treat by identifying treatment readiness or engagement, a key responsivity question using a modified Stages of Change (SOC) model (Prochaska, Diclemente, & Norcross, 1992). The VRS/VRS-SO SOC model is also used to assess treatment change by documenting the person's movement through the SOC, which serves as a proxy for risk reduction. The two tools share many common features and can be used also as standalone risk assessment and prediction tools. To avoid repetition, they are discussed together where appropriate.

VRS Description

The VRS uses 6 static and 20 dynamic predictors to assess risk for violence (see Table 10.1 for brief item descriptions). The VRS/VRS-SO static predictors remain unchanged regardless of treatment interventions. The VRS/VRS-SO dynamic and static predictors are rated on 4-point ordinal scales (0, 1, 2, or 3) after completing a file review and a semi-structured interview. In general, higher ratings signal a closer link to violence in lifetime functioning. Higher ratings on the static predictors signal more extensive criminality and dysfunctional upbringing. Dynamic predictors closely linked to violence (rated 2 or 3) are appropriate targets for treatment. The total VRS/VRS-SO score (the sum of static and dynamic predictor ratings) indicates the level of violence risk; the higher the score, the higher the risk. The psychometric properties and predictive efficacy of the tools were assessed based on clearly articulated scoring rubrics and accepted psychometric practices. The VRS/VRS-SO is a dynamic empirical actuarial risk assessment tool (Hanson & Morton-Bourgon, 2009), given that the items are summed to generate a numeric score that is then linked to risk levels and recidivism estimates.

Table 10.1 A Brief Description of VRS Static and Dynamic Items and What They Assess

Static Items

S1 Current age: age at assessment.
S2 Age at first violent conviction: age at first violent criminal conviction.
S3 Number of young offender convictions: number of convictions before age of majority.
S4 Violence throughout lifespan: extent of violence throughout lifespan.
S5 Prior release failures: escapes or breaches of conditional release(s).
S6 Stability of family upbringing: stability of the person's upbringing and family environment.

Dynamic Items

D1   Violent lifestyle: assesses the level of violence in the person's overall lifestyle.
D2   Criminal personality: assesses the presence of callous unemotional personality (e.g. PCL-R Factor 1) features.
D3   Criminal attitudes: does the person's criminal attitudes facilitate violence?
D4   Work ethic: value working for a living or prefer socially inappropriate ways for financial gains.
D5   Criminal peers: are violent behaviors associated with negative peer influences?
D6   Interpersonal aggression: does the person habitually use aggression/violence in interpersonal interactions?
D7   Emotional control: assesses the link between violence and the regulation of affect.
D8   Violence during institutionalization: assesses the proneness to violence while in custody.
D9   Weapon use: assesses the link between the possession of weapons and violence.
D10 Insight into violence: assesses the level of insight or understanding regarding past violence.
D11 Mental disorder: assesses the association of mental disorder and violence.
D12 Substance abuse: assesses the association of substance use and violence
D13 Stability of relationships: assesses the ability to maintain stable, supportive marital or similar relationships.

(Continued)

Table 10.1 (Continued)

D14 Community support: assesses the level of positive community support.
D15 Release to high-risk situations: assess if release plans could expose the person to high-risk situations.
D16 Violence cycle: assesses the presence of a pattern or cycles of violent behaviors.
D17 Impulsivity: assesses the extent of impulsive behaviors.
D18 Cognitive distortions: assesses the use of distorted thinking to justify or rationalize offending behaviors.
D19 Compliance with community supervision: assesses willingness to cooperation with community supervision.
D20 Security level at release: assesses the security level of the institution from which the person will likely be released.

Note: All items are rated on a 4-point (3, 2, 1, 0) scale. Item descriptions are abbreviated examples of the originals and are not intended to be used for clinical or research purposes. Please consult the VRS rating manual (Wong & Gordon, 1999–2003) for more detailed descriptions, stages of change ratings, and scoring instructions.

Both VRS/VRS-SO use a modified transtheoretical or SOC model to assess the individual's readiness for treatment and treatment change. Dynamic variables identified as treatment targets (rated 2 or 3) are also rated to determine the individual's SOC that include *Precontemplation, Contemplation, Preparation, Action*, and *Maintenance*. Persons in the Precontemplation stage show no intention to change, are in denial, and often externalize blame. Those in the Contemplation stage might acknowledge their problems but there is no behavioral evidence of change: "all talk, no walk." Those in the Preparation stage can talk and show some walk, but changes tend to be recent and/or quite unstable. Those in the Action stage actively and consistently work to improve their behaviors and to address their problems. In the Maintenance stage, gains are consolidated, strengthened and generalized to multiple novel situations. The operationalizations of the SOC measure the extent to which newly learned positive coping abilities are stable, sustainable, and generalizable. Progression from a less advanced to more advanced SOC for each treatment target indicates improvement leading to risk reduction which can be measured for each treatment target. Progression through the SOC can be assessed based on what has been termed offense analog/paralleling (negative or offense-like) behaviors and offense reduction (positive or prosocial) behaviors observable in custodial settings (see Gordon & Wong, 2010).

Progression from one stage to the next is set as equivalent to 0.5 points in risk reduction with the exception of progressing from the Precontemplation to the Contemplation stage as no behavioral change is required other than expressing an intention to change in the latter. The pretreatment rating for each of the dynamic risk variables (e.g., rating 3) minus the change in risk based on the individual's progress through the stages (e.g., −1 when progressing two stages from Contemplation to Action) provides the post-treatment level of risk (i.e., 3 − 1 = 2). Each dynamic variable targeted for treatment is so rated to determine the total reduction in risk at the end of treatment.

Development of the VRS

The VRS static predictors are gleaned from the theoretical and research literature reflecting the person's history of violence and criminality and parallel what the PCC refers to as antisocial behavioral history. The age variable was selected based on the well-established link between age and criminality (Hirschi & Gottfredson, 1983).

The VRS dynamic predictors or variable risk factors (see Kraemer et al., 1997) are changeable or potentially changeable predictors that can be affected by psychological, social, or physiological means, such as psychological treatment. Changes in the dynamic predictors should be linked to changes in recidivism. The VRS dynamic predictors are aligned with various domains of the PCC. The antisocial attitude domain is captured by seven VRS predictors, *D3, D6, D7, D9, D10, D16, D17, and D18* (see Table 10.1); the antisocial associate domain by *D5*; the antisocial personality domain by *D2*; and the domains of home, school, work, and leisure by *D1, D4, D12, D13, D14, D15,* and *D19*. Three VRS predictors not represented in the PCC, *D8, D11,* and *D20*, are well supported by research (Duncan, Kennedy, & Patrick, 1995; Hann & Harman, 1992; Lattimore, Visher, & Linster, 1995; Warburton & Stahl, 2016; Wong & Gordon, 2006). In sum, there is good theoretical or empirical support for the selection of the VRS static and dynamic variables.

Ratings of the VRS dynamic predictors, in most cases, reflect the association of the various problem areas with violence. For example, the endorsement of the substance abuse predictor (ratings of 2 or 3) signals a consistent link of substance abuse with violence rather than the mere presence of substances abuse problems.

Validation of the VRS

The VRS has been validated on adult male offenders in Canada (Burt, 2000, 2003; Burt, Olver & Wong, 2016; Gordon, 1998; Lewis, 2004; Wong & Gordon, 2006; Valliant, Gristey, Pottier, & Kosmyna, 1999; Wong & Burt, 2007) many with significant histories of criminality and a substantial number of them being of Indigenous ancestry. The studies even included a small sample ($n = 17$) of university students. The VRS has also been validated on adult male or mixed-gender forensic psychiatry inpatients in the United Kingdom (Dolan & Fullam, 2007; Doyle, Carter, Shaw, & Dolan, 2012), the Netherlands (De Vries Robbé, Weenink, & De Vogel, 2006), China (mixed gender sample; Zhang, Chen, Cai, & Hu, 2012), and Canada (males; Hogan & Olver, 2016, 2018, 2019; Wilde & Wong; 2000). The VRS has also been validated in two samples of high-risk and personality-disordered offenders, many with significant psychopathic characteristics (Coupland & Olver, 2018; Lewis, Olver, & Wong, 2013), Canadian female federal offenders (Stewart, 2011), and offenders on community supervision (Wong & Parhar, 2011).

Reliability of the VRS

The VRS has demonstrated strong reliability across several independent investigations. Interrater reliability evaluations showed strong intraclass correlation (ICC) values for independent ratings of the static (ICC = .96–.98), dynamic (ICC = .85–.96), and total (ICC = .82–.96) scores (Coupland & Olver, 2018; de Vries Robbé et al., 2006; Dolan & Fullam, 2007; Doyle et al., 2012; Lewis et al., 2013; Stewart, 2011; Valliant et al., 1999; Wong & Gordon, 2006). Internal consistency as measured via Cronbach's alpha for VRS total scores has ranged from .79 to .94 across samples that reported these values.

Validity of the VRS

Factor Structure

An exploratory factor analysis on the primary VRS validation sample produced three correlated factors that accounted for 56% of the total variance (Wong & Gordon, 2006). Factor 1 included 2 static and 10 dynamic predictors and tended to measure attitudes and behaviors specific to interpersonal violence. Factor 2 was comprised of 3 static items and 2 dynamic predictors that tended to reflect issues more typical for younger offenders (e.g., antisocial peers, impulsivity). Finally, Factor 3 consisted of 1 static and 9 dynamic predictors broadly indicative of an antisocial lifestyle. Factors 1 and 3 were quite highly correlated ($r = .55$) and more closely linked to violent reconviction ($r = .38$ and $.32$, respectively) than Factor 2 ($r = .13$). The results of the preliminary factor analysis suggest that Factors 1 and 3, which have most of the dynamic variables, have more in common with each other than with Factor 2 and provide some evidence for the separation of the static and dynamic predictors.

Convergent Validity

The convergent validity of the VRS has been demonstrated through associations with other empirically validated risk assessment tools or schemes, including the PCL-R total and factor scores (.62–.83), LSI-R (.83), GSIR (−.63) and HCR-20 (.83–.84) across a series of independent studies and offender samples (de Vries Robbé et al., 2006; Dolan & Fullam, 2007; Hogan & Olver, 2016; Lewis et al., 2013; Valliant et al., 1999; Wong & Gordon, 2006).

Predictive Validity

As the VRS was designed to predict violence, we only report the tool's predictive efficacy for violent reoffending, although good prediction of nonviolent and general reoffending were also obtained in many samples. The VRS static, dynamic, and total scores showed medium to high predictive validity for community and institutional violence in 12 international studies of male and female samples (see Table 10.2). The correspondence of AUC values (.56, .64, and .71) to effect size (low, medium, and high, respectively) was based on criteria reported in Rice and Harris (2005). Across 11 international samples, VRS total scores (i.e., static + dynamic) have demonstrated broadly high predictive validity for violent recidivism and institutional misconduct (median AUC = .75), including a large incarcerated male Canadian correctional sample (Wong & Gordon, 2006); Canadian female federal offenders (Stewart, 2011); psychiatric inpatients in Canada (Hogan & Olver, 2016, 2018, 2019), UK (Dolan & Fullam, 2007; Doyle et al., 2012), and the Netherlands (De Vries Robbé et al., 2006); high-risk-treated violent offenders with significant psychopathic features from programs in Canada (Coupland & Olver, 2018; Lewis et al., 2013), New Zealand (Polaschek, Yesberg, Bell, Casey, & Dickson, 2016), and Australia (O'Brien & Daffern, 2017); and a sample of Canadian parolees (Wong & Parhar, 2011). VRS scores were also negatively correlated with positive community outcomes such as good employment, housing, relationships, successful supervision, and involvement in prosocial activities ($r = -.26$ to $-.51$, $p < .001$; Coupland & Olver, 2020) in a male offender sample.

Dynamic Predictive Validity

Some dynamic risk predictors, such as age, though changeable, cannot be purposely manipulated. In contrast, *causal* dynamic predictors, if purposely manipulated, as in treatment, should produce predictable changes in outcomes such as recidivism reduction. To establish causality, the dynamic predictors must be measured prospectively in at least two time points, and changes in risk should be linked to changes in recidivism in the predicted direction (see Kraemer et al., 1997).

Dynamic predictive validity of the VRS for violent recidivism has been investigated in at least four studies with treated violent offenders. Using Cox regression survival analysis, two Canadian samples of high risk treated violent offenders from the Aggressive Behavioural Control (ABC) program demonstrated VRS change scores to be associated with decreased violent recidivism after controlling for baseline risk (i.e., pretreatment total scores) (Lewis et al., 2013; Coupland & Olver, 2018). The studies generated hazard ratios (e^B) ranging from .92 to .94 indicating a 6%–8%

Table 10.2 VRS: Summary of Predictive Validity Findings (AUC Unless Otherwise Indicated) for Violent Recidivism

VRS Study	Sample and Setting	N	Static	Dynamic	Total
Coupland & Olver, 2018	Treated violent offenders, ABC Program, RPC	155	.65	.65	.66
Coupland & Olver, 2018	Same as above with institutional outcome	178	.59[NS]†	.59[NS]†	.59[NS]†
de Vries Robbé et al., 2006	Forensic inpatients, the Netherlands	50	–	–	.78†
Doyle et al., 2012	Forensic patients, UK hospital	114	.61[NS]	–	.66
Dolan & Fullam, 2007	Forensic inpatients, UK hospital	136	.62†	.72†	.71†
Hogan & Olver, 2016	Forensic inpatients, western Canada hospital	77	.58†	.69†	.68†
Hogan & Olver, 2018	Forensic inpatients, western Canada hospital	18	.65[NS]†	.79†	.78†
Hogan & Olver, 2019	Same as Hogan and Olver (2016) with community follow-up	62	.78	.81	.82
Lewis et al., 2013	Treated violent offenders, ABC Program, RPC	150	.60	.66	.64
O'Brien & Daffern, 2017	Treated violent offenders, Australia Corrections	82	–	–	.64††
Stewart, 2011	Female, CSC	101	–	–	.84
Wong & Gordon, 2006	Prison inmates, CSC Prairies	918	.75	.75	.75
Wong & Parhar, 2011	Parolees, CSC	60	–	–	.83
Polaschek et al., 2016	Treated and untreated violent offenders, New Zealand Corrections	275	.51[NS]††	.61††	–
	Median AUC community recidivism		.62	.66	.70
	Median AUC institutional recidivism		.59	.70	.69

Note: All AUC values significant at *p* < .05 or better except for NS = not significant. ABC = Aggressive Behaviour Control Program; RPC = Regional Psychiatric Centre, Canada; CSC = Correctional Service of Canada; † institutional violence/aggression; †† AUC values converted using other effect size information provided in the study.

reduction in the hazard of violence for every 1-point increase in change score after controlling for pretreatment risk. Similar trends were found in a New Zealand prison-based study of within-treatment change (Yesberg, 2015) in a sample of 123 high-risk violent offenders. Although the change did not attain significance, its magnitude ($e^B = .89$) was consistent with the hazard ratios from the larger Canadian samples. A recent Australian study using a small sample ($n = 61$) of treated violent offenders did not find VRS change scores to be associated with reductions in violent recidivism (O'Brien & Daffern, 2017). Of note, 15 additional men who did not complete violent offender treatment (and who would have received low or no change from pre- to post-treatment) were excluded from the change-outcome analyses. This could create a confound through the inclusion only of those men who successfully completed and hence fared well in treatment; in such circumstances, any change score would be less likely to discriminate recidivists from non-recidivists.

VRS-SO Description

The Violence Risk Scale-Sexual Offense Version (VRS-SO; Wong, Olver, Nicholaichuk, & Gordon, 2003, 2017) integrates sexual offender risk assessment and treatment planning, including the assessment of change, within a single instrument. It can be used with adult sexual offenders who may vary in their risk level, victim preferences, or whether they commit contact or noncontact offenses. The VRS-SO, modeled closely after the VRS, uses both static and dynamic variables to assess sexual offending recidivism risk, whereas dynamic variables are used to identify treatment targets and measure changes in risk as a result of treatment or other change agents. The VRS-SO comprises 7 static and 17 dynamic items that are empirically, theoretically, or clinically related to sexual reoffending risk (see Table 10.3). As with the VRS, the VRS-SO assesses and measures change using a modified application of the TM operationalized for each of the 17 dynamic items, with criminogenic items receiving such ratings pre- and post-treatment to arrive at a quantitative index of change.

The VRS-SO initial validation sample consisted of a range of treated federal offenders varying from low to very high risk with a slightly negatively skewed distribution; the sample also consisted of a number of sexual offenders of Indigenous descent. The validity of the tool has been examined using separate samples in New Zealand (Beggs & Grace, 2010, 2011) and Austria (Eher, Olver, Heurix, Schilling, & Rettenberger, 2015; Olver & Eher, 2019) with very similar results. Over three quarters of the sexual offenders in the inaugural VRS-SO validation sample had an intake diagnosis of some type of personality disorder, and over half received a diagnosis of antisocial personality disorder or had antisocial personality traits (Olver & Wong, 2011).

The VRS-SO also has potential applicability within special sexual offender evaluation contexts including Dangerous Offender (DO) evaluations in Canada and sexually violent predator (SVP) evaluations in the United States. For these evaluations, the VRS-SO can be used both in the pre-detention assessment to provide information concerning risk and treatment readiness, as well as in post-detention assessment for purposes of identifying any treatment-related changes and reassessing risk. A New Zealand pilot prison-based program with high-risk rapists may be seen as a proxy to similar special high-risk populations, the results of which demonstrated that changes on the variables can occur with intensive treatment, and this may translate into incremental reductions in risk level (e.g., from high to moderate-high and so on) (Wilson, Kilgour, & Polaschek, 2013). Future investigative efforts would be well served to examine if such treatment-related changes in these and other special populations translate into reductions in sexual reoffending and other violent behavior.

Method of and Rationale for Development of the VRS-SO

The static items of the VRS-SO were developed using statistical-actuarial procedures. A pool of 24 static variables identified from the literature were initially coded and correlated with sexual reoffending on approximately half of a randomly selected sample ($n = 152$) of medium- to high-risk treated sexual offenders. Nonredundant variables with consistent and significant univariate associations (there was no minimum effect size threshold) with binary and/or continuously measured sexual recidivism were retained and rescaled to a 4-point format. The items were then cross-validated on the remainder of the sample ($n = 169$) through examining univariate associations. The dynamic component was developed through a detailed review of the sexual offender prediction and treatment literature including meta-analytic reviews (Hanson & Bussière, 1998), individual studies identifying dynamic predictors (e.g., Hanson & Harris, 2000), and theoretical contributions from the relapse prevention literature (Pithers, 1990; Ward & Hudson, 1998) and the PCC (Andrews & Bonta, 1994, 1998).

Table 10.3 VRS-SO Static and Dynamic Items and Brief Item Descriptions

Static Items

S1 Age at release: < age 25; 25–34; 35–44; 45 years and up.
S2 Age at first sex offense: < age 20; 20–24; 25–34; 35 and up.
S3 Sex offender victim profile: mixed offender; child molester; rapist; incest offender.
S4 Prior sex offenses: 4 or more prior sexual charges/convictions; 2–3 prior; 1 prior; 0 prior.
S5 Unrelated victims: 4 or more unrelated victims; 2–3 unrelated; 1 unrelated; 0 unrelated (all related).
S6 Victim gender: 2+ male victims; 1 male and 1 female/or 2+ female; 1 male victim only; 1 female victim only.
S7 Prior sentencing dates: 11+ prior sentencing dates; 5–10 prior; 2–4 prior; 0–1 prior.

Dynamic Items

D1 Sexually deviant lifestyle: lifestyle hobbies, interests, work, or relationships involve sexually deviant behaviors.[SD]
D2 Sexual compulsivity: strong sex drive and high frequency of sexual behavior and cognitions.[SD]
D3 Offense planning: victim grooming and premeditation involved in sexual offending.[SD]
D4 Criminal personality: interpersonal and emotional attributes conducive to criminal behavior (e.g., lack of remorse).[C]
D5 Cognitive distortions: attitudes and distorted thinking supportive of sexual offending.[TR]
D6 Interpersonal aggression: physically and/or verbally aggressive behavior in interpersonal interactions.[C]
D7 Emotional control: tendency to overcontrol or undercontrol emotions linked to sexual offending.[DNL]
D8 Insight: poor understanding of causes of sexual offending and unwillingness to discuss/explore sexual offending.[TR]
D9 Substance abuse: substance use problems linked specifically to sexual offending.[C]
D10 Community support: lack of positive support people, services, or plans in community (or unwilling to use).[C]
D11 Released to HRS: offender seems likely or has shown pattern of returning to situations linked to sex offending.[TR]
D12 Sexual offending cycle: pattern of interpersonal, situational, and personal factors linked to sexual offending.[SD]
D13 Impulsivity: behavior displays tendency to "act first, think later" and lacks reflection or forethought.[C]
D14 Compliance with community supervision: poor attitude and/or cooperation with community supervision.[C]
D15 Treatment compliance: poor attitude and/or cooperation with sex offender treatment.[TR]
D16 Deviant sexual preference: interests or preferences for deviant sexual stimuli or behavior (e.g., children, violence).[SD]
D17 Intimacy deficits: incapacity to form or maintain adult romantic relationships.[DNL]

Note: All items are rated on a 4-point (3, 2, 1, 0) scale. Item descriptions are abbreviated examples of the originals and are not intended to be used for clinical or research purposes. Please consult the VRS-SO rating manual (Wong et al., 2003) for more detailed item descriptions, stages of change ratings, and scoring instructions. Note: SD = loading on the Sexual Deviance factor; C = loading on the Criminality factor; TR = loading on the Treatment Responsivity factor; DNL = did not load.

Source: Adapted from Olver, Wong, Nicholaichuk, and Gordon (2007) with permission.

An important practical limitation in assessing reoffense risk among sexual offenders is that, while in custody, their ability to access potential victims or engage in other sexually deviant behaviors (e.g., viewing child pornography) is quite limited. As such, consideration of offense paralleling, analog, or proxy behaviors is necessary to assess the continued presence of dynamic risk markers. Though the need to use offense-paralleling behaviors to assess sexual offenders is more obvious, the same also applies to some criminogenic needs for nonsexual offenders, such as family violence or use of specific weapons. The VRS-SO includes, where appropriate, offense paralleling and proxy behaviors in the rating descriptions of the items and the stage of change to assess risk and to evaluate change. Some behavioral proxies, such as deviant sexual fantasies of children, violence, and coercive sex, can occur both in the community and within the institution. Some sexual offenders may engage in inappropriate fantasies about staff and may even try to establish personal liaisons with them as a substitute for sexually deviant behaviors they engage in outside the institution. Other offense analog behaviors may include using child images available in shopping catalogs or magazines, engaging in lusty and sexually degrading talk, or developing indiscriminate casual homosexual liaisons. In sum, the VRS-SO makes use of many of these offense-paralleling behaviors to assess the presence or absence of dynamic risk factors and treatment change.

Reliability of the VRS-SO

The VRS-SO has demonstrated strong reliability across several independent investigations. In terms of its interrater reliability, strong intraclass correlation (ICC) values have been obtained for independent ratings of the static (ICC = .97), dynamic (ICC = .74–.92), and total (ICC = .86–.90) scores (Beggs & Grace, 2010; Beyko & Wong, 2005; Olver et al., 2007; Sowden & Olver, 2017). Internal consistency as measured via Cronbach's alpha for VRS-SO dynamic and total scores has ranged from .81 to .95 across these samples.

Validity of the VRS-SO

Factor Structure

Several studies have examined the factor structure of the VRS-SO, with emphasis placed on identifying latent constructs underpinning the dynamic items. The inaugural work by Olver et al. (2007) found 15 out of 17 items loaded on three oblique factors labeled Sexual Deviance, Criminality, and Treatment Responsivity. Sexual Deviance taps a pattern of deviant sexual interests, preoccupations, and behavior, while Criminality measures a general antisocial orientation (e.g., impulsivity, aggressiveness, substance abuse, and criminal personality), and Treatment Responsivity assesses sexual offender attitudes and cognitions, including insight and openness toward treatment. Subsequent factor analyses have yielded some variability in solutions depending on the sample. In a prospective multisite investigation, Olver, Neumann, Kingston, Nicholaichuk, and Wong (2018) found the traditional three factors to emerge and demonstrated stability in the factor loadings over time through longitudinal factor analysis. The three-factor model was also replicated through confirmatory factor analysis in an Austrian prison sample of adult and child contact sexual offenders (Olver & Eher, 2019). In two samples of child sexual abusers, slightly different solutions have been found including four factors (Beggs & Grace, 2010) as well as a variation on the three-factor model (Goodman-Delahunty & O'Brien, 2012).

Convergent Validity

Evidence for convergent validity has been obtained in a number of VRS-SO studies. First, the VRS-SO static items have demonstrated high convergence with the Static-99 and 99R (r = .70–.80; Olver et al., 2007; Olver, Klepfisz, Stockdale, Kingston, Nicholaichuk, & Wong, 2016), while the dynamic items have yielded high convergence with STABLE 2000 (r = .68; Olver, Neumann et al., 2018) and 2007 (r = .66–.75; Sowden & Olver, 2017). The three broad factors have also converged with theoretically relevant measures in important ways. For instance, the Sexual Deviance factor correlates highly with self-report measures of deviant sexual fantasy (Beggs & Grace, 2010), phallometric measurements of arousal to child visual stimuli (Canales, Olver, & Wong, 2009),

Child Pornography Offender Risk-Tool (C-PORT; Seto & Eke, 2015) ratings (Maltais & Sribney, 2018), clinical ratings of sexual deviance and emotional identification with children (Olver, Neumann et al., 2018), and deficits in socioemotional functioning (Olver, Nicholaichuk, & Wong, 2014). Moreover, the Criminality factor correlates highly with Factor 2 totals of Hare's (2003) Psychopathy Checklist-Revised (Olver & Wong, 2009) and self-report measures of aggression, anger, hostility toward women, and rape myth acceptance (Beggs & Grace, 2011; Olver, Neumann et al., 2018; Olver, Nicholaichuk, & Wong, 2014). Finally, the Treatment Responsivity factor correlates highly with PCL-R Factor 1 totals (Olver & Wong, 2009), and clinical and self-report ratings of sexual offender attitudes, empathy, acceptance of responsibility, and social anxiety (Beggs & Grace, 2011; Olver, Neumann et al., 2018; Olver, Nicholaichuk, & Wong, 2014).

Predictive Validity

The predictive validity of the VRS-SO for sexual and violent reoffending has been examined in three federal Canadian correctional samples (Olver et al., 2007, Olver, Nicholaichuk, Kingston, & Wong, 2014; Sowden & Olver, 2017) as well as samples in New Zealand (Beggs & Grace, 2010, 2011), Australia (Goodman-Delahunty & O'Brien, 2012), Austria (Eher et al., 2015; Olver & Eher, 2019), and the United States (Johnson, 2014). Predictive validity findings, sample characteristics, and study features are provided for eight samples and 2,104 offenders (Table 10.4). Although this research has demonstrated that VRS-SO scores predict both sexual and nonsexual reoffending, as with the VRS, the results are prioritized in terms of the criterion of primary interest (sexual reoffending). The median AUC value ranged from .67 to .72 for the static, dynamic, and total scores on the measures, representing moderate to high predictive validity using the Rice

Table 10.4 VRS-SO: Summary of Predictive Validity Findings (AUC Value) for Sexual Recidivism

VRS-SO Study	Sample and Setting	N	Static	Dynamic	Total
Beggs & Grace, 2010	Treated child sex offenders, Kia Marama Program, New Zealand	218	.70	.81	.81
Eher et al. 2015	Child sex offenders, Austria, prison setting	189	.76	.67	.76
Goodman-Delahunty & O'Brien 2012	Treated and untreated incest offenders, Cedar Cottage, Western Australia	172	.54[NS]	.49[NS]	.56[NS]
Johnson, 2014	Treated adult and child contact sex offenders, Kentucky USA, prison setting	290	.66	.61	.67
Olver & Eher, 2019	Mixed sample, child and adult contact sex offenders, Austria, prison setting	351	.80	.70	.79
Olver et al., 2007	Treated adult and child contact sexoffenders, Clearwater Program, RPC	321	.74	.67	.72
Olver et al., 2020; Olver et al., 2016	Treated adult and child contact sexual offenders, National Sex Offender Program, CSC	564	.69	.70	.72
Sowden & Olver, 2017	Treated adult and child contact sexual offenders, Clearwater Program, RPC	180	.53[NS]	.64	.62
	Median AUC		.69	.67	.72

Note: All AUC values significant at $p < .05$ or better except for except for NS = not significant. RPC = Regional Psychiatric Centre; CSC = Correctional Service of Canada and Harris (2005) interpretive rubric. These prediction magnitudes are also entirely in line with the Hanson and Morton-Bourgon (2009) meta-analysis, which found median d values of .66–.67 for static and dynamic actuarial measures (corresponding to an AUC of .68).

Although the VRS-SO significantly predicted sexual reoffending across most of the samples, it demonstrated poor predictive validity for this outcome in a sample of Australian incest offenders (Goodman-Delahunty & O'Brien, 2012) although it did predict nonsexual violent and general recidivism. We attribute this in part to range restriction on one of the item constellations, the Sexual Deviance factor, which had an extremely high mean (13.1 out of a maximum 15 points) and very tight range ($SD = 1.9$), especially compared to other child sexual abuser samples with a lower mean and greater variability (e.g., Beggs & Grace, 2010, 2011; $M = 9.1$, $SD = 2.7$).

In the six studies that have examined incremental validity of static and dynamic scores for sexual reoffending, four of these (Beggs & Grace, 2010; Olver et al., 2007; Olver Nicholaichuk, Kingston et al., 2014; Olver Nicholaichuk, Kingston, & Wong, 2020; Olver & Eher, 2019; Sowden & Olver, 2017) have found VRS-SO dynamic scores to significantly add to the predictive efficacy of static measures (Static-99/99R or VRS-SO static) through Cox regression survival analysis. Although incremental validity data may be informative, such analyses do not demonstrate that dynamic variables can change or that potential changes are meaningful; only that these attributes explain unique variance in outcome.

Dynamic Predictive Validity

Several of the studies summarized in Table 10.4 have examined the dynamic predictive validity of VRS-SO scores; that is, the extent to which the dynamic items can change whether such changes are linked to changes in recidivism. Across the treatment programs from which the VRS-SO has been rated, the amount of change has ranged from 2.5 points on average (i.e., about one stage of change improvement on five criminogenic items) to 4 or more points (e.g., Beggs & Grace, 2011; Olver, Nicholaichuk, Kingston et al., 2014; Olver et al., 2020; Sowden & Olver, 2017). Residualized change scores are examined in these analyses, given that high-risk offenders have more room to change, but remain higher risk compared to low-risk offenders even after making strides in treatment. Most typically Cox regression survival analysis has been used controlling for pretreatment score to examine the association of VRS-SO measured treatment change, to reductions in recidivism over time. The four studies (Beggs & Grace, 2011; Olver et al., 2007; Olver, Nicholaichuk, et al., 2014; Olveret al., 2020; Sowden & Olver, 2017) that have used this design have consistently arrived at a change score hazard ratio (eB) of approximately .90, interpreted to mean a predicted 10% decrease in the hazard for a new sexual offense for every 1-point increase in change score after controlling for baseline risk. The results point to a small in magnitude but robust change effect for the VRS-SO dynamic items with respect to risk reduction, supporting the dynamic predictive validity of the instrument for sexual violence risk.

VRS/VRS-SO Summary

The VRS/VRS-SO were developed as specialized risk assessment tools for violent and sexual offending that integrated risk assessment with treatment and change. Research evidence has demonstrated their robust psychometric characteristics including predictive efficacy in independent studies with international samples. A growing body of research supports the notion that the dynamic variables on the VRS/VRS-SO can change, and that positive changes (i.e., improvement) on these variables are associated with reductions in violent and sexual offending even after controlling for baseline risk. These findings, interpreted with caution, suggest that the VRS/VRS-SO dynamic predictors could be deemed "causal risk factors" using Kraemer et al.'s (1997,

p. 341) criteria and terminology as outlined in the discussion of the VRS. Kraemer et al. (1997) correctly pointed out that "when causal risk factors are identified for an outcome, questions may still remain about the mechanism or process by which those causal risk factors operate," identifying the relevant causal risk factors "might provide inspiration about where to look for the cause" (p. 341), whether this be completing treatment, enhancing community supports, aging, or so forth.

Case Illustration Using the VRS-SO

The following clinical case was developed to illustrate the use of the VRS-SO for risk assessment, treatment planning, and evaluating change. Although this case has been informed by previous cases, the details including the subject's name, history, and treatment responses are fictitious and are intended for illustration purposes only.

Bill, a 36-year-old White man, was serving his first 4-year prison sentence for sexual assault against two teenage boys, aged 13 and 14 years. Bill came from a middle-class background with no reported abuse or neglect growing up. He first learned about sex through erotic magazines he hid around his home. Bill reported being sexually attracted to and having had crushes on school-age boys. His first sexual experience occurred when he was about 13 with a neighborhood boy who was about 11. He was also involved in mutual fondling and oral sex with other neighborhood boys. Bill occasionally dated girls in high school, but these relationships were generally short-lived. In his 20s and early 30s, Bill reported living a marginalized existence, using alcohol heavily, being frequently unemployed, and remaining sexually attracted to boys.

Bill was first convicted of a sexual offense against children at age 22, when he enticed an 11-year-old who was riding his bike home and performed fellatio on him. Bill used a similar modus operandi with other boys. Bill remained socially isolated, with the exception of the company of the estranged boys he would invite into his home. Here he would entice them with alcohol and drugs, and, should they offer little or no resistance, he would sexually assault them. Bill rationalized that he was pleasuring the victims because they occasionally ejaculated and they "freely" consented. Even after his fourth conviction, Bill maintained that he had not harmed the victims because they "wanted it," and, if anybody was to blame, it was the irresponsible parents who failed to provide proper supervision. When Bill was arrested, police found a cache of photos of naked boys on his computer.

Following his sentencing and referral to treatment, Bill maintained a cautious and skeptical stance toward the prospect of therapy. In the pretreatment assessment, Bill reported that most of his sexual fantasies involved boys between the ages of 10 and 15, although he reported also having some attraction to young men. He reported masturbating almost daily to these fantasies and admitted to having more victims over the years than he had been convicted for. Despite his drug and alcohol use, Bill reported that he was seldom intoxicated during his sexual offenses and generally used substances to establish relationships with the victims. Bill denied having problems with aggression and anger although he reported a history of other emotional problems, including depression and anxiety. Although he reported having had some short-lived gay relationships, Bill never cohabitated with a lover for any meaningful period of time and was frequently lonely and socially withdrawn. Bill reported that the victims filled an emptiness within him through their social contacts.

Figure 10.1 (left-hand side) presents the first page of a VRS-SO score sheet illustrating Bill's ratings on the static items during pretreatment. Bill's item scores reflect the fact that he is a 36-year-old man serving a 4-year sentence, meaning that he will at most be 40 years old when he is released. He was charged for his first sexual offense at age 22, has an extrafamilial child victim profile, and has in excess of four prior sexual offense charges or convictions. All his victims were unrelated males, and he has four prior sentencing dates. Bill's VRS-SO static score was 15.

VRS:SO Score Sheet ©

Name: Bill

Client #:

Pre-Treatment Rater: Dr. M. Olver　　Pre-Treatment Rating Date: 2007 01 15

Post-Treatment Rater: Dr. M. Olver　　Post-Treatment Rating Date: 2007 09 14

Static Factors

Risk Factor[1]		Codes	Score	1 or N
S1	Age at Time of Release	Under 25 years	3	
		25 to 34 years	2	
		35 to 44 years	①	
		45 years or older	0	
S2	Age at First Sexual Offense	Under 20 years	3	
		20 to 24 years	②	
		25 to 34 years	1	
		35 years or older	0	
S3	Sex Offender Type	Mixed (both adult and child victims)	3	
		Child molester (child victims only)	②	
		Rapist (adult victims only)	1	
		Incest (related victims predominantly)	0	
S4	Prior Sexual Offenses	4-4+ prior arrests/charges/convictions for a sexual offense	③	
		2-3 prior arrests/charges/convictions for a sexual offense	2	
		1 prior arrests/charge conviction for a sexual offense	1	
		No prior arrests/charges/convictions for a sexual offense	0	
S5	Unrelated Victims	4 or more unrelated victims	③	
		2-3 unrelated victims	2	
		1 unrelated victim	1	
		No unrelated victims (related victims only)	0	
S6	Number and Gender of Victims	2 or more male victims & any number of female victims	③	
		2 or more female victims or 1 female and 1 male victim	2	
		1 male victim only	1	
		1 female victim only	0	
S7	Prior Sentencing Dates	11 or more prior sentencing occasions	3	
		5-10 prior sentencing occasions	2	
		2-4 prior sentencing occasions	①	
		0-1 prior sentencing occasions	0	
Total Static Factor Score		Before Treatment	15	
		After Treatment	15	

[1] If it is necessary to omit a Static or Dynamic Factor, the rater should indicate whether the omission is because there is insufficient information (I) or because the item is not applicable (N).

© 2000 Stephen Wong, Mark Olver, Terry Nicholaichuk, & Audrey Gordon

---

For Stage Of Change:
PrC = PreContemplation/Contemplation
P = Preparation
A = Action
M = Maintenance

Use these symbols to indicate the Stage of Change:
O = Pre-treatment
X = Post-treatment

# of Stages changed:
no change = 0
1 stage = .5
2 stages = 1.0
3 stages = 1.5

DYNAMIC FACTORS AND TOTAL SCORES

		Pre-Tx (a)	F 1[*]	F 2	F 3	Stage of Change[††]	# of Stages changed x .5 (b)	Post-Tx (a-b)[†††]	F 1	F 2	F 3	1 or N
D1	Sexually Deviant Lifestyle	0 1 2 ③	3			PrC X A M	1.5 1 ⑤ 0	2.5	2.5			
D2	Sexual Compulsivity	0 1 ② 3	2			PrC X A M	1.5 1 ⑤ 0	1.5		1.5		
D3	Offense Planning	0 1 2 ③	3			PrC X A M	1.5 1 ⑤ 0	2.5	2.5			
D4	Criminal Personality	0 ① 2 3		1		PrC P A M	1.5 1 .5 0	1			1	
D5	Cognitive Distortions	0 1 2 ③			3	PrC P A M	1.5 1 ⑤ 0	3			3	
D6	Interpersonal Aggression	⓪ 1 2 3	0			PrC P A M	1.5 1 .5 ⓪	0			0	
D7	Emotional Control	0 1 ② 3				PrC P A M	1.5 1 ⑤ 0	1.5		1.5		
D8	Insight	0 1 ② 3			2	PrC P A M	1.5 1 .5 ⓪	2			2	
D9	Substance Abuse	0 1 2 3	1			PrC P A M	1.5 1 ⑤ 0	1		1		
D10	Community Support	0 1 ② 3		2		PrC X A M	1.5 1 ⑤ 0	1.5		1.5		
D11	Release to High Risk Situations	0 1 ② 3			2	PrC X A M	1.5 1 ⑤ 0	1.5			1.5	
D12	Sexual Offending Cycle	0 1 2 ③	3			PrC X A M	1.5 1 ⑤ 0	2.5	2.5			
D13	Impulsivity	⓪ 1 2 3	0			PrC P A M	1.5 1 .5 ⓪	0			0	
D14	Compliance with Community Supervision	0 1 ② 3		2		PrC X P A M	1.5 1 ⑤ 0	2		2		
D15	Treatment Compliance	0 ① 2 3				PrC P A M	1.5 1 ⑤ 0	1		1		
D16	Deviant Sexual Preference	0 1 2 ③	3			PrC X A M	1.5 1 .5 0	2.5	2.5			
D17	Intimacy Deficits	0 1 2 ③			3	PrC P A M	1.5 1 ③ 0	3			3	
Total Dynamic Factor Score		Pre-Tx 33	14	6	8	Total Dynamic Factor Score →		Post-Tx 29	11.5	5.5	7.5	
Total Static Factor Score From Previous Page →		15				Total Static Factor Score From Previous Page →		15				
Total Static + Total Dynamic Factor Score →		48				Total Static + Total Dynamic Factor Score →		44				

Indicate if Clinical Override was used:　Yes O　No X

[†] To calculate scores for Factors 1 (Sexual Deviancy), 2 (Criminality), & 3 (Treatment Responsivity): Place Pre-Tx score in the corresponding shaded box to the right (Note: D7 is excluded). Tally each column (F1, F2, F3) and enter total score in appropriate box.
[††] For treatment purposes, specify whether the client is in Pre-contemplation or Contemplation stage by circling (O) the 'P' or 'C' stage for pre- and post-treatment, respectively.
[†††] If there is a deterioration during treatment, 'b' score is added to 'a' score for the corresponding Dynamic Factor

Figure 10.1 VRS-SO Static and Dynamic Items Score Sheet and Ratings for the Case of Bill

Figure 10.1 (right-hand side) also presents the second page of Bill's VRS-SO score sheet with his ratings on the dynamic items pre- and post-treatment. Bill's VRS-SO dynamic items profile at pretreatment (left-hand side of the form) indicated that many dynamic items were criminogenic. For the sake of brevity, the scoring rationale for a few representative items on each factor is discussed in detail. First, all the items on the sexual deviance factor were criminogenic for Bill (i.e., receiving a 2- or 3-point rating). For instance, given that Bill reported that he was sexually preoccupied with preteen boys, fantasized about this group predominantly, and had a child pornography collection, he received a score of 3 on the deviant sexual preference item. As well, because he masturbated and fantasized quite frequently, he received a score of 2 on sexual compulsivity; a higher reported frequency of sexual thoughts and behaviors would have generated a score of 3.

Bill had a mixture of high and low scores on items comprising the criminality and treatment responsivity factors. Bill received low scores on several criminality factor items: given that he had basically no concerns with physically or verbally aggressive interpersonal behavior and impulsivity, he received a score of 0 on interpersonal aggression and 0 on impulsivity. Although Bill had some contact with his family, by and large they were estranged, and, having few meaningful supports, Bill received a score of 2 on community support. Although he also abused substances, this consumption did not seem to have a strong link to sexual offending. In terms of items on the treatment responsivity factor, Bill had clear attitudes and cognitions supportive of sexual offending, thus receiving a score of 3 on cognitive distortions. Given his level of cooperation with treatment and limited understanding of the issues and events contributing to his offending, he received a score of 1 on treatment compliance and a 2 on insight.

After rating Bill's static and dynamic items pretreatment, he received a total score of 48, placing him in the above-average risk range for recidivism. On each of the items deemed criminogenic (i.e., 2- or 3-point rating), Bill was rated as being in the precontemplative or contemplative stage of change given that he had yet to acknowledge his problems or was aware of his problems but reluctant to make changes. For instance, given that Bill was very reluctant to change his deviant fantasies despite their maladaptive nature, he was rated as being in the pre-contemplative stage of change on deviant sexual preference. Moreover, although Bill knew he was depressed, anxious, and lonely and that such emotional states were linked to his sexual offending, he had yet to make any positive change in his emotional functioning at the outset of treatment, and, as such, he was rated as being in the contemplative stage on emotional control.

The VRS-SO can be used to assist case conceptualization and treatment planning. The static items provide an empirical-actuarial estimate of the offender's risk, reflect the extensiveness of past sexual and nonsexual misconduct, and should show no change with treatment. The dynamic items, on the other hand, although also summable to generate an actuarial estimate of risk, can be used to elucidate the various elements involved in the persistence and maintenance of sexual offending. Specifically, dynamic items dubbed criminogenic can be used to create a dynamic risk profile of individual needs and, hence, areas that should be targeted for intervention.

Treatment for Bill consisted of a 12-month high-intensity inpatient sexual offender program and a combination of group and individual therapy. Bill had the opportunity to disclose his offenses in group and benefit from feedback from other treatment participants. He completed a detailed crime cycle and learned about the cognitive, behavioral, and emotional dynamics of his sexual offending. Although at first rationalizing and minimizing his sexual abuse of boys, the feedback and challenges he received from other group members, coupled with the constructive and accepting group environment and individual psychotherapy, gradually increased his acceptance of responsibility and accountability for his offenses. Bill also completed a detailed relapse prevention plan that articulated his reoffense pathways, high-risk situations, and strategies to circumvent relapse. Bill further completed treatment modules that specifically addressed cognitive distortions and attitudes related to sexual offending, healthy relationships and attachments, assertiveness and social skills, victim empathy, and fantasies/healthy sexuality.

Bill made modest gains in a number of areas. Bill's fantasy monitoring records demonstrated a decrease in the frequency of deviant fantasies and an increase in appropriate adult male homosexual fantasies, and the frequency with which he masturbated decreased as well. In his work, Bill noticed that when he experienced negative emotional states (e.g., loneliness, stress, feeling overwhelmed) he sometimes retreated into his fantasy world. Over the course of treatment, he became better at disclosing and discussing his feelings and using other, more appropriate coping strategies to manage them. Bill was able to identify cognitive distortions he used to justify his sexual offending and used some effective strategies to challenge them; however, he frequently struggled with relinquishing his justifications and at times dwelled on the physiological displays of sexual excitement shown by his victims to excuse and minimize his behavior. Bill's case management team also worked hard to establish supports for him in the community, and he reestablished some contact with an older sibling who committed to supporting him.

Following the completion of treatment, Bill was considered to have made varying gains in all of his criminogenic need areas. However, Bill was judged to have advanced to the preparation stage on several of his dynamic risk factors, given that his changes were relatively recent (i.e., made over the course of a 12-month treatment program) and he had not yet had any opportunity to practice his skills in real-world contexts. As illustrated in Figure 10.1, at post-treatment, Bill's VRS-SO score changed by 4 points (roughly one-half of a standard deviation) as he moved to the preparation stage on eight of the criminogenic items. An online VRS-SO Excel calculator can generate logistic regression based estimates based on combinations of risk and change scores (Olver, Mundt et al., 2018). This amount of change, coupled with his initial baseline score, is associated with an estimated sexual reoffending rate of 23% after 5 years and 34.6% after 10 years. A continued reduction in Bill's risk would be anticipated if he completed a maintenance sexual offender group and continue to demonstrate sustained behavior change in his dynamic risk factors into the community. For Bill to move into action stages for most of the criminogenic factors, he would have to demonstrate sustained changes over a significant period of time. Moving into the maintenance stage would further require the generalization of the changes to real-life situations and for Bill to have withstood significant challenges with little or no relapse.

References

Andrews, D. A., & Bonta, J. (1994, 1998). *The psychology of criminal conduct* (2nd ed.). Cincinnati, OH: Anderson.

Beggs, S. M., & Grace, R. C. (2010). Assessment of dynamic risk factors: An independent validation study of the violence risk scale: Sexual offender version. *Sexual Abuse: A Journal of Research and Treatment, 22,* 234–251.

Beggs, S. M., & Grace, R. C. (2011). Treatment gains for sexual offenders against children predicts reduced recidivism: A comparative validity study. *Journal of Consulting and Clinical Psychology, 79,* 182–192.

Beyko, M. J., & Wong, S. C. P. (2005). Predictors of treatment attrition as indicators for program improvement not offender shortcomings: A study of sex offender treatment attrition. *Sexual Abuse: A Journal of Research and Treatment, 17,* 375–389.

Bonta, J., & Andrews, D. A. (2017). *The psychology of criminal conduct* (6th ed.). New York: Routledge.

Burt, G. N. (2000). *Predicting violent recidivism of treated violent offenders using the psychopathy checklist-revised and the violence risk scale* (Unpublished Master's thesis). University of Saskatchewan, Saskatoon.

Burt, G. N. (2003). *Investigating characteristics of the non-recidivating psychopathic offender* (Unpublished doctoral dissertation). University of Saskatchewan, Saskatoon.

Burt, G. N., Olver, M., & Wong, S. C. P. (2016). Investigating characteristics of the nonrecidivating psychopathic offender. *Criminal Justice and Behavior, 40,* 1326–1348.

Canales, D. D., Olver, M. E., & Wong, S. C. P. (2009). Construct validity of the violence risk scale-sexual offender version for measuring sexual deviance. *Sexual Abuse: A Journal of Research and Treatment, 21*, 474–492.

Coupland, R. B. A., & Olver, M. E. (2018). Assessing dynamic violence risk in a high risk treated sample of violent offenders. *Assessment*, 1–15. Epub ahead of print. doi:10.1177/1073191118797440

Coupland, R. B. A., & Olver, M. E. (2020). Assessing protective factors in treated violent offenders: Associations with recidivism reduction and positive community outcomes. *Psychological Assessment, 32*.

de Vries Robbé, M., Weenink, A., & de Vogel, V. (2006, June). *Dynamic risk assessment: A comparative study into risk assessment with the violence risk scale (VRS) and the HCR-20*. Paper presented at the annual conference of the International Association of Forensic Mental Health Services, Amsterdam, The Netherlands.

Dolan, M., & Fullam, R. (2007). The validity of the violence risk scale second edition (VRS-2_ in a British forensic inpatient sample. *The Journal of Forensic Psychiatry & Psychology, 18*, 381–393.

Doyle, M., Carter, S., Shaw, J., & Dolan, M. (2012). Predicting community violence from patients discharged from acute mental health units in England. *Social Psychiatry and Psychiatric Epidemiology, 47*, 627–637.

Duncan, R. D., Kennedy, W. A., & Patrick, C. J. (1995). Four-factor model of recidivism in male juvenile offenders. *Journal of Child Clinical Psychology, 24*, 250–257.

Eher, R., Olver, M. E., Heurix, I., Schilling, F., & Rettenberger, M. (2015). Predicting reoffense in pedophilic child molesters by clinical diagnoses and risk assessment. *Law and Human Behavior, 39*, 571–580.

Goodman-Delahunty, J., & O'Brien, K. (2012). *Reoffense risk in intrafamilial child sexual offenders*. Report to the Criminology Advisory Research Council, Sydney.

Gordon, A. E. (1998). *The interrater reliability, internal consistency and validity of the violence risk scale—experimental version 1* (Unpublished Master's thesis). University of Saskatchewan, Saskatoon.

Gordon, A. E., & Wong, S. C. P. (2010). Offense analogue behaviours as indicator of criminogenic need and treatment progress in custodial settings. In M. Daffern, L. Jones, & J. Shine (Eds.), *Offence paralleling behaviour: An individualized approach to offender assessment and treatment* (pp. 171–183). Chichester: Wiley.

Hann, R. G., & Harman, W. G. (1992). *Predicting violent risk for penitentiary inmates* (User Report No. 1992-08). Ottawa: Department of the Solicitor General of Canada.

Hanson, R. K., & Bussière (1998). Predicting relapse: A meta-analysis of sexual offender recidivism studies. *Journal of Consulting and Clinical Psychology, 66*, 348–362.

Hanson, R. K., & Harris, A. J. R. (2000). Where should we intervene? Dynamic predictors of sexual offense recidivism. *Criminal Justice and Behavior, 27*, 6–35.

Hanson, R. K., & Morton-Bourgon, K. E. (2009). The accuracy of recidivism risk assessments for sexual offenders: A meta-analysis of 118 prediction studies. *Psychological Assessment, 21*, 1–21.

Hare, R. D. (2003). *The Hare psychopathy checklist-revised* (2nd ed.). Toronto, ON: Multi-Health Systems.

Hirschi, T., & Gottfredson, M. (1983). Age and the explanation of crime. *American Journal of Sociology, 83*, 552–584.

Hogan, N. R., & Olver, M. E. (2016). Assessing risk for aggression in forensic psychiatric inpatients: An examination of five measures. *Law and Human Behavior, 40*, 233–243.

Hogan, N. R., & Olver, M. E. (2018). A prospective examination of the predictive validity of five structured instruments in the assessment of inpatient violence risk in a secure forensic hospital setting. *International Journal of Forensic Mental Health, 17*, 122–132.

Hogan, N. R., & Olver, M. E. (2019). Static and dynamic assessment of violence risk among discharged forensic patients. *Criminal Justice and Behavior, 46*, 923–938.

Johnson, R. C. (2014). *The violence risk scale—sex offender version: Construct and predictive validity using a Kentucky Department of Corrections sample* (Unpublished dissertation). Spalding University, Louisville, KY.

Kraemer, H. C., Kazdin, A. E., Offord, D. R., Kessler, R. C., Jensen, P. S., & Kupfer, D. J. (1997). Coming to terms with the terms of risk. *Archives of General Psychiatry, 54*, 337–343.

Lattimore, P. K., Visher, C., & Linster, R. L. (1995). Predicting arrest for violence among serious youthful offenders. *Journal of Research in Crime and Delinquency, 32*, 54–83.

Lewis, K. (2004). *The relationship between the URICA and correctional treatment in a sample of violent male offenders* (Unpublished doctoral dissertation). University of Saskatchewan, Saskatoon.

Lewis, K., Olver, M. E., & Wong, S. C. P. (2013). The violence risk scale: Predictive validity and linking treatment changes with recidivism in a sample of high risk offenders with psychopathic traits. *Assessment, 20*, 150–164.

Maltais, N., & Sribney, C. (2018, October). *Assessing the convergent validity of the VRS-SO and the C-PORT with a community sample*. Poster presented at the 37th annual meeting of the Association for the Treatment of Sexual Abusers, Vancouver, BC.

McGuire, J. (2008). A review of effective interventions for reducing aggression and violence. *Philosophical Transactions of the Royal Society, 363*(1503), 2483–2622.

O'Brien, K., & Daffern, M. (2017). Treatment gain in violent offenders: The relationship between proximal outcomes, risk reduction and violent recidivism. *Psychiatry, Psychology and Law, 24*, 244–258.

Olver, M. E., & Eher, R. (2019). Predictive properties and factor structure of the VRS-SO in an Austrian sample. *European Journal of Psychological Assessment*. Epub ahead of print. doi:10.1027/1015-5759/a000551

Olver, M. E., Klepfisz, G., Stockdale, K. C., Kingston, D. A., Nicholaichuk, T. P., & Wong, S. C. P. (2016). Some notes on the validation of VRS-SO static scores. *Journal of Sexual Aggression, 22*, 147–160.

Olver, M. E., Mundt, J. C., Thornton, D., Beggs Christofferson, S. M., Kingston, D. A., Sowden, J. N., . . . Wong, S. C. P. (2018). Using the violence risk scale-sexual offense version in sexual violence risk assessments: Updated risk categories and recidivism estimates from a multisite sample of treated sexual offenders. *Psychological Assessment, 30*, 941–955.

Olver, M. E., Neumann, C. S., Kingston, D. A., Nicholaichuk, T. P., & Wong, S. C. P. (2018). Construct validity of the violence risk scale-sexual offender version instrument in a multisite sample of treated sexual offenders. *Assessment, 25*, 40–55.

Olver, M. E., Nicholaichuk, T. P., Kingston, D. A., & Wong S. C. P. (2014). A multisite examination of sexual violence risk and therapeutic change. *Journal of Consulting and Clinical Psychology, 82*, 312–324.

Olver, M. E., Nicholaichuk, T. P., Kingston, D. K., & Wong, S. C. P. (2020). A prospective multisite examination of dynamic sexual violence risk: Extension and update to Olver, Nicholaichuk, Kingston, and Wong (2014). *Journal of Consulting and Clinical Psychology*. Epub ahead of print. doi:10.1037/ccp0000478

Olver, M. E., Nicholaichuk, T. P., & Wong, S. C. P. (2014). The predictive and concurrent validity of a psychometric battery used to assess sex offenders in a treatment program: An 18-year follow up. *Journal of Sexual Aggression, 20*, 216–239.

Olver, M. E., & Wong, S. C. P. (2009). Therapeutic responses of psychopathic sexual offenders: Treatment attrition, therapeutic change, and long term recidivism. *Journal of Consulting and Clinical Psychology, 77*, 328–336.

Olver, M. E., & Wong, S. C. P. (2011). Predictors of sex offender treatment dropout: Psychopathy, sex offender risk, and responsivity implications. *Psychology, Crime, and Law, 17*, 457–471.

Olver, M. E., Wong, S. C. P., Nicholaichuk, T., & Gordon, A. (2007). The validity and reliability of the violence risk scale-sexual offender version: Assessing sex offender risk and evaluating therapeutic change. *Psychological Assessment, 19*, 318–329.

Pithers, W. D. (1990). Relapse prevention for sexual aggressors: A method for maintaining therapeutic gain and enhancing external supervision. In W. L. Marshall, D. R. Laws, & H. E. Barbaree (Eds.), *Handbook of sexual assault: Issues, theories, and treatment of the offender* (pp. 343–361). New York: Plenum Press.

Polaschek, D. L. L., Yesberg, J. A., Bell, R. K., Casey, A. R., & Dickson, S. R. (2016). Intensive psychological treatment of high-risk violent offenders: Outcomes and pre-release mechanisms. *Psychology, Crime & Law, 22*, 344–365.

Prochaska, J. O., DiClemente, C. C., & Norcross, J. C. (1992). In search of how people change: Applications to the addictive behaviors. *American Psychologist, 47*, 1102–1114.

Rice, M. E., & Harris, G. T. (2005). Comparing effect sizes in follow-up studies: ROC area, Cohen's d, and r. *Law and Human Behavior, 29*, 615–620.

Seto, M. C., & Eke, A. W. (2015). Predicting recidivism among adult male child pornography offenders: Development of the child pornography offender risk tool (CPORT). *Law and Human Behavior, 39*, 416–429.

Sowden, J. N., & Olver, M. E. (2017). Use of the violence risk scale sexual offender version and the stable 2007 to assess sexual offender treatment change. *Psychological Assessment, 29*, 293–303.

Stewart, C. A. (2011). *Risk assessment of federal female offenders* (Unpublished dissertation). University of Saskatchewan, Saskatoon.

Valliant, P., Gristey, C., Pottier, D., & Kosmyna, R. (1999). Risk factor in violent and non-violent offenders. *Psychological Reports, 85*, 675–680.

Warburton, K. D., & Stahl, S. (2016). *Violence in psychiatry*. Cambridge: Cambridge University Press.

Ward, T., & Hudson, S. M. (1998). A model of the relapse process in sex offenders. *Journal of Interpersonal Violence, 13*, 700–725.

Wilde, S., & Wong, S. (2000). *The predictive and congruent validity of the violence risk scale (Version 2) with mentally disordered offenders*. Paper presented at the Annual Convention of the Canadian Psychological Association, Ottawa.

Wilson, N. J., Kilgour, G., & Polaschek, D. L. L. (2013). Treating high-risk rapists in a New Zealand intensive prison programme. *Psychology, Crime, & Law, 19*, 527–547.

Wong, S. C. P., & Burt, G. N. (2007). The heterogeneity of incarcerated psychopaths: Differences in risk, need, recidivism and management approaches. In H. Herve & J. C. Yuille (Eds.), *The psychopath: Theory, research, and practice* (pp. 461–484). New York: Taylor & Francis.

Wong, S. C. P., & Gordon, A. E. (1999–2003). *The violence risk scale*. Unpublished manuscript, University of Saskatchewan, Saskatoon.

Wong, S. C. P., & Gordon A. E. (2006). The validity and reliability of the violence risk scale: A treatment-friendly violence risk assessment tool. *Psychology, Public Policy, and Law, 12*, 279–309.

Wong, S. C. P., Gordon, A. E., & Gu, D. (2007). Assessment and treatment of violence-prone forensic clients: An integrated approach. *British Journal of Psychiatry, 190*, s66–s74.

Wong, S. C. P., Olver, M. E., Nicholaichuk, T. P., & Gordon, A. (2003, 2017). *The violence risk scale: sexual offense version (VRS-SO)*. Saskatoon: Regional Psychiatric Centre and University of Saskatchewan.

Wong, S. C. P., & Parhar, K. K. (2011). Evaluation of the predictive validity of the Violence Risk Scale in a paroled offender sample: A seven-year prospective study. *Journal of Forensic Psychiatry and Psychology, 22*, 790–808.

Yesberg, J. A. (2015). *Exploring mechanisms of change in the rehabilitation of high risk offenders* (Unpublished doctoral dissertation). Victoria University of Wellington, Wellington, NZ.

Zhang, X., Chen, X., Cai, W., & Hu, J. (2012). Reliability of the violence risk scale Chinese version. *Journal of Forensic Medicine, 28*, 32–35.

Structured Professional Judgment Measures

Chapter 11

The Early Assessment Risk Lists for Boys (EARL-20B) and Girls (EARL-21G)

*Leena K. Augimeri, Margaret Walsh, Pia Enebrink,
Depeng Jiang, Andrea Blackman, and Areti Smaragdi*

Introduction

Antisocial behavior during childhood is an important warning sign for continued behavior problems (e.g., delinquency or conduct disorder) in adolescence and adulthood (Loeber & Farrington, 2001; Moffitt, Caspi, Harrington, & Milne, 2002). Moreover, it is linked with increased risk for becoming a chronic offender (Howell, Lipsey, Wilson, Howell, & Hodges, 2019). This can lead to substantial personal and familial suffering and societal costs; the average male offender between 12 and 21 years of age will require allocation of between $1.5 and $2.5 million in public service dollars for associated costs, and this figure may exceed $6 million for a serious offender (Public Safety Canada, 2016). Children can engage in a range of antisocial behaviors; however, for the purposes of this chapter, we are defining antisocial behavior as acts that could lead to criminal charges if adults. Some examples of antisocial behavior include: assault, aggression, fighting, physically attacking people, theft, cruelty to animals, vandalism, and serious violations of rules. However, since many children show variability and desistance from such behaviors over time (Lipman, Bennett, Racine, Mazumdar, & Offord, 1998), it is difficult to predict which children will continue or discontinue with their antisocial behavior.

One way to enhance predictions of antisocial behavior is to concentrate on risk factors that are present in the child's life. Over the past two decades, rigorous research on risk factors that contribute to antisocial behavior has been conducted. As a result, there is a fairly comprehensive and documented understanding about factors that place antisocial children at risk for engaging in delinquent behavior and continued offending (e.g., Howell, 2003; Lahey, Moffit, & Caspi, 2003; Loeber, Farrington, & Petechuk, 2003; Loeber, Burke, & Lahey, 2002). Lately, a number of structured professional judgment tools, utilized in risk assessment and based on descriptions of evidence-based risk factors for antisocial behaviors, have been developed for use with adults (e.g., Historical, Clinical and Risk Management—HCR-20 V3; Douglas, Hart, Webster, & Belfrage, 2013), and for youth (e.g., Structured Assessment of Violence Risk in Youth—SAVRY; Borum, Bartel, & Forth, 2002). These have advanced the field and benefited correctional and forensic mental health systems of care (Bloom, Webster, Hucker, & De Freitas, 2007; Webster, Martin, Brink, Nicholls, & Middleton, 2004). However, prior to 1998, there were no assessment schemes available to identify specific domains of risk for antisocial children under the age of 12 (Augimeri, Koegl, Ferrante, & Slater, 2006). The importance of developing such a tool cannot be overstated. The middle years, denoted as ages 6 to 12, are a critical window in time when children are particularly responsive to intervention and prevention efforts (Piquero, Jennings, Farrington, Diamond, & Reingle Gonzalez, 2016; Moffit et al., 2011).

The ability to identify or predict which antisocial pre-adolescent children will continue to engage in such behavior in adolescence and/or adulthood represents one of the most important challenges in the fields of developmental criminology and forensic psychology. It is based on the tantalizing proposition that the careful identification of risk factors will lead to the development of effective prevention and intervention strategies for children (Augimeri, Webster, Koegl, & Levene, 1998). Addressing this gap in professional practice, researchers and practitioners at the Centre for Children Committing Offences (CCCO) housed at the Child Development Institute (CDI) in Toronto, Canada, were the first to develop a comprehensive psychosocial risk assessment framework focused on young children with antisocial behavior (Borum et al., 2002). The first assessment tool for boys, under the age of 12, appeared as a "consultation edition" in 1998 (Augimeri et al., 1998), and has since been updated to the Early Assessment Risk List for Boys, Version 2 (EARL-20B; Augimeri, Koegl, Webster, & Levene, 2001). A parallel assessment tool for girls was also developed in 2001, the Early Assessment Risk List for Girls, Version 1 Consultation Edition (EARL-21G; Levene et al., 2001).

The tools are currently going through their second iteration for girls and third for boys. While retaining all the key principles and original structure, the new versions have updated the items according to the latest scientific research, and accordingly, also place a greater focus on how culture and ethnicity may affect risk factors. Similarly, based on the currently available literature and clinical expertise, gender differences and similarities have taken a greater focus in the new tools. In keeping with the scientist-practitioner framework and a core principle of the CCCO and CDI, the revision process involved both clinicians and internal and external researchers, as well as external culture experts, and involved extensive literature reviews, focus groups, surveys, piloting, and numerous revisions before approving the final tools, which should be available in the beginning of 2021.

Method of and Rationale for Development

Early identification and targeted interventions are considered key when helping troubled children and their families, and are equally important for the communities and service providers who bear responsibility for the healthy development of children. Given the focus of the CCCO at CDI (i.e., research, training, and dissemination of evidence-based, gender-specific practices pertaining to young children in conflict with the law), its work in the past decade focused on the development of a comprehensive and remarkably straightforward children's mental health and crime prevention strategy for dealing with these young at-risk children. This three-stage mental health and crime prevention strategy includes: (1) *centralized community referral protocols* that bring together community stakeholders such as police, child welfare workers, school administrators, and children's mental health partners to help navigate at-risk children through the system in a timely manner to appropriate service providers; (2) *structured professional judgment clinical risk assessment* approach utilizing the EARL-20B for boys and EARL-21G for girls that gauges the risk of future antisocial potential and treatment needs for targeted children and their families; and (3) *gender-specific STOP NOW AND PLAN (SNAP®) evidence-based, trauma informed programs* that are tailored to meet the clinical needs of children with serious disruptive behavior problems (e.g., aggression, rule-breaking, and conduct) and their families.

As service providers, researchers, and policy makers have a good understanding of the importance of early interventions in supporting children who are at risk for future antisocial behavior (Brestan & Eyberg, 1998; Frick, 1998; Farrington & Welsh, 2007), a structured, early assessment risk tool would help to facilitate and allocate resources and services according to identified risk and need. Early intervention has been associated with vast improvement both in the realm of social change and the monetary burden that society faces in the absence of such measures (Cohen, Piquero, & Jennings, 2010). It is especially relevant for aggressive and antisocial children because early age at first offense is one of the strongest and most robust predictors of reoffending (Loeber et al., 2003). The savings associated with such early identification and intervention could be realized not only for the individual child, but also for family and community (Hoge & Andrews, 1996).

Recognizing that the practice of risk assessment is increasingly becoming a standard part of mental health professional practice (Berman et al., 2012), the development of a comprehensive risk assessment scheme to help clinicians identify young children who are considered to be at risk for continued antisocial behavioral problems (see Augimeri, Koegl, Levene, & Webster, 2005) made sense. In fact, the U.S. Office of Juvenile Justice and Delinquency Prevention Study Group on Serious and Violent Offenders recommended the development and validation of screening instruments to identify children at risk of becoming serious and violent offenders (Loeber & Farrington, 1998).

To illustrate the importance of early identification and intervention of risk factors, Koegl and Farrington recently conducted the first evaluation of the monetary costs associated with childhood risk factors for boys between the ages of 6 and 11. The calculation included costs to victims, as well as the correctional and other criminal justice systems, during the time the boys were 12 to 20 years old. Boys that fell into the highest risk group based on their EARL-20B scores (quartile range) incurred an average cost of CAN$878,460, as compared to the lowest risk group, which incurred costs of CAN$361,581 (Koegl & Farrington, 2019). The majority of the costs were incurred during the ages of 15–17, which is not surprising given that the age-crime curve peaks in mid-to-late adolescence (Piquero, Farrington, & Blumstein, 2007). Early risk assessment is a crucial first step in prevention of criminal behavior, and this study neatly shows the benefits of such assessments.

Early works by leading researchers (e.g., Rolf Loeber, David Farrington, James C. Howell, Magda Stouthamer-Loeber, and Gerald Patterson) investigating risk factors associated with serious violent and chronic offending by children and juveniles and senior researchers at CDI (Christopher D. Webster, Debra Pepler, David Day, Leena K. Augimeri, Christopher Koegl, and Margaret Walsh) helped to shape the CCCO's thinking about structured risk assessment as it pertained to young children (for a detailed history of the rationale for the development of the EARLs see Augimeri et al., 2005; Augimeri, 2019.)

The EARL assessment covers a wide range of variables related to the child, their family, neighborhood, responsiveness to treatment, and other social factors (e.g., poverty, negative peer influence) that are related to subsequent antisocial behavior. As previously indicated, even though there is no shortage of dependable information on this subject (see, for example, Burke, Loeber, Mutchka, & Lahey, 2002; Loeber & Farrington, 2001; Loeber & Stouthamer-Loeber, 1998), there are still relatively few assessments that have harnessed this information and made it available to clinicians in a practical and useable way (Hrynkiw-Augimeri, 2005).

Description of Measure

The EARL-20B and EARL-21G (currently available versions until 2021, when the newly revised EARLs will be ready for distribution) are validated, gender-specific, structured professional judgment (SPJ) risk assessment tools. The SPJ model emerged from the actuarial and clinical debate that seems to pull the best from both approaches (see Webster, Hucker, & Bloom, 2006) as it is "systematic, consistent, and grounded in research" (Borum & Verhaagen, 2006, p. 75).

The EARL framework, modeled after an SPJ violence risk assessment instrument for use with adults in civil, forensic, and correctional settings (HCR-20 V3; see Chapter 12, this volume), outlines empirically recognized risk processes that relate to the development and maintenance of aggressive and antisocial behavior among children. The EARL-20B and EARL-21G were developed to: (1) provide a platform for increasing clinicians' and researchers' general understanding of early childhood risk factors; (2) offer a structure that helps clinicians systematically identify and manage risks in order to plan appropriate treatment to improve clinical outcomes; and (3) improve the reliability and validity in predicting the likelihood of antisocial children engaging in antisocial behavior (Augimeri et al., 2005). Thus, the EARLs aim to balance clinical utility (e.g., service planning, resource allocation) with prediction and are best considered "decision-enhancing" tools (Enebrink, Långström, & Gumpert, 2006).

The EARL items are divided into three main categories: Family, Child, and Responsivity (referred to as Barriers to Treatment in the latest version) factors. Family items assess the extent to which the child has or has not been effectively nurtured, supported, supervised, and encouraged by his or her parents or caregivers. Assessors also must gauge the level of support and amount of stress family members are encountering, and the extent to which they may or may not endorse or participate in antisocial activities. Under the Child items, the focus is on individual risk factors associated with the child and the extent to which he or she performs his or her social role and acts responsibly and sensibly. The third (two-item) category, Responsivity, focuses on the ability and willingness of the child and family to engage in treatment and benefit from planned interventions. Table 11.1 lists the items included the EARL-20B, Version 2 and EARL-21G, Version 1. The revised version 3 and 2, for boys and girls, respectively, will further include an additional item in the Responsivity category, which focuses on responsivity from the community level and addresses some of the prejudice and discrimination often experienced by minority populations.

Similar to other SPJ measures, each of the 20 EARL-20B and 21 EARL-21G items are rated zero (0), one (1) or two (2). A rating of 0 indicates that the characteristic or circumstance is not evident. A rating of 2 indicates that the characteristic or circumstance is present, and a rating of 1 indicates that there is some, but not complete, evidence for the factor. This rating system is identical in meaning to more recent SPJ measures such as the HCR-20 V3 that have dropped the numbers, and simply rate items as Not Present, Possibly/Partially Present, or Present. The scores from each item can be summed up into a total score ranging between 0 and 40 for the boys' tool and between 0 and 42 for the girls' tool. A "Critical Risk" checkbox is included beside each item (described in more detail in the next section). An evaluation of the total sum, risk factor pattern, and case-specific factors and conducting an overall estimate of "low," "moderate," or "high" risk of antisocial behavior complete the assessment. The updated versions are rated in the same manner, with the addition of a "confidence in rating" question, scored similarly as "low," "moderate," or "high" confidence.

Table 11.1 Items in the Early Assessment Risk List for Boys (EARL-20B) and Girls (EARL-21G)

Family (F) Items	Child (C) Items	Responsivity (R) Items
Household Circumstances	Developmental Problems	Family Responsivity
Caregiver Continuity	Onset of Behavioral Difficulties	Child Responsivity
Supports	Abuse/Neglect/Trauma	
Stressors	Hyperactivity/Impulsivity/Attention Deficits (HIA)	
Parenting Style	Likeability	
Antisocial Values and Conduct	Peer Socialization	
Caregiver-Daughter Interaction (*)	Academic Performance	
	Neighborhood	
	Authority Contact (⁺)	
	Antisocial Attitudes	
	Antisocial Behavior	
	Coping Ability	
	Sexual Development (*)	

(⁺) Item specific to the EARL-20B; (*) Item specific to the EARL-21G

Interpreting Risk

The clinical challenge, of course, is to be able to predict which boys and girls will persist in their antisocial patterns, describe how these patterns may establish over time, and plan as well as implement interventions that can break the vicious circles of antisocial behavior.

In general, the higher the total score (i.e., a higher number of risk factors), the more likely a child is at risk for engaging in ongoing antisocial behavior. This relationship is based on the presumption that scores on risk factors are additive, and with data averaged across many cases, this is usually true (Hall, 2001). In reality, risk factors are probably both cumulative and interactive (Monahan et al., 2001). Since there are no algorithms or cutoff scores that dictate final risk ratings, it is important to focus on each child's individual presentations of items across the risk summary as the total score. No single risk factor can sufficiently predict future antisocial behavior, but it is possible that a single risk factor may play a disproportionate role in contributing to a particular child's overall level of risk. For example, a child could achieve a relatively low total EARL-20B or EARL-21G score yet display one category of behaviors (e.g., antisocial friends, abuse, neglect, trauma) so salient that he or she is actually at great risk for embarking on an antisocial trajectory. For this reason, and to assist with matching intervention resources to level of need, a "Critical Risk" checkbox is included beside each item. In this way, the EARL-20B and EARL-21G afford the opportunity to adapt assessment and treatment to meet the requirements of a particular case, a feature viewed as essential to evidence-based clinical practice (American Psychological Association on Evidence-Based Practice, 2006).

The tool can be completed by a single clinician or by a clinical team, with or without access to a parent or other informant. The assessor must evaluate carefully each of the items based on the information obtained through a structured interview, case conference, or, for research purposes, a case file review. To inform a structured approach to clinical judgment (see Borum, 1996), evaluators are expected to obtain and assess information from multiple agents (e.g., teachers, parents, child care givers, doctors) and multiple sources (e.g., clinical records, school reports, standardized tests; American Academy of Child and Adolescent Psychiatry, 1997). This process ensures that the evaluator has available the most current and accurate information before rendering a clinical risk judgment and before recommending particular interventions and treatments.

This tool was designed for clinicians and professionals experienced in, and knowledgeable about, working with children who display serious antisocial behavior. It is vital that assessor(s) score the items exactly as described in the coding sections of the manual. As noted in Webster and Hucker (2007), "risk assessments should lead to risk management" (p. 130), and the developers of the EARLs intend the tools to be used only by individuals who understand this principle. In addition, they should not be used in a strictly mechanical way to determine the availability, nature, or intensity of treatment using the individual or total score. Training to gain a better understanding of the tools' utility is highly recommended:

> It is possible to discern whether or not each and every participant has grasped the essential essence of the scheme, thus being able to provide trainees or agencies with a training score card that can be used to show which trained staff has mastered the use of the instrument and which have not.
>
> (Webster et al., 2014, pp. 127–128)

In regards to assessing risk and using the completed EARL Summary Sheet as a "prescription" to determine effective clinical risk management plans, see the case example at the end of this chapter.

Gender-Specific Approach to Risk Assessment

It is increasingly recognized that boys and girls who present with serious antisocial behaviors may require different types of intervention (Moffitt, Caspi, Rutter, & Silva, 2001), and the presentation of these behaviors as well as future outcomes may vary partly due to these differences. Many risk factors for antisocial behavior are similar for boys and girls, for example: academic challenges (Metsäpelto et al., 2015), negative peer influences (Ettekal & Ladd, 2015), and family violence (Fox et al., 2015). But it has been consistently demonstrated that family relationships play a larger role in the development and prevention of antisocial behavior for girls relative to boys (Ehrensaft, 2005; Lösel & Farrington, 2012; Pepler et al., 2010; Pepler, Craig, Jiang, & Connolly, 2011).

Similarly, while traumatic childhood experiences are risk factors for both boys and girls, the type and rate of traumatic experiences differs between the genders. For example, although boys are more likely to experience community violence, girls are significantly more likely to experience sexual abuse—the most severe form of childhood trauma (Begle et al., 2011; Kerig & Becker, 2015). It is also likely that while the type and rate of a risk factor are comparable for boys and girls, they may nevertheless have different consequences depending on gender. For example, boys act more aggressively than girls in response to neglect (Logan-Greene & Jones, 2015). Indeed, it is likely that gender differences in risk factors for antisocial behavior is qualitative rather than quantitative in nature. As a consequence, and to encourage assessors to be mindful of the complex and sometimes subtle differences between the genders, the creators of the EARLs have kept the tools gender-specific. The separation further enhances treatment planning and evaluation for boys and girls. In contrast to other risk assessment tools, such as the SAPROF and SAVRY, which have mostly been developed and researched in male populations (de Vogel, de Vries Robbé, de Ruiter, & Bouman, 2011; Klein, Yoon, Briken, Turner, & Spehr, 2012; Lodewijks, de Ruiter, & Doreleijers, 2010), the EARL-21G is unique in that it was designed specifically for use with female populations, and separate reliability and validity assessments have been conducted on the tool.

Reliability: EARL-20B

The first reliability study was conducted on the EARL-20B Version 1. The study measured basic interrater reliability through a prospective study of 21 boys and their families admitted into the SNAP® Boys Program (formerly the SNAP® Under 12 Outreach Project; SNAP ORP). The SNAP® Boys is housed at the CDI, an accredited, multi-service, and mental health agency for children under the age of 12 years who exhibit serious antisocial behavior (i.e., having police contact for engaging in these behaviors/activities) and their families. Results showed moderate-to-good interrater agreement based on the total score on pre-treatment assessment (ICC_1 = .64) to post-treatment assessment (ICC_1 = .88; Hrynkiw-Augimeri, 1998). Qualitative findings further suggested that the tool was especially helpful in providing clinicians "with a thorough assessment procedure, a guide to gear the treatment interventions, and a barometer to evaluate whether a child was still considered high-risk at post intervention" (Hrynkiw-Augimeri, 1998, p. 31).

As part of a more stringent evaluation, the reliability and predictive validity of the EARL-20B (see later in this chapter) was assessed through a follow-up of a large sample of SNAP® Boys-treated children (Hrynkiw-Augimeri, 2005). Files from 379 boys who received the SNAP® Boys between 1985 and 1999 were retrospectively coded using Version 1 of the EARL-20B. Each of three raters were randomly assigned 193 files to code. Of these, 100 were common (all three raters rated these files) and 93 were unique to each of the three raters. Raters were blind as to which files were common and all outcome data. Analyses revealed excellent agreement between the three raters on the total EARL-20B score for the 100 common files (ICC_1 = .82) as well as the Family Items subscale (ICC_1 = .78). In addition, there was good agreement on the EARL-20B

Child Items (ICC$_1$ = .73) subscale and lower though moderately acceptable agreement on the Responsivity Items (ICC$_1$ = .53) subscale. An examination of the individual items in the right-hand column of Table 11.2 indicated the range of agreement.

Overall, results from this study indicate acceptable inter-reliability for the EARL-20B assessments, especially for the total EARL-20B score with values comparable to other SPJ tools such as the .SAVRY, START, and HCR-20 (see Chapter 12).

Research conducted on the EARL-20B, Version 2, by researchers in Sweden has yielded similarly encouraging findings. Enebrink, Långström, Hultén, and Gumpert (2006) examined the interrater reliability of the EARL-20B with boys referred to nine child and adolescent psychiatric units across Sweden. For most of the individual EARL-20B items, Kappa statistics indicated good agreement (mean = .62, range = .30–.87; only two items were poor, between .30 and .40), whereas intraclass correlation coefficients for Total, Child, and Family subscale scores indicated excellent agreement (.90–.92). The overall estimate of high, medium, or low risk for antisocial behavior received an acceptable value of 0.48.

Interrater reliability was also examined using a Dutch translation of the EARL-20B in a non-treatment sample of boys with a first-time arrest (de Ruiter & van Domburgh, unpublished manuscript). ICCs were good for both Total Score (single measure ICC = .74; CI = .58–.84; average measure ICC = .85; CI = .74–.92) and Final Risk Judgment (single measure ICC = .79; CI = .65–.87; average measure ICC = .88; CI = .79–.93).

Table 11.2 EARL-20B Item, Subscale, and Total Scores: Descriptive Statistics and Interrater Reliability

EARL-20B Items	Descriptive Statistics	Interrater Reliability
	M (SD)	ICCI (95% CI)
Family Items	6.12 (2.71)	.78 (.71–.84)
F1 Household Circumstances	1.06 (0.82)	.61 (.50–.70)
F2 Caregiver Continuity	0.73 (0.75)	.47 (.35–.58)
F3 Supports	0.81 (0.79)	.53 (.42–.64)
F4 Stressors	1.49 (0.63)	.48 (.36–.59)
F5 Parenting Style	1.39 (0.62)	.60 (.50–.69)
F6 Antisocial Values and Conduct	0.65 (0.71)	.61 (.51–.70)
Child Items	12.99 (3.77)	.74 (.66–.81)
C1 Developmental Problems	0.28 (0.52)	.54 (.44–.65)
C2 Onset of Behavioral Difficulties	1.60 (0.51)	.60 (.49–.69)
C3 Trauma	0.88 (0.88)	.63 (.53–.72)
C4 Impulsivity	0.77 (0.66)	.62 (.52–.71)
C5 Likeability	0.43 (0.57)	.46 (.35–.58)
C6 Peer Socialization	1.31 (0.69)	.43 (.31–.55)
C7 School Functioning	1.39 (0.65)	.61 (.50–.70)
C8 Structured Community Activities	1.13 (0.83)	.53 (.42–.64)
C9 Police Contact	1.39 (0.83)	.71 (.62–.78)
C10 Antisocial Attitudes	1.08 (0.69)	.51 (.39–.62)
C11 Antisocial Behavior	1.68 (0.49)	.17 (.05–.30)
C12 Coping Ability	1.04 (0.73)	.52 (.41–.63)
Amenability Items	1.85 (1.22)	.53 (.42–.64)
A1 Family Responsivity	1.08 (0.78)	.51 (.39–.62)
A2 Child Treatability	0.77 (0.70)	.44 (.32–.56)
Total Score	20.28 (6.13)	.82 (.75–.87)

Note: For descriptive statistics, N = 379 boys; for reliability analyses, n = 100.

Reliability: EARL-21G

To date, a number of studies have been completed on the EARL-21G—all of which have produced similar positive findings to the EARL-20B in terms of the clinical utility, reliability, and validity of the tool. The first of these studies (Levene, Walsh, Augimeri, & Pepler, 2004) was a retrospective examination of the reliability and validity of the EARL-21G. Intraclass correlation coefficients were calculated for total scores derived from three coders who assessed 30 common files. Encouragingly, modest agreement between raters was found, with statistically significant positive Pearson correlations of .64, .65, and .84, of the EARL total sum scores and intraclass correlation coefficients of .67 (single measure) and .86 (average measure).

We subsequently repeated the interrater reliability coding exercise prospectively using seven clinicians who rated 12 common case files (see Levene et al., 2004). In this study, a higher rate of agreement was achieved with an overall Pearson correlation of .81 of total sum scoring and intraclass correlation coefficients of .80 (single measure) and .96 (average measure) were obtained.

Further, a team of researchers and clinicians generated pre-admission EARL-21G profiles for 162 girls who received the SNAP® Girls (Walsh, Yuile, Jiang, Augimeri, & Pepler, 2007). Trained coders read each girl's case file using an EARL-21G manual to assign risk ratings. All files were assessed using a detailed research codebook developed to specify the criteria outlined in each of the EARL-21G risk items (Levene et al., 2001). Interrater reliability was calculated by randomly selecting 47 common cases for all coders to read and code. Mean agreement on classifying girls into no (0), low (1), and high (2) risk categories for each of the 21 risk factors ranged from .34 to .88 (Kappa; Cohen, 1960) with an averaged item level agreement on the individual items of .55. Landis and Koch (1977) suggest that kappa values from .41 to .60 are moderate, and that values above .60 are substantial. Reliability scores for four risk factors were too low (i.e., .36 to .40); those items most difficult to assess through the case reviews were Supports, Peer Socialization, Academic Performance, and Antisocial Attitudes. Therefore, to improve reliability, all risk factors were collapsed into two binary groups from a 3-point scale to a 2-point scale. Collapsing each risk factor also helped to define two groups of girls that would be meaningful for interpretation and statistically suitable for comparison. For the majority of risk factors (i.e., 7 Family risks and 7 Child risks), collapsing allowed a comparison between girls rated high-risk (score of 2), with low-risk girls (scores of 0 or 1). By collapsing this way, high-risk versus moderate and low-risk, it provided two groups of girls each with a sufficient sample size to make a valid comparison as the number of girls at low risk (0) was too small to be a meaningful group. In contrast, 5 Child risk factors did not receive as many high-risk ratings, and so the distribution of scores was not adequate for collapsing into a low/moderate risk group (0 and 1) and a high risk group (2). Consequently, the scores were collapsed into 0 (no risk) versus 1 and 2 (moderate to high risk). The interrater agreement on scores using this dichotomous classification reached an acceptable range (Kappa .40 to .89, mean of .67).

Validity: EARL-20B

Concurrent Validity

Another study tested whether the EARL-20B total scores at intake were predictive, or more accurately *post*dictive, of the Child Behavior Checklist (CBCL; Achenbach & Rescorla, 2001) delinquency score at discharge (Augimeri, Enebrink, Walsh, & Jiang, 2010). There was a positive correlation between the CBCL Delinquency Subscale scores at discharge and the EARL-20B total score, $r = .34$, $p < .001$. Two regression models were fitted to examine the relationship between the CBCL Delinquency Subscale Score at discharge and the EARL-20B total score.

Model 1 examined the overall association without controlling for the other candidate factors (i.e., CBCL delinquency admission score, age, and treatment effects). Model 2 examined the relationship controlling the CBCL delinquency score at admission, age, and treatment effects (number of ORP sessions attended). The results of the two models are shown in Table 11.3.

Results indicated that the EARL-20B total scores postdicted the CBCL Delinquency Subscale at discharge. This conclusion held after controlling for the admission CBCL delinquency subscale score, age, and treatment effects. The relatively low value for R^2 (.12) for Model 1 suggests that these results, though significant, leave much of the variance (88%) of CBCL delinquency discharge scores unexplained. Controlling for admission CBCL delinquency subscale score, age, and treatment effects in Model 2 increased the variance explained to 41%. Results from Model 2 also indicated that the effect of the number of ORP group sessions attended on the CBCL delinquency discharge score approached significance ($p = .10$) after controlling for delinquency admission score and EARL-20B total score.

Predictive Validity

Results from longitudinal studies have shown that the EARL-20B total score and summary risk rating predict early onset of criminal activity (Augimeri, Walsh, Woods, & Jiang, 2012), as well as type (Koegl, Farrington, & Augimeri, 2019), prevalence, and frequency of convictions (Augimeri, Pepler, Walsh, Jiang, & Dassinger, 2010; Koegl, 2011).

In the Dutch study by de Ruiter and van Domburgh (unpublished manuscript) described earlier, the predictive validity of the EARL-20B was tested for the first time in a non-treatment sample of 199 boys. All of the participants had experienced their first arrest prior to the onset of the study. Outcome data were collected at 1- and 2-year follow-up periods and included measures of delinquency (the Observed Antisocial Behavior Questionnaire—OAB; Slot, Orobio de Castro, & Duivenvoorden, 1998), behavioral problems and hyperactivity (Strengths and Difficulties Questionnaire—SDQ; Goodman, 1997; van Widenfelt, Goedhart, Treffers, & Goodman, 2003), reactive and proactive aggression (Reactive-Proactive Aggression Questionnaire—RPQ; Raine et al., 2006), bullying (Social and Health Assessment; Schwab-Stone et al., 1995, 1999; Weisberg, Voyce, Kasprow, Arthur, & Shriver, 1991), and externalizing behavior disorders (Diagnostic Interview Schedule for Children—DISC; Shaffer et al., 1996).

The majority of the EARL-20B scales correlated with the antisocial markers at the 1- and 2-year follow-ups ($p = .17–.48$). Scores on the Child domain, Total score, and summary risk rating subscales correlated with all parent and self-reported externalizing behaviors tested at 2-year follow-up, with the exception of child-reported pro-active aggression ($p = .19–.45$). Furthermore, Receiver Operating Characteristic (ROC) analysis using Area Under the Curve (AUC) values

Table 11.3 Results from Regression of CBCL Delinquency Discharge Score

Model	B	SEB		t value	sr^2	pr^2
Model 1						
EARL-20B Total Score	0.56	0.10	.34	5.49***		
Model 2						
EARL-20B Total Score	0.24	0.09	.15	2.65**	.17	.14
CBCL Delinquency Admission Score	0.65	0.06	.57	10.32***	.57	.53
Number of ORP Group Sessions	−0.22	0.14	−.09	−1.63	−.11	−.08
Age at Follow-up	−0.18	0.17	−.06	−1.05	−.07	−.05

Note: * $p < .05$; ** $p < .01$; *** $p < .001$.

revealed that all EARL scales, except for Child Domain on General Recidivism (AUC = .58; p = .06) and Total Score on violent offending (AUC = .59; p = .11), significantly predicted self-reported delinquency at 1- and 2-year follow-up, a Disruptive Behavior Disorder (DBD) at 2-year follow-up (range AUCs = .70 to .79), and new police registrations (range AUCs = .60 to .61), as well as new police registrations for violent offending (range AUCs = .62 to .69). These AUCs, while still relatively small, are higher than in previous studies, which is likely reflective of increased predictive value due to the non-treatment sample. Previously, in a retrospective file study, Hrynkiw-Augimeri (2005) reported an AUC value of .56 (p < .05) for Total Score on offending. However, it should also be noted that the follow-up period in the Hrynkiw-Augimeri study was 8 years vs. 2 years in the Dutch study.

The first follow-up (8 years) of a sample of 379 boys who participated in the SNAP® Boys included a search of correctional records to determine whether each boy had subsequent criminal charges (Hrynkiw-Augimeri, 2005). In Canada, children under 12 are not held liable for criminal offenses. Therefore, the criterion for participation was that the child had to have reached the age of 12 years by the time the review of criminal records began. This way, all participants would have reached the age of criminal liability and would be eligible for youth or adult court contact. The mean EARL-20B total scores of boys who were found guilty of an offense were significantly higher than for those boys who were not found guilty of an offense, 21.62 (SD = 5.94) and 20.32 (SD = 6.23), respectively (t (377) = 2.07, p < .05, Cohen's d = .21). To illustrate this relationship further, logistic regression analyses were conducted on the probability of being found guilty of an offense as a function of EARL-20B total scores. Two models were fitted to examine the relationship between the EARL-20B score and the probability of being found guilty of a future offense. Model 1 examined the relationship without considering raters' confidence level in their EARL-20B scores. Model 2 includes the interaction between raters' confidence level and EARL-20B scores. The results of these analyses are shown in Table 11.4.

Again, results indicated that as EARL-20B scores increased, the probability of being found guilty of a future offense rose significantly. On average, the estimated odds of being guilty of future offenses increased by 1.03 for each unit increase in EARL-20B scores. Figure 11.1 shows how the association between EARL-20B total scores and being found guilty of a future criminal offense was moderated by the raters' confidence level (determined by the amount and quality of information contained in the clinical file).

Results of ROC analyses supported this finding—albeit generally with small effect sizes—with higher total scores postdicting findings of guilt at levels greater than expected by chance,

Table 11.4 Results From Logistic Regression Model of Being Found Guilty of an Offense

Model					95% CI	
	B	SE	Wald	Odds Ratio	Lower	Upper
Model 1						
EARL-20B Total Score	0.03	0.02	3.86*	1.03	1.00	1.08
Model 2						
EARL-20B Total Score	−0.03	0.04	0.65	0.97	0.89	1.05
Confidence Level						
Medium vs. Low	−2.21	0.98	5.05*	0.11	−1.81	2.41
High vs. Low	−2.77	1.20	4.38*	0.06	−2.28	2.41
Confidence Level × EARL-20B Score						
Medium vs. Low	0.09	0.05	3.13	1.09	0.99	1.19
High vs. Low	0.11	0.05	3.99*	1.11	1.00	1.22

Note: * p < .05; ** p < .01; *** p < .001.

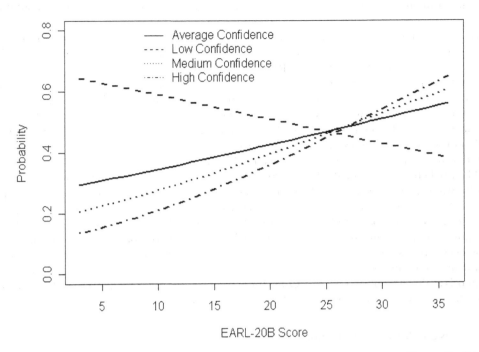

Figure 11.1 Predicted Probability of Future Offense by EARL-20B Score as a Function of Rater Confidence

AUC = .56, *95%* CI = .51–.62, SE_{AUC} = .03, *p* < .05. We then considered the severity of outcomes for those 164 boys found guilty of an offense at follow-up. As expected, as EARL-20B total scores increased in magnitude, boys were more likely to be found guilty of committing offenses, *r* = .16, *p* < .05, and more likely to appear in court to receive a disposition, *r* = .18, *p* < .05. These relationships held after controlling for length of follow-up. Using a median split on EARL-20B total scores to group boys into low (EARL-20B total scores = 0–21) and high (EARL-20B scores = 22–40) risk categories, a chi-square analysis revealed that more boys in the high-risk group were found guilty of an offense (49%) than boys in the low-risk group (38%), χ^2 (1) = 4.87, p < .05. Of the 164 boys who were found guilty, 88 were identified at high-risk (having high EARL-20B scores, true positives), and 76 were not identified as being at risk (false negatives). This resulted in a sensitivity of 54%. Of the 215 boys with no future offense, 123 were identified as being at low risk (true negatives), resulting in a specificity of 57%. Of the 180 boys identified at risk by high EARL-20B scores, 92 had no future offence at follow-up (false positives), resulting in a Positive Predictive Value (boys classified at high risk with future offenses at follow-up) of 49%. Of the 199 children identified as low risk by the EARL-20B, 123 had did not offend, resulting in a Negative Predictive Value (boys classified at low risk with no future offenses at follow-up) of 62%. These results demonstrate that the higher the total EARL-20B score, the more likely the boy would be found guilty of committing an offence.

Importantly, the association between EARL-20B and future offending became stronger as the raters became more confident in their assessments (i.e., had better information available in the file). Table 11.4 demonstrates that when raters had little or no confidence in their ratings, there was no significant association between the EARL-20B score and future offending. As a consequence, the updated versions of the EARLs require assessors to rate their level of confidence in their scores and direct them to withhold final judgment and acquire more information if their confidence is low.

Koegl, Farrington, and Augimeri (2019) used the same sample of 379 boys and 67 girls (mean age 9) to predict criminal convictions between the ages of 12 and 21 using criminal records from provincial and national databases. EARL-20B total scores predicted conviction status for boys for total offending (AUC = .64) and three offense subtypes (i.e., property, person, or administration of justice—failure to appear in court or breach of probation) with AUC values ranging between .60 and .63. The most salient individual predictors for boys were antisocial values and conduct, followed by the risk factors of having antisocial parents, failing school, and associating with antisocial peers. Interestingly, the predictive validity was higher for older (10–11 years) compared to younger (6–9 years) boys (Koegl et al., 2019).

The predictive validity of the EARL-20B was also assessed in a prospective multi-center project in Sweden, using a sample of 76 clinic-referred boys (Enebrink, Långström, & Gumpert, 2006). The total summary score and short-term risk (evaluated as low, medium, or high risk) showed moderately good predictive validity when compared to parent/teacher-ratings of reactive and proactive aggression and disruptive behaviors at the 6-month (total score r's: .31–.53; short-term risk r's: .47–.58) and 30-month (total score r's: .20–.38; short-term risk r's: .31–.50) follow-ups. The total summary score was also significantly related to a conduct disorder (CD) diagnosis at the 30-month outcome (Odds Ratio total sum 1.33, 95% CI (1.11–1.59), short-term risk 6.67 CI (1.49–29.91), long-term risk 15.75 CI (2.18–113.56).

Predictive Validity of Subscales

In addition to the predictive validity of the EARL-20B total score and summary risk rating, it has been demonstrated that all EARL subscales (Family, Child, and Responsivity) predict antisocial outcomes (Augimeri et al., 2012). In an analysis conducted by Hyrnkiw-Augimeri (2005), the 20 items in the EARL-20B were clustered into subscales using exploratory and confirmatory factor analyses to determine if the factors would form subscales other than the existing Family, Child, and Responsivity domains. They first conducted Exploratory Factor Analysis (EFA) to extract latent factor structures that underlie the 20 items in the EARL-20B device and examine how these items cluster into common factors. The clusters were termed "Child," "Family," and "Biological" factors. Confirmatory Factor Analysis (CFA) was then used to clarify the factor structure that emerged from the EFA. Both EFA and CFA identified a three-factor structure for the EARL-20B. It has been shown the three subscales are good predictors of an antisocial or violent outcome (Hrynkiw-Augimeri, 2005).

As valid and reliable indices of risk, and based on their ability to predict future antisocial conduct in the form of official youth and adult criminal convictions (Hrynkiw-Augimeri, 2005), these subscales were used as predictor variables. Figure 11.2 depicts the three-subscale structure of the EARL-20B, and the interrelationships between individual items (for complete details, see Hrynkiw-Augimeri, 2005). Subsequent analysis on the later version (version 2) of the EARL-20B revealed the same three factors as for the previous version, with the exception that Neighborhood moved from a Child to a Family factor. These three clusters further predicted entry into the criminal justice system (Augimeri et al., 2010).

Another study (Augimeri, Jiang, Koegl, & Carey, 2006) used growth mixture modeling to investigate whether treatment intensity (number of SNAP sessions attended) and severity of risk (based on the EARLs) could predict severity of behavioral symptoms (based on CBCL). The study used three time points of behavioral measures and found that the greater the number of EARL risks, the higher the probability that the boys would fall in a high delinquency class. This was particularly evident if the boy scored high on Child and Biological risk factors. Treatment

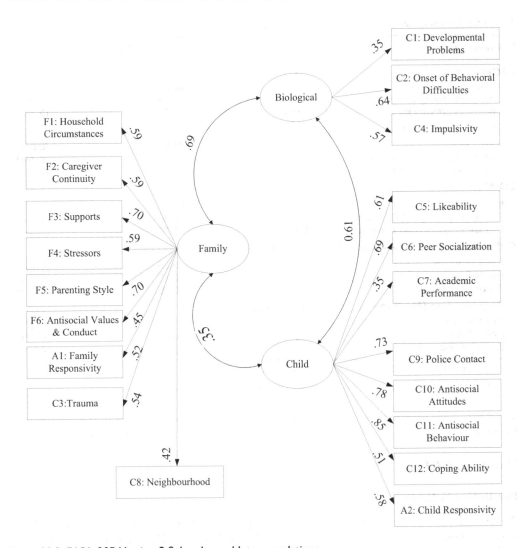

Figure 11.2 EARL-20B, Version 2 Subscales and Intercorrelations

intensity moderated effects only for high delinquent boys, indicating that the SNAP program is particularly useful for high-risk children. Table 11.5 displays the estimated results from the extended growth mixture model.

In terms of risk as assessed by the EARL-20B, results indicate that the tool, and in particular the Child and Biological subscales, significantly distinguished between delinquency class (high versus low, and medium versus low). These factor-derived scales are not meant to substitute the Family, Child, and Responsivity domains within the EARL-20B manual but are meant to further enhance clinical risk management decisions about the type and amount of services that are offered to children with conduct problems. Based on the pattern of results from the analysis, we know that children who score higher on the Child and Biological subscales of the EARL-20B are more likely to engage in delinquent behavior (i.e., be a member of the high delinquency class). If their measured level of CBCL delinquency places them in the high-risk class, it would be important,

Table 11.5 Enhanced SNAP® Boys Treatment Effects by Delinquency Class

Delinquency Class	Estimate (SE)+	SIG
HIGH (N = 37)		
Initial Level	82.6	(1.34)***
Change following SNAP® Boys	2.64	(1.99)
Change Regressed on Enhanced SNAP® Boys	−8.01	(2.34)***
MODERATE (N = 219)		
Initial Level	74.5	(0.64)***
Change following SNAP® Boys	−3.96	(0.76)***
Change Regressed on Enhanced SNAP® Boys	−1.98	(1.00)*
LOW (N = 63)		
Initial Level	60.9	(1.89)***
Change following SNAP® Boys	−2.24	(1.93)
Change Regressed on Enhanced SNAP® Boys	−1.76	(1.76)
C Regressed on (High- vs. Low-delinquency)		
Child Subscale	0.60	(0.15)***
Family Subscale	0.17	(0.11)
Biological Subscale	0.89	(0.31)**
C Regressed on (Medium- vs. Low-delinquency)		
Child Subscale	0.21	(0.07)**
Family Subscale	0.07	(0.07)
Biological Subscale	0.55	(0.22)*

Significance (SIG): ***$p < 0.001$; ** $p < 0.01$; * $p < 0.05$

+Estimates are estimated regression coefficients from growth mixture modeling.

if not necessary, to offer these boys enhanced services such as individual mentoring (or befriending in the SNAP program), school advocacy, academic tutoring, and family counseling.

Validity: EARL-21G

Predictive Validity

An investigation has been completed on the efficacy of the EARL-21G in predicting girls' offending convictions (Levene et al., 2001). Using a median split, the EARL total score from 67 SNAP® Girls case files were separated into high and low risk. Official conviction data showed that, overall, only 18 out of 67 (27%) of the girls committed an offense during the follow-up period. Although higher EARL-21G scores were related to more offending (34% vs. 20%), the difference between the two groups failed to reach statistical significance. However, the fact that the participants in this study were enlisted in treatment may have mitigated future offenses and reduced differences between girls that were high versus low risk at the start of the study.

In a manner similar to the boys' tool, a factor analysis of the girl's tool by Augimeri and colleagues found a "Relational Disturbance" factor that was made up of items pertaining to a girl's inability to develop a strong relational capacity. As depicted in Figure 11.3, the factor included the items *Caregiver Continuity, Abuse/Neglect/Trauma, Antisocial Values and Conduct*, and *Sexual Development*, and was found to significantly predict future criminal offenses for girls (Augimeri et al., 2010).

The most recent investigation of the predictive power of the EARLs was conducted by Koegl et al. (2019), and described earlier. The study included 67 girls with an EARL assessment and

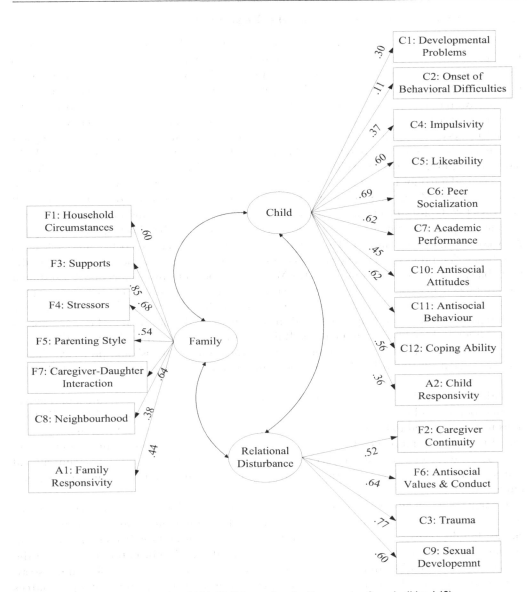

Figure 11.3 Three-Factor Model in EARL-21G Items for the Prospective Sample (*N* = 148)

subsequent criminal records up to the age of 21, The authors found that, as opposed to boys, the total EARL score for girls predicted only property offending (AUC = .70). However, when comparing results to boys, it is important to know that the number of girls was lower than the number of boys (369 boys and 67 girls). Looking at the individual items, manifesting antisocial behavior was the strongest predictor for any offence for girls (*OR* = 6.00). Following antisocial behavior, the most salient predictors of any conviction for girls were poor coping ability, actively manifesting ADHD or related symptoms, being unlikable to adults, and family responsivity. Interestingly, compared to boys, academic performance, poor peer socialization, or being exposed to maladaptive parenting styles did not predict future offending for girls (Koegl et al., 2019).

Limitations and Necessary Future Research

Two key aspects of the EARL tools require consideration by both clinicians and researchers. First, users need to be aware of the setting in which the EARLs were developed: for use with children engaging in antisocial behavior, under the age of 12, who were referred to a children's mental health center in a large multicultural city. The authors of the EARLs have attempted to bring awareness to possible differences in cultural values, attitudes, and gender norms in the overview and coding sections of the manuals (particularly in the newest version). However, users should always demonstrate an awareness and knowledge of the cultural context influencing how information is gathered and understood during an EARL assessment. At this time, the EARLs have been translated into Swedish, Norwegian, Finnish, Dutch, Japanese, and French and have been adapted for use in both urban and rural settings across Europe, Canada, the United States, and New Zealand. Second, at present, like most risk assessment tools, the EARL-20B and EARL-21G assessment framework focuses solely on risk factors and does not capture the presence of protective and promotive factors (see Stouthamer-Loeber, Loeber, Wei, Farrington, & Wikström, 2002; Farrington, Ttofi, & Piquero, 2016). Stouthamer-Loeber and colleagues (2002) describe protective factors as "processes that interact with risk factors in reducing the probability of a negative outcome" (p. 112). Yet inclusion of protective factors in risk assessment has several benefits. For example, integrating protective factors creates a more balanced and less stigmatized view of offenders (Rogers, 2000). Clinically, the added consideration of protective factors allows clinicians to help clients find their strengths and motivation and develop appropriate strengths-based treatment plans (de Ruiter & Nicholls, 2011). In addition, predictions of long-term antisocial outcomes are more accurate when using both risk and protective factors (Lodewijks et al., 2010; Loeber, Pardini, Stouthamer-Loeber, & Raine, 2007; de Vries Robbé, de Vogel, & Douglas, 2013).

With this in mind, the authors of the EARLs are currently working to create a protective-factors tool for children under the age of 12 to be used in combination with the EARLs. This tool is expected to be available in 2021. It is imperative that the EARLs undergo continual review and improvement in light of new research findings, for example the impact of protective factors, in order to keep them current and able to address relevant clinical issues, as well as ongoing evaluation of how the EARLs improve treatment planning and implementation.

Though validated and reliable clinical assessment tools, use of the original EARLs demands significant time, resources, and a knowledge of developmental and contextual factors (individual, family, peers, and community) pertaining to young children's mental health and antisocial risk. Moreover, it requires a wide range of detailed information concerning the target child. This limits utility outside of a clinical setting, where the need for rapid assessment may preclude the user from gathering extensive information from multiple sources and agents.

Conclusion

The early prediction of juvenile delinquency represents an important challenge in the field. Key to this challenge is the consideration of whether it is realistic to assume that delinquent behavior can be predicted, especially with very young children. Researchers and clinicians have to deal with extremely short histories (maximum 11 years) and long follow-up periods (until these children are considered youths or adults). From when children are assessed to the time they become adolescents or adults, a multitude of factors can affect their life course. Therefore, the overarching goal of the EARLs is not *only* to assess risk but to play a pivotal role in helping clinicians determine effective clinical risk management plans that may buffer risk and prevent these high-risk children from eventually entering the juvenile and/or adult justice systems. In light of the findings presented in this chapter (e.g., Augimeri et al., 2006, 2010, 2012), it would be beneficial if long-term risk management plans were implemented for the high-risk children to ensure continued support and prevent criminal behavior in the long term. As children grow, other age-appropriate tools, such as the SAVRY (Borum et al., 2002) for adolescents and HCR-20 V3 (Douglas, Hart, Webster, & Belfrage, 2013) for adults, should be utilized. Balancing clinical utility with prediction, the EARL-20B and EARL-21G join other devices designed to help professionals make practical day-to-day decisions about prioritizing treatment and understanding children on a case-by-case basis.

Case Example

[The following case example is provided to illustrate how the EARL-20B Summary Sheet is used by trained clinicians to rate and summarize risk issues; and the EARL Case Planning Eco-Systemic Assessment Form used to identify clinical risk management strategies based on the EARL-20B assessment with a focus on "clinical risk" items as a starting point for treatment planning.]

Finn is a 6-year-old feisty and sad looking boy who physically looks like a "stout little man." He met all his developmental milestones on time (e.g., walked, talked, and was toilet trained) and is currently in a regular grade one class. However, he is withdrawn from the classroom on a daily basis so that he can receive remedial help for reading and math. He has been placed on waiting list for an Identification Placement Review Committee (IPRC) meeting. This process will determine if he will need to be placed in a specialized learning program and/or has psychosocial deficits. In addition, the teacher is extremely concerned about his explosive behavior and inattention. He is constantly getting into fights with peers and has had numerous altercations involving teachers and administrative staff—including the principal. When he gets angry, he threatens others, is verbally abusive and has major temper tantrums (dad reports that this kind of behavior began when he was just 3 or 4 years old). This has resulted in a number of in- and out-of-school suspensions. On a number of occasions, he has described himself as being "out of control" and feeling very sad to the point of wanting to hurt himself when he is angry and upset. Given his difficult temperament, he is ostracized, bullied, and isolated from other children. They find it hard to like him, and he also indicates that "no one likes me." Adults also report that Finn is an anxious and defiant boy who is difficult to engage which make it "hard to like him." He displays self-defeating thinking and has a misplaced sense of entitlement; however, he does know right from wrong and can be empathetic.

Since he was a toddler Finn has lived with his dad most of his life in a modest home in a neighborhood described as being "tough." He lived with his biological mom for a short period of time when he was just over a year when his parents separated. This arrangement fell apart and Finn was returned to his dad. He has little contact with his mother given the strained relationship between his parents. His mother has since remarried and has had two other children. Finn talks about his mother fondly but also indicates he resents her for leaving him behind. Dad reports that Finn sometimes cries himself to sleep when he thinks about her. Dad is in his 40s and has indicated that he has "tried his best" with his son. He is able to acknowledge that Finn has had to "grow up fast and raise himself" given he is always at work as finances are tight and has some issues of his own that he needs help with (e.g., he indicates he is a "social alcoholic" who also has relied on pain medication to deal with his back problems).

Finn's dad was also able to report that he has used punitive discipline (e.g., severe spanking) and on other occasions is very "easy going" with his parenting as he lets Finn do what he wants. He also indicated that he has neglected him on occasion when he left him unattended when he went out or was "drunk." Dad acknowledges this behavior is not appropriate and has decided he needs to get help for him and his son. This became evident for him when the police brought Finn home after he was caught shoplifting at the local grocery store. The Children's Aid Society (child welfare) was also called when the police brought Finn home late at night and no one was home. They referred the family to a local children's mental health center (Child Development Institute) for services. Dad was very responsive to this and indicated it was like a "call for help" as he felt his life was getting "out of control." He reported he felt pretty isolated (even though he had a stable girlfriend who helped at times) and needed help to get things back on track in order to help his son and himself. Although Dad sees this as a big support, Finn on the other hand is a bit more guarded about getting help.

Case Discussion

The attached EARL-20B Summary Sheet summarizes all relevant information obtained from the various sources and informants in order to render a summary risk rating. The more confident raters are in the information they have, the better the risk prediction (Hrynkiw-Augimeri, 2005). Although there are no cutoff scores, Finn's *Total Score* (27/40) is considered high given the normal distribution of scores ranged from 3 to 36 with a mean of 20.9 and a median of 21 ($SD = 6.1$, $n = 378$) (Augimeri et al., 2001). In addition to the total score, Finn received a number of "2" ratings, especially under the *Child Items*.

Based on the information presented and the corresponding EARL-20B risk assessment, it is suggested that this child and his dad be engaged in high-intensity children's mental health services specializing in latency-aged children with disruptive behavior problems. The suggested cognitive behavioral multi-modal services recommended for Finn and his Dad is the SNAP® Boys program at the Child Development Institute. This programs offers the following recommended service components (SNAP® Boys Group, a self-control and problem-solving group; SNAP® Parent Group that focuses on effective parent management strategies; Individual Befriending/Mentoring and connections to structured community recreation activities; SNAP Parenting and Individual Family Counselling; School Support/Advocacy to assist the child in school; and Academic Tutoring to booster the child's academics through a tutoring club). Psycho-Educational and Psychological assessments are critical to address the academic issues, self-harming, trauma and identified depressive symptomology. Given issues regarding potential barriers for treatment engagement as noted in the Family Responsivity (R1) risk item, treatment delivery needs to be flexible to diminish all possible barriers to engage this family in service. To further ensure treatment success, establishing a strong therapeutic alliance/connection with both Finn and his Dad are important. Ongoing treatment reviews (every six months) to ensure treatment compliance and outcome monitoring needs to be conducted.

The EARL-20B Version 2 Summary Sheet

(To be used in association with the EARL-20B, Version 2 Manual)

Child's Name or ID#: _____ Date: _____

(First name SURNAME)   (YYYY-MM-DD)

Assessor: _____ Child's DOB: _____ Age: _____

Family Items	Rating (0–1–2)	Critical Risk
F1	**Household Circumstances** *finances tight, adequate space, modest*	1
F2	**Caregiver Continuity** *Dad (primary)—lived with bio-mom when he was 1 year old—he misses her*	1
F3	**Supports** *Child Development Institute, isolated (no extended family), Dad's partner*	1
F4	**Stressors** *dad's back problems, strained relationship w/ ex-wife, raising son on his own, dad feels "out of control"*	2
F5	**Parenting Style** *punitive, lax, inconsistent, lacks nurturance, parents self*	2
F6	**Antisocial Values and Conduct** *Dad (drinking & abusing his prescription drugs—pain medication)*	1

Child Items	Rating (0–1–2)	Critical Risk
C1	**Developmental Problems** *met all developmental milestones on time*	0
C2	**Onset of Behavioral Difficulties** *age 3 (serious temper tantrums)*	2
C3	**Abuse/Neglect/Trauma** *neglect, abuse (severe spanking), abandonment issues*	2
C4	**HIA (Hyperactivity/Impulsivity/Attention Deficits)** *attention problems, NO diagnosis*	1
C5	**Likeability** *difficulty w/ adults, hard to engage, difficult temperament, feels "no one likes me"*	2
C6	**Peer Socialization** *ostracized, isolated, bullies, excluded, bullies, gets into lots of fights*	2
C7	**Academic Performance** *Grade 1, receiving w/drawl, struggling-math & reading, waiting for IPRC*	1
C8	**Neighborhood** *lived in same neighborhood most of his life, considered a 'tough' community*	1
C9	**Authority Contact** *principals, teachers, police*	2
C10	**Antisocial Attitudes** *self-defeating thinking, defiant, misplaced sense of entitlement, empathetic, knows right from wrong*	1

(Continued)

(Continued)

C11	**Antisocial Behavior**	2
	problems—*multiple settings, school suspensions, assault, threatens, verbally abusive, stealing, explosive*	
C12	**Coping Ability**	2
	depressive symptomotoly, feels out of control, anxious, self-harm	

Responsivity Items	Rating (0–1–2)	Critical Risk
R1	**Family Responsivity**	0
	Dad willing to get help, active, seems committed	
R2	**Child Responsivity**	1
	interested but guarded	

	LOW	MOD	HIGH
Overall Clinical Judgment			

Notes (Clinical Risk Management Plan): *Finn has experienced a lot of negative life circumstances. He is extremely angry and as a result is explosive at times and has major abandonment issues. Based on the EARL risk summary and the noted critical risk factors, the following treatment recommendations are suggested:(1) Finn attend the SNAP®Boys Groups—learn self-control and problem-solving strategies to help control his anger and deal more effectively with his problems; (2) Dad attend the SNAP®Parent Group—learn effective parent management strategies; (3) connect Finn to a structured community activity where he will have access to positive mentors and activities with children his age; (4) Finn receive individual befriending with the SNAP®Group Leader to work on his individual goals, his academics and behavioral issues; (5) further assessment to investigate—depression, anxiety, and attention issues; (6) connect Dad to community supports to help him deal with alcohol and prescription drug misuse; and (7) ensure Dad and Finn continue to be engaged in services (concern whether Dad's job, health, and/or addiction issues will impeded his ability to attend services.*

EARL CASE PLANNING ECO-SYSTEMIC ASSESSMENT FORM

NAME: *Finn Robbes* (fictitious)

BIRTHDATE: *August 14, 2013*

SCREENING DATE(S): *February 18, 2019*

TOTAL EARL SCORE: *27*

ID #: *02226*

ASSESSOR: *Leena K. Augimeri*

SERVICE COORDINATOR: *Nicola Slater*

OVERALL CLINICAL JUDGMENT:

CRITICAL RISK ITEM(S)	REASON	TREATMENT FOCUS	
F2	Caregiver Continuity	Even though Dad has been the stable caregiver and Finn sees Mom periodically—he resents her for leaving and sometimes cries himself to sleep when he thinks about her (abandonment issues)	Self-Esteem Building Strengthening Dad and Finn's attachment
F3	Supports	Family has few identified supports in place (CDI and Dad's partner)	Community connections Engagement Broadening the scope of the family supports

F4	Stressors	Dad has a number of health issues, raising his son on his own (strained relations with Finn's mom) and feels "out of control" at times	Engage Dad in SNAP services as a support
			Dad to learn how to use SNAP (deal with his own emotion arousal)
			Help Dad find appropriate medical services to deal with his medical issues
F6	Antisocial Values and Conduct	Dad's alcohol and addiction (misuse of prescription drugs) issues	Help Dad find appropriate Addiction Services
F5	Parenting Style	Parent is inconsistent, does not adequately monitoring child and uses punitive discipline and enmeshed boundaries (treats son like a friend)	Parent Management Training
C3	Abuse/Neglect/ Trauma	Child has experienced physical, emotional abuse and neglect.	Trauma work
C4	HIA (Hyperactivity/ Impulsivity/ Attention Deficits)	Issues noted in regards to impulsivity and concentration problems. No formal testing/ assessment has been conducted. Not sure if this is in relation to HIA or possible anxiety or depression.	Psycho-Educational & Psychological Assessment
C5	Likeability	Adults find it difficult to "like" Finn and he acknowledges that "no one likes him."	Engagement and developing a therapeutic alliance
			Social Skills Training
			Cognitive Restructuring
C6	Peer Socialization	History of strained peer relationships with peers (bullied and bullies).	SNAP (self-control and problem solving)
			Social Skills Training
			Building Healthy Relationships
C12	Coping Ability	Finn is displaying depressive symptoms. He is withdrawn, sad, and feels unloved. He sometimes also self-harms and is anxious.	Psychological Assessment
			Self-Esteem building
			Cognitive restructuring
R1	Family Responsivity	This item received a rating of "0"—however there are a number of factors that can impede Dad's ability to follow through which could result in disengagement from service.	Developing a therapeutic alliance with Dad
			Providing flexible service delivery
			Build strong supports

SUGGESTED CLINICAL RISK MANAGEMENT STRATEGIES—BASED ON EARL ASSESSMENT

CHILD:

Psychiatric Consult (assess depression and suicide ideation—determine if additional specialized mental health services are warranted at this time)

PARENT/FAMILY:

TYPE OF SERVICE RECOMMENDED BASED ON OVERALL CLINICAL JUDGMENT LEVEL

RECOMMENDED SERVICE:

PLANNING

NEAREST INTERSECTION TO CHILD'S HOME: *Weston Road & St. Clair Avenue West, Toronto*

CLOSEST APPROPRIATE SERVICE PROVIDER(S): *Child Development Institute*

AGENCY REFERRED TO: *Child Development Institute*

DESIGNATED PROGRAM: *SNAP Boys Program*
(if applicable)

CONTACT PERSON: *CDI Intake*

PHONE NUMBER:
416–603–1827

AGENCY ADDRESS:
46 St. Clair Gardens, Toronto, Ontario, M6E 3V4

DATE: *February 18, 2020*

TITLE: *Intake Worker*

EMAIL ADDRESS:
snap@childdevelop.ca

FOLLOW-UP PLAN: *Ensure family is actively participating in treatment; suggested recommendations have been implemented; ongoing treatment reviews; and monitoring of treatment outcomes.*
EARL ASSESSOR SIGNATURE: *Leena K. Augimeri*

References

Achenbach, T. M., & Rescorla, L. A. (2001). *Manual for the ASEBA school age forms and profile.* Burlington, VT: University of Vermont, Research Center for Children, Youth and Families.

American Academy of Child and Adolescent Psychiatry. (1997). Practice parameters for the assessment and treatment of children and youth with conduct disorder. *Journal of American Academy of Child and Adolescent Psychiatry, 36,* 122S–139S.

American Psychological Association Presidential Task Force on Evidence-Based Practice. (2006). Evidence-based practice in psychology. *American Psychologist, 61,* 271–285.

Augimeri, L. K. (2019). Early assessment of risks and their amelioration by the stop now and plan (SNAP) model: National and international research. In D. Eaves, C. D. Webster, Q. Haque, & J. Thalken-Eaves (Eds.), *Structured professional judgment of violence risks: A practical introduction.* West Sussex: Pavilion Publishing and Media Ltd.

Augimeri, L. K., Enebrink, P., Walsh, M., & Jiang, D. (2010). Gender-specific childhood risk assessment tools: Early assessment risk lists for boys (EARL-20B) and girls (EARL-21G). In R. K. Otto & K. S. Douglas (Eds.), *Handbook of violence risk assessment* (pp. 43–62). Oxford: Routledge, Taylor & Francis.

Augimeri, L. K., Jiang, D., Koegl, C. J., & Carey, J. (2006). *Differential effects of the under 12 outreach project (ORP) associated with client risk & treatment intensity.* Program Evaluation Report Submitted to the Centre of Excellence for Child and Youth Mental Health at CHEO, Ottawa.

Augimeri, L. K., Koegl, C. J., Ferrante, P., & Slater, N. (2006, Fall). Why and how: Conducting effective clinical risk assessments with children with conduct problems. *Canada's Children, 12*(2), 24–27 (English); 28–32 (French).

Augimeri, L. K., Koegl, C. J., Levene, K. S., & Webster, C. D. (2005). Early assessment risk list for boys and girls. In T. Grisso, G. Vincent, & D. Seagrave (Eds.), *Mental health screening and assessment in juvenile justice* (pp. 295–310). New York: Guilford Press.

Augimeri, L. K., Koegl, C. J., Webster, C. D., & Levene, K. S. (2001). *Early assessment risk list for boys: EARL-20B* (Version 2). Toronto, ON: Earlscourt Child and Family Centre.

Augimeri, L. K., Pepler, D., Walsh, M. M., Jiang, D., & Dassinger, C. R. (2010). *Aggressive and antisocial young children: Risk prediction, assessment, and clinical risk management.* Provincial Centre of Excellence Program Evaluation Grant, Toronto, ON.

Augimeri, L. K., Walsh, M., Woods, S., & Jiang, D. (2012). Risk assessment and clinical risk management for young antisocial children: The forgotten group. *Universitas Psychologica, 11,* 1147–1156.

Augimeri, L. K., Webster, C. D., Koegl, C. J., & Levene, K. S. (1998). *Early assessment risk list for boys: EARL-20B* (Version 1, consultation ed.). Toronto, ON: Earlscourt Child and Family Centre.

Begle, A. M., Hanson, R. F., Danielson, C. K., McCart, M. R., Ruggiero, K. J., Amstadter, A. B., . . . Kilpatrick, D. G. (2011). Longitudinal pathways of victimization, substance use, and delinquency: Findings from the national survey of adolescents. *Addictive Behaviors, 36*(7), 682–689.

Berman, J., Minne, C., Attard, S., & Oyebode, O. (2012). 31—forensic psychiatry. In P. Wright, J. Stern, & M. Phelan (Eds.), *Core psychiatry* (3rd ed., pp. 471–486). London: W.B. Saunders.

Bloom, H., Webster, C., Hucker, S., & De Freitas, K. (2007). The Canadian contribution to violence risk assessment: History and implementations for current psychiatric practice. In H. Bloom & C. Webster (Eds.), *Essential writings in violence risk assessment and management* (pp. 77–92). Toronto, ON: Centre for Addiction and Mental Health.

Borum, R. (1996). Improving the clinical practice of violence risk assessment: Technology, guidelines and training. *American Psychologist, 51,* 945–956.

Borum, R., Bartel, P., & Forth, A. (2002). *Manual for the structured assessment of violence risk in youth (SAVRY)* (Version 1, consultation ed.). Tampa, FL: University of South Florida.

Borum, R., & Verhaagen, D. (2006). *Assessing and managing violence risk in juveniles*. New York: Guilford Press.

Brestan, E. V., & Eyberg, S. M. (1998). Effective psychosocial treatments of conduct-disordered children and adolescents: 29 years, 82 studies, and 5,272 kids. *Journal of Clinical Child Psychology, 27*, 180–189.

Burke, J. D., Loeber, R., Mutchka, J. S., & Lahey, B. B. (2002). A question for DSM-V: Which better predicts persistent conduct disorder—delinquent acts or conduct symptoms? *Criminal Behavior and Mental Health, 12*, 37–52.

Cohen, J. (1960). A coefficient of agreement for nominal scales. *Educational and Psychological Measurement, 20*, 37–46.

Cohen, M. A., Piquero, A. R., & Jennings, W. G. (2010). Studying the costs of crime across offender trajectories. *Criminology and Public Policy, 9*(2), 279–305.

de Ruiter, C., & Nicholls, T. (2011). Protective factors in forensic mental health: A new frontier. *International Journal of Forensic Mental Health, 10*, 160–170. doi:10.1090/14999013.2011.600602

de Ruiter, C., & van Domburgh, L. (2016). *Predictive validity of the early assessment risk list for boys (EARL-20B) after first police contact: Differences between Western and Non-Western boys in The Netherlands*. Manuscript in preparation.

de Vogel, V., de Vries Robbé, M., de Ruiter, C., & Bouman, Y. H. A. (2011). Assessing protective factors in forensic psychiatric practice: Introducing the SAPROF. *International Journal of Forensic Mental Health, 10*, 171–177.

de Vries Robbé, M., de Vogel, V., & Douglas, K. S. (2013). Risk factors and protective factors: A two-sided approach to violence risk assessment. *The Journal of Forensic Psychiatry and Psychology, 24*, 440–457.

Douglas, K. S., Hart, S. D., Webster, C. D., & Belfrage, H. (2013). *HCR-20 (Version 3): Assessing risk of violence—user guide*. Burnaby, BC: Mental Health, Law, and Policy Institute, Simon Fraser University.

Ehrensaft, M. K. (2005). Interpersonal relationships and sex differences in the development of conduct problems. *Clinical Child and Family Psychology Review, 8*, 37–63. doi:10.1007/s10567-005-2341-y

Enebrink, P., Långström, N., & Gumpert, C. H. (2006). Predicting aggressive and disruptive behavior in referred 6- to 12-year-old boys: Prospective validation of the EARL-20B risk/needs checklist. *Assessment, 13*, 356–367.

Enebrink, P., Långström, N., Hultén, A., & Gumpert, C. H. (2006). Swedish validation of the early assessment risk list for boys (EARL-20B), a decision-aid for use with children presenting with conduct-disordered behavior. *Nordic Journal of Psychiatry, 60*, 468–446.

Ettekal, I., & Ladd, G. W. (2015). Developmental pathways from childhood aggression-disruptiveness, chronic peer rejection and deviant friendships to early-adolescent rule breaking. *Child Development, 86*(2), 614–631.

Farrington, D. P., Ttofi, M. M., & Loeber, R. (2014). Facteurs de protection contre la delinquance [Protective factors against delinquency]. *Revue Francaise de Criminologie et de Droit Penal, 2*, 39–64.

Farrington, D. P., Ttofi, M. M., & Piquero, A. R. (2016). Risk, promotive, and protective factors in youth offending: Results from the Cambridge study in delinquent development. *Journal of Criminal Justice, 45*, 63–70.

Farrington, D. P., & Welsh, B. C. (2007). *Saving children from a life of crime*. New York: Oxford University Press.

Fox, B. H., Perez, N., Cass, E., Baglivio, M. T., & Epps, N. (2015). Trauma changes everything: Examining the relationship between adverse childhood experiences and serious, violent and chronic juvenile offenders. *Child Abuse & Neglect, 46*, 163–173.

Frick, P. J. (1998). *Conduct disorders and severe antisocial behavior*. New York: Plenum Press.

Goodman, R. (1997). The strengths and difficulties questionnaire: A research note. *Journal of Child Psychology and Psychiatry, 38*, 581–586.

Hall, H. V. (2001). Violence prediction and risk analysis: Empirical advances and guides. *Journal of Threat Assessment, 1*, 1–39.

Hart, S. D. (2001). Assessing and managing violence risk. In K. S. Douglas, C. D. Webster, S. H. Hart, D. Eaves, & J. R. P. Ogloff (Eds.), *HCR-20 violence risk management companion guide* (pp. 13–26). Burnaby, BC: Mental Health Law, and Policy Institute, Simon Fraser University.

Hoge, R. D., & Andrews, D. A. (1996). *Assessing the youthful offender: Issues and techniques*. New York: Plenum Press.

Howell, J. C. (2003). *Preventing & reducing juvenile delinquency: A comprehensive framework*. Thousand Oaks, CA: Sage.

Howell, J. C., Lipsey, M. W., Wilson, J. W., Howell, M. Q., & Hodges, N. J. (2019). *A handbook for evidence-based juvenile justice systems* (revised ed.). London: The Rowman & Littlefield Publishing Group, Inc.

Hrynkiw-Augimeri, L. K. (1998). *Assessing risk for violence in boys: A preliminary risk assessment study using the early assessment risk list for boys (EARL-20B)* (Unpublished Master's thesis). Ontario Institute for Studies in Education, University of Toronto, ON.

Hrynkiw-Augimeri, L. K. (2005). *Aggressive and antisocial young children: Risk prediction, assessment and management utilizing the early assessment risk list for boys (EARL-20B)* (Unpublished doctoral dissertation). Ontario Institute for Studies in Education, University of Toronto, Toronto, ON.

Kerig, P. K., & Becker, S. P. (2015). 12 early abuse and neglect as risk factors for the development of criminal and antisocial behavior. In *The development of criminal and antisocial behavior* (pp. 181–199). Cham, Switzerland: Springer.

Klein, V., Yoon, D., Briken, P., Turner, D., & Spehr, A. (2012). Assessment of accused juvenile sex offenders in Germany: A comparison of five different measures. *Behavioral Sciences and the Law, 30,* 181–195. doi:10.1002/bsl.2006

Koegl, C. J. (2011). *High-risk antisocial children: Predicting future criminal and health outcomes* (Unpublished doctoral dissertation). University of Cambridge, Cambridge.

Koegl, C. J., & Farrington, D. P. (2019). Estimating the monetary cost of risk factors for crime in boys using the EARL-20B. *Psychological Services.* doi: 10.1037/ser0000401

Koegl, C. J., Farrington, D. P., & Augimeri, L. K. (2019). Predicting future criminal convictions of children under age 12 using the early assessment risk lists. *Journal of Developmental and Life-Course Criminology,* 1–24.

Lahey, B. B., Moffit, T. E., & Caspi, A. (2003). *Causes of conduct disorder and juvenile delinquency.* New York: Guilford Press.

Landis, R., & Koch, G. G. (1977, March). The measurement of observer agreement for categorical data. *Biometrics, 33*(1), 159–174.

Levene, K. S., Augimeri, L. K., Pepler, D., Walsh, M., Webster, C. D., & Koegl, C. J. (2001). *Early assessment risk list for girls: EARL-21* (Version 1, consultation ed.). Toronto, ON: Earlscourt Child and Family Centre.

Levene, K. S., Walsh, M. M., Augimeri, L. K., & Pepler, D. J. (2004). Linking identification and treatment of early risk factors for female delinquency. In M. M. Moretti, C. L. Odgers, & M. A. Jackson (Eds.), *Girls and aggression: Contributing factors and intervention principles* (pp. 147–163). New York: Kluwer Academic.

Lipman, E. L., Bennett, K. J., Racine, Y. A., Mazumdar, R., & Offord, D. R. (1998). What does early antisocial behavior predict? A follow-up of 4- and 5-year-olds from the Ontario child health study. *Canadian Journal of Psychiatry, 43,* 605–613.

Lodewijks, H. P. B., de Ruiter, C., & Doreleijers, T. A. H. (2010). The impact of protective factors in desistance from violent reoffending: A study in three samples of adolescent offenders. *Journal of Interpersonal Violence, 25,* 568–587. doi:10.1177/0886260509334403

Loeber, R., Burke, J. D., & Lahey, B. B. (2002). What are adolescent antecedents to antisocial personality disorder? *Criminal Behavior and Mental Health, 12,* 24–36.

Loeber, R., & Farrington, D. P. (Eds.). (1998). *Serious and violent juvenile offenders: Risk factors and successful interventions.* Thousand Oaks, CA: Sage.

Loeber, R., & Farrington, D. P. (Eds.). (2001). *Child delinquents: Development, interventions and service needs.* Thousand Oaks, CA: Sage.

Loeber, R., Farrington, D. P., & Petechuk, D. (2003, May). *Child delinquency: Early intervention and prevention.* Child Delinquency Bulletin Series. Washington, DC: U.S. Department of Justice.

Loeber, R., Pardini, D. A., Stouthamer-Loeber, M., & Raine, A. (2007). Do cognitive, physiological, and psychosocial risk & promotive factors predict desistance from delinquency in males? *Development & Psychopathology, 19,* 867–887.

Loeber, R., & Stouthamer-Loeber, M. (1998). Development of juvenile aggression and violence: Some common misconceptions and controversies. *American Psychologist, 53,* 242–259.

Logan-Greene, P., & Jones, A. S. (2015). Chronic neglect and aggression/delinquency: A longitudinal examination. *Child Abuse & Neglect, 45,* 9–20.

Lösel, F., & Farrington, D. P. (2012). Direct protective and buffering protective factors in the development of youth violence. *American Journal of Preventive Medicine, 43,* S8–S23. doi:10.1016/j.amepre.2012.04.029

Metsäpelto, R. L., Pakarinen, E., Kiuru, N., Poikkeus, A. M., Lerkkanen, M. K., & Nurmi, J. E. (2015). Developmental dynamics between children's externalizing problems, task-avoidant behavior, and academic performance in early school years: A 4-year follow-up. *Journal of Educational Psychology, 107*(1), 246–257.

Moffitt, T. E., Caspi, A., Harrington, H., & Milne, B. J. (2002). Males on the life-course-persistent and adolescence-limited antisocial pathways: Follow-up at age 26 years. *Development and Psychopathology, 14,* 179–207.

Moffit, T.E., Arseneault, L., Belsky, D., Dickson, J., Hancox, R., Harrington, H. L., . . . Capsi, A. (2011). A gradient of childhood self-control predicts health, wealth, and public safety. *Proceedings of the National Academy of Sciences, 108*(7), 2693–2698.

Moffitt, T. E., Caspi, A., Rutter, M., & Silva, P. A. (2001). *Sex differences in antisocial behavior: Conduct disorder, delinquency, and violence in the Dunedin longitudinal study*. Cambridge: Cambridge University Press.

Monahan, J., Steadman, H. J., Silver, E., Appelbaum, P. S., Robbins, P. C., Mulvey, E. P., . . . Banks, S.(2001). *Rethinking risk assessment: The MacArthur study of mental disorder and violence*. New York: Oxford University Press.

Pepler, D. J., Craig, W., Jiang, D., & Connolly, J. (2011). Girls' aggressive behavior problems: A focus on relationships. In M. Kerr, H. Stattin, C. M. E. Engels, G. Overbeek, & A. K. Andershed (Eds.), *Understanding girls' problem behavior: How girls' delinquency develops in the context of maturity and health, co-occurring problems, and relationships* (pp. 167–185). West Sussex: John Wiley & Sons Ltd.

Pepler, D. J., Walsh, M., Yuile, A., Levene, K., Jiang, D., Vaughan, A., & Webber, J. (2010). Bridging the gender gap: Interventions with aggressive girls and their parents. *Prevention Science, 11*, 229–238. doi:10.1007/s/1121-009-0167-4

Piquero, A. R., Farrington, D. P., & Blumstein, A. (2007). *Key issues in criminal career research: New analyses of the Cambridge study in delinquent development*. Cambridge: Cambridge University Press.

Piquero, A. R., Jennings, W. G., Farrington, D. P., Diamond, B., & Reingle Gonzalez, J. M. (2016). A meta-analysis update on the effectiveness of early self-control improvement programs to improve self-control and reduce delinquency. *Journal of Experimental Criminology*, 1–16.

Public Safety Canada. (2016). *Tyler's troubled life: The story of one young man's path towards a life of crime* (Research Report 2016-R005). Ottawa: Public Safety Canada. ISBN:978-0-660-05425-4.

Raine, A., Dodge, K., Loeber, R., Gatzke-Kopp, L., Lynam, D., Reynolds, C., . . . Liu, J. (2006). The reactive–proactive aggression questionnaire: Differential correlates of reactive and proactive aggression in adolescent boys. *Aggressive Behavior, 32*, 159–171. doi:10.1002/ab.20115

Rogers, R. (2000). The uncritical acceptance of risk assessment in forensic practice. *Law and Human Behavior, 24*, 595–605. doi:10.1023/A:1005575113507

Schwab-Stone, M. E., Ayers, T. S., Kasprow, W., Voyce, C., Barone, C., Shriver, T., & Weissberg, R. P. (1995). No safe haven: A study of violence exposure in an urban-community. *Journal of the American Academy of Child and Adolescent Psychiatry, 34*, 1343–1352.

Schwab-Stone, M. E., Chen, C. S., Greenberger, E., Silver, D., Lichtman, J., & Voyce, C. (1999). No safe haven II: The effects of violence exposure on urban youth. *Journal of the American Academy of Child and Adolescent Psychiatry, 38*, 359–367.

Shaffer, D., Fisher, P., Dulcan, M. K., Jensen, P. S., Fisher, P., Bird, H. R., Goodman, S. H., Lahey, B. B. . . . Rae, D. S. (1996). The NIMH diagnostic interview for children version 2.3 (DISC-2.3): Description, acceptability, prevalence rates, and performance in the MECA study. *Journal of the American Academy of Child and Adolescent Psychiatry, 35*, 865–877.

Slot, N. W., Orobio de Castro, B., & Duivenvoorden, Y. (1998). *The WAS-instruments: Observed antisocial behavior questionnaire for parents, teachers and children [de WASlijsten: Vragenlijsten Waargenomen Antisociaal Gedrag voor ouders, leerkrachten en kinderen]*. Duivendrecht: Paedologisch Instituut.

Stouthamer-Loeber, M., Loeber, R., Wei, E., Farrington, D. P., & Wikström, P. O. H. (2002). Risk and promotive effects in the explanation of persistent serious delinquency in boys. *Journal of Consulting and Clinical Psychology, 70*, 111–123.

Walsh, M., Yuile, A., Jiang, D., Augimeri, L. K., & Pepler, D. (2007). *Early Assessment Risk List for Girls (EARL-21G): Predicting antisocial behaviours and clinical implications*. Manuscript in preparation.

Webster, C. D., Haque, Q., Augimeri, L., Brink, J., Cree, A., Desmarais, S., . . . Snowden, R. (2014). Teaching and researching SPJ guides. In C. D. Webster, Q. Haque, & S. J. Hucker (Eds.), *Violence risk-assessment and management: Advances through structured professional judgement and sequential redirections* (2nd ed., pp. 123–137). West Sussex: John Wiley & Sons, Ltd.

Webster, C. D., & Hucker, S. J. (2007). *Violence risk assessment and management*. West Sussex: John Wiley & Sons Ltd.

Webster, C. D., & Hucker, S. J., & Bloom, H. (2006). Transcending the actuarial versus clinical polemic in assessing risk for violence. *Criminal Justice and Behavior, 29*, 659–665.

Webster, C. D., Martin, M. L., Brink, J., Nicholls, T. L., & Middleton, C. (2004). *Short-term assessment of risk and treatability (START)*. Hamilton, ON: St. Joseph's Healthcare, Forensic Services.

Weisberg, R. P., Voyce, C. K., Kasprow, W. J., Arthur, M. W., & Shriver, T. P. (1991). *The social and health assessment*. New Haven, CT: Yale Child Study Center.

van Widenfelt, B. M., Goedhart, A. W., Treffers, P. D. A., & Goodman, R. (2003). Dutch version of the strengths and difficulties questionnaire (SDQ). *European Child and Adolescent Psychiatry, 12*, 281–289.

Chapter 12

The Science of and Practice with the HCR-20 V3 (Historical-Clinical-Risk Management-20, Version 3)

Kevin S. Douglas and Catherine S. Shaffer

Description of Measure

The Historical-Clinical-Risk Management-20 (HCR-20) was first published in 1995 (Webster, Eaves, Douglas, & Wintrup, 1995) and revised shortly thereafter with the publication of Version 2 (Webster, Douglas, Eaves, & Hart, 1997). Given developments in the risk assessment field generally (see Cook & Hart, 2017; Douglas, 2019a, 2019b; Hart, Douglas, & Guy, 2017; Monahan, 2013), and the growth of research on Version 2 (see Douglas et al., 2020, with summaries of hundreds of studies on Version 2—with roughly 100 at the time of revising the instrument), Version 3 was published in 2013 (Douglas, Hart, Webster, & Belfrage, 2013). This chapter will focus almost entirely on Version 3 because Version 2 is no longer recommended for use, and there are numerous published reviews of Version 2 (see Douglas & Reeves, 2010, in the first edition of this book).

Definition and Elements of "Violence" in the HCR-20 V3

The HCR-20 V3 defines violence as "*actual, attempted, or threatened infliction of bodily harm on another person*" (p. 36). Further, "[b]odily harm includes both physical and serious psychological harm, so long as it 'substantially interferes with the health or well-being of an individual' (R. v. McCraw, 1991, p. 81, Supreme Court of Canada)" (p. 36). Acts such as stalking, extortion, kidnapping, or threats of violence typically would meet the definition of violence.

This definition is only slightly modified from, although considerably more elaborated upon compared to, Version 2. It has several notable features. First, it is broad enough to be adapted to the various contexts in which the HCR-20 V3 is used, discussed in this chapter. Users can focus on severe violence if need be (say, in some civil commitment jurisdictions) but could also focus on broader forms of violence that are relevant in certain settings (i.e., outpatient supervision; workplace settings), or considered clinically relevant (i.e., as possible warning signs for more serious violence). Second, both short-term (days to weeks) and longer-term (months to years) violence is captured by the definition. Third, the definition includes attempted violence, not merely completed violence. Often the difference between the two is that in one instance, the perpetrator "failed," and in the other they "succeeded." But, the active risk factors and motivations behind the behavior are identical.

Moreover, for an act to meet the definition of violence, there must be some degree of intentionality present in the perpetrator. That is, the act must not be reflexive or accidental—the person must have intended the act, been negligent, careless, or willfully blind. Whether the act occurred when a person was in an altered cognitive state due to mental disorder or intoxication does not disqualify the act from meeting the definition of violence. The definition of violence is characterized in the HCR-20 V3 User Guide as follows, in Figure 12.1 (see Douglas et al., 2013, Table 3.1, p. 37):

Violence Occurred When:	
A.	A person engaged in an act (or omission)
B.	with some degree of willfulness that
C.	caused or had the potential to cause
D.	physical or serious psychological harm to
E.	another person or persons.

Figure 12.1 HCR-20 V3 Definition of Violence

There are several exclusionary criteria. As shown in Figure 12.1, acts or omissions must be directed against humans (that is, not against property or animals). If property is damaged, that would be considered violence if, for instance, it reasonably caused fear of harm in a person (i.e., smashing a chair beside a person while glaring at them angrily), or could reasonably harm a person (i.e., arson). If an animal is harmed, of course evaluators would need to understand any implications that has for risk against humans (i.e., sadistic tendencies), but it would not be considered violence for the purpose of completing the HCR-20 V3, unless, again, it reasonably caused fear of harm in a person (i.e., harming an animal while saying "this is what I am going to do to you"). We also exclude acts that occur within the allowable rules of sport or are *legally justified* within an employment context (law enforcement, military, hospital, prison, or other relevant workplaces).

As with other SPJ instruments, we encourage evaluators to consider not only whether violence has occurred, but its other dimensions. The purpose of this is to foster a comprehensive understanding of the role that violence has played in a person's life, in terms of its nature and course. For instance, evaluators might consider severity, frequency, trajectory (is it getting worse over time?), nature of victims, weapon use, context, and whether it has been present across developmental domains. Detailed discussion of these issues is included within the User Guide.

Type of Measure

The HCR-20 V3 embodies and exemplifies the structured professional judgment (SPJ) approach to violence risk assessment and management. As described in detail in Heilbrun and colleagues' opening chapter of this book, SPJ approaches provide a systematic, structured, comprehensive approach to risk assessment and management, without requiring the evaluator to use algorithms or formulae to estimate risk levels. Heilbrun et al. also clearly describe the core differences between the SPJ approach and the actuarial approach to risk assessment. As Heilbrun et al. point out, the predictive validity of the SPJ approach is at least as strong as the actuarial approach, despite their many developmental, philosophical, and pragmatic differences.

As with all SPJ measures, the HCR-20 V3 guides evaluators through the following steps of conducting violence risk assessments (see Figure 12.2): (1) gathering and documenting information; (2) rating the presence and (3) individual relevance of operationally defined violence risk factors; (4) developing a formulation of violence risk, or why a person has acted violently, by considering what motivates, disinhibits, and destabilizes a person; (5) forecasting future likely scenarios of violence, or specifying the nature of violence, its motivations, potential victims of violence, and situational elements likely to be present in possible future acts of violence; (6) specifying risk management plans tied to a person's risk factors, and informed by the evaluator's formulation and scenario plans; and (7) estimating degree of risk for violence generally, serious violence, and imminent violence. Although other SPJ measures might not have the same precise number of steps, or use of language, the process is the same.

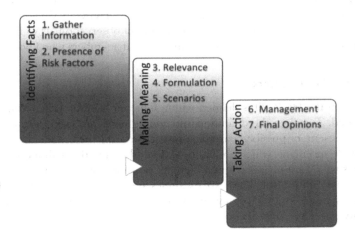

Figure 12.2 HCR-20 V3 Steps at a Glance

Using the HCR-20 V3 in Practice

The HCR-20 V3 is intended to structure a comprehensive violence risk assessment. Users must have appropriate experience, education, and knowledge, which is described in the User Manual (Douglas, Hart, Webster, & Belfrage, 2013). The administration of HCR-20 Version 3 is intended to represent the natural flow of activities and decision-making that professionals undertake not only for risk assessment, but for most assessment tasks. That is, professionals must gather information, identify important and relevant facts, make sense of that information, consider the implications of the information for the future, and recommend future steps to best handle any future concerns. In the violence risk assessment context, evaluators gather information, reduce that to risk factors, try to make sense of why a person has acted violently in the past, consider how and under what circumstances they might act violently in the future, and recommend management strategies to reduce risk.

Because human beings generally make better decisions when the decision-making process is structured, the general decision-making process outlined earlier is structured into seven steps. The purpose of providing structure to the entire risk assessment (decision-making) process is to avoid, as much as possible, reliance on heuristics, bias, consideration of task-irrelevant information, and ignoring task-relevant information. The seven administration steps of the HCR-20 Version 3 follow, and are depicted in Figure 12.2 (Figure 3.1 from the HCR-20 V3 User Guide, p. 40).

This Figure captures three essential tasks of violence risk assessment: gathering case facts and organizing them according to risk factors ("Identifying Facts"); trying to understand *why* a person has been violent, and what they might do in the future ("Making Meaning"); and determining the best way to reduce risk and communicate one's findings ("Taking Action").

Step 1: Case Information

This step involves gathering and documenting enough relevant information to inform a comprehensive risk assessment. The HCR-20 Version 3 authors recommend that if at all possible the minimum information base should consist of a thorough review of case records (consisting of correctional, police, health, employment, and school files, as available) and an interview with the person of interest. Under some circumstances, information will be limited, or unavailable, in which case the evaluator must decide whether to use the HCR-20 Version 3. Where possible and indicated, other sources of information include direct observation, as well as interviews with collateral sources such as family members, victims, or staff members who know the person well.

Step 2: Presence of Risk Factors

Each risk factor on the HCR-20 is defined within Chapter 4 of the User Manual, and coding notes are provided. Together, the definition and coding notes are used to rate whether the risk factor is present, absent, or possibly/partially present. Some of the broader or more complicated risk factors include sub-items, which are optional. In addition to the definition and coding notes, each item comes with a list of indicators, which are possible ways in which the risk factor might manifest at the idiographic level. These are examples and are not meant to be coded. In addition to rating the 20 standard risk factors, evaluators can specify case-specific risk factors, so long as they can identify case facts to justify doing so.

Step 3: Relevance of Risk Factors

One of the novel features of the HCR-20 Version 3 is rating the idiographic relevance of risk factors. The 20 standard risk factors on the HCR-20 Version 3 have support at the sample or population level. Their presence should be treated as hypotheses to be confirmed by the evaluator, because not all risk factors affect all people in the same manner. Further, risk factors for violence do not have the same strength or potency for all people equally. As such, if a risk factor is determined to be present (or possibly/partially present) at Step 2, the evaluator must determine whether it elevates the risk *for the person under evaluation*. That is, has it played a causal role in a person's violence? Does it interfere with the deployment of risk reduction strategies? This step is intended to optimize the individualization of the assessment, and to bridge the nomothetic and idiographic levels of analysis. It is also a mechanism for evaluators to determine what risk factors really are most important in understanding a given case.

Most actuarial measures pre-weight risk factors. That is, they presume that, even before an evaluator has met an evaluee, certain risk factors are more important than others. In clinical reality, however, the situation is typically not so neat and tidy. For some people, substance use or mental illness might be the most important risk factors, and for others, they may be peripheral. It is a mistake to presume that all risk factors operate equally for all people.

Relevance is defined as whether a risk factor is casual at the individual level (that is, did it drive or motivate violence, or disinhibit a person, such as violent ideation or intoxication might?), whether it impairs a person's decision-making about violence (that is, does it impair or destabilize careful decision-making, such as intellectual impairment or executive dysfunction might?), or whether it is otherwise critical to manage (that is, does it allow other risk factors to persist or perpetuate, such as poor treatment plans or lack of social support might?). This process helps to answer the question "why" a person did what she did, and to make sense of the case.

Step 4: Risk Formulation

Risk formulation furthers the process of making sense of a case. Like formulation in other contexts (i.e., therapy), risk formulation involves the application or theory or conceptual models to integrate and condense case information into a set of smaller conceptual units that explain why, in this context, a person has been violent. As such, rather than having, say, 15 risk factors to deal with, the evaluator may now have three interconnected themes that explain a person's violent behavior. The purpose is to develop an individual theory of violence, in order to understand why a person might be violent in the future, and what be done to reduce risk. Formulation in the risk assessment context, as in any other decision-making context, is vital for understanding the reasons behind the violence. It offers a mechanism to explain, rather than merely describe and forecast, violence. Greater explication of violence risk formulation can be found in recent literature (Guy, Douglas, & Hart, 2015; Hart, Douglas, & Guy, 2017; Hart & Logan, 2011; Logan, 2016, 2017).

Step 5: Risk Scenarios

This step asks evaluators to specify plausible concerns for the future with respect to a person's violence. If a person were violent again, what might he or she do? What might the warning signs be? Scenario planning has been used for well over a century in other disciplines, such as military planning, and more recently for emergency preparedness, engineering, business, law enforcement, and public health (Amer, Daim, & Jetter, 2013; Chermack & Lynham, 2002; Hart, 2003; Hart & Logan, 2011; Ringland, 1998; Robbins, 1995; van Notten, Rotmans, van Asselt, & Rothman, 2003). It is ideal for planning in the face of uncertainty, which aptly describes the risk assessment and management context (Hart, 2003). Typically, a small number of scenarios is specified (say, a repeat, twist, and worst-case scenario), a process that leads logically to the question, "What can be done to identify and manage risk under these plausible scenarios?"

Step 6: Management Strategies

Stemming from the previous steps, risk management should address the most important dynamic risk factors (present and relevant—Steps 2 and 3), why a person acts violently (Step 4), and what they might do in the future (Step 5). Management strategies are specified under four categories: monitoring (how often, by whom, where?); supervision (how restrictive should conditions be?); treatment (what ameliorative or skills-based programming make sense?); and victim safety planning (what can be done to help potential victims enhance their safety?). Not only should strategies be specified, but so too should their details (if anger management is recommended, what specific program should it be?) and logistics (can we ensure that the timing of this program does not conflict with other programming, or with employment?). Consistent with the Risk-Need-Responsivity model (see Wormith & Bonta, Chapter 8, this volume; and Hoge, Chapter 9, this volume), risk management intensity should be commensurate with risk level.

Step 7: Conclusory Opinions

The final step is simply for the evaluator to communicate her summary opinions about level of risk. Several such judgments are called for. A judgment of future risk, or case prioritization, is a statement that reflects the evaluator's opinion about the level of risk (how likely is it, based on the preceding steps, that this person will commit some form of violence in the next 6–12 months?) and concomitant degree of effort required to mitigate risk. A simple judgment of low, moderate, or high is provided. Evaluators are also asked, using the same logic, to make a risk judgment for serious (life-threatening) and imminent violence (in the coming hours, days to weeks).

As stated in the HCR-20 V3 User Guide (p. 62):

- "Low" or "Routine" means the person is not considered in need of any special intervention or supervision strategies designed to manage violence risk, and that there is no need to monitor the person closely for changes in risk.

- "Moderate" or "Elevated" means that the person requires some special management strategies, including at the very least, an increased frequency of monitoring.
- "High" or "Urgent" suggests that there is an urgent need to develop a risk management plan for the person, which typically would involve (at a minimum) advising staff, increasing supervision levels, placing the person on a high priority list for available treatment resources, and scheduling regular reassessments. Some high-risk cases will require an emergency response (e.g., hospitalization, suspension of conditional release).

The User Guide provides additional guidance for making these judgments. For instance,

> generally, the more risk factors that are present and relevant, the higher the risk for future violence. A greater number of risk factors typically will require more urgent or intensive management strategies in order to mitigate risk. Similarly, if there are fewer risk factors present and relevant, risk generally will be lower, and risk management will be less urgent and intensive.

> (p. 62)

Users are cautioned to provide justification for providing high-risk estimates in the face of few risk factors, or low-risk estimates in the face of many risk factors. Additionally, as part of this narrative form of communication, evaluators are encouraged to explain which risk factors are present and relevant, how they contribute to a person's risk, and the nature and intensity of risk management required to manage risk.

These summary risk ratings have been studied extensively in research. As we review in the following, and as is reviewed in Heilbrun et al.'s Chapter 1 in this volume, they have considerable support in terms of predictive validity, and incremental validity relative to numeric sums or combinations of risk factors (that is, actuarial indices). In the vast majority of research evaluations, they perform comparably or better than numerically (that is, actuarially) derived risk estimates.

Description of Items

As with its predecessors, the HCR-20 V3 contains 20 violence risk factors distributed across three scales: Historical (10 items); Clinical (5 items); Risk Management (5 items). The Historical (H) Scale, as its name indicates, focuses on past experiences, behaviors, and challenges, across the lifespan, up to the time of the evaluation. The Clinical (C) Scale focuses on recent emotional, behavioral, and mental health adjustment, typically in the past 6–12 months. The Risk Management (R) Scale considers challenges in the coming 6–12 months. These scales and their risk factors are shown in Table 12.1. As can be seen, some risk factors contain sub-items. Typically, the risk factors with sub-items are broad in nature, or more complex than others. Each risk factor is defined in the User Guide, as described earlier. Presence is coded (in Step 2) as being absent, partially present, or present, and Relevance as low, moderate, or high. Detailed instructions and explanations are provided in the User Guide.

Given that one of the purposes of the HCR-20 V3 is to help monitor changes over time in a person's risk, in such contexts the more dynamic items (those on the C and R Scales) should be re-evaluated periodically, to monitor change. Moreover, although the H Scale is, by definition, comprised of past risk factors, these generally are not considered static, or unchanging. The only way in which they are static is that, once a person has had one of those risk factors, he or she will always have had it. However, these risk factors *must* form an important part of management and intervention. We also encourage evaluators to track any changes (recent worsening or improvements) of the H Scale risk factors. For example, it is very different if a person's substance

Table 12.1 HCR-20 Version 3 Risk Factors

Historical Scale (History of Problems with . . .)

H1.   Violence
    a.   As a Child (12 and Under)
    b.   As an Adolescent (13–17)
    c.   As an Adult (18 and Over)
H2.   Other Antisocial Behavior
    a.   As a Child (12 and Under)
    b.   As an Adolescent (13–17)
    c.   As an Adult (18 and Over)
H3.   Relationships
    a.   Intimate
    b.   Non-Intimate
H4.   Employment
H5.   Substance Use
H6.   Major Mental Disorder
    a.   Psychotic Disorder
    b.   Major Mood Disorder
    c.   Other Major Mental Disorders
H7.   Personality Disorder
    a.   Antisocial, Psychopathic, and Dissocial
    b.   Other Personality Disorders
H8.   Traumatic Experiences
    a.   Victimization/Trauma
    b.   Adverse Childrearing Experiences
H9.   Violent Attitudes
H10.   Treatment or Supervision Response

Clinical Scale (Recent Problems with . . .)

C1.   Insight
    a.   Mental Disorder
    b.   Violence Risk
    c.   Need for Treatment
C2.   Violent Ideation or Intent
C3.   Symptoms of Major Mental Disorder
    a.   Psychotic Disorder
    b.   Major Mood Disorder
    c.   Other Major Mental Disorders
C4.   Instability
    a.   Affective
    b.   Behavioral
    c.   Cognitive
C5.   Treatment or Supervision Response
    a.   Compliance
    b.   Responsiveness

Risk Management Scale (Future Problems with . . .)

R1.   Professional Services and Plans
R2.   Living Situation
R3.   Personal Support
R4.   Treatment or Supervision Response
    a.   Compliance
    b.   Responsiveness
R5.   Stress or Coping

Source: Reprinted with permission of the Authors.

use problems were contained to some period of time many years ago, or if a person is currently experiencing serious problems with substance use.

Contexts and Populations in Which the HCR-20 V3 Is Appropriate to Use

Broadly, the HCR-20 V3 can be used with men or women, 18 and above, if there is a clinical or legal reason to estimate a person's risk. Most commonly, it is used and has been evaluated in forensic psychiatric, civil psychiatric, and correctional populations. The most common applications are for pre-release decisions (i.e., forensic conditional release; parole; discharge from psychiatric facility), and institutional planning (i.e., risk within hospital or correctional facility). It can be used "part way" through a community or institutional period of supervision (for instance, if a person has been in prison for some years but has not yet received a comprehensive assessment of risk and intervention needs).

Other common applications include use by law enforcement. For instance, it has been used to help select participants for gang exiting programs, and to gather information on risk factors and motivations for "persons of interest" who police must interact with either on an ongoing basis, or in one potentially high-risk situation (i.e., duty to warn a person that his or her life is in danger, where that person might be criminally involved). It is used in workplace violence situations as well. Cawood (2017) evaluated the validity of the HCR-20 V3 in a workplace context, as we review later.

We stress that it is *not* necessary that a person has a mental illness in order for the HCR-20 V3 to be used. Mental illness is but one potential risk factor covered by the instrument. Similarly, it is *not* necessary that a person has a history of violence in order to use it. If there is a legal or clinical rationale to make decisions about violence risk (i.e., threats of violence have been uttered; or a person appears to be psychiatrically deteriorated, hostile, and experiencing violent ideation), then it is appropriate to use the HCR-20 V3.

The HCR-20 V3 should not be used with children. Generally, caution should be exercised if used with older adolescents, given the presence of measures that were developed specifically for that age group. However, there is a transition period (say, ages 16–20) where either the HCR-20 V3 or an adolescent-specific measure like the SAVRY (see Borum et al., Chapter 18, this volume)—or both—would be appropriate to use. For instance, for a somewhat more mature adolescent, living independently, the HCR-20 V3 might be preferred; for a less mature, dependent 19-year-old, the SAVRY might be preferred.

User Qualifications

As explained in the User Guide, evaluators should meet three basic criteria: (a) knowledge of "the professional and scientific literatures on the nature, causes, and management of violence" (p. 38); (b) "expertise in individual assessment" (p. 38), such as interviewing, record review, and, although not necessary, but helpful, understanding how to administer and interpret standardized tests; and (c) "expertise in mental disorder" (p. 38) in terms of assessment and diagnosis of not only mental illness but personality disorder and substance-related disorders. Users without the third criterion can still use the HCR-20 V3 if they do so with consultation or under supervision of a person who meets that criterion (say, as part of a team that includes a person legally entitled to make diagnoses); or if they rely upon previously established diagnoses, if they code the relevant items provisionally, subject to confirmation by a qualified professional; or if they omit those risk factors, and state the limitations of doing so.

The HCR-20 V3 authors do not require training, but strongly recommend that potential users receive training by a qualified trainer (who can be, but does not have to be, one of the HCR-20

V3 developers), engage in self-study, and engage in practice cases. Further, if the instrument is being used within a legal context, users should have full understanding and knowledge of the legal criteria relevant to risk that evaluees will be subject to, as well as the broader legal context and legal procedure. These recommendations are not unique to the HCR-20 V3, but instead are consistent with well-established ethical guidelines of most professionals who would be potentially engaged in risk assessment.

There is no requirement that a person holds an advanced degree such as a doctoral or medical degree, or holds a certain professional position, such as a psychologist or psychiatrist. The criteria would often be met through such means; however, other combinations of education, experience, or training can suffice, so long as the criteria are met. This principled approach is consistent with laws surrounding the demonstration of expertise for qualification as an expert witness. For this reason, the HCR-20 V3 is used not only by psychologists or psychiatrists, but also by nurses, law enforcement officers, case managers, social workers, threat assessment professionals within workplaces, or other such professionals.

Sources of Information

The two most important sources of information, in order of importance, are records or files, and interviews. Ideally, evaluators should strive hard to have access to both, for all evaluations. We understand and acknowledge that in some circumstances this will be impossible (for instance, if an evaluee simply refuses to be interviewed), or difficult (records cannot be accessed, are incomplete, or are very scant). Yet, a risk assessment may still be required. In such circumstances, the evaluator may offer an opinion, with caveats and limitations prominently included, stating that his or her opinion could change subject to more information. Or, the evaluator could decide that the information base is simply too thin to offer an opinion. This is a matter of professional judgment and is similar whether the HCR-20 V3 is being used or not.

With respect to the HCR-20 V3 specifically, however, if the evaluator cannot code many, or perhaps the majority of, risk factors and is unable to determine which risk factors are most relevant, or cannot derive a coherent formulation, then use of the HCR-20 V3 *qua* HCR-20 V3 is likely not advisable. It would still be possible to code whatever risk factors can be coded, so that at least there are some guidelines and operational definitions (and hence likely reliability) used to do so. However, the evaluator would still need to decide whether a clinical opinion about risk was advisable, and should state that the HCR-20 V3 item definitions were relied upon to inform any clinical opinions, but the opinions were not derived from a complete use of the HCR-20 V3 process.

Method of and Rationale for Development

The HCR-20 V3 drew on general development principles common to all SPJ instruments and explained in their manuals. Generally, risk factors are selected based on a thorough review of the scientific and professional literatures; a reasonable number of risk factors is selected that provides comprehensive coverage of the violence literature but is not overwhelming to users. For that reason, risk factors tend not to be highly specific (say, delusions involving persecution), but rather are moderately broad (for instance, item C3—Recent Problems with Symptoms of Major Mental Disorder). The evaluator can then specify under this category exactly how the risk factor manifests for an individual, and, of course, whether it is relevant to that person's violence.

The rationale for this method of item selection—called rational or logical item selection—is multifold, and has been reviewed by us and others many times, including in the HCR-20 V3 User Guide (Douglas et al., 2013; see also Douglas, 2019a, 2019b; Douglas, Hart,

Webster, Belfrage, Guy, & Wilson, 2014; Hart et al., 2017). In general, this method avoids pitfalls associated with relying on a single, or small number, of specific samples, to select risk factors, which many actuarial instruments do (though not all—see the instruments within Part III, "Rational-Actuarial Measures," in this volume). Such reliance can lead to sample dependence (certain risk factors are significant, or not, within certain samples); the exclusion of risk factors (if they were not measured to begin with, were not codable from case files, or simply were not predictive in a given sample); the inclusion of generally irrelevant risk factors (if significant in this but few other samples); over-optimization of weights (that tend to break down in new samples); dependence on statistical weaknesses of data peculiar to a given sample (restricted range; multicollinearity; unreliable measurement of certain risk factors; skewed distributions of risk factors or outcomes; unique or idiosyncratic definitions of risk factors); and exposure to past human error (errors or omissions in entering information into case files). These are but a few of the many challenges associated with reliance on single, or a small number of, samples.

By relying on the larger literature, as SPJ instruments do, these potential problems are not compounded, but rather are minimized. Robust associations between variables will emerge across multiple studies, all of which have their own unique set of weaknesses and peculiarities. But any given sample might fail to show an association that appears robustly elsewhere in the literature. This is why robust risk factors like problematic illicit drug use appear on the HCR-20 V3 but not on some actuarial instruments, such as the VRAG.

Additionally, like other SPJ instruments, the HCR-20 V3 was developed to be comprehensive, not only in its coverage of violence risk factors but also in terms of the entire assessment process, from gathering information to making final risk estimates (as represented in its seven steps). The rationale for these choices was to provide an optimal amount of structure throughout the decision-making process, to promote actual understanding of the causes of violence within individual cases, and to ensure that an assessment is complete (that is, not systematically excluding content, in the form of risk factors, or process, in the form of decision steps).

There were some features of development that were unique to the revision and development of HCR-20 V3. These are described in detail in the User Guide (Douglas et al., 2013) and elsewhere (Douglas et al., 2014) and are summarized briefly here. Given that Version 2 was already well established and broadly used, we consulted a wide variety of professionals about their opinions of its strengths and weaknesses. We also canvassed the professional and scientific literatures for any need to modify the risk factors on the instrument. One result of this process was a 300-page report that reviewed the violence literature, specifically in terms of the degree of support for the existing V2 risk factors (Guy & Wilson, 2007). We reviewed the empirical literature on V2, in terms of whether there were any obvious weaknesses. And, of course, we integrated our own experience and reflections on V2 over the years.

After this process, we produced a Draft Version of V3, in 2008. Then, we presented this to well over 50 experienced users and received written feedback. We asked certain groups to test it out and provide written feedback. In total, roughly 30 clinicians tested it with about the same number of cases. We received extensive feedback, and we made some revisions to the Draft at that time. We then produced what we hoped was the penultimate draft and asked various groups of researchers if they were interested in testing its reliability and validity. We also performed our own testing of its interrater reliability (Douglas & Belfrage, 2014) and predictive validity within correctional and civil psychiatric samples (Strub, Douglas, & Nicholls, 2014). In total, there were tests of reliability and predictive validity across six countries and seven samples, involving over 600 participants, the results of which were peer-reviewed and published in a special issue of the *International Journal of Forensic Mental Health* (Douglas, 2014). Being satisfied with the general findings from these studies, we did not make further substantive changes, and we published the

HCR-20 V3 in 2013 (Douglas et al., 2013). (We published the manual after learning of the results of the studies, but before the special issue was ultimately produced).

Interrater Reliability

The most important index of reliability for the HCR-20 V3—or any SPJ instrument—is interrater reliability. In gauging the adequacy of reliability, we rely on the oft-cited benchmarks posed by Fleiss, Levin, and Paik (1981) and Landis and Koch (1977). For instance, Fleiss et al. (1981) proposed that for single measure intraclass correlation coefficients (ICCs), values .75 and above be considered "excellent," those from .60 to .74 "good," between .40 and .59 "moderate" and under .40 "poor." Landis and Koch (1977) suggest the following guidelines: below 0 is "poor," .00 to .20 is "slight," .21 to .40 is "fair," .41 to .60 is "moderate," .61 to .80 is "substantial," and .81 to 1.00 is "almost perfect."

Our chapter in the First Edition of this *Handbook* demonstrated acceptable interrater reliability for Version 2 of the HCR-20 (Douglas & Reeves, 2010). Based on roughly 20–25 samples, median interrater reliability indices for Version 2 were .85 (Total), .86 (H), .74 (C), and .68 (R), indicating a range of good/substantial to excellent/almost perfect. The median ICC_1 value of the summary risk rating for Version 2, across nine effects from five samples, was .65 ("good" to "substantial").

There have been at least 17 separate published evaluations of the interrater reliability of HCR-20 V3 at the point of writing. This includes ten amongst forensic patient samples, and seven across civil psychiatric samples, correctional and mixed psychiatric/correctional samples, and workplace samples. We review these next.

Forensic Samples

Douglas and Belfrage (2014) conducted an in-depth study devoted solely to interrater reliability. Three experienced, professional clinician raters independently reviewed 32 files of patients within a Swedish forensic hospital, then jointly interviewed each patient. They then independently completed ratings of the presence and relevance of HCR-20 V3 risk factors, and of SRRs. Single rater ICC_1 for total and scale scores ranged from 0.69 to 0.94 (averaging 0.85). Most ICC_1 values were in the "excellent" (Fleiss et al., 1981) or "almost perfect" (Landis & Koch, 1977) range, with one (.69) being in the "good" or "substantial" range. Values of ICC_2, expectedly, were higher, with all but one (.87) being .90 or above, and three reaching .98. Most individual risk factors had ICC_1 values that were 0.75 or greater. Relevance Ratings' ICC_1 values ranged from 0.60 to 0.80 (averaging 0.70), and hence were primarily in the "good" (Fleiss et al., 1981) or "substantial" (Landis & Koch, 1977) range. ICC_2 values, of course, were higher, ranging from .82 to .93.

IRR (ICC_1) for summary risk ratings was 0.81 (risk of institutional violence) and 0.75 (risk for community violence). ICC_2 values were .93 and .90, respectively. Across a total of 138 paired ratings, 86.15% were in perfect agreement (i.e., low-low; moderate-moderate; high-high), and in only 1 out of 138 paired ratings (0.65%) was there a low-high disagreement. The single low-high disagreement was for risk of institutional violence. There were no such disagreements for risk for community violence.

Kötter et al. (2014) reported the results from another in-depth interrater reliability study, in which 5 separate raters each rated 30 male German forensic psychiatric patients. The raters were completing or had completed MA degrees in psychology. They had no previous experience in violence risk assessment and had undergone a two-day training on the HCR-20 V3. Ratings were based on 10- to 20-page written synopses of actual cases. Raters were required to complete the ratings within one week, and hence averaged six cases per day. The authors reported item-level ICC_1 values, including for sub-items. The mean item-level ICC_1 values were described as "good," or "substantial" using the guidelines of Fleiss et al. (1981) and Landis and Koch (1977), respectively. They were as follows: .65 (H), .66 (C), and .73 (R-Out). For the SRRs, ICC_1 was .86—"excellent" to "almost perfect." The authors noted that lack of variability might have substantially lowered mean item-level ICC_1 indices. For instance, H3 had an ICC_1 of .06, but a percent agreement of 80.5%. Moreover, requiring novice raters with minimal training to complete six cases per day, using paper-only synopses, might have limited reliability.

Using 50 male and 17 female insanity acquittees in the Northeastern United States as participants, and eight graduate-level coders, Green et al. (2016) reported that for "both men and women, reliability was excellent for the Historical, Clinical, Risk Management, and Total scale scores" (p. 55). Pairwise-derived ICC_2 values for male patients were .91 (H), .88 (C), .87 (R-In), and .94 (Total), and for female patients .80 (H), .89 (C), .92 (R-In), and .90 (Total). The item-level average ICC_2 values for men were .74 (H), .79 (C), and .72 (R-In), and for women they were .41 (H), .80 (C), and .59 (R-In). Values for R-Out and SRRs were not reported. There was greater variability in item-level reliability for women; however, these indices were based on only 17 cases, relative to 50 for men, and hence greater variability would be expected. More research, based on comparable sample sizes, is necessary prior to drawing conclusions about reliability differences for men and women.

Cabeldue et al. (2018) reported item- and scale-level interrater reliability based on paired ratings of 74 male and female forensic patients in New York State. Using file review methods, the authors randomly selected the interrater reliability subsample from a larger sample of 140 participants. The gender breakdown of the interrater subsample was not specified, although 81% of the full sample consisted of men. Reliability (ICC_1) was excellent at the scale level: H (.87), C (.88), and R (.87). Item-level reliability was also very strong: H range (.50–1.0), C range (.62–.92), and R range (.60–.79). The authors did not code SRRs.

In another interrater reliability evaluation, Mastromanno et al. (2018) reported excellent ICC_1 and ICC_2 values based on chart reviews of 30 forensic psychiatric inpatients in Australia. For the C and R-In Scale Presence Ratings respectively, ICC_1 was .85 and .89 (ICC_2 was .92 and .94). For C and R-In Relevance Ratings respectively, ICC_1 was .76 and .74. ICC_2 was .86 and .85. Although the larger sample contained 32 men and 8 women, gender breakdown was not provided for the reliability subsample. Similarly, information about raters was not provided.

In a Canadian study, Penney, Marshall, and Simpson (2016) used a subsample of 12 forensic patients from their larger sample of 87 such patients. The full sample was 84% male, although the gender composition of the reliability subsample was not specified. Raters were graduate level. The authors reported ICC_1 values at the baseline (hospital) assessment as well as at a 6-month community follow-up. Reliability was "good to excellent" (p. 378) at both timeframes. The range of ICC_1 values at baseline, for Presence Ratings of the scales, was .85 to .94, and at the community follow-up it was .72 to .93. The ICC_1 for the SRR at baseline was 1.0, and at the community follow-up, it was .72.

Based on ten Canadian forensic psychiatric inpatients, Hogan and Olver (2016) reported a range of ICC (type not indicated) indices from .73 to .86 across all HCR-20 V3 components, both for pre-treatment and post-treatment ratings. In the larger sample of 99 patients, 86% were male. There were two graduate-level raters. In another Canadian study of forensic patients, Cook et al. (2018) used a subsample of 11 patients to test the interrater reliability of SRRs, and reported an ICC_1 of .80 at two time points, two months apart, within the hospital. A further Canadian study used four raters, each of whom rated 32 male and female forensic patients (Haag, Hogan, & Cheng, 2017, unpublished data analyses cited in Cheng, Haag, & Olver, 2019). They reported ICC_1 values of .97 for the total score, and high values for the Future Violence/Case Prioritization (.88), Serious Physical Harm (.90), and Imminent Violence (.83) SRRs as well.

Based on a larger sample of 409 medium secure forensic patients discharged from custody over the course of a year from all UK facilities responsible for medium secure patients, Doyle et al. (2014; see also Coid et al., 2015) had four raters each complete independent HCR-20 V3 protocols. ICC values (type unspecified) were consistently high for the rating of the Presence of risk factors: H (.91), C (.90), R-Out (.93), and Total (.92). No information was provided on the raters or the gender of the reliability subsample, although roughly 90% of the larger sample was male. The HCR-20 V3 was coded on the basis of file information plus interviews with a clinical staff member who knew the patient well.

Civil Psychiatric

Howe, Rosenfeld, Foellmi, Stern, and Rotter (2016) evaluated the interrater reliability of the HCR-20 V3 using 35 male and female civil psychiatric patients hospitalized within a large public state hospital in the Northeastern United States. The sample was 69% Black. Raters reviewed medical file information, and "when possible, brief interviews with the patient's treatment team" were conducted. No information was provided about the proportion of patients for whom interviews with the treatment were conducted. Four raters (one forensic psychologist and three MA-level graduate students) provided ratings, with reliability indices being calculated on pairwise ratings between two independent raters. Reliability was somewhat lower in this study compared to most others, with the majority of ICC_1 indices being in the moderate to good range, as follows (all for Presence Ratings): H (.71), C (.55), R-Out (.48), Total (.64). Summary risk ratings were as follows: Future Violence/Case Prioritization (.51), serious physical violence (.57), and imminent violence (.77).

Correctional

Using 15 male offenders detained in a Southwestern U.S. jail drawn randomly from their larger sample, Smith, Kelley, Rulseh, Sörman, and Edens (2014) reported ICC_1 values for the Presence Ratings for the H, C, R-In, and R-Out Scales of .92, .67, .68, and .88, respectively. For the Relevance Ratings ICC_1 values were .85 (H), .77 (C), R-In (.48), and R-Out (.67). The authors noted that the lower R-In reliability was attributable primarily to R2, R4, and R5. For six SRR ratings (In and Out, for each of overall violence, imminent violent, and serious violence), weighted kappa was .66 (range of .43 to .85). Only one of the 90 comparisons included a high-low disagreement. This study protocol used both participant interviews and file reviews, with trained graduate-level evaluators and one PhD-level evaluator providing ratings.

In a Dutch sample of 25 male forensic patients,[1] three raters completed a draft version of the HCR-20 V3 (de Vogel, van den Broek, & de Vries Robbé, 2014). Reported ICC values (type unspecified), based on file review, were .84 for the Total Scale Presence Ratings and .72 for the SRRs. Rater training and background were not specified, although they were drawn from a larger group of raters described as "seven researchers/diagnosticians and three treatment supervisors" (p. 112).

Sea, Hart, and Douglas (2020) conducted a large-scale evaluation of the field interrater reliability of the authorized Korean version of the HCR-20 V3. A total of 32 correctional psychologists, employed across 18 prisons, participated as raters. Teams of four raters each rated 80 male offenders detained within the Korean Corrections System, with one rater taking the lead in the interview and the other three observing. All raters independently reviewed case files and provided HCR-20 V3 Presence and Relevance Ratings as well as summary risk ratings. The authors reported both single and average reliability estimates (ICC_1 and ICC_2) at the item and scale levels for Presence and Relevance Ratings as well as for each of the summary risk ratings (Future Violence/Case Prioritization; serious physical violence; imminent violence).

For the scale-level Presence ratings, ICC_1 ratings were primarily in the "excellent" or "almost perfect" range, with one scale (H-Presence) being somewhat lower—albeit still "good" or "substantial"—at .73. Values for the C, R, and Total scales were .89, .86, and .79 respectively. All ICC_2 values for the Presence ratings were above .90: H (.91), C (.97), R (.96), Total (.93). ICC_1 and ICC_2 for the summary risk ratings were also very good, at .83 and .97, respectively.

Mixed Psychiatric and Correctional

In a sample of 200 men and women undergoing pre-trial forensic psychiatric evaluations in Sweden, Persson, Belfrage, Fredriksson, and Kristiansson (2017) used a subsample of 10 participants to determine interrater reliability. A forensic psychiatric and forensic social worker conducted interviews and reviewed file information for this study. The gender of the reliability subsample was not stated. Just under half of the complete sample was deemed to have a major mental disorder, and hence would have been sentenced to treatment in a forensic hospital, with the remainder sentenced to prison. Persson et al. reported excellent ICC_1 values for both the HCR-20 V3 Total Scale Presence Ratings (.81) as well as the SRR of low, moderate, and high risk (.80). Sub-scale and item-level reliability was not reported.

The interrater reliability of the official Chinese translation of the HCR-20 V3 was evaluated within a larger prospective study of 152 (94 male and 58 female) civil psychiatric patients and offenders with mental disorders (Chen et al., 2020). Three raters each independently rated a randomly selected subset of 33 participants. Both ICC_1 and ICC_2 were reported. ICC_1 for the Presence Ratings for the H, C, R-Out, and Total Scales were .90, .63, .69, and .82, respectively. For the Relevance Ratings ICC_1 values were .93 (H), .72 (C), .58 (R-Out), and .88 (Total). ICC_2 values were of course larger, all above .80. ICC_2 for the Presence Ratings for the H, C, R-Out, and Total Scales were .96, .83, .87, and .93, respectively. For the Relevance Ratings ICC_2 values were .98 (H), .89 (C), R-Out (.80), and Total (.96). The ICC_1 for the summary risk rating was .90, and ICC_2 was .96.

Workplace Settings

Cawood (2017) tested the interrater reliability, using ICC_1, of 40 workplace cases, each rated by three doctoral-level graduate students. The raters had access to case files that had been developed from industry (i.e., businesses; higher education) cases by non-mental health threat assessment professionals. ICC_1 for the SRRs was .72. No other indices were reported.

Summary of Interrater Reliability

The interrater reliability for the HCR-20 V3 appears to be acceptable, with the majority of ICC_1 values in the high .70s to .80+, and most ICC_2 values being .80 to .90+. Findings are based on 17 samples and 465 participants, across multiple settings and nine different countries, with different methods and raters used across studies. This holds true for Presence Ratings and SRRs, as well as for Relevance Ratings, although there are fewer evaluations of these latter indices.

Concurrent Validity

Concurrent validity is of moderate importance in the validation process of a risk assessment instrument. The primary purpose of a risk assessment instrument is not to predict other risk assessment or related instruments. However, to the extent that the HCR-20 V3 (or any other risk assessment instrument) correlates well with instruments that themselves are associated with violence, this provides at least indirect support for its validity.

Association Between Version 2 and Version 3 of the HCR-20

Given the well-established link between Version 2 of the HCR-20 and violence, perhaps the most important test of Version 3's concurrent validity is its correlation with V2. Four such studies have been conducted within forensic psychiatric settings. Bjørkly, Eidhammer, and Selmer (2014) evaluated the concurrent validity between V2 and V3 through internal consistency indices derived jointly between the two measures, based on ratings of 20 Norwegian forensic patients rated by two mental health nurses. They reported joint V2–V3 Cronbach alpha values of .85 (H), .59 (C), .81 (R), and .84 (Total) for the Presence Ratings, and .85 (H), .58 (C), .79 (R), and .84 (Total) for the Relevance Ratings. Citing Nunnally and Bernstein (1994), the authors stated that these values reflect moderate to good levels of internal consistency for early stages of measure development. Moreover, the authors reported Pearson correlations between the measures' Total Scales of .58 (Presence) and .55 (Relevance). The authors also reported mean score differences between V2 and V3. They concluded, "the concurrent validity of the second and third versions of the HCR-20 is significant and solid" (p. 240).

The correlation between the Total scores on V2 and V3 in a sample of 86 Dutch forensic patients (similar to correctional offenders, as described earlier) was .93 (de Vogel et al., 2014). Douglas and Belfrage (2014) reported V2–V3 correlations based on their interrater reliability study of Swedish forensic patients, described earlier, as follows: (all r's significant at $p < .001$): H (.87), C (.76), R (In) (.67), and R (Out) (.82), Total Score (In) (.85), and Total Score (Out) (.90). SRRs on V2 were not available, thus concurrent validity between SRRs on V3 and V2 was not reported. De Vogel, Bruggeman, and Lancel (2019), as part of a larger predictive validity study of 78 female forensic patients, reported intercorrelations between each scale on V3 with its counterpart on V2. Correlations ranged from .83 (H Scale) to .94 (Total Scale).

Strub et al. (2014) examined concurrent validity between Version 2 and Version 3 amongst Canadian civil psychiatric patients and criminal offenders. Concurrent validity between the HCR-20 Version 2 and 3 was as follows (all p's $< .001$): H ($r = .89$), C ($r = .76$); R ($r = .81$), HCR-20 Total ($r = .91$), and SRR ($r = .98$). In a U.S. sample of civil psychiatric patients, in Howe et al. (2016) evaluated the associations between V2 and V3 as a function of whether the same or different raters completed the instruments. Not surprisingly, correlations were meaningfully higher when the same rater completed both instruments. It should be noted that using different raters introduces an additional source of variance—raters—to the analysis, and hence any departure from perfect interrater reliability will be reflected in the inter-measure correlations.

First, the authors compared Version 2 and Version 3 ratings when two independent raters rated both instruments. Correlations between Total scores on Version 2 and Version 3 ($r = .62, p < .001$) as well as H ($r = .68, p < .001$), C ($r = .48, p < .01$), and R subscales were significant ($r = .46, p < .01$, respectively). In addition, Version 2 SRRs were significantly correlated with all three SRRs on Version 3 including Future Violence/Case Prioritization ($r = .40, p < .05$), Serious Physical Harm ($r = .39, p < .05$), and Imminent Violence ($r = .58,$ p $< .001$). Second, the authors compared the association between Version 2 and Version 3 rated by the same rater. Correlations between Total scores ($r = .90, p < .001$) as well as correlations between the H ($r = .84, p < .001$), C ($r = .80, p < .001$), and R subscales ($r = .85, p < .001$) were significant. Version 2's SRR was also significantly correlated with that rater's Version 3's Future Violence/Case Prioritization ($r = .67, p < .001$), Serious Physical Harm ($r = .71, p < .001$), and Imminent Violence ratings ($r = .75, p < .001$).

Association Between HCR-20 V3 Items/Scales and Summary Risk Ratings

Several studies have evaluated whether, and which, HCR-20 V3 scales are predictive of its summary risk ratings. This is an index of the extent to which the non-algorithmic ratings of violence risk that are used with the HCR-20 V3 are influenced by the linear combination of sums of risk factors. In that way, these studies test one of the assumptions of the SPJ model broadly, and the HCR-20 V3 specifically, that, in general, the more risk factors that are present, the greater the risk posed. Of course, within the SPJ framework, allowance is made for a non-linear association between risk factors and risk estimates (that is, a small cluster of risk factors could result in a legitimate high-risk rating). This assumption is not tested by the current analyses.

Howe et al. (2016), in their U.S. sample of 64 civil psychiatric patients, found that 14 of the 20 V3-item Presence Ratings (including 4 of 5 for both the C and R Scales) were correlated with the SRR of Future Violence/Case Prioritization, with a range of $r = .26$ to .53. Although fewer item Relevance Ratings were also correlated with these SRRs, there were many (13) significant Presence × Relevance interactions (r's $= .26–.61$) Intuitively, this confirms that risk factors that are both present and highly relevant are most likely to influence evaluators' judgments about risk. Similar findings were reported for SRRs of serious physical violence and imminent violence.

In a U.S. sample of 84 male pre-trial jail detainees, Smith et al. (2014) focused on the interaction between Presence and Relevance Ratings at the scale level (sums of item-level Presence × Relevance interaction scores). They reported, based on discriminant function analyses, that, for the Future Violence/Case Prioritization SRR, the interaction terms between Presence and Relevance Ratings of the C and R Scales were uniquely predictive. Indeed, only the interaction terms were predictive of all SRRs. Consistent with Howe et al. (2016), this indicates that risk factors that are not only present but also deemed to be relevant to an individuals' violence influence their ratings about violence risk.

In a Scottish file review study of 75 forensic patients, Neil, O'Rourke, Ferreira, and Flynn (2019) reported correlations between V3 scales and an integrated SRR based on the HCR-20 V3 and the SAPROF. Correlations for the C (.68), R (.52), and Total Scales (.44) were large, whereas for the H Scale it was small and unexpectedly negative (−.21). The behavior of the H Scale in this study was unusual and, as the authors noted, could be attributable to limited range in scores.

In another study of this issue, Cheng, Haag, and Olver (2019) evaluated which HCR-20 V3 items, along with a number of covariates (i.e., age; gender; nature of index offense) were predictive of SRRs, within a sample of 32 forensic patients each rated by 4 raters. They constructed regression equations for each rater separately to evaluate differences across raters. Ratings were based on file material only. In general, the authors reported that SRRs were largely, and strongly, predicted by HCR-20 V3 subscales. Using the outcome of Future Violence/Case Prioritization as an example, the Multiple R values across the four raters ranged from .67 to .85. There were differences between raters in terms of which items were most strongly predictive of SRRs. For two raters, H2 (Other Antisocial Behavior) was most predictive, whereas R1 (Treatment or Supervision Response) and H9 (Violent Attitudes) were most predictive for the other two raters. A series of multiple regression analyses used the subscales, along with various demographic and historical variables, to predict SRRs for each rater. The Historical and Clinical Scales commonly entered the predictive models, but variables such as gender, race, seriousness of index offense, and age at first insanity acquittal entered some models as well. These variables tended to have more inconsistent and weaker associations with SRRs than did the HCR-20 V3 subscales.

Association Between HCR-20 V3 and Other Risk Assessment Instruments

Two studies have evaluated the associations between the HCR-20 V3 and Level of Service instruments (see Wormith & Bonta, Chapter 8, this volume). In Persson et al.'s (2017) Swedish sample of 200 male and female forensic pre-trial evaluees, the HCR-20 V3 and Level of Service-Revised (Andrews & Bonta, 1995) total scores were highly correlated (.78–.81, depending on whether the participant was evaluated to have a severe mental disorder at the time of the offence), as were HCR-20 V3 SRRs and LSI-R categorical ratings (.57–.69). In a study of 80 Korean offenders,

Sea et al. (2020) reported somewhat lower correlations between total scores on the Korean translation of these instruments (.58, for Presence Ratings; .53, for Relevance Ratings). The H Scale was mostly strongly related to the LSI-R Total scale (.68, for Presence Ratings; .67 for Relevance Ratings). The C Scale was not significantly correlated with the LSI-R Total scale (r's < .20), whereas the R Scale was (r's = .46). Both the H and R Scales correlated with most LSI-R subscales, whereas the C Scale correlated with only two (Emotional/Personal, and Attitudes/Orientation). These analyses indicate a robust shared variance between much of the HCR-20 V3 and LSI-R, with the C Scale seemingly capturing risk-relevant variance not captured by the LSI-R.

Similarly, four studies have reported concurrent validity between the HCR-20 V3 and a measure of protective factors, the Structured Assessment of Protective Factors (SAPROF; see de Vries Robbé et al., Chapter 17, this volume). In Persson et al.'s (2017) Swedish study, cited earlier, there was an expected negative association between these measures' total scores (−.76 to −.79) and SRRs (−.48 to −.53). In a Scottish file review study of 75 forensic patients, the correlation between total score was −.55 (Neil et al., 2019). The H Scale, oddly, did not correlate with any of the SAPROF indices (perhaps due to limited range, according to the authors), whereas the C and R Scales tended to correlate with moderate to large inverse effect sizes with SAPROF scales. Coid et al. (2015) reported moderate-sized average inverse item-level correlations between HCR-20 V3 and SAPROF items in a sample of 409 male and female medium-security forensic patients in the UK. In a Dutch forensic sample of 78 female patients, de Vogel et al. (2019) reported scale and total level correlations between the instruments. The total scores correlated at −.69, whereas the HCR-20 V3 Total Scale scores correlated between −.49 and −.64 with SAPROF subscales. The range of correlations at the sub-scale level between instruments was from a low of −.12 (*ns*) between the C Scale and the SAPROF External Scale, and −.63 between both the H and C Scales and the SAPROF Motivation Scale.

Two studies have evaluated associations between HCR-20 V3 and the Short-Term Assessment of Risk and Treatability (START; see Nicholls et al., Chapter 15, this volume). In Hogan and Olver's (2016; see also Hogan & Olver, 2019) Canadian study of 99 forensic patients, the total HCR-20 V3 Scale correlated .77 with the START Vulnerability Scale for V3 Presence Ratings, and .61 for Relevance Ratings. For Presence Ratings, V3 scale score correlations ranged from .53 (H) to .72 (C), and for Relevance Ratings, from .46 (H) to .63 (C). In terms of HCR-20 V3 SRRs, correlations with the START Vulnerability Scale were large for Future Violence/Case Prioritization (.45) and Imminent Violence (.57), but small and non-significant for Serious Physical Violence (−.14). Expectedly, HCR-20 V3 indices showed inverse associations with the START Strengths Scale. The total Presence and Relevance scores correlated −.55 and −.42, respectively, with this START index. Scale-level Presence scores correlated from −.35 (C) to −.55 (R) with the START Strengths Scale, whereas scale-level Relevance scores correlated from −.27 (C) to −.45 (R). The Future Violence/Case Prioritization SRR was correlated −.42 with the START Strengths Scale, and the Imminent Risk SRR at −.25. The Serious Physical Violence SRR was not significantly correlated with the START Strengths Scale (−.06). In de Vogel et al.'s (2019) Dutch study of 78 female forensic patients, HCR-20 V3 indices (Presence) were robustly associated with START Vulnerability (Total = .80; scale range = .55 [H] to .82 [C]) and Strengths Scales (Total = −.79; scale range = −.55 [H] to −.81 [C]).

Two studies have used the HCR-20 V3 SRRs as outcome variables to test a violence screening instrument consisting of a small number of risk factors (previous violence; violent threats; violent thoughts; agitation; paranoia; treatment resistance) (Rotter & Rosenfeld, 2018; Rosenfeld et al., 2017), and have reported robust associations between the screening instrument and the HCR-20 V3 SRRs.

A number of studies have reported associations between the HCR-20 V3 and other risk assessment measures. For instance, Cook et al. (2018) tested the concurrent validity between the

HCR-20 V3 and the Hamilton Anatomy of Risk Management: Forensic Version (HARM-FV; Chaimowitz & Mamak, 2011) in a forensic psychiatric sample. The HARM-FV is a 14-item risk assessment instrument developed for use in forensic inpatient settings to assess change in dynamic risk factors and facilitate risk management. The study sample consisted of 39 participants found unfit to stand trial (8%, $n = 3$) or NCRMD (92%, $n = 36$). HCR-20 V3 SRRs—including Future Violence/Case Prioritization, Serious Physical Harm, and Imminent Violence—were significantly associated with HARM-FV Immediate and Short Term Professional Support ratings at 1- and 3-month follow-ups ($r = .50$–.62, p < .01). Kappa coefficients were also reported for HCR-20 and HARM-FV. There was significant rater agreement between HCR-20 Future Violence/Case Prioritization ratings and HARM-FV Immediate and Short Term Professional Support at 1 and 3 months ($κ = .32$–.46, $p < .001$).

Hogan and Olver (2016; see also Hogan & Olver, 2019), in their study of 99 forensic patients, reported correlations between the HCR-20 V3 and the Violence Risk Scale (VRS; see Olver & Wong, Chapter 10, this volume) and the Violence Risk Appraisal Guide-Revised (VRAG-R; see Hilton et al., Chapter 7, this volume). The HCR-20 V3 Total Scale Presence and Relevance scores were very highly correlated with the VRS Dynamic and Total Scales (.77–.83), and somewhat less so with VRS Static and VRAG-R scores (.56–.69). The H Scale (Presence and Relevance) had very high correlations with all VRS indices and the VRAG-R (.71–.85). The C Scale (Presence and Relevance) had primarily moderate correlations with the VRS Dynamic and Total Scale scores (.30–.49) and was not significantly correlated with the VRS Static Scale or the VRAG-R. The R Scale (Presence and Relevance) showed moderate to large correlations with all VRS indices and the VRAG-R (.40–.67). In terms of SRRs, the Future Violence/Case Prioritization was highly correlated with the VRS Dynamic (.78) and Total Scale scores (.76), and also robustly correlated with the VRS Static (.52) and VRAG-R scores (.56). The Serious Physical Violence SRR was not significantly correlated with any VRS index or the VRAG-R, whereas the Imminent Violence SRR was moderately correlated with the VRS Dynamic Scale (.33) and Total Scale (.28), and not significantly correlated with the VRS Static Scale or the VRAG-R.

In a total cohort of 327 forensic patients from New South Wales, Australia, Adams, Thomas, Mackinnon, and Eggleton (2018) reported large correlations between the HCR-20 V3 Total score and indices from the DUNDRUM Quartet (Kennedy, O'Neil, Flynn, & Gill, 2010), a measure of risk and recovery (.61–.81). The C Scale similarly had large correlations with this instrument (.60–.88), whereas the H and R Scales had moderate to large associations (.33–.62 and .33–.74, respectively). Associations with a measure of needs within forensic settings (the forensic version of the Camberwell Assessment of Need; Thomas et al., 2003) were more variable (.10–.71) but primarily in the moderate to large range. In this same study, several HCR-20 V3 indices (H Scale; C Scale) differentiated groups of patients in high secure settings from those in lower secure settings or the community, although a consistent pattern did not emerge.

In Persson et al.'s (2017) Swedish study of forensic evaluees, the HCR-20 V3 Total Scale had moderate to large correlations (.33–.53, depending on whether evaluees had been deemed to have had a serious mental disorder at the time of their offense) with the actuarial Classification of Violence Risk (COVR; see Monahan, Chapter 5, this volume). Sea et al. (2020) reported primarily moderate to large correlations (.23–.51, with one non-significant outlier of .14) between the HCR-20 V3 Total and subscale Presence and Relevance scores and a Korean correctional risk assessment measure. De Vogel et al. (2019) reported correlations ranging from .52 to .66 between V3 indices and the Female Additional Manual (FAM; de Vogel, de Vries Robbé, van Kalmthout, & Place, 2014), a measure meant to supplement SPJ measures for evaluating risk amongst women.

Association Between HCR-20 V3 and Measures of Psychopathy

Measures of psychopathy are not risk assessment instruments, but they are frequently used within risk assessment because psychopathy is relevant to risk and often studied within risk assessment studies. Three studies have reported the associations between the HCR-20 V3 and the *Hare Psychopathy Checklist-Revised* (PCL-R Hare, 2003; see DeMatteo et al., Chapter 2, this volume). Across these studies (de Vogel et al., 2019; Hogan & Olver, 2016; Sea et al., 2020)—from the Netherlands, Canada, and Korea—total scores on both instruments were highly correlated (.44 in Korea, .60–.67 in the Netherlands and Canada). The H Scale was also highly correlated with the PCL-R total score (.49–.54 in Korea, .66–.76 in the Netherlands and Canada), whereas C and R showed more variability and a smaller upper end (for the C Scale, .17–.24 in Korea, .23–.45 in the Netherlands and Canada; and for the R Scale, .29–.37 in Korea, .35–.53 in the Netherlands and Canada). In each study, correlations tended to be higher (moderate to large) for the behavioral aspects of the PCL-R compared to the interpersonal and affective aspects, where they were small to moderate, and sometimes not significant. Both Sea et al. and Hogan and Olver reported large correlations with the Future Violence/Case Prioritization SRR and the PCL-R total. Sea et al. also reported primarily moderate correlations with the Comprehensive Assessment of Psychopathic Personality (CAPP; Cooke, Hart, Logan, & Michie, 2004, 2012).

Summary of Concurrent Validity

There is a strong association between Versions 2 and 3 of the HCR-20. The range of correlations between V2 and V3 total scores, when the same rater is used, is .85–.94. For the scales, it is .83–.89 (H), .76–.90 (C), and .81–.89 (R-Out). Summary risk ratings are also highly correlated (.67–.75 in one study, and .98 in another). Correlations are expectedly lower though still substantial in the two studies that used different raters. Together, these findings indicate substantial content overlap in terms of risk domains. Despite some changes to items, the implication is that there ought to be consistency between V2 and V3 in terms of capturing risk level and risk domains of evaluees. Further, studies indicate that the rater-generated SRRs—the indices intended to communicate judgments of risk level and hence management need—are strongly rooted in the risk factors contained on the instrument.

Moreover, in terms of concurrent validity with other risk assessment measures, the literature would indicate that the HCR-20 V3 is strongly associated with other established—and emerging—instruments. Patterns of association make conceptual sense, in that its dynamic elements tend to be more strongly correlated with the dynamic elements of other instruments. It is also inversely associated with protective factors and with strengths, as it should be. Finally, the HCR-20 V3 is associated in conceptually meaningful ways with measures of psychopathy.

Clinical Utility

A number of investigations have reported on aspects of the perceived clinical utility of the HCR-20 V3. Indeed, one of the goals of revising V2 was to enhance professional decision-making when using the HCR-20. Numerous changes were made to accomplish this goal, reviewed elsewhere in this chapter. Studies in this section include surveys of professionals, evaluations of the quality of risk assessment reports generated using V3, and the association between V3 and release decisions.

de Vogel et al. (2014) conducted a user satisfaction survey of 192 professionals who attended 11 workshops on HCR-20 V3 in the Netherlands. The main purpose of the survey was whether V3 was perceived to be "user-friendly and having additional value for risk assessment and management in daily practice" (p. 112). The majority of the sample thought the following components of V3 were useful: sub-items (89%, $n = 163$), indicators (80%, $n = 145$), Relevance Ratings (76%, $n = 140$), risk formulation (74%, $n = 134$), scenario planning (75%, $n = 136$), and additional SRRs of imminent and serious violence (67%, $n = 118$). Roughly two-thirds responded that V3 was as easy as or easier to code than V2 (64%, $n = 87$).

A UK study compared the quality of case formulations that used either Version 2 or 3 of the HCR-20 (Hopton, Cree, Thompson, Jones, & Jones, 2018). Drawing on 58 V2 and 63 V3 reports generated in the field across 17 forensic services, the authors tested formulation quality using the Case Formulation Quality Checklist-Revised (CFQC-R; McMurran & Bruford, 2016). This measure draws from Hart, Sturmey, Logan, and McMurran's (2011) article on the quality of formulation, and contains ratings for 10 aspects of formulation quality. The authors reported that formulations based on V3 were rated as being of significantly higher quality than those based on V2, on six of ten scales and overall quality, despite not being longer in length. None of the V2-based formulations were rated as being of better quality than V3 formulations. Specifically, formulations were rated as being of higher quality on the domains of narrative, external coherence, factual foundation, internal coherence, events being understood over time, and completeness. For a detailed example and discussion of formulation using the HCR-20 V3, see Logan (2014).

Belfrage (2015) described the process of implementing the HCR-20 V3 into two large Swedish forensic hospitals that previously had been using Version 2. Despite some obstacles, he reported that once implemented, use of the V3 resulted in: risk assessments that were more individualized; treatment plans that drew more comprehensively from the risk assessments; more systematic risk assessments; an electronic risk database that encouraged risk assessments to be conducted every six months; greater involvement of physicians within risk-relevant treatment planning; enhanced communication with courts with respect to risk factors and hence targets for intervention; greater involvement of patients in the risk assessment process, and their understanding of their formulation (essentially, their motivators, disinhibitors, and destabilizers for violence); and greater appreciation amongst staff of patient formulations.

A team from Norway completed 20 cases using HCR-20 V3 (Bjørkly et al., 2014) and reported their opinions regarding its clinical utility. They concluded that the risk factors are "more elaborated on, detailed, and more thoroughly explained" and that its new administration method "provide[s] a very robust platform and guide for violence risk management" (p. 240). Further, it "may substantially reduce the risk for empirically unfounded conclusions" (p. 241), that the addition of individual relevance ratings "informs the development of a tailor-made and recognizable risk management plan" (p. 241), and finally that V3

> contribute[s] to a more systematic and detailed violence risk assessment, with reinforced guidance to integrate development and evaluation of risk management strategies. The requirement in the seven-step procedure to introduce and discuss future risk directly in relation to a risk management plan is a significant step forward emphasizing one of the key facets of the SPJ tradition.
>
> (p. 241)

Finally, in terms of release decisions, Cabeldue et al. (2018), in their New York sample of 140 male and female insanity acquittees, evaluated which HCR-20 V3 items and scales predicted clinicians' recommendations for transfer to less secure civil psychiatric facilities, or retention within a secure forensic psychiatric hospital. The mean H, C, and R Scale scores were significantly lower in the "transfer" group relative to the "retain" group. However, effect sizes were substantially larger for C (Cohen's $d = 1.90$) and R (Cohen's $d = 1.97$) relative to H (Cohen's $d = 0.57$). Moreover, in multivariate analyses, the C and R Scale were uniquely predictive of "transfer" decisions, whereas the H Scale was not. Analyses controlled for time since the index offense and violence within the hospital, which at a bivariate level predicted these decisions.

Summary of Clinical Utility

In summary, work done of relevance to the clinical utility of the HCR-20 V3 suggests that it is perceived as clinically useful by practitioners, that it improves violence risk formulation, that it improves patient treatment planning and involvement of key stakeholders, and that it informs key clinical-legal decision-making. In the next section, the extent to which it is associated with future violence will be the focus.

Predictive Validity

In evaluating the validity of the HCR-20 V3, it is important to focus on its core assumptions. To that end, research has evaluated: (a) whether the Presence and Relevance Ratings of the risk factors are associated with future violence; (b) whether the summary risk ratings are associated with future violence; (c) whether summary risk ratings add incremental predictive validity beyond Presence and/or Relevance Ratings of risk factors; and (d) whether changes over time in Presence and/or Relevance Ratings are associated with future changes in violence. In addition, some research has evaluated (e) how the HCR-20 V3 has fared vis-à-vis other risk assessment instruments, and (f) whether it is moderated by factors such as gender or setting. We review these topics in turn.

Predictive Validity of the Presence and Relevance of Risk Factor Ratings

The predictive validity of the risk factors contained on the HCR-20 V3 has been studied in forensic psychiatric, civil psychiatric, and correctional settings. Most have been within forensic settings, estimating risk in the community post-discharge, whereas some have estimated inpatient risk. Studies have been conducted in Australia, Canada, China, the Netherlands, Scotland, Sweden, the United Kingdom (England and Wales), and the United States. We will differentiate these applications as we review the literature.

Predictive Validity of HCR-20 V3 Risk Factors for Post-Discharge Community Violence Amongst Forensic Psychiatric Patients

Two Canadian studies have evaluated the predictive validity of various HCR-20 V3 indices in this context. In their sample of 87 forensic patients (83% male) who had been found not criminally responsible, Penney et al. (2016), using a repeated-measures prospective design, evaluated the HCR-20 V3, PCL-R, Brief Psychiatric Rating Scale (BPRS), State-Trait Anxiety Inventory (STAI), State-Trait Anger Expression Inventory (STAXI-2), Perceived Stress Scale (PSS), and Positive and Negative Affect Scale (PANAS). Measures were assessed before hospital discharge, and in the case of dynamic measures, at one and six months post-discharge.

Multinomial ordinal logistic regression was conducted to examine the incremental predictive efficacy of static and dynamic risk indicators measured at baseline for violence perpetration, victimization, and re-hospitalization. First, whether dynamic risk factors added to the capacity of the Historical (H) subscale on HCR-20 V3 to predict outcomes was examined. Neither symptom- nor affect-based dynamic risk indicators accounted for additional variance in these models above and beyond H subscale scores ($p > .05$). In addition, neither C nor R subscale scores accounted for additional variance in these models above and beyond H subscale scores ($p > .05$). Logistic regression odds ratios for the H Scale, with respect to violence, ranged from 1.50 to 1.58 (50% to 58% increase in the odds of violence for every point increase on the H Scale). The PCL-R was unrelated to violence in all models. Findings regarding summary risk ratings and dynamic risk are reported in the pertinent sections that follow.

In Hogan and Olver's (2019) study of 82 forensic patients released into the community and followed for an average of eight years, the authors reported both bivariate and multivariate findings and also compared the HCR-20 V3 to other commonly used instruments, all of which have chapters devoted to them in this book (VRS; PCL-R; START; VRAG-R). The authors reported findings from risk ratings made at pretreatment, as well as those made at post-treatment. The AUCs for the HCR-20 V3 were generally strong and significant. The Total, H, C, and R Scale scores produced significant AUCs at pretreatment of .85, .80, .75 and .68, respectively, and at post-treatment, .81, .79, .72, and .73. This study was one of the few to also test the predictive validity of the Relevance Ratings, which fared comparably to the Presence Ratings. The Total, H, C, and R Scale scores produced significant AUCs at pretreatment of .80, .80, .73, and .69, respectively, and at post-treatment, .83, .78, .76, and .78. Tests of the SRRs, incremental validity, and dynamic validity are reported later in this chapter.

In a UK study of all medium secure forensic patients released in the UK over a course of a year ($n = 387$), Doyle et al. (2014) completed the HCR-20 V3 at baseline (discharge from forensic facilities), and follow-up violence data was collected at 6 and 12 months post-discharge using clinical records and information obtained through interview with a social supervisor and/or care coordinator who knew the patient well. Violence was defined and measured using the MacArthur Community Violence Instrument, using sources of official police data, case file review, and interviews of participants and collaterals. Of the sample, 14% ($n = 54$) committed an act of violence at 6 months and 23% ($n = 89$) committed an act of violence at 12 months. For 6 months post-discharge AUC values were .73, .63, .75, and .67 for the Total, H, C, and R Scales, respectively. For 12 months post-discharge, AUC values were .70, .63, .71, and .63 for the Total, H, C, and R Scales, respectively. Although total scores are not recommended for clinical practice in an algorithmic manner, patients whose number of risk factors surpassed the median were two to five times more likely to be violent compared to those under the median.

In the same sample, although with slightly more patients ($n = 409$), Coid, Kallis, Doyle, Shaw, and Ullrich (2015) tested item-level associations with subsequent violence. They compared what they labeled a "predictive approach" and a "causal approach." The former used risk factors rated in one 6-month window to predict violence in the next 6-month window. The latter used the same 6-month window for both predictors and outcome. It should be stated that, despite being labeled "causal," these analyses were not able to test causality, but rather merely closer proximity in time between predictors and outcomes. The threat, of course, is that the outcomes preceded the predictors, which, then, by definition means that the predictors could not have caused the outcomes.

Despite these limits, Coid et al. (2015) found that a considerable number of HCR-20 V3 risk factors—and SAPROF protective factors—were associated with violence. More than half of HCR-20 V3 individual risk factors (and SAPROF individual protective factors) were predictive of violence. In multivariate analyses involving only ostensibly dynamic risk and protective items (C, R, and the SAPROF dynamic items), as would be expected, a smaller set of individual factors was predictive. In particular, for the HCR-20 V3, Violent Ideation or Intent (C2), Instability (C4), and Stress or Coping (R5) were each uniquely predictive of violence, and the remaining risk factors became non-significant.

The core problem with research of this type is the presumption that each individual risk factor will be uniquely significant in any given study, which would indeed be a rare phenomenon. Risk factors for SPJ measures are selected on the basis of broad empirical support across many studies—not a single study. Hence, Coid et al. made the same error that some actuarialists make—over-emphasizing a single sample in the development (or, here, evaluation) of a risk assessment measure. Despite that, in this particular sample, three of the ten dynamic risk factors were uniquely predictive of violence. A number of other risk factors were also associated with violence, and with the other risk factors, suggesting that there may be mediation of some risk factors by others with respect to their links to violence. This possibility is feasible and expected, and indeed forms the basis for formulation, in which evaluators integrate risk factors at the individual level and determine which play the most crucial role.

Two studies on predictive validity have been conducted in the Netherlands. De Vogel et al. (2014) tested the penultimate draft version of the HCR-20 V3 in 86 forensic patients who had been released to the community and followed for three years. Predictive validity of the HCR-20 V2 and HCR-20 V3 were evaluated with respect to violent recidivism after discharge at 1-, 2-, and 3-year follow-ups using Receiver Operating Characteristic (ROC) analyses. Area Under the Curve (AUC) values of the HCR-20 V3 Total score (all p's < .05) were as follows: .77 (1-year follow-up); .75 (2-year follow-up); and .67 (3-year follow-up). For the HCR-20 V2 Total score, AUC values were comparable and not significantly different (AUCs = .80, .74, and .67 at 1-, 2-, and 3-year follow-ups, respectively).

In their sample of 78 female forensic patients, de Vogel et al. (2019) reported AUC values at both 3- and 12-year follow ups. Total score AUCs were significant, at .71 and .67, respectively. Scale scores ranged from .64 (*ns*) to .68. This study compared five risk assessment instruments plus the PCL-R. None of the instruments was particularly strongly related to violence. However, the authors concluded that the most promising indices were the HCR-20 V3 Clinical Scale and the START Vulnerability Scale.

In Persson et al.'s (2017) Swedish sample of 200 male and female forensic pre-trial evaluees followed for one year, the AUC for the HCR-20 V3 total score was significant, at .79. The authors did not report effect sizes for subscales. They did report outcomes for other instruments, however, including the COVR (AUC = .61), LSI-R (.70), and SAPROF (.78). All values were significant. The highest AUC—though not significantly higher than the HCR-20 V3 or SAPROF alone—was for the HCR-SAPROF index (AUC = .81).

Finally, Mastromanno et al. (2018) reported the predictive validity of the combined C and R Scales, coded from files soon after entry to a forensic hospital in Australia, in terms of post-release violent and nonviolent recidivism (obtained from a police database), in a sample of 40 patients (32 male). Ratings were made, on average, 2 years prior to discharge, and the sample was followed in the community for an average of 12 years and 10 months. In logistic regression analyses, the combined C and R Presence Ratings were significant predictors of violent recidivism, despite such a lengthy follow-up period. For each 1-point increase on this index, there was a 26% increase in the odds of observing violence. Similar findings were reported for the PCL-R. However, when both the C-R index and the PCL-R were entered together in the model, neither were significant. This is likely due to the analyses being underpowered and the indices being highly correlated (r = .73).

Predictive Validity of HCR-20 V3 Risk Factors for Inpatient Violence in Forensic and Other Secure Psychiatric Settings

Four studies have been published on the association between the HCR-20 V3 and violence within forensic and other secure psychiatric settings: one from Canada; one from the United States; and two from Scotland. Hogan and Olver (2016) used archival data to evaluate this association amongst 99 patients (86% male) within a secure forensic setting. Roughly half had been adjudicated Not Criminally Responsible, and the other half were offenders with mental disorders, or patients referred to the facility (reasons not specified). The mean length of stay was roughly 19 months.

The authors reported AUC values both for Presence and Relevance Ratings of the risk factors, summed across scales. They also included the START, VRS, VRAG-R, and PCL-R. Effect sizes were largest for the Total Scale (Presence AUC = .76; Relevance AUC = .70), C Scale (Presence AUC = .76; Relevance AUC = .72), and R Scale (Presence AUC = .76; Relevance AUC = .72). They were smaller, though still significant, for the H Scale (Presence and Relevance AUCs = .64). Findings for the VRS and START—both of which also contain dynamic variables—were comparable to the HCR-20 V3 Total, C, and R Scales. The PCL-R total score and VRAG-R were not significantly predictive of violence.

Green et al. (2016) completed the HCR-20 V3 from the files of 100 male and 24 female insanity acquittees in New York and were interested in comparing the HCR-20 V3 across gender (despite the small N for female patients). Over a 15.5-month average follow-up, the point-biserial correlations for men ranged from small (R Scale r_{pb} = .18, ns) to large (C Scale r_{pb} = .48). The H Scale and Total Scale produced moderately sized, significant correlations (.33 and .41, respectively). For the female patients, none of the HCR-20 V3 indices were significantly correlated with violence, stemming from the small subsample size of 24. Three of the correlations were moderate in size (H, C, and Total, ranging from .27 to .31), whereas one (R) was near zero and negative (−.08). Given the small number of female patients, these particular findings should be interpreted with caution.

Neil et al. (2019) conducted a file-based, pseudo-prospective study of 75 male patients from the State Hospital in Edinburgh, Scotland (which also services Northern Ireland). Patients were resident for at least 2 years, and the follow-up period was 12 months. The authors also coded the SAPROF for protective factors. They reported AUC values that were higher, and significant, for the dynamic C and R Scales (.71 for C; .69 for R). The H Scale was not significantly predictive of violence. Multivariate logistic regression analyses indicated that the SAPROF did not add incrementally to the C and R Scales, entered together.

In another Scottish study, Smith, O'Rourke, and Macpherson (2020) recruited 167 male patients from three secure hospitals in Scotland (two medium secure and one high secure). The design was prospective for the majority of the sample, with some cases collected using a pseudo-prospective design. Also using a maximum of 12-month follow-up (range from 2–12 months), the authors, similar to Neil et al. (2019), found larger effects for the dynamic C and R Scales relative to the H Scale. For any violence, the (significant) AUC values for C and R were .72 and .64, whereas for the H Scale it was non-significant (.51). The Total Scale produced a significant AUC of .69. For physical violence, the C Scale, specifically, produced the largest AUC (.77), with the R Scale being lower, although still significant and of moderate size (.67). Again, the H Scale was not predictive of violence (.50). The Total Scale produced a significant AUC of .70.

Predictive Validity of HCR-20 V3 Risk Factors for Post-Discharge Community Violence in Civil Psychiatric and Correctional Settings

Two studies have been published using both civil psychiatric and correctional samples, evaluating the predictive validity of the HCR-20 V3 for post-release violence. In their Canadian study, Strub et al. (2014) evaluated both shorter-term violence (4–6 weeks post-discharge) and longer-term violence (6–8 months post-discharge) in a prospective study of 106 participants (56 offenders and 50 patients; 59% male). Baseline and community follow-up data were collected from multiple file sources, interviews, and self-report sessions with participants, and from collaterals, when possible. In general, the HCR-20 V3 indices were predictive of both shorter- and longer-term violence with moderate to large effect sizes, for both participant groups.

The authors tested the predictive utility of the HCR-20 V3 using point biserial correlation coefficients and Receiver Operating Characteristic (ROC) analyses. In the combined sample analyses, all Presence Ratings sums (i.e., H, C, R, and HCR-20 Total) were significantly associated with violence (all p's < .05). Correlations ranged from .26 to .46 and averaged .36. AUC values ranged from .71 to .78 and averaged .74. Similarly, for the combined sample analyses, all Relevance Ratings sums were significantly associated with violence (all p's < .05). Correlations ranged from .21 to .32 and averaged .27. Area Under the Curve (AUC) values ranged from .63 to .72 and averaged .68. Point biserial correlations and AUC values were also reported separately for each subsample and follow-up length. Relevance Ratings did not add incrementally to Presence Ratings for the H, C, R, and Total Scales (p > .05).

There were some differences in effect sizes across subsamples. For instance, the AUC values were stronger for the HCR-20 V3 Total Scale in the psychiatric sample (AUC = .88) than the correctional sample (AUC = .70) for shorter-term violence, whereas the contrary was true for longer-term violence (psychiatric AUC = .70; correctional AUC = .79). However, a series of logistic regression analyses revealed almost no formal moderation by sample, indicating, in general, comparable performance for patients and offenders.

Chen et al. (2020) performed a similar prospective study involving file reviews and interviews with 152 Chinese patients and offenders, using the authorized Chinese translation of the HCR-20 V3. Similar to Strub et al. (2014), they used both shorter-term (6 weeks) and longer-term (6 months) follow-up periods. They also reported effect sizes for the time period between 7 weeks and 6 months, although we do not focus on that here. As with Strub et al., the authors evaluated the Relevance Ratings in addition to the Presence Ratings.

At the 6-week follow-up, for Presence Ratings, AUC values were large for the patient subsample (all values significant unless otherwise noted): Total (.84), H (.77), C (.72), and R (.73). There was somewhat more variability for the offender subsample: Total (.75), H (.74), C (.58, ns), and R (.70), although most indices were strong. For Relevance Ratings at the 6-week follow-up, AUC values for the patient subsample were mainly large—Total (.80), H (.80), C (.68), and R (.73)—as they were for the offender subsample: Total (.76), H (.69), C (.71), and R (.74).

At the 6-month follow-up, for Presence Ratings, AUC values were large for the patient subsample for Total (.83) and H (.78), and moderate for C (.67) and R (.68). They were generally smaller for the offender subsample: Total (.67), H (.65, ns), C (.59, ns), and R (.69). For Relevance Ratings at the 6-month follow-up, AUC values for the patient subsample were again mainly large: Total (.81), H (.79), C (.73), and R (.76). There was again more variability within the offender subsample: Total (.72), H (.65, ns), C (.66), and R (.74).

Usefully, the authors reported mean effect sizes, across all combinations of follow-ups. For patients, the average r_{pb} for Presence Ratings was .35, and the average AUC was .74. The average r_{pb} for Relevance Ratings was .37, and the average AUC was .77. For offenders, the average r_{pb} for Presence Ratings was .25, and the average AUC was .68. The average r_{pb} for Relevance Ratings was noticeably higher, at .34, and the average AUC was .71.

The authors went further to test sample difference, reporting significant differences between mean effect sizes. AUC values were significantly higher for patients than offenders for H (Presence and Relevance) and Total (Presence), but they were higher for offenders for R (Relevance). In addition, in a series of logistic regression analyses in which subsample was tested for its moderation effects, only one analysis showed that the interaction between HCR-20 V3 index and sample added incrementally to the baseline model. Hence, on average, as with Strub et al. (2014), the subsample differences on average were neither systematic nor strong.

One primary difference in findings between this study and Strub et al. (2014) is the finding that Relevance Ratings tended to add incremental predictive validity to Presence Ratings. As noted in the HCR-20 V3 User Guide (Douglas et al., 2013), this is not a requirement for the validation of the instrument, as Relevance Ratings are intended primarily to inform practitioners' formulations. However, they are intended to do so by requiring evaluators to indicate which factors are most important in any given individual case. The following incremental effects (that is, significant improvement to logistic regression model fit upon entry of Relevance Ratings, once Presence Ratings were already in the model) were reported: R Scale, for 6-week follow-up; C, R, and Total Scales, at the 7-week to 6-month follow-up; and H, C, R, and Total Scale, at the 6-month follow-up.

Predictive and Incremental Validity of Summary Risk Ratings

Bivariate Association Between SRRs and Violence

One of the more important tests for SPJ instruments is whether the final risk estimate of Low, Moderate, or High Risk, or summary risk rating (SRR), is predictive of future violence. Proponents of the actuarial approach have for decades asserted that human judgment cannot equal, or surpass, algorithmic predictions (see, for example, Hilton et al., Chapter 7, this volume). Research on Version 2 of the HCR-20 and some other SPJ instruments, however, has soundly refuted these assertions. As reviewed by Heilbrun and colleagues in Chapter 1 of this volume, 39 of 45 such studies of SRRs have supported their predictive validity, and indeed, 16 of 18 studies that have tested the incremental predictive validity of these judgments vis-à-vis the predictive validity of the sums of risk factors (which, when used in such a manner, constitute actuarial prediction) have found incremental validity.

The pattern of findings for the HCR-20 V3 is consistent with these established findings in the risk assessment literature. Eight published studies have reported basic bivariate associations between SRRs and subsequent violence, mostly focusing on the omnibus rating Risk for Future Violence/Case Prioritization. As shown in Table 12.2, most AUC values have fallen in the .70s or .80s (with .71+ indicating a large effect size according to Rice & Harris, 2005). First averaging within sample, and then across samples, the average AUC for all SRRs is .73. For the "Risk for Future Violence" ratings (the omnibus rating), the average is .75.

Percent Violent Within Low-, Moderate-, and High-Risk Categories

Four of the aforementioned studies, plus an additional one (Penney et al., 2016), have evaluated the proportion of people within the Low, Moderate, or High Risk categories who have then subsequently committed acts of violence. These findings are shown in Figure 12.3. In the Low Risk category, the average is 7%; in the Moderate Risk category, it is 31%, and in the High Risk Category, it is 58%. Of course, these observations are influenced by factors such as follow-up length, base rates of violence, definitions of violence, and the number of methods used to detect violence. Despite these study differences, the results are clear—there are meaningful differences between judgments of low, moderate, and high risk in terms of expectations for violence that might follow.

It is worth noting that these analyses merely test the basic SPJ assumption that professionals are able to make sound decisions about risk level using measures such as the HCR-20 V3. They are not intended to represent probabilistic estimates of a given person's risk for violence, should he or she be judged to be low, moderate, or high risk. For instance, it would be inappropriate to state that Patient X, having been determined to be high risk, has a 58% probability of being violent. Rather, the take-home message is that there are meaningful and clear differences between risk categories in terms of expected future violence, and that professionals ought to have confidence in making such decisions and basing recommendations upon them. The research on the SRRs using the HCR-20 V3 is highly consistent with Version 2—as described in Heilbrun et al.'s opening chapter in this volume, 39 of 45 studies have found support for SRRs using V2, and 16 of 18 that tested their incremental validity against the actuarial use of the instruments' subscales found support for such incremental validity. We turn to this topic with respect to V3 now.

Table 12.2 Predictive Validity of HCR-20 V3 Summary Risk Ratings

Study	Sample	Index	AUC	r
Cawood (2017)	Workplace	Risk for Serious Violence	.70	
Chen et al. (2020)	Offenders, community, 6 weeks	Risk for Violence	.81	.45
	Offenders, community, 6 months	Risk for Violence	.77	.46
	Patients, community, 6 weeks	Risk for Violence	.82	.48
	Patients, community, 6 months	Risk for Violence	.82	.59
de Vogel et al. (2014)	Forensic, community, 1 year	Risk for Violence	.72	
	Forensic, community, 2 years	Risk for Violence	.67	
	Forensic, community, 3 years	Risk for Violence	.64	
	Forensic, community, 1 year	Risk for Violence (5-point)	.82	
	Forensic, community, 2 years	Risk for Violence (5-point)	.74	
	Forensic, community, 3 years	Risk for Violence (5-point)	.71	
Hogan and Olver (2016)	Forensic, inpatient	Risk for Violence	.68	
	Forensic, inpatient	Risk for Serious Violence	.44	
	Forensic, inpatient	Risk for Imminent Violence	.75	
Hogan and Olver (2019)	Forensic, community, pre-tx	Risk for Violence	.69	
	Forensic, community, pre-tx	Risk for Serious Violence	.53	
	Forensic, community, pre-tx	Risk for Imminent Violence	.68	
	Forensic, community, post-tx	Risk for Violence	.73	
	Forensic, community, post-tx	Risk for Serious Violence	.48	
	Forensic, community, post-tx	Risk for Imminent Violence	.66	
Neil et al. (2019)	Forensic, inpatient	HCR-SAPROF IFRJ, Violence	.80	.55
Persson et al. (2017)	Forensic, community	Risk for Violence	.74	
Strub et al. (2014)	Offenders, community, 4–6 weeks	Risk for Violence	.72	.34
	Offenders, community, 6–8 months	Risk for Violence	.68	.33
	Patients, community, 4–6 weeks	Risk for Violence	.91	.51
	Patients, community, 6–8 months	Risk for Violence	.74	.48

Note: AUCs of .44 (Hogan & Olver, 2016) and .53/.48/.66 (Hogan & Olver, 2019) are not significant. All other AUCs and r's are significant. The HCR-SAPROF IFRJ is the "Integrated Final Risk Judgment" of Low, Moderate, or High risk based on the combined analysis of the HCR-20 V3 and the SAPROF (Neil et al., 2019). In de Vogel et al. (2014), the authors, in addition to the traditional SRR of Low, Moderate, or High, also tested a 5-point system that included "Low-Moderate" and "Moderate-High" ratings.

Incremental Predictive Validity of SRRs Compared to Numeric Totals of Scales

Several studies have tested whether the HCR-20 V3 SRRs improve significantly on the use of its subscales, used in a numeric or actuarial manner. The basic logic of such tests is to first enter the total or subscales into a regression model (linear, logistic, etc., depending on the distribution of the outcome), which thereby optimizes the statistical association between the numeric value of the total or subscale scores, and the outcome of violence. This is an actuarial use of the instrument, in that such an analysis can produce weights that define an estimated numeric probability of violence, depending on a person's score on the scale. Then, the human judgments of low, moderate, or high risk are entered on a subsequent step of the regression model. If they enter the model, adding significantly to it (and thereby explaining a significantly higher proportion of the variance than the scales alone), then the SRRs are said to have incremental validity. An additional evaluative step is to observe which of the predictors in the final model (that is, the scales and the SRRs) are individually significant. In many instances, only the SRRs remain significant and hence solely account for the instrument's predictive validity.

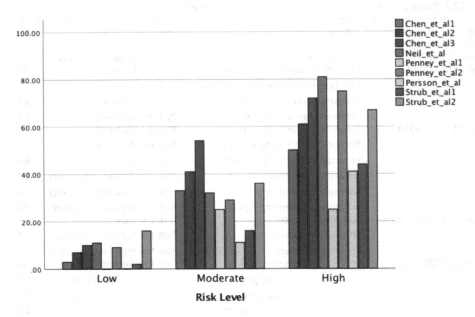

Figure 12.3 Percent of Violence Within Low, Moderate, and High Risk Categories

Chen et al. (2020) tested the incremental predictive validity of SRRs against the total scores on the HCR-20 V3, as well as against the subscales (both Presence and Relevance Ratings in separate analyses), in their Chinese sample of offenders and patients. In a series of logistic regression analyses, SRRs added incrementally to each analysis and were significant in each final model. In a number of analyses, the numeric use of the HCR-20 V3 was no longer significant once the SRRs were in the model. Similarly, Strub et al. (2014), in their Canadian sample of offenders and patients, reported that SRRs added incrementally to all analyses, both of Presence and Relevance Ratings for short-term (4–6 weeks) and longer-term (6–8 months) follow-ups. Neil et al. (2019) tested the incremental validity of the SAPROF and the HCR-SAPROF Integrated Final Risk Judgment (IFRJ)—a SRR based on the combined use of the HCR-20 V3 and the SAPROF—against the numeric use of the C and R Scales. Although the SAPROF numeric score did not add incrementally to the C and R index, the IFRJ did.

Dynamic Predictive Validity

A core assumption of the HCR-20 V3—and indeed a hallmark of the SPJ model—is that its putatively changeable, or dynamic, risk factors, are indeed capable of indexing change over time. Moreover, when changes occur on these risk factors, it should be the case that the occurrence of violence follows suit. Several studies of the HCR-20 V3 have tested these assumptions. Two studies by Hogan and Olver on the same sample, one for forensic inpatient violence (2016) and the other for post-discharge community violence (2019), reported evidence for dynamic predictive validity. The Presence and Relevance Ratings of both the C and R Scales significantly declined across pre- and post-treatment. Further, in both studies, changes in both the Presence and Relevance Ratings of the C and R Scales added incremental validity to the prediction of subsequent violence, relative to baseline HCR-20 V3 scores, with the exception of one analysis (change in R Scale Presence Ratings for inpatient violence).

Penney et al. (2016) reported that C and R Scale scores declined over time in their sample of 87 forensic patients discharged to the community, for those who were higher than the median on the H Scale (that is, had higher "historical" risk). They also reported that over time, significantly more patients were rated as low risk at follow-up (38%) relative to baseline (18%), and fewer were rated as moderate risk (76% vs. 54%). Changes on the C and R Scales significantly predicted both future violence and rehospitalization, adding incrementally to scores on the H Scale.

Coid et al. (2015) used multilevel modeling to account for multiple measurement periods, and reported that, at a bivariate level, most C and R risk factors were predictive of violence within the same 6-month period. Using multivariate analyses, three dynamic HCR-20 V3 factors (Violent Ideation or Intent; Instability; Stress/Coping) were uniquely associated with violence, with large odds ratios (6.98, 5.41, and 8.35, respectively) and accounted for the other items' associations with violence as well.

Finally, Mastromanno et al. (2018) measured changes in the C and R Scales across two time-frames (first 2 months and last 2 months of treatment), in their sample of 40 forensic inpatients. Although there were significant changes in the C and R Scales across time (the former improving and the latter worsening), these changes were not associated with violence either on their own in bivariate analyses, or in multivariate analyses that included HCR-20 V3 baseline scores as well. Given that studies that have used larger samples have reported dynamic validity, it is possible that the combination of file-only ratings (which makes the rating of C and R items more challenging) and a small sample contributed to the null findings. It could also be that the changes that were observed were too far detached from outcomes (the follow-up period was up to 13 years).

Potential Moderating Effects (Gender; Setting)

Several studies have tested whether the HCR-20 V3 performs comparably across gender or setting. Findings are consistent with evidence for Version 2 of the HCR-20 that predictive validity does not appear to vary across gender or settings. For instance, Strub et al. (2014; see also Strub, Douglas, and Nicholls, 2016), in their sample of 106 male and female offenders and patients, conducted formal moderation analyses both for gender, and for setting (patient vs. offender sample)—in neither instance did the predictive validity vary across groups. Similarly, Chen et al. (2020), in their sample of 152 male and female offenders and patients, reported the absence of moderation effects. De Vogel et al. (2019) did not test moderation per se, but rather tested the predictive validity of the HCR-20 V3 in an all-female sample of 78 forensic patients. As reviewed earlier, AUCs for the total score ranged from .67 to .71, depending on the follow-up length, and the authors concluded that the C Scale (along with the START Vulnerability Scale) was amongst the more promising predictive indices. Finally, Green et al. (2016) compared correlations between the HCR-20 V3 and violence for 24 female and 100 male forensic patients. As reviewed earlier, although some predictive indices were smaller for women than men, none of the differences were significant. Given the small number of women in this study, it is difficult to draw firm conclusions one way or the other.

Summary of Predictive Validity

The pattern of validity findings reviewed herein are highly similar to the pattern of validity findings with Version 2 of the HCR-20. There is strong evidence that HCR-20 V3 risk factors are predictive of future violence, with some indication that the C and R Scales might be more strongly related to institutional or perhaps shorter-term violence. This finding makes conceptual sense, given that these risk factors are more likely to change in the short-term relative to the H Scale factors. There is emerging evidence that the Relevance Ratings—which form the basis for formulation—also have predictive validity, and indeed may show incremental effects above and beyond Presence Ratings. More research is needed on this point, however. There is clear support for the validity of the human-generated summary risk ratings, both in terms of their simple bivariate association with future violence as well as their incremental validity above and beyond the linear, algorithmic, combination of sums of risk factors. This finding is consistent with the conclusions drawn by Heilbrun and colleagues in their chapter with respect to the SPJ model more broadly. Further, there is good evidence from several studies that the C and R Scales can capture change, and that this change is predictive of subsequent violence, hence supporting the dynamic predictive validity of the instrument. Finally, there is little evidence that the validity of the HCR-20 is affected by gender, or by setting. In total, then, the primary assumptions of the HCR-20 V3 all appear to have solid empirical backing.

Limitations and Necessary Future Research

Although the research conducted to date on the HCR-20 V3 supports a number of its most important basic tenets (interrater reliability and predictive validity of risk factor ratings and SRRs; incremental validity of SRRs; dynamic predictive validity, or the predictive validity of changes in HCR-20 V3 risk factor presence and relevance), a number of areas warrant more attention. Of course, we will always recommend and welcome additional research and evaluation of basic tenets in additional samples and contexts.

Research on formulation and scenario planning is sparse in the risk assessment field, despite each topic having considerable evidence outside of the field. Establishing their reliability is a first step. Evaluations of formulation could focus on the extent to which they improve risk management plans—i.e., are risk management plans more closely tailored to key risk factors? Are a greater proportion of relevant risk factors addressed compared to when formulation is not used? Do key stakeholders consider them useful? Further, it is possible that formulation increases evaluators' understanding of individual cases, which could enhance predictive validity. This could be evaluated in a research design that compared decision-making with and without the use of formulation. Similarly, to the extent that formulation might produce more informed risk management plans, researchers could test whether the use of formulation leads to lower rates of violence in the future.

Many of the topics that can be evaluated vis-à-vis formulation could also be evaluated with respect to scenario planning (i.e., improved quality of risk management; increased validity). Studies could also address whether posited scenarios actually are more likely to come to fruition compared to non-posited scenarios. This, of course, is very complicated if people are specifically acting to prevent scenarios from unfolding. Hence, unobtrusive measurement would be key. For instance, scenarios would have to be constructed without influencing actual practice, preferably using archived cases. Subsequent acts of violence would be compared to the scenarios that were constructed.

Another key purposes of the SPJ approach is to prevent subsequent violence through risk management. Evaluating risk management should consist of whether using V3 increases the quality of risk management plans. The ultimate test is whether the use of V3 to construct management plans actually reduces violence compared to assessment/management approaches that do not use V3.

As reviewed in Slobogin's Chapter 4 in this volume, there has been a great deal of attention paid recently to whether risk assessment instruments unfairly over-estimate the risk of ethnic minority people (see also Starr, 2014). In some instances, certain instruments are described as containing "proxies for race," to use the phrase offered by former Attorney General Eric Holder in a speech on the topic. As Slobogin describes, there have been unsuccessful attempts to abolish the use of certain instruments. In Canada, the use of the PCL-R and certain actuarial instruments (such as the VRAG) with Indigenous offenders was declared impermissible by the highest court in Canada, the Supreme Court of Canada, because they were not adequately validated with these offenders (*Ewert v. Canada*, 2018; see also Hart, 2016).

Regardless of legal objections or outcomes, the field simply has the obligation to ensure that its instruments are indeed fair across different groups of people. SPJ instruments—being highly focused on individual understanding of people—might be well suited to ensure that evaluees' culture, ethnicity, race, gender, sexual orientation, and other personal characteristics and lived experiences are well integrated into the understanding and formulation of their risk, possible scenarios of concern, and risk-relevant management and intervention plans. As such, we would strongly encourage more research on the HCR-20 V3 with fairness and diversity at the forefront.

Finally, we would encourage research on the "real world" reliability and validity, and the implementation of the HCR-20 V3, into systems and agencies. As is well known in the field of implementation science, a great many factors that are seemingly irrelevant to the assessment or task at hand influence whether it works in the way it is intended to work (Damschroder et al., 2009; Vincent, Guy, & Grisso, 2012). Principles of implementation science must be brought to bear on the next generation of violence risk assessment research.

Case Example (Condensed)

Referral Questions and Sources of Information

Janice Hodgson is a 26-year-old White female admitted to the Secure Forensic Hospital (SFH) on February 23, 2015, after being found Not Guilty by Reason of Insanity (NGRI) for a charge of Assault Causing Bodily Harm and Failure to Comply with a Restraining Order. She is diagnosed with Paranoid Schizophrenia. This was her first admission to SFH. She has a Review Board hearing scheduled for August 29, 2016.

A comprehensive violence risk assessment was conducted to inform the decision of the Review Board. The key referral questions were: (a) What is the level of risk posed by Ms. Hodgson, should she be released into the community? (b) What risk management strategies would mitigate this risk? The risk assessment included an interview of three hours' duration with Mr. Hodgson, and a review of her institutional files.

Background Information

Family History

Ms. Hodgson was born in Sometown, Michigan. Her parents separated when she was 7 years old and she and her older brother spent time with both parents while growing up. Ms. Hodgson recalls witnessing occasional verbal and physical abuse between her parents prior to their separation. She can recall two instances when her father physically abused her mother—once he slapped her across the face during a heated argument (she cannot recall what the argument was about), and the second time her father grabbed her mother by the arms and pushed her against the wall after he questioned her about money issues. Following the separation, her parents were on mainly amicable terms and made decisions regarding both children together. She had a good relationship with both parents as well as her brother, and there is no evidence of any abuse being perpetrated against the children.

Education History

Ms. Hodgson enjoyed school as a child and received good grades (A's and B's). She did not have any problems at school and did not cause trouble. She was not involved in fighting or bullying and was never suspended or expelled. She graduated from high school with honors and has taken courses in art and writing since then.

Employment History

Following high school, Ms. Hodgson worked with her father at his restaurant as a waitress for approximately one year. She left that job when she was able to find employment where she felt she could use her artistic and creative talent, including painting work and various art projects. Both the painting and art project employment was sporadic, dependent upon work available. She was able to hold both jobs at the same time and left after approximately one year due to the inconsistency of her schedule. She was unemployed for 2 months until she found a job at a law office. She enjoyed this job as it provided her with a steady Monday-to-Friday schedule, but she was laid off after almost two years due to cutbacks. Ms. Hodgson claims she was a good worker, was always on time, did not skip work, did not use drugs or alcohol while on the job, and never had any conflicts with coworkers or her employer.

Since being laid off (age 22), Ms. Hodgson has not been employed and has lived off of her disability benefits. She ran into money troubles a few months after she lost her job, was unable to pay rent, was evicted from her apartment and returned home to live with her mother. She had two jobs in offices as a clerk, but was somewhat unreliable, missing some shifts, and quitting shortly after starting. Over the next few years she moved back and forth between living with her mother and living with her boyfriend. Prior to her index offense, Ms. Hodgson was unemployed, collecting social assistance and living with her mother.

Substance Abuse History

Ms. Hodgson first tried alcohol at the age of 15. There is no evidence that she had a significant problem with her alcohol use, and she also denies that she had any problems (e.g., fights, crime) when drinking. Her heaviest alcohol use was from 15 to 16 years old, but even at this time her drinking was restricted to weekend use only. After age 16, she drank only on occasion in social settings.

Ms. Hodgson first used drugs (marijuana) at age 16. She later tried LSD and mushrooms, but used these on only one occasion. Her marijuana use was more of a problem in her life. She felt that marijuana made her telepathic, and she became temporarily obsessed with it, using a heavy quantity on a daily basis from age 17 to 19 and again from age 23 until the time of her index offense (age 25). She states that her marijuana use contributed to her inability to pay her rent and eviction from her apartment.

Relationship History

Ms. Hodgson has had one significant relationship that lasted for approximately four years off and on, from the ages of 20 to 24. Over these years, the couple lived together and became engaged. The relationship was noted as being both verbally and physically abusive, with each perpetrating abuse against the other. This partner is the victim of her index offense (described later) and the two are no longer in contact (as a result of a court-ordered restraining order against Ms. Hodgson). She admits that she still has feelings for him and would like to get back together.

Mental Health History

Ms. Hodgson has had mental illness problems since she was a child. Her first contact with a mental health professional was when she was 8 years old, when she developed a fear of food and putting anything into her mouth. She was hospitalized for two weeks. Following her release from the hospital, Ms. Hodgson met with an art therapist because she was withdrawn and was still having trouble eating.

Ms. Hodgson claims that she was fine for several years after this initial episode, but in her late teens, her symptoms began to re-emerge. At the age of 18, she was admitted to a hospital for one week due to active symptoms such as auditory and visual hallucinations, slowed speech and physical movement, and emotional instability. She was diagnosed with Schizophrenia during this admission. After her release, she was followed by a community mental health team. Reports from her treatment team indicate that Ms. Hodgson struggled with medication compliance and her mental health continued to deteriorate.

In April 2012, Ms. Hodgson was admitted to the hospital at the request of her father. This admission was a result of her bizarre behavior. Following a verbal fight with her sister-in-law, she left for a walk. When she returned back to the house, she refused to talk and threw a "temper tantrum"—crying and banging her fists on the walls and ground. She then went into a fit of rage and had a physical scuffle with her father. Following this admission, she was accepted into an Early Psychosis Program. Throughout the summer of 2012 she reported to her community treatment team and complied with her medications. While reporting to the treatment team, she expressed paranoid ideations about demons inhabiting her partner and her mother. Her medications were adjusted and her paranoid delusions decreased.

In October 2012, Ms. Hodgson began to complain to her partner that someone was trying to poison her. Consequently, she was again admitted to a psychiatric hospital. On admission, her speech was disorganized with loosening of logical associations. She was having persecutory delusions of being poisoned and auditory hallucinations of a male and female talking to each other in a derogatory fashion. She was released after nine days.

In January 2013, Ms. Hodgson was again noncompliant with her medications and her symptoms re-emerged. She lost her motivation to complete the art course in which she was enrolled. By March 2013, she had discontinued all of her medications and was smoking marijuana daily. She began to experience auditory hallucinations. Her treatment team attempted to restart her on her medications, but when they would not support her idea for a vitamin-only treatment she discontinued meeting with them.

Eventually, she started on her medications again, but in May 2014 she discontinued them because she felt they were poisoning her. Her mental state deteriorated and she exhibited decreased appetite and weight loss. She had delusions that she had special powers and that she was Jennifer Aniston's twin (actor). She was experiencing auditory hallucinations, thought insertion, thought broadcasting, and referential ideation involving TV and radio. She was admitted to hospital on June 1, 2014, and released June 15, 2014. At discharge, she denied any auditory hallucinations. Her next contact with a mental health professional occurred as a result of her index offense (described next).

Criminal History

Ms. Hodgson's index offense occurred after discontinuing medications, and while she was experiencing acute symptoms including persecutory delusions. Prior to the index offense, she had no formal criminal history; this was her first contact with police (age 25), although as mentioned previously, she had both perpetrated and been the victim of minor physical aggression with her partner, and, as described next, she had two more serious acts of violence against her partner shortly before the index offense. The victim of her index offense was her on-again, off-again partner. The first assault against her partner occurred in October 2014 when Ms. Hodgson slapped her partner and threw a knife at him, causing him minor wounds (she was not charged for this).

In December 2014, the victim had gone for a vacation to a family cottage. She followed her partner to the cottage, snuck in, and ran up behind him with a large stick. She hit him on the head; he turned around and she hit him again, causing bruises and a black eye. He ran out of the cottage, left in his vehicle, and called the police. Following this assault, a restraining order was granted and she was to have no contact with her partner. At this time Ms. Hodgson again moved back with her mother and continued to experience delusions.

From December 2014 to February 2015, Ms. Hodgson did not contact her partner, but continued to experience active symptoms. On February 23, 2015, she severely attacked her ex-partner. Ms. Hodgson still had a key for his apartment, and let herself in when she knew he wasn't there. Once he returned home, she surprised him and sprayed him in the face with cooking spray. She then hit and kicked him numerous times in the face, head, back, and arms as he was holding his face in pain. The assault was stopped when police arrived at the apartment shortly after the assault commenced. A neighbor had heard the yelling and called the police immediately after she knocked on the victim's door and did not receive a response. Fortunately, there was a police officer in the immediate vicinity. The victim suffered lacerations in his facial area which required stitches and will likely leave permanent scarring on his forehead and cheek. He required treatment to the retinas of both eyes to repair damage in them caused by the impact of the assault.

After being arrested, she was immediately brought to SFH for an assessment (February 23, 2005). At trial, she was found NGRI on the charges of Assault Causing Bodily Harm and Failure to Comply with Restraining Order, and has been committed to SFH since her admission on February 23, 2015. She had remained at SFH throughout her trial, which was short and took place quickly after the index offense.

Adjustment After Hospitalization

On admission to hospital, Ms. Hodgson was yelling and complaining that her partner was an alien, and that she was going to harm him again. When she arrived at the hospital, she was secluded due to her agitated state. When the psychiatrist was finally able to interview Ms. Hodgson, she noted that her affect was blunted, she had poor eye contact and her responses were delayed and vague. She told the psychiatrist she attacked the victim because she feared that he was an alien and was going to hurt her, but she denied that she was still experiencing delusions or hallucinations. She also reported that she had special powers such as telepathy, telekinesis, and astral travel. She told the psychiatrist that she knew karate and astrophysics without being taught either of them. It was later learned that Ms. Hodgson had discontinued her medications yet again a few weeks prior to the last assault.

In her first few months on the unit, Ms. Hodgson was cooperative with the routine, but needed multiple prompts before she would respond. She did not socialize with anyone and spent a lot of time sitting in the dark staring out the window. In June 2015, it appeared that her mental state was deteriorating again as she reported that others could read her thoughts and that she was allergic to the protein in milk. She felt that it is why she had been catatonic while in the hospital.

However, as of August 2015, Ms. Hodgson has steadily improved. She continued to be cooperative with the unit routine but no longer required multiple prompts to respond. Ms. Hodgson's last Review Board hearing was on January 5, 2016. Her next hearing is scheduled for August 29, 2016.

Recent Functioning (January 2016–August 2016)

At Ms. Hodgson's January 2016 Review Board hearing, the Board acknowledged that Ms. Hodgson had made significant improvements during her months at SFH but was concerned because she had only shown these improvements in the past 6 months. The Board decided that 6 months was too short a time to be convinced that she posed little risk if released and decided to continue her hospitalization. Following her Review Board, the staff noted that she reacted well to their decision. She did not suffer any relapse and remained motivated with her treatment plan.

Since January 2016, the staff have found Ms. Hodgson to be polite and quiet, and have noted that she gets along well with other patients. There have been no problems with medication non-compliance and Ms. Hodgson appears to understand that the medications are important for her health. She has become involved in the programs recommended by her treatment team. She is currently attending a relapse prevention program and successfully completed a symptom management program (June 2016). Her summary report from the symptom management program indicates that Ms. Hodgson was a good participant: she contributed to group discussions, attended all sessions, and completed all homework assignments.

Ms. Hodgson's brother and mother visit frequently, as do a few of her friends from the community. Over the past 6 months, Ms. Hodgson has spent a significant amount of time with family members away from the hospital and has not had any problems. There is only one occasion where Ms. Hodgson returned late from a day leave, but she called the hospital in advance to inform the staff. Ms. Hodgson spends a great deal of her leisure time writing or doing artwork. She has recently started attending a recreation center and swims laps three times a week. In March 2016, she expressed interest in obtaining a part-time job. However, she learned about a creative writing class being offered and decided to participate in this instead, stating that she thought it would be too stressful to try to do both the course and work part-time.

Ms. Hodgson feels her mental illness is to blame for her violence, and realizes the impact that using marijuana and not complying with her required medications has had on her mental state, symptoms, and behavior. She stated that she believes that it is necessary for her to continue on her medications. She is described by staff as very motivated to return to the community, but with some anxiety about stressors involved when this occurs. Marijuana use has not been a problem for Ms. Hodgson. She was been subjected to five drug screens since January 2016 and all have returned negative.

Release Plans

Ms. Hodgson has made a number of plans for her release from hospital. She will live with her mother, who is very supportive, and she has already made arrangements for her rent to be transferred from her disability benefits to her mother each month. She would like to resume courses at college, but it is not in her immediate plan because of stress limits. She would like to re-establish herself in the community, start her treatment, and then look into the courses of interest.

Plans have been made for Ms. Hodgson to attend an NGRI group at the outpatient clinic nearest to her residence. She will be assigned a case manager and a psychiatrist at this location and will attend appointments as recommended by them. At the moment, she does not plan to attend any special programming (beside the NGRI group). She states that will continue to comply with her medications, which she now finds easier to do since they are given by injection every couple of weeks and she now suffers few side effects.

She is aware that if she stops her medications, her symptoms will return. If her symptoms begin to worsen, she states that her plan is to contact her psychiatrist. She also has a verbal agreement with her mother that if she notes any deterioration in her mental state, she will immediately notify her treatment team at the outpatient clinic.

Ms. Hodgson is close with her parents, her stepmother, and brother. Her stepmother and mother have been very involved in her current admission and have met with her treatment team on two occasions to understand how to help her while in the community. Both have expressed their willingness to support Ms. Hodgson on release, as has the rest of her family. Her brother has offered an opportunity for her to work part-time in his garden landscaping company once she is settled in the community and ready to work.

Ms. Hodgson also has the support of a few close friends who have remained in touch while she was in hospital. Her friends evidently are prosocial and not involved in any criminal activity or drugs. In particular, she has one close friend who also suffers from a mental illness, and the two have been a source of support for each other while dealing with their illness.

Ms. Hodgson reports feeling anxious about the future and not knowing what will happen, but has tried to arrange her post-release life so it does not have too many stressors. She plans to spend her leisure time running, swimming, writing, and being with her close friends or family. She does not think she will have a problem staying away from drugs and alcohol as she has a better understanding of the effect drugs have on her mental state and she will be associating with individuals who do not use drugs. The main source of her stress will be trying to deal with her ex-partner's family.

Ms. Hodgson does not feel that she is at risk of committing a new crime when released to the community.

Risk Assessment

In order to inform my judgment of risk, I used the HCR-20 Version 3 (Historical-Clinical-Risk Management-20) violence risk assessment instrument. This instrument has been shown through research to facilitate consistency in clinical evaluations of risk for violence, and that its risk factors and judgments of risk based upon them help evaluators to determine whether an individual poses a low, moderate, or high level of future risk for violence. This HCR-20 V3 includes 20 risk factors to consider (see Table 12.1), along with standard instructions for how to rate them; I determined whether each of these risk factors was present for Ms. Hodgson, and if so, how relevant they are in terms of explaining her past violence, or whether they would interfere with management strategies in the future.

The HCR-20 V3 includes 10 Historical risk factors—past events, experiences, or conditions that are known to increase the risk for violence. I determined that there were definite problems in six areas (i.e., risk factors): previous violence (H1), relationships (H3), employment (H4), substance use (H5), major mental illness (H6), and treatment or supervision response (H10: she violated a restraining order and was noncompliant with medication while in hospital). There were partial problems in two areas: other antisocial behavior (H2), and some potentially traumatic experiences within relationships, such as experiencing physical altercations between parents, and suffering minor acts of aggression from her former partner (H8). The most important, or relevant, risk factors in this domain include previous violence (H1), relationship problems (H3), mental disorder (H6), and substance use problems (H5). Risk factors of moderate relevance include treatment or supervision response (H10) and traumatic experiences (H8).

In terms of recent functioning, the HCR-20 V3 includes five risk factors on its Clinical scale that are intended to summarize a person's recent emotional, behavioral, and cognitive functioning. I determined whether these risk factors were present within the past six months—since Ms. Hodgson's last Review Board Hearing. I determined that none of the risk factors was definitely present, and one was partially present: insight problems (C1), in that she tends to blame her mental illness entirely for her offense, she may still want to get back together with the past boyfriend she assaulted, and she feels she poses "no risk."

The HCR-20 V3 Risk Management scale includes five risk factors that pertain to an individual's possible future living circumstances. I rated these risk factors as if Ms. Hodgson were to be released into the community, rather than for continued hospitalization. That is, I determined, given her current release planning, whether the risk factors would be present if she were released into the community by the Review Board next month. I used a 6- to 12-month timeframe for these ratings. I determined that four of the five Risk Management risk factors were partially present: problems with her plans for professional supervision, in that substance use problems are not adequately addressed (R1); living situation (R2), in that she plans to live with her mother, who, though supportive, has been a subject of her delusional beliefs in the past, a fact which has not been dealt with adequately; treatment or supervision response (R4), in that she has been noncompliant in the past and could benefit explicitly from interventions geared toward ensuring compliance; and stress and coping (R5), in that she has had problems in the past in this area, and is feeling somewhat anxious about her transition to the community. Of the C and R factors, the most relevant are insight problems, professional services, and living situation.

It is clear that, despite these areas of concern, Ms. Hodgson has made considerable progress, and in many ways is doing well, even within her areas of risk. For instance, she has recently been compliant, and her symptoms have subsided. She has not been using substances. She has good and reasonable plans after discharge, and support from friends and relatives. However, there do appear to be further opportunities to improve Ms. Hodgson's prospects for success, such as adding substance use treatment, further collaboration and education with her mother concerning signs and symptoms of mental disorder, and awareness raising in terms of her possible tendency to be noncompliant, and to underestimate her risk.

In terms of explaining her previous violence, Ms. Hodgson's mental disorder (schizophrenia [H6], including paranoid delusions [C3]), exacerbated historically through substance use problems (H5), and relationship troubles (H8) have led to some past difficulties establishing trusting relationships with care providers, authorities, and employers, as well as with family members, prospective friends, and intimate partners (H3, H4, H10). In particular, she has had a conflictual, distrustful, and somewhat unstable relationship with her past intimate partner. When acutely psychotic (H6, C3), and not coping well with stress (C4, R5), she would have thoughts of harming her partner (C2), motivated by a perceived need to defend herself against prospective harm, and to assert control over her partner through acts of violence (H1).

Currently, moderate insight problems (C1) may have contributed to a somewhat underdeveloped community risk management plan, in terms of certain aspects of intervention (R1, she should consider substance use treatment), her living situation (R2, her mother should be educated on early warning signs of psychosis), her potential for noncompliance (R4, she should consider counseling sessions devoted to compliance), and stress and coping (R5, although currently not experiencing serious difficulties, she could benefit from counseling focusing on problem solving and coping with stress).

If Ms. Hodgson were to act violently in the future, the most likely scenario would be a repeat of her past violence, against her former, or a new, intimate partner. In this scenario, there would be a relapse into psychosis, likely preceded by stress, substance use, or noncompliance with medication, and she would feel a need to protect herself from her partner. The harm could be severe. The risk for this currently is low, and not imminent. It is also possible that, should she relapse into psychosis and is without an intimate partner, then another person with whom she is in close contact, such as her mother, or a treatment provider, might become part of her delusional thinking, and hence be at risk to be victimized. Again, the risk for this scenario currently is low.

In terms of management plans, there are a number of features of her plans that are strong, including supportive counseling, assignment of a case manager, presence of personal support, and a reasonable degree (that is, not too demanding) of vocational and recreational activities. In terms of *monitoring*, she should be seen at least once per week to start by her case manager, as well as by a psychiatrist, to monitor her medication. Her support network should be further educated on common signs of deterioration, and how these might manifest specifically for her, so they can provide feedback to the treatment team. Any signs of stress, arguments, change in demeanor, suspicion, contact with her former boyfriend, establishment of a new relationship, should lead to a re-evaluation of risk. In terms of *supervision*, there does not appear to be a need for her to remain in a secure hospital facility, or even in a supervised staffed home; that is, her plans to live—for now—with her mother, appear reasonable. However, should any of the warning signs listed above emerge, there should be plans in place to provide a living situation where her mother, and her past or (if applicable) new partner, would be safe. In terms of *treatment*, although her supportive group counseling will be helpful, she should also consider counseling for substance use, medication compliance, and coping with stress. Finally, as mentioned, her personal support network should all be educated on signs of decompensation, how to interact with her should she begin to decompensate, and what steps to take if these emerge (i.e., immediately contact case manager; assist her in making her appointments; if need be, not being in close physical proximity).

Currently, Ms. Hodgson's risk for violence in the community over the coming 12 months must be considered moderate, but manageable. Her risk for imminent violence over the coming days to weeks is low, because her most relevant risk factors are, for the most part, being adequately managed, and she has had a good period of time with healthy functioning. However, her overall risk must be considered moderate because there are a number of risk factors that currently are not explicitly addressed by her management plans (substance use; noncompliance; coping with stress). The prospects for Ms. Hodgson's overall risk to move from moderate to low appear good, pending the further development of her management plans.

Note

1. This study is included under the "Correctional" section because in the Netherlands, most forensic patients do not have a major mental illness. Indeed, in the current larger sample of 86 patients, only 20% had a psychotic diagnosis, with 63% having personality disorder (primarily Cluster B) as the primary diagnosis. As such, despite being a "legal" forensic sample, in reality it is more akin to a correctional sample.

References

Adams, J., Thomas, S. D. M., Mackinnon, T., & Eggleton, D. (2018). The risk, needs and stages of recovery of a complete forensic patient cohort in an Australian state. *BMC Psychiatry, 18*, 35.

Amer, M., Daim, T. U., & Jetter, A. A. (2013). Review of scenario planning. *Futures Elsevier Ltd., 46*, 23–40.

Andrews, D. A., & Bonta, J. (1995). *Level of service inventory-revised*. Toronto, ON: Multi-Health Systems.

Belfrage, H. (2015). Upgrading the practical use of the historical clinical risk management—20 in forensic psychiatric treatment: The process of going from version 2 to version 3 at two forensic psychiatric hospitals. *Journal of Threat Assessment and Management, 2*, 33–39.

Bjørkly, S., Eidhammer, G., & Selmer, L. E. (2014). Concurrent validity and clinical utility of the HCR-20V3 compared with the HCR-20 in forensic mental health nursing: Similar tools but improved method. *Journal of Forensic Nursing, 10*(4), 1–9, 234–242.

Cabeldue, M., Green, D., Griswold, H., Schneider, M., Smith, J., Belfi, B., & Kunz, M. (2018). Using the HCR-20V3 to differentiate insanity acquittees based on opinions of readiness for transfer. *Journal of the American Academy of Psychiatry and Law, 46*, 339–350.

Cawood, J. S. (2017). The interrater reliability and predictive validity of the HCR-20V3 in common workplace environments. *Journal of Threat Assessment and Management, 4*(1), 1–11. doi:10.1037/tam0000071

Chaimowitz, G., & Mamak, M. (2011). *Companion guide to the aggressive incidents scale and the Hamilton anatomy of risk management*. Hamilton, ON: St. Joseph's Healthcare.

Chen, Y., Douglas, K. S., Yu, Y., Zhang, Z., Liu, X., Xiao, C., . . . Ma, A. (2020). *Evaluating the HCR-20V3 violence risk assessment measure with mentally disordered offenders and civil psychiatric patients in China*. Manuscript under review.

Cheng, J., Haag, A. M., & Olver, M. E. (2019). Predictors of historical clinical risk management-20 version 3 (HCR-20: V3) summary risk ratings. *Psychiatry, Psychology and Law, 26*, 682–692.

Chermack, T. J., & Lynham, S. A. (2002). Definitions and outcome variables of resource planning. *Human Resource Development Review*, *1*, 366–383.

Coid, J. W., Kallis, C., Doyle, M., Shaw, J., & Ullrich, S. (2015). Identifying causal risk factors for violence among discharged patients. *PLoS One*, *10*(11), e0142493.

Cook, A. N., & Hart, S. D. (2017). Violence risk assessment across nations and across cultures: Legal, clinical, and scientific considerations. In R. Roesch & A. N. Cook (Eds.), *Handbook of forensic mental health services* (pp. 131–152). New York: Routledge, Taylor & Francis Group.

Cook, A. N., Moulden, H. M., Mamak, M., Lalani, S., Messina, K., & Chaimowitz, G. (2018). Validating the Hamilton anatomy of risk management—forensic version and the aggressive incidents scale. *Assessment*, *25*, 432–445.

Cooke, D. J., Hart, S. D., Logan, C., & Michie, C. (2004). *Comprehensive assessment of psychopathic personality—institutional rating scale (CAPP-IRS)*. Unpublished manuscript, Glasgow Caledonian University, Glasgow.

Cooke, D. J., Hart, S. D., Logan, C., & Michie, C. (2012). Explicating the construct of psychopathy: Development and validation of a conceptual model, the comprehensive assessment of psychopathic personality (CAPP). *International Journal of Forensic Mental Health*, *11*, 242–252.

Damschroder, L. J., Aron, D. C., Keith, R. E., Kirsh, S. R., Alexander, J. A., & Lowery, J. C. (2009). Fostering implementation of health services research findings into practice: A consolidated framework for advancing implementation science. *Implementation Science*, *4*, 50.

de Vogel, V., Bruggeman, M., & Lancel, M. (2019). Gender-sensitive violence risk assessment: Predictive validity of six tools in female forensic psychiatric patients. *Criminal Justice and Behavior*, *46*, 528–549.

de Vogel, V., de Vries Robbé, M., van Kalmthout, W., & Place, C. (2014). *Female additional manual (FAM): Additional guidelines to the HCR-20 V3 for assessing risk for violence in women*. Utrecht, The Netherlands: Van der Hoeven Kliniek.

de Vogel, V., van den Broek, E., & de Vries Robbé, M. (2014). The use of the HCR-20V3 in Dutch forensic psychiatric practice. *International Journal of Forensic Mental Health*, *13*, 109–121.

Douglas, K. S. (2014). Introduction to the special issue of the HCR-20 version 3. *International Journal of Forensic Mental Health*, *13*, 91–92.

Douglas, K. S. (2019a). Evaluating and managing risk for violence using structured professional judgment. In A. Day, C. Hollin, & D. Polaschek (Eds.), *Handbook of correctional psychology* (pp. 427–445). Chichester: Wiley.

Douglas, K. S. (2019b). Structured professional judgment model of criminal risk assessment. In R. D. Morgan (Ed.), *Sage encyclopedia of criminal psychology*. Thousand Oaks, CA: Sage.

Douglas, K. S., & Belfrage, H. (2014). Interrater reliability and concurrent validity of the HCR-20 version 3. *International Journal of Forensic Mental Health*, *13*, 130–139.

Douglas, K. S., Blanchard, A., & Hendry, M. (2013). Violence risk assessment and management: Putting structured professional judgment into practice. In C. Logan & L. Johnstone (Eds.), *Risk assessment and management: Clinical guidelines for effective practice* (pp. 29–55). New York: Routledge, Taylor & Francis Group.

Douglas, K. S., Hart, S. D., Webster, C. D., & Belfrage, H. (2013). *HCR-20 V3: Assessing risk for violence—user guide*. Burnaby, BC: Mental Health, Law, and Policy Institute, Simon Fraser University.

Douglas, K. S., Hart, S. D., Webster, C. D., Belfrage, H., Guy, L. S., & Wilson, C. (2014). Historical-clinical-risk management-20, version 3 (HCR-20 V3): Development and overview. *International Journal of Forensic Mental Health*, *13*, 93–108.

Douglas, K. S., & Reeves, K. (2010). The HCR-20 violence risk assessment scheme: Overview and review of the research. In R. Otto & K. S. Douglas (Eds.), *Handbook of violence risk assessment*. Oxford: Routledge, Taylor & Francis.

Douglas, K. S., Shaffer, C., Blanchard, A., Guy, L. S., Reeves, K., & Weir, J. (2020). *HCR-20 violence risk assessment scheme: Overview and annotated bibliography*. HCR-20 Violence Risk Assessment White Paper Series, #1. Burnaby, BC: Mental Health, Law, & Policy Institute, Simon Fraser University. Retrieved from HCR-20.com

Doyle, M., Power, L. A., Coid, J., Kallis, C., Ullrich, S., & Shaw, J. (2014). Predicting post-discharge community violence in England and Wales using the HCR-20^{V3}. *International Journal of Forensic Mental Health*, *13*(2), 140–147.

Ewert v. Canada (2018); SCC 30, 2018, 2 S.C.R. 165.

Fleiss, J. L., Levin, B., & Paik, M. C. (1981). The measurement of interrater agreement. In *Statistical methods for rates and proportions* (2nd ed., pp. 212–236). Hoboken, NJ: Wiley.

Green, D., Schneider, M., Griswold, H., Belfi, B., Herrera, M., & Deblasi, A. (2016). A comparison of the HCR-20[V3] among male and female insanity acquittees: A retrospective file study. *International Journal of Forensic Mental Health, 15*(1), 48–64.

Guy, L. S., Douglas, K. S., & Hart, S. D. (2015). Risk assessment and communication. In B. Cutler & P. Zapf (Eds.), *APA handbook of forensic psychology* (Vol. 1., pp. 35–86). Washington, DC: American Psychological Association.

Guy, L. S., & Wilson, C. M. (2007). *Empirical support for the HCR – 20: A critical analysis of the violence literature.* HCR-20 Violence Risk Assessment White Paper Series, #2. Burnaby, BC: Mental Health, Law, & Policy Institute, Simon Fraser University. Retrieved from HCR-20.com

Hare, R. D. (2003). *Manual for the Hare Psychopathy Checklist-Revised* (2nd ed.). Toronto, ON: Multi Health Systems.

Hart, S. D. (2003). Violence risk assessment: An anchored narrative approach. In M. Vanderhallen, G. Vervaeke, P. J. Van Koppen, & J. Goethals (Eds.), *Much ado about crime: Chapters on psychology and law* (pp. 209–230). Brussels: Uitgeverij Politeia NV.

Hart, S. D. (2016). Culture and violence risk assessment: The case of *"Ewert v. Canada"*. *Journal of Threat Assessment and Management, 3*, 76–96.

Hart, S. D., Douglas, K. S., & Guy, L. S. (2017). The structured professional judgment approach to violence risk assessment: Origins, nature, and advances. In M. Rettenberger & L. Craig (Series Eds.) & D. Boer (Vol. Ed.), *The Wiley-Blackwell handbook on the assessment, treatment and theories of sexual offending: Volume 1. Assessment* (pp. 643–666). Oxford: Wiley-Blackwell.

Hart, S. D., & Logan, C. (2011). Formulation of violence risk using evidence-based assessments: The structured professional judgment approach. In P. Sturmey & M. McMurran (Eds.), *Forensic case formulation* (pp. 83–106). Chichester: Wiley-Blackwell.

Hart, S. D., Sturmey, P., Logan, C., & McMurran, M. (2011). Forensic case formulation. *International Journal of Forensic Mental Health, 10*, 118–126.

Hogan, N. R., & Olver, M. E. (2016). Assessing risk for aggression in forensic psychiatric inpatients: An examination of five measures. *Law and Human Behavior, 40*, 233–243.

Hogan, N. R., & Olver, M. E. (2019). Static and dynamic assessment of violence risk among discharged forensic patients. *Criminal Justice and Behavior, 46*, 923–938.

Hopton, J., Cree, A., Thompson, S., Jones, R., & Jones, R. (2018). An evaluation of the quality of HCR-20 risk formulations: A comparison between HCR-20 Version 2 and HCR-20 Version 3. *International Journal of Forensic Mental Health, 17*, 195–201.

Howe, J., Rosenfeld, B., Foellmi, M., Stern, S., & Rotter, M. (2016). Application of the HCR-20 version 3 in civil psychiatric patients. *Criminal Justice and Behavior, 43*(3), 398–412.

Kennedy, H. G., O'Neill, C., Flynn, G., & Gill, P. (2010). *The Dundrum toolkit: Dangerousness, understanding, recovery and urgency manual (the Dundrum quartet). Four structured professional judgement instruments for admission triage, urgency, treatment completion and recovery assessments.* Dublin: Trinity College Dublin.

Kötter, S., Von Franqué, F., Bolzmacher, M., Eucker, S., Holzinger, B., & Müller-Isberner, R. (2014). The HCR-20[V3] in Germany. *International Journal of Forensic Mental Health, 13*(2), 122–129.

Landis, J., & Koch, G. G. (1977). The measurement of observer agreement for categorical data. *Biometrics, 33*, 159–174.

Logan, C. (2014). The HCR-20 version 3: A case study in risk formulation. *International Journal of Forensic Mental Health, 13*, 172–180.

Logan, C. (2016). Risk formulation: The new frontier in risk assessment and management. In R. D. Laws & W. O'Donohue (Eds.), *Treatment of sex offenders: Strengths and weaknesses in assessment and intervention* (pp. 83–105). New York: Springer.

Logan, C. (2017). Formulation for forensic practitioners. In R. Roesch & A. N. Cook (Eds.), *Handbook of forensic mental health services* (pp. 153–178). New York: Routledge, Taylor & Francis Group.

Mastromanno, B., Brookstein, D. M., Ogloff, J. R. P., Campbell, R., Chu, C. M., & Daffern, M. (2018). Assessing change in dynamic risk factors in forensic psychiatric inpatients: Relationship with psychopathy and recidivism. *The Journal of Forensic Psychiatry & Psychology, 29*, 323–336.

McMurran, M., & Bruford, S. (2016). Case formulation quality checklist: A revision based upon clinicians' views. *Journal of Forensic Practice, 18*, 31–38.

Monahan, J. (2013). Violence risk assessment. In R. K. Otto & I. B. Weiner (Eds.), *Handbook of psychology: Forensic psychology* (Vol. 11, 2nd ed., pp. 541–555). Hoboken, NJ: John Wiley & Sons Inc.

Neil, C., O'Rourke, S., Ferreira, N., & Flynn, L. (2019). Protective factors in violence risk assessment: Predictive validity of the SAPROF and HCR-20^{V3}. *International Journal of Forensic Mental Health, 19*(1). Online first.

Nunnally, J. C., & Bernstein, I. H. (1994). *Psychometric theory* (3rd ed.). New York: McGraw-Hill.

Penney, S. R., Marshall, L. A., & Simpson, A. I. F. (2016). The assessment of dynamic risk among forensic psychiatric patients transitioning to the community. *Law and Human Behavior, 40*, 374–386.

Persson, M., Belfrage, H., Fredriksson, B., & Kristiansson, M. (2017). Violence during imprisonment, forensic psychiatric care, and probation: Correlations and predictive validity of the risk assessment instruments COVR, LSI-R, HCR-20^{V3} and SAPROF. *International Journal of Forensic Mental Health, 16*, 117–129.

R. v. McCraw, 1991 3 SCR 72.

Rice, M. E., & Harris, G. T. (2005). Comparing effect sizes in follow-up studies: ROC Area, Cohen's d, and r. *Law and Human Behavior, 29*, 615–620.

Ringland, G. (1998). *Scenario planning: Managing for the future.* Chichester: Wiley.

Robbins, G. C. (1995). Scenario planning: A strategic alternative. *Public Management, 77*, 4–8.

Rosenfeld, B., Foellmi, M., Khadivi, A., Wijetunga, C., Howe, J., Nijdam-Jones, A., . . . Rotter, M. (2017). Determining when to conduct a violence risk assessment: Development and initial validation of the Fordham Risk Screening Tool (FRST). *Law and Human Behavior, 41*, 325–332.

Rotter, M., & Rosenfeld, B. (2018). Implementing a violence risk screening protocol in a civil psychiatric setting: Preliminary results and clinical policy implications. *Community Mental Health Journal, 54*, 245–251.

Sea, J., Hart, S. D., & Douglas, K. S. (2020). *The interrater reliability and concurrent validity of the HCR-20 version 3 among South Korean correctional offenders: A field research.* Manuscript under review.

Smith, S. T., Kelley, S. E., Rulseh, A., Sörman, K., & Edens, J. F. (2014). Adapting the HCR-20V3 for pretrial settings. *International Journal of Forensic Mental Health, 13*, 160–171.

Smith, K. J., O'Rourke, S., & Macpherson, G. (2020). The predictive validity of the HCR20v3 within Scottish forensic inpatient facilities: A closer look at key dynamic variables. *International Journal of Forensic Mental Health, 19*, 1–17.

Starr, S. B. (2014). Evidence-based sentencing and the scientific rationalization of discrimination. discrimination. *Stanford Law Review, 66*, 803–872. Retrieved from https://repository.law.umich.edu/law_econ_current/90/?utm_source=repository.law.umich.edu%2Flaw_econ_current%2F90&utm_medium=PDF&utm_campaign=PDFCoverPages

Strub, D. S., Douglas, K. S., & Nicholls, T. L. (2014). The validity of version 3 of the HCR-20 violence risk assessment scheme amongst offenders and civil psychiatric patients. *International Journal of Forensic Mental Health, 13*, 148–159.

Strub, D. S., Douglas, K. S., & Nicholls, T. L. (2016). Violence risk assessment of civil psychiatric patients with the HCR-20: Does gender matter? *International Journal of Forensic Mental Health, 15*, 81–96.

Thomas, S., Harty, M. A., Parrott, J., McCrone, P., Slade, M., & Thornicroft, G. (2003). *The forensic CAN: A needs assessment for forensic mental health service users.* London: Gaskell.

van Notten, P. W. F., Rotmans, J., van Asselt, M. B. A., & Rothman, D. S. (2003). An updated scenario typology. *Futures, 35*, 423–443.

Vincent, G. M., Guy, L. S., & Grisso, T. (2012). *Risk assessment in juvenile justice: A guidebook for implementation.* Chicago, IL: John D. & Catherine T. MacArthur Foundation.

Webster, C. D., Douglas, K. S., Eaves, D., & Hart, S. D. (1997). *HCR-20: Assessing risk for violence* (Version 2). Burnaby, BC: Mental Health, Law, and Policy Institute, Simon Fraser University.

Webster, C. D., Eaves, D., Douglas, K. S., & Wintrup, A. (1995). *The HCR-20 scheme: The assessment of dangerousness and risk.* Burnaby, BC: Simon Fraser University and Forensic Psychiatric Services Commission of British Columbia.

Chapter 13

The Juvenile Sex Offender Assessment Protocol-II (J-SOAP-II)

Robert A. Prentky and Sue Righthand

Description of Measure

The Juvenile Sex Offender Assessment Protocol-II Manual (Prentky & Righthand, 2003) describes J-SOAP-II as a checklist whose purpose is to aid in the systematic review of risk factors that have been identified in the professional literature as being associated with sexual and criminal offending. It is designed to be used with boys in the age range of 12 to 18 who have been adjudicated for sexual offenses, as well as non-adjudicated youths with a history of sexually coercive behavior. Decisions about reoffense risk should *not* be based exclusively on the results from J-SOAP-II. J-SOAP-II should always be used as part of a comprehensive risk assessment. Like any scale that is intended to assess risk, J-SOAP-II requires ongoing validation and possible revision, as we learn more about how J-SOAP-II works and about how best to assess the risk of youths who have sexually offended.

Development of the J-SOAP

The original version of this risk assessment scale was developed at Joseph J. Peters Institute (JJPI) in Philadelphia in 1994–1995. The impetus was the need to assess risk for juveniles in a newly developed, community-based treatment program. After several phone calls to colleagues with extensive experience working with juvenile sex offenders revealed that they were not aware that any protocol for assessing risk existed, we set out to develop one. The risk assessment variables were developed after reviews of the extant literature covering five areas: (1) clinical studies of juvenile sex offenders; (2) risk assessment/outcome studies of juvenile sex offenders; (3) risk assessment/outcome studies of adult sex offenders; (4) risk assessment/outcome studies from the general juvenile delinquency literature; and (5) risk assessment studies on mixed populations of adult offenders.

In all, 23 items representing 4 subscales were developed. These scales were intended to capture the two major historical (static) domains that are of importance for risk assessment with this population (Scale 1: Sexual Drive/Sexual Preoccupation and Scale 2: Impulsive, Antisocial Behavior), and the two major dynamic areas that could reflect behavior change (Scale 3: Clinical/Treatment and Scale 4: Community Adjustment). The latter two subscales were of particular importance, because the protocol was developed to assess not only risk at discharge but change as a function of treatment.

Our understanding of the factors associated with increased risk for sexual offending was derived primarily from studies of adjudicated juveniles and adults that have reoffended with new sexual offenses. One of the factors occasionally associated with sexual reoffending among youths who have committed sexual offenses involves sexual preoccupation and atypical sexual interests and behaviors. As such, multiple and frequent sexual offenses, persistent sexual offending following legal sanctions, excessive sexual activity and sexual preoccupation beyond what may be developmentally expected are factors that are associated with repeat offending. Scale 1 of the J-SOAP assesses high sex drive and sexual preoccupation beyond what would be expected developmentally. A second factor associated with increased risk for sexual offending, and especially nonsexual offending, is impulsive antisocial and delinquent behavior, which is assessed by Scale 2 (Impulsive/Antisocial Behavior). This domain is important, since most youth that reoffend do so by committing a nonsexual offense.

Although Scale 1 and Scale 2 are comprised predominantly of historical items that cannot reflect change, *the domains themselves are fluid*. For example, although a *history* of impulsive, antisocial, or delinquent behavior is fixed, the probability of such behavior in the future is likely to change as a result of maturation and treatment. Scales 3 and 4 are comprised of dynamic items that can reflect change over time with the potential for depicting mitigation or aggravation of risk. Scale 3 is an Intervention scale and measures an array of factors typically addressed in sex offense specific treatment, whereas Scale 4 items pertain to the youth's recent adjustment in the community and the availability and use of positive supports.

No *a priori* item weightings were used. All items are trichotomized and assumed, absent empirical data to suggest otherwise, to be of equal importance. The coding for each item provided, to whatever extent possible, behavioral anchors to increase clarity and reliability. As we explain in the Validation section of this chapter, a construction/validation study in 1995 led to revisions. This revised scale was completed in 1998 and was referred to as J-SOAP (Prentky, Harris, Frizzell, & Righthand, 2000).

In the Validation section of this chapter, we review the validity studies leading to the J-SOAP and the subsequent validity studies leading, in turn, to the revised J-SOAP-II. In this chapter's Appendix, we have highlighted the major changes, such as item additions and deletions, at both stages of scale development. In addition to the detailed changes, there were numerous more minor changes, such as item wording and scoring criteria.

J-SOAP Scales and Constituent Items

Scale/Item 1	Sexual Drive/Preoccupation Scale:	Scale/Item 3	Clinical Intervention Scale:
1.	Prior Legally Charged Sex Offenses	17.	Accepting Responsibility for Offense(s)
2.	Number of Sexual Abuse Victims	18.	Internal Motivation for Change
3.	Male Child Victim	19.	Understands Risk Factors
4.	Duration of Sex Offense History	20.	Empathy
5.	Degree of Planning in Sexual Offense(s)	21.	Remorse and Guilt
6.	Sexualized Aggression	22.	Cognitive Distortions
7.	Sexual Drive and Preoccupation	23.	Quality of Peer Relationships
8.	Sexual Victimization History		
		Scale/Item 4	**Community Stability-Adjustment Scale**
Scale/Item 2	**Impulsive/Antisocial Behavior Scale:**	24.	Management of Sexual Urges and Desire
9.	Caregiver Consistency	25.	Management of Anger
10.	Pervasive Anger	26.	Stability of Current Living Situation
11.	School Behavior Problems	27.	Stability in School
12.	History of Conduct Disorder	28.	Evidence of Positive Support Systems
13.	Juvenile Antisocial Behavior		
14.	Ever Charged or Arrested Before Age 16		
15.	Multiple Types of Offenses		
16.	History of Physical Assault/Exposure to Family Violence		

Summarizing and Reporting J-SOAP-II Ratings

As noted, the J-SOAP-II does not use cutoff scores for mechanical assignment to risk bins (e.g., low, moderate, high). The reasons are threefold: (1) providing empirically determined cutoff scores requires a very large and diverse database that accounts for potential age and racial/ethnic differences, and includes excellent follow-up information on sexual recidivism; (2) cutoff scores rarely apply with comparable accuracy across samples unless the samples are very similar to the reference group with respect to potentially critical risk considerations, such as age and extent of nonsexual delinquency; (3) the presence of cutoff scores encourages conclusions about risk based exclusively on the score from the risk scale. It is for that reason that J-SOAP-II has avoided use of cutoff scores for risk levels. In that regard, J-SOAP would not be regarded as structured professional judgment. As pointed out by Vincent, Guy, and Grisso (2012), the MacArthur Foundation guide for assessing risk in juvenile justice settings cautions that risk assessment is not simply a matter of administering a risk assessment scale; it is a *process*.

We do not take this last point as an idle exhortation. We have always maintained that the only truly valid evaluation of risk with juveniles derives from an idiographic or comprehensive evaluation that includes the results from nomothetic sources, such as a risk assessment scale, but also includes all other risk-relevant information for a particular individual. Rather than assigning cutoff scores (or empirically unsupported clinical judgments), we concluded that the most prudent and responsible approach is to recommend the use of ratios to convey the findings, requiring no clinical inferences or judgment about the ratings, requiring users to integrate those findings into an idiographic evaluation.

As such, the score of each scale is divided by the total possible score for that scale. The total J-SOAP-II score can also be reported as a ratio. These ratios reflect the observed proportion (or "amount") of risk rated as present for each scale and for the total score *at a given point in time*. As alluded to earlier, we intentionally provided no procedure for converting a proportion of risk into a categorical classification (i.e., low, moderate, high). Conclusions about risk (low, moderate, high) must derive from a comprehensive (idiographic) evaluation that includes J-SOAP-II but is not based exclusively on J-SOAP-II. Users report their findings from J-SOAP-II according to the proportion of risk observed on the date of testing (e.g., Scale 1: 4/16 (25%) or Full Scale: 18/56 (32%). These proportions are illustrated in the following table.

J-SOAP-II Scales	Add	Range	Calculate
Static Scales:			
Sexual Drive/ Preoccupation	#1–#8	0–16	Scale 1 tot / 16 =
Impulsive/Antisocial Behavior	#9–#16	0–16	Scale 2 tot / 16 =
Static Sub-Score	#1–#16	0–32	Scale 1 + 2 / 32 =
Dynamic Scales:			
Clinical intervention	#17–#23	0–14	Scale 3 tot / 14 =
Community Stability	#24–#28	0–10	Scale 4 tot / 10 =
Dynamic Sub-Score	#17–#28	0–24	Scale 3 + 4 / 24 =
TOTAL J-SOAP Score	#01–#28	0–56	Scale 1 – 4 / 56 =

Users and Caveats

As we discuss in the Manual, it is imperative that clinicians who assess adolescents' risk for offending be knowledgeable about the significant risk-relevant challenges involved in assessing this population. As is well accepted by now, adolescent functioning is very much "in flux."

No aspect of their adolescent development, including their cognitive, social, and emotional development, can be assumed "fixed" or permanent; *change* is a defining feature of adolescent development. In addition, the life circumstances of those we evaluate often are very unstable. In a very real sense, we are trying to assess the risk of "moving targets." Since risk status may change, sometimes dramatically, in a brief period of time, we strongly recommend that youths be reassessed for risk at a *minimum* of every 6 months. At the very least, Scales 3 and 4 should be rescored every 6 months because, although new events may impact the static scales, the dynamic scale items are expected to change over time. Certainly, reassessments should be done even more frequently if life circumstances dictate (i.e., if the examiner is aware of risk-relevant changes that have occurred).

Prior to using J-SOAP-II, users should have training and experience in assessing juveniles who commit sexual offenses and risk assessment in general, and users should be knowledgeable about the relevant and evolving research regarding risk assessment as it pertains to juvenile offending (sexual as well as nonsexual). In addition, prior to using J-SOAP-II, users should read the manual and be familiar with its contents. Further, before using the scale in any professional capacity, users should complete several practice cases and compare their scores with qualified others who have scored the same case to identify and resolve any scoring inconsistencies. It is also recommended that J-SOAP-II users periodically consult with each other about their scoring and attend continuing education workshops on juvenile sex offense risk and needs assessment.

Adjusting J-SOAP-II Scores

Users have been known to "adjust" J-SOAP-II scores by changing the way they rated one or more items, because the score was not consistent with their clinical impression of the juvenile. This would, in effect, be changing the criteria for scoring that item, and that clearly is *not* acceptable. The scores for individual items, as well as the overall scale scores, should never be changed or adjusted other than when new information dictates the necessity for correcting an initial rating (not an *adjustment*). "Adjustment" of one's initial clinical impressions about risk is perfectly legitimate and indeed often necessary based on risk-relevant information not included in J-SOAP-II, but the "adjustment" is not to a J-SOAP-II score. The "adjustment" is one's conclusions based on a far wider range of risk-relevant information than any risk assessment scale could possibly cover. Such risk-relevant information would most likely take the form of dynamic risk factors not included in the assessment scale that can mitigate or aggravate risk.

Using J-SOAP-II Scores in Treatment

Although the explicit purpose of J-SOAP-II is to facilitate risk assessment, it may be particularly useful for informing and guiding legal and clinical decision-making with regard to risk management. For example, if a youth has a relatively high proportion of risk on Scale 1 but a relatively low proportion on Scale 2, the youth may require more sex offense-specific treatment interventions and less of a focus on delinquency interventions. In fact, mixing such a youth with more "hard-core" juvenile offenders may be detrimental. *In our experience*, most juvenile sex offenders seem to have a Scale 1 proportion in the range of 20%–35%, and sometimes lower, not reflecting a high sexual drive or high degree of preoccupation. A marked difference between Scale 1 and Scale 2, with an elevation on Scale 1, clearly alerts the examiner to a youngster that is sexually preoccupied.

In contrast, a youth who has a relatively high percentage on Scale 2 but a relatively low percentage on Scale 1 may have sexually offended as part of a more general pattern of antisocial behavior. In such cases, the sexual offense may not reflect serious issues involving management of sexually deviant or sexually coercive behavior. This youngster may require delinquency-focused treatment interventions, perhaps with some limited psychoeducational interventions that address appropriate sexual boundaries, non-abusive sexual behavior, impulse control, and healthy masculinity.

Youth who have high percentages on *both* Scale 1 and Scale 2 may well require more intensive supervision, perhaps in a secure residential placement, and need sex-offense-specific treatment as well as delinquency-focused interventions. Low percentages on *both* Scales 1 and 2, on the other hand, may suggest that the offending behavior was more situational and requires only limited and brief interventions, such as psychoeducational approaches that address human sexuality, appropriate sexual behavior, social skills training and dating skills. Additionally, youth with a high proportion on Scale 3 may have never been in treatment or are in the early stages of treatment; they may not admit their offenses because they are scared and fear getting in more trouble, or may just be *talking the talk* (i.e., learned what to say). Others may lack empathy and/or remorse, traits that may be associated with a more entrenched antisocial personality style. Scale 4, Community Adjustment, is rated only if the juvenile has been living in or having unrestricted access to the community for some or all of the preceding 6 months. Youth with high percentages on this scale may be having difficulty managing their behavior appropriately and/or may have minimal or negative supports. These youth may require more intensive supervision and interventions, perhaps in a residential setting. Specific interventions, of course, depend on the overall risk/needs picture and findings from the comprehensive assessment.

Sex-Offense-Specific Treatment Needs and Progress Report

We have long held the belief that assessment of risk among juveniles with sex offenses (JSO) must embrace a continuum of care and not shine a spotlight exclusively on the youngster's potential *dangerousness*. To that end, Righthand (2005) first developed the Treatment Needs and Progress Report (TNPR) in 2002 to complement J-SOAP. The intent of the TNPR was to track changes in critical treatment needs from baseline (intake) through subsequent therapy sessions and assist in assessing readiness for discharge. The TNPR focused on those areas deemed most important for the youngster's course of treatment. The advantage of the TNPR was that it enabled a large number of risk-relevant dynamic factors to be assessed systematically during the course of treatment.

Initial findings indicated important programmatic risk-reduction effects documented by the TNPR (Righthand, Boulard, Cabral, & Serwik, 2011). When J-SOAP Scale 3 and the TNPR were administered at the beginning and conclusion of treatment, there was a decline in risks and needs associated with recidivism (Scale 4 could not be re-administered in accordance with J-SOAP scoring rules since the youths in this sample had not been in the community). A study with 187 juveniles adjudicated for sexual offenses indicated that interrater reliability was excellent (.82) and internal consistency (a = 0.72) was good (Righthand, Hecker, & Dore, 2012). Predictive validity for sexual recidivism was moderate (AUC = .71; 95% CI .50, .91) but not statistically significant given that only 6 youths, less than 4% of the sample, reoffended with a sexual offense (Righthand et al., 2012, Righthand, Vincent, & Huff, 2017).

Validation of J-SOAP

The construction/validation sample consisted of 96 juvenile sexual offenders, ranging in age from 9 to 20 (average age was 14), who were referred to JJPI beginning in 1994 for assessment and treatment (Prentky et al., 2000). The risk assessment protocol was completed on all 96 juvenile sex offenders as part of a comprehensive intake battery at JJPI. The protocol was completed again at time of discharge, on average 24 months later. The protocol was coded independently by two clinicians entirely from archival documents and data obtained from the intake battery. After the ratings were completed, the clinicians discussed disagreements, and the agreed-upon ratings were used to examine outcomes. Twelve-month follow-up data on sexual and nonsexual reoffending were obtained on 75 of the 96 youths in the study. The short-term [12-month] recidivism rate of 11% included only 3 youths that committed another sexual offense, 4 youths that committed a nonsexual victim-involved offense, and 1 youth who committed a nonsexual, victimless offense.

The interrater reliability (IRR) for all items, except for Caregiver Instability, was good to excellent, ranging from .75 to .91, with an average IRR of .83. The reliability for Caregiver Instability was poor (.59), and that item has since been revised. Three of the subscales had moderate internal consistency, with alphas ranging from .68 to .73. The Clinical/Treatment scale had a high degree of internal consistency (.85). Three of the four subscales comprised items with high item-total correlations ($r > .30$). Seven of the 9 items in Scale 2, 4 of the 5 items in Scale 3, and all items in Scale 4 exceeded this benchmark. The exception was Scale 1. The *only* Scale 1 item with a reasonably high item-total correlation was Prior Charged Sex Offenses.

Overall, there was an average raw total scale score at intake was *21* (21/46 = .46) for those juveniles who did *not* reoffend and an average raw scale score of *30* (30/46 = .65) for those *three juveniles who committed another sexual offense*. These results were obviously based on an extremely small sample of eight recidivists, only three of whom were sexual recidivists. For that reason, we applied no inferential statistics, and observed group differences were not confirmed by statistical significance.

This study was informative in pointing to areas that required revision and clarification. The scoring criteria for every item were carefully examined for ambiguity, including a pilot review by probation officers and forensic examiners in Maine. As a result, behavioral examples and anchors were added. Two changes were made to Scale 1. First, the Scale 1 item that included offense planning (History of Predatory Behavior) was replaced with a more clearly defined Offense Planning item. The new Offense Planning item was behaviorally anchored and easier to code from file data than the History of Predatory Behavior item, which required difficult inferences and judgments about behaviors such as grooming and exploitation. Second, a fifth item was added to Scale 1 that was intended to capture the degree to which the juvenile sexualized his victims (for example, use of pornography in the offense, filming the victim, engaging in unusual or ritualized sexual acts with the victim). Two changes were also made to Scale 2. A Juvenile Antisocial Behavior item was added that was intended to assess general delinquency, and a History of Expressed Anger item was added that was designed to assess disruptions due to poorly controlled and poorly managed anger.

The revised scale, completed in 1998 and referred to as J-SOAP, was examined with a sample of 153 juveniles who committed sex offenses (Righthand, Prentky, Hecker, Carpenter, & Nangle, 2000). The juveniles had an average age of 16 and had been adjudicated for a sex offense, *or* had been adjudicated for another offense but had a documented sex offense in their records. The victims ranged in age from 1 year to 36 years, with an average age of 8.6 years. Interrater reliabilities for the four subscales ranged from .80 to .91. Internal consistency continued to be quite high for Scale 2 ($\alpha = .88$), Scale 3 ($\alpha = .95$), and Scale 4 ($\alpha = .80$), with Scale 1 evidencing moderate internal consistency ($\alpha = .64$).

We looked at the factor structure of the 26 items comprising J-SOAP using principal component analysis (PCA) (Righthand et al., 2000). The four-factor solution provided strong empirical support for the four J-SOAP scales. The first factor, accounting for slightly over 20% of the variance, was the equivalent of Scale 2 (Impulsive, Antisocial Behavior) of J-SOAP. The first factor mapped Scale 2 precisely, with all items on Scale 2 falling on it. The loadings for these 11 items ranged from .44 to .77. The second factor, also accounting for 20% of the variance, was the equivalent of Scale 3 (Clinical Intervention) on J-SOAP. All five Scale 3 items loaded on this factor along with one item (Quality of Peer Relations) that was from Scale 4. The loadings for the five Scale 3 items ranged from .83 to .88. The third factor, accounting for about 9% of the variance, was the precise equivalent of Scale 1 (Sexual Drive & Preoccupation) on the J-SOAP. All five Scale 1 items loaded on this factor, with item loadings ranging from .51 to .72. The fourth factor, accounting for about 8.5% of the variance, was the equivalent of Scale 4 (Community Adjustment). Four of the five Scale 4 items loaded on this component, with item loadings ranging from .46 to .78.

The concurrent validity of J-SOAP was explored by examining how well it correlated with the Youth Level of Service/Case Management Inventory (YLS/CMI; see Hoge, Chapter 9, this volume; Righthand et al., 2000). In addition, we examined the relationship between the J-SOAP static scales (Scales 1 and 2) and criminal history variables coded from the juveniles' files. The coded variables were: (1) Total Offenses, the total number of offenses of any type committed by the youth; (2) Sexual Offenses, the total number of sexual offenses committed by the youth; (3) Sex Offense Victims, the number of victims of contact sexual offenses; and (4) Sexual Aggression, the degree of aggression displayed by the youth during any and all sexual activities throughout his life.

The YLS/CMI was highly correlated with the total J-SOAP score ($r = .91$), as well as the individual scales: Scale 1, $r = .37$; Scale 2, $r = .81$; Scale 3, $r = .88$; Scale 4, $r = .91$. Scale 1 was uncorrelated with Total Offenses ($r = .08$) but significantly correlated with Number of Sex Offenses ($r = .36$), Number of Sex Offense Victims ($r = .64$), and Degree of Sexual Aggression ($r = .27$). Scale 2 was uncorrelated with Number of Sex Offenses ($r = .03$) but significantly correlated with Total Offenses ($r = .30$), Number of Sex Offense Victims ($r = .27$), and Degree of Sexual Aggression ($r = .29$).

The placements of 134 of 153 of the youths in the study could be coded. The validity of J-SOAP was also examined by comparing 45 residential and 89 community juveniles on J-SOAP scales (Righthand, Carpenter, & Prentky, 2001). Since Scale 4 is not scored for youths who have been in secure care for 6 months or longer, Scale 4 was not examined. The other three J-SOAP scales discriminated between the two groups, with the residential juveniles rated as significantly higher risks than the community juveniles on all three scales.

Hecker, Scoular, Righthand, and Nangle (2002) examined juvenile and adult arrest and conviction data for a period spanning 10 to 12 years on a sample of 54 male adolescent sex offenders. Twenty of the juveniles committed a nonsexual offense (37%) and 6 of the juveniles committed a sexual offense (11%) during the follow-up period. Although the total J-SOAP score was not correlated with sexual reoffending, Scale 1 alone significantly improved the prediction of sexual recidivism above chance in receiver operator characteristic analyses (Area Under the Curve, or AUC = .79). A serious caveat, however, is that there were only 6 sexual recidivists. The very low rate of sexual recidivism has been a methodological impediment that has seriously hindered our ability to examine in greater depth the predictive validity of J-SOAP.

Waite, Pinkerton, Wieckowski, McGarvey, and Brown (2002) reported on a 9-year follow-up study of 253 high-risk juvenile sex offenders. Although the detected rate of sexual recidivism was, once again, very low (4.3%, 11 youths were arrested for a new sexual offense), roughly 60% of the sample was arrested for other offenses. Using a modified Scale 2 from the J-SOAP (8 of the 11 items were coded), the juveniles were split into two groups: Low Impulsive/Antisocial ($n = 118$) and High Impulsive/Antisocial ($n = 135$). The proportions of the Low and High groups arrested for any new offense was 52.6% and 74.8%, respectively ($p < .001$). Although the numbers were very small, it is noteworthy that the High Scale 2 juveniles were three times more likely to be rearrested for a new sexual offense (9.8%) than juveniles with Low Scale 2 scores (2.9%).

Righthand, Knight, and Prentky (2002) tested four theoretical models using structural equation modeling. This study reported on a sample of 153 youth comprising a subset of a larger sample ($n = 208$) drawn from the Maine Department of Corrections, ranging in age from 7 to 20. More than one-quarter (29%) of the youth had open cases with child welfare. The study explored (a) the relationship of antecedent adverse life experiences to J-SOAP Scales 1, 2, and 3, and (b) the relationship of J-SOAP to sex offense outcome variables. The six key findings from this study were:

- a strong relationship between a history of sexual abuse and Scale 1 (after the Scale 1 item "sexual abuse history" was removed);
- the *severity* of the sexual abuse was the most important facet of sexual abuse for predicting outcome;
- family violence/trauma and caregiver instability were both related to scores on Scale 2 (after the Scale 2 item "caregiver instability" was removed);
- scores on Scale 1 were strongly related to the number of victims (the higher the score, the greater the number of victims) (after the Scale 1 item "# of victims" was removed);
- scores on Scale 2 was related to victim age (higher Scale 2 scores were associated with older victims (teenage or older);
- scores on Scales 1 and 2 were associated with the amount of force used in the sexual offenses.

Development of J-SOAP-II

The J-SOAP was revised again based on the results of the research summarized in the previous section (Righthand et al., 2005). In all, the revised scale (J-SOAP-II) has 28 items, 2 more than the original J-SOAP. An attempt was made to better anchor all of the items using clear, behavioral language. Numerous, more subtle, changes were also made to item wording and scoring criteria and are addressed in more detail in the Appendix.

Where J-SOAP-II "Fits" Methodologically

The most commonly used risk scales developed for juveniles who commit sex offenses are methodologically quite different, and these differences should be noted by users. For illustrative purposes, we compare J-SOAP-II with two other well-known risk scales designed for these youth—ERASOR and JSORRAT-II. Although all three scales primarily employ empirically supported risk factors, some items, such as Empathy, Motivation for Change, and Taking Responsibility, are theoretically driven and lack empirical support. For all three tools, archival data often are used to rate the risk factors, occasionally complemented by an interview. This is where similarities end. The *Estimate of Risk of Adolescent Sexual Offense Recidivism* (ERASOR; Worling & Curwen, 2001) is a good example of a structured professional judgment (SPJ) measure. After the individual risk factors are rated, the examiner assigns a Low, Moderate, or High classification based on her/his professional judgment. Since there are no numeric cutoff scores, it is up to the examiner to determine level or degree of risk.

By contrast, the Juvenile Sex Offender Assessment Protocol-II (J-SOAP-II; Prentky & Righthand, 2003; Prentky, Harris, Frizzell, & Righthand, 2000) and the Juvenile Sexual Offense Recidivism Risk Assessment Tool-II (JSORRAT-II; Epperson, Ralston, Fowers, & DeWitt, 2005, 2012) are hybrids; neither is an SPJ measure. J-SOAP-II is not a traditional SPJ scale like the ERASOR, since, unlike the ERASOR, there is no categorical assignment for purposes of risk classification (low, moderate, high), hence no "professional judgment" is required to reach a classification.

Both the J-SOAP-II and the JSORRAT-II are methodologically quite dissimilar, however. With the J-SOAP-II, all of the individual risk factors are rated, after which the examiner evaluates and may report the proportion of risk for each of four scales, as well as the total score for all four scales. In this way, the examiner considers only the quantum risk rated as present on the items included in the scale without employing any clinical judgment to infer *level* of risk. Like the ERA-SOR, the J-SOAP-II has no cutoff scores, but unlike the ERASOR, the J-SOAP-II also has no risk-level classification groups (Low, Moderate, or High). The JSORRAT-II, by contrast, provides life tables for two states—Iowa and Utah. These life tables are unique to those states and presumably could not be used elsewhere. The JSORRAT-II thus is "actuarial," but only in two states (Epperson et al., 2012). In any other state, the total score from the 12 items on the JSORRAT-II is assigned a risk level using numeric cutoffs (Low = 0, Low-Moderate = 1–3, Moderate = 4–7, Moderate-High = 8+).

Validation: J-SOAP-II

Although several studies have reported good to excellent interrater reliability for the J-SOAP (Caldwell, Ziemke, & Vitacco, 2008; Viljoen et al., 2008), the reliability of Scale 4 was poor in at least one study (Martinez, Rosenfeld, & Flores, 2007). Scale 4, which assesses community adjustment and availability of positive supports, is particularly sensitive to the quality (clarity and consistency) of the data upon which judgments are made. Martinez et al. (2007) further reported high Cronbach alphas (strong internal consistency) for the Total and the combined static (scales 1 and 2) and dynamic (scales 3 and 4), as well as variability among the individual scales, ranging from .69 (Scale 4) to .90 (Scale 3).

Predictive validity studies have yielded mixed findings. In the Martinez et al. (2007) study, the Total J-SOAP-II score predicted both general and sexual recidivism (AUC values of .76 and .78, respectively). Notably, the dynamic scales (3 and 4) were much more robust predictors of sexual recidivism (AUC = .86) than the static scales (1 and 2) (AUC = .63). In an earlier study, however, Parks and Bard (2006) found that it was Scale 2 that predicted both sexual and nonsexual reoffending. Juveniles in the Parks and Bard study, however, had been released from a secure correctional facility, thus explaining the efficacy of Scale 2 which assesses antisocial and delinquent behavior. Although Powers-Sawyer and Miner (2009) reported strong predictive accuracy for sexual recidivism (AUC = .75), they had only seven recidivists in their sample of 96 incarcerated juvenile sex offenders (7.3%). In contrast to Parks and Bard, Powers-Sawyer and Miner found that the J-SOAP-II was a weak predictor of nonsexual violent reoffense and nonsexual general reoffense. Not surprisingly, Powers-Sawyer and Miner found Scale 1 (AUC = .72) to be a stronger predictor than Scale 2 (AUC = .64).

Prentky et al. (2010) examined the predictive validity of J-SOAP-II in samples of 331 preadolescent boys (age ≤ 11) and 220 adolescent boys (age 12–17), all of whom were wards of the Massachusetts Department of Social Services. Two independent, "masked" raters coded a random 15% of both samples, yielding high interrater reliability on most variables (Scale 1, M = .88, range = .98–.78); Scale 2, M = .88, range = .97–.75; Scale 3, M = .86, range = .91–.79; Scale 4, M = .85, range = .93–.80. Three variables fell below a benchmark of .80: Sexualized Aggression (.78), Conduct Disorder before age 10 (.75), and Quality of Peer Relationships (.79). Survival functions were estimated using the Kaplan-Meier product-limit method. Sexual reoffending within the 7-year follow-up period was higher than generally reported in the literature, since new incidents were not limited to official charges but included incidents substantiated by case workers and documented in the records: Adolescents (13.9%) and Preadolescents (24.7%) [−2 log(LR) = .009].

A subsample of both groups had been considered "high risk" and assigned to treatment. These high-risk youth had been in more residential placements (p < .001) and spent more time in their residential placements (p < .005). This high-risk subsample also had slightly higher reoffense rates: Adolescents (15.7%) and Preadolescents (27.9%) [−2 log(LR) = .016]. As noted, the reoffense rates discussed elsewhere in this chapter generally reported lower sexual reoffense rates, likely reflecting the substantial variability subject to methodological differences in how reoffense is defined and data are gathered (cf., Prentky, Lee, Knight, & Cerce, 1997).

Estimates of hazard rates using Cox Proportional Hazard Model yielded the following significant chi-squares:

> *Adolescents*: Scale 1, $\chi^2 = 18.7$, HR $= 13.9$, $p < .0001$; Scale 2, $\chi^2 = 5.7$, HR $= 3.0$, $p < .02$, Scale 4, $\chi^2 = 13.5$, HR $= 5.0$, $p < .0002$
>
> *Pre- Adolescents*: Scale 1, $\chi^2 = 28.8$, HR $= 6.7$, $p < .0001$; Scale 4, $\chi^2 = 28.8$, HR $= 3.8$, $p < .0002$].

Among those in the higher risk subsample,

> *Adolescents*: Scales 1 (HR $= 12.1$), 2 (HR $= 2.8$), and 4 (HR $= 5.5$)
>
> *Pre-Adolescents*: Scales 1 (HR $= 7.4$), 3 (HR $= 3.9$), and 4 (HR $= 4.0$)

A logistic regression model predicted the binary dependent outcome variable (sexual reoffense). Predictors were the individual J-SOAP-II scales. The largest ORs (calculated from the estimate) were for Scales 1 and 4 for both *Adolescents* (Scale, 1, Wald $= 26.6$, OR $= 1.6$; and Scale 4, Wald $= 22.7$, OR $= 1.7$) and *Pre-Adolescents* (Scale 1, Wald $= 48.5$, OR $= 1.6$; and Scale 4, Wald $= 42.5$, OR $= 1.5$). By way of interpretation, with an OR of 1.6, the odds of a sexual reoffense in 7 years of exposure will be 60% higher if the value of J-SOAP-II Scale 1 increases by *one* point. As noted, this was the case both for the adolescents and the pre-adolescents.

Receiver operating characteristic (ROC) curve estimates of predictive accuracy were derived. Scale 3 was calculated only for the high-risk (treatment) subsample for whom treatment information was available.

The AUC values for the *full sample* were:

> *Adolescents*: Scales 1, 2, and 4, respectively, .83, .66, .81. Scale 3 was calculated only for the high-risk (treatment) subsample.
>
> *Pre-Adolescents*: Scales 1, 2, 4, respectively, .78, .56, .76. The very low AUC values for Scale 2 with the pre-adolescents, both full and high-risk analyses may simply reflect the inappropriateness of a scale focused on juvenile delinquency and juvenile justice consequences with pre-adolescents.

The AUC values for the *high-risk sample* were:

> *Adolescents*: Scales 1, 2, 3, and 4, respectively, .80, .67, .68, .82.
>
> *Pre-Adolescents*: Scales 1, 2, 3, 4, respectively, .77, .56, .74, .77.

Rajlic and Gretton (2010) examined the moderating effect of offender type on the predictive validity of the J-SOAP-II and the ERASOR, in 286 juvenile sex offenders. Sex offense-only adolescents were compared with those who committed sex offenses and other offenses. Rajlic and Gretton (2010) found that both the ERASOR and J-SOAP-II predicted sexual recidivism and nonsexual recidivism in the combined sample (AUC values: ERASOR .71/.71; J-SOAP-II .69/.77, respectively). However, when the two subsamples were examined separately, both scales predicted sexual reoffense with a large effect size but *only* in the sex-offense-only group (AUC values: .86 and .80). By marked contrast, however, neither risk scale predicted sexual recidivism beyond chance levels in the sex offense plus delinquency group (AUC values: .54 and .51). The Rajlic and Gretton (2010) study is one of the very few to provide empirical evidence for the need to consider taxonomic heterogeneity, addressed over 20 years ago (Knight & Prentky, 1993), highlighting why studies of mixed samples may yield discrepant and suboptimal results. In the present study, three sets of strikingly different findings on prediction of *sexual* reoffending might have been presented for the J-SOAP-II: Combined Sample (AUC = .69), Sex-Offense Only Sample (AUC = .80), Delinquency-Sex Offense Sample (AUC = .51). The same pattern, of course, would have true for the ERASOR.

Chu, Ng, Fong, and Teoh (2012) compared the J-SOAP-II and the YLS/CMI in a sample of 104 Singaporean youth. Although the intraclass correlation coefficients (reflecting similarity between values for items within the same group) were deemed "excellent" for the J-SOAP-II total score (.77), "fair" for the ERASOR total score (.49), "fair" for the ERASOR overall clinical rating (.43), and "good" for the YLS/CMI total score (.67), *only* the ERASOR predicted sexual reoffense (AUC = .83 for clinical rating and .74 for total score). The J-SOAP-II total score (AUC = .51) predicted no better than chance. The AUC value for the YLS/CMI was reported to be .29, that is, inversely related to outcome. All of the scales (ERASOR overall clinical rating and total score, J-SOAP-II total score, and YLS/CMI total score) significantly predicted *nonsexual* recidivism.

In a similar finding, Viljoen et al. (2008) compared the Juvenile Sexual Offense Recidivism Risk Assessment Tool—II (JSORRAT-II, Epperson, Ralston, Fowers, & Dewitt, 2005), and the Structured Assessment of Violence Risk in Youth (SAVRY, Borum, Bartel, & Forth, 2002) (see Borum et al., Chapter 18, this volume), and the J-SOAP-II in a residential sample of 169 youth. Although the SAVRY and the J-SOAP-II total scores significantly predicted *nonsexual* violent reoffense, none of the three scales predicted sexual reoffense (sexual reoffense rate was 8.4%). Both the J-SOAP-II and the SAVRY were more effective in predicting violent reoffending in older youth (16 and older). Caldwell, Ziemke, and Vitacco (2008) also reported non-significance for the J-SOAP-II Total score and the Static score in their study of post-treatment sexual reoffense. Consistent with Viljoen et al. and Chu et al., however, Scale 2 of the J-SOAP-II predicted violent nonsexual reoffense and other nonsexual reoffense. Notably, Scale 3 predicted sexual reoffense.

A key meta-analysis conducted by Viljoen and her colleagues (Viljoen, Mordell, & Beneteau, 2012) compared the J-SOAP-II, ERASOR, J-SORRAT-II, and Static-99 using 33 studies with a total of 6,196 male juveniles. Although 15 studies of the J-SOAP-II were identified, not all met their criteria for inclusion and thus were omitted from their analyses. The nine studies that investigated the J-SOAP-II total score yielded an average AUC of .67 (95% CI = .59–.75). Equivalent findings for the subscales were: Scale 1 (AUC = .61; 95% CI = .53–.69), Scale 2, (AUC = .63; 95% CI .58–.69), Scale 3, (AUC = .60; 95% CI = 54–.66), and Scale 4, (AUC = .70; 95% CI = .60–.80).

The total scores for all four risk assessment scales compared in this meta-analysis significantly predicted sexual reoffense, with aggregated AUC values ranging from .64 to .67, and there were no differences between the scales in predictive accuracy. Moreover, these AUC values reflecting the predictive accuracy of these scales are roughly equivalent to the AUC values typically reported for the adult sex offender risk assessment and general delinquency scales. Although all of these AUC values significantly predicted sexual recidivism, for all practical purposes (i.e., application in forensic settings), the results should be considered suboptimal.

Translating these AUC values into more common indices of effect size, an AUC value of .64 translates to a Cohen's d value of .52 and a point-biserial correlation (r_{pb}) of .25; an AUC value of .67 translates into a d value of .62 and an r_{pb} of .30 (Rice & Harris, 2005). Using Cohen's (1977) guidelines, the effect sizes for all four of the risk scales compared in the meta-analysis are in the *moderate* range. Our common goal should be reaching an AUC $\geq$ .70, which more closely approximates a large effect size (d = .74). It should be noted that although these guidelines provide a benchmark for gauging progress, Baguley (2009) and others have argued against using "canned effect sizes" (p. 613), noting that the *practical significance* of the scale's accuracy should drive the degree of accuracy demanded by its application. Given the *practical* significance in the present context (i.e., its application in legal decision-making regarding such determinations as community vs. residential placement for juvenile sex offenders), the ballpark correlations between the score of these risk assessment scales and recidivism (.25–.30) are not adequate. To be clear, however, we are *not* arguing against the use of structured risk assessments like the J-SOAP. Indeed, structured risk assessment protocols are integral to an evaluation and must be integrated into a comprehensive (idiographic) evaluation. Reliance on unstructured clinical judgments of risk has proven to be folly. We are simply rebutting the use of structured risk assessment *in isolation* with a mindful eye on the impact of our management decisions.

Since the Viljoen et al. (2012) meta-analysis, at least five additional studies examined the predictive validity of the J-SOAP-II. Ralston and Epperson (2013) included the J-SOAP-II in a large, comparative analysis of two juvenile and two adult sexual offense-specific risk assessment tools that investigated 636 juveniles who had offended sexually. Scales 3 and 4 were omitted because the records were archival and quite old, hence dynamic information was inadequate. Ralston and Epperson (2013) reported that Scale 1 significantly predicted juvenile sexual recidivism with an AUC value of .76 (99.9% CI .67–.85) and juvenile *violent* sexual recidivism with an AUC of .78 (99.9% CI .69–.87).[1] Scale 2 predicted juvenile sexual recidivism with an AUC value of .75 (99.9% CI = .66–.84) and juvenile *violent* sexual recidivism with an AUC value of .77 (99.9% CI = .67–.87). Scales 1 and 2 did not predict nonsexual violent recidivism. Scale 1 significantly predicted sexual recidivism occurring in adulthood with an AUC value of .65 (99.9% CI = .51–.79), as did Scale 2 with an AUC value of .66 (99.9% CI = .53–.80). Reduced predictive accuracy of the J-SOAP-II in predicting recidivism in adulthood underscores the importance of using such adolescent measures for short-term risk assessments only (i.e., we recommend that, at minimum, the J-SOAP-II be repeated every 6 months).

Martinez, Rosenfeld, Cruise, and Martin (2015) compared the predictive validity of the J-SOAP-II with samples of youth in a medium security facility ($n = 70$) and an unlocked residential treatment center ($n = 86$). The predictive validity for the full Total Score, including or excluding Scale 4, was moderate but not statistically significant (AUC .64, .63, respectively). As commonly found with follow-up studies of this population, the known sexual reoffense rates were very low ($n = 5$ and 8 for the two subsamples). Thus, the true positive target was 13 out of 156. Martinez and his colleagues further reported noteworthy sample differences. Youth at the residential (unlocked) facility were significantly higher on Scale 1 and significantly lower on Scales 2 and 3. Although only 5 (out of 86) reoffended sexually (5.8%), the AUC value for the Total J-SOAP score (.63) was higher than the AUC value for the locked facility (.58) with a higher sexual reoffense rate (8, 11.4%). Ordinarily, one would expect improved predictive accuracy (higher c value) with a higher reoffense base rate. The authors speculated that superior treatment at the unlocked facility may have contributed to the lower Scale 3 score and possibly the lower reoffense rate, noting that "Although far from definitive, these findings may reflect the greater intensity of sex offender treatment at unlocked facilities, as this setting focused much more intensively on sex offender programming than did the other. The significantly lower scores on J-SOAP-II Scale III (Intervention), reflecting fewer intervention-based risk factors, supports this hypothesis but is clearly insufficient to "test" the differences in treatment programming across the two sites" (Martinez et al., 2015, p. 63).

Viljoen et al. (2017) examined the utility of dynamic variables in the J-SOAP-II and the SAVRY in a sample of 163 juvenile sex offenders that had been discharged from a residential, cognitive-behavioral treatment program. Interestingly, although half of the boys evidenced decreases on the J-SOAP-II's Dynamic Risk Total Score, and one third evidenced a decrease on the SAVRY's Dynamic Risk Total Score after treatment, an apparent drop in risk and an increase in protective factors did *not* predict a significant reduction in reoffending (no matter how reoffending was examined). Thus, although both the J-SOAP-II and the SAVRY were capturing change, it was *not* change that translated into a reduction in reoffense. Viljoen et al. (2017) went on to note that, "One exception to this was that reliable decreases in risk factors on the J-SOAP-II Intervention scale significantly predicted lower rates of sexual reoffending" (p. 363). During the follow-up period only 12 youth were arrested for a sexual reoffense (7.4%).

Barra, Bessler, Landolt, and Aebi (2018) compared the J-SOAP-II, ERASOR, and Violence Risk Appraisal Guide-Revised (VRAG-R; Harris et al., 2015; see Hilton et al., Chapter 7, this volume) on a sample of 597 juvenile sex offenders, examining sexual, nonsexual violent, and general criminal recidivism at three exposure periods: 0.5–3.0 years and in adulthood (>18 years). Recidivism rates by exposure time and offense type were: *Sexual*: 0.5 = 3.5%, 3.0 years = 7.4%, >18 = 3.1%; *Nonsexual Violent*: 0.5 = 8.0%, 3.0 years = 18.5%, >18 = 8.7%; *General*: 0.5 = 21.6%, 3.0 years = 43.4%, >18 = 32.5%. The sexual reoffense AUC values for the ERASOR (0.76, 0.78, 0.70) and the J-SOAP-II (0.74, 0.74, 0.70) appeared comparable at all three exposure periods while the VRAG-R was somewhat less predictive (0.67, 0.69, 0.69). The latter findings for the VRAG might be assumed given that it was not intended specifically for sexual offenders and it was not intended for use with juveniles. Not surprisingly, the VRAG-R did better at predicting nonsexual reoffense (for which the VRAG was intended) and predicting reoffense for those over 18 (again, for which the scale was intended). Barra et al. (2018) concluded, as many others have, that juvenile sex offender risk assessment should not be based solely on scores from psychometric scales but rather on idiographic evaluations.

Wijetunga, Martinez, Rosenfeld, and Cruise (2018) examined age and sexual drive on J-SOAP-II ratings in a sample of 156 male juvenile sexual offenders. Follow-up was an average of about five years (M = 63.70 months) with an overall sexual recidivism rate of 8.3% (*n* = 13). Overall, Wijetunga et al. (2018) found that the J-SOAP-II had greater predictive efficacy (higher AUC values) with young juveniles (ages 14–16) than the older youth (ages 17–19) and somewhat greater efficacy with youth higher in sexual drive. Notably, the sexual recidivism rate was the same for the younger youth (8.47%) and the older youth (8.25%). Sexual Drive, moreover, was not significantly associated with age or sexual recidivism (High Sexual Drive: 10%; Low Sexual Drive: 11.32%). Although the former age-related finding is consistent with findings reported by Ralston and Epperson (2013), it is not consistent with results reported by Viljoen et al. (2008). It should be noted, however, that the age groupings in the two studies did not overlap. Although Scales 2, 3, and 4 significantly predicted outcome for the younger youth, none of the individual scales predicted outcome for the older youth. In addition, Scale 3 (Clinical/Intervention) significantly predicted time to reoffense but only for the younger youth. Wijetunga et al. speculated about changes in efficacy of risk factors over the course of adolescence. Although the impact of age of onset of intervention (Scale 3) is complexly related to development, with psychosocial maturity, capacity to resist impulses, and increased volitional control coming with age, earlier intervention may, in some cases, be salutary by addressing some problems before they become entrenched (e.g., negative effects of trauma).

Schwartz-Mette, Righthand, Hecker, Dore, and Huff (2019) reported on a long-term follow-up (M = 10.75 years) of 166 juvenile sex offenders that had been scored on the J-SOAP-II. Once again, the number of identified sexual recidivists within the exposure period was very small (6, 3.7%), although the number of nonviolent, nonsexual reoffenders (82, 50%) and violent, nonsexual reoffenders (39, 23.8%) was considerable.

The AUC values for prediction of a new *sexual offense* was 0.76 for the total J-SOAP-II score, .77 for Scale 1 and .79 for the combined Static score. Although statistically significant, predictive efficacy dropped and was moderate with violent nonsexual offenses: Total Score (AUC = .68), Scale 2 (AUC = .68), combined Static score (AUC = .64), Scale 3 (AUC = .66), Scale 4 (AUC = .66), combined Dynamic score (AUC = .70) and was "moderate" as well. Predictive accuracy with *nonviolent, nonsexual* offenses was technically significant although, practically speaking, weak: Scale 2 (AUC = .63), Scale 3 (AUC = .60), combined Dynamic score (AUC = .60).

Overview of Predictive Validity Research

We have learned a great deal over the past two decades, including the importance of a primary focus on risk-relevant dynamic factors that, when addressed effectively in treatment, may not only mitigate risk, but promote protective factors that enhance strengths and facilitate positive youth development.

The preceding review is noteworthy in part due to the large number of research studies that have included J-SOAP-II. The mixed findings are consistent with what Viljoen et al. (2012) and others (e.g., Hempel, Buck, Cima, & Hjalmar van Marle, 2013) have pointed out regarding studies of juvenile sex offender risk assessment scales in general. As with all scales addressing risk with juvenile sex offenders, there is considerable variability in reports of predictive validity. In the case of J-SOAP-II, some studies find clear support for the Total score and Scale 1, while other studies have provided support for Scales 2, 3, and 4. Other studies report null findings.

Such inconsistency is invariably due to sampling differences (e.g., Scale 2 is likely to have greater efficacy with samples of more delinquent youth, while Scale 3 is likely to have greater efficacy with samples of treated youth) and, importantly, methodological problems (e.g., small sample size, low base rates of sexual reoffending, length of follow-up and relatedly adequacy of follow-up data, and samples with deficient or insufficient data for rating the items reliably, fidelity to scale directions, as well as studies that included youth that the risk scale was not intended for, such as sexual harassers in Aebi, Plattner, Steinhausen, & Bessler, 2011). The length of follow-up and quality of outcome data undoubtedly are significant contributors to disparate findings. Variability in quality of archival data used for the ratings and presence or absence of an interview are contributing factors as well. It should be noted, however, that Rajlic and Gretton (2010) reported that most studies of J-SOAP-II and the ERASOR have found interrater reliability to be adequate or better. The single most daunting methodological problem, however, has always been the low base rates for sexual reoffending, generally averaging around 10–15% (Caldwell, 2016; Finkelhor, Ormrod, & Chaffin, 2009). Such low (known) base rates for sexual reoffense result in high false positive rates, posing a formidable obstacle to improving accuracy.

Nevertheless, considerable user feedback suggests that the subscale scores of J-SOAP-II can provide valuable information. As noted earlier, youth with a relatively high score on Scale 1 and a relatively low score on Scale 2 require more sex offense-specific interventions and less of a focus on delinquency interventions. In fact, mixing such a youth with more "hard-core" delinquents may do more harm than good. In contrast, a youth who has a high score on Scale 2 and a relatively low score on Scale 1 may have sexually offended as part of a general pattern of antisocial behavior, requiring a primary, if not exclusive, focus on delinquency interventions. Youth who have high scores on both Scales 1 and 2 may require more intensive supervision, perhaps in a secure residential placement, and need sex offense-specific treatment as well as delinquency-focused interventions. Low scores on Scales 1 and 2, on the other hand, may suggest that the offending behavior was situational, requiring limited interventions, such as a psychoeducational focus on human sexuality, social skills training, and dating skills.

Additionally, some youth with relatively high scores on Scale 3 may be presentence or pretreatment or in the early stages of treatment and scared to discussed their offenses, fearful of getting in more trouble, and afraid of loss of support from family and friends. Other youth with high Scale 3 scores may lack empathy and/or remorse, traits that may be associated with a more entrenched antisocial personality style; other youth with mid-range scores may just be *talking the talk* (i.e., having learned what to say), and still others with relative low scores may have limited treatment needs to begin with or may have made progress in treatment. Because most items on the current J-SOAP-II Scale 3 are addressed in treatment (McGrath, Cumming, Burchard, Zeoli, & Ellerby, 2010), ratings on Scale 3 are likely to decrease as youth engage in treatment, necessitating re-evaluations on Scale 3 rather than relying on the intake evaluation. Relying solely on the intake assessment is likely to increase invalidity, even when youth have not been in treatment (i.e., changes may occur even in the absence of treatment simply as a result of aging, parental response, and exposure to counselors and other staff). With youth in treatment, we recommend re-visiting Scale 3 every three months. Even when youth have not been in treatment, Scale 3 should be re-visited when discharge is being considered.

Limitations and Research Needs

Improving Reliability

As Vincent et al. (2012) stressed, good interrater reliability is crucial. One of the most important factors contributing to unreliability is the lack of information or the ambiguity of information that is used to score the items. How incomplete or ambiguous the information is may vary enormously from one case to another and of course from one site to another. There are no simple or easy methods for dealing with this problem, other than employing multiple sources of archival information and interviewing the youth and collateral informants. Not only is there a greater likelihood of finding additional information, but multiple sources provide a cross-check of existing information.

To enhance reliability, we strongly recommend that examiners use as many different sources of information as possible when scoring J-SOAP-II. In addition, although it is often not feasible, we also recommend that the J-SOAP-II be scored by two independent clinicians or a treatment team who then compare and discuss their scores. The agreed-upon ("consensus") scores should be used. When the available information is limited or incomplete, items should always be scored "conservatively" (in the direction of lower risk), and it should be noted that the resulting findings may underestimate the risk. If data are absent or so poor or contradictory that rating the item cannot be done reliably, the item should not be rated and the proportion for that scale can be changed accordingly (reflecting the omitted item/s).

Addressing Methodological Problems Related to Validity

As we alluded to earlier and discussed on many prior occasions, there are numerous methodological challenges of follow-up studies with juveniles examining the predictive efficacy of risk assessment tools (e.g., Prentky, Pimental, Cavanaugh, & Righthand, 2009; Prentky, Righthand, & Lamade, 2016; Righthand, Vincent, & Huff, 2017; Schwartz-Mette, Righthand, Hecker, Dore, & Huff, 2019). The problems plaguing risk assessment with juveniles were excellently reviewed by Vincent et al. (2012) in their MacArthur Foundation Guidebook. In what follows, we offer a few highlights and how we have sought to address them in our current project (Prentky, Righthand, & Lamade, 2015, described in the following):

- Perhaps the number "1" limitation is the base rate of sexual reoffense, hovering around 10–15% when arrest or adjudication for a sex offense is used as the criterion (e.g., Caldwell, 2016; Finkelhor et al., 2009; Gretton, McBride, Hare, O'Shaughnessy, & Kumka, 2001; Righthand & Welch, 2001; Viljoen et al., 2012; Worling & Curwen, 2000). In their meta-analysis of 33 studies ($n = 6,196$), Viljoen et al. (2012) reported a sexual reoffense rate of

10.9% after an average of 71 months (6 years) exposure. As has frequently been reported, Viljoen et al. (2012) found a much higher *non*sexual (general) reoffense rate (49%). Less than a half dozen studies appear to be outliers regarding known incidence of sexual reoffense, mostly with very small samples (e.g., Borduin et al., 1990, *n* = 16, 44%; Langstrom & Grann, *n* = 46, 20%; Milloy, 2006, *n* = 21, 385; Rubenstein et al., 1993, *n* = 19, 37%. The one exception was the study of 303 youth by Nisbet, Wilson, and Smallbone (2004), reporting a sexual reoffense rate of 25%.

All of these studies used as outcome an arrest, an adjudication, or re-incarceration for a new sex offense. To address this, we have expanded the scope of the dependent variable to include a wider range of "outcomes" beyond sexual reoffense. In keeping with our goal of shifting the focus from negative outcomes (sexual reoffense) to positive outcomes, we treated facets of healthy adjustment as "dependent" variables (e.g., educational achievement, improvement in social skills, degree of commitment to all recommended interventions, and indices of change as a function of treatment).

- The near exclusive focus on risk factors and concomitant exclusion of presumptive protective and responsivity factors (responsiveness to interventions) has been inconsistent with the present state of the art (Vincent et al., 2018). In our current project, we have included a number of protective factors that may serve potentially to mitigate risk, not merely to reflect the absence of risk, as well as responsivity factors that may improve efficacy of our interventions.

- Thus far, all juveniles have generally been deposited into a common, undifferentiated subject pool in research studies. The marked heterogeneity of juvenile sex offenders (Chaffin, 2008; Hunter, 2006; Hunter et al., 2003; Knight & Prentky, 1993) necessitates taxonomic differentiation, as suggested in Figure 13.1. As Chaffin (2008) pointed out,

> the term *juvenile* sex *offender*, as a taxonomic category has virtually no value other than as an administrative classification for crimes. Taxonomically, the term misleads more often than it informs . . . it has little value as a risk marker, as a prognostic indicator, or prescriptively for intervention purposes.
>
> (p. 117)

It is clear that decision-making, whether it is about intervention planning or risk management, will be improved with taxonomic models, the simplest of which, as a starting point, were developed by Hunter and his colleagues (Hunter et al., 2003). A valid taxonomic model can yield homogeneous subtypes that lead to improved decision-making. To that end, we are testing the utility of Hunter's 4-subgroup classification depicted in Figure 13.1. This goal is all the more critical if our ultimate objective is improving risk management and remediation. As it stands, the heterogeneity of the category *juvenile sex offender* leads only to suboptimal policies, procedures, and outcomes.

- To our knowledge, almost all risk assessment scales, both for adult as well as juvenile offenders, utilize a 3-point scale in which "0" is the apparent absence of the factor and "2" is the clear presence of the factor, resulting in a heterogeneous lumping of all other individuals that are not clearly 0 or 2 as "1." Knight, Ronis, and Zakireh (2009), in offering recommendations for future research on risk assessment with juvenile sex offenders, pointed out that such a scale, while optimizing interrater reliability, sacrifices variance associated with severity, detracting from accuracy (validity). If the goal is improving risk management rather than risk prediction, more differentiated scales are required. By creating a more differentiated rating scale (avoiding the de facto unsure or unclear ("1") option), we may improve content validity as well as sensitivity. In our current project we have adopted a 4-point scale defined in terms of degree of intervention required for that factor, ranging from 0 (no intervention needed) to

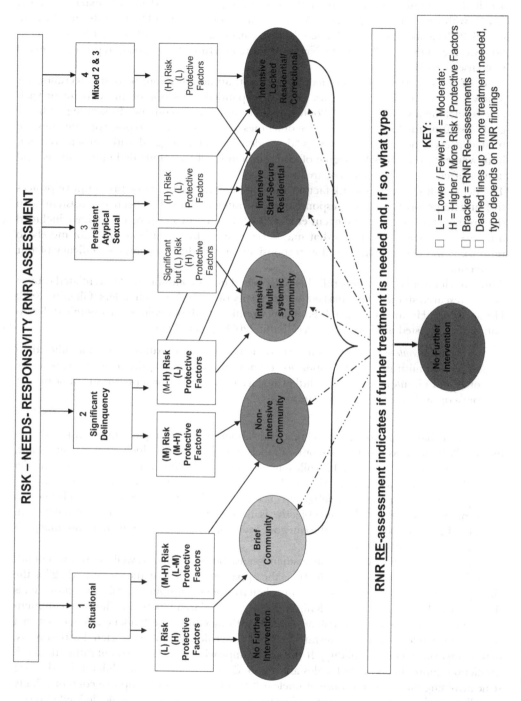

Figure 13.1 Risk-Need-Responsivity (RNR) Assessment

3 (intervention clearly required). All four levels for each item are defined in terms of degree of intervention required.

- Scale 3 has illustrated the complexity of assessing change as a function of treatment, raising a range of methodological issues, from the operationalization of the items, focusing, for example, on remorse, guilt, or empathy as it directly pertains to one's victims rather than as a global personality trait, the necessity of evaluating treatment progress over time to assess change, and quality of data used to assess the items. Additionally, the items for Scale 3 were selected and operationalized 25 years ago, well before almost all of the current literature on dynamic risk assessment with juvenile sex offenders was published. In 1995, most of the treatment literature and treatment programming was on adult sex offenders and derived from experiments with civil commitment.

- Further, Scale 4 is problematic for two reasons: (a) as the items are presently operationalized, the scale cannot be used for discharge planning; and (b) the scale includes items that pertain to the individual as well as his social ecology. Both problems have been addressed in the current project. Items have now been operationalized so they can be rated in advance of discharge, and a principal components analysis yielded three components, two of which correspond to these concerns (i.e., two are more intra-personal and one is composed entirely of community supports and resources. We intend to explore the substitution of these two factors with the existing Scale 4.

Overall, although relatively few studies have found clear evidence for the efficacy of Scales 3 and 4, it does not mean that the scales are without merit; it means that the scales must be revised consistent with the state of the art guided by empirical inquiry and the extant literature. Some requirements (for both Scales 3 and 4) are unrelated to the items themselves and would seem transparently obvious (e.g., not relying solely on archival data; whenever possible conducting one or more clinical interviews of the youth; if the youth is in treatment or participating in other services [e.g., probation], inquire about the quality of participation in such services, and repeat scale item ratings at appropriate time intervals). There is no substitute for the breadth and quality of the sources of data relied upon for the ratings.

Current Project

The TNPR described earlier in this chapter, in connection with J-SOAP, antedated our current project, which is designed to develop, implement, and test a dynamic risk and needs (intervention) scale intended for risk *management* as well as *guidance* in treatment. Prentky, Righthand, and Lamade (2015) set forth an agenda to *integrate* rational management policies with assessment of risk that parallels and informs individualized strategies for risk management and intervention. We did so diagrammatically by illustrating a hypothetical integration of four subtypes based on the work of Hunter (2006, 2008; Hunter et al., 2003; see Figure 13.1), each characterized by hypothetical levels of risk and availability of protective factors, leading to an optimal case management plan. The Venn diagram (Figure 13.2) illustrates a continuum of treatment intensity as well as a range of placement options. Decision-makers, such as judges, ultimately determine management settings, and these decisions must be informed by competent clinical input regarding the current assessment of the individual and socio-ecological risk and recommended interventions, including treatment intensity. As the Association for the Treatment of Sexual Abusers' (ATSA) Policies and Practices (2017) suggest, these decisions should *always* favor, whenever possible, the *least* restrictive placement.

We recommended that a youth-centered, developmentally sensitive agenda replace the current punitive, offender-centered agenda. The "good news" is that children and adolescents do *not* present the stark threat to reoffend that they are assumed to. The "bad news" is that "good news" is not always welcome news. Chaffin (2008) wrote,

> Vested political or financial interests and highly emotional advocacy agendas complicate healthy skepticism about the facts or their dispassionate consideration. Moral panic, righteous indignation, and truthiness have their own allure and satisfaction. The sound bite that we should put our kids' safety before the rights of sexual offenders, adult or juvenile, sounds so intuitively correct that it is a guaranteed political winner, even if the policy it promotes is ultimately destructive and fails to deliver the child protection goods.
>
> (p. 120)

The bulk of empirical data thus far point to the same conclusions: (1) when defined as re-arrest or re-adjudication for another sex offense, recidivism rates are typically so low that risk-related probabilistic estimates often cannot be reliably determined (i.e., the false positive rates are too high); (2) *all* adolescents are subject to an extended period (roughly a decade) of pervasive cognitive, social/interpersonal, and emotional growth—growth equates to change, and change challenges all prognostications about risky behavior; and (3) compared with adults, adolescents tend to be more amenable to interventions, including treatment.

Prentky et al. (2015) contended, "The research tasks going forward are vastly more encompassing than testing the latest version of a new risk assessment scale. No risk assessment scale, no matter what its presumptive predictive accuracy, will solve the systemic problem of how youngsters who have committed sexual offenses should be safely managed and treated. The quintessential issue may be seen as the interminable debate over retributive versus restorative justice for juveniles," (pp. 665–666). The most prudent answer transcends this conundrum, and can be resolved less contentiously by adopting the most data-informed, cost-effective (viable) responses to the problem. The logic is simple. By doing a credible individualized assessment of risk-relevant factors, we can tailor an intervention plan designed to mitigate those risk factors, thereby accomplishing the twin objectives of fostering healthier adjustment and mitigating the likelihood of any further inappropriate sexual behavior.

The larger agenda for our current project dictated that a critical focus must be on addressing the problems discussed in this chapter. We set out to develop a model that constituted a shift in paradigm, moving from a risk prediction-based scheme to an intervention-based scheme. The

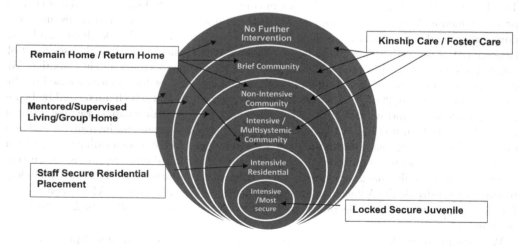

Figure 13.2 Continuum of Treatment Intensity and Level of Placement

model alluded to in this chapter was developed, implemented, and tested over the past three years with support from the Department of Justice (cf. Kang et al., 2019). This risk-based, intervention driven model (interventions determined by assessed risk factors) benefitted by a wonderful advisory board, extensive feedback from site users, and a close, collegial working relationship among the four core staff—Righthand, Worling, Kang, and Prentky. The net result was a risk-based intervention needs scale that included, in test version, 27 items, primarily dynamic risk factors, with a lesser number of protective, socio-ecological, and responsivity factors. The finalized scale was programmed in REDCap and sited at public and private juvenile justice agencies in five states that provide cognitive-behavioral treatment. REDCap permitted automated scale scoring that facilitated rating scale items and data collection. At the end of the 1-year trial period, 1,602 assessments (and reassessments) were completed on 604 youth. Of the 604, 188 youth were assessed 4 or more times (every 3 months) during treatment. Items with the greatest efficacy were selected for the final iteration.

Case Study: Maxwell

Maxwell is a 14-year-old boy who was recently adjudicated delinquent after acknowledging that he sexually abused his 10-year-old sister over a number of years, beginning with touching and progressing to penetration. Incidents involving penetration occurred multiple times over a 12-month period, beginning when she was 9 and he was 12. His reports of the offenses are generally consistent with those of the victim, but he indicates the incidents were less frequent than reported by his sister and occurred only over a single year. They both reported that initially the contact was limited to genital touching but in recent years had become more invasive and included penetration. The victim told her mother about the abuse when she learned that Maxwell had offered to babysit their 5-year-old stepsister and had touched her genitals over her clothes. Maxwell was referred for evaluation to assist the court with dispositional decisions.

Maxwell and his sister's early years were characterized by significant abuse and neglect. Both parents engaged in heavy substance abuse, and the children often were left to fend for themselves. The two children were exposed to violent arguments between their parents. Their father left the family when Maxwell was 5 years old. Their mother continued to abuse substances and had a series of live-in boyfriends, one of whom sexually abused Maxwell. When Maxwell began school, reports to child welfare authorities described him as hungry, dirty, and dressed in tatters. After coming to school with unexplained bruises, Maxwell and his sister were placed in foster care. Maxwell was 6.

There were several attempts to reunify the children with their mother. Their father could not be located. Within a year, efforts to reunify the children with their parents were discontinued. After a pre-adoptive placement of 6 months or more, the placement was disrupted as the pre-adoptive parents decided they could not manage the children's oppositional and unruly behaviors and Maxwell's temper outbursts. Fortunately, another pre-adoptive home was found for both siblings within a short period of time.

After the children were placed with the new family, there was a "honeymoon" period, and the adoption was finalized, problems ensued. Maxwell, age 8, assumed a parental role with his sister, and she was inclined to listen to him rather than their new caregivers. Their adoptive mother became pregnant for the first time. Maxwell became increasingly defiant and angry when the parents attempted to set normative behavior limits. They sought out individual counseling which focused on anger management for Maxwell.

At school, Maxwell received special education services due to delays in speech, language, and academics. He was teased by children and rejected by most of his peers. Sometimes other boys started fights, but sometimes he initiated them. By age 10, Maxwell was suspended twice for fighting and once for bringing a knife to school. Maxwell was caught on a couple of occasions stealing items, games, and electronics from other children. These problems were addressed internally by the school.

As a pre-teen, Maxwell continued to be socially isolated from his peers. At his parents' encouragement he participated in a youth group at church; he enjoyed guitar lessons taught by a local college student. He had become less argumentative at home. He seemed to enjoy family outings and camping trips. He still struggled academically at school but had made some important gains. He spent a lot of time alone in his room, playing video games.

After he was adjudicated as having sexually abused his sister, Maxwell participated in a comprehensive forensic assessment involving clinical interviews, psychological testing, interviews with his parents, and a review of police, social service, and school records. The Juvenile Sex Offender Assessment Protocol II was used as a component of this evaluation. Referral questions included Maxwell's risk of repeat sex offending as identification of any factors that could promote healthy and positive development. Questions were also raised about specific treatment needs and placement options. Maxwell presented as somewhat downcast, which appeared appropriate given the nature and seriousness of this evaluation and its potential consequences. Yet he was responsive to questions and appeared able to fully participate in the evaluation.

When discussing the offenses, Maxwell stated he touched his sister the first time after other boys had been boasting about such pursuits with their girlfriends, and he reported vague memories of adults doing such things at parties with each other at his biological parents' home. He said he had not thought of doing such a thing with his sister, but it happened. There were other times after that the thought occurred to him but he did not act on it, and sometimes he did. His sister confirmed that the abuse sometimes happened once or twice a week, but other times weeks would pass without any incidents even though there were times they were alone together. As time passed and she became increasingly reluctant to comply, Maxwell pressured his sister by telling her they would both be in trouble if she told and sometimes set her up by finding out something she had done wrong and would not want their parents to know, and threatening to tell them. Maxwell stated that although he initiated the sexual encounters, his sister sometimes willing and enjoying them. When asked why she disclosed her abuse, Maxwell acknowledged that he had begun to pressure her and "people don't like to be pushed to do things they don't want." He also admitted that his sister was very put off by his touching her private area and seemed upset. He noted that both of them seem over it now. Maxwell said he was sorry for the problems he caused everyone.

Like many youth who have not yet begun treatment for sexually abusive behavior, Maxwell was not able to articulate specific risk factors associated with his sexual misconduct. He seemed to have a vague sense that feeling lonely may be involved and said that in the future he could go to talk to his parents when feeling alone. When asked about talking with friends, he said his peers are just a bunch of jerks. He said there was one girl who seemed nice, but she turned out just like all the others. Maxwell did not justify his sexually abusive behavior except to say that he did not realize how bad it was or that it was against the law.

Although Maxwell said he will never get in trouble like this again and does not need counseling, he indicated his willingness to participate if it would help his family. He said he liked going to counseling when he was little, because the counselor was nice and taught him ways to control his anger better. Maxwell reported he rarely experiences sexual feelings anymore. His family reported there is no indication that, aside from the offenses, he has difficulty managing sexual urges. Like Maxwell, his family also reported it has been a long time since his temper has flared, but they noted he often seems subdued and somber, which they have attributed to normal teenage angst.

Maxwell continues to attend school. He is staying at his adoptive grandmother's home at night, but has daily contact with his parents and supervised visits with his siblings, all of whom want him to return home. Maxwell's family and extended family are strong supports, and he continues to participate in his church's youth group. However, Maxwell does not appear to have actively used such positive supports to help him address his difficulties in the past and will need encouragement to do so, as well as to expand his social contacts to include more rewarding peer relationships and prosocial activities.

Maxwell's scale and total ratings reflected the following:

Total J-SOAP-II	24/56	43%
Sexual Drive/Preoccupation Scale	06/16	38%
Impulsive-Antisocial Behavior	09/16	56%
Clinical Intervention Scale	08/14	57%
Community Stability Scale	01/10	10%

On Scale 1, the Sex Drive/Preoccupation Scale, Maxwell has just over a third of possible risk factors present. These risk factors were related to the duration of his offense history, multiple victims, planning some of the sexual offenses, and his own history of victimization. Other risk factors often associated with sexual reoffending, such as sexual preoccupation, reoffending following charged sex offenses, are absent. Further, this is Maxwell's only adjudication for a sexual or any other type of offense, and assessment findings suggest it has provided him with a clear message about the seriousness of such abusive behavior.

Scale 2, the Antisocial/Impulsive Scale, is comprised of historical items that cannot change. Maxwell's J-SOAP II Scale 2 scores reflect a moderate number of risk factors, just over half. However, a review of Maxwell's social history indicates that these difficulties were more pronounced when he was younger and have dissipated to a large extent in recent years (e.g., diminished temper outbursts and fighting). Maxwell's early history of abuse, neglect, and caregiver instability may have been strong contributors to these early difficulties. Yet, clinical interviews and psychological test findings (not reported here) suggest Maxwell may struggle with depression. On a positive note, Maxwell does not appear to have clear antisocial attitudes and beliefs, or a persistent history of poor impulse control and antisocial behavior.

Findings for Scale 3, the J-SOAP II Intervention scale, are consistent with other evaluation findings indicating that Maxwell evidences a moderate number (just over one-half) of risk factors which, when combined with findings from Scale 1 and 2, suggest the need for sex offense-specific treatment. Scale 3 items reflect Maxwell's acceptance of responsibility for his sexual offenses, his genuine remorse and empathy, and his motivation to avoid reoffending. Although research has not demonstrated the significance of these individual factors, studies show treatment completion is related to lower rates of repeat offending, and these individual factors are typically addressed in sex offense-specific treatment. Further, in cases involving sibling abuse and family reunification, factors such as accepting responsibility for the abuse, remorse, and empathy are very relevant to ensure the victim is not re-victimized by being blamed for the sexual abuse in any way. An important risk factor noted throughout this evaluation and on Scale 3 is Maxwell's social isolation and absence of a positive peer group.

Scale 4, the Community Stability/Adjustment score, reflects some important strengths and protective factors evidenced by Maxwell and his family. Overall, Maxwell's community adjustment in the past 6 months has been positive, with only 10% of possible scale-assessed "risk" indicated (i.e., 1 of 10 possible points), and this single point reflected Maxwell's previously reported need for more positive peer relationships, social connections, and prosocial supports. Scale 4 results also are consistent with other evaluation findings in indicating that Maxwell's adoptive family continues to be invested in him and is committed to reunifying their family if and when it is safe to do so. They have used therapeutic resources in the past and are willing to do so now.

Although Maxwell shares some characteristics with juveniles who have committed sex offenses and who have reoffended with a new sexual offense, it should be noted that many risk factors appear absent, and some have remitted over time. There is no evidence that Maxwell engages in sexual fantasies involving young children, nor does he appear sexually preoccupied. Importantly, as described earlier, he presents with important factors that may help to reduce the risk of repeat sexual offending, including a willingness to engage in treatment.

Multisystemic Therapy for Problematic Sexual Behavior (MST-PSB) may be an excellent intervention for Maxwell and his family. MST-PSB is an intensive, family- and community-based intervention, with good research support, for youths with problematic sexual behavior. It addresses risk factors associated with sexually abusive behavior while promoting strengths and protective factors. It combines social learning, cognitive-behavioral, and family therapy interventions, youth and parenting skill building, and school and community engagement to provide individualized interventions that facilitate safe and positive family relationships and community safety. Intervention targets for Maxwell and his family include: (a) safety planning that can facilitate family reintegration in the home when appropriate; (b) clarification of responsibility to ensure Maxwell's victim understands she is not responsible for the abuse; and (c) increasing positive communication between Maxwell and his parents, assisting the parents in providing healthy sexual education to Maxwell, promoting increased prosocial peer association and positive school and community engagement. Further assessment of Maxwell's apparent struggles with depression may be required and, if indicated, appropriate intervention should be provided. Timely intervention is important to ensure that depression does not interfere with treatment engagement.

Note

1. Ralston and Epperson (2013) reported they selected a 99.9% Confidence Interval, a more narrowly defined level of significance to reduce the risk of a Type I error, i.e., reduce the risk of false positives and identifying individuals as recidivists when they are not, thereby increasing the significance of their findings.

References

Aebi, M., Plattner, B., Steinhausen, H.C., & Bessler, C. (2011). Predicting sexual and nonsexual recidivism in a consecutive sample of juveniles convicted of sexual offences. *Sexual Abuse: Journal of Research and Treatment, 23,* 456–473.

ATSA. (2017). *Practice guidelines for the assessment, treatment, and intervention with adolescents who have engaged in sexually abusive behavior.* Beaverton, OR: Author.

Baguley, T. (2009). Standardized or simple effect size: What should be reported? *British Journal of Psychology, 100,* 603–617.

Barra, S., Bessler, C., Landolt, M. A., & Aebi, M. (2018). Testing the validity of criminal risk assessment tools in sexually abusive youth. *Psychological Assessment, 30,* 1430–1443. doi:10.1037/pas0000590

Borduin, C. M., Henggeler, S. W., Blaske, D. M., & Stein, R. J. (1990). Multisystemic treatment of adolescent sexual offenders. *International Journal of Offender Therapy and Comparative Criminology, 34,* 105–113.

Borum, R., Bartel, P., & Forth, A. (2002). *SAVRY: Manual for the structured assessment of violence risk in youth.* Tampa, FL: Florida Mental Health Institute, University of South Florida.

Caldwell, M. F. (2016). Quantifying the decline in juvenile sexual recidivism rates. *Psychology, Public Policy, and Law, 22,* 414–426.

Caldwell, M. F., Ziemke, M. H., & Vitacco, M. J. (2008). An examination of the sex offender registration and notification act as applied to juveniles: Evaluating the ability to predict sexual recidivism. *Psychology, Public Policy, and Law, 14,* 89–114.

Chaffin, M. (2008). Our minds are made up—don't confuse us with the facts: Commentary on policies concerning children with sexual behavior problems and juvenile sex offenders. *Child Maltreatment, 13*, 110–121.

Chu, C. M., Ng, K., Fong, J., & Teoh, J. (2012). Assessing youth who sexually offended: The predictive validity of the ERASOR, J-SOAP-II, and YLS/CMI in a non-western context. *Sexual Abuse, 24*, 153–174. doi:10.1177/1079063211404250

Cohen, J. (1977). *Statistical power analysis for the behavioral sciences.* New York: Routledge.

Epperson, D. L., Ralston, C. A., Fowers, D., & Dewitt, J. (2005). *Development of the juvenile sexual offense recidivism risk assessment tool-II (JSORRAT-II).* Retrieved from www.psychology.iastate.edu/faculty/epperson/jsorrat-ii-download.htm

Epperson, D. L., Ralston, C. A., Fowers, D., & DeWitt, J. (2012, October, 22). *Scoring guidelines for the juvenile sexual offense recidivism risk assessment tool—II (JSORRAT—II).* Pullman, WA: Washington State University.

Finkelhor, D., Ormrod, R., & Chaffin, M. (2009). Juveniles who commit sex offenses against minors. *Juvenile Justice Bulletin.* Retrieved from unh.edu/ccrc/pdf/CV171.pdf

Gretton, H. M., McBride, M., Hare, R. D., O'Shaughnessy, R., & Kumka, G. (2001). Psychopathy and recidivism in adolescent sex offenders. *Criminal Justice and Behavior, 28*, 427–449.

Harris, G. T., Rice, M. E., Quinsey, V. L., & Cormier, C. A. (2015). *Violent offenders: Appraising and managing risk* (3rd ed.). Washington, DC: American Psychological Association. doi:10.1037/14572000

Hecker, J., Scoular, J., Righthand, S., & Nangle, D. (2002, October). *Predictive validity of the JSOAP over 10-plus years: Implications for risk assessment.* Paper presented at the Annual Meeting of the Association for Treatment of Sexual Abusers, Montreal, Quebec.

Hunter, J. A. (2006). Understanding diversity in juvenile sexual offenders: Implications for assessment, treatment, and legal management. In R. E. Longo & D. S. Prescott (Eds.), *Current perspectives: Working with sexually aggressive youth and youth with sexual behavior problems* (pp. 63–77). Holyoke, MA: NEARI Press.

Hunter, J. A. (2008). The sexual crimes of juveniles. In R. R. Hazelwood & A. W. Burgess (Eds.), *Practical aspects of rape investigation* (4th ed., pp. 409–427). New York: CRC Press.

Hunter, J. A., Figueredo, A. J., Malamuth, N., & Becker, J. V. (2003). Toward the development of a typology. *Sexual Abuse: A Journal of Research and Treatment, 15*, 27–48.

Kang, T., Beltrani, A., Manheim, M., Spriggs, S., Nishimura, B., Sinclair, S., . . . Prentky, R. A. (2019). Development of a risk/treatment needs and progress protocol for juveniles with sex offenses. *Translational Issues in Psychological Science, 5*, 154–169. doi:10.1037/tps0000191

Knight, R. A., & Prentky, R. A. (1993). Exploring characteristics classifying juvenile sexual offenders. In H. E. Barbaree, W. L. Marshall, & S. M. Hudson (Eds.), *The juvenile sexual offender* (pp. 45–83). New York: Guilford Press.

Knight, R. A., Ronis, S. T., & Zakireh, B. (2009). Bootstrapping persistence risk predictors for juveniles who sexually offend. *Behavioral Sciences and the Law, 27*, 878–909. doi:10.1002/bsl.908

Langstrom, N., & Grann, M. (2000). Risk for criminal recidivism among young sex offenders. *Journal of Interpersonal Violence, 15*, 855–871.

Martinez, R., Rosenfeld, B., Cruise, K., & Martin, J. (2015). Predictive validity of the J-SOAP-II: Does accuracy differ across settings? *International Journal of Forensic Mental Health, 14*, 56–65, doi:10.1080/14999013.2015.1019683

Martinez, R., Rosenfeld, B., & Flores, J. (2007). Validity of the juvenile sex offender assessment protocol II (J-SOAP-II) in a sample of urban minority youth. *Criminal Justice and Behavior, 34*, 1284–1295.

McGrath, R., J., Cumming, G. F., Burchard, B. L., Zeoli, S., & Ellerby, L. (2010). Current practices and emerging trends in sexual abuser management: The Safer Society 2009 North American Survey. Brandon, VT: Safer Society Press.

Milloy, C. D. (2006). Juveniles Who Commit Sexual Offenses Recommended For Commitment Under Washington's Sexually Violent Predator Law, Where No Petition Was Filed. Olympia, WA: Washington State Institute for Public Policy. Retrieved from: www.wsipp.wa.gov.

Nisbet, I.A., Wilson, P.H. & Smallbone, S.W. (2004). A prospective longitudinal study of sexual recidivism among adolescent sex offenders. *Sexual Abuse: A Journal of Research and Treatment, 16*, 223–234.

Parks, G. A., & Bard, D. E. (2006). Risk factors for adolescent sex offender recidivism: Evaluation of predictive factors and comparison of three groups based upon victim type. *Sexual Abuse: A Journal of Research and Treatment, 18*, 319–342.

Powers-Sawyer, A. B., & Miner, M. H. (2009). Actuarial prediction of juvenile recidivism: The static variables of the juvenile sex offender assessment protocol-II (J-SOAP-II). *Sexual Offender Treatment, 4.* Retrieved from www.sexual-offender-treatment.org/2-2009_02.html

Prentky, R. A., Harris, B., Frizzell, K., & Righthand, S. (2000). Development and validation of an actuarial instrument for assessing risk among juvenile sex offenders. *Sexual Abuse: A Journal of Research and Treatment, 12,* 71–93.

Prentky, R. A., Lee, A. F. S., Knight, R. A., & Cerce, D. (1997). Recidivism rates among child molesters and rapists: A methodological analysis. *Law and Human Behavior, 21,* 635–659.

Prentky, R. A., Li, N. C., Righthand, S., Schuler, A., Cavanaugh, D., & Lee, A. F. (2010). Assessing risk of sexually abusive behavior among youth in a child welfare sample. *Behavioral Sciences and the Law, 28,* 24–45.

Prentky, R. A., Pimental, A., Cavanaugh, D. J., & Righthand, S. (2009). Predicting risk of sexual recidivism in juveniles: Predictive validity of the J-SOAP-II. In A. R. Beech, L. A. Craig, & K. D. Browne (Eds.), *Assessment and treatment of sex offenders: A handbook.* Hoboken, NJ: John Wiley & Sons, Inc.

Prentky, R. A., & Righthand, S. (2003). *Juvenile sex offender assessment protocol-II: J-SOAP-II manual.* Bridgewater, MA: Author.

Prentky, R. A., Righthand, S., & Lamade, R. (2015). Juvenile sexual offending: Assessment and intervention. In K. Heilbrun, D. DeMatteo, & N. Goldstein (Eds.), *Handbook of psychology and juvenile justice* (pp. 641–672). Washington, DC: American Psychological Association.

Prentky, R. A., Righthand, S., & Lamade, R. (2015). Juvenile Sexual Offending: Assessment and Intervention. Eds., K. Heilbrun, D. DeMatteo, & N. Goldstein (pp. 641–672). Invited Chapter in *Handbook of Psychology and Juvenile Justice.* Washington, D.C.: American Psychological Association.

Prentky, R. A., Righthand, S., & Lamade, R. (2016). Sexual offending: Assessment and intervention. In K. Heilbrun, D. DeMatteo, & N. Goldstein (Eds.), *Handbook of psychology and juvenile justice.* Washington, DC: American Psychological Association.

Rajlic, G., & Gretton, H. M. (2010). The moderating effect of offender type an examination of two sexual recidivism risk measures in adolescent offenders: The moderating effect of offender type. *Criminal Justice and Behavior, 37,* 1066–1085. doi:10.1177/0093854810376354

Ralston, C. A., & Epperson, D. L. (2013). Predictive validity of adult risk assessment tools with juveniles who offended sexually. *Psychological Assessment, 25,* 905–916. doi:10.1037/a0032683

Rice, M. E., & Harris, G. T. (2005). Comparing effect sizes in follow-up studies: ROC Area, Cohen's d, and r. *Law and Human Behavior, 29,* 615–620. doi:10.1007/s10979-005-6832-7

Righthand, S. (2005). *Treatment needs and progress report.* Retrieved from www.csom.org

Righthand, S., Boulard, N., Cabral, J., & Serwik, A. (2011). Reducing sexual offending among juveniles in Maine: A systems approach. *Corrections Today,* 24–27.

Righthand, S., Carpenter, E. M., Prentky, R. A. (2001, November). *Risk assessment in a sample of juveniles who have sexually offended: A comparative analysis.* Poster presented at the Annual Conference of the Association for the Treatment of Sexual Abusers, San Antonio, TX.

Righthand, S., Hecker, J., & Dore, G. (2012, October). *Using assessments to guide effective interventions & preliminary findings of the treatment needs and progress report.* Paper presented at the Association for the Treatment of Sexual Abusers' 31st Annual Research and Treatment Conference, Denver, CO.

Righthand, S., Knight, R., & Prentky, R. (2002, October). *A path analytic investigation of proximal antecedents of J-SOAP risk domains.* Paper presented at the Annual Meeting of the Association for Treatment of Sexual Abusers, Montreal, Quebec.

Righthand, S., Prentky, R., Hecker, J. E., Carpenter, E., & Nangle, D. (2000, November). *JJPI-maine juvenile sex offender risk assessment schedule (J-SOAP).* Poster presented at the Association for the Treatment of Sexual Abusers 19th Annual Research and Treatment Conference, San Diego, CA.

Righthand, S., Prentky, R., Knight, R., Carpenter, E., Hecker, J., & Nangle, D. (2005). Factor structure and validation of the juvenile sex offender assessment protocol (J-SOAP). *Sexual Abuse: A Journal of Research and Treatment, 17*(1), 13–30.

Righthand, S., Vincent, G., & Huff, R. (2017). Assessing risks and needs with adolescents who have sexually offended: Research-based guidelines. In S. Righthand & W. Murphy (Eds.), *The safer society handbook of assessment and treatment with adolescents who have sexually offended.* Brandon, VT: Safer Society Press.

Righthand, S., & Welch, C. (2001, March). *Juveniles who have sexually offended a review of the professional literature* (OJJDP Report). Washington, DC: Office of Juvenile Justice and Delinquency Prevention, Office of Justice Programs, Department of Justice.

Rubenstein, M., Yeager, M.A., Goodstein, B.A., & Lewis, D.O. (1993). Sexually assaultive male juveniles: A follow-up. *American Journal of Psychiatry, 150,* 262–265.

Schwartz-Mette, R. A., Righthand, S., Hecker, J., Dore, G., & Huff, R. (2019). Long-term predictive validity of the juvenile sex offender assessment protocol—II: Research and practice. *Sexual Abuse.* doi:10.1177/1079063219825871

Viljoen, J. L., Gray, A. l., Shaffer, C., Latzman, N. E., Scalora, M. J., & Ullman, D. (2017). Changes in J-SOAP-II and SAVRY scores over the course of residential, cognitive-behavioral treatment for adolescent sexual offending. *Sexual Abuse: A Journal of Research and Treatment, 29,* 342–374.

Viljoen, J. L., Mordell, S., & Beneteau, J. L. (2012). Prediction of adolescent sexual reoffending: A meta-analysis of the J-SOAP-II, ERASOR, J-SORRAT-II, and Static-99. *Law and Human Behavior, 36,* 423–438. doi:10.1037/h0093938

Viljoen, J. L., Scalora, M., Cuadra, L., Bader, S., Chavez, V., Ullman, D., & Lawrence, L. (2008). Assessing risk of violence in adolescents who have sexually offended: A comparison of the J-SOAP-II, J-SORRAT-II, and SAVRY. *Criminal Justice and Behavior, 35,* 5–23. doi:10.1177/0093854807307521

Vincent, G., Guy, L. S., & Grisso, T. (2012). *Risk assessment in juvenile justice: A guidebook for implementation.* Models for Change: System Reform in Juvenile Justice: John D. and Catherine T. MacArthur Foundation. Retrieved from www.modelsforchange.net/publications/346

Vincent, G., Sullivan, C. J., Sullivan, C., Guy, L., Latessa, E., Tyson, J., & Adams, B. (2018, December). *Studying drivers of risk and needs assessment instrument implementation in juvenile justice.* Juvenile Justice Bulletin. Washington, DC: Office of Juvenile Justice and Delinquency Prevention, Office of Justice Programs, U.S. Department of Justice.

Waite, D., Pinkerton, R., Wieckowski, E., McGarvey, E., & Brown, G. L. (2002, October). *Tracking treatment outcome among juvenile sexual offenders: A nine year follow-up study.* Paper presented at the Annual Meeting of the Association for Treatment of Sexual Abusers, Montreal, Quebec.

Wijetunga, C., Martinez, R., Rosenfeld, B., & Cruise, K. (2018). The influence of age and sexual drive on the predictive validity of the juvenile sex offender assessment protocol—revised. *International Journal of Offender Therapy and Comparative Criminology, 62,* 150–169. doi:10.1177/0306624X16650681

Worling, J. R., & Curwen, T. (2000). Adolescent sexual offender recidivism: Success of specialized treatment and implications for risk prediction. *Child Abuse & Neglect, 24,* 965–982.

Worling, J. R., & Curwen, T. (2001). Estimate of risk of adolescent sexual offense recidivism (ERASOR; Version 2.0). In M. C. Calder (Ed.), *Juveniles and children who sexually abuse: Frameworks for assessment* (pp. 372–397). Lyme Regis: Russell House.

Worling, J. R., Litteljohn, A., & Bookalam, D. (2010). 20-year prospective follow-up study of specialized treatment for adolescents who offended sexually. *Behavioral Sciences and the Law, 28,* 46–57.

Appendix
Revisions Leading to the J-SOAP

Scale 1

Six substantial changes were made. These changes include the addition of four new items, the deletion of one item, and an extensive revision of another. The decision to add several items was based on weaknesses in Scale 1 and recent research suggesting the potential importance of these items in assessing the risk of sexual reoffending. The four new items are: (1) Number of Sexual Abuse Victims, which measures the number of victims the juvenile has ever sexually abused; (2) Male Child Victim, which assesses the juvenile's history of sexually abusing a substantially younger male child; (3) Sexualized Aggression, which assesses the presence of gratuitous or expressive aggression that goes beyond what was required to complete the sexual offense; and (4) Sexual Victimization History, which assesses the juvenile's own history of sexual victimization and the complexity and severity of the abuse.

The *deleted* item is High Degree of Sexualizing the Victim. This item had a very low frequency of occurrence and appeared of limited utility. One item, Evidence of Sexual Preoccupation/Obsessions, was replaced with a more clearly defined Sexual Drive and Preoccupation item. The new Sexual Drive and Preoccupation item was behaviorally anchored with a range of examples making it easier to code from file data. Scale 1 in the J-SOAP-II now has a total of eight items.

Scale 2

Five substantial changes were made, affecting six items. (1) Two items, History of Substance Abuse and History of Parental Substance Abuse, were eliminated. Several studies consistently indicated that these were weak items and were not contributing to the predictive ability of Scale 2. (2) The item School Suspensions or Expulsions was combined with the item School Behavior Problems to reduce the obvious overlap between those two items. (3) The item Impulsivity was dropped. As a risk predictor, lifestyle impulsivity appears to be more effective with adults than with juveniles. The J-SOAP item, Juvenile Antisocial Behavior, provides a much better assessment of impulsivity in adolescence. (4) An item, Physical Assault History/Exposure to Family Violence, was added based on the empirical literature as well as our recent path analysis looking at the developmental antecedents of J-SOAP scales. (5) The item Caregiver Consistency was revised. In order to provide a more sensitive assessment of caregiver changes that might impact adversely affect the development of attachments and relationships, the item was changed to assess caregivers prior to age 10 rather than 16. J-SOAP-II Scale 2 now has a total of eight items.

Scale 3

Because J-SOAP-II may be useful for assessing nonsexual recidivism as well as sexual recidivism, relevant Scale 3 Intervention items were revised to include changes in attitudes and behaviors related to nonsexual offending as well as sexual offending. In addition, because empathy and remorse are really distinct attitudes and feelings, the J-SOAP item Evidence of Empathy, Remorse, and Guilt was divided into two items, one simply entitled Empathy, and the other entitled Remorse and Guilt. Finally, based on Principal Components Analyses findings, the item Quality of Peer Relationships was moved from Scale 4 to Scale 3, where it appears to fit conceptually as an important target of treatment interventions. These changes result in J-SOAP-II Scale 3, the Intervention Scale, having a total of seven items.

Scale 4

Two substantial changes were made to Scale 4. One new item, Management of Sexual Urges and Desire, was added to assess the extent to which the juvenile manages his sexual urges and desires in socially appropriate and healthy ways. Also, as noted previously, the item Quality of Peer Relationships was moved from Scale 4 to Scale 3. These changes resulted in Scale 4 having a total of five items.

Chapter 14

Structured Professional Judgment Guidelines for Sexual Violence Risk Assessment

The Sexual Violence Risk-20 (SVR-20) Versions 1 and 2 and Risk for Sexual Violence Protocol (RSVP)

Stephen D. Hart and Douglas P. Boer

In this chapter, we review two related sets of structured professional judgment guidelines for assessing risk for sexual violence. The *Sexual Violence Risk-20* actually exists in two editions, Version 1 (Boer, Hart, Kropp, & Webster, 1997) and Version 2 (Boer, Hart, Kropp, & Webster, 2017), hereinafter abbreviated SVR-20 V1 and V2, respectively. Although V2 is intended to supersede V1, we review V1 here because a number of English-language evaluators have not yet switched to V2 and most evaluators working in other languages cannot use V2 because translations are not yet completed. The *Risk for Sexual Violence Protocol*, abbreviated herein as RSVP, is currently available only in one version (Hart et al., 2003), with Version 2 scheduled for release by December 2020.

This chapter updates our contribution to the first edition of the book (Hart & Boer, 2010). The SVR-20 V1 or RSVP have been reviewed by others, most often as part of narrative or meta-analytic reviews of multiple sexual violence risk assessment tools (e.g., Hanson & Morton-Bourgon, 2009). Our review is unique in three major respects. First, we provide a full description of the administration process of the SVR-20 V1/V2 and RSVP. We discuss the guidelines together because they are similar in format and content and to that extent that we consider them to be parallel forms; yet, there are some noteworthy differences between them, primarily with respect to the complexity of their administration procedures. Second, we provide a narrative summary of all the major disseminations to date we could locate that evaluated the interrater reliability and criterion-related validity of judgments made using the guidelines. Third, we illustrate the use of the guidelines—and the differences between them—using a case example.

Description

Type of Instrument

The SVR-20 V1/V2 and RSVP are structured professional judgment (SPJ) guidelines for conducting comprehensive assessment of risk for sexual violence. They are intended to help evaluators to make two major decisions about risk for sexual violence (Hart, Douglas, & Guy, 2016). The first decision concerns identifying the evaluee's potential for harm with respect to the nature, seriousness, imminence, frequency or duration, and likelihood of any future sexual violence the evaluee may commit. This decision is predictive in the sense that it involves forecasting or anticipating an uncertain future, rather than predictive in the sense of calculating or estimating the absolute, precise, quantitative probability of an event or occurrence in the future. The second decision concerns identifying feasible and effective means of mitigating the risks posed by the evaluee. This decision involves developing action plans that are strategic, tactical, and logistical in nature.

Guidelines, most generally, are "pronouncements, statements, or declarations that suggest or recommend specific professional behavior, endeavor, or conduct" (American Psychological Association, 2002, p. 1052). The development of guidelines is one of the primary methods used to promote best practice in health care professions (Reed, McLaughlin, & Newman, 2002). Consistent with recommendations for health care guidelines (e.g., American Psychological Association, 2002), development of SPJ guidelines such as the SVR-20 V1/V2 and RSVP is based in part on a systematic review of the existing scientific research, standards of practice, ethical codes, and relevant law. Accordingly, the SVR-20 V1/V2 and RSVP may be considered research products (Addis, 2002). They fall within the definition of evidence-based, empirically guided, or empirically supported guidelines to the extent that their use reflect "the conscientious, explicit and judicious use of current best evidence in making decisions about the care of individual patients" (Sackett, Rosenberg, Gray, Haynes, & Richardson, 1996, p. 71; see also Hart, 2009; Hart et al., 2016). They may also be accurately characterized as best practice guidelines, consensus guidelines, or clinical practice parameters, in health care; or, using terms more common in correctional psychology, as management-focused, risk-need-responsivity, or fourth-generation risk assessment instruments (e.g., Bonta & Andrews, 2017; Andrews, Bonta, & Wormith, 2006).

The SVR-20 V1/V2 and RSVP differ from some guidelines in two important ways. First, they reflect the opinions and recommendations of the authors, rather than the official position or policy of any agency, organization, or association. Second, they are not practice standards, as they are not binding on and do not restrict the practice of any professional groups.

Criterion Assessed

As stated previously, the SVR-20 V1/V2 and RSVP are intended to guide assessment of *risk for sexual violence*. Below, we divide this criterion into two parts for the purposes of defining it: *sexual violence* versus *risk*.

Definition of Sexual Violence

The SVR-20 V1/V2 and RSVP define sexual violence as the "actual, attempted, or threatened sexual contact with another person that is nonconsensual" (Hart et al., 2003, p. 2; see also Boer et al., 1997, p. 9, and Boer et al., 2017, p. 2). The sexual contact can be direct or indirect. Direct sexual contact involves one or more of the following: sexual touching of a victim by the perpetrator either physically or with an object; communication of a sexual nature between the perpetrator and victim, either verbal or nonverbal, that does not use an intermediary; or other interaction of a sexual nature between perpetrator and victim while they are in close physical proximity. The sexual contact may be nonconsensual because it occurred despite the victim's explicit refusal to consent, without the explicit consent of the victim, or with the assent of a victim who was legally unable to give consent due to immaturity, infirmity, or (perceived) duress. Put another way, sexual violence is interpersonal behavior of a sexual nature (e.g., with respect to motivation or behavioral topography) that is inherently coercive and thus has the potential to cause people reasonable fear of physical or grave psychological harm.

The definition just presented is broad and includes a wide range of acts that would constitute violations of criminal or civil law in most jurisdictions, although acts need not result in findings of culpability to be considered sexual violence. It excludes some forms of unusual, problematic, or even illegal sexual behavior that do not involve sexual contact with other people or that are consensual (e.g., sex with animals, sadomasochistic sex with a consenting partner). Of course, conduct that does not fall within the definition of sexual violence per se may fall within the definition of various risk factors for sexual violence and may constitute reasonable grounds for suspecting that the person has a history of sexual violence or is at risk for sexual violence.

With respect to the definition of sexual violence, two types of conduct require special discussion. The first is conduct that involves the production, consumption, or distribution of pornography. When the evaluee was a party to production of pornography that included depiction of sexual violence as defined earlier, the conduct constitutes sexual violence. If the evaluee was a party to consumption or distribution of pornography that included depiction of sexual violence as defined earlier, the conduct constitutes sexual violence. The second type of conduct involves human trafficking and pimping. If the evaluee was party to the commission of sexual violence perpetrated by others by procuring potential victims (i.e., knew or ought reasonably to have known that the people were intended victims of sexual violence) or using duress to force victims to have sexual contact with others, the conduct constitutes sexual violence.

Definition of Risk

The SVR-20 V1/V2 and RSVP, like all SPJ guidelines, conceptualize risk broadly in terms of the nature, severity, imminence, frequency, and likelihood of future sexual violence. According to this definition, risk is about uncertainty—what we do not know about the future, not what we do know. With respect to risk for sexual violence (and, in our view, all forms of violence), that uncertainty is unbounded. We don't know precisely how to conceptualize or define sexual violence (linguistic uncertainty). We don't know exactly what causes sexual violence (epistemic uncertainty). We don't know how to measure causal factors precisely (evaluative uncertainty). We don't know how to apply findings from group-based research to make precise predictions about individuals (ludic uncertainty).

The definition of risk used in SPJ guidelines, with its focus on uncertainty, is consistent with that of major international organizations such as ASIS International and The Risk and Insurance Management Society (2015), the International Standards Organization (2018), and the Society for Risk Analysis (2018), and also consistent with that used in the law in various countries (e.g., in Canada, *Smith v. Jones*, 1999). But it is in stark contrast to the definition used by actuarial tests of risk for sexual violence. They define risk solely in terms of frequentist probabilities, either relative or absolute, based on statistical profiles of recidivism in various reference groups of offenders or forensic mental health patients. We have discussed the problems with such an impoverished definition of risk at length elsewhere (e.g., Hart & Douglas, 2019; Hart et al., 2016), but for the purpose of this chapter it will suffice to say the fundamental problem is that it pretends a degree of certainty—linguistic, epistemic, evaluative, and ludic—that simply does not exist (for a more extensive discussion, see Hart, 2004/2011).

Structure

SPJ guidelines such as the SVR-20 V1/V2 and RSVP are structured in two ways. First, they have administration procedures that comprise specific steps. Second, they identify and define a set of risk factors that should be considered, at a minimum, in all evaluations. Below, we discuss these two types of structure in greater detail. As will be clear from the discussion, the structural differences between the guidelines are relatively minor, and we expect that evaluators could and should reach more or less identical overall decisions about risks posed and management of risks in a given case regardless of which set of guidelines they use. This is the reason why we consider them to be equivalent or parallel forms.

Administration Procedure

As noted previously, the SVR-20 V1/V2 focus primarily on description of risks for sexual violence posed by evaluees and so have a relatively simple administration procedure that comprises four steps. In Step 1, evaluators gather information about the case via document review and interviews with evaluees and collateral sources. The guidelines discuss the sorts of information that evaluators should attempt to gather and the methods they should consider for gathering it. The goal is to establish an information base that is reasonably comprehensive and trustworthy and will permit evaluators to reach findings and opinions with a reasonable degree of professional confidence or certainty.

In Steps 2 and 3, evaluators determine the presence of each of 20 standard risk factors according to two timeframes: Past, or prior to last 12 months; and Recent, or within the last 12 months. (As will be discussed, there are some differences in the standard risk factors included in the SVR-20 V1 versus V2.) Evaluators also have the ability to specify the presence of any case-specific or idiosyncratic risk factors that are not already included in the standard 20. Judgments of presence are based on the existence of evidence in the information base and are made on a 3-point ordinal scale (Yes = *evidence the risk factor is present*, Possibly/Partially = *evidence the risk factor is possibly or partially present*, No = *no evidence the risk factor is present*), except that judgments of Recent presence in the SVR-20 V1 use slightly different anchors and focus on change (*evidence that the risk factor has worsened, no evidence that the risk factor has changed, evidence that the risk factor has improved*). Presence ratings may be omitted if there is not sufficient information with which to make a judgment. The distinction between Past and Recent is intended to oblige evaluators to consider changes over time in the status or level of risk factors.

In Step 4, evaluators express global opinions about the nature of the risks posed by evaluees, in light of the pattern of risk factors present. Both the SVR-20 V1 and V2 include a summary risk rating that reflects judgments about the degree of effort or intervention that would be required to prevent future sexual violence by evaluees under assumed conditions of release. It is equivalent to a judgment of the likelihood that evaluees would commit future sexual violence if released without any special release conditions or interventions. The SVR-20 V2 also includes additional ratings. Serious Physical Harm reflects judgments about the degree to which evaluees pose a risk for sexual violence that includes lethal, life-threatening, or severe bodily harm. Need for Immediate Action reflects judgments about whether evaluees pose a risk for imminent sexual violence (i.e., pose a clear and present danger). Other Risks Indicated reflects judgments about whether evaluees may pose a risk of harm other than sexual violence that may be worthy of follow-up assessment. Finally, Case Review reflects judgments concerning how soon evaluees should undergo reassessment of risk for sexual violence and what "red flags" (i.e., specific events or occurrences) should trigger an immediate reassessment. Summary risk ratings, as well as ratings of Serious Physical Harm and Need for Immediate Action, are made on a 3-point ordinal scale (*Low, Moderate, High*); ratings of Other Risks Indicated are also made on a 3-point ordinal scale (*No, Possibly, Yes*); and ratings of Case Review are made in terms of a recommended timeframe or date for case review in the absence of red flags.

The administration procedure for the RSVP is a bit more complex, comprising six steps, due to its focus on the development of detailed case management plans. Step 1, in which evaluators gather information about the case via document review and interviews with evaluees and collateral sources, is identical to that in the SVR-20 V1/V2.

Step 2, in which evaluators making presence ratings for 22 standard risk factors (see the following) Past and Recent, is a combination of Steps 2 and 3 in the SVR-20 V2. (As will be discussed, there are some differences in the way the domain of risk factors was captured in the RSVP versus the SVR-20 V1/V2.)

In Step 3, evaluators determine the causal or functional relevance of each of the 22 standard risk factors with respect to the perpetration and management of risk for future sexual violence. These judgments are made on the basis of an integrative case formulation (also known as a case conceptualization) of the evaluee's history of sexual violence made using a theoretical framework, either Action Theory (the one most often discussed with respect to SPJ guidelines; see Hart et al., 2003; Hart & Logan, 2011; Hart et al., 2016) or the evaluator's preferred alternative. Relevance is coded on the same 3-point ordinal scale used for presence ratings.

In Step 4, the evaluator identifies the most plausible scenarios of future sexual violence based on the evaluee's history of sexual violence, the evaluator's case formulation of the evaluee, and the evaluator's knowledge and experience. Scenarios are brief narrative descriptions of what kinds of sexual violence the evaluee is most likely to perpetrate, for which kinds of motivations, resulting in what kinds of psychological and physical harm, against which kinds of victims, and at which times or in which situations, as well as a judgment of the perceived likelihood that evaluees will commit sexual violence of that sort given their anticipated living situation (e.g., planed or likely conditions of confinement or community residence). The process of developing scenarios in the RSVP was based on principles and methods of scenario planning, a planning method used widely in other fields (see discussion by Hart et al., 2016).

In Step 5, evaluators develop a detailed case management plan in light of the identified scenarios that details the critical strategies, tactics, and logistics required to effectively manage or mitigate the person's risk for future sexual violence. The strategies and tactics are divided into four categories, according to whether they focus on monitoring (surveillance), supervision (restriction of freedoms), intervention (assessment, treatment, and rehabilitation), or victim safety planning (enhancing the security resources of likely victims).

Step 6, in which evaluators express global opinions about the nature of the risks posed by evaluees, is almost identical to that in the SVR-20 V2, with two exceptions: first, the SVR-20 V2 summary risk rating is referred to as the Case Prioritization Rating in the RSVP; second, the SVR-20 V2 Need for Immediate Action rating is referred to as the Immediate Action Required rating in the RSVP, where it is coded (*No, Possibly, Yes*).

Of the various global judgments regarding risk included in the SVR-20 V1/V2 and RSVP, the most important is the summary risk rating or Case Prioritization rating. A judgment that the overall risk or prioritization in a case is *Low* indicates the evaluee does not appear to need any special intervention or supervision strategies designed to manage violence risk, and there is no need to monitor the evaluee closely for changes in risk. A judgment of *Moderate* indicates a risk management plan should be developed for the evaluee, which typically would involve (at a minimum) systematic reassessment of risk. A judgment of *High* indicates an urgent need to develop a risk management plan for the evaluee, which typically would involve (at a minimum) advising staff, increasing supervision levels, placing the individual on a high-priority list for available treatment resources, scheduling regular reassessments, or even an emergency response (e.g., hospitalization, suspension of conditional release). But making global judgments of risk is neither necessary nor sufficient to conduct a comprehensive risk assessment. From the SPJ perspective, the most important task is the development of plans to manage or mitigate risk, and this can be done without the need for making global judgments in some contexts.

Content

The standard 20 risk factors in the SVR-20 V1 are presented in Table 14.1. As the table indicates, they are divided into three domains on a purely rational or practical (i.e., not statistical) basis. The *Psychosocial Adjustment* domain comprises 11 risk factors that reflect the evaluee's history of personal problems with respect to such things as employment and education, relationships, antisocial conduct, and various aspects of mental health. The *Sexual Offences* domain comprises seven risk factors that reflect the evaluee's history of sexual violence, both in terms of past acts of sexual violence and cognitions related to sexual violence. The *Future Plans* domain comprises two risk factors that reflect the evaluee's general ability to develop plans to cope with personal problems and work with professionals to mitigate risk for sexual violence.

The risk factors in the SVR-20 V1 were modified slightly in V2 in light of the updated literature review, as well as the experience of the authors and feedback from other evaluators. (The revision process is discussed in detail below.) The SVR-20 V2 still includes 20 risk factors divided into three domains on a rational basis: *Psychosocial Adjustment*, 10 risk factors; *History of Sexual Offending*, 7 risk factors; and *Future Plans*, 3 risk factors. They are presented in Table 14.2.

The 22 standard risk factors in the RSVP are presented in Table 14.3. They are divided into five domains on a rational basis. The *Sexual Violence History* domain comprises five risk factors that reflect the evaluee's history of sexually violent acts. The *Psychological Adjustment* domain comprises five risk factors that reflect problems with general mental well-being or functioning. The *Mental Disorder* domain comprises five risk factors that directly reflect specific mental health problems. The *Social Adjustment* domain comprises four risk factors that reflect general problems with social integration or functioning. Finally, the *Manageability* domain comprises three risk factors that reflect the evaluee's general ability to develop plans to cope with personal problems and work with professionals to mitigate risk for sexual violence

Intended Applications

Purposes

The primary intended purpose of the SVR-20 V1/V2 and RSVP is to assist evaluators to undertake sexual violence risk assessment. For this purpose, they can be used in several different ways. First, they can function as reference texts, documents that can be read in advance of conducting

Table 14.1 Risk Factors in the SVR-20 V1

Domain	Risk Factor
Psychosocial Adjustment	1. Sexual deviation
	2. Victim of child abuse
	3. Psychopathy
	4. Major mental illness
	5. Substance use problems
	6. Suicidal/homicidal ideation
	7. Relationship problems
	8. Employment problems
	9. Past nonsexual violent offences
	10. Past nonviolent offences
	11. Past supervision failure
History of Sexual Offenses	12. High density
	13. Multiple types
	14. Physical harm
	15. Weapons/Threats
	16. Escalation in frequency or severity
	17. Extreme minimization/denial
	18. Attitudes that support or condone
Future Plans	19. Lacks realistic plans
	20. Negative attitude toward intervention

Note: SVR-20 V1 = Sexual Violence Risk-20.

Source: Boer et al. (1997).

Table 14.2 Risk Factors in the SVR-20 V2

Domain	Risk Factor
Psychosocial Adjustment	1. Sexual deviation
	2. Sexual health problems
	3. Victim of child abuse
	4. Psychopathic personality disorder
	5. Major mental disorder
	6. Substance use problems
	7. Suicidal/homicidal ideation
	8. Relationship problems
	9. Employment problems
	10. Nonsexual offending
Sexual Offending	11. Chronic sexual offending
	12. Diverse sexual offending
	13. Physical harm in sexual offending
	14. Psychological coercion in sexual offending
	15. Escalation in sexual offending
	16. Extreme minimization/denial of sexual offending
	17. Attitudes that support or condone sexual offending
Future Plans	18. Lacks realistic plans
	19. Negative attitude toward intervention
	20. Negative attitude toward supervision

Note: SVR-20 V2 = Version 2 of the Sexual Violence Risk-20.

Source: Boer et al. (2017).

Table 14.3 Risk Factors in the RSVP

Domain	Risk Factor
History of Sexual Violence	1. Chronicity of sexual violence
	2. Diversity of sexual violence
	3. Escalation of sexual violence
	4. Physical coercion in sexual violence
	5. Psychological coercion in sexual violence
Psychological Adjustment	6. Extreme minimization or denial of sexual violence
	7. Attitudes that support or condone sexual violence
	8. Problems with self-awareness
	9. Problems with stress or coping
	10. Problems resulting from child abuse
Mental Disorder	11. Sexual deviance
	12. Psychopathic personality disorder
	13. Major mental illness
	14. Problems with substance use
	15. Violent or suicidal ideation
Social Adjustment	16. Problems with intimate relationships
	17. Problems with non-intimate relationships
	18. Problems with employment
	19. Nonsexual criminality
Manageability	20. Problems with planning
	21. Problems with treatment
	22. Problems with supervision

Note: RSVP = Risk for Sexual Violence Protocol.

Source: Hart et al. (2003).

sexual violence risk assessments to enhance the knowledge and skills of evaluations. Second, they can function as *aides mémoire* or memory aids, documents that can be referred to in the course of conducting sexual violence risk assessments to ensure that evaluators practice in a systematic, thorough manner. Finally, to the extent that evaluators follow closely the recommendations outlined in the guidelines, they function as psychological tests—that is, documents that constitute evaluative devices or procedures (e.g., American Educational Research Association, American Psychological Association, & National Council on Measurement in Education, 1999). Like all tests, the SVR-20 V1/V2 and RSVP attempt to structure the process of assessment. Unlike many psychological tests, however, they were not intended to quantify behavior in the form of scores that can be interpreted with respect to norms or other criteria. Similar tests have been developed for use in a wide range of psycholegal assessments and have been referred to as *forensic assessment instruments* or *forensically relevant assessment instruments* (Grisso, 2003; Heilbrun, 2001; Heilbrun, Rogers, & Otto, 2002).

Secondary intended purposes of the SVR-20 V1/V2 and RSVP are to assist research, education, and training with respect to sexual violence and risk assessment as well to judge the quality and adequacy of sexual violence risk assessments conducted by others (e.g., as part of routine quality assurance audits or critical incident reviews).

The SVR-20 V1/V2 and RSVP should not be used to determine whether evaluees have committed an act of sexual violence in the past. Nor should they be used to determine whether evaluees "fit the profile of a sex offender," given the heterogeneity of people who commit sexual violence. Finally, they should not be used to assess risk of nonsexual violence, other forms of violence such as (nonsexual) intimate partner violence and stalking, or nonviolent criminal conduct. If there is any evidence that evaluees may be at risk of antisocial behavior other than sexual violence, evaluators should document their opinions in this regard.

Contexts

The SVR-20 V1/V2 and RSVP are intended for use in a wide range of civil and criminal justice contexts. These contexts include but are not limited to: pretrial and sentencing evaluations; correctional intake and discharge evaluations; post-sentence civil commitment (i.e., sexually violent predator) evaluations; duty to protect, community notification, and sex offender registration evaluations; child protection or custody/access evaluations; bullying, sexual harassment, and sexual violence evaluations in workplaces or institutions of higher education; and investigations such as fatality inquests, critical incident reviews, ethical or professional standard complaints, and civil suits related to professional negligence or wrongful death.

Populations

The SVR-20 V1/V2 and RSVP are most appropriate for use with people who self-identify as cisgender male or female, are adults or emerging adults (age 18 and older), and were raised or reside in countries with developed economies, regardless of their sexual orientation and their history of physical or mental health problems. This is because the scientific and professional literature that served as the basis for constructing the guidelines focused primarily on this group.

The SVR-20 V1/V2 and RSVP are of uncertain appropriateness for the evaluation of some people. One example is people who self-identify as transgender, including those who are transsexual or non-binary, regardless of sexual orientation. Other examples are people who were raised in countries with developing economies, or who self-identify as members of understudied cultures or subcultures. When an evaluation is necessary but involves unusual or even novel group differences, we recommend that evaluators proceed using the SVR-20 V1/V2 and RSVP as a general framework but explicitly acknowledge its limitations (due to the absence of a well-developed evidence base) and take steps to ensure the evaluation is comprehensive and individualized. This may require evaluators to become familiar with authoritative treatises concerning the group differences, consult with people who are acknowledged as experts in the group differences, and discuss directly with evaluees whether and how the group differences may be relevant to risk for sexual violence.

The SVR-20 V1/V2 and RSVP are inappropriate for evaluations of children and young adolescents (i.e., age 15 and younger). Sexual misbehavior by children and young adolescents differs in important ways from the sexual violence committed by older adolescents and adults. For example, the former is targeted primarily at same-aged victims, is less likely to involve physical coercion, and may also be related to different causal processes, such as delayed social maturation.

Cautions Regarding Use

By their very nature, SPJ guidelines like the SVR-20 V1/V2 and RSVP are neither exhaustive nor fixed. In any given evaluation, there may be case-specific factors that are crucial to professional judgments concerning risk. The existence or use of professional guidelines does not obviate the need to exercise professional judgment (Addis, 2002; American Psychological Association, 2002; Reed et al., 2002).

Also by their nature, SPJ guidelines like the SVR-20 V1/V2 and RSVP cannot be used to estimate the specific likelihood or absolute probability that a given evaluee will commit sexual violence in the future. Indeed, as discussed previously, making estimates of this sort with any reasonable degree of certainty probably lies beyond the ability of science (Hájek & Hall, 2002; Hart, 2004/2011; Hart & Cooke, 2013; Hart, Michie, & Cooke, 2007).

Like all guidelines, the SVR-20 V1/V2 and RSVP have a natural lifespan and must be updated (e.g., American Psychological Association, 2002; Reed et al., 2002). Version 2 of the SVR-20 was released in 2018 (albeit with a 2017 publication date), and a revision of the RSVP is currently in preparation with publication anticipated in late 2020.

The SVR-20 V1/V2 and RSVP focus on the risks posed by the evaluee, rather than on the risks posed to a specific potential victim. Victim-focused risk assessments—sometimes referred to as victim safety planning or victim lethality assessments—differ from perpetrator-focused risk assessments in important ways, including consideration of psychological, social, and environmental factors that may increase the victim's vulnerability to sexual violence (Krug, Dahlberg, Mercy, Zwi, & Lozano, 2002). Evaluators should consider expanding their risk assessments to include consideration of victim vulnerability factors in cases where any future sexual violence is likely to be targeted at a specific person.

User Qualifications

According to the SVR-20 V1/V2 and RSVP, evaluators should meet two general requirements. First, they should have a good understanding of sexual violence, including at least a basic familiarity with the professional and scientific literatures on its nature, causes, and management. Second, evaluators should have training and experience in individual assessment, including interviewing and reviewing third-party information; training and experience in the administration and interpretation of standardized tests can also be helpful.

The guidelines include risk factors related to mental disorder. Evaluators who are not trained or qualified to assess and diagnose mental disorder have four options. First, they can assess risk factors related to mental disorder in consultation with or under the supervision of qualified evaluators. Second, they can assess risk factors related to mental disorder by referring to the results of psychodiagnostic assessments conducted by qualified evaluators. Third, they can assess risk factors related to mental disorder provisionally, document this, and discuss the importance of having their provisional assessments confirmed by qualified evaluators. Finally, they can decide not to assess risk factors related to mental disorder, document this, and discuss how the incomplete assessment limits their opinions regarding risk.

It is completely acceptable, and even desirable, for the SVR-20 V1/V2 and RSVP to be administered with the involvement of a team. We recommend, however, that one member of the team take formal and primary responsibility for collating information, recording consensus regarding findings and opinions, and authoring reports.

The SVR-20 V1 and V2 manuals do not discuss the training of evaluators. The RSVP manual states that evaluators do not need to complete any specific training program, but rather can accomplish adequate training in a number of different ways, including self-study, supervised practice, and attendance at lectures or workshops. It recommends about 16 to 32 hours of training that includes the following components: a review of the manual, with particular emphasis on basic information and administration issues; a review of any critical advances in knowledge regarding sexual violence or risk assessment subsequent to publication of the RSVP manual; completion of practice cases based on file review; and completion of actual cases under supervision of or in consultation with experienced colleagues.

Method and Rationale for Development

Principles of Development

As noted previously, the SVR-20 V1/V2 and RSVP were based on a systematic review of the scientific and professional literature on sexual violence. The literature reviewed included a wide range of empirical reports, reviews, and previous guidelines that were published in journals and books or as reports available from government agencies. The administration procedures in the SVR-20 V1/V2 and RSVP were based primarily on publications from the professional literature: reviews and previous guidelines published in journal articles, in books, or as agency reports. In contrast, the risk factors in the SVR-20 V1/V2 and RSVP were drawn from the scientific literature, including quantitative and narrative reviews of the empirical literature, individual empirical studies, and theoretical reviews.

The literature reviews were broad in scope. We searched multiple computerized databases covering medicine (primarily psychiatry) and social science (primarily psychology and criminology) to identify disseminations (books, articles, chapters, government reports, conference papers, and graduate dissertations and theses) related to sexual violence, sexual violence risk assessment and management, and cognate terms. We included all disseminations in English, as well as some disseminations in other languages that we were able to comprehend without the need for professional translation, but we excluded publications that focused solely on sexual misbehavior in children or young adolescents (i.e., younger than 15 years old). We then inspected the reference lists of the included disseminations to identify additional studies of potential relevance. Our literature reviews we conducted were greatly assisted by reviewing the meta-analytic and narrative reviews prepared by others, as well as by encyclopedic works (e.g., Boer, 2016).

Our literature review had two major goals. The first was to identify the types and sources of information generally considered important for conducting a comprehensive assessment of risk for sexual violence. The second was to synthesize a list of risk factors. We attempted to identify individual risk factors that were: (a) supported by scientific research; (b) consistent with major theories and previous professional recommendations; and (c) legally acceptable, that is, consistent with human or civil rights. (Some examples of legally problematic or unacceptable factors include ascribed factors such as age, sex, and race; reliance on such factors may be considered problematic or even a violation of constitutional or human rights.) We also attempted to make sure the list or set of factors was: (a) reasonably comprehensive; (b) not unduly long; and (c) couched in the basic language of practitioners, that is, neither too general nor too specific.

There are differences in the risk factors included in the guidelines. We consider these differences to be minor. The (surprisingly small) differences between the SVR-20 V1 and V2 can be attributed to the fact that the literature on sexual violence reviewed as part of their development evolved between 1997 and 2017. The differences between the SVR-20 V1/V2 and RSVP can be attributed to the fact that the latter places a greater emphasis on the development of case management plans. The RSVP therefore conceptualizes a few risk factors in a more granular and treatment-relevant way than does the SVR-20 V1/V2.

Interrater Reliability

In this section, we summarize the findings of studies that have evaluated the interrater reliability of risk judgments made using the SVR-20 V1/V2 and RSVP. We do not discuss the structural properties of ratings made using the SVR-20 V1/V2 and RSVP. As the SVR-20 V1/V2 and RSVP are formative evaluative devices (i.e., are intended to assist the forecasting of future sexual violence) rather than reflective measures (i.e., indicators of a latent trait or taxon), there is no good reason to expect that the covariance among ratings of individual risk factors in the guidelines will have a specific pattern that is stable across samples. We therefore view research on such things as the internal consistency, homogeneity, or factor structure of risk factor ratings (e.g., Kanters et al., 2017; Walters, Knight, & Thornton, 2009) to be of little relevance in evaluating SPJ guidelines.

With respect to interrater reliability, we review research (publications and conference presentations) for each set of guidelines in chronological order, from oldest to newest. We have attempted to eliminate redundancy by reviewing only a single dissemination (typically, the published or most recent version) when multiple disseminations were based on the same dataset. For the purpose of evaluating interrater reliability, it is conventional for researchers to convert the various ratings of risk made using the guidelines from ordered categories into numerical scores (i.e., 0 = *No*, *Low*, or *Routine*; 1 = *Possibly or Partially*, *Moderate*, or *Elevated*; 2 = *Yes*, *High*, or *Urgent*). Many researchers also create total or domain scores by summing numerical scores for the presence or relevance of risk factors. Also, in research on the RSVP, some researchers combine numerical scores for the presence-past and presence-recent ratings of each risk factor by taking the maximum of the two values to create a single score reflecting presence-ever (i.e., "ever present"). Except where noted otherwise, interrater reliability in the studies reviewed in this section was indexed using single rater intraclass correlation coefficients, abbreviated herein as ICC_1, calculated for absolute agreement using a mixed effects model. ICC_1 is most appropriate for true continuous variables but can also be used with ordinal categorical variables and is mathematically equivalent to another popular index, weighted *kappa* or κ_W. Following Fleiss (1981), we interpreted ICC_1 coefficients as follows: < .39 = *poor*, .40 to .49 = *fair*, .50 to .74 = *good*, and > .75 = *excellent*.

Ideally, the interrater reliability of risk factors should be evaluated individually. In some studies and disseminations, however, this is not feasible due to sample size or page limitations, and so the interrater reliability of risk factors is evaluated as an ensemble by analyzing composite scores. Although this is acceptable for research purposes, we emphasize that this is not the manner in which the SVR-20 V1/V2 and RSVP are intended to be used in practice, and also that such composite scores are not mathematically optimized measures of risk.

SVR-20 V1/V2

Sjöstedt and Långström (2003) evaluated interrater reliability between two independent raters in two subsamples of 15 cases each, randomly selected from a larger sample of 51 adult male rapists who underwent presentence forensic psychiatric evaluations in Sweden between 1988 and 1990. SVR-20 V1 ratings were made on the basis of file information. Presence ratings for individual risk factors had generally poor to fair interrater reliability in the first subsample of 15 people, $M\kappa = .36$. The authors speculated this may have been due to variation among raters in experience and repeated the analyses in a second set of 15 people after additional training. Interrater reliability for presence ratings increased: κ ranged from .08 to 1.00, with $M = .51$ and $Mdn = .57$. In the second subsample, the interrater reliability of summary ratings of risk for sexual violence was fair, $\kappa = .50$.

De Vogel, de Ruiter, van Beek, and Mead (2004) evaluated agreement between two independent raters in a subsample of 30 cases, randomly selected from a larger sample of adult male sex offenders admitted to a Dutch forensic psychiatric hospital between 1974 and 1996. SVR-20 V1 ratings were made on the basis of file information. Interrater reliability was fair or better for 18 of 20 individual risk factors. Two risk factors had poor interrater reliability: 1 (*Sexual deviance*), $ICC_1 = .38$; and 7 (*Relationship problems*), $ICC_1 = .29$. According to the authors, the low reliability for ratings of 1 (*Sexual deviance*) was due to lack of clinical experience for one of three clinicians who made ratings; interrater reliability was good for the two experienced clinicians, $ICC_1 = .68$. Also according to the authors, the low reliability of ratings for 7 (*Relationship problems*) was due to lack of variance. Presence ratings for individual risk factors were also recoded and summed to create total and domain scores. Interrater reliability for total scores was excellent: $ICC_1 = .75$. For domain scores, it was good to excellent: $ICC_1 = .74$ for *Psychosocial Adjustment*, $ICC_1 = .74$ for *Sexual Offences*, and $ICC_1 = .78$ for *Future Plans*. Finally, interrater reliability of the summary risk rating for sexual violence was fair: $ICC_1 = .48$. In 2 of 30 cases (7%), one rater judged "high risk" whereas another rater judged "low risk."

Hildebrand, de Ruiter, and de Vogel (2004) evaluated the interrater reliability between two independent raters for a single SVR-20 V1 risk factor, 1 (*Sexual deviance*), in a subsample of 24 cases randomly selected from a larger sample of 94 adult male rapists admitted to a Dutch forensic psychiatric hospital. Ratings were made on the basis of file information. Presence ratings were dichotomized, *Absent* versus *Possibly/Partially Present* or *Present*. The interrater reliability of the dichotomized ratings was fair, $\kappa = .59$. Raters agreed on the presence or absence of sexual deviance in 19 of the 24 cases (79%).

Zanatta (2005) evaluated interrater reliability between independent raters in a subsample of 15 cases, randomly selected from a larger sample of 164 adult male sex offenders in Canada, 82 offenders who had received indeterminate sentences as Dangerous Offenders and a control group of 82 repeat sex offenders. SVR-20 V1 ratings were based on file information. Presence ratings were recoded and summed to create *Psychosocial Adjustment* and *Sexual Offences* domain scores. The interrater reliability of both section scores was excellent: $ICC_1 = .87$.

Rettenberger and Eher (2007) evaluated interrater reliability between two independent raters in a subsample of 10 cases, randomly selected from a larger sample of 254 adult male sex offenders admitted to the Austrian federal correctional system in 2002 or 2003. SVR-20 V1 ratings were made on the basis of file information. Presence ratings were recoded and summed to create Total scores, which had excellent interrater reliability: $ICC_1 = .84$.

Pérez Ramírez, Redondo Illescas, Martínez García, García Forero, and Andrés Pueyo (2008) evaluated agreement between two independent raters in 30 adult male offenders, randomly selected from a larger sample of a subsample of 163 sex offenders in Spain. SVR-20 V1 ratings were made on the basis of file information. They reported that interrater reliability for ratings of the presence of individual risk factors, indexed using κ, was good to excellent, ranging from 0.73 to 1.00 with $M = 0.95$.

Barbaree, Langton, Blanchard, and Boer (2008), following on Langton (2003), evaluated agreement between two independent raters in a subsample of 63 cases, randomly selected from a larger sample of adult sex offenders who completed prison-based treatment in Canada. SVR-20 V1 ratings were made on the basis of file information. Raters coded the presence for all individual risk factors for 99.5% of the subsample. Presence ratings were recoded and summed to create total scores. The interrater reliability of total scores, indexed using Spearman *rho*, was 0.75, which the authors interpreted as "moderate-high" (Barbaree et al., 2008, p. 52).

Hill, Habermann, Klusmann, Berner, and Briken (2008) evaluated interrater reliability between two independent raters in a sample of 166 adult male sexual homicide offenders in Germany. SVR-20 V1 ratings were based on forensic psychiatric reports, except for 19 (*Lacks realistic plans*), which could not be coded. Presence ratings for individual risk factors were recoded and summed to create total scores. The interrater reliability of total scores was excellent: $ICC_1 = .87$.

Rettenberger, Boer, and Eher (2011) studied 430 adult males convicted of sexual offenses and incarcerated in Austrian prisons. Two independent evaluators completed the SVR-20 V1 for a randomly selected subsample of 10 offenders. The interrater reliability of total scores was excellent: $ICC_1 = .84$.

Jackson (2016) evaluated interrater reliability between two independent evaluators in a sample of 100 adult male sex offenders who had completed a community-based sex offender treatment program in Canada. SVR-20 V1 ratings were based on files. Evaluators met after completing each series of 5 to 10 cases to review and discuss their ratings before coding the next series of cases. For individual risk factors, the interrater reliability of presence ratings was generally excellent, ranging from $ICC_1 = .64$ to .96, with *Mdn* = .81. The interrater reliability of total scores was excellent, with $ICC_2 = .96$ (which corresponds to an estimated ICC_1 of .93). The reliability of section scores was also excellent: *Psychosocial Adjustment*, $ICC_2 = .95$ (estimated $ICC_1 = .90$); *Sexual Offences*, $ICC_2 = .94$ (estimated $ICC_1 = 88$); and *Future Plans*, $ICC_2 = .86$ (estimated $ICC_1 = .75$).

Tsao and Chu (in press) studied 134 adult male offenders convicted of sexual offenses in Singapore. SVR-20 V2 ratings were made on the basis of file information. Interrater reliability was examined in a subsample of 10 offenders who were assessed by two evaluators working independently. The interrater reliability of total scores was good: $ICC_1 = .70$.

RSVP

Hart (2003) evaluated interrater reliability in a sample of 50 adult male sex offenders at an outpatient forensic psychiatric clinic in Canada. RSVP ratings were made by two independent evaluators based on file information. Only limited interrater reliability analyses were conducted. The interrater reliability of presence-ever total scores was excellent, $ICC_1 = .91$, and the interrater reliability of Case Prioritization ratings was good, $ICC_1 = .68$.

Watt, Hart, Wilson, Guy, and Douglas (2006) evaluated interrater reliability in a sample of 50 high-risk adult male sex offenders who were under community supervision in Canada. RSVP ratings were made by two independent raters based on file information. For individual risk factors, interrater reliability was calculated for presence ratings, both past and recent, as well as for relevance ratings. Interrater reliability for presence-past ratings was generally excellent, ranging from $ICC_1 = .58$ to .97, with *Mdn* = .91. For presence-recent ratings, one risk factor could not be evaluated due to lack of variance; interrater reliability for the remaining 21 risk factors ranged from .62 to 1.00, with *Mdn* = .87. For relevance ratings, interrater reliability ranged from .65 to .94, with *Mdn* = .88. Item-level ratings were recoded and summed to create total and domain scores. For presence-past ratings, the interrater reliability of composite scores was excellent: $ICC_1 = .99$ for total, .98 for *Sexual Violence History*, .92 for *Psychological Adjustment*, .96 for *Mental Disorder*, .96 for *Social Adjustment*, and .98 for *Manageability*. For presence-recent ratings, the interrater reliability of composite scores was excellent: $ICC_1 = .96$ for total, .93 for *Sexual Violence History*, .88 for *Psychological Adjustment*, .96 for *Mental Disorder*, .90 for *Social Adjustment*, and .93 for *Manageability*. For relevance ratings, the interrater reliability of summary scores was also excellent: $ICC_1 = .98$ for total, .93 for *Sexual Violence History*, .91 for *Psychological Adjustment*, .95 for *Mental Disorder*, .90 for *Social Adjustment*, and .93 for *Manageability*. Finally, the interrater reliability of Case Prioritization ratings was excellent, with $ICC_1 = .92$.

Sutherland et al. (2012) recruited 28 forensic mental health or intellectual disability professionals, to rate six case vignettes using the RSVP. Interrater reliability for presence-past ratings of individual risk factors ranged from $ICC_1 = .13$ to .77 (*Mdn* = .59); for presence-recent ratings, from .09 to .78 (*Mdn* = .48); and for relevance ratings, from .48 to .92 (*Mdn* = .74). (Sutherland et al. did not calculate total and domain scores for presence or relevance in the usual way, so they are not reported here.) The interrater reliability of summary judgments ratings was: Case Prioritization, $ICC_1 = .62$; Serious Physical Harm .69; Immediate Action Required, .43; and Other Risks Indicated, .66. An innovative aspect of the Sutherland et al. (2012) study was that it also examined the interrater reliability of scenarios for future violence and scenario-based management plans identified by evaluators. They were asked to make a series of closed-ended ratings for two specific scenarios, "repeat" and "escalation." The interrater reliability of ratings for the repeat scenarios ranged from $ICC_1 = .46$ to .85 (*Mdn* = .56); for the escalation scenario, it ranged from .25 to .78 (*Mdn* = .48); and for the recommended level of supervision, it was .87. In other analyses, Sutherland et al. (2012) found that the ratings made by professionals also had moderate agreement with "gold standard" ratings by experts; this was particularly true for raters with more extensive training in the use of the RSVP.

Wilson (2013) conducted a study similar to Sutherland et al. (2012). She recruited 17 professionals to take online training in the use of the RSVP and complete six practice cases, selected at random from a pool of 10 cases. For individual risk factors, the interrater reliability of presence-ever ratings ranged from $ICC_1 = .11$ to .91 (*Mdn* = .42); and for relevance ratings, from .18 to .61 (*Mdn* = .39). The interrater reliability of total scores for presence-ever and relevance was $ICC_1 = .56$ and .55, respectively; interrater reliability of domain scores for presence-ever ratings ranged from .07 to .78 (*Mdn* = .48) and for relevance ratings it ranged from = .12 to .60 (*Mdn* = .53). The interrater reliability of summary judgments ratings was: Case Prioritization, $ICC_1 = .29$; Serious Physical Harm, .44; and Immediate Action Required, .21. Wilson (2013) also had researchers rate the overall similarity of integrative case formulations, scenarios of future sexual violence, and management plans between two randomly selected sets of ratings: one set of 69 similarity ratings was made within cases (i.e., for the RSVP evaluations conducted by different evaluators of the same case), and another set of 69 similarity ratings was between cases (i.e., for evaluations conducted by different evaluators of different cases). The researchers were blind to whether the set of evaluations was from the within- or between-case set. Multivariate analyses indicated that the similarity ratings were significantly higher for the within-case set than for the between-case set. In other analyses, Wilson (2013) found that the ratings made by professionals also had fair agreement with "gold standard" ratings by experts.

Darjee et al. (2016) studied 109 people referred to a community-based program for sex offenders in Scotland. They examined the interrater reliability of RSVP ratings in a subsample of 11 who were independently rated by two evaluators. For individual risk factors, the interrater reliability for presence-past ratings ranged from $ICC_1 = .09$ to 1.00 (*Mdn* = .83); for presence-recent, from .00 to 1.00 (*Mdn* = .83); and for relevance, from .08 to 1.00 (*Mdn* = .72). The interrater reliability of total scores for presence-past, presence-recent, and relevance was $ICC_1 = .81, .91,$ and .83, respectively. The summary judgment ratings also had excellent interrater reliability: Case Prioritization, $ICC_1 = 1.00$; Serious Physical Harm, .95; and Immediate Action Required, .95.

Vargen, Jackson, and Hart (2020), in a study of 100 adult male sex offenders who had completed a community-based sex offender treatment program in Canada, examined the interrater reliability of RSVP ratings made by two independent raters based on file information. Interrater reliability for presence-ever (i.e., combined presence-past and presence-recent) ratings of individual risk factors ranged from $ICC_1 = .58$ to .94 ($Mdn = .78$); and for relevance ratings, ranged from .48 to .92 ($Mdn = .74$). The interrater reliability of total presence and relevance scores was excellent, $ICC_1 = .93$ and .90, respectively; interrater reliability of domain scores for presence ratings ranged from .75 to .92 ($Mdn = .87$), and for relevance ratings it ranged from = .75 to .89 ($Mdn = .82$). The interrater reliability of summary judgments ratings was: Case Prioritization, $ICC_1 = .74$; Serious Physical Harm, .85; and Immediate Action Required, .80.

Sea and Hart (in press) conducted a field study specifically to examine the interrater reliability of ratings made using the RSVP. A sample of 47 adult male sexual offenders in Korea was evaluated by 32 experienced correctional psychologists who completed training in the use of the RSVP. The psychologists worked in teams of 4, per standard practice in the corrections service, and so reviewed the same information and conducted a joint interview, but afterward made ratings independently. Interrater reliability for presence-ever ratings of individual risk factors ranged from $ICC_1 = .71$ to .91 ($Mdn = .84$); and for relevance ratings, from .65 to .96 ($Mdn = .81$). The interrater reliability of total presence and relevance scores was excellent, $ICC_1 = .95$ and .98, respectively; interrater reliability of domain scores for presence ratings ranged from .87 to .93 ($Mdn = .89$) and for relevance ratings it ranged from .84 to .91 ($Mdn = .90$). The interrater reliability of summary judgments was: Case Prioritization, $ICC_1 = .71$; Serious Physical Harm, .67; and Immediate Action Required, .51. Following Sutherland et al. (2012), Sea et al. and Hart also examined the interrater reliability of a series of ratings made for two repeat and escalation scenarios of future sexual violence. The interrater reliability of ratings for the repeat scenarios ranged from $ICC_1 = .49$ to .85 ($Mdn = .65$); and for the escalation scenario, it ranged from .20 to .78 ($Mdn = .58$).

Criterion-Related Validity

In this section we review research on the criterion-related validity of risk judgments made using the SVR-20 V1/V2 and RSVP, which is the facet of validity most relevant to the use of the guidelines in practice. We do not discuss the content-related validity of the guidelines, which in this case is a function of the adequacy of the literature reviews on which they were based. There has been no systematic analysis of or research regarding this issue. Finally, we do not discuss construct-related validity more generally. As the SVR-20 V1/V2 and RSVP are formative rather than reflective in nature, there is no good reason to expect that risk ratings made using the guidelines will have a specific, theoretically meaningful pattern of associations with reflective measures of various constructs or even formative measures of adverse behavioral outcomes other than sexual violence (i.e., a nomological network). Also, although we support the use of the guidelines in more general research endeavors such as to study a specific risk factor for sexual violence (e.g., Hildebrand et al., 2004; Jackson, Read, & Hart, 2008; Nunes et al., 2007), understand clinician's views of the dynamic nature of risk factors (e.g., Sweller, Daffern, & Warren, 2016), evaluate risk communication (e.g., Jung, Pham, & Ennis, 2013; Storey, Watt, & Hart, 2015) and treatment decisions (Smid, Kamphuis, Wever, & Van Beek, 2013), and explore the neurobiological correlates of sexual offending (e.g., Schiltz et al., 2007; Walter et al., 2007), we do not believe such studies to provide strong, clear, or direct evidence of the validity of the guidelines per se.

As in the previous section, we review disseminations (publications and conference presentations) concerning each set of guidelines in chronological order, oldest to newest, and relying on a single dissemination for each dataset whenever possible. Below, we divide our review of research into studies that examined two aspects of criterion-related validity: concurrent validity, that is, the association of risk ratings made using the SVR-20 V1/V2 and RSVP with ratings made using other assessment procedures; and predictive validity, that is, studies that compared those who did versus did not engage in sexual violence following assessment. Some of these studies were truly predictive in design, whereas others were quasi-predictive or retrospective.

Concurrent Validity

SVR-20 V1/V2 vs. RSVP

As noted earlier, we consider the guidelines to be parallel forms. The association between risk ratings made using the SVR-20 V1 and RSVP was examined in detail originally by Jackson (2016), and more recently in Vargen et al. (2020). The SVR-20 V1 and RSVP both were completed on the basis of file information by two evaluators in a sample of 100 adult male sex offenders who had completed a community-based sex offender treatment program in Canada. Although the evaluators worked blind to each other, their SVR-20 V1 and RSVP ratings were not independent. After making their ratings, the evaluators met to review each case and made a final set of consensus ratings for each set of guidelines. SVR-20 V1 presence total scores were correlated $r = .97$ with RSVP presence-ever total scores and $r = .93$ with RSVP relevance total scores. SVR-20 V1 presence domain scores were correlated between .12 and .92 ($Mdn = .46$) with RSVP presence-ever and between .19 and .85 ($Mdn = .51$) with RSVP relevance domains scores; the correlations were highest between corresponding domains (e.g., *Sexual Offences* on the SVR-20 V1 versus *History of Sexual Violence* on the RSVP).

SVR-20 V1/V2 vs. Other Procedures

Langton (2003) studied 468 adult male sex offenders, the same sample subsequently studied by Barbaree et al. (2008). The SVR-20 V1 was coded from institutional files. Presence total scores on the SVR-20 V1 were correlated with total scores on various actuarial tests of risk for sexual violence: the Rapid Risk Assessment for Sexual Offense Recidivism (RRASOR; Hanson, 1997), $r = .20$; the Static-99 (Hanson & Thornton, 1999), .36; and the Minnesota Sex Offender Screening Tool-Revised (MnSOST-R; Epperson, Kaul, & Hesselton, 1998), .46. The correlations with tests of risk for general (i.e., nonsexual) violence were somewhat higher: Violence Risk Appraisal Guide and Sex Offender Risk Appraisal Guide (VRAG and SORAG; Quinsey et al., 1998), .53 and .58, respectively.

   Zanatta (2005) studied 82 adult male sex offenders given indeterminate sentences under Canadian criminal law and compared them to a group of 82 adult male sex offenders who received determinate sentences. The SVR-20 V1 was coded on the basis of institutional records. Presence total scores were correlated $r = .71$ with VRAG total scores and .72 with SORAG total scores.

   Dietiker, Dittmann, and Graf (2007) studied 64 sex offenders in Switzerland. They coded the SVR-20 V1 on the basis of institutional records. Presence total scores on the SVR-20 V1 were strongly associated with expert clinical ratings of sexual violence risk, with Area Under the Curve (AUC) = .89, as well as with numerical presence total scores on Version 2 of the Historical-Clinical-Risk Management-20 (HCR-20; Webster, Douglas, Eaves, & Hart, 1997), Spearman $rho = .85$.

   Parent, Guay, and Knight (2011) studied 503 adult males who were evaluated at the Massachusetts Treatment Center for Sexually Dangerous Persons (MTC) in Bridgewater, Massachusetts, between 1959 and 1984. They reported the concurrent validity of nine risk-relevant assessment instruments. The correlation (r) between total presence scores on the SVR-20 V1 and total scores on the other instruments were as follows: the Hare Psychopathy Checklist-Revised (PCL-R; Hare, 1991, 2003), .75; VRAG, .63; SORAG, .69; RRASOR, .28; Static-99, .55; Static-2002, a revision of the Static-99 (Hanson & Thornton, 2003), .43; Risk Matrix 2000, an actuarial test used in the

UK that yields total scores related to risk for sexual violence and general violence (RM2000S and RM2000V; Thornton et al., 2003), .33 and .37, respectively; and MnSOST-R, .57.

Rettenberger, Matthes, Boer, and Eher (2010) studied 394 adult male sex offenders in Austria. SVR-20 V1 total scores had moderate to large correlations with total scores on German-language translations of several risk-related measures: RRASOR, $r = .37$; Static-99, .63; SORAG, .79; and PCL-R, .77 (these findings updated those previously reported by Rettenberger & Eher, 2006, 2007).

Kanters et al. (2017) reported analyses of sex offenders in the Netherlands who were assessed using both the SVR-20 V1 and the PCL-R. The correlation between total presence scores on the SVR-20 V1 and total scores on the PCL-R was $r = .61$ in 24 child molesters and .60 in 32 rapists.

Tsao and Chu (in press), in their study of 134 adult male offenders convicted of sexual offenses in Singapore, examined correlations between SVR-20 V2 ratings and scores on several other risk-relevant measures. SVR-20 V2 total scores were correlated $r = .41$ with total scores on the Static-99R; .48 with total scores on the STABLE-2007, a measure of dynamic risk factors for sexual violence often used in conjunction with the Static-99 (Fernandez, Harris, Hanson, & Sparks, 2014); .72 with total scores on the PCL-R; and .75 with total scores on the Level of Service/Case Management Inventory, a measure of risk for general recidivism (Andrews, Bonta, & Wormith, 2004). SVR-20 V2 summary risk ratings for sexual violence were made on the basis of file information.

RSVP vs. Other Procedures

Kropp (2001) studied two samples of sex offenders, including a subsample of 53 offenders from the larger sample collected by Dempster (1998) and a subsample of 39 from Klaver, Watt, Kropp, and Hart (2002) and Hart (2003). The RSVP was coded on the basis of institutional files in both samples. Presence-ever total scores on the RSVP had large correlations with total scores on other risk-related measures: MnSOST-R and Static-99, both $r = .53$; SORAG, $r = .63$; and PCL-R, $r = .75$. Case Prioritization ratings of overall risk for sexual violence on the RSVP had moderate to large correlations with total scores on other measures: MnSOST-R, $r = .41$; Static-99, $r = .50$; SORAG, $r = .33$; and PCL-R, $r = .40$.

Hart (2003), in his study of 50 adult male sex offenders at an outpatient forensic psychiatric clinic, reported that presence-ever total scores on the RSVP had moderate to large correlations with total scores on other risk-related measures: MnSOST-R, $r = .51$; Static-99, $r = .31$; and SORAG, $r = .45$. Case Prioritization ratings of overall risk for sexual violence on the RSVP had moderate to large correlations with total scores on other measures: MnSOST-R, $r = .50$; Static-99, $r = .41$; and SORAG, $r = .46$.

Watt et al. (2006), in their study of 50 high-risk adult male sex offenders under community supervision in Canada, found that total scores on the Static-99 were correlated $r = .73$ with presence-past total scores on the RSVP, $r = .69$ with presence-recent ratings, $r = .77$ with relevance ratings, and $r = .77$ with Case Prioritization ratings. Total scores on the VRAG were correlated $r = .80$ with presence-past total scores on the RSVP, $r = .76$ with presence-recent total scores, $r = .82$ with relevance total scores, and $r = .65$ with Case Prioritization ratings.

Darjee et al. (2016), in their study of 109 people referred to a community-based program for sex offenders in Scotland, examined the concurrent validity of the RSVP. RSVP presence-past total scores were correlated $r = .77$ with PCL-R total scores, $r = .41$ with RM2000S total scores, and $r = .47$ with RM2000V total scores. RSVP presence-recent total scores were correlated $r = .45$ with PCL-R total scores, $r = .31$ with RM2000S total scores, and $r = .24$ with RM2000V total scores. Finally, RSVP relevance total scores were correlated $r = .75$ with PCL-R total scores, $r = .43$ with RM2000S total scores, and $r = .48$ with RM2000V total scores.

Vargen et al. (2020), in their study of 100 adult male sex offenders who completed a community-based sex offender treatment program in Canada, reported concurrent validity with respect to two actuarial tests. RSVP presence-ever and relevance total scores were correlated $r = .68$ and .66, respectively, with total scores on the SORAG; and .51 and .43, respectively, with total scores on the Static-99R. With respect to summary judgments of risk, Case Prioritization ratings were correlated $r = .65$ with total scores on the SORAG and .63 with total scores on the Static-99R; Serious Physical Harm ratings, .44 with total scores on the SORAG and .24 with total scores on the Static-99R; and Immediate Action Required ratings, .44 with total scores on the SORAG and .51 with total scores on the Static-99R.

Sea and Hart (in press), in their study of 47 sex offenders in Korea, reported concurrent validity of the RSVP with respect to two actuarial tests. RSVP presence-ever and relevance total scores were correlated $r = .67$ and .52, respectively, with total scores on the Hallym Assessment Guide for Sex Offender Risk (HAGSOR; Joe, 2010); and .67 and .49, respectively, with total scores on the Static-99R. With respect to summary judgments of risk, Case Prioritization ratings were correlated $r = .10$ with total scores on the HAGSOR and .11 with total scores on the Static-99R; Serious Physical Harm ratings, .57 with total scores on the HAGSOR and .35 with total scores on the Static-99R; and Immediate Action Required ratings, $-.18$ with total scores on the HAGSOR and $-.16$ with total scores on the Static-99R.

Predictive Validity

SVR-20 V1/V2

Using a retrospective case-control design, Dempster (1998) studied a sample of 95 adult males in Canada who were released to the community following incarceration for serious sexual offenses. Based on review of official records (police reports and criminal records) at the end of a follow-up period lasting several years, the offenders were divided into three groups: 42 non-recidivists, 29 nonsexual violent recidivists, and 24 sexually violent recidivists. The SVR-20 was coded from files. Dempster examined summary risk ratings and then numerically recoded items and summed them to yield total scores. According to ROC analyses, both SVR-20 summary risk ratings and total scores significantly discriminated between sexually violent recidivists and non-recidivists, AUC = .77 and .74, respectively, $p < .001$. Summary risk ratings significantly discriminated between sexually violent and nonsexually violent recidivists, AUC = .68, $p < .05$, but total scores did not, AUC = .55, $n.s.$ The predictive validity of the SVR-20 was equal or superior to that of other risk assessment instruments, including the RRASOR, SORAG, and VRAG. Finally, incremental validity analyses indicated that summary risk ratings had unique predictive power with respect to recidivism, even after controlling for numerical risk scores on the SVR-20.

Dempster and Hart (2002), following on Dempster (1998), studied a sample of 95 adult males who were released into the community upon completion of sentences for serious sexual offenses. The SVR-20 V1 was coded on the basis of pre-release correctional files, blind to case outcome. Based on review of police reports and criminal records at the end of a follow-up period lasting several years, the offenders were divided into three groups: 42 non-recidivists, 29 nonsexual violent recidivists, and 24 sexually violent recidivists. Dempster and Hart (2002) calculated the correlation between lifetime presence ratings for the 20 individual risk factors and recidivism, coded dichotomously (0 = No, 1 = Yes). The correlations between SVR-20 V1 item presence ratings and sexual violence ranged from $-.06$ to .50, with $Mdn = .23$; 18 of 20 correlations were positive in sign, and 9 of 20 were both positive and statistically significant ($p < .05$). The item with the lowest validity was 6 (Major mental illness), which was correlated $-.05$ with nonsexual violence and $-.06$ with sexual violence; this is due primarily to the fact that very few of the offenders suffered from serious psychopathology aside from substance use or personality disorders.

Lennings (2003) studied 27 males, aged 16 to 68, charged with sexual offenses. He completed the SVR-20 V1 on the basis of complete clinical evaluations. He divided the sample into two groups: 18 who were found or pleaded guilty, and 9 who were not found guilty (including one whose charges were dismissed due to health reasons). Despite the small sample size, the offenders who were found or pleaded guilty had presence total scores that were significantly higher than those of the offenders not found guilty on 9 of 20 items; none of the items had presence ratings that were significantly lower on offenders not found guilty.

McPherson (2003) studied a sample of 40 sexual offenders assessed or treated at a forensic psychiatric outpatient clinic. The SVR-20 V1 was coded on the basis of clinical records. All were convicted of non-contact sexual offenses, completed assessment and treatment, and then reoffended. Based on the nature of their new sexual offenses, they were divided into two groups: 20 committed a second sexual offense that also was non-contact, whereas the other 20 escalated to commit contact sexual offenses. McPherson reported that offenders who subsequently escalated had significantly higher presence ratings on 10 of 20 individual risk factors; none of the items had presence ratings that were significantly lower in offenders who escalated.

Sjöstedt and Långström (2003) studied 51 adult male rapists who underwent presentence forensic psychiatric evaluations in Sweden between 1988 and 1990. The SVR-20 V1 was coded on the basis of file information. Recidivism (new convictions for sexually violent offenses) was coded from official records during a follow-up period that averaged about 9.5 years after release. According to ROC analyses, neither presence total scores nor summary risk ratings on the SVR-20 V1 significantly predicted recidivism, all $.47 \leq AUC \leq .56$. VRAG scores also were not significantly predictive of recidivism, $AUC = .58$, but RRASOR total scores were $AUC = .71$. According to correlational analyses, none of the risk assessment measures was significantly predictive of recidivism.

de Vogel et al. (2004) studied 122 adult male sex offenders admitted to a forensic psychiatric hospital in the Netherlands. Dutch translations of the SVR-20 V1 and Static-99 were completed on the basis of file information. Using a retrospective design, they coded recidivism (new convictions for sexually violent offenses) from official records during an average follow-up period of about 11.5 years. ROC analyses indicated that the SVR had good predictive validity: for presence total scores, $AUC = .80$; summary risk ratings, $AUC = .83$. The predictive validity of total scores on the Static-99 was lower, although not significantly so, at .71. Finally, incremental validity analyses indicated that summary risk ratings had some unique predictive power with respect to recidivism, even after controlling for numerical risk scores on the SVR-20 V1.

Craig, Browne, Beech, and Stringer (2006) evaluated the predictive validity of several risk assessment measures, including the SVR-20 V1, Static-99, and RM2000S, in a sample of 85 sexual offenders in the UK. The risk assessment measures were coded from files. Using a retrospective design, they determined recidivism (reconviction for new sexual offenses) over a follow-up period that averaged about 8.5 years. The base rate of recidivism was estimated to be 7% at 2 years, 12% at 5 years, and 18% at 10 years after release. According to ROC analyses, none of the risk assessment measures, including SVR-20 V1 total scores, significantly predicted sexually violent recidivism at 2, 5, or 10 years after release in the group of sexual offenders, with AUCs ranging from .46 to .68.

Stadtland et al. (2005, 2006) studied 134 treated sex offenders in Germany, all adult males. The SVR-20 V1 was coded on the basis of institutional files. Using a retrospective follow-up design, they examined the association between the risk assessment instruments and recidivism. Recidivism was defined as new convictions for sexually or nonsexually violent offenses during a post-release follow-up period lasting an average of 9 years. SVR-20 V1 ratings were available for

119 men who successfully completed treatment. The rate of recidivism among 67 offenders with SVR-20 V1 presence total scores of 20 or lower was 16% ($n = 11$); the rate among 52 offenders with scores of 21 or higher was 38% ($n = 20$). According to Kaplan-Meier survival analyses, the difference between these two groups in recidivism as a function of time was statistically significant, with Log rank and Breslow tests both $p < .001$. According to ROC analyses, the AUC for SVR-20 V1 presence total scores was .68, which was lower than that of Static-99 total scores (.72) but slightly higher than that of HCR-20 numeric total scores and PCL-R total scores (.65 and .64, respectively), although none of the differences was statistically significant.

Barbaree et al. (2008), following on Langton (2003), evaluated the predictive validity of the SVR-20 in 468 adult sex offenders who completed a prison-based sex offender treatment program in Canada. SVR-20 V1 ratings were made on the basis of file information. Using a retrospective design, they coded recidivism, defined as any new conviction for a sexual or violent offense during a follow-up that averaged 5.1 years after release. According to ROC analyses, SVR-20 V1 presence total scores significantly predicted recidivism, with AUC = .63.

Hill et al. (2008) examined the association between SVR-20 V1 ratings and recidivism in 166 adult male sexual homicide offenders in Germany. SVR-20 V1 ratings were based on forensic psychiatric reports; one risk factor, 19 (Lacks realistic plans), could not be coded. Recidivism was defined as new convictions for sexually violent offenses, according to official records, during a lengthy follow-up period. Presence total scores were dichotomized, low (≤ 24) and high (≥ 25). SVR-20 V1 scores were not significantly associated with recidivism: the rate of sexually violent recidivism in both the low and high groups was 24%. Total scores on the Static-99 were also not significantly associated with recidivism. In other studies based on the same dataset, it was reported the sexual homicide perpetrators detained in forensic hospital received significantly higher summary risk ratings on the SVR-20 V1 than did sexual homicide perpetrators detained in prison (Ujeyl, Habermann, Briken, Berner, & Hill, 2008), but there were no significant differences between sexual homicide perpetrators whose victims were children versus those whose victims were adults with respect to SVR-20 V1 presence total scores (Spehr, Hill, Habermann, Briken, & Berner, 2010).

Pérez Ramírez et al. (2008) studied 163 adult male offenders in Spain. The SVR-20 V1 was coded on the basis of file information. Using a retrospective design, they coded recidivism from official records; the base rate of new sexual offenses was 15% over a follow-up that averaged about five years. ROC analyses indicated that SVR-20 presence total scores had a statistically significant association with recidivism; AUC = .83.

Parent et al. (2011) studied 503 adult males who were evaluated at the Massachusetts Treatment Center for Sexually Dangerous Persons (MTC) in Bridgewater, Massachusetts, between 1959 and 1984. Using a retrospective design, they examined recidivism (defined as new charges or convictions for sexual offenses) over a 15-year follow-up period. They compared the predictive validity of nine risk-relevant assessment instruments, including the SVR-20 V1, PCL-R, VRAG and SORAG, RRASOR, Static-99 and Static-2002, RM2000S and RMS000V, and MnSOST-R. All of the instruments had moderate and statistically significant predictive validity with respect to new charges or convictions for hands-on sexual offenses, $.65 \leq$ AUC $\leq .71$, with the exception of the RM2000V which had small and non-significant predictive validity, AUC = .52. The predictive validity of the SVR-20 V1 presence total scores was AUC = .66. All of the instruments had small and non-significant predictive validity with respect to sexual offenses that were not hands-on (i.e., "nuisance" offenses), all AUC $\leq .61$. Predictive validity tended to be slightly higher in extrafamilial child molesters than in rapists; for the SVR-20 V1, AUC = .67 and .68, respectively.

Rettenberger et al. (2010) studied 394 adult male sex offenders in the Austrian Prison System. They examined the predictive validity of five risk-relevant assessment instruments—including the

PCL-R, RRASOR, Static-99, SORAG, and SVR-20 V1—with respect to recidivism (defined as reconvictions) over a follow-up period that averaged about 36 months. All of the instruments had moderate and statistically significant predictive validity with respect to any new convictions for sexual offenses, $.69 \leq AUC \leq .74$, with the exception of the PCL-R which had small and non-significant predictive validity, $AUC = .59$. The predictive validity of the SVR-20 V1 presence total scores was $AUC = .71$. Predictive validity was higher in extrafamilial child molesters; for the SVR-20 V1, $AUC = .75$, which was higher than that of the other instruments, although not significantly so. The findings of Rettenberger et al. (2010) were extended in two studies published subsequently. In the first, Rettenberger et al. (2011) examined the predictive validity of the SVR-20 V1 in an expanded sample totaling 493 adult male sex offenders studied over a follow-up that averaged more than 4 years. The predictive validity of presence total scores was $AUC = .72$ for convictions for any new sexual offense and .71 for any new hands-on sexual offense; among extrafamilial child molesters, predictive validity was .77 for any new sexual offense and .72 for any new hands-on sexual offense; whereas among rapists predictive validity was .71 for any new sexual offense and .74 for any new hands-on sexual offense. For the prediction of any new sexual offense, 16 of 20 individual risk factor presence ratings had $AUC > .50$ (7 of them significantly so) and 4 had $AUC < .50$ (none of them significantly so), and the average (*Mdn*) AUC was .59. For the prediction of any new hands-on sexual offense, 18 of 20 individual risk factor presence ratings had $AUC > .50$ (4 of them significantly so) and 2 had $AUC < .50$ (none of them significantly so), and the average (*Mdn*) AUC was .60. In the second, Yoon et al. (2018) examined whether protective factors had incremental predictive validity with respect to risk ratings made using the SVR-20 V1; they did not.

Blacker, Beech, Wilcox, and Boer (2011) studied 88 sex offenders, 44 of whom had intellectual impairment and 44 of whom did not. They examined the predictive validity of four risk assessment instruments, including the RRASOR, RM2000V, SVR-20 V1, and the Stable and Acute scales of the Assessment of Risk and Manageability of Individuals with Developmental and Intellectual Limitations Who Offend—Sexually (ARMIDILO-S; Boer et al., 2012). Recidivism was coded from records over a follow-up period that averaged more than 9 years. In offenders with special needs, only ARMIDILO-S Stable and Acute scores had significant predictive validity; but in the other offenders, the SVR-20 V1 total presence scores had the highest predictive validity. When recidivism was defined broadly as any sexually motivated misbehavior, including non-criminal acts, the predictive validity of SVR-20 V1 presence total scores was $AUC = .40$ in offenders with special needs and .70 in the other offenders; when recidivism was defined more narrowly as any new convictions for sexual offenses, predictive validity was .45 in offenders with special needs and .73 in the other offenders.

Smid, Kamphuis, Wever, and Van Beek (2014) studied 397 sex offenders in the Netherlands. They examined recidivism, defined as any new charges or convictions, over a follow-up period that averaged about 12 years. They compared the predictive validity of nine risk-relevant instruments, including the RRASOR, Structured Anchored Clinical Judgment Minimum (SACJ-Min; Grubin, 1998), Static-99R, Static-2002R, RM2000S, SORAG, and SVR-20 V1. The predictive validity of SVR-20 V1 total presence scores was lower than that of total scores on the other instruments: $AUC = .58$ at 5 years, .61 at 10 years, and .61 overall.

Jackson (2016) studied 100 adult males who completed a community-based sex offender treatment program. She examined recidivism, defined as any new police contact (including investigation, charge, and conviction) for sexual offenses, over a follow-up period of 10 years post-treatment. She reported the predictive validity of presence scores for individual risk factors on the SVR-20 V1 and also compared the predictive validity of SVR-20 V1 presence total scores to total scores on the Static99R, Static-2002R, and SORAG. (Comparisons of the predictive validity of the SVR-20 V1 and RSVP are summarized in the next section.) With respect to presence scores for individual risk factors, 19 of 20 individual risk factor presence ratings had AUC > .50 (2 of them significantly so) and 1 had AUC < .50 (not significantly so); the average (*Mdn*) AUC was .56. The predictive validity of presence total scores was AUC = .68, which was the same as that of the Static-99R and slightly (but not significantly) smaller than that of Static-2002R and SORAG total scores, both AUC = .71.

Kanters et al. (2017) studied 70 sex offenders in the Netherlands who were released following treatment in a forensic mental health facility. They examined the predictive validity of SVR-20 V1 ratings made before and after treatment. Recidivism was defined as any new conviction over a follow-up period that averaged about five years. SVR-20 V1 ratings presence total scores had small and nonsignificant predictive validity with respect to any new convictions for sexual offenses: for ratings made before treatment, AUC = .62; and for ratings after treatment, .60. The predictive validity of summary risk ratings made before treatment was also small and nonsignificant, .58; but for ratings made after treatment was moderate and significant, .76.

Tsao and Chu (in press), in their study of 134 adult male sex offenders in Singapore, examined the predictive validity of SVR-20 V2 ratings. Recidivism was defined as any new offenses and any new sexual offenses during a follow-up that averaged 3.7 years after conviction. (All offenders received community sentences.) SVR-20 V2 total scores and summary risk ratings for sexual violence had large and statistically significant predictive validity with respect to any new sexual offenses, AUC = .76 and .78, respectively. The predictive validity of the SVR-20 total scores and summary risk ratings was slightly (but not significantly) higher than that of total scores on the Static-99R, STABLE-2007, PCL-R, and LS/CMI.

RSVP

Kropp (2001) studied a subsample of 53 offenders from the larger sample collected by Dempster (1998) that included 15 sexually violent recidivists and 38 non-recidivists or nonsexually violent recidivists. The RSVP was coded from files; "past" and "recent" presence ratings on the RSVP were recoded into numeric scores, combined, and summed to yield total scores. RSVP case prioritization ratings were significantly correlated with sexually violent recidivism, $r = .40, p < .05$; the correlation between total scores and sexually violent recidivism was not significant, $r = .23$. In comparison, total scores on the MnSOST-R, Static-99, and SORAG were correlated $r = .18, .30,$ and .33 with sexually violent recidivism; the latter two correlations were statistically significant, $p < .05$. Turning to case prioritization ratings, 8 of 15 offenders (53%) rated as high priority were sexually violent recidivists, compared to 5 of 20 offenders (20%) rated as moderate priority and 2 of 19 offenders (11%) rated as low priority.

Darjee et al. (2016) conducted a field study of 109 people who were assessed using the RSVP by various professionals working for a community-based program. They examined recidivism (new investigations, charges, or convictions) with respect to both any new sexual offenses and serious sexual offenses over a follow-up period of a little over 3 years. According to ROC analyses, total presence-past, presence-recent, and relevance scores on the RSVP had small but nonsignificant predictive validity vis-à-vis any sexual offenses, AUC = .58, .61, and .60, respectively; but higher predictive validity vis-à-vis serious sexual offenses, AUC = .68, .71, and .66, respectively. In comparison, the predictive validity of Case Prioritization, Serious Physical Harm, and Immediate Action Required ratings vis-à-vis any sexual offenses was .59, .53, and .55, respectively; and vis-à-vis serious sexual offenses was .63, .60, and .68, respectively. According to survival analyses, Case Prioritization ratings were associated with time to new sexual offenses. Interestingly, there was a good match between scenarios of future sexual violence identified by evaluators and the actual sexual offenses that were (allegedly) committed; according to Darjee et al., the match was 96% for victim gender, 77% for victim age, 69% for relationship to victim, and 62% for seriousness of harm.

Vargen et al. (2020) and Jackson (2016) reported the predictive validity of RSVP ratings from Jackson's study of 100 adult males who completed a community-based sex offender treatment program. Recidivism was defined as any new police contact (including investigation, charge, and conviction) for sexual offenses over a follow-up period of 10 years post-treatment. Looking first at the predictive validity of individual risk factors in the RSVP, according to the Cox regression survival analyses, for both presence-ever and relevance ratings, 20 of 22 had Hazard Ratios (HRs) greater than 1 (3 significantly so for presence-ever ratings and 6 for relevance ratings) and only 2 had HRs less than 1 (none significantly so for either presence-ever or relevance ratings); the *Mdn* HR was 1.33 for presence-ever ratings and 1.30 for relevance ratings. Looking next at Case Prioritization ratings, there was a strong association with recidivism. The proportion of recidivists among those rated *Low*, *Moderate*, and *High* was .17, .32, and .62, respectively; using those with *Low* ratings as a reference group, the odds of recidivism was 2.20 times greater among those with *Moderate* ratings and 8.60 times higher among those with *High* ratings. Finally, a series of analyses compared the predictive validity of RSVP Case Prioritization ratings and presence-ever total scores (divided into quintiles, i.e., five equal-sized groups) to that of total scores on the Static-99R and SORAG (both of the latter also divided into quintiles, to permit direct comparison with RSVP presence-ever scores). The predictive validity of RSVP presence-ever, Static-99R, and SORAG total scores was HR = 1.61, 1.56, and 1.66, respectively, all somewhat lower than that of RSVP Case Prioritization ratings but still statistically significant. Incremental validity analyses indicated that neither Static-99R nor SORAG total scores significantly improved the predictive validity of RSVP presence-ever total scores or Case Prioritization ratings.

Limitations of Supporting Research

What We Know: Conclusions Based on Research to Date

Based on the research reviewed, we offer three general conclusions regarding judgments of risk for sexual violence made using the SVR-20 V1 and RSVP. First, research supports the view that judgments of risk for sexual violence made using the SVR-20 V1 and RSVP typically have interrater reliability that may be characterized as *good* to *excellent* in absolute terms. Second, judgments of risk for sexual violence made using SPJ guidelines have concurrent validity with respect to actuarial tests of risk for sexual violence and other risk-related measures that is moderate to high in absolute terms. Third, judgments of risk for sexual violence made using the SVR-20 V1 and RSVP typically have predictive validity with respect to sexual violence that is moderate in absolute terms and, in relative terms, equal to that of actuarial tests of risk for sexual violence. This last conclusion is similar to that reached by others in meta-analyses. For example, in the meta-analyses by Hanson and Morton-Bourgon (2009) and Singh, Grann, and Fazel (2011), the SVR-20 V1 had the highest predictive validity among the various sexual violence risk assessment tools evaluated.

What We Don't Know: Problems With Past Research and Recommendations for Future Research

In our chapter in the first edition of this book, we identified four major problems with research on SPJ guidelines for sexual violence. As they are still relevant, we provide an updated discussion of them. We recognize that all studies (including, of course, our own) have flaws or limitations, many of which reflect strategic decisions or operational limitations. The point here is not to blame researchers for being imperfect, but rather to enhance their awareness of problems they may be able to avoid.

Inadequate File Information

Most researchers made ratings on the basis of file information. It is difficult or even impossible to code some risk factors when institutional records are limited in quality and quantity, especially when the original assessments summarized in the records were themselves restricted in breadth or depth. The risk factors that seem to be adversely impacted most often by reliance on files are those related to mental health problems and future plans. Best practice when evaluating the SVR-20 V1/V2 and RSVP is to conduct risk comprehensive assessments *de novo* following the administration procedures set out in the guidelines. In disseminations, researchers should describe the file information that was available to evaluators in their studies and identify any systematic or substantial limitations of the file information.

Inadequate Training and Experience of Evaluators

Some researchers acknowledged use of evaluators who lack adequate training and experience in the use of the SVR-20 V1/V2 and RSVP, and others failed to provide information about the training and experience of evaluators. Although the guidelines are written in plain language, it is not a simple matter for evaluators to make judgments about such things as sexual deviance, psychopathy, or the chronicity of an offender's history of sexual violence; to develop formulations of risk for sexual violence; or develop scenario-based management plans. Best practice when evaluating the SVR-20 V1/V2 and RSVP is to recruit evaluators who meet the criteria outlined in the guidelines, provide them with standardized training, and then provide them with regular supervision or booster training. In disseminations, researchers should provide a clear summary of how evaluators were recruited, trained, and supervised to use the guidelines.

Inadequate Evaluation of Risk Ratings

This is perhaps the most serious problem. Researchers have tended to limit their evaluations of the reliability and validity of judgments made using the SVR-20 V1/V2 and RSVP to presence ratings of individual risk factors, composited into numerical total scores reflecting lifetime presence. This does not reflect the manner in which the guidelines are intended to be used in practice. First, the administration procedures of the guidelines do not require evaluators to convert ratings into numbers or composites; indeed, evaluators are specifically advised not to engage in such practices. Second, such ratings are of limited importance. Rating the presence of individual risk factors is only the second step of the administration procedures of the SVR-20 V1/V2 and RSVP; in subsequent steps, evaluators consider the dynamic nature of the risk factors (i.e., fluctuations in their presence or severity over time), as well as their relevance to the person's overall risk for sexual violence and management of those risks. Best practice when evaluating the SVR-20 V1/V2 and RSVP is to follow the administration procedures outlined in the guidelines as closely as possible and, whenever possible, to focus on presence ratings for individual risk factors or, alternatively, global judgments of risk (e.g., Summary Risk or Case Prioritizations ratings) rather than on numerical presence total scores. In disseminations, researchers should note any deviations from the administration procedures outlined in the guidelines.

Inadequate Assessments in Follow-up Studies

Most evaluations of the predictive validity of judgments made using the SVR-20 V1/V2 and RSVP focus on recidivism status at the endpoint of a long-term follow-up. In research of this sort, risk assessments conducted at the start of the follow-up are used to forecast recidivism over a period of years, in the absence of any reassessments of risk or any control over case management tactics implemented. Best practice when evaluating the SVR-20 V1/V2 and RSVP is to conduct reassessments on a regular basis (e.g., from every 1 or 2 months up to once or twice per year) and also to record and control such things as monitoring and supervision conditions, treatment received, and so forth. In disseminations, researchers should identify any limitations in their ability to assess recidivism (e.g., failure to take into account emigration, institutionalization, mortality, and so forth) and implementation of case management tactics.

Directions for Future Research

In light of discussions in this chapter and elsewhere (e.g., Hart et al., 2016), we have a number of recommendations concerning avenues for future research on the SVR-20 V1/V2 and RSVP.

Consumer Satisfaction Research

Previously, we (Hart & Boer, 2010) called for research in the form of surveys, focus groups, and so forth on the extent to which various stakeholders—evaluators and other interested parties—view the guidelines as acceptable, useful, in need of improvement, and so forth. We are pleased to report that, in addition to one review and two studies known to us when we prepared the original chapter (Archer, Buffington-Vollum, Stredny, & Handel, 2006; Lally, 2003; Witt, 2000), two others became known to us immediately thereafter (Bengtson & Pedersen, 2008; Khiroya, Weaver, & Maden, 2009), and others have been published in the intervening years (e.g., Judge, Quayle, O'Rourke, Russell, & Darjee, 2014; Kelley, Ambroziak, Thornton, & Barahal, 2020; Viljoen, McLachlan, & Vincent, 2010). These studies have found that at least a substantial minority of practitioners across various countries and within various agencies use the SVR-20 V1/V2 and RSVP regularly and also view them as useful. But key issues remain unexplored by the existing research. These include:

- *Training of evaluators.* What background knowledge, skills, or experience best prepare evaluators to use the SVR-20 V1/V2 and RSVP? What do evaluators with different levels of experience perceive to be critical needs that would prepare them to use the SVR-20 V1/V2 and RSVP? Which training curricula, delivered by which methods, do evaluators find most helpful in helping them to acquire the knowledge and skills required to make good use of the SVR-20 V1/V2 and RSVP?
- *Usefulness of guidelines according to evaluators.* How often are the SVR-20 V1/V2 and RSVP considered by experienced evaluators to be clearly appropriate, clearly inappropriate, or questionably appropriate for use in practice in various settings? For what decision-making purposes or with which types of evaluees are they considered to be especially helpful or unhelpful? What kinds of revisions or modifications would make the guidelines easier to use or more useful?
- *Acceptability of guidelines according to other stakeholders.* How are the guidelines perceived by evaluees, correctional or forensic mental health administrators, legal professionals, and laypeople with respect to such issues as face validity, fairness, and relevance to decision-making? What could be done to improve the perceived acceptability of the guidelines? Surveys of this sort

could also include reviews of case law in various decisions focusing specifically on the SVR-20 V1/V2 and RSVP, similar to previous reviews focusing on other SPJ guidelines such as the HCR-20. For example, a brief search conducted at the time this chapter was being prepared returned more than 120 reported decisions by Canadian courts in which the SVR-20 V1/V2 was cited and more than 100 in which the RSVP was cited.

Judgments Related to Relevance of Risk Factors, Formulation, and Scenarios

Most research on SPJ guidelines, including the SVR-20 V1/V2 and RSVP, has focused on presence ratings and global judgments of risk in the form of Summary Risk or Case Prioritization ratings made on a 3-point ordinal scale. This is understandable, as the presence rating and overall judgments of risk are simple to code and analyze; but it is also unfortunate, as they reflect only one part of the process of risk assessment. Research is needed to explore how evaluators and stakeholders make sense of risk factors—how they develop mental models of what caused the past sexual violence of evaluees and what might cause them to be sexually violent in the future, as well as how they determine what steps could be taken to prevent sexual violence. The RSVP is particularly well suited to this sort of research, as it includes steps in which evaluators make explicit formulation-based ratings of the relevance of each risk factor with respect to past sexual violence, as well as describe what they consider to be the plausible scenarios of possible future sexual violence. (Indeed, the RSVP was the first set of SPJ guidelines to include these steps.) We have followed with great interest the research of several groups on formulation generally, including several studies focusing specifically on formulation using the RSVP (e.g., Sea & Hart, in press; Sutherland et al., 2012; Wilson, 2013), and eagerly await further research on topics such as:

- *Process of making judgments.* How do evaluators construct mental models of the sexual violence risk of evaluees? For example, how do they decide which risk factors are most relevant and how they act synergistically to cause sexual violence? What implicit theories guide the judgments of untrained or novice versus trained or experienced evaluators? Can evaluators be trained to use different theories to make formulations and, if so, which theories appear to be most useful for constructing good formulations? What makes a formulation "good"? How do training and experience influence the scenarios identified by evaluators? What features of scenarios are most helpful for the development of management plans? What are the best models for conceptualizing, developing, and communicating about management plans? To answer questions of this sort, it would be helpful to use qualitative research methods, for example, to observe evaluators conducting risk assessments in real-world settings; ask them to "talk aloud" while or immediately after making judgments; and conduct in-depth interviews with them (individually or in focus groups) to explore how they understand their own judgment processes or evaluate the adequacy of their own judgments. Research could also use quantitative methods to examine the impact of training, experience, or varying decision-making processes on the quality of judgments.
- *Interrater reliability of judgments.* To what extent do evaluators agree on judgments about formulation-based relevance and scenario-based management plans? This is a tricky question. There are two basic approaches to answering it. The first is to deconstruct the judgments into a series of highly structured ratings and then use conventional methods to analyze them. For example, Sutherland et al. (2012) and Sea and Hart (in press) asked evaluators to identify specific scenarios of future sexual violence (e.g., repeat, escalation) and make a series of ratings about them (e.g., characteristics of victims). The second is to find novel ways to analyze the judgments more holistically. For example, Wilson (2013) asked evaluators to write short narrative formulations for a series of cases, and then asked blind raters to judge the

overall similarity of two pairs of narrative formulations: either by different evaluators for the same case or by different evaluators for different cases. Each approach has its own strengths and limitations, of course, and so both approaches should be used.

- *Impact of judgments on evaluators' management plans.* Do complex judgments enhance the ability of evaluators to develop case management plans? Do they increase the quality of those plans with respect to detail, feasibility, sequencing of interventions, and so forth? One way to answer these questions is to ask evaluators to conduct risk assessments with versus without making judgments related to the relevance of risk factors, formulations, and scenarios to determine the impact of such judgments on the management plans they recommend as well as their overall ratings of risk for sexual violence. Research could also examine different ways to increase the usefulness of complex judgments.

Field Studies of Sexual Violence Risk Assessments

Research on risk assessment tends to be conducted under conditions that do not closely resemble actual practice. For example, it is common that the evaluators are researchers with specific training in the use of one or more tools and limited experience in assessment, rather than by actual practitioners; the evaluations are based solely on file information collected by others, rather than on complete clinical data (including interviews) collected by evaluators; or the evaluations are focused on assessment of risk at a very specific point in time, rather than on the process of risk assessment and management over time. This also holds true for the SVR-20 V1/V2 and RSVP. There are notable exceptions, of course, such as the studies by Darjee et al. (2016) and Sea and Hart (in press). But more evidence is needed concerning the extent to which findings observed in research settings or under controlled conditions generalize to the "field"—that is, practice settings or more open conditions. Put differently, there is a need to determine the effectiveness of sexual violence risk assessments, rather than their efficacy (e.g., Hart & Logan, 2011). Key topics here include:

- *Interrater reliability in field settings.* What level of agreement or consistency is observed across evaluators with respect to the various ratings and judgments they make using the guidelines? To what degree is the level of agreement or consistency affected by factors such as the training or experience of evaluators, the adequacy or completeness of the information base for assessments, and so forth?
- *Impact on case management decisions.* Do risk judgments made using the guidelines, including complex judgments, influence (i.e., were incorporated into) the management plans recommended or implemented in cases?
- *Predictive validity of risk judgments made in the field settings.* Are risk judgments made using the guidelines associated with actual case outcomes—that is, the nature, seriousness, imminence, and frequency of future sexual violence? More importantly, is there evidence that implementation of the management plans recommended for cases lead to a reduction in risk for future sexual violence?
- *Other facets of the utility of guidelines.* What policies, initial and continuing education, and quality assurance procedures support successful agency-wide adoption of the guidelines in field settings? In what proportion of cases do evaluators actually complete risk assessments using the guidelines? How long does it take evaluators to complete their risk assessments? What is the fidelity of those assessments with respect to the administration procedures outlined in the guidelines? What case characteristics are associated with failure to complete risk assessments, undue length of time to completion, or low-fidelity risk assessments? Does use of the

guidelines influence—and, more specifically, improve—risk communication (written reports, expert evidence), reassessment of risk, and the development, implementation, and revision of case management plans? To what extent does the utility of the SVR-20 V1/V2 and RSVP vary across settings and, if so, what factors appear to be related to this variability? To answer these questions, it may be helpful to conceptualize the adoption of the SVR-20 V1/V2 and RSVP in field settings as a novel intervention (in contrast to alternative methods of risk assessment, including "risk assessment as usual"), and to study it using methods from implementation science and treatment outcome research (e.g., Hart, 2003).

Diversity and Risk Assessment

There is increased awareness of the potential susceptibility of risk assessments to bias on the basis of diversity, including group differences related to gender (e.g., biological sex, gender identity, gender role, gender expression, or sexual interest), age (e.g., development or maturity), ethnicity (e.g., race, culture, nationality, language, religion, or other aspects of heritage), and physical or mental disability (e.g., health problems, limitations, or differences). Although there has been some development work on specific guidelines for assessing sexual violence risk in, for example, male adolescents, it is simply not feasible to develop and validate a new assessment tool for each potential subgroup of interest (e.g., for evaluating a transgender adolescent of European heritage with intellectual disability). Is it possible to develop frameworks that can be used with risk assessment guidelines that will help evaluators identify and respond to the full range or potentially important diversity? Does the use of such frameworks lead to increases in the interrater reliability, predictive validity, and utility of risk judgments? And does it lead to increases in consumer satisfaction with risk assessments (i.e., a perception that they are unbiased or less biased)?

Case Example

Here, we present a more detailed version of a case presented elsewhere (Hart & Kropp, 2008). Key details have been omitted or changed to protect the privacy of people involved.

Overview

Mr. V was 84 years old at the time he was assessed. His heritage was German, but his family immigrated to the United States three generations ago and he was born and raised in the rural area of a midwestern state. He was referred for a comprehensive sexual violence risk assessment to help determine whether, four years after being declared a sexually violent predator, he continued to meet statutory criteria for civil commitment or should be granted a conditional or unconditional discharge.

Psychosocial History

Sexual Offenses

Mr. V had a history of 6 sexual offenses that involved noncoercive sexual touching and oral sex with and by prepubescent boys, aged 10 to 12. In each instance, Mr. V approached the boys, who were previously unknown to him, in public places and offered them money to engage in sex. The offenses occurred over an extended period of time: The first offense occurred when Mr. V was about 46 years old, and the most recent offense occurred when he was about 72 years old.

Past Functioning

Mr. V's development and social adjustment were positive until he reached the age of 46. His childrearing experiences were unremarkable, with the exception of unwanted sexual touching by his brother for a brief period of time when he was about 7 years old. He had no problems at school or work. He graduated from high school and completed 2 years of college. He served in the military during World War II and received an honorable discharge. He operated a successful business for many years. His social attitudes and orientation were prosocial, and he had no problems with the law. He had a stable marriage for many years and together with his wife raised four children, despite the fact that his wife had serious physical and emotional health concerns until her death when he was 46 years old. He was actively involved in a local church. Finally, during this period of his life, Mr. V no serious problems related to physical or mental health.

Mr. V's psychosocial adjustment decreased markedly following his wife's death. There was no indication from any source that Mr. V had engaged in sexually deviant behavior or had experienced sexually deviant thoughts, images, urges, or fantasies prior to his wife's death. But afterward, he became sexually interested in and sought out sexual contact with boys. As noted earlier, this resulted in convictions for sexual offenses on three occasions, each time as a result of sexual contact with boys aged about 10 or 11 years old. Although Mr. V consistently minimized his personal responsibility for sexual contact with boys in a highly defensive manner, it was clear from available evidence that after the death of his wife he also began to experience thoughts and urges involving sex with boys, and in fact masturbated to such thoughts on many occasions. Based on his history, Mr. V was diagnosed by health care providers with a paraphilic disorder, specifically, pedophilia. Concurrent with the onset of his paraphilic disorder and subsequent convictions, Mr. V. had serious employment and financial problems, as well as problems with his personal relationships, including the dissolutions of a second marriage and strained relationships with his children.

Recent Functioning

Mr. V's adjustment following his civil commitment as a sexually violent predator, when he was about 70 years old, was generally positive. There is no indication that he exhibited serious behavior problems, including problems related to sexual behavior. He participated actively in treatment, including related activities such as polygraphic evaluations, and made progress (albeit limited) in some areas.

Mr. V's physical health was generally good, given his advanced age. He suffered from mild heart disease. His mobility was mildly restricted. He had an enlarged prostate gland. He reported a significant decline in sexual appetite, functioning, and behavior over the previous 5 years, and in particular during the previous 3 years (e.g., said he did not masturbate, did not experience sexual urges, was no longer able to achieve an erection). He was not upset or distressed by the decline in his functioning, which he accepted as a foreseeable consequence of normal aging and his physical health problems.

Mr. V's mental health also was generally good. He exhibited mild symptoms of dysthymia (e.g., periods of feeling distressed and irritable). He also exhibited some signs of mild cognitive impairment, which likely reflected normal aging but also may have reflected the early stages of dementia. He did not exhibit signs or report symptoms of paraphilic disorder over the previous 5 years, and in particular during the previous 3 years (e.g., reported he no longer had sexual fantasies, urges, or behavior involving sexual contact with boys).

Mr. V's self-reported decline in sexual functioning and appetite were consistent with reports by institutional staff: Mr. V was not observed masturbating in his room, engaging in sexual talk or sexual activity with other patients, or attempting to acquire or make pornographic materials. Mr. V's reports also were consistent with the results of medical testing, which indicated that he was suffering from heart disease and prostate problems that would likely cause erectile difficulties, and with the results of polygraphic interviews, which indicated that he was not lying about his decreased sexual functioning and behavior.

Plans for the Future

Mr. V developed plans for his release from civil commitment that were reasonably detailed, feasible, and confirmed by collateral informants. He intended to seek accommodation at an approved facility, where the management had experience housing registered sex offenders. He arranged for volunteer and other activities, on a limited scale, that would allow him to make appropriate use of public transit (e.g., not on routes or at times where he was likely to encounter unaccompanied minors). He also made arrangements for financial support and plans for developing positive social relationships (i.e., with peers at suitable locations).

Analysis Using SVR-20 V1

There was evidence that seven risk factors were definitely present in Mr. V's case by history: 1 (*Sexual deviation*), 2 (*Victim of child abuse*), 7 (*Relationship problems*), 8 (*Employment problems*), 12 (*High density sex offences*), 17 (*Extreme minimization/denial of sex offences*), and 18 (*Attitudes that support or condone sex offences*). There was also possible or partial evidence of 20 (*Negative attitude toward intervention*). But in each of these areas, Mr. V had demonstrated some capacity for good adjustment over extended periods of time, that is, up until the age of about 46.

In terms of recent change, there was evidence that four of the risk factors present by history had improved to some extent over the previous 12 years, including: 1 (*Sexual deviation*), 17 (*Extreme minimization/denial of sex offences*), 18 (*Attitudes that support or condone sex offences*), and 20 (*Negative attitude toward intervention*). There was no good evidence that the remaining factors had improved or worsened significantly over time, which for 2 (*Victim of child abuse*) was due to its fixed nature and for 12 (*High density sex offences*) was due to lack of opportunity to commit sexual violence.

No case-specific risk factors were coded as present in the case. The evaluator considered Mr. V's physical health problems to be risk reducing rather than risk enhancing, as they would likely reduce both his motivation and his capacity to perpetrate sexual violence.

With respect to the summary risk rating, given the overall pattern of risk factors, both in terms of lifetime presence and recent change, the evaluator considered Mr. V to pose a *Low* risk for future sexual violence. It seemed as though little effort or intervention would be required to prevent further offending in Mr. V's case, at least relative to other cases.

Analysis Using SVR-20 V2

It is a simple matter to recast the findings and opinions obtained with the SVR-20 V1 into those using the SVR-20 V2. There was evidence that seven SVR-20 V2 risk factors were definitely present in Mr. V's case in the past, that is, prior to the past year: 1 (*Sexual deviation*), 3 (*Victim of child abuse*), 8 (*Relationship problems*), 9 (*Employment problems*), 11 (*Chronic sexual offending*), 16 (*Extreme minimization/denial of sexual offending*), and 17 (*Attitudes that support or condone sexual offending*). There was also possible or partial evidence of 19 (*Negative attitude toward intervention*). Recently—that is, in the past year—only two of these risk factors appeared to be definitely present: 3 (*Victim of child abuse*) and 8 (*Relationship problems*). The remaining risk factors possibly or partially present, with the exception of 11 (*Chronic sexual offending*) which was rated as absent due to lack of opportunity to commit sexual violence. As Mr. V's physical health problems were considered risk-reducing rather than risk-enhancing, 2 (*Sexual health problems*) was not coded present either recently or in the past.

With respect to the overall judgments of risk, the evaluator considered Mr. V to pose a *Low* risk for future sexual violence on the summary risk rating. Serious Physical Harm and Need for Immediate Action were also rated *Low*. Other Risks Indicated was rated *No*. Case Review was recommended for a month after release into the community, as more rapid case review or reassessment did not appear necessary.

Analysis Using the RSVP

In Mr. V's case, there was evidence that eight RSVP risk factors were definitely present in the past: 1 (*Chronicity of sexual violence*), 5 (*Psychological coercion in sexual violence*), 6 (*Extreme minimization or denial of sexual violence*), 7 (*Attitudes that support or condone sexual violence*), 8 (*Problems with self-awareness*), 11 (*Sexual deviance*), 16 (*Problems with intimate relationships*), and 18 (*Problems with employment*). There was possible or partial evidence of a further two risk factors: 10 (*Problems resulting from child abuse*) and 21 (*Problems with treatment*). The remaining risk factors appeared to be absent. Recently, in the past year, there was definite evidence of 16 (*Problems with intimate relationships*) and possible or partial evidence of 6 (*Extreme minimization or denial of sexual violence*), 7 (*Attitudes that support or condone sexual violence*), 8 (*Problems with self-awareness*), 18 (*Problems with employment*), and 21 (*Problems with treatment*).

The evaluator's formulation of Mr. V's past sexual offending was that the death of his wife led to loneliness and a blockage of his normal or appropriate sexual outlets. The blockage apparently allowed an underlying sexual deviance to emerge, which until that point had been managed by a combination of internal and external controls (e.g., adequate self-regulation, active engagement in conventional social relationships and activities). He apparently did not actively search for potential victims, but on the few occasions in which he was alone with children who resembled his preferred sexual stimulus, he experienced a strong desire to have sex with boys, projected this sexual desire onto them (i.e., convinced himself that the boys wanted to have sex with him, rather than vice versa), and opportunistically engaged them in sexual activity. According to this formulation, the risk factors with highest relevance in the past were 16 (*Problems with intimate relationships*), 11 (*Sexual deviance*), 8 (*Problems with self-awareness*), and 21 (*Problems with treatment*). But in light of the changes in Mr. V's life circumstances, his needs for intimacy and sexuality appeared to have declined, and so the evaluator considered 8 (*Problems with self-awareness*) and 21 (*Problems with treatment*) to be the most relevant risk factors with respect to his risk for future sexual violence. Mr. V's intact interpersonal skills and his general prosocial attitudes and orientation appeared to the evaluator to be areas of personal strength (i.e., resource or resilience factors).

The evaluator developed two primary scenarios of future sexual violence. In the first, a "repeat" scenario, Mr. V is released into the community and has good initial adjustment, but becomes increasingly lonely, misses intimate and sexual contact with others, begins to visit locations frequented by young boys (such as parks or schoolyards), and eventually tries to convince a young boy to have sex with him. In this scenario, the primary motivation is to reduce feelings of loneliness. The most likely victims are young boys, aged 10 to 12, strangers targeted in an opportunistic manner. The nature of the sexual activity is likely to be non-coercive sexual touching. There is some chance of an escalation to threats of psychological or physical harm, but the likelihood of serious physical harm seems remote, given the absence of any relevant history of such violence and Mr. V's declining physical health. The risk of the scenario seems chronic or long-term, rather than acute or imminent, and possible warning signs of escalating risk include increasing complaints of dysthymia or loneliness and increasing time spent outside in outdoor activities (i.e., not in his residence).

In the second scenario, a "twist" scenario, Mr. V's mild cognitive impairment worsens progressively over the months following his release, his behavior becomes increasingly disinhibited, and he tries to sexually touch another person—probably a young boy aged 10 to 12, but possibly a male of female of any age, once again strangers targeted opportunistically. In this scenario, the primary motivation is sexual gratification; it is not so much that Mr. V's urge to engage in sex is strong, but rather that he is so disinhibited he acts out on even mild urges. If his behavior is disorganized by dementia, the chances of physical harm to victims may be even lower than in the first scenario. The risk appears to be distant or remote rather than acute or imminent, and warning signs of increasing include noticeable worsening of cognitive functions (e.g., declining memory, impaired abstract thinking) and seriously disinhibited behavior (e.g., walking around naked, making grossly inappropriate sexual comments). The evaluator did not perceive any other plausible scenarios of future violence, such as alternative "twist" scenarios (e.g., obscene phone calls to young boys) or "escalation" scenarios (e.g., rape of an adult female, sexual homicide of a young boy). In contrast, the evaluator found it easy to develop an "improvement" or "desistence" scenario in which Mr. V is released, his decline in sexual appetite and function continues, and he develops a routine of activities that help him fulfill his personal needs in an appropriate manner. In this scenario, Mr. V does not experience any significant desire for contact—sexual or otherwise—with young boys and develops coping strategies that are sufficient to control any urges he experiences.

Based on the scenarios, the evaluator made detailed recommendations for case management plans. Briefly, these included developing strategies for: (1) caregivers and supervisors to monitor Mr. V's mood and social contacts, his cognitive functioning, and any evidence of disinhibited sexual behavior; (2) restricting Mr. V's residence and travel to limit his contact with children, whether intentional or accidental; and (3) increasing Mr. V's involvement in appropriate activities that included daily social contact with age-appropriate peers.

Finally, the evaluator reached a number of conclusory opinions to assist communication of the findings of the risk assessment. The rating of Case Prioritization was *Low*, as the evaluator believed it was feasible to develop and implement the case management plan with little effort and good chance of success. The rating of risk for Serious Physical Harm also was *Low*, as the evaluator did not perceive any grounds to believe Mr. V would escalate to any sort of physical violence, let alone life-threatening violence. The rating of Immediate Action Required was *No*, as the evaluator did not see any special management activities that would require implementation prior to or immediately upon release. The rating of Other Risks Indicated was *No*, as the evaluator did not perceive Mr. V to pose a risk for other interpersonal or self-directed violence. Finally, in terms of date for Case Review, the evaluator recommended that if Mr. V was released, his risk should be reassessed within a month, and immediate reassessment should be triggered by any sign that Mr. V's sexual appetite or functioning are, in fact, still active.

Case Discussion

This brief case example illustrates some of the key features of the SVR-20 V1/V2 and RSVP. The most important lesson to be learned is that both sets of guidelines help evaluators reach findings and form opinions regarding the risks for sexual violence posed by an evaluee and the management of those risks. The SVR-20 V1/V2 and RSVP do this in somewhat different ways—the SVR-20 V1/V2 are simpler but provide less structure for developing management plans than does the RSVP—yet none relies on quantification, reference to norms, or specific probability estimates that the evaluee will commit sexual violence. The decisions made using the guidelines can be framed, justified, and challenged in narrative terms. They are grounded in the scientific literature, but not cloaked in a mantle of science that makes them invisible or inaccessible to people who are not statisticians. As forecasts or predictions of the future they are, admittedly, educated guesses—much preferable to wild, ill-informed, or ignorant guesses, but guesses nonetheless. Yet they have great potential utility for guiding action in a manner that is both reasoned and reasonable. We believe this is the best science can offer to decision-makers at this time, given the inchoate state of our knowledge about sexual violence.

References

Addis, M. E. (2002). Methods for disseminating research products and increasing evidence-based practice: Promises, obstacles, and future directions. *Clinical Psychology: Science and Practice, 9*, 367–378.

American Educational Research Association, American Psychological Association, & National Council on Measurement in Education. (1999). *Standards for educational and psychological testing.* Washington, DC: American Psychological Association.

American Psychological Association. (2002). Criteria for practice guideline development and evaluation. *American Psychologist, 57*, 1048–1051.

Andrews, D. A., Bonta, J., & Wormith, S. J. (2004). *Manual for the level of service/case management inventory (LS/CMI).* Toronto, ON: Multi-Health Systems.

Andrews, D. A., Bonta, J., & Wormith, S. J. (2006). The recent past and near future of risk and/or need assessment. *Crime & Delinquency, 52*, 7–27.

Archer, R. P., Buffington-Vollum, J. K., Stredny, R. V., & Handel, R. W. (2006). A survey of psychological test use patterns among forensic psychologists. *Journal of Personality Assessment, 87*, 84–94.

ASIS International & The Risk and Insurance Management Society. (2015). *Risk assessment.* ANSI/ASIS/RIMS RA.1-2015. Alexandria, VA: ASIS International.

Barbaree, H. E., Langton, C. M., Blanchard, R., & Boer, D. P. (2008). Predicting recidivism in sex offenders using the SVR-20: The contribution of age-at-release. *International Journal of Forensic Mental Health, 7*, 47–64.

Bengtson, S., & Pedersen, L. (2008). Implementation of evidence-based practices in forensic psychiatric clinical practice in Denmark: Are we there? *Scandinavian Journal of Forensic Sciences, 2*, 47–52.

Blacker, J., Beech, A. R., Wilcox, D. T., & Boer, D. P. (2011). The assessment of dynamic risk and recidivism in a sample of special needs sexual offenders. *Psychology, Crime & Law, 17*, 75–92.

Boer, D. P. (Series Ed.). (2016). *The Wiley handbook on the theories, assessment, treatment of sexual offending.* Oxford: Wiley.

Boer, D. P., Haaven, J. L., Lambrick, F., Lindsay, W. R., McVilly, K., Sakdalan, J., & Frize, M. (2012). *ARMIDILO-S manual: Web version 1.0.* Retrieved from www.armidilo.net

Boer, D. P., Hart, S. D., Kropp, P. R., & Webster, C. D. (1997). *Manual for the sexual violence risk—20: Professional guidelines for assessing risk of sexual violence.* Burnaby, BC: Mental Health, Law, & Policy Institute, Simon Fraser University.

Boer, D. P., Hart, S. D., Kropp, P. R., & Webster, C. D. (2017). *Manual for version 2 of the sexual violence risk—20: Structured professional judgment guidelines for assessing and managing risk of sexual violence.* Vancouver, BC: Protect International Risk and Safety Services Inc.

Bonta, J., & Andrews, D. A. (2017). *The psychology of criminal conduct* (6th ed.). New York: Routledge.

Craig, L. A., Browne, K. D., Beech, A., & Stringer, I. (2006). Differences in personality and risk characteristics in sex, violent and general offenders. *Criminal Behaviour and Mental Health, 16*, 183–194.

Craig, L. A., Browne, K. D., & Stringer, I. (2004). Comparing sex offender risk assessment measures on a UK sample. *International Journal of Offender Therapy and Comparative Criminology, 48*, 7–27.

Darjee, R., Russell, K., Forrest, L., Milton, E., Savoie, V., Baron, E., . . . Stobie, S. (2016). *Risk for sexual violence protocol (RSVP): A real world study of the reliability, validity and utility of a structured professional judgement instrument in the assessment and management of sexual offenders in South East Scotland.* Edinburgh: NHS Lothian Sex Offender Liaison Service. Retrieved from www.rma.scot/wp-content/uploads/2018/04/Risk_for_Sexual_Violence_Protocol_-_RSVP.pdf

Dempster, R. J. (1998). *Prediction of sexually violent recidivism: A comparison of risk assessment instruments* (Unpublished Master's thesis). Department of Psychology, Simon Fraser University, Burnaby, BC.

Dempster, R. J., & Hart, S. D. (2002). The relative utility of fixed and variable risk factors in discriminating sexual recidivists and nonrecidivists. *Sexual Abuse: A Journal of Research and Treatment, 41,* 121–138.

de Vogel, V., de Ruiter, C., van Beek, D., & Mead, G. (2004). Predictive validity of the SVR-20 and static-99 in a Dutch sample of treated sex offenders. *Law and Human Behavior, 28,* 235–251.

Dietiker, J., Dittmann, V., & Graf, M. (2007). Gutachterliche Risikoeinschätzung bei Sexualstraftätern Anwendbarkeit von PCL-SV, HCR-20 + 3 und SVR-20 [Risk assessment of sex offenders in a German-speaking sample: Applicability of PCL-SV, HCR-20 + 3, and SVR-20]. *Nervenarzt, 78,* 53–61.

Epperson, D. L., Kaul, J. D., & Hesselton, D. (1998). *Final report on the development of the Minnesota sex offending screening tool-revised (MnSOST-R).* St. Paul: Minnesota Department of Corrections.

Fernandez, Y., Harris, A. J. R., Hanson, R. K., & Sparks, J. (2014). *STABLE-2007 coding manual: Revised 2014.* Unpublished manual, Public Safety Canada, Ottawa.

Fleiss, J. L. (1981). *Statistical methods for rates and proportions* (2nd ed.). New York: Wiley.

Grisso, T. (2003). *Evaluating competencies: Forensic assessments and instruments* (2nd ed.). New York: Kluwer Academic, Plenum Press.

Grubin, D. (1998). *Sex offending against children: Understanding the risk.* Police Research Series Paper 99. London: Home Office.

Hájek, A., & Hall, N. (2002). Induction and probability. In P. Machamer & M. Silberstein (Eds.), *The Blackwell guide to the philosophy of science* (pp. 149–172). London: Blackwell.

Hanson, R. K. (1997). *The development of a brief actuarial scale for sexual offense recidivism.* Ottawa: Public Works and Government Services Canada.

Hanson, R. K., & Morton-Bourgon, K. E. (2009). The accuracy of recidivism risk assessments for sexual offenders: A meta-analysis. *Psychological Assessment, 21,* 1–21.

Hanson, R. K., & Thornton, D. M. (1999). *Static-99: Improving actuarial risk assessment for sexual offenders* (Corrections Research User Report 1999-02). Ottawa: Solicitor General of Canada.

Hanson, R. K., & Thornton, D. (2003). *Notes on the development of Static-2002* (Corrections Research User Report 2003-01). Ottawa: Solicitor General of Canada.

Hare, R. D. (1991). *The Hare psychopathy checklist—revised.* Toronto, ON: Multi-Health Systems.

Hare, R. D. (2003). *The Hare psychopathy checklist—revised* (2nd ed.). Toronto, ON: Multi-Health Systems.

Hart, S. D. (2003, April). *Assessing risk for sexual violence: The risk for sexual violence protocol (RSVP).* Paper presented at the Annual Meeting of the International Association of Forensic Mental Health Services, Miami, FL.

Hart, S. D. (2011). Complexity, uncertainty, and the reconceptualization of violence risk assessment. In R. Abrunhosa (Ed.), *Victims and offenders: Chapters on psychology and law* (pp. 57–69). Brussels: Politeia (Original work published 2004).

Hart, S. D. (2009). Evidence-based assessment of risk for sexual violence. *Chapman Journal of Criminal Justice, 1,* 143–165.

Hart, S. D., & Boer, D. P. (2010). Structured professional judgment guidelines for sexual violence risk assessment: The sexual violence risk—20 (SVR-20) and risk for sexual violence protocol (RSVP). In R. K. Otto & K. S. Douglas (Eds.), *Handbook of violence risk assessment* (pp. 269–294). Milton Park: Routledge.

Hart, S. D., & Cooke, D. J. (2013). Another look at the (im-) precision of individual risk estimates made using actuarial risk assessment instruments. *Behavioral Sciences and the Law, 31,* 81–102.

Hart, S. D., & Douglas, K. S. (2019). Violence risk assessment and management—from prediction to prevention. In D. Eaves, C. D. Webster, Q. Haque, & J. Thalken-Eaves (Eds.), *Risk rules: A practical guide to structured professional judgment and violence prevention* (pp. 87–92). Hove: Pavilion Publishing and Media Ltd.

Hart, S. D., Douglas, K. S., & Guy, L. S. (2016). The structured professional judgment approach to violence risk assessment: Origins, nature, and advances. In L. Craig & M. Rettenberger (Vol. Eds.) & D. Boer (Series Ed.), *The Wiley handbook on the theories, assessment, treatment of sexual offending: Volume II. Assessment* (pp. 643–666). Oxford: Wiley.

Hart, S. D., & Logan, C. (2011). Formulation of violence risk using evidence-based assessments: The structured professional judgment approach. In P. Sturmey & M. McMurran (Eds.), *Forensic case formulation* (pp. 83–106). Chichester: Wiley-Blackwell.

Hart, S. D., Michie, C., & Cooke, D. J. (2007). Precision of actuarial risk assessment instruments: Evaluating the "margins of error" of group v. individual predictions of violence. *British Journal of Psychiatry, 190,* 60–65.

Hart, S. D., & Kropp, P. R. (2008). Sexual deviance and the law. In D. R. Laws & W. O'Donohue (Eds.), *Sexual deviance* (2nd ed., pp. 557–570). New York: Guilford Press.

Hart, S. D., Kropp, P. R., Laws, D. R., Klaver, J., Logan, C., & Watt, K. A. (2003). *The risk for sexual violence protocol (RSVP): Structured professional guidelines for assessing risk of sexual violence.* Burnaby, BC: Mental Health, Law, and Policy Institute, Simon Fraser University.

Heilbrun, K. S. (2001). *Principles of forensic mental health assessment.* New York: Kluwer Academic, Plenum Press.

Heilbrun, K. S., Rogers, R., & Otto, R. K. (2002). Forensic assessment: Current status and future directions. In J. R. P. Ogloff (Ed.), *Taking psychology and law into the twenty-first century* (pp. 37–59). New York: Kluwer Academic, Plenum Press.

Hildebrand, M., de Ruiter, C., & de Vogel, V. (2004). Psychopathy and sexual deviance in treated rapists: Association with sexual and nonsexual recidivism. *Sexual Abuse: A Journal of Research and Treatment, 16,* 1–24.

Hill, A., Habermann, N., Klusmann, D., Berner, W., & Briken, P. (2008). Criminal recidivism in sexual homicide perpetrators. *International Journal of Offender Therapy and Comparative Criminology, 52,* 5–20.

International Standards Organization. (2018). *Risk management: Principles and guidelines* (2nd ed.). Geneva: Author. ISO 31000:2018.

Jackson, K. J. (2016). *Validation of the Risk for sexual violence protocol in adult sexual offenders* (Unpublished doctoral dissertation). Department of Psychology, Simon Fraser University, Burnaby, BC.

Jackson, K. J., Read, J. D., & Hart, S. D. (2008, March). *The co-occurrence of psychopathy and sexual deviance as risk factors for sexual violence.* Paper presented at the annual meeting of the American Psychology-Law Society (Div. 41 of the American Psychological Association), Jacksonville, FL.

Joe, U. K. (2010). *Hallym assessment guide for sex offender risk.* Seoul: Korean Correctional Service.

Judge, J., Quayle, E., O'Rourke, S., Russell, K., & Darjee, R. (2014). Referrers' views of structured professional judgment risk assessment of sexual offenders: A qualitative study. *Journal of Sexual Aggression, 20,* 94–109.

Jung, S., Pham, A., & Ennis, L. (2013). Measuring the disparity of categorical risk among various sex offender risk assessment measures. *Journal of Forensic Psychiatry & Psychology, 24,* 353–370.

Kanters, T., Hornsveld, R. J., Nunes, K. L., Zwets, A. J., Muris, P., & van Marle, H. C. (2017). The sexual violence risk-20: Factor structure and psychometric properties. *Journal of Forensic Psychiatry & Psychology, 28,* 368–387.

Kelley, S. M., Ambroziak, G., Thornton, D., & Barahal, R. M. (2020). How do professionals assess sexual recidivism risk? An updated survey of practices. *Sexual Abuse, 32,* 3–29.

Khiroya, R., Weaver, T., & Maden, T. (2009). Use and perceived utility of structured violence risk assessments in English medium secure forensic units. *Psychiatric Bulletin, 33,* 129–132.

Klaver, J., Watt, K., Kropp, P. R., & Hart, S. D. (2002, August). *Actuarial assessment of risk for sexual violence.* Paper presented at the annual meeting of the American Psychological Association, Chicago, IL.

Kropp, P. R. (2001, April). *The risk for sexual violence protocol (RSVP).* Paper presented at the Founding Conference of the International Association of Forensic Mental Health Services, Vancouver, BC.

Krug, E. G., Dahlberg, L. L., Mercy, J. A., Zwi, A. B., & Lozano, R. (Eds.). (2002). *World report on violence and health.* Geneva: World Health Organization.

Lally, S. J. (2003). What tests are acceptable for use in forensic evaluations? A survey of experts. *Professional Psychology: Research and Practice, 34,* 491–498.

Langton, C. M. (2003). *Contrasting approaches to risk assessment with adult male sexual offenders: An evaluation of recidivism prediction schemes and the utility of supplementary clinical information for enhancing predictive accuracy* (Unpublished doctoral dissertation). Institute of Medical Science, University of Toronto, Toronto, ON.

Lennings, C. J. (2003). The use of the SVR-20 in a forensic sample: A research note. *International Journal of Forensic Psychology, 1,* 147–153.

McPherson, G. J. D. (2003). Predicting escalation in sexually violent recidivism: Use of the SVR-20 and PCL: SV to predict outcome with non-contact recidivists and contact recidivists. *Journal of Forensic Psychiatry & Psychology, 14,* 615–627.

Nunes, K. L., Hanson, R. K., Firestone, P., Moulden, H. M., Greenberg, D. M., & Bradford, J. M. (2007). Denial predicts recidivism for some sexual offenders. *Sexual Abuse, 19,* 91–105.

Parent, G., Guay, J. P., & Knight, R. A. (2011). An assessment of long-term risk of recidivism by adult sex offenders: One size doesn't fit all. *Criminal Justice and Behavior, 38,* 188–209.

Pérez Ramírez, M., Redondo Illescas, S., Martínez García, M., García Forero, C., & Andrés Pueyo, A. (2008). Predicción de riesgo de reincidencia en agresores sexuales. *Psicothema, 20*, 205–210.

Quinsey, V. L., Harris, G. T., Rice, M. E., & Cormier, C. A. (1998). *Violent offenders: Appraising and managing risk.* Washington, DC: American Psychological Association.

Reed, G. M., McLaughlin, C. J., & Newman, R. (2002). American Psychological Association policy in context: The development and evaluation of guidelines for professional practice. *American Psychologist, 57*, 1041–1047.

Rettenberger, M., Boer, D. P., & Eher, R. (2011). The predictive accuracy of risk factors in the sexual violence risk—20 (SVR-20). *Criminal Justice and Behavior, 38*, 1009–1027.

Rettenberger, M., & Eher, R. (2006). Actuarial assessment of sex offender recidivism risk: A validation of the German version of the static-99. *Sexual Offender Treatment, 1*, 1–11.

Rettenberger, M., & Eher, R. (2007). Predicting reoffence in sexual offender subtypes: A prospective validation study of the German version of the sexual offender risk appraisal guide (SORAG). *Sexual Offender Treatment, 2*, 1–12.

Rettenberger, M., Matthes, A., Boer, D. P., & Eher, R. (2010). Prospective actuarial risk assessment: A comparison of five risk assessment instruments in different sexual offender subtypes. *International Journal of Offender Therapy and Comparative Criminology, 54*, 169–186.

Sackett, D. L., Rosenberg, W. M. C., Gray, J. A. M., Haynes, R. B., & Richardson, W. S. (1996). Evidence-based medicine: What it is and isn't. *British Medical Journal, 312*, 71–72.

Sea, J., & Hart, S. D. (in press). The interrater reliability and concurrent validity of the Risk for Sexual Violence Protocol in Korean sexual offenders. *International Journal of Offender Therapy and Comparative Criminology.*

Schiltz, K., Witzel, J., Northoff, G., Kathrin Zierhut, K., Gubka, U., Fellmann, H., . . . Bogerts, B. (2007). Brain pathology in pedophilic offenders: Evidence of volume reduction in the right amygdala and related diencephalic structures. *Archives of General Psychiatry, 64*, 737–746.

Singh, J. P., Grann, M., & Fazel, S. (2011). A comparative study of violence risk assessment tools: A systematic review and metaregression analysis of 68 studies involving 25,980 participants. *Clinical Psychology Review, 3*, 499–513.

Sjöstedt, G., & Långström, N. (2003). Assessment of risk for criminal recidivism among rapists: A comparison of four different measures. *Psychology, Crime & Law, 8*, 25–40.

Smid, W. J., Kamphuis, J. H., Wever, E. C., & Van Beek, D. (2013). Treatment referral for sex offenders based on clinical judgment versus actuarial risk assessment: Match and analysis of mismatch. *Journal of Interpersonal Violence, 28*, 2273–2289.

Smid, W. J., Kamphuis, J. H., Wever, E. C., & Van Beek, D. J. (2014). A comparison of the predictive properties of nine sex offender risk assessment instruments. *Psychological Assessment, 26*, 691–703.

Smith v. Jones, 1 S.C.R. 455 (1999).

Society for Risk Analysis. (2018). *Society for risk analysis glossary.* Retrieved from https://sra.org/sites/default/files/pdf/SRA%20Glossary%20-%20FINAL.pdf

Spehr, A., Hill, A., Habermann, N., Briken, P., & Berner, W. (2010). Sexual murderers with adult or child victims: Are they different? *Sexual Abuse, 22*, 290–314.

Stadtland, C., Hollweg, M., Kleindienst, N., Dietl, N., Reich, U., & Nedopil, N. (2005). Risk assessment and prediction of violent and sexual recidivism in sex offenders: Long-term predictive validity of four risk assessment instruments. *Journal of Forensic Psychiatry & Psychology, 16*, 92–108.

Stadtland, C., Hollweg, M., Kleindienst, N., Dietl, N., Reich, U., & Nedopil, N. (2006). Rückfallprognosen bei Sexualstraftätern—Vergleich der prädiktiven Validität von Prognoseinstrumenten. *Nervenarzt, 77*, 587–595.

Storey, J. E., Watt, K. A., & Hart, S. D. (2015). An examination of violence risk communication in practice using a structured professional judgment framework. *Behavioral Sciences and the Law, 33*, 39–55.

Sutherland, A. A., Johnstone, L., Davidson, K. M., Hart, S. D., Cooke, D. J., Kropp, P. R., . . . Stocks, R. (2012). Sexual violence risk assessment: An investigation of the interrater reliability of professional judgments made using the risk for sexual violence protocol. *International Journal of Forensic Mental Health, 11*, 119–133.

Sweller, T., Daffern, M., & Warren, N. (2016). Challenges in determining how dynamic risk factors manifest in incarcerated sexual offenders. *Psychiatry, Psychology and Law, 23*, 765–781.

Thornton, D., Mann, R., Webster, S., Blud, L., Travers, R., Friendship, C., & Erikson, M. (2003). Distinguishing and combining risks for sexual and violent recidivism. In R. Prentky, E. Janus, M. Seto, &

A. W. Burgess (Vol. Eds.), *Annals of the New York academy of science: Vol. 989. Understanding and managing sexually coercive behavior* (pp. 225–235). New York: New York Academy of Science.

Tsao, I. T., & Chu, C. M. (in press). An exploratory study of recidivism risk assessment instruments for individuals convicted of sexual offenses in Singapore. *Sexual Abuse.* Doi:10.1177/1079063219884575

Ujeyl, M., Habermann, N., Briken, P., Berner, W., & Hill, A. (2008). Sexuelle Tötungsdelikte: Vergleich von Tätern im Straf- und im Maßregelvollzug [Comparison of sexual murderers in forensic psychiatric hospitals and in prison]. *Nervenarzt, 79,* 587–593.

Vargen, L., Jackson, K. J., & Hart, S. D. (2020). Interrater reliability, concurrent validity, and predictive validity of the risk for sexual violence protocol. *Law and Human Behavior, 44,* 37–50.

Viljoen, J. L., McLachlan, K., & Vincent, G. M. (2010). Assessing violence risk and psychopathy in juvenile and adult offenders: A survey of clinical practices. *Assessment, 17,* 377–395.

Walter, M., Witzel, J., Wiebking, C., Gubka, U., Rote, M., Schiltz, K., . . . Northoff, G. (2007). Pedophilia is linked to reduced activation in hypothalamus and lateral prefrontal cortex during visual erotic stimulation. *Biological Psychiatry, 62,* 698–701.

Walters, G. D., Knight, R. A., & Thornton, D. (2009). The latent structure of sexual violence risk: A taxometric analysis of widely used sex offender actuarial risk measures. *Criminal Justice and Behavior, 36,* 290–306.

Watt, K. A., Hart, S. D., Wilson, C., Guy, L., & Douglas, K. S. D. (2006, March). *An evaluation of the risk for sexual violence protocol* (RSVP) *in high risk offenders: Interrater reliability and concurrent validity.* Paper presented at the annual meeting of the American Psychology-Law Society (Division 41 of the American Psychological Association), St. Petersburg, FL.

Webster, C. D., Douglas, K. S., Eaves, D., & Hart, S. D. (1997). *HCR-20: Assessing risk for violence* (Version 2). Burnaby, BC: Simon Fraser University.

Wilson, C. M. (2013). *Reliability and consistency of risk formulations in assessments of sexual violence risk* (Unpublished doctoral dissertation). Department of Psychology, Simon Fraser University, Burnaby, BC.

Witt, P. H. (2000). A practitioner's view of risk assessment: The HCR-20 and SVR-20. *Behavioral Sciences and the Law, 18,* 791–798.

Witte, T., Di Placido, C., & Wong, S. (2001). *How dangerous are dangerous sex offenders? An estimation of recidivism and level of risk using a matched control group.* Saskatoon: Regional Psychiatric Centre.

Yoon, D., Turner, D., Klein, V., Rettenberger, M., Eher, R., & Briken, P. (2018). Factors predicting desistance from reoffending: A validation study of the SAPROF in sexual offenders. *International Journal of Offender Therapy and Comparative Criminology, 62,* 697–716.

Zanatta, R. (2005). *Risk of violence and sexual recidivism: A comparison of dangerous offenders and repetitive sexual offenders* (Unpublished doctoral dissertation). Department of Psychology, Simon Fraser University, Burnaby, BC.

Author Notes

The authors declare a conflict of interest: They benefit from sales of SVR-20 V1/V2 and RSVP and conducting training workshops in the use of them. The views expressed herein are those of the authors and do not necessarily reflect those of organizations for which they work or with which they are affiliated.

Thanks to Yan Lin Lim and Sungil Bang for assistance in updating literature reviews used to prepare this chapter.

Address correspondence via the Internet to hart@sfu.ca or via surface mail to Professor Stephen D. Hart, Department of Psychology, Simon Fraser University, Burnaby, British Columbia, Canada, V5A 1S6.

Short-Term Assessment of Risk and Treatability (START)

Rationale, Application, and Empirical Overview

Tonia L. Nicholls, Karen Petersen, Madison Almond, and Cameron Geddes

People entering public institutions, be it prisons, tertiary or forensic psychiatric hospitals, homeless shelters, or community mental health clinics often present with complex, intermingled physical health, mental health and associated risks and needs. The Centre for Mental Health in the UK estimates that 90% of prisoners have a mental health or substance misuse problem and that many have more than one (Durcan, Allan, & Hamilton, 2018). Furthermore, individuals with mental illness are at greater risk of self-harm, suicide, substance abuse, and victimization compared to the general population (Haw, Hawton, Houston, & Townsend, 2001; Nordentoft, Mortensen, & Pedersen, 2011; Swendsen et al., 2010; Hiday, Swartz, Swanson, Borum, & Wagner, 1999), and these adverse outcomes are related to one another (Vaughn et al., 2010; Poorolajal, Haghtalab, Farhadi, & Darvishi, 2016). Violent behaviours directed at oneself and others, as well as victimization, often co-occur and represent precipitating and/or predisposing factors for one another (Strub, Douglas, & Nicholls, 2016). Thus, a comprehensive approach is needed to assess and effectively prevent diverse adverse outcomes in populations of individuals with mental illness and criminal justice involvement.

The *Short-Term Assessment of Risk and Treatability* (START) (Webster, Martin, Brink, Nicholls, & Middleton, 2004; Webster, Martin, Brink, Nicholls, & Desmarais, 2009) is an empirically and theoretically informed structured professional judgment (SPJ) guide for the dynamic assessment of risks and treatability in adults (also see START: Adolescent Version; Viljoen, Nicholls, Cruise, Desmarais, & Webster, 2014) with mental illness and/or criminal justice needs. The START has become the most widely adopted and researched inpatient risk assessment and treatment planning tool (O'Shea & Dickens, 2014) and has been recognized as a means of supporting best practices (e.g., BC Patient Safety & Quality Council, 2011; Haute Authorité de Santé, 2011; Health Standards Organization, 2011; Risk Management Authority, 2019).[1]

The START is intended to assist mental health professionals in providing comprehensive care plans to address the needs of individuals with complex needs while meeting the legal and ethical responsibilities of evaluating and preventing risk to patients, staff, and the community (i.e., violence, self-harm, suicide, unauthorized leave, substance abuse, self-neglect, and victimization). The measure allows for the differential coding of 20 dynamic items as both Strengths and Vulnerabilities over a relatively short period of time (3 months) compared to other risk assessment measures, making the START a tool of choice for integrating risk assessment with treatment planning (Crocker et al., 2011; Dickens, 2015; Doyle & Logan, 2012; Doyle, Lewis, & Brisbane, 2008; Khiroya, Weaver, & Maden, 2009; Kroppan et al., 2011; Levin, Nilsen, Bendtsen, & Bülow, 2018; Nicholls, Brink, Desmarais, Webster, & Martin, 2006; Quinn, Miles, & Kinane, 2013). The START was developed by an interdisciplinary clinical team—led by nurses, occupational therapists, psychiatrists, psychologists, recreational therapists, social workers, and vocational/rehabilitation workers (Webster, Nicholls, Martin, Desmarais, & Brink, 2006). Results of several studies indicate it is a user-friendly tool with good practical utility and face validity for qualified mental health professionals of all disciplines (Doyle et al., 2008; Khiroya et al., 2009) and that it increases multidisciplinary participation in treatment planning (Crocker et al., 2011; Kroppan, Nonstad, Iversen, & Søndenaa, 2017).

Description of Measure

The START is an assessment and treatment planning guide that supports clinicians in simultaneously evaluating an individual's Strengths and Vulnerabilities. It comprises 20 dynamic items (i.e., changeable) that were identified through a consideration of theory and research across diverse populations (corrections, tertiary psychiatry, forensic mental health) and contexts (inpatient/community). This assessment is intended to inform a short-term estimation (generally forecasting 3 months into the future) of an individual's risk on seven domains and guide comprehensive interdisciplinary treatment planning. In light of the intermingled risks that many individuals with mental health needs and criminal justice involvement present with, the START does not solely assess the risk of a single outcome of concern (e.g., interpersonal violence). Rather, the START guides a short-term estimate of risk for a variety of interrelated concerns commonly encountered in day-to-day clinical practice with individuals who have mental health and criminal justice-related needs: suicide, self-harm, self-neglect, unauthorized absence (AWOL), substance abuse, and victimization. The intent of the START is to guide comprehensive care planning.

Purpose

The START was developed in direct response to four primary gaps in the risk assessment and forensic mental health fields.

Overlapping Risks

First, given the extent to which individuals with mental illness and criminal justice involvement present with diverse and intermingled risks (e.g., self-harm and general offending; violence, substance abuse and victimization, etc.), a comprehensive assessment and treatment planning guide is needed. The START structures clinical assessments of risk to self and others and aids treatment providers in practical day-to-day decision-making around a variety of matters (e.g., security levels and privileges within institutions, day passes, visit leaves) (see Webster et al., 2006).

Dynamic Variables

Second, although the risk estimates and case formulation are firmly grounded in a consideration of static and historical information ("Key Items," "Critical Items," and the "Hx" column in Risk Estimates; see Figure 15.1), the START is comprised of 20 dynamic variables. As such, the START is consistent with leading practice in risk assessment which calls for consideration of dynamic variables (Douglas & Skeem, 2005; Wilson, Desmarais, Nicholls, Hart, & Brink, 2013), recovery-oriented treatment (de Vries Robbé, de Vogel, & Douglas, 2013), and alignment with the ultimate goals of care providers (i.e., supporting change, providing patients with hope) (Viljoen, Viljoen, Nicholls, & de Vries Robbé, 2017). A consideration of dynamic variables is consistent with a growing body of literature demonstrating that dynamic variables may hold promise in risk assessments (Douglas & Skeem, 2005), particularly in the short term (Wilson et al., 2013) and as a measure of resiliency to future violent offending (de Vries Robbé, de Vogel, Douglas, & Nijman, 2015; Desmarais, Nicholls, Wilson, & Brink, 2012). Specifically, dynamic variables may contribute a unique predictive validity for offending when combined with static factors (de Vries Robbé, de Vogel, & de Spa, 2011; Olver, Wong, Nicholaichuk, & Gordon, 2007).

BC MENTAL HEALTH & SUBSTANCE USE SERVICES
RESEARCH INSTITUTE

St. Joseph's Healthcare Hamilton

Name	Mr. L
MRN	20200707
Sex: M	D.O.B: 10.10.1990

START Summary Sheet ©

Diagnoses: ☒ DSM-5 ☐ ICD-10   **1.** Schizophrenia (Paranoid)   **2.** Substance Use (Cannabis)

3.   4.   5.

STATUS:	☒ HOSPITAL Specify: Forensic Psychiatric	☐ COMMUNITY Specify:	☐ CORRECTIONS Specify:
PURPOSE:	☐ REFERRAL ☐ ADMISSION	☐ REVIEW Specify:	☒ OTHER Specify: Recent Behav. Change

START Time Frame: 3 Months (or behavioural change)

days/weeks/months

Key Item	Strengths 2 1 0	START Items	Vulnerabilities 0 1 2	Critical Item
○	☐ ☒ ☐	1. Social Skills	☐ ☒ ☐	○
○	☐ ☒ ☐	2. Relationships (TA: Y ☐ /N ☒)*	☐ ☒ ☐	○
○	☐ ☒ ☐	3. Occupational	☐ ☐ ☒	○
○	☐ ☐ ☒	4. Recreational	☐ ☐ ☒	○
○	☐ ☒ ☐	5. Self-Care	☐ ☒ ☐	○
○	☐ ☒ ☐	6. Mental State	☐ ☐ ☒	◉
○	☐ ☒ ☐	7. Emotional State	☐ ☒ ☐	○
○	☐ ☐ ☒	8. Substance Use	☐ ☐ ☒	○
○	☐ ☒ ☐	9. Impulse Control	☐ ☒ ☐	○
○	☐ ☒ ☐	10. External Triggers	☐ ☒ ☐	○
◉	☐ ☒ ☐	11. Social Support (PPS: Y ☐ /N ☒)‡	☐ ☐ ☒	○
○	☐ ☒ ☐	12. Material Resources	☒ ☐ ☐	○
○	☐ ☐ ☒	13. Attitudes	☐ ☒ ☐	○
○	☐ ☐ ☒	14. Med Adherence (N/A ☐)†	☐ ☐ ☒	◉
○	☐ ☐ ☒	15. Rule Adherence	☐ ☐ ☒	○
○	☐ ☐ ☒	16. Conduct	☐ ☒ ☐	○
○	☐ ☐ ☒	17. Insight	☐ ☐ ☒	◉
○	☐ ☒ ☐	18. Plans	☐ ☐ ☒	○
○	☐ ☒ ☐	19. Coping	☒ ☐ ☐	○
○	☐ ☐ ☒	20. Treatability	☐ ☐ ☒	◉
○	☐ ☒ ☐	21. Case Specific Item: Intelligence	☐ ☐ ☒	○
○	☐ ☐ ☐	22. Case Specific Item:	☐ ☐ ☐	○

SIGNATURE RISK SIGNS

1st episode QUERY: wearing same T-shirt for several days; expressing belief his genius is being thwarted; believing he can insert video game into tooth cavity.

SPECIFIC RISK ESTIMATES

Hx∘	Risks	T.H.R.E.A.T	Low	Mod	High
☒	Violence	No ☒ Yes ☐	☐	☐	☒
☐	Self-Harm	No ☒ Yes ☐	☒	☐	☐
☐	Suicide	No ☒ Yes ☐	☒	☐	☐
☐	Unauthorized Leave		☐	☐	☒
☒	Substance Abuse		☐	☐	☒
☒	Self-Neglect		☐	☒	☐
☐	Being Victimized		☒	☐	☐
☒	Case Specific Risk: Hospital Internet Breach		☐	☐	☒

CURRENT MANAGEMENT MEASURES

Current Privilege Level: 3 ▼

Recommended Privilege Level: 2 ▼

Med secure unit; limit access to funds; IM medications; weekly urine screens; privileges on hold.

Health Concerns/Medical Tests: Dental pain; patient is presently refusing care

Risk Formulation: What factors predict/explain/which person/will carry out/what act/when?

If non-compliant with medications, patient may become increasingly paranoid and/or delusional, with increased agitation. Potential for violence towards caregivers and/or those he believes are involved in his delusion-based conspiracy network. Absent the secure setting, Mr. L is unlikely to be compliant with conditions or his orders (meds, SU).

Psychiatrist: Dr. D. F.	CMC: Ms. S. J.	Social Worker: Ms. S. L.
Primary Nurse: Ms. K. R.	Nurse(s): Ms. J. R.; Mr. R. O.	Other (pls specify position): Pharmacist: Dr. A. A.
Date Completed: 11.10.2020	Time to Complete: 40min	

*TA - Therapeutic Alliance   ‡PPS - Positive Peer Support   †N/A - Not Applicable   ∘Hx - Historical   FPSC Version 1.0 Electronic

Figure 15.1 START Summary Sheet for the Case of Mr. L

Integrating Strengths and Risks

Third, the START was the first SPJ measure to equitably consider individual's Strengths and Vulnerabilities; it guides a balanced assessment of a person's capacities, talents, and resources while also acknowledging a person's challenges and deficits. This even-handed assessment facilitates risk amelioration through implementation of effective management strategies and engagement of clients in programs of targeted treatment and intervention ("push" and "pull"). The equalized consideration of strengths and risks and attentiveness to recovery-oriented practice has led the measure to be described as "highly compatible with notions of person-centeredness and recovery-oriented practice" (Dickens, 2015, p. 461).

The risk assessment field has demonstrated a movement towards the side-by-side inclusion of risks and strengths, evidenced by the recent creation of tools with equally balanced strength and risk items (e.g., the START) and tools assessing either risks or strengths that are meant to operate in tandem (e.g., the HCR-20 and the SAPROF; de Vogel, de Ruiter, Bouman, & de Vries Robbé, 2012), and has been well documented in the literature (Barnao, 2013; Ward, Mann, & Gannon, 2007; Rogers, 2000; Seligman, 2002). These objectives are consistent with recommendations regarding the consideration of strengths by the Mental Health Commission of Canada (2015). Finally, although further research is needed, there is some evidence combining consideration of strength and risk variables in assessments can increase predictive validity for violence recidivism over assessing solely for risk variables (de Vries Robbé et al., 2011; Kashiwagi, Kikuchi, Koyama, Saito, & Hirabayashi, 2018). Even when the presence of strengths does not increase predictive validity, they continue to act as protective factors for violence (Wilson, Desmarais, Nicholls, & Brink, 2010) and may still be valuable information for clinical treatment planning. Furthermore, clinicians have expressed the benefits of integrating protective factors (strengths) into clinical assessments as a well-rounded snapshot of client treatment progress and the inclusion of strengths can facilitate a therapeutic alliance, treatment motivation, and skills acquisition (de Vries Robbé, de Vogel, & Stam, 2012; Dumas & Ward, 2016; Ray & Simpson, 2019).

Treatment Relevant

Finally, given all of these considerations, the START is uniquely positioned to facilitate treatment planning in diverse populations (Kroppan et al., 2011). The measure provides a comprehensive 360-degree view of the patient, is attentive to the range of adverse outcomes of concern when caring for mentally ill and justice-involved individuals, and supports attention to progress and deterioration in both strengths and risks. Legislation (e.g., Section 16, *Criminal Code of Canada*, 1985) clearly intends mental health, forensic, and correctional care providers to prepare people to return the community in an expeditious and safe fashion. Theory (Andrews, 2011; Andrews & Bonta, 2010) and research evidence (Dvoskin, Skeem, Novaco, & Douglas, 2011) strongly advocate for a shift in practice from punitive approaches to supporting recovery (e.g., through education, occupational opportunities, and social support).

Further, several countries have passed legislation endorsing the recovery model as a guiding principle of mental health services and education (Rufener, Depp, Gawronska, & Saks, 2015). The START also lends itself well to monitoring patient progress (e.g., changes in behaviours, attitudes, and emotional state) over time. Clinicians, along with patients, family, and other stakeholders (Review Boards) can monitor risk and track patient progress with the START. The measure can also be used to inform critical decision-making, including: (1) placement (e.g., inpatient vs. community, max/med/min security unit), (2) privilege levels (e.g., level of supervision for hospital programming, community access), (3) referrals for assessments, and (4) treatment and care planning (e.g., recommendations for programming and treatment). Implementation research suggests that completing the START is a useful undertaking (e.g., Khiroya et al., 2009) and assists treatment teams with documentation and organizing information (Doyle et al., 2008). For instance, Levin et al. (2018) concluded that the assessment increased consensus in defining risks and communicating treatment needs. Similarly, results of several studies (Crocker et al., 2011; Doyle et al., 2008; Kroppan et al., 2011) indicate that assessments and care plans are more systematic and structured when the START is employed. The use of the START has been found to have increased the knowledge of the patients' risk and protective factors for violence and to lead to a broader, more nuanced understanding of the patient (Crocker et al., 2011; Kroppan et al., 2011).

Populations and Settings

The START is intended for assessing risks and treatment planning with adults with mental health, substance use, and criminal justice-related needs. However, following publication and dissemination, there was considerable interest and perceived value in using the measure with youth. Thus, several of the original START authors (Webster, Desmarais, and Nicholls) collaborated with experts in developmental psychology, trauma, and forensic mental health (Professors/Drs. Jodi Viljoen and Keith Cruise) to develop the START: Adolescent Version (START:AV; Viljoen et al., 2014).[2] Generally, we would consider individuals appropriate for a START assessment if they are 18 to 25 years of age or older. In some circumstances, a young person (e.g., 16 or 17 years of age) may be living independently and thus the care team may determine it would be more appropriate to complete an adult START than to use the START:AV. Similarly, given the adolescent version is attentive to the extent to which young people are embedded within the family network and financially dependent on others, it may be more appropriate to evaluate a young person (25 years or younger) who remains in the family home with the START:AV.

The START can be used in both inpatient and community settings for mental health, forensic, and correctional clients (Gray et al., 2011; O'Shea & Dickens, 2014) and has been used with diverse populations (e.g., individuals who are homeless). The measure supports transparency, consistency, and accuracy in communication among colleagues and between units, agencies, and other primary stakeholders (e.g., with the individual and their family). The START is considered particularly helpful for handovers; for instance, when a patient leaves an inpatient setting and returns to the community or when care providers are on vacation.

User Qualifications

The START is designed to integrate the expertise of mental health specialists of various disciplines, preferably working together as a team (Webster et al., 2009). In this fashion, it is assumed that professionals using the measure will possess the typical qualifications for the various mental health disciplines, as well as START-specific training (Webster et al., 2004, p. 169, 2009, p. 79). The START can be used by a diverse range of experienced clinical staff members; this includes but is not limited to social workers, nurses, psychiatrists, and psychologists. The rationale is that most mental health settings integrate multidisciplinary teams and acknowledges that it is typically nurses, occupational therapists, and rehabilitation staff who spend the most time with patients and are thus well positioned to comment on the person's behaviour. Professionals of various backgrounds are able to provide unique contributions to assessing specific items. For example, social workers are often most knowledgeable about a patient's social support and material resources; nurses, occupational therapists, and rehabilitation therapists can provide unique observations about the person's day-to-day conduct; psychiatrists may have more insight into the individual's emotional state and medication adherence. In addition, it is recommended that the individual who is the focus of the START assessment should be involved in the assessment process, as appropriate (Nyman, Hofvander, Nilsson, & Wijk, 2019). Research demonstrates the potential benefits of collaborative decision-making and treatment planning. For instance, Livingston et al. (2016) concluded that even when forensic psychiatric patients disagree with the disposition determination, provided they felt respected through the process, they are more likely to be cooperative.

Timeframe

A virtue of the START, particularly for treatment decision-making purposes and monitoring patient progress, is that while it is attentive to the past, it is a short-term dynamic risk assessment. As such, ratings for the 20 Strengths and Vulnerabilities are to be based upon the patient's behaviour and presentation in the prior 3 months, or since the last START assessment. However, the START also allows for the inclusion of static and historical information in every aspect of the measure. The coding of Key Items and Critical Items can include anything the team knows about the patient (past or present). Similarly, the future-oriented Specific Risk Estimates have a foundation on past evidence that the person has engaged in that behaviour (e.g., self-harm, suicidal ideation, violence, substance abuse) or that the outcome has been a concern previously (e.g., victimization, self-neglect). It is suggested that assessors forecast up to 3 months into the future for the Specific Risk Estimates.

START assessments provide a snapshot of patient risk over the future 3 months, unless otherwise clinically indicated. For instance, if a patient was admitted to hospital with acute psychotic symptoms and placed in seclusion/on a locked unit but had a history of responding well to medications, the team would logically want to re-evaluate the person once the symptoms had cleared and consider moving them to a less restrictive environment. Conversely, if a patient was noted to be pacing and uttering threats under his breath during an outpatient appointment, staff would logically want to re-evaluate and reassess, specifically to determine if a return to hospital was required. This 3-month timeframe reflects two primary considerations: (1) the dynamic nature of the items, and (2) the purpose of the START—to be intentional about using risks/needs to inform placement, programming, and privileges. Since, for example, a person's risk of violence can diminish rapidly once severe symptoms of mental illness are treated and can increase just as quickly if he or she stops taking prescribed medications or is exposed to destabilizers, the shorter period of time for which a START rating is considered valid aims to convey that risk is a changing phenomenon that is heavily influenced by variable internal and external factors.

Description of Content and Items

The START is comprised of 20 dynamic items that were identified through a consideration of theory, empirical research, and clinical expertise across related areas of research and practice (e.g., violence, unauthorized leave, suicide, and self-harm risk assessment literature; inpatient and community treatment literature; tertiary, forensic, and correctional research). Each item is evaluated simultaneously for vulnerabilities and strengths. Items are scored 0/No (minimal/low), 1/Possible (partial/moderate), or 2/Yes (clear/definite/high) as demonstrated by the individual in the recent past (generally, the last 3 months). In addition, assessors can include static and historical information as Key Items and Critical Items (see Figure 15.1).

Key and Critical Items

In addition to evaluating the individual's current presentation, each of the 20 items can be coded as "Key Items" or "Critical Items" (see far left and far right columns of the items, Figure 15.1). This allows one or more assessors (preferably a clinical team) to communicate that the item has been especially important historically and/or is of considerable relevance to treatment planning and/or future outcomes.

A Critical Item reflects a "red flag" (e.g., substance use relapse; return to an antisocial peer group; noncompliance with treatment/medication). If this is present, the team is concerned that the patient has already relapsed or could deteriorate, and/or that his or her risk level(s) may increase (e.g., for suicide, offending, self-neglect, respectively). This allows assessors to communicate how the patient is doing presently, without losing sight of the fact that the person may have demonstrated substantial Strengths and/or Vulnerabilities on an item previously. For instance, Mental State may be coded as a Critical Item for an individual who exhibited paranoid delusions that were directly related to his index offense and subsequent Not Criminally Responsible on account of Mental Disorder (NCR-MD) finding and forensic hospital admission 6 months ago, even if the person has been asymptomatic over the last 3 months and has a "0" Vulnerability score on that item presently.

Conversely, Key Items reflect "therapeutic levers," which are opportunities to engage the patient or an acknowledgement of past or present skills or supports. Flagging an item as a Key Item indicates that it is an area in which the individual has demonstrated strength in the past or where the treatment team may want to focus support for the individual on their road to recovery, regardless of how the person presents on the item currently. To be clear, an individual may receive a low or high score on an item and still have that item coded as a "Key Item." For example, if an individual received significant recreational or occupational benefit from writing, the treatment team may want to consider incorporating journaling or other forms of creative expression into recovery planning. Similarly, a person may presently be reluctant to have contact with supportive friends and family due to feelings of shame (avoiding contact with prosocial supports demonstrates some Vulnerabilities) but treatment providers may want to support reunification with a prosocial support network; thus, it would be useful to code Social Support as a Key Item.

The START authors recommend that teams be reasonably parsimonious in their use of Key and Critical items (Webster et al., 2009). Key and Critical items can provide guidance or the "action items" for the next care planning meeting and it can be difficult or overwhelming when the patient has many Vulnerabilities and few Strengths. Identifying Key Items or Critical Items can help to identify the current priorities of the treatment plan, which should reflect the shared goals of the patient and treatment team, whenever possible (Nicholls, Desmarais, Martin, Brink, & Webster, 2019).

Case-Specific Items

In addition to the 20 standard START items, a minority of individuals will have Strengths and/or Vulnerabilities in other areas that assessors may wish to document. The content of these items can vary widely depending on the individual being assessed, but some areas that are commonly encountered are cognitive abilities, culture, and/or trauma.[3]

Case-Specific Risk Estimates

Case specificity is also a feature of the START Specific Risk Estimates. In addition to the seven outcomes listed in the Specific Risk Estimates, users may wish to include additional patient safety concerns or antisocial behaviours. Common examples include reckless driving, driving under the influence, or engaging in unprotected sex despite having a diagnosis of HIV. The authors also encourage assessors to use this space to provide additional information about the type of outcome of concern. For instance, hostage taking, stalking, intimate partner violence, child abuse, or gang involvement would be addressed under the Violence Specific Risk Estimate. The START is first and foremost intended to be a communication tool, a means of identifying and documenting risk to prevent adverse outcomes. While being attentive to the value of a "one-pager," the team is mindful that documentation and clarity that will efficiently convey critical information is of the utmost importance; the START should form the foundation of an integrated treatment plan .[4]

There Is No Silver Bullet; However . . .

The primary intention of a risk assessment is to prevent harm; the priority is to keep the patient, staff, and the community safe and to promote recovery. However, human behaviour is complex and risk is often highly dynamic. For example, a patient and their care provider may both leave a productive treatment session feeling quite positive but upon returning home the patient could receive a distressing phone call, relapse to substance use, and subsequently hurt themselves or someone else. No matter how good the measure or the clinician, there is no silver bullet, and unfortunately, adverse events will occur. However, seasoned clinicians are also likely aware that using measures such as the START, and other forensic measures, such as those covered in this book, also serve to protect the best interests of the assessor. START supports evidence-based practice, transparency, and accountability, which can be essential to prevent liability. A senior colleague at the BC Forensic Psychiatric Hospital, Mr. Peter Parnell, Director of Access, Transitions, and Risk, often shares with direct care staff and people engaged in START Workshops how he was called in to testify at an inquiry into a forensic community patient's suicide. He describes how he was able to use the START to demonstrate precisely how and why he had made his determination and was relieved to promptly be thanked for his time and complete his testimony in just ~10 minutes.

Overview of the START Summary Sheet and Recommendations for the Organization of the Assessment

There are six distinct sections of the START Summary Sheet: (1) Identifying information, (2) 20 Items, including two separate columns to code Key Items and Critical Items, (3) Signature Risk Signs, (4) Specific Risk Estimates, (5) Health Concerns, and (6) Current Management Measures and Risk Formulation (see Figure 15.1).

As with any assessment, the clinician will always want to begin by ensuring that the correct Identifying Information is linked to the patient being assessed, and to be clear about the purpose of the evaluation. The patient's past and current presentation and associated needs on the Items should then be considered. That information, gleaned from file reviews, interviews with the patient and collaterals, administrative records, etc., should help to determine if there are any signature risk signs and if the person has any physical health concerns. Finally, a comprehensive consideration of the individual's mental health, substance use, and criminal justice involvement will inform the "Hx" column. All of this information is then used to inform the Risk Estimates.

When using the START Summary form, assessors should work from top to bottom and left to right, much like reading a book. Thus, START assessments can be used to justify necessary limitations put on a patient's civil liberties (e.g., it is useful to help explain to the patient or a family member why the patient is living in a locked unit; or why the treatment team has recommended a Custody disposition or a Conditional Discharge). It can be helpful when providing expert testimony before a tribunal[5] and as a rationale to other stakeholders as to why other care planning and referrals have been made (e.g., referrals for assessments, treatment).

Identifying Information

Similar to other health care documentation, the START Summary Sheet allows for information such as name, sex, identification number, and date of birth to ensure a correct match between the evaluation and the individual being assessed. DSM or ICD diagnoses should also be included for easy reference for the treatment team and other stakeholders (e.g., tribunals, units/agencies receiving a patient upon transfer/discharge). In addition, assessors are able to indicate the setting by choosing between options of "hospital," "community," or "corrections," and can write in the reason for the assessment (e.g., upcoming court date/annual review/change in patient presentation) and the person's current legal status (e.g., involuntary, NCRMD, remand, etc.).

START Items: Scoring Strengths and Vulnerabilities

The assessment can proceed with any item, meaning it is not important to complete the items in the order they are presented on the form (i.e., 1–20). Further, there are no concrete guidelines about completing the coding for all of the Vulnerabilities versus all of the Strengths first, for instance. That being said, given the importance of being attentive to the item anchors and operational definitions, it may be the case that assessors find it helpful to complete the assessment of both Strengths *and* Vulnerabilities for each item to be more efficient than coding all Strengths for the 20 items and then returning to each item to evaluate Vulnerabilities. As we will expand on in the following sections, there may also be value in considering all 20 items before determining which items should be coded as Key or Critical.

As mentioned earlier, a unique facet of the START is its equal focus on both the individual's Vulnerabilities and Strengths. The measure is comprised of 20 items that are each rated twice—the patient's Vulnerabilities (or risk factors—challenges, deficits) regarding the item on one "side," and the patient's Strengths (or protective factors—capacities, skills) related for the item on the other. Borrowing from pre-existing measures, such as the HCR-20 (Webster, Douglas, Eaves, & Hart, 1997; Webster, Eaves, Douglas, & Wintrup, 1995), the START employs a 3-level scale. A maximum rating can be given to each of the 20 items if there is strong evidence that the factor is present and relevant to the individual's risks or needs. A moderate score is given when the factor is possibly evident or evident to some (but not the full) extent, or when there is partial evidence that the factor has relevance for the client. The person being assessed would receive a low score if there is no support for the presence of the item or if there is clear evidence the item is irrelevant to the person's risks and needs. The value of a scale that considers an individual's Strengths as well as his or her Vulnerabilities has been established (Barnao, 2013; Ward et al., 2007; Rogers, 2000; Seligman, 2002; de Vries Robbé et al., 2012; see the "Overview of Research" section later in this chapter). When using risk assessment tools that focus solely on risk/vulnerabilities, evaluators can be led to conceptualize that a score of 0 is the "full stop" point, as it is the highest possible positive score. Allowing the scale to reach in the opposite, protective direction aims to help assessors consider what positive aspects of the individual's life may be interwoven into intervention and treatment planning to uniquely contribute to risk reduction efforts (Borum, Bartel, & Forth, 2003).

The inclusion of a separate Strengths scale should not influence coding of the Vulnerability scale, and vice versa. Separating Strengths and Vulnerabilities into two discrete scales was done to encourage evaluators to conceptualize an individual's ability to have both Strengths and Vulnerabilities in one domain, and to plan for the buffering of Vulnerabilities and the promotion of Strengths, simultaneously. For example, a person may be highly motivated to stop using drugs/alcohol, recognize that he has a significant substance use problem, and willingly attend various treatment programs, but still frequently relapse, at least initially. Similarly, a patient may easily form strong relationships with her female peers and have a prosocial and supportive family, but may be taken advantage of in abusive romantic relationships with men. In each of these case examples the patient exhibits both Strengths and Vulnerabilities, and the assessment provides the treatment team with insights into how to proceed to support the person's Strengths and address their needs.

Consideration of these two case examples can demonstrate the clinical utility of considering Strengths and Vulnerabilities separately when it comes to treatment planning. In the first case, if the assessment had only considered the patient's deficits, it would reflect ongoing Vulnerabilities because the person continues to relapse. If substance use was associated with a risk estimate (e.g., the person committed thefts to support their habit or had a history of aggression when high/ drunk) it should also be coded a Critical Item. Often the first response for people with substance use disorders is to recommend motivational interviewing. In this scenario, the care team likely would not want to engage the patient in motivational interviewing but rather might want to work with the patient to identify any stressors or circumstances that precede a relapse. In fact, to pursue motivational interviewing might be a waste of limited resources and could detract from the therapeutic alliance by making the patient feel that he was not being heard and that the treatment was not addressing his present needs. In the second scenario, to code the patient's social support as having Vulnerabilities would clearly be accurate, and it might again be coded a Critical Item. However, simply acknowledging that the patient has an antisocial romantic partner and to neglect that she has a substantial prosocial network would offer substantially fewer insights into how the team might want to proceed. Working with the patient to develop healthy boundaries and healthy romantic relationships would be a critical therapeutic goal. If the patient was in an inpatient environment, the staff may want to consider close monitoring or even limiting access to grounds during periods when male patients are also outside. Similarly, the wisdom of placing the patient on a mixed-sex unit would be an important topic for discussion and might be delayed until the patient demonstrated some insight.

Signature Risk Signs

A particularly unique contribution of the START is the inclusion of what the manual refers to as Signature Risk Signs (Webster et al., 2009). The idea is similar to the serial sexual homicide literature, in that a detective coming across a crime scene might recognize a pattern of behaviour (e.g., a body displayed in a certain, precise manner; a "trophy" removed; or something identifiable left at the crime scene). Our colleague Dr. Emlene Murphy (then medical director of the BC Forensic Psychiatric Hospital) drew the team's attention to the notion that among a minority, yet perhaps substantial number of persons with mental illness, the emergence of psychotic, depressive, or other symptoms or behaviours may signal a relapse. The indicators may be subtle and initially appear to be unrelated to the individual's mental health or risk to self or others, or initially even could be perceived to indicate therapeutic progress or recovery. However, an anamnestic clinical approach and growing familiarity with the person during repeated relapses may shed light on seemingly irrelevant symptoms that represent a "signature risk sign" which is invariant for that specific person and may serve as an extremely reliable predictor of impending relapse and elevated risk for violence to self or others (Melton, Petrila, Poythress, Slobogin, Otto, & Mossman, 2018, p. 298).

The START Summary Sheet includes a space for "Signature Risk Signs" to ensure that they are communicated to all other persons involved in the patient's care.[6] For example, an individual's fixation on Armageddon may be a Signature Risk Sign for violence risk when in the past this fixation has preceded murder committed within the context of a delusional belief of saving the victims from Armageddon. Signature Risk Signs can be as simple as wearing a certain article of clothing or a person licking his fingers and smoothing out his eyebrows, when doing so has been found to consistently precede aggression. To unaware treatment providers, the behaviours may initially seem irrelevant or benign, or may even be characterized as a prosocial leisure pursuit (e.g., making paper flowers or paper airplanes) but they can be very helpful to indicate that supervision, management and monitoring should be revisited (e.g., serum levels should be checked, urine drug screens completed, one-on-one observation, delaying a day leave).

Examples of Signature Risk Signs:

- Becomes preoccupied with an identified individual
- Becomes paranoid about an entire population of individuals (e.g., blonde-blue eyed women)
- Wears excessive jewelry and "gangster clothing"
- Becomes preoccupied with health/fitness
- Makes a crucifix out of chicken bones and wearing it as a necklace
- Reports smelling "unicorn exhaust"
- Grows a beard
- Becomes fixated on numbers and number sequences
- Develops an unusual accent
- Reports fatigue due to alien blood transfusion
- Taking showers with clothing on and wetting hair repeatedly

---

T.H.R.E.A.T.

Although the START is designed to aid professionals in synthesizing vast amounts of historical and current clinical information about the individual to inform their assessment and care plan, it is important to always be aware of imminent and serious risks that must be addressed immediately. In these cases, when there often is no time for the systematic collection of information, the START communicates T.H.R.E.A.T.: a *T*hreat of *H*arm that is *R*eal, *E*nactable, *A*cute, and *T*argeted. That is, a significant risk of harm to self or to others that is credible (e.g., the assessee has known motivation to harm), effectible (e.g., the individual has adequate means to harm, such as a weapon), immediate (e.g., staff and/or co-patients may be in imminent danger), and specific (e.g., targeted to a particular person and/or group) (Webster et al., 2004, 2009). In this section of the START Summary Sheet, the T.H.R.E.A.T. box is indicated in relation to the individual's risk for violence, self-harm, and/or suicide. If it is deemed that a threat of this nature exists, it is expected that the ordinary START assessment process will be suspended in order for the threat to be addressed and managed.

Specific Risk Estimates

The START includes seven Specific Risk Estimates that point to both risks to self and others. These risks are to be scored as if the client were living independently in the community with no supervision. Thus, the main question asked by these estimates is "What is the risk, over the specified timeframe, if the client was given the opportunity?" A rating of "low" refers to the absence of risk, or to minimal risk. Therefore, no unique management strategies are required, and the patient can continue to be monitored as per usual (Webster et al., 2004, 2009). "Moderate" ratings refer to a greater-than-average risk, and as such require a risk management plan, with identification of strategies that target reduction of risks and enhancement of strengths. A timetable for monitoring and evaluating the effectiveness of these strategies should also be developed.

A "high" rating refers to risks that are a serious and imminent threat. Risk management strategies should be implemented immediately and should be focused on pressing needs. The plan should also consider short- and long-term[7] risk reduction and strength enhancement.

The START also allows for inclusion of historical lifetime risk of each Specific Risk Estimate. This is to ensure that a thorough client history has been completed. However, historical risk is simply one piece of information; it does not necessarily reflect the individual's current risk level. A person can have a history of engaging in violence, substance use, suicide, etc., but presently be "low" risk; on the other hand, a person can also have a "high" current level of risk while having no history of that particular behaviour.

Timeframe Considerations

On average START assessors are forecasting 3 months into the future. However, the START is intended to support clinical practice and the long-term success of the patient. Moreover, the authors acknowledge that each patient's profile and care trajectory will vary.

CASE EXAMPLE

Sarah is a bright, young, first-year university student admitted to hospital. She has a pro-social and engaged family. In the immediate future the team is focused on alleviating her depressed mood through a combination of medications and psychosocial rehabilitation (engaging her in activities she has enjoyed in the past such as yoga, cooking, and movie nights).

Nonetheless, the team is mindful that Sarah has responded well to medications in the past and her length of stay is expected to be short. Sarah's longer-term goals involve supporting her in remaining close with her family and doing whatever possible to prevent her from falling behind in her studies. This includes arranging family visits, referring Sarah to work with the hospital teacher and cooking with the rehab staff, as well as supporting her in her desire to initiate a book club for her fellow female patients. The plan might also include discussions with the patient, and family as appropriate, about the potential need to re-evaluate Sarah's courseload as a mechanism to reduce unnecessary anxiety and depression as a strategy to prevent a relapse.

Risk Management and Treatment Planning

After an individual's risks have been identified, it is important for assessors to develop a plan to manage those risks. The START provides space for brief risk management planning—it is recommended that a detailed plan should also be documented elsewhere (contact START@phsa.ca for an Integrated Treatment Planning form). The START Summary Sheet includes prompts for treatment planning (e.g., privilege levels) and additional documents are available that integrate the START assessment with routine treatment planning (see Figure 15.2; also see START:AV; Viljoen et al., 2014).

Although the START focuses on a 3-month window, we recognize that in clinical practice the clinician and the patient may be contemplating multiple timeframes and acute, short-term, and longer-term needs and treatment plans. The START is intended to support quality patient-centred care; thus the 3-month timeframe is a guideline. For instance, at the BC Forensic Psychiatric Hospital, the START policy requires that the measure is completed as soon as an NCR

Substance Use

Key Item	Strengths		Items	Vulnerabilities		Critical Item
☐	2 ☐	1 ☐ 0 ☒	**8. Substance Use**	☐ 0 ☐ 1	☒ 2	☐

Supporting Evidence for Strengths

There is currently no evidence of any Strengths. Mr. L does not abstain, nor does he express any insight into the risks associated with using in hospital (e.g., violating rules, the conditions of his order results in limits to his privileges; mixing non-prescription drugs with his meds). He does not demonstrate any efforts to quit using THC.

Supporting Evidence for Vulnerabilities

Mr. L is testing positive for THC in a controlled environment. He denies use despite + testing and he will not disclose how he is accessing. He advocates for use of cannabis in place of his antipsychotic medications. Team believes patient may use cannabis as a means of coping with SX.

Supporting Evidence for Key Items

There is no evidence that Substance Use is a Key Item.

Supporting Evidence for Critical Items

There is insufficient evidence that this is a Critical Item. There is not a long history of severe and/or persistent drug use. Mr. L's THC use did not appear to play a significant role in the index offence and his use has not been associated with any recent risks to himself or others.

Priorities for Substance Use

GOALS: Team, particularly primary nurse, will increase collaboration and engagement with patient and family to inform understanding of what it is that motivates Mr. L to use THC. Reduce access/use of THC. Increase motivation to stop using THC and his insight into the importance of not using non-prescribed drugs given it is a condition of his Review Board order and thus, could interfere with his application for additional privileges, community outings.

Case Management Plan

MONITORING:

1. Mr. L will undergo irregularly scheduled urine drug screens ~2x/weekly (per the Matrix program standard).
2. His behaviour will be monitored for evidence of use of THC, particularly upon return from grounds.
3. The team will work with Mr. L to identify/understand triggers, if his use is linked to any particular stressors (e.g., some staff have postulated that his mother's visits cause anxiety), and if so, how best to support him.

SUPERVISON:

1. Mr. L's grounds privileges will be immediately suspended for 1 week. Each time he tests positive for THC he will lose grounds privileges for 1 week, for the next 2 months.
2. The team will ask the forensic security officers to monitor video surveillance tapes of the hospital grounds to determine how Mr. L is obtaining THC and discuss with grounds staff and patients, as appropriate.
3. Staff will ask facilities management staff to trim the trees near Mr. L's favourite spot on the grounds and change the type and location of chairs to decrease unobserved spaces.

ASSESSMENT and TREATMENT:

1. Mr. L's mental state, his lack of insight, and minimal response to antipsychotic medications are critical items on his START assessment and all remain considerable Vulnerabilities. The psychiatrist and pharmacist will consider increasing Mr. L's medications and/or examining alternatives (clozapine).

(Continued)

2. Refer Mr. L to concurrent disorders counsellor to assess using motivational interviewing and MI treatment. To determine what function marijuana currently has for him and identify treatment goals to address same.

3. Mr. L is difficult to engage in programming. In the absence of intrinsic motivation, the team will implement extrinsic motivation. Each time Mr. L attends NA or SMART recovery program, he will receive I hour of time playing the computer game of his choice (given the risk associated with his computer use in the past, this will be on a non-networked television).

Other Actions/Notes:

I. **Follow up with concurrent disorders counsellor (CDC):** Counsellor recently interviewed Mr. L. and recommended individual Motivational interview sessions to prepare him for entry into the hospital's substance use program (Matrix).

2. **Matrix program:** Mr. L should be added to the waitlist pending approval of CDC.

3. Long term, the team will continue to build Mr. L's motivation through various pursuits:
   — **Recreational:** latest Marvel movie is to be released in a few months, and Mr. L has repeatedly expressed an interest in seeing it in theatre. The team can encourage him to refrain from substance use and work to increase his privilege level with the goal of planning a Staff Supervised Community Outing.
   — **Occupational:** With supervision to ensure he is not accessing the internet, Mr. L should be given opportunity to obtain continuing education credits and long term to take part in a work placement relevant to his interests in programming.
   — **Relationships and Social Support:** Mr. L and his family will be encouraged to take part in family counselling sessions, when appropriate.

Figure 15.2 Portion of a START Risk Assessment, Risk Management, and Treatment Planning Form

determination is made and an assessment patient becomes a treatment patient, but within the first 3 months at a maximum. Further, consistent with recovery-oriented practice, we also encourage staff to be planning for community release immediately from the time of admission. Thus, while the START assessment and treatment plan is "focused" on the short term, the intention is to encourage teams to use the assessment and care plan as a foundation for longer-term success. This can serve to provide patients with an understanding of the anticipated care pathway and support the individual and their support network in maintaining hope and developing insight, goals, and concrete plans for achieving their goals (see the "Timeframe Considerations" textbox).

Overview of Research

Systematic Review and Meta-Analysis

A systematic review and meta-analysis of the START, comprised of 23 and 9 studies, respectively, was conducted by O'Shea and Dickens (2014). The authors examined the psychometric properties of the measure and the validity of each of the seven distinct risk domains (i.e., violence, self-harm, suicide, unauthorized leave, substance abuse, self-neglect, and victimization). Evidenced by the systematic review, the START is well received by users; mental health professionals find it both clinically useful and efficient to complete (O'Shea & Dickens, 2014). The internal consistency of the START Vulnerabilities scale ranged from .80 to .95 across the seven studies and the Strengths scale ranged from .76 to .95 (considered good or acceptable to excellent; O'Shea & Dickens, 2014). The authors reported significant positive correlations between the START Vulnerability scale scores and the total and subscale scores of the HCR-20 (.46 to .83; Douglas et al., 2013), the Suicide Risk Assessment and Management Manual (.58; Bouch & Marshall, 2003), and the PCL:SV (.21; Hart et al., 1995) (O'Shea & Dickens, 2014). O'Shea and Dickens (2014) also reported the total Strengths scale scores and total scores of the Structured Assessment of Protective Factors (SAPROF; de Vogel et al., 2012) showed a significant positive correlation (.81) and, as would be expected, the Vulnerabilities scale scores had a significant negative correlation with the SAPROF (−.78; Abidin et al., 2013). The START Strengths and Vulnerabilities scales fell within the good to excellent interrater reliability range in the seven studies examined (ICC: .78–.86; Spearman's r: .69–.83; Kappa: .07–.13; O'Shea & Dickens, 2014).

As is often the case with SPJ measures, although the items on the START are not intended to be summed to determine an individual's risk, many researchers have examined the association between the START Vulnerability total score/Strength total score and various outcomes of relevance. In their review, O'Shea and Dickens (2014) concluded that the Vulnerability scale total score was significantly associated with multiple outcomes of relevance, including verbal aggression, physical aggression, unauthorized leave, and substance use in the majority of studies examined. However, one study found the Vulnerabilities scale significantly predicted aggression to objects but not aggression against individuals (Morris, 2013), and in no study did the scale predict suicidality, self-harm, or victimization. The Strengths scale total score predicted the absence of all forms of measured aggression (verbal and/or physical aggression against objects and individuals) in most research, and in one study it significantly predicted unauthorized leaves and substance abuse (Braithwaite, Charette, Crocker, & Reyes, 2010), and in another study it was significantly associated with self-neglect (Gray et al., 2011). Larger AUC values were observed in most examined studies for the Vulnerabilities scale compared to the Strengths scale (O'Shea & Dickens, 2014).

O'Shea and Dickens (2014) reported on two studies that had examined the incremental validity of the START Strengths and Vulnerabilities scale total scores over the HCR-20 Historical scale in regards to predicting physical aggression against others: in one, the Vulnerabilities scale demonstrated significant incremental validity, as did the C and R Scales of the HCR-20 (Wilson et al., 2013). In the other, the Strengths scale predicted physical aggression against others more strongly than the HCR-20 Historical scale and the PCL:SV, while the Vulnerabilities scale demonstrated incremental validity over the same measures for the prediction of amalgamated aggression and verbal aggression (Desmarais, Nicholls, et al., 2012). Within a third study, the START scales did not demonstrate incremental validity over each other, evidencing comparable predictivity (Wilson et al., 2010).

Finally, the authors concluded that the meta-analysis was consistent with the systematic review: both subscales were predictive for some risk domains (O'Shea & Dickens, 2014). Specifically, the Specific Risk Estimates predicted each of their respective risk outcomes at a rate that exceeds chance (weighted mean AUC values = .60 to .76), while the Strengths and Vulnerabilities scales consistently predicted measures of aggression (.70 to .78) but did not have significant associations with some risk estimates, including self-harm, victimization, and self-neglect (.53 to .61). The O'Shea and Dickens (2014) systematic review and meta-analysis provided an overview of the utility of the START in both clinical and research settings, most strongly for the prediction of diverse measures of aggression. In the sections that follow, we provide a detailed examination of literature on the START, including research published subsequent to O'Shea and Dickens (2014).

Internal Consistency

A total of nine distinct studies that have examined the internal consistency of the START were identified. Consistency for the total Strength and Vulnerabilities scales, measured using Cronbach's alpha values, has ranged from .86 to .95 (Nicholls et al., 2006; Timmins, Evans, & Tully, 2018). More specifically, in a study conducted by Nicholls and colleagues (2006) within a forensic inpatient sample in Canada, the internal consistency for independent ratings was .86 across psychiatrists, case managers, and social workers. The Vulnerabilities scale displayed an alpha value ranging between .76 and

.95 while the Strengths scale ranged from .80 to .95 in forensic inpatient, civil secure inpatient, and community settings with sample sizes ranging from 50 to over 1000 patients (Abidin et al., 2013; Desmarais, Van Dorn, et al., 2012; Lowder, Desmarais, Rade, Coffey, & Van Dorn, 2017; Lowder, Desmarais, Rade, Johnson, & Van Dorn, 2019; Nicholls et al., 2011; Nonstad et al., 2010; Timmins et al., 2018; Viljoen, Nicholls, Greaves, Ruite, & Brink, 2011). Internal consistency for the Specific Risk Estimates has only been examined in one study conducted in the United Kingdom which engaged a variety of mental health professionals (psychiatrists, psychologists, occupational therapists, and registered mental health nurses) as raters and was reported to be .74 (Timmins et al., 2018).

Interrater Reliability

In the first study to examine the interrater reliability (IRR) of the START, an intraclass correlation coefficient (ICC_2) of .87 was found across groups of psychiatrists ($n = 42$), case managers ($n = 37$), and social workers ($n = 32$) who completed 111 total START assessments independently (Nicholls et al., 2006). Studies that came after have reported ICCs ranging from .64 to .90 for the Vulnerabilities scale and .49 to .85 for the Strengths scale and have examined the reliability of researcher and case manager START ratings across up to 29 independent raters (Troquete et al., 2015; Viljoen et al., 2011; Wilson et al., 2010, 2013).

The Specific Risk Estimates have been evaluated less frequently. One Canadian study reported an ICC_1 of .81 combined across all risk estimates, rated by graduate-level research assistants (Wilson et al., 2010). The START Strengths and Vulnerabilities scales and Specific Risk Estimates have been found to have Kappas ranging from .64 to 1.00 (Gunenc, O'Shea, & Dickens, 2018; Marriott, O'Shea, Picchioni, & Dickens, 2017; O'Shea, Picchioni, & Dickens, 2016). Specifically, a study by Marriott and colleagues (2017) in which two researchers independently rated 20 inpatients in a secure psychiatric unit found the lowest IRR for a Specific Risk Estimate was for self-neglect ($\kappa = .64$) and the highest to be for aggression (including physical and verbal aggression; $\kappa = 1.00$). Similarly, investigators in another study conducted in a psychiatric inpatient setting reported the lowest IRR value of the START Specific Risk estimates, when rated by patients' multidisciplinary teams, to be for the unauthorized leave Specific Risk Estimates ($\kappa = .86$) and the highest to be the substance use Specific Risk Estimates (Kappa = .89) (O'Shea & Dickens, 2015). Finally, using Spearman's correlation coefficients, Abidin and colleagues (2013) found an r of .85 and .69 for the START Vulnerabilities and Strengths scales, respectively, when 21 inpatients were rated at two separate times by two researchers.

Predictive Validity

The START is unique from other measures in that it is intended to guide assessments and treatment across multiple risks: violence, self-harm, suicide, unauthorized leave, substance use, self-neglect, and victimization. Overall, studies evaluating predictive validity of the START Vulnerabilities scale, Strengths scale, and Specific Risk Estimates have most often examined violence to self and others, and the other Specific Risk Estimates, including unauthorized leave and substance abuse, have been examined in a smaller body of literature.

The START Vulnerabilities scale has been found to be consistently predictive of aggression and violence to others; AUCs for inpatient aggression range from .58 to .95 over 16 studies (Dickens & O'Shea, 2015; Finch, Gilligan, Halpin, & Valentine, 2017). However, the START was not intended to predict minor forms of aggression (such as off-handed, antagonistic remarks) and rather is intended to evaluate an individual's risk of violence on principles of severity, imminence, and likelihood (Webster et al., 2009). When aggression is disaggregated into physical aggression, verbal aggression, and aggression against objects, AUC values ranging from .58 to .94 (Dickens &

O'Shea, 2015; Finch et al., 2017), .60 to .93 (Dickens & O'Shea, 2015; Finch et al., 2017), and .84 to .90 (Cartwright, Desmarais, Hazel, Griffith, & Azizian, 2018; Desmarais, Nicholls, et al., 2012) have been found for each type of aggression respectively, with the vast majority being significantly predictive. It is noteworthy that these studies spanned diverse civil, forensic, and combined inpatient settings in the United Kingdom, Canada, the United States, and Australia and employed a mix of assessors, including mental health professionals and research assistants; further studies in the community/outpatient context are required. The Vulnerabilities scale has been found to predict physical aggression and verbal aggression at 1-, 3-, and 6-month follow-up periods in the same settings (AUCs of .69 to .95; Cartwright et al., 2018; Chu, Thomas, Ogloff, & Daffern, 2011; Finch et al., 2017). It was also significantly predictive of number of arrests at 9, 12, and 18 months (Walden chi-square values of 4.17 to 17.27) and number of jail days at 6, 9, 12, and 18 months (Walden chi-square values of 4.17 to 68.75) in a sample of clients involved in a mental health jail diversion program in the United States (Lowder et al., 2017).

Researchers have also found the Vulnerabilities scale to be predictive of unauthorized leave (AUC of .64 to .66; Braithwaite et al., 2010; O'Shea & Dickens, 2015), self-harm, and suicide (.70; Marriott et al., 2017) while the association with substance use (.63 to .67; Braithwaite et al., 2010; O'Shea & Dickens, 2015), self-neglect (.52 to .75; Braithwaite et al., 2010; Marriott et al., 2017), and victimization (.55 to .61; Braithwaite et al., 2010; Marriott et al., 2017) has been more variable. In a small sample of intellectually disabled offenders in the United Kingdom ($N = 28$), the Vulnerabilities scale (coded by a multidisciplinary mental health team) was associated with aggression (.66 to .71), property theft/damage (.69 to .73), noncompliance (.61 to .63), stalking/intimidation (.66 to .68), and self-harm (.62 to .69) at 30- and 90-day follow-up periods (Inett, Wright, Roberts, & Sheeran, 2014). Only at the 90-day follow-up mark was the measure predictive for suicide (.67). The Vulnerabilities scale was predictive of female verbal (.75) and general aggression (.74) and self-harm/suicide in a combined forensic and civil sample in the United Kingdom (.68; O'Shea & Dickens, 2015). A study in an outpatient forensic setting in the Netherlands asked clients to self-report their START scores and their case managers to simultaneously score the START for their clients; the average of the critical Vulnerabilities, as rated by patients, was not significantly predictive of future violent or criminal behaviour (.62), as well as the sum of the Vulnerabilities scale, as rated by the patients' case managers (.63; van den Brink et al., 2015).

The predictive validity of the START Strengths total scores has also been assessed in a variety of studies. Given the outcomes studied are typically negative in nature, it is standard practice to assess the predictive validity of the Strengths scale for individuals abstaining from these outcomes, or conversely to use participants' inverted Strengths score to predict negative outcomes. Predictive validity investigations of the START Strengths total scores for general aggression has produced AUCs ranging from .61 to .78 over 18 studies (Abidin et al., 2013; Van den Brink et al., 2015). All but one of these 18 studies found the START Strengths total score was significantly associated with at least one of the outcomes of concern. These studies included secure forensic and civil inpatient and forensic outpatient settings in many European and North American countries and examined the START Strengths scale predictive validity in a combined total of over 2500 individuals. Research methods ranged from file-based retrospective coding conducted by trained research assistants to teams of mental health clinicians completing the START as part of their routine clinical practice, demonstrating the strength of the START within research and clinical contexts. While typically significantly predictive, the AUCs for the Strengths scale have generally been lower than the AUCs for the Vulnerabilities scale, with AUCs ranging from .63 to .80 for physical aggression and .64 to .75 for verbal aggression across civil and forensic inpatient settings (Desmarais, Nicholls, et al., 2012; Dickens & O'Shea, 2015). The Strengths scale score has also been found to be significantly predictive of property damage (.77; Desmarais, Nicholls, et al., 2012). Specifically, when different lengths of follow-up periods were assessed, Strengths scores are predictive of physical aggression and verbal aggression at 1-, 2-, and 3-month follow-up periods (AUCs from .63 to .75; Cartwright et al., 2018; Dickens & O'Shea, 2015) and predictive of arrests and jail days at 3, 6, 9, 12, and 18 months when U.S.-based forensic outpatient participants self-rated their own START Strengths and their case-mangers rated their START Strengths (AUCs from .83 to .96; Lowder et al., 2017).

A wide range of other risk outcomes have also been found to be associated with the START Strengths scale. At 30- and 90-day follow-up periods, the Strengths scale was inversely significantly predictive of property damage (.30), noncompliance (.40), and stalking behaviours (.32) in a UK forensic low-security inpatient sample of 27 mentally disordered offenders assessed by their clinical teams (Inett et al., 2014). Research by Dickens and O'Shea (2015) examining 231 civil psychiatric patients in the United Kingdom assessed as part of regular clinical care found that self-neglect was predicted at 1- and 2-month follow-up periods (AUCs of .69); however, in two other studies of civil inpatient participants in Canada and the United Kingdom, victimization was not significantly predicted (Braithwaite et al., 2010; Gray et al., 2011). Braithwaite et al. (2010) reported the Strengths scale predicted unauthorized leave (AUC of .66) and substance abuse (AUC of .63) but did not predict self-harm or suicidal ideation.

Lastly, the predictive validity of the START Specific Risk Estimates (i.e., violence, self-harm, suicide, UAL, substance abuse, self-neglect, victimization), particularly the Specific Risk Estimate for violence, have been examined. Investigation of these aspects of the measure is particularly crucial, because the START is an SPJ measure and it is the Specific Risk Estimates in which the risk assessor consolidates all information into an assessment of risk (low, medium, or high) to inform management and care plans. The START violence Specific Risk Estimate has been found to be predictive of diverse forms of aggression across a variety of studies: any aggression (.62 to .80; Desmarais, Nicholls, et al., 2012; Van den Brink et al., 2015), verbal aggression (.62 to .78; Desmarais, Nicholls, et al., 2012; Marriott et al., 2017), physical aggression towards others (.68 to .85; Desmarais, Nicholls, et al., 2012; Marriott et al., 2017), and physical aggression towards objects (.84; Desmarais, Nicholls, et al., 2012) in civil and forensic secure inpatient settings in Canada, the United Kingdom, and the Netherlands, using file review, clinical team ratings, and self-report methods. The violence Specific Risk Estimate was predictive for verbal and physical aggression at one- (.65, .71), two (.62, .68), and three- (.62, .88) month follow-up periods in a civil sample (Dickens & O'Shea, 2015) and for any aggression (.83) and physical aggression (.85) in females within a combined civil and forensic sample (O'Shea & Dickens, 2015).

Additionally, the Specific Risk Estimates for self-harm and suicide (combined in many studies) were predictive for self-harming behaviours and suicide at one (.65 to .77), two (.67 to .78), and three (.69 to .81) months (Dickens & O'Shea, 2015; O'Shea et al., 2015; Marriot et al., 2017). Unauthorized leave was predicted by the Specific Risk Estimate for unauthorized leave (.66; O'Shea & Dickens, 2015) and substance use was predicted by the Specific Risk Estimate for substance use (.72 to .78; Braithwaite et al., 2010; O'Shea & Dickens, 2015). The START Specific Risk Estimate for victimization was predictive of victimization at 3 months in one study conducted within a secure civil inpatient hospital (.65; Dickens & O'Shea, 2015) but was not predictive in another secure civil inpatient unit (Marriot et al., 2017). A file-based research conducted in a secure forensic hospital in Canada did not find predictive validity for the violence, self-harm, suicide, unauthorized leave, self-neglect, and victimization Specific Risk Estimates; however, the authors reported large confidence intervals on AUCs and odds ratios (Braithwaite et al., 2010).

One study (Troquete et al., 2015) conducted with forensic outpatient participants as part of a larger randomized controlled trial (RCT) in the Netherlands included an intervention group of 310 clients and 29 case managers who assessed their patients using the START. Clients assigned to the control group did not have their case managers use the results of a START assessment to inform subsequent treatment planning. This research tested the predictive validity of models that combined the START Strengths scale, Vulnerabilities scale, violence SRE, and the Historical scale of the HCR-20 Version 2 (Webster et al., 1997). All models listed were significantly predictive. When the model included the Historical HCR-20 scale and the sum of the Vulnerabilities scale, the AUC was .62. The AUC remained at .62 when the sum of the Strengths scale was added to the model and increased to .65 when the violence SRE was added (Troquete et al., 2015). When another model consisting of the Historical HCR-20 scale and the mean number of critical Vulnerabilities was tested, the AUC was .61. The AUC remained consistent when the mean number of key Strengths was added to the model and increased significantly to .67 when the violence SRE was added (Troquete et al., 2015). However, it is important to note that this RCT involved an intention to treat and the authors reported there was sub-optimal implementation of the intervention (i.e., 35% of the intervention group did not receive the intervention) which may have influenced the results. Future RCTs with stronger fidelity are required to clarify these issues.

Incremental Validity

A particularly unique aspect of the START is that assessors are prompted to consider both the Strengths and the Vulnerabilities of the examinee; thus, both scales should add to each other and have unique independent effects when both are considered. Several studies have examined the START scales and Specific Risk Estimates and have found evidence of incremental validity for a variety of outcomes in forensic and civil inpatient settings. The START Strengths scale showed significant incremental validity over the Vulnerabilities scale for general aggression, verbal aggression, and physical aggression with changes in chi-square values ranging from 4.25 to 6.36 (O'Shea et al., 2015) and over the Historical scale of the HCR-20 for physical aggression (chi-square change of 4.67; Desmarais, Nicholls, et al., 2012) within forensic samples, using both research assistant file-based and clinical team assessments. These results are likely due to the higher responsivity of dynamic risk factors (e.g., the items of the START Strengths and Vulnerabilities scales) versus static risk factors to changes in individual risk of violence (Wilson et al., 2013). Similarly, the START Vulnerabilities scale showed significant incremental validity over VRAG-R, length of institutional stay, and HCR-20 Historical scale scores for inpatient aggression and specifically verbal aggression (4.05 to 10.11; Desmarais, Nicholls, et al., 2012; Wilson et al., 2013). However, the Strengths and Vulnerabilities scales have not demonstrated incremental validity over each other for all outcomes (Desmarais, Nicholls, et al., 2012; Wilson et al., 2010). Further examination of the interrelationship between the Strengths and the Vulnerabilities scales and the potential impact on incremental validity (e.g., multicollinearity) would be informative.

Given that the START is an SPJ measure, the expectation is that the Specific Risk Estimates should outperform the predictive accuracy of the total scores. The rationale is that the particular interrelation of items might lend themselves to suggesting different results than would simply be indicated by summing up items. For instance, a man with no history of mental health problems or criminal behaviours and a strong prosocial upbringing may have considerable Strengths and minimal Vulnerabilities. However, if that same young man becomes psychotic and is convinced that his partner is cheating on him, he may become determined to kill an innocent neighbour. Thus, he may be considered high risk by the treating clinician and thus coded High on the Violence Risk Estimate. Therefore, it is critical that the incremental validity of the START Specific Risk Estimates be studied.

The Specific Risk Estimate for violence had incremental validity over the Vulnerabilities and Strengths scales for general aggression perpetrated by men and women (increases in model fit were 4.71 and 9.83 respectively) and for physical aggression for men (increase of model fit to 10.08) in one study of START ratings completed in routine clinical practice in a combined forensic and civil inpatient secure unit (O'Shea et al., 2015). The suicide Specific Risk Estimate showed incremental validity over lifetime history of suicide attempts for the prediction of self-injurious behaviour within a sample of maximum-security forensic psychiatric inpatients who were rated on the START within 2 weeks of admission (Lam, 2014). Furthermore, incremental validity was demonstrated within a sample of civil psychiatric inpatients who were interviewed by research assistants for START coding purposes (4.68; Gatner, Douglas, & Nicholls, 2016) as well as over the Vulnerability scale for women's suicidal behaviour in a combined civil and forensic secure setting (8.86; O'Shea & Dickens, 2015). The self-harm Specific Risk Estimate demonstrated incremental validity over the Vulnerability scale when the outcome of interest was self-harming behaviour in a sample of women (chi-square increase of 6.01; O'Shea & Dickens, 2015) and a sample of both genders (11.75 to 12.53; Gatner et al., 2016). The violence Specific Risk Estimate predicted general aggression (chi-square increase of 4.71) and physical aggression (10.08) in men over the Strengths scale and general aggression in women (9.83) over the Vulnerabilities scale (O'Shea & Dickens, 2015). Furthermore, Desmarais, Nicholls, and colleagues (2012) concluded that general, physical, and verbal aggression, as well as aggression against objects, was predicted more strongly by the violence Specific Risk Estimate than by the Strengths and Vulnerabilities scales combined with the HCR-20 Historical scale (7.61, 12.52, 6.04, 8.11, respectively).

International Uptake, User-Friendliness, and Perceived Clinical Relevance

The START has been adopted widely into practice and implemented in diverse contexts (e.g., community probation, homeless shelters). The measure has been translated into eight languages: Danish, Dutch, Finnish, French, German, Italian, Norwegian, and Swedish, and a Japanese manual is in preparation. The START:AV has been translated into Dutch and Norwegian, and Finnish and Italian translations are in progress. Users advocate for the START's general clinical utility, particularly focusing on the value of its dynamic nature (Desmarais, Nicholls, et al., 2012), the integration of strengths, and the capacity to increase multidisciplinary collaboration (Crocker et al., 2011; Kroppan et al., 2017; Levin et al., 2018).

Case Example

Background

Mr. L is a 30-year-old Caucasian male with a primary diagnosis of schizophrenia and a comorbid substance use disorder (cannabis). He was found Not Criminally Responsible on account of Mental Disorder (NCRMD) after killing his father and gravely injuring his mother 5 years ago. He is currently being treated in a high-secure forensic hospital.

Collateral reports indicate that Mr. L had an unremarkable childhood. He grew up in Vancouver, Canada, and is the youngest of three siblings raised by his biological parents. He is described as a quiet child who often went unnoticed. Mr. L was not very athletic, and children called him "geeky." His older sisters provided significant social support, helping Mr. L choose "cool" clothing and attempting to assist him to fit in at school, for instance. In high school he attended classes, rarely contributed to class discussions, had a few friends with whom he enjoyed playing video games, and earned acceptable, but unremarkable grades (B's and C's). He did not fail any grades or get into trouble in school. Mr. L's family reports a strong and supportive family dynamic. Mr. L had a loving relationship with his sisters and mother. His relationship with his father was more distant; however, their interest in computers brought them together.

As an adolescent, Mr. L spent much of his free time in his room playing video games and reading comic books. He had a small group of friends with whom he would engage in activities related to his interests. For example, they would plan weeks in advance to attend the latest superhero movie premiere. After graduating from high school, Mr. L registered for a computer programming course at a community college and continued working 10 hours a week at his long-standing part-time job at a comic book and memorabilia store.

Mr. L's parents became concerned when he started missing his classes and then stopped attending them altogether. He called in sick at his job for several shifts and a few weeks later quit his job. His parents also noticed a steep decline in his hygiene. They noted that he would rarely join the family for meals and was subsisting mostly on junk food. Mr. L had not seen his friends within the weeks leading up to the index offence; however, he did continue to interact with them through online multiplayer video games.

One day his father came home unexpectedly in the middle of the day and smelled cannabis coming from the basement. When asked about the odour, Mr. L loudly and vehemently denied drug use, and when asked to explain his isolation and lack of any social, educational, or occupational pursuits, Mr. L said he was spending his time developing a video game and did not want to risk someone stealing his groundbreaking ideas. To his father's knowledge, Mr. L had no history of using substances.

Over the next couple of months Mr. L become increasingly irritable and hostile towards his father in particular. He also exhibited increasing paranoia; he was frequently overheard muttering to himself that family members and people walking down the street in front of his home were part of a large-scale conspiracy to suppress his genius or steal his creations. Mr. L continued to use cannabis on a regular basis.

Mr. L's parents visited their family doctor to ask for advice. They were advised that because Mr. L was an adult and was not seeking help himself, there was very little anyone could do unless he was an overt danger to himself or others. When questioned further about Mr. L's behaviour, his parents noted that despite escalating irritability and hostility toward others, he had no history of physical aggression and had made no overt threats to harm anyone. Similarly, despite his deteriorating self-care and weight gain, his mother and father both agreed he exhibited only very minimal risk to his own well-being. Specifically, they acknowledged he had no history of suicide or self-harm, nor had he expressed any ideation or plans to their knowledge.

Over the several weeks leading up to the attack on his parents, Mr. L's family noted a further increase in his symptoms including greater frequency of cannabis use and a heightened level of paranoia. His hostility continued to escalate into minor violent acts such as muttering threats towards his family under his breath (e.g., "vengeance will be mine," "you will pay for your betrayal") and shaking his fists in his mother's face when she refused to give him money. On one occasion, Mr. L and his mother were having a confrontation in the kitchen when Mr. L pushed her; she lost her balance and fell backwards hitting her head on the kitchen table. Mr. L's father came into the room moments later (having heard the yelling and the fall) and convinced his son to help him take his mother to the emergency room. Although his mother was not hurt badly, based on Mr. L's agitated behaviour and his parents' reports of recent behaviour, emergency room staff called the police and requested the emergency room psychiatrist assess Mr. L. As a result, Mr. L was held in hospital for a 24-hour psychiatric assessment. Mr. L was released early the next morning as his mental state was stable and the emergency room psychiatrist did not deem him a further risk. A few hours after arriving home, he brutally beat his parents with a baseball bat while they were asleep in their bed. His father died as a result of his injuries and, although his mother survived, she received life-changing injuries (e.g., severe and persistent headaches, difficulty sleeping). Mr. L was arrested and subsequently underwent a series of psychological assessments. He was eventually found NCRMD by the provincial Supreme Court and was admitted to a high security forensic psychiatric hospital.

Course in Hospital

Upon admission to hospital, Mr. L initially presented as extremely paranoid and hostile. He believed he was hospitalized as part of a conspiracy to suppress his brilliance and steal the video game he had created. He went through phases of refusing to eat and even attempted to convince other patients that the food was being poisoned. For similar reasons, he also initially refused all medication. When injections were presented as the alternative if he continued to refuse, he grudgingly agreed to take oral medication. However, in the ensuing weeks his behaviour failed to improve and his delusions remained firmly intact. Staff soon discovered he only appeared to be cooperating with medication and treatment. In fact, he was using multiple creative means to avoid ingesting the medications. A few weeks after injection medications were implemented, his behaviour and mental state improved. He has not behaved aggressively since admission to hospital. Since the injectable medications were initiated, he is also less hostile and paranoid. After several months on a maximum-secure unit without any incidents of aggression, Mr. L was moved to a medium-security unit so that he could receive access to more programming, where he remains.

Recent Developments (the Last 3 Months)

Mr. L has remained withdrawn, has received no visits from friends that the treatment team is aware of, and isolates from other patients. When he is encouraged by staff, or internally motivated to engage in conversation, he is articulate and able to express his needs and desires clearly. His two older sisters have expressed an interest in being kept abreast of his progress, but they are not ready to have contact with Mr. L at this time. Mr. L's mother has been through extensive physical and psychological rehabilitation. In the last couple of months she has started visiting with her son for short periods with supervision. Although initially distant in these meetings, Mr. L has recently become more animated and warm and looks forward to his mother's visits. Mr. L's mother has expressed a desire to rebuild her relationship with her son and a willingness to eventually consider supervising him when he is allowed to leave the hospital. Staff are happy to see Mr. L bonding with his mother but remain cognizant that she was a target of violence in the index offence.

Mr. L attends programming when he feels like it and when the activity interests him. For example, his treatment team has encouraged him to attend a substance abuse group and a mental health awareness program, intended to enhance his insight into his illness and the offences, yet he rarely attends either. His excuses range from feeling tired to not having the right T-shirt to wear. Overall, Mr. L spends the majority of his time idle and rarely engages in unit programming and recreation. The only exception is that he had been attending a computer literacy program regularly that he seemed to enjoy. Mr. L interacted well with other patients in the program and had recently been displaying mentorship skills in his interactions. In addition, Mr. L had a more expressive relationship with his instructor than he has developed with other treatment providers. However, his participation in the program ended when staff discovered that he had successfully disabled security measures on the computer he used during the class, allowing him access to the internet. He downloaded contact information for approximately 50 highly placed authorities, to whom he wrote letters asking for their help to get him released from the hospital. He also created a GoFundMe page to collect money for his "legal fees" and created a blog where he documented what he believed to be his mistreatment by the hospital staff and a conspiratorial group working to suppress his genius. After this activity was uncovered, it took IT security personnel a month to discover how he disabled the security protocols on the computer without detection.

Mr. L appears to have above average intelligence, although this is based on observation as Mr. L has not cooperated with testing. Despite this evidence that his delusional thoughts persist, he does not display signs of disorganized thinking.

Mr. L maintains his basic hygiene at socially appropriate levels; however, he has idiosyncratic behaviours surrounding his self-care. For example, he will only wear one T-shirt for weeks at a time and will wear a hospital-issued PJ top (only because staff refuse to allow him to go topless) while the T-shirt is at laundry. Then for no apparent reason that he is willing or able to articulate he will destroy the much-worn T-shirt and switch to a different outfit. Sometimes his clothing choices are socially appropriate and sometimes they are unusual (e.g., wearing two different shoes). Staff is unsure if this behaviour stems from psychosis or is his own form of rebellion.

Mr. L appears to be suffering from dental pain, yet he refuses to see a dentist. He told staff that he is developing video game technology that can be miniaturized to fit into a cavity and he will endure his tooth pain until he is released from hospital and can test this technology on himself.

In recent months, Mr. L has consistently presented as calm, contained, and deliberate. When there is a source of frustration (e.g., another patient acting childishly), he gets up and walks away. Yet, he remains emotionally withdrawn. He rarely engages in conversations or expresses any thoughts or emotions without prompting. However, on occasion, if staff can engage him in a conversation related to his delusional beliefs, the underlying anger he feels at staff, the hospital, society at large, and the members of the conspiracy to keep him detained, is very apparent.

Mr. L has tested positive for cannabis three times in the last month, yet he denies any use. Staff have not discovered how he is getting the drug. The only time they believe he can obtain cannabis is when he is given access to grounds. However, during these times he always sits in the same chair and is never observed socializing with other patients. Alternative explanations such as patients or staff supplying it on the unit remain unexplored.

Mr. L has been displaying worrisome behaviours with regard to money. A couple of weeks ago, his treatment team gave him access to a small amount of his money. Although his expressed intent was to spend the money on snacks, staff recently discovered that he was in fact hoarding it in his room. There is a general consensus among staff that he may be planning to attempt an unauthorized leave as he has been watching the door and paying special attention to staff schedules.

Mr. L continues to demonstrate a lack of insight into his illness and his index offences. He continues to receive his medications by injection and presents evidence at every treatment team meeting to support his request to discontinue his injection medication and start a trial of medicinal cannabis to treat his "supposed schizophrenia," noting that he has done his research and he does not "fit the bill for that diagnosis." He states he did not assault his parents and that someone from the conspiracy network committed the crime and planted evidence implicating him in order to get him hospitalized and out of their way. Mr. L has detailed plans to get out of the hospital. They involve getting access to the money he raised through GoFundMe (an investigation indicated that few funds were raised, and these were returned to the donators) and engaging a detective and legal team to get him released from hospital at which time he will continue his groundbreaking work.

Integrating the START Risk Assessment, Risk Management, and Treatment Planning

As a result of the recent changes in Mr. L's behaviour, the treatment team met to complete an updated START assessment (see Figure 15.1) and discuss whether that indicated a need for any changes in his risk management and treatment plan (see a portion of the treatment plan in Figure 15.2). Because team members were concerned about the possibility that Mr. L was planning to escape from the hospital, they limited his access to his funds and increased monitoring of his behaviour on the unit, particularly when he was near exits. Mr. L has proven to be adept at eluding staff while engaging in restricted activities (e.g., computer hacking). The treatment team plans to focus on working with Mr. L to develop a recovery plan. Mr. L is intelligent, young, and healthy. He has demonstrated an ability to develop relationships with a small group of friends and his family. Staff would like to support increased visitation with his mother and continue to speak with his sisters in hopes that they may eventually want to rebuild a relationship with Mr. L. There is some indication that during the time Mr. L had access to the internet, he reached out to his old friends. Through conversations with Mr. L and the family, staff are attempting to determine if encouraging this contact could be appropriate. Mr. L has a clear aptitude with technology that his treatment team would like to explore this with him—both from an educational as well as an occupational perspective. Technology might also be an important tool for increasing Mr. L's therapeutic alliance with treatment team members. It is possible that mentorship and/or leadership abilities could be nurtured if staff can develop a plan that would allow Mr. L to safely teach other patients computer skills. The treatment team has also put in a referral for Mr. L to the book club. The group is currently reading a graphic novel that might serve as a good introduction to the group and its activities.

Specific Risk Estimates

Readers are reminded that the START Specific Risk Estimates should be coded as if the person is living in the community, without any restrictions/professional support, similar to the general population. The assessment should justify the management measures and treatment plan. Thus, a patient should not be coded as low risk for violence or substance abuse because they are on a locked unit and/or detained in a secure hospital; rather, a person who is believed to be at risk to themselves or others would require hospitalization. It is recommended that anytime a patient is considered Moderate of High risk for any of the outcomes of concerns a risk management strategy is documented and enacted (see Specific Risk Estimates, Figure 12.1 START Summary Sheet).

VIOLENCE

Mr. L's risk for future violence is presently high. The team believes that should he be in the community unsupervised, there is every reason to be concerned he would stop taking medications, cannabis use would persist or escalate, his delusions and paranoia might intensify, and violence could result, as evidenced by his history and his current mental state and behavior. Specifically, he has a history of *verbal aggression* ("vengeance will be mine", "you will pay"), *physical aggression* (pushing mother, resulting in minor-mod injuries), and *severe violence* (index offence—beat parents w/baseball bat while sleeping; father died and mother sustained grievous, life-altering injuries). Moreover, while he has been on injectable medications in hospital and has remained free of any incidents of violence for 5 years, he continues to express anger, distrust, and paranoia toward staff and society, generally ("the members of the conspiracy"). In addition, although his hostility and aggression are being well managed in hospital, this is believed to be, in large part, due to the moderately successful use of antipsychotic medication. His treatment team remains concerned that Mr. L continues to lack insight into his mental illness. He does not acknowledge the usefulness of antipsychotic medications in supporting recovery, nor the role his mental illness played in his index offence. Moreover, Mr. L does not accept responsibility for the index offence, which involved severe violence against family members, and continues to verbalize his distrust of others. Of note, he communicates psychotic beliefs consistent with those that preceded the index offence. The treatment team is implementing the use of incentives to help motivate Mr. L to attend and participate in an insight-oriented CBT group. In addition, Mr. L's mother, and to a lesser extent his sisters, are being integrated into the treatment planning.

UNAUTHORIZED LEAVE

Mr. L's behaviour (e.g., monitoring secure doors and staffing schedules; hiding money in his room and misleading staff about his intended use of funds), lack of insight into his mental health needs (e.g., denies he has a mental illness; believes he is being hospitalized unjustly), and remaining psychotic symptoms (e.g., continues to verbalize that there is a conspiracy to have him detained in hospital, to steal his proprietary creation(s)) suggest he remains at high risk for UAL.

SUBSTANCE ABUSE

Mr. L continues to use THC in the hospital and thus is considered high risk for substance use should he be discharged. The treatment team has decided to temporarily suspend his privileges and investigate why and how Mr. L has been accessing marijuana. This portion of the START risk assessment, risk management, and treatment plan is shown in Figure 15.2.

SELF-NEGLECT

Mr. L has a history of neglecting his self-care and presently remains at moderate risk. His mental state has not stabilized, and thus it would be expected that he would slip into old patterns of poor sleep, an unhealthy diet, and sedentary lifestyle if released to the community. Of note, he is in need of dental care but is presently adamant he will not see the dentist.

CASE SPECIFIC

Mr. L was found to be abusing his computer and internet access (emailing strangers, setting up a GoFundMe page). There is no evidence to suggest that he may not pursue similar endeavours in the future given he continues to believe his hospitalization is unjustified, remains untrusting of care providers, and is eager to depart hospital.

Case Comment

In the year that followed the START assessment, Mr. L's treatment team continued to update and refine his START, risk management, and treatment plans. Mr. L responded well to being an active participant in his recovery plan. He enjoyed being a mentor to other patients, and this role accentuated some strengths that the treatment team had not seen in Mr. L, (e.g., empathy toward others) as well as provided a prosocial outlet for skills that had previous been directed towards antisocial activities (e.g., organization and planning). Mr. L's institutional cannabis use ended when a staff member was fired for selling cannabis to several patients. His treatment team remained concerned about his continued interest in using cannabis. Mr. L's behaviour and insight continued to improve sufficiently so that his treatment team granted increased privileges and access to programs. They are planning to provide staff escorted access to the community in the near future, with an eye towards a possible trial of living in the community in the years to come.

Notes

1. The START has been recognized as a Leading Practice by the Health Standards Organization (formerly Accreditation Canada, 2011). The British Columbia START team (BC Mental Health and Substance Use Services (BCMHSUS) won a Quality Award in the "Living With Illness" category from the BC Patient Safety and Quality Council (2011). The START is one of two recommended measures to support clinical judgement by the Quebec Ministry of Health (2011). The measure has been recognized as a validated risk assessment tool by Scotland's Risk Management Authority and is included in their Risk Assessment Tool Evaluation Directory (2012–present).
2. There is a START:AV Knowledge Guide (the evidence base for the measure) and a START:AV User Guide that is intended for clinicians implementing the measure into practice.
3. The START adult and adolescent teams both considered the importance of being attentive to Adverse Childhood Experiences and other forms of victimization, violence, and trauma. Careful consideration was given to including ACEs/Trauma as an item; however, the challenge of coding that variable as a

"Strength" could not be resolved. Thus, we encourage assessors to be mindful that prior victimization including child abuse should be recorded in the "Hx" column of the Risk Estimate and consideration should be given to including relevant concerns as a "Case Specific Item."
4. The START Summary Sheet (Figure 15.1) is recommended to be supplemented with coding notes (see Figure 15.2 for a sample) and an integrated treatment plan (contact start@phsa.ca for more information).
5. See the "There Is No Silver Bullet" textbox.
6. Patients and family members may provide particularly valuable insights into signature risk signs. Alternatively, if the team is not certain that patients and family are aware of these indicators it may be important information to share to help prevent relapse and adverse outcomes.
7. See the Risk Management section and the "Timeframe Considerations" textbox.

References

Abidin, Z., Davoren, M., Naughton, L., Gibbons, O., Nulty, A., & Kennedy, H. G. (2013). Susceptibility (risk and protective) factors for in-patient violence and self-harm: Prospective study of structured professional judgement instruments START and SAPROF, DUNDRUM-3 and DUNDRUM-4 in forensic mental health services. *BMC Psychiatry, 13*(197). doi:10.1186/1471-244X-13-197

Andrews, D. A. (Don.). (2011). The risk-need-responsivity (RNR) model of correctional assessment and treatment. In J. A. Dvoskin, J. L. Skeem, R. W. Novaco, & K. S. Douglas (Eds.), *Using social science to reduce violent offending.* (pp. 127–156). Oxford: Oxford University Press.

Andrews, D. A., & Bonta, J. (2010). Rehabilitating criminal justice policy and practice. *Psychology, Public Policy, and Law, 16*(1), 39–55. doi:10.1037/a0018362

Barnao, M. (2013). The good lives model tool kit for mentally disordered offenders. *The Journal of Forensic Practice, 15*(3), 157–170. doi:10.1108/JFP-07-2012-0001

BC Patient Safety & Quality Council (2011). *BC Mental Health and Addictions START Program.* Retrieved from https://bcpsqc.ca/quality-awards/winners/bc-mental-health-and-addictions-start-program/

Borum, R., Bartel, P., & Forth, A. (2003). *Manual for the structured risk assessment of violence in youth (SAVRY)* (Version 1.1). Tampa, FL: University of South Florida.

Bouch, J., & Marshall, J. J. (2003). *S-RAMM: Suicide risk assessment and management manual* (Research ed.). Vale of Glamorgan: Cognitive Centre Foundation.

Braithwaite, E., Charette, Y., Crocker, A. G., & Reyes, A. (2010). The predictive validity of clinical ratings of the short-term assessment of risk and treatability (START). *The International Journal of Forensic Mental Health, 9*, 271–281. doi:10.1080/14999013.2010.534378

Cartwright, J. K., Desmarais, S. L., Hazel, J., Griffith, T., & Azizian, A. (2018). Predictive validity of HCR-20, START, and Static-99R assessments in predicting institutional aggression among sexual offenders. *Law and Human Behavior, 42*(1), 13–25. doi:10.1037/lhb0000263

Chu, C. M., Thomas, S. D. M., Ogloff, J. R. P., & Daffern, M. (2011). The predictive validity of the short-term assessment of risk and treatability (START) in a secure forensic hospital: Risk factors and strengths. *The International Journal of Forensic Mental Health, 10*, 337–345. doi:10.1080/14999013.2011.629715

Criminal Code, R.S.C., c.46, s.16 (1985).

Crocker, A. G., Braithwaite, E., Laferrière, D., Gagnon, D., Venegas, C., & Jenkins, T. (2011). START changing practice: Implementing a risk assessment and management tool in a civil psychiatric setting. *International Journal of Forensic Mental Health, 10*(1), 13–28. doi:10.1080/14999013.2011.553146

Desmarais, S. L., Nicholls, T. L., Wilson, C. M., & Brink, J. (2012). Using dynamic risk and protective factors to predict inpatient aggression: Reliability and validity of START assessments. *Psychological Assessment, 24*(3), 685–700. doi:10.1037/a0026668

Desmarais, S. L., Van Dorn, R. A., Telford, R. P., Petrila, J., & Coffey, T. (2012). Characteristics of START assessments completed in mental health jail diversion programs. *Behavioral Sciences & the Law, 30*(4), 448–469. doi:10.1002/bsl.2022

de Vogel, V., de Ruiter, C., Bouman, Y., & de Vries Robbé, M. (2012). *SAPROF: Guidelines for the assessment of protective factors for violence risk* (2nd ed., English version). Utrecht, The Netherlands: Forum Educatief.

de Vries Robbé, M., de Vogel, V., & de Spa, E. (2011). Protective factors for violence risk in forensic psychiatric patients: A retrospective validation study of the SAPROF. *International Journal of Forensic Mental Health, 10*(3), 178–186. doi:10.1080/14999013.2011.600232

de Vries Robbé, M., de Vogel, V., & Douglas, K. S. (2013). Risk factors and protective factors: A two-sided dynamic approach to violence risk assessment. *Journal of Forensic Psychiatry & Psychology, 24*(4), 440–457. doi:10.1080/14789949.2013.818162

de Vries Robbé, M., de Vogel, V., Douglas, K. S., & Nijman, H. L. I. (2015). Changes in dynamic risk and protective factors for violence during inpatient forensic psychiatric treatment: Predicting reductions in postdischarge community recidivism. *Law and Human Behavior, 39*(1), 53–61. doi:10.1037/lhb0000089

de Vries Robbé, M., de Vogel, V., & Stam, J. (2012). Protective factors for violence risk: The value for clinical practice. *Psychology, 3*(12), 1259–1263. doi:10.4236/psych.2012.312A187

Dickens, G. L. (2015). Re-focusing risk assessment in forensic mental health nursing. *Journal of Psychiatric and Mental Health Nursing, 22*(7), 461–462. doi:10.1111/jpm.12256

Dickens, G. L., & O'Shea, L. E. (2015). How short should short-term risk assessment be? Determining the optimum interval for START reassessment in a secure mental health service. *Journal of Psychiatric and Mental Health Nursing, 22*(6), 397–406. doi:10.1111/jpm.12232

Douglas, K. S., Hart, S. D., Webster, C. D., & Belfrage, H. (2013). *HCR-20V3: Assessing risk of violence—user guide.* Burnaby, BC: Mental Health, Law, and Policy Institute, Simon Fraser University.

Douglas, K. S., & Skeem, J. L. (2005). Violence risk assessment: Getting specific about being dynamic. *Psychology, Public Policy, and Law, 11*(3), 347–383. doi:10.1037/1076-8971.11.3.347

Doyle, M., Lewis, G., & Brisbane, M. (2008). Implementing the short-term assessment of risk and treatability (START) in a forensic mental health service. *Psychiatric Bulletin, 32,* 406–408. doi:10.1192/pb.bp.108.019794

Doyle, M., & Logan, C. (2012). Operationalizing the assessment and management of violence risk in the short-term: Short-term risk management. *Behavioral Sciences & the Law, 30*(4), 406–419. doi:10.1002/bsl.2017

Dumas, L. L., & Ward, T. (2016). The good lives model of offender rehabilitation. *The Behavior Therapist, 39*(5), 175–177.

Durcan, G., Allan, J., & Hamilton, I. S. (2018). *From prison to work: A new frontier for individual placement and support.* Retrieved from www.centreformentalhealth.org.uk/publications/prison-work

Dvoskin, J., Skeem, J. L., Novaco, R., & Douglas, K. S. (2011). *Using social science to reduce violent offending.* Oxford: Oxford University Press. doi:10.1093/acprof:oso/9780195384642.001.0001

Finch, B., Gilligan, D. G., Halpin, S. A., & Valentine, M. E. (2017). The short- to medium-term predictive validity of static and dynamic risk-of-violence measures in medium- to low-secure forensic and civil inpatients. *Psychiatry, Psychology and Law, 24*(3), 410–427. doi:10.1080/13218719.2016.1247640

Gatner, D. T., Douglas, K. S., & Nicholls, T. L. (2016, June). *Examining the short-term assessment of risk and treatability (START) predictive validity of prospective suicide related behaviour and self-harm.* Paper presented at the Annual Conference of the International Association of Forensic Mental Health Services, New York.

Gray, N. S., Benson, R., Craig, R., Davies, H., Fitzgerald, S., Huckle, P., . . . Snowden, R. J. (2011). The short-term assessment of risk and treatability (START): A prospective study of inpatient behavior. *The International Journal of Forensic Mental Health, 10,* 305–313. doi:10.1080/14999013.2011.631692

Gunenc, C., O'Shea, L. E., & Dickens, G. L. (2018). Structured risk assessment for reduction of multiple risk outcomes in a secure mental health setting: Use of the START. *Criminal Behaviour and Mental Health, 28*(1), 61–71. doi:10.1002/cbm.2036

Hart, S., Cox, D., & Hare, R. (1995). *Manual for the Psychopathy Checklist: Screening Version (PCL: SV).* Toronto, ON: Multi-Health Systems.

Haute Autorité de Santé (2011). *Dangerosité psychiatrique: étude et évaluation des facteurs de risque de violence hétéro-aggressive chez les personnes ayant des troubles schizophréniques ou des troubles de l'humeur.* Retrieved from https://www.has-sante.fr/upload/docs/application/pdf/2011-07/evaluation_de_la_dangerosite_psychiatrique_-_recommandations_2011-07-06_15-48-9_213.pdf

Haw, C., Hawton, K., Houston, K., & Townsend, E. (2001). Psychiatric and personality disorders in deliberate self-harm patients. *The British Journal of Psychiatry, 178*(1), 48–54. doi:10.1192/bjp.178.1.48

Health Standards Organization (2011). *Short-Term Assessment of Risk and Treatability (START).* Retrieved from https://healthstandards.org/leading-practice/short-term-assessment-of-risk-and-treatability-start/

Hiday, V. A., Swartz, M. S., Swanson, J. W., Borum, R., & Wagner, H. R. (1999). Criminal victimization of persons with severe mental illness. *Psychiatric Services*, *50*(1), 62–68. doi:10.1176/ps.50.1.62

Inett, A., Wright, G., Roberts, L., & Sheeran, A. (2014). Predictive validity of the START with intellectually disabled offenders. *Journal of Forensic Practice*, *16*(1), 78–88. doi:10.1108/JFP-12-2012-0029

Kashiwagi, H., Kikuchi, A., Koyama, M., Saito, D., & Hirabayashi, N. (2018). Strength-based assessment for future violence risk: A retrospective validation study of the structured assessment of protective factors for violence risk (SAPROF) Japanese version in forensic psychiatric inpatients. *Annals of General Psychiatry*, *17*(1), 5–8. doi:10.1186/s12991-018-0175-5

Khiroya, R., Weaver, T., & Maden, T. (2009). Use and perceived utility of structured violence risk assessments in English medium secure forensic units. *Psychiatric Bulletin*, *33*(4), 129–132. doi:10.1192/pb.bp.108.019810

Kroppan, E., Nesset, M. B., Nonstad, K., Pedersen, T. W., Almvik, R., & Palmstierna, T. (2011). Implementation of the short-term assessment of risk and treatability (START) in a forensic high secure unit. *International Journal of Forensic Mental Health*, *10*(1), 7–12. doi:10.1080/14999013.2011.552368

Kroppan, E., Nonstad, K., Iversen, R. B., & Søndenaa, E. (2017). Implementation of the short- term assessment of risk and treatability over two phases. *Journal of Multidisciplinary Healthcare*, *10*, 321–326. doi:10.2147/JMDH.S133514

Lam, J. (2014). *Use of the short-term assessment of risk and treatability in a forensic facility: Examining the impact of suicide behavior on multiple risk outcomes* (UMI No. 3643381) (Doctoral Dissertation). ProQuest Dissertations Publishing, Fordham University, New York.

Levin, S., Nilsen, P., Bendtsen, P., & Bülow, P. (2018). Staff perceptions of facilitators and barriers to the use of a short- term risk assessment instrument in forensic psychiatry. *Journal of Forensic Psychology Research and Practice*, *18*(3), 199. doi:10.1080/24732850.2018.1466260

Livingston, J. D., Crocker, A. G., Nicholls, T. L., & Seto, M. C. (2016). Forensic mental health tribunals: A qualitative study of participants' experiences and views. *Psychology, Public Policy, and Law*, *22*(2), 173–184. doi:10.1037/law0000084

Lowder, E. M., Desmarais, S. L., Rade, C. B., Coffey, T., & Van Dorn, R. A. (2017). Models of protection against recidivism in justice-involved adults with mental illnesses. *Criminal Justice and Behavior*, *44*(7), 893–911. doi:10.1177/0093854817710966

Lowder, E. M., Desmarais, S. L., Rade, C. B., Johnson, K. L., & Van Dorn, R. A. (2019). Reliability and validity of START and LSI-R assessments in mental health jail diversion clients. *Assessment*, *26*(7), 1347–1361. doi:10.1177/1073191117704505

Marriott, R., O'Shea, L. E., Picchioni, M. M., & Dickens, G. L. (2017). Predictive validity of the short-term assessment of risk and treatability (START) for multiple adverse outcomes: The effect of diagnosis. *Psychiatry Research*, *256*, 435–443. doi:10.1016/j.psychres.2017.07.009

Melton, G. B., Petrila, J., Poythress, N. G., Slobogin, C., Otto, R. K., & Mossman, D. (2018). *Psychological evaluations for the courts: A handbook for mental health professionals and lawyers* (4th Ed.). New York: Guildford Press.

Mental Health Commission of Canada. (2015). *Guidelines for recovery-oriented practice*. Retrieved from www.mentalhealthcommission.ca/sites/default/files/MHCC_RecoveryGuidelines_ENG_0.pdf

Morris, D. (2013). The predictive validity of the Short-Term Assessment of Risk and Treatability in an inpatient female forensic population (Master's thesis, University of Birmingham, Birmingham, United Kingdom).

Nicholls, T. L., Brink, J., Desmarais, S. L., Webster, C. D., & Martin, M. (2006). The Short-Term Assessment of Risk and Treatability (START): A prospective validation study in a forensic psychiatric sample. *Assessment*, *13*(3), 313–327. doi:10.1177/1073191106290559

Nicholls, T. L., Desmarais, S., Martin, M. L., Brink, J., & Webster, C. M. (2019). Short-Term Assessment of Risk and Treatability (START). In R. D. Morgan (Ed.), *The Sage encyclopedia of criminal psychology* (pp. 1385–1389). Thousand Oaks, CA: Sage.

Nicholls, T. L., Petersen, K. L., Brink, J., & Webster, C. (2011). A clinical and risk profile of forensic psychiatric patients: Treatment team STARTs in a Canadian service. *International Journal of Forensic Mental Health*, *10*(3), 187–199. doi:10.1080/14999013.2011.600234

Nonstad, K., Nesset, M. B., Kroppan, E., Pedersen, T. W., Nøttestad, J. A., Almvik, R., & Palmstierna, T. (2010). Predictive validity and other psychometric properties of the short-term assessment of risk and treatability (START) in a Norwegian high secure hospital. *International Journal of Forensic Mental Health*, *9*(4), 294–299. doi:10.1080/14999013.2010.534958

Nordentoft, M., Mortensen, P. B., & Pedersen, C. B. (2011). Absolute risk of suicide after first hospital contact in mental disorder. *Archives of General Psychiatry*, *68*(10), 1058–1064. doi:10.1001/archgenpsychiatry.2011.113

Nyman, M., Hofvander, B., Nilsson, T., & Wijk, H. (2019). Mental health nurses' experiences of risk assessments for care planning in forensic psychiatry. *The International Journal of Forensic Mental Health*. doi:10.1080/14999013.2019.1646356

Olver, M. E., Wong, S. C. P., Nicholaichuk, T., & Gordon, A. (2007). The validity and reliability of the violence risk scale-sexual offender version: Assessing sex offender risk and evaluating therapeutic change. *Psychological Assessment*, *19*(3), 318–329. doi:10.1037/1040-3590.19.3.318

O'Shea, L. E., & Dickens, G. L. (2014). Short-term assessment of risk and treatability (START): Systematic review and meta-analysis. *Psychological Assessment*, *26*(3), 990–1002. doi:10.1037/a0036794

O'Shea, L. E., & Dickens, G. L. (2015). Predictive validity of the START for unauthorised leave and substance abuse in a secure mental health setting: A pseudo-prospective cohort study. *International Journal of Nursing Studies*, *52*(5), 970–979. doi:10.1016/j.ijnurstu.2015.02.007

O'Shea, L. E., Picchioni, M. M., & Dickens, G. L. (2016). The predictive validity of the short-term assessment of risk and treatability (START) for multiple adverse outcomes in a secure psychiatric inpatient setting. *Assessment*, *23*(2), 150–162. doi:10.1177/1073191115573301

Poorolajal, J., Haghtalab, T., Farhadi, M., & Darvishi, N. (2016). Substance use disorder and risk of suicidal ideation, suicide attempt and suicide death: A meta-analysis. *Journal of Public Health*, *38*(3), 282–291. doi:10.1093/pubmed/fdv148

Quinn, R., Miles, H., & Kinane, C. (2013). The validity of the short-term assessment of risk and treatability (START) in a UK medium secure forensic mental health service. *International Journal of Forensic Mental Health*, *12*(3), 215–224. doi:10.1080/14999013.2013.832714

Ray, I., & Simpson, A. I. F. (2019). Shared risk formulation in forensic psychiatry. *The Journal of the American Academy of Psychiatry and the Law*, *47*(1), 22–28. doi:10.29158/JAAPL.003813-19

Risk Management Authority (2019). *Short-Term Assessment of Risk and Treatability (START)*. Retrieved from https://www.rma.scot/wp-content/uploads/2019/09/RATED_START_July-2019_Hyperlink-Version.pdf

Rogers, R. (2000). The uncritical acceptance of risk assessment in forensic practice. *Law and Human Behaviour*, *24*, 595–605. doi:10.1023/A:1005575113507

Rufener, C., Depp, C., Gawronska, M., & Saks, E. (2015). Recovery in mental illnesses. In D. V. Jeste & B. W. Palmer (Eds.), *Positive psychiatry: A clinical handbook*. Arlington, VA: American Psychiatric Association Publishing. doi:10.1176/appi.books.9781615370818.dj05

Seligman, M. E. P. (2002). *Authentic happiness*. New York: Free Press.

Strub, D. S., Douglas, K. S., & Nicholls, T. L. (2016). Violence risk assessment of civil psychiatric patients with the HCR-20: Does gender matter? *International Journal of Forensic Mental Health*, *15*(1), 81–96. doi:10.1080/14999013.2016.1141438

Swendsen, J., Conway, K. P., Degenhardt, L., Glantz, M., Jin, R., Merikangas, K. R., . . . Kessler, R. C. (2010). Mental disorders as risk factors for substance use, abuse and dependence: Results from the 10-year follow-up of the national comorbidity survey. *Addiction*, *105*(6), 1117–1128. doi:10.1111/j.1360-0443.2010.02902.x

Timmins, K. L. E., Evans, L., & Tully, R. J. (2018). Inter-rater reliability of the short-term assessment of risk and treatability (START). *The Journal of Forensic Psychiatry & Psychology*, *29*(6), 968–988. doi:10.1080/14789949.2018.1523945

Troquete, N. A. C., van den Brink, R. H. S., Beintema, H., Mulder, T., van Os, T. W. D. P., Schoevers, R. A., & Wiersma, D. (2015). Predictive validity of the short-term assessment of risk and treatability for violent behavior in outpatient forensic psychiatric patients. *Psychological Assessment*, *27*(2), 377–391. doi:10.1037/a0038270

van den Brink, R. H. S., Troquete, N. A. C., Beintema, H., Mulder, T., van Os, T. W. D. P., Schoevers, R. A., & Wiersma, D. (2015). Risk assessment by client and case manager for shared decision making in outpatient forensic psychiatry. *BMC Psychiatry*, *15*(1), 120. doi:10.1186/s12888-015-0500-3

Vaughn, M. G., Fu, Q., Delisi, M., Beaver, K. M., Perron, B. E., & Howard, M. O. (2010). Criminal victimization and comorbid substance use and psychiatric disorders in the United States: Results from the NESARC. *Annals of Epidemiology*, *20*(4), 281–288. doi:10.1016/j.annepidem.2009.11.011

Viljoen, J., Nicholls, T. L., Cruise, K., Desmarais, S. L., & Webster, C. D. (2014). *Short-Term Assessment of Risk and Treatability (START): Adolescent version—user guide.* Burnaby, BC: Mental Health & Addiction Services, Simon Fraser University.

Viljoen, S., Nicholls, T., Greaves, C., Ruiter, C., & Brink, J. (2011). Resilience and successful community reintegration among female forensic psychiatric patients: A preliminary investigation: Resilience and successful community reintegration. *Behavioral Sciences & the Law, 29*(5), 752–770. doi:10.1002/bsl.1001

Viljoen, S., Viljoen, J. L., Nicholls, T. L., & de Vries Robbé, M. (2017). The role of protective factors in forensic risk assessments. In R. Roesch & A. N. Cook (Eds.), *Handbook of forensic mental health services* (pp. 179–215). London: Routledge. doi:10.4324/9781315627823-7

Ward, T., Mann, R. E., & Gannon, T. A. (2007). The good lives model of offender rehabilitation: Clinical implications. *Aggression and Violent Behavior, 12*(1), 87–107. doi:10.1016/j.avb.2006.03.004

Webster, C. D., Douglas, K. S., Eaves, D., & Hart, S. D. (1997). *HCR-20: Assessing the Risk for Violence (Version 2).* Vancouver, BC: Mental Health, Law, and Policy Institute, Simon Fraser University.

Webster, C. D., Eaves, D., Douglas, K. S., & Wintrup, A. (1995). *The HCR-20 Scheme: The Assessment of Dangerousness and Risk.* Vancouver, BC: Mental Health, Law, and Policy Institute, and Forensic Psychiatric Services Commission of British Columbia.

Webster, C. D., Martin, M. L., Brink, J., Nicholls, T. L., & Desmarais, S. (2009). *Manual for the short-term assessment of risk and treatability (START)* (Version 1.1). Hamilton, ON: Forensic Psychiatric Services Commission, St. Joseph's Healthcare.

Webster, C. D., Martin, M. L., Brink, J., Nicholls, T. L., & Middleton, C. (2004). *Manual for the short-term assessment of risk and treatability (START)* (Version 1.0, consultation ed.). Hamilton, ON: Forensic Psychiatric Services Commission, St. Joseph's Healthcare.

Webster, C. D., Nicholls, T. L., Martin, M., Desmarais, S. L., & Brink, J. (2006). Short-term assessment of risk and treatability (START): The case for a new structured professional judgment scheme. *Behavioral Sciences & the Law, 24*(6), 747–766. doi:10.1002/bsl.737

Wilson, C. M., Desmarais, S. L., Nicholls, T. L., & Brink, J. (2010). The role of client strengths in assessments of violence risk using the short-term assessment of risk and treatability (START). *International Journal of Forensic Mental Health, 9*(4), 282–293. doi:10.1080/14999013.2010.534694

Wilson, C. M., Desmarais, S. L., Nicholls, T. L., Hart, S. D., & Brink, J. (2013). Predictive validity of dynamic factors: Assessing violence risk in forensic psychiatric inpatients. *Law and Human Behavior, 37*(6), 377–388. doi:10.1037/lhb0000025

Chapter 16

The Spousal Assault Risk Assessment Guide (SARA)

P. Randall Kropp and Andrea Gibas

Overview of the SARA

The first two versions of the Spousal Assault Risk Assessment Guide (SARA and SARA-Version 2; Kropp, Hart, Webster, & Eaves, 1994, 1995) were developed in the early 1990s during a time of increased recognition of the social and economic tolls caused by spousal violence in our society. A special edition of the SARA-Version 2 (SARA-V2) soon followed, employing normative tables to assist evaluators in making professional judgments of risk (Kropp, Hart, Webster, & Eaves, 1999). Since that time there has been a proliferation of research and commentaries on domestic violence risk assessment (Abramsky et al., 2011; Bennett Cattaneo & Goodman, 2005; Capaldi, Knoble, Shortt, & Kim, 2012; Dutton & Kropp, 2000; Hilton & Harris, 2005; Kropp, 2008; Riggs, Caulfield, & Street, 2000; Schumacher, Feldbau-Kohn, Slep, & Heyman, 2001; Vest, Catlin, Chen, & Brownson, 2002; Stith, Smith, Penn, Ward, & Tritt, 2004), and there is increasing evidence of the validity of a number of risk assessment tools including the SARA-V2 (Kropp & Hart, 2000), the Danger Assessment (DA; Campbell, 1995; Campbell, Webster, & Glass, 2009), the Domestic Violence Screening Instrument-Revised (DVSI-R; Williams & Houghton, 2004; Williams, 2012), and the Ontario Domestic Assault Risk Assessment (ODARA: Hilton, Harris, & Rice, 2010). Within this growing field, the SARA guides remain popular risk assessment and case management tools for those working with perpetrators and victims of domestic violence. Indeed, various versions of the SARA have now been translated into at least ten languages and are being used in at least 15 countries on six continents. This chapter will review the content and development of the third and most recent version of the guide, the SARA-Version 3 (SARA-V3: Kropp & Hart, 2015). The chapter will also summarize existing reliability and validity studies on all versions of the SARA, and conclude with a case study to illustrate the use of the SARA-V3.

Success of early versions of the SARA led to the development of the Brief Spousal Assault Form for the Evaluation of Risk (B-SAFER; Kropp, Hart, & Belfrage, 2010). The B-SAFER is based upon the SARA-V2 and parallel in structure to the SARA-V3 (e.g., with the inclusion of victim vulnerability factors). It is intended as a shorter, simpler risk assessment instrument. First developed for use by law enforcement, it is now used in a variety of settings and contexts that require more time-limited assessments. The B-SAFER is now well established in the literature, but space does not allow a full description of these guidelines in this chapter. We refer the interested reader to a number of publications available on the B-SAFER (see, for example: Belfrage & Strand, 2014; Kropp, Hart, & Belfrage, 2010; Loinaz, 2014; Serie, van Tilburg, van Dam, & de Ruiter, 2017; Storey & Strand, 2013; Storey, Kropp, Hart, Belfrage, & Strand, 2014; Thijssen & de Ruiter, 2011).

SARA-V3

Description

The SARA-V3 is a set of structured professional judgment (SPJ) guidelines for the assessment and management of risk for intimate partner violence (IPV). IPV is defined as any actual, attempted, or threatened physical harm perpetrated by a man or woman against someone with whom he or she has, or has had, an intimate, sexual relationship. This definition is inclusive: It is not limited to acts that result in physical injury or death; it is not limited to relationships where the partners are or have been legally married; and it is not limited by the gender of the victim or perpetrator. Also, it is consistent with the observation that violence between intimate partners is pandemic in our societies regardless of the nature of their relationship. In these ways it has a potentially wider application than some other risk assessment instruments that employ narrower definitions of spousal assault.

Consistent with recommendations for guidelines in the field of health care, such as those made by the American Psychological Association (APA, 2002), development of the SARA-V3 was based in part on a systematic review of the existing research. Accordingly, use of the SARA-V3 may be considered evidence-based, empirically guided, or empirically supported practice. Also consistent with APA's recommendations, its development took into consideration existing standards of practice, ethical codes, and relevant law. The SARA-V3 helps evaluators to exercise their best judgment; it is not a replacement for professional discretion. Its purpose is to introduce a systematic, standardized, and practical framework for gathering and considering information when making decisions about IPV risk.

Format

The factors considered in the SARA-V3 are divided into three domains (see Table 16.1 for a summary). Nature of IPV includes 8 factors related to the pattern of any IPV behavior perpetrated by the evaluee. Perpetrator Risk Factors are 10 factors reflecting the psychosocial adjustment and background of the evaluee. Victim Vulnerability Factors are 6 factors reflecting the psychosocial adjustment and background of the (potential) victim. In general, factors in the first domain help the evaluator characterize the seriousness of the evaluee's IPV; those in the second domain, characteristics of the evaluee that may be associated with decisions to engage in IPV; and those in the third domain, characteristics of the victim that may be associated with decisions to engage in self-protective behavior. Evaluators also have the ability to document "other considerations," which are rare or unusual risk factors relevant to the case at hand.

Development

Building on the popularity and success of the SARA-V2, a revision and expansion of the guidelines was deemed necessary for four primary reasons. First, the empirical and professional literatures on IPV risk assessment technology and risk factors have expanded tremendously in the 16 years since the SARA-V2 was published. The SARA-V3 reflects these advancements in knowledge. Second, recent years have also seen significant developments in the SPJ approach to risk assessment in general. For example, SPJ guidelines, such as the Risk for Sexual Violence Protocol (RSVP; Hart, Kropp, Laws, Klaver, Logan, & Watt, 2003), the Guidelines for Stalking Assessment and Management (SAM; Kropp, Hart, & Lyon, 2008), and the Historical-Clinical-Risk Management-20, Version 3 (HCR-20 V3; Douglas et al., 2013), incorporated steps related to the formulation of violence perpetration and management plans and also introduced worksheets

Table 16.1 Factors in the SARA-V3

Nature of IPV: History Includes:	Perpetrator Risk Factors: Problems With:	Victim Vulnerability Factors: Problems With:
N1. Intimidation	P1. Intimate Relationships	V1. Barriers to Security
N2. Threats	P2. Non-Intimate Relationships	V2. Barriers to Independence
N3. Physical Harm	P3. Employment/Finances	V3. Interpersonal Resources
N4. Sexual Harm	P4. Trauma/Victimization	V4. Community Resources
N5. Severe IPV	P5. General Antisocial Conduct	V5. Attitudes or Behavior
N6. Chronic IPV	P6. Major Mental Disorder	V6. Mental Health
N7. Escalating IPV	P7. Personality Disorder	
N8. IPV-Related Supervision Violations	P8. Substance Use	
	P9. Violent/Suicidal Ideation	
	P10. Distorted Thinking About IPV	

to assist administration. Thus, these steps were also incorporated into the SARA-V3. Third, a review of the literature, as well as work on the SAM, B-SAFER, and other SPJ guidelines, convinced the authors that it was both important and feasible to incorporate vulnerability factors that reflect common barriers to victims' ability, opportunity, or motivation to engage in self-protective behavior; inclusion of victim vulnerability factors in the SARA-V3 would facilitate a more realistic and comprehensive analysis of risk and enhance ability to develop safety plans. Fourth, in a more practical sense, the authors hoped to revise the SARA to incorporate more than 20 years of experience conducting spousal violence risk assessments and the feedback we have received during hundreds of SARA training workshops for diverse professionals around the world—indeed, on every continent except Antarctica.

The changes made to the SARA-V3 were done with considerable effort to preserve the integrity of the SARA-V2. Thus, none of the core content of the SARA-V2 was lost. Rather, risk factors of the SARA-V2 were simply reorganized (and relabeled in some cases) into the Nature of IPV and Perpetrator Risk Factors domains. The authors used a logical and intuitive approach to organizing the risk factors. We were also aided by the research of colleagues in Scotland (Cooke & Michie, 2003), who analyzed data from 2796 male offenders from Canada in an attempt to identify possible redundancy among the 20 SARA-V2 risk factors. Briefly, factor analyses suggested that the statistical association among the ratings of the SARA-V2 items could be modeled adequately using a smaller number of factors, with each factor comprising multiple items. The seven factors, all carefully represented in the SARA-V3, were interpreted as follows: history of spousal violence, life-threatening spousal violence, escalation of spousal violence, attitudes supportive of spousal violence, general antisocial behavior, failure to obey court orders, and mental disorder.

Applications

The SARA-V3 is intended for use by criminal justice, victim support, security, post-secondary, health, and mental health professionals working in a variety of contexts where complaints of IPV arise. In the *criminal justice system*, risk assessment is relevant at a number of junctures: during police investigation, prior to trial, prior to sentencing of the offender, and prior to release of the offender. In the *civil justice system*, risk assessment is relevant to protection of potential victims, especially in the context of family court, child protection, and occupational health and safety matters. In *health care settings*, risk assessment is relevant when attempting to prioritize or triage cases for service delivery. Also, it may be useful when decisions are being made regarding which interventions are most appropriate and most likely to be effective in a case.

Intended Populations

The SARA-V3 is intended for use in cases in which there are reasonable grounds to believe an evaluee poses a risk for IPV, including but not limited to those in which the evaluee has a known or suspected history of IPV. The SARA-V3 is intended for use in cases where the evaluee is aged 18 and older. Given the unfortunate absence of validated IPV risk assessment tools intended for use with those below the age of 18, the SARA-V3 may be of some assistance when evaluating adolescents, especially those between the ages of 15 and 18; however, evaluators are cautioned that research on this age group is limited (Capaldi, Knoble, Shortt, & Kim, 2012; Leen, Sorbring, Mawer, Holdsworth, Helsing, & Bowen, 2013; Richards & Branch, 2012; Rothman, Johnson, Azrael, Hall, & Weinberg, 2010).

The SARA-V3 is intended for use with both male and female evaluees, regardless of sexual orientation or culture. The primary risk factors for perpetration of IPV are the same across gender, sexual orientation, and culture (e.g., Archer, 2000; Capaldi et al., 2012; Magdol et al., 1997; Robertson & Murachver, 2009; Stith, Smith, Penn, Ward, & Tritt, 2004). Of course, the nature of IPV may differ markedly across the same factors, which highlights the need for evaluators to have familiarity with or competence related to them.

Finally, the SARA-V3 is intended for use with the most common or typical forms of IPV. The nature of common or typical IPV includes threats, physical assault, and sexual assault of victims who are intimate partners currently, were intimate partners until recently, or who are closely acquainted with current or former intimate partners (e.g., their parents, children, coworkers, or new intimate partners). It may be advisable to expand the assessment beyond the use of the SARA-V3 to include additional SPJ guidelines when the IPV has unusual or special characteristics. For example, if the IPV appears to be related to a history of physical assault outside of intimate relationships, the evaluator should consider also using the HCR-20 V3. If the IPV includes sexual assault that appears to be related to a history of sexual violence outside of intimate relationships, and especially if it appears the sexual assault may be related to paraphilic disorders, the evaluator should consider also using the RSVP. If the IPV involved group action (e.g., conspiracy or multiple perpetrators), including by members of the same family or cultural community, the evaluator should consider also using the PATRIARCH (Kropp, Belfrage, & Hart, 2013) or Multi-Level Guidelines (Cook, Hart, & Kropp, 2015). If the IPV involved targeting of a victim long (e.g., months or years) after the final dissolution of the intimate relationship, and especially if it involves proxy perpetrators and secondary victims, the evaluator should consider using the SAM.

Evaluator Qualifications

Evaluators are responsible for ensuring that their evaluation conforms to relevant laws, regulations, and policies. Evaluators should meet the following minimal qualifications: (1) expertise in individual assessment (e.g., training or work-related experience with perpetrators or victims of IPV); and (2) expertise in the area of IPV (e.g., coursework, knowledge of the relevant literature, work-related experience).

Assessment Procedure

The SARA-V3 administration procedure comprises six steps. In Step 1, SARA-V3 evaluators gather and document basic case information. In Step 2, evaluators identify the presence of 24 factors in the three domains as well as any additional case-specific factors. In Step 3, evaluators assess the relevance of the factors with respect to the perpetration or prevention of future IPV. In Step 4, evaluators identify and describe the most likely scenarios of future IPV. In Step 5, evaluators recommend plans for managing IPV risk in light of the relevant risk factors and scenarios of risk. Finally, in Step 6, evaluators document their judgments regarding overall risk. Each step is discussed in more detail in this section. To facilitate documentation, the authors developed the SARA-V3 Rating Sheet and Worksheet. The Rating Sheet is designed for evaluators who want to record only basic information (i.e., findings and opinions from Steps 2, 3, and 6); and the Worksheet, for evaluators who want to record complete information. The SARA-V3 may be administered without completing a Rating Sheet or Worksheet, but the Rating Sheet and Worksheet should be used always and only in conjunction with the SARA-V3 User Manual.

Step 1: Case Information

Evaluators should begin by identifying people who are the subject of the risk assessment, that is, people about whom the evaluators have reasonable grounds that they might pose a risk for IPV. In the majority of cases, this is a single person who has a known, suspected, or alleged history of IPV and may be referred to as the primary perpetrator or simply as the perpetrator (P). If a primary perpetrator uses accomplices, referred to as proxy perpetrators, their actions are also considered when coding the risk factors.

Also, evaluators should identify people who they believe might be the likely target of any future IPV committed by the perpetrator or evaluee. In the majority of cases, this is a single person who is the victim of known, suspected, or alleged IPV by the perpetrator or evaluee and may be referred to as the primary victim or simply the victim (V). If a perpetrator expands the scope of the IPV to target the primary victim's friends, acquaintances, or family members (i.e., violence toward others in the context of IPV), these people are typically referred to as secondary victims.

To make judgments about risk for IPV using the SARA-V3, evaluators must have access to information about the presence of and the changes over time in the Nature of IPV, Perpetrator Risk Factors, and Victim Vulnerability Factors. Ideally, the following methods of gathering information are used: (1) an interview with the primary perpetrator and any secondary perpetrators; (2) an interview with the primary victim and any secondary victims; (3) interviews with collateral informants, including family members and friends of the primary perpetrator and victim; (4) a review of collateral records, including police reports, victim statements, statements made by the perpetrator, the perpetrator's criminal record, and so forth; and (5) a psychological or psychiatric assessment, when it appears that the perpetrator may have a history of mental health problems. Evaluators are reminded that the information they gather may be sensitive in nature. It is important that evaluators respect the rights of interviewees by obtaining informed consent and protecting their privacy, in accordance with relevant law and policy. Every effort should be made to keep information private when it could jeopardize the victim's safety.

Steps 2 and 3: Presence and Relevance of SARA-V3 Risk Factors

After information has been gathered and documented, evaluators should code the presence of individual factors. Ratings are made for each of the individual factors in each of the three domains. Evaluators also can identify "other considerations," that is, case-specific factors not included among the standard factors. The presence of factors is coded using a 3-point response format that reflects the certainty of the evaluator's opinion. To reflect possible changes over time, the factors are coded *Recent* versus *Past*. *Recent* is the 1 year (52 weeks) prior to the evaluation, whereas *Past* is any time prior. If no information is available concerning a given factor or the information obtained is unreliable, the factor should be left uncoded (i.e., omitted).

Next, evaluators rate on a 3-point scale the relevance of the Perpetrator Risk Factors and Victim Vulnerability Factors with respect to the development of future risk management plans. A factor is relevant if it is an important consideration when making plans about monitoring, treatment, supervision, or victim safety planning in the case at hand, or the factor is critical to the evaluator's formulation of what caused the perpetrator to commit IPV and how best to prevent future IPV.

Step 4: Risk Scenarios

Determining which risk management plans are appropriate in a given case depends on the risks posed by the individual. Before taking preventive action, the evaluator must first answer the question, what am I trying to prevent? Or, to put another way, what exactly is it that I am worried this person might do? In this step, the evaluator presents what might happen in the future in light of the factors identified as present and relevant in Steps 2 and 3. These descriptions of "possible futures" are often referred to as scenarios, short narratives designed to simplify complex issues in a way that facilitates their communication to decision-makers. Scenario-based risk assessment is a form of scenario planning, a management strategy used for more than 50 years in fields such as business, health care, and the military (Ringland, 1998; Schwartz, 1990; van der Heijden, 1997).

Step 5: Management Plans

In this step, the evaluator recommends risk management plans. The strategies are based on consideration of the presence and relevance of factors in Steps 2 and 3 as well as the various scenarios of IPV identified in Step 4. The SARA-V3 encourages users to think about risk management in terms of four basic activities: *monitoring, treatment, supervision,* and *victim safety planning* (Douglas et al., 2013; Kropp, Hart, Lyon, & LePard, 2002). The goal of *monitoring* is to evaluate changes in risk over time so that risk management plans can be revised as appropriate, and to identify any "triggers" or "red flags" that might warn the person's risk for IPV is imminent or escalating. *Treatment* involves the provision of habilitative or rehabilitative services. The goal of treatment is to improve deficits in the individual's psychosocial adjustment or functioning. *Supervision* involves restriction of the perpetrator's rights or freedoms. The goal of supervision is to make it (more) difficult for the individual to engage in further IPV. Finally, *victim safety planning* involves improving the victim's dynamic and static security resources, a process sometimes referred to as "target hardening." The goal is to ensure that if IPV reoccurs—despite all monitoring, treatment, and supervision efforts—any negative impact on the psychological and physical well-being of victims is minimized. Optimally, developing risk management plans requires familiarity with and cooperation among a number of professionals working in different agencies and clinics, each with a different skill set and mandate (e.g., Hart et al., 2001; Kropp, Hart, Lyon, & LePard, 2002; Robinson, 2006; Robinson & Tregidga, 2007).

Step 6: Conclusory Opinions

The final step is to document summary judgments in a clear, simple manner that facilitates appropriate action. These opinions address the following issues: *Case Prioritization, Risk for Serious Physical Harm, Immediate Action Required, Other Risks Indicated,* and the *Date for Case Review. Case Prioritization* is coded using a 3-point response format, according to the degree of effort or intervention it will require to prevent the person from committing IPV. *Risk of Serious Physical Harm* reflects the severity of IPV the person might commit, and is also coded using a 3-point response format: Low, Moderate, or High risk. The *Imminent Violence* rating, also coded as Low, Moderate, or High, reflects the imminence of any IPV the person might commit. *Other Risks Indicated* allows evaluators to note whether other risks are present and should be the focus of further evaluation. These may take the form of specialized forms of violence (e.g., sexual assault, child physical abuse) or other harmful activities such as suicidal behavior or self-harm. Finally, the evaluator is asked to recommend a date for regular *Case Review* (i.e., reassessment of risk) as well as any warning signs that should trigger an earlier reassessment.

Research on the SARA Guidelines

Overview

Considerable support for the SARA guidelines can be found in the empirical literature. A number of independent peer-reviewed studies, government reports, conference papers, a master's thesis, and at least two doctoral dissertations have provided some evidence for the reliability and validity of the SARA tools when used in law enforcement, forensic mental health, and correctional settings (i.e., Belfrage et al., 2012; Cairns, 2004; Gibas, Kropp, Hart, & Stewart, 2008; Grann & Wedin, 2002; Heckert & Gondolf, 2004; Hilton et al., 2004; Jung & Buro, 2016; Kropp & Hart, 2000; Mowat-Léger, 2001; Olver & Jung, 2017; Ryan, 2016; Rudd, Skilling, & Nonemaker, 2010; Schafers, 2019; Williams & Houghton, 2004; Wong & Hisashima, 2008). These studies are reviewed in detail in this section. Further, the SARA-V2 is supported by narrative reviews of IPV risk assessment instruments (Bowen, 2011; Helmus, & Bourgon, 2011; Nicholls, Pritchard, Reeves, & Hilterman, 2013). Finally, at least four meta-analytic studies have shown good results for the SARA-V2 (Guy, 2008; Hanson, Helmus, & Bourgon, 2007; Messing & Thaller, 2013; Singh, Grann, & Fazel, 2011). For example, in the Singh et al. analysis, the SARA-V2 ranked third out of nine commonly used violence risk assessment instruments with respect to overall predictive validity.

Our own narrative review revealed a number of methodological problems with many of the studies utilizing the SARA guidelines. Many of the important validation studies of the SARA guidelines did not administer the instruments according to the manuals, excluded or "simulated" many of the risk factors due to inadequate information, or did not incorporate summary risk ratings (i.e., the SPJ method). These problems make interpretation of results difficult. Nonetheless, each of the studies is described and reviewed in detail in this section with particular reference to the reliability and validity of the SARA; major methodological limitations are noted where relevant. The studies are listed here chronologically.

Kropp and Hart (2000)

The first systematic evaluation of the reliability and validity of the SARA-V2 was reported by two of its authors. The study involved 2681 male offenders (671 probationers and 1010 inmates) in the Canadian criminal justice system. A variety of corrections (e.g., probation officers), mental health (e.g., treatment staff), and trained research staff (e.g., doctoral-level clinical psychology students) were responsible for providing SARA-V2 ratings for the sample. At the individual item-level, intraclass correlation coefficients (ICC) ranged between 0.45 and 0.86 (*Mdn* ICC = 0.65). The interrater reliability ICC for the SARA-V2 total score was 0.84. The reliability was higher for Part 1 of the SARA-V2 (i.e., related to criminal history and psychosocial adjustment; ICC = 0.87) than for Part 2 (i.e., related to spousal assault history; ICC = 0.68). The summary risk ratings (Low, Moderate, High) also demonstrated statistically significant interrater reliability (ICC = 0.63), even when dichotomized (Low/Moderate risk vs. High risk; ICC = 0.57). Lastly, interrater reliability for the SARA-V2 Critical Items was relatively low, but these items were also infrequently endorsed and had a restricted range.

To test concurrent validity, the SARA-V2 was compared to three general risk-related measures: The Psychopathy Checklist: Screening Version (PCL:SV; Hart, Cox, & Hare, 1995) the General Statistical Information on Recidivism Scale (GSIR; Nuffield, 1982), and the Violence Risk Assessment Guide (VRAG; Quinsey, Harris, Rice, & Cormier, 1998). The total SARA-V2 score ($r = 0.43$), Part 1 ($r = 0.45$) and Part 2 ($r = 0.30$) scores, respectively, exhibited moderate correlations with the PCL:SV. Both the GSIR ($r = -0.40$) and VRAG ($r = 0.50$) correlated to a moderate and large degree with the general violence risk factors of the SARA-V2 (Part 1). Correlations with the spousal assault-specific items and summary risk ratings were not statistically significant. These results are evidence of the good convergent and discriminant validity of the SARA-V2 when compared to validated measures of general violence risk.

In addition, group comparisons were made between recidivistic ($n = 52$) and non-recidivistic ($n = 50$) spousal assaulters. Significant group differences were found between the groups using actuarial analog measures of risk derived from the SARA-V2 (i.e., the total score and number of factors present). Individuals who were rated as high risk on the SARA-V2 tended to be spousal assault recidivists, and those rated low risk were more likely to be non-recidivists ($\chi^2_{(2, 102)} = 13.69, p = 0.001$). A similar pattern was found when the risk ratings were dichotomized into high versus moderate/low risk ($\chi^2_{(1, 102)} = 7.82, p = 0.005$). After controlling for treatment suitability, time at risk, and continuous (i.e., actuarial) scores on the SARA-V2, the summary risk ratings continued to significantly differentiate between recidivist and non-recidivist spousal assaulters. Receiver Operating Characteristic (ROC) analysis indicated that the AUC for the SARA-V2 was 0.70. Overall, the results suggest that the SARA-V2 is able to discriminate between recidivists and non-recidivists. Regarding the latter finding, the results indicated that structured professional judgment ratings of risk method outperformed the actuarial method in postdicting recidivism.

Mowat-Léger (2001)

Interrater reliability of the SARA-V2 was measured on 16 subjects. The intraclass correlation coefficients ranged between 0.95 and 0.99 for all four sections of the SARA-V2 (e.g., 0.95 for Psychosocial Adjustment). Similarly, the SARA-V2 total, Part 1, and Part 2 scores had reported intraclass correlation coefficients greater than 0.90 (SARA-V2 total, ICC = 0.99; SARA-V2 Part 1, ICC = 0.98; SARA-V2 Part 2, ICC = 0.93). Within the sample under study, the SARA-V2 exhibited impressive interrater reliability.

Mowat-Léger also examined the concurrent validity of the SARA-V2 when compared to two other domestic violence risk instruments—the Abusive Behavior Inventory (ABI; Shepard & Campbell, 1992), and the Inventory of Beliefs about Wife Beating (IBWB; Saunders, Lynch, Grayson, & Linz, 1987). The results indicate that the SARA-V2 total score was strongly and significantly correlated with the total score of the ABI ($r = 0.46$) and IBWB ($r = -0.30$), and the two subscales of the ABI (Physical Abuse: $r = 0.59$ and Emotional Abuse: $r = 0.36$). Part 2 (Spousal Assault History) evidenced a stronger correlation with the domestic violence risk assessment instruments than Part 1 (Criminal History) of the SARA-V2 (e.g., $r = 0.60$ vs. $r = 0.37$ for ABI physical abuse). Further, all components of the SARA-V2 were significantly correlated with the PCL:SV; Part 1 showed a higher correlation ($r = 0.59$) than Part 2 ($r = 0.37$).

Grann and Wedin (2002)

A sample of male offenders who underwent a forensic psychiatric evaluation was selected. The 88 cases involved offenders who had been convicted of a violent spousal assault or homicide and had been diagnosed with a personality disorder. The researchers examined interrater reliability and the concurrent and predictive validity of the SARA-V2 ratings that were completed by a bachelor's-level psychology student who has been trained on use of the tool. Because of the retrospective file-based design of the study, material required to complete the SARA-V2 was sometimes unavailable and thus omitted. In particular, 4 of the 20 items were deemed too difficult to rate reliably from file information. Although the missing items were prorated (i.e., replaced with the expected mean), the measurement reliability of the SARA-V2 was likely diluted as a result. Further, the authors noted that the SARA-V2 was used as "an actuarial tool in the strict sense" (p. 10), and summary risk ratings were not applied. This procedure thus appeared to violate the fundamental assumption, stated in the SARA-V2 manual, that risk is not a simple function of the number of risk factors present (although, in general, SPJ approaches acknowledge that the more risk factors present, typically, the higher the risk).

On a subsample of 18 randomly selected cases rated independently by a doctoral-level psychologist, the results indicated that the reliability of the SARA-V2 was acceptable; at an individual item level, Cohen's kappa ranged from between 0.30 and 1.00 (average kappa = 0.58). Intraclass correlation coefficients for the SARA-V2 total, Part 1, and Part 2 scores were statistically significant at 0.85, 0.88, and 0.74, respectively.

Using a retrospective design, postdictive validity of the SARA-V2 was assessed in the 88 cases with a follow-up period of approximately 10 years. Three SARA-V2 risk factors were identified as being important in influencing risk for partner violence recidivism: Past Violation of Conditional Release or Community Supervision, Personality Disorder with Anger, Impulsivity or Behavioral Instability, and Extreme Minimization or Denial of Spousal Assault History. ROC analyses were conducted using the SARA-V2 total, Part 1, and Part 2 scores for the four distinct post-detainment time periods (6 months, 1 year, 2 years, and 5 years). Inclusive of all time periods, the AUCs ranged from between 0.49 and 0.65, representing minimal improvements over chance in predicting spousal violence recidivism. However, the authors acknowledged that the results of the study were appreciably limited by the retrospective design, the questionable reliability of the SARA-V2 due to its simulation, and the use of a small, but highly selective sample (i.e., male offenders diagnosed with a personality disorder).

To examine concurrent validity, Grann and Wedin compared SARA-V2 total scores with five measures of general violence recidivism. The SARA-V2 total score correlated significantly with all five measures: (1) number of previous convictions ($r = 0.39$); (2) number of previous violent convictions ($r = 0.29$); (3) ratings on the PCL-R ($r = 0.59$); (4) the Historical items of the HCR-20 (Webster, Douglas, Eaves, & Hart, 1997; $r = 0.46$); and (5) the VRAG ($r = 0.33$). The researchers' hypothesis that Part 1 of the SARA-V2 would correlate more strongly with measures of general recidivism than Part 2 of the SARA-V2 was substantiated (e.g., for the VRAG; Part 1 of the SARA-V2, $r = 0.49$ and Part 2, $r = -0.01$). The SARA-V2 thus exhibited both convergent (Part 1) and divergent (Part 2) validity with established measures of general violence risk prediction.

Heckert and Gondolf (2004)

This study attempted to examine the incremental predictive power of female spousal violence victims' perceptions of risk for future violence over the use of conventional risk assessment instruments. The sample comprised 840 men from four U.S. cities, 82% of whom were court-mandated to attend domestic violence treatment. Three risk assessment instruments were used in the study (SARA-V2, Danger Assessment, and the Kingston Screening Instrument for Domestic Violence (K-SID; Gelles & Tolman, 1998), and all risk factor scores were derived from the researchers' comprehensive dataset. It was acknowledged that most potential risk factors were included in their dataset, but only "simulated" (p. 787) versions of all of the risk instruments could be ascertained. However, only 10 items of the SARA-V2 were used as recommended by the authors of the tool, with 6 items of the SARA-V2 being "similar" to and 4 items "unavailable" in the file information provided; it could be argued that only 50% of the SARA-V2 items were reliably applied. Summary risk ratings were not used and "simulated" actuarial scores served as the only measure of risk. This estimated SARA-V2 total score demonstrated modest predictive capability (AUC = 0.64). The SARA-V2 AUC was greater than the K-SID (AUC = 0.57), but lower than that DA (AUC = 0.70) in predicting multiple outcomes, but the authors did not indicate if these differences were statistically significant.

Hilton, Harris, Rice, Lang, and Cormier (2004)

Hilton and her colleagues included the SARA-V2 in their validation research of Ontario Domestic Assault Risk Assessment Guide (ODARA). The development sample data for the ODARA was obtained from the Ontario Provincial Police, and the sample was considered typically representative of aggressive spousal assaulters. A total of 589 offenders were included in the construction sample, and an additional 100 offenders were used in the cross-validation sample. The measures were coded from files by individuals with "extensive" risk assessment experience and graduate research assistants who were trained and closely supervised. The authors noted that "the integrity of . . . SARA scores cannot be guaranteed because the interviews and clinical judgments recommended by their authors were not available" (p. 271).

In the timeframe under review, one third of the subjects in the study recidivated violently against a female partner. The ROC Area Under the Curve (AUC) for the SARA-V2 was reported to be 0.64, which was less than the ODARA (AUC = 0.77) but greater than another risk assessment instrument, the Danger Assessment (AUC = 0.59). ROC analyses were repeated with a cross-validation sample ($n = 100$), but the SARA-V2 total score was not significantly related to recidivism in that sample. Finally, the total score on the SARA-V2 was correlated with the ODARA ($r = 0.60$), providing evidence of concurrent validity between the SARA and the newly developed actuarial instrument.

Williams and Houghton (2004)

This study focused primarily on the concurrent and predictive validity of the Domestic Violence Screening Instrument (DVSI; Williams & Houghton, 2004), but SARA-V2 results were included for comparison purposes. The research was conducted with a sample of 1465 men arrested within a 9-month period for committing an act of violence against female intimate partners. The SARA-V2 was administered post-adjudication by probation officers trained by staff that had attended a training workshop by the developers of the tool. The SARA-V2 ratings were completed on a subsample of 434 offenders using all relevant sources of information (i.e., interview with the perpetrator and victim, and collection of collateral material).

ROC analyses were used to determine the predictive validity of the two instruments. The total SARA-V2 scores and a weighted version of the SARA-V2, which incorporated a summary risk rating (i.e., risk for violence against a partner), were used in the analyses. Both the SARA-V2 total scores (AUC = 0.65) and the weighted SARA-V2 scores (AUC = 0.65) predicted spousal violence recidivism significantly better than chance. The SARA-V2 total score and weighted SARA-V2 score AUCs were 0.70 and 0.71, respectively, when predicting general recidivism. The authors reported that the predictive accuracy of the DVSI was slightly less than that of the SARA-V2, but this difference was not statistically significant. It was also noted that the predictive accuracy of both the actuarial and structured judgment (i.e., summary risk ratings) components of the SARA-V2 performed equally well.

Williams and Houghton also assessed the concurrent validity of the SARA-V2 by correlating the total scores of the SARA-V2 and the DVSI. The level of agreement between the two instruments was moderate ($r = 0.54$). Additionally, when comparing the DVSI and the SARA-V2 summary risk ratings, the level of agreement was slightly greater ($r = 0.57$).

Cairns (2004)

The SARA-V2 was included in a comprehensive evaluation of a domestic violence treatment program in Alberta, Canada. In this prospective research, 231 spousal assaulters were assessed with the SARA-V2 using all available information, including an interview with the offender, at intake to the program. Predictive validity of the SARA-V2 was measured by recording new breach of release conditions immediately before or during the treatment program. The average follow-up period was approximately six months. Of 39 documented breach cases considered, one (2.5%) was assessed as low risk on the SARA-V2, 17 (45.9%) at moderate risk, and 21 (55.3%) at high risk. These rates are in comparison to proportions of 17% low, 47% moderate, and 36% high risk in the total sample. Odds ratios indicated high-risk offenders were 2.5 times more likely to breach conditions than a combined low/moderate-risk group. Alternatively, moderate/high-risk offenders were 9.4 times more likely than low-risk offenders to breach conditions. The AUC for partner reported IPV recidivism over a 10-month follow-up was 0.69 for SARA-V2 summary risk ratings. The statistical significance of the AUC was not reported.

Wong and Hisashima (2008)

This was primarily a concurrent and predictive validity study using the SARA-V2 and the DVSI (Domestic Violence Screening Instrument) in the State of Hawaii. In total, 196 SARA-V2 assessments were completed on IPV perpetrators between 2003 and 2007. The assessments were completed by probation officers who had received training on the SARA-V2. Approximately 440 DVSI assessments were also completed during this time interval. A 3-month minimum follow-up period for recidivism was included.

In terms of concurrent validity, the correlation between the SARA-V2 and DVSI was significant ($r = 0.54$, $p < 0.01$). An additional comparison to the Level of Service Inventory-Revised (LSI-R; see Wormith & Bonta, Chapter 8, this volume) revealed a moderate correlation with the SARA-V2 ($r = 0.43$, $p < 0.01$). These results were suggestive of adequate concurrent validity of the SARA-V2. Regarding predictive validity analyses, 32% of a high-risk SARA-V2 group and 17% of a combined low/moderate-risk SARA-V2 group were re-arrested for an IPV offense, $\chi2 = 4.75$, $p < 0.05$. Overall, the authors recommended the use of the SARA-V2 and the DVSI in Hawaii, albeit with caution due to the small sample size (due to lowered completion rates of the SARA-V2 by probation officers) and brief follow-up period for recidivism.

Andrés-Pueyo, López, and Álvarez (2008)

This was the first validation study of the Spanish version of the SARA-V2. A retrospective design was used, with file review of a sample of 102 couples that were involved with the Barcelona Provincial Criminal Court in 2004 and 2005. Legal and technical reports were reviewed in order to complete the SARA-V2. Additionally, the couples were followed for a period of 12 months to assess for IPV recidivism. Once again, a limitation of this study was that summary risk ratings were not produced; analyses used only total SARA-V2 scores.

Sixty percent of the aggressors reoffended in the follow-up period. The authors noted that the SARA-V2 provided "high predictive capacity" in terms of correctly classifying 85% of the aggressors and 72% of the non-aggressors. Individuals whose score was above the mean total score for the sample were six times more likely to offend than those below the mean ($\chi2 = 16.8$,

$p < 0.0001$; OR = 5.77). The authors concluded by noting that the SARA-V2 allows for decision-making that permits the adjustment of interventions to ensure the management of an IPV aggressor and protects the victim in an ongoing dynamic manner.

Gibas, Kropp, Hart, and Stewart (2008)

Using a correctional sample, 108 male IPV offenders were assessed using the SARA-V2 shortly before their release into the community. The offenders were followed in the community for at least 6 months. Summary risk ratings were initially identified pre-release as: low (27%), moderate (28%), or high (45%).

Summary risk ratings and IPV-related recidivism were strongly related, $\chi2 = 18.7$, $p < 0.001$. That is, 8% in the low-risk group, 17% in the moderate-risk group, and 31% in the high-risk group committed new spousal offenses during the follow-up period. Part I ($r = 0.17$, $p < 0.05$), Part II ($r = 0.33$, $p < 0.01$), and the SARA-V2 total scores ($r = 0.31$, $p < 0.01$) were also significantly associated with IPV recidivism. The summary risk ratings and spousal recidivism evidenced the strongest association, with $r = 0.40$, $p < 0.01$. Incremental validity was demonstrated, with the SARA-V2 total score predicting new spousal offenses above that predicted with the Statistical Information on Recidivism Scale (SIR) score, which is a measure of general recidivism risk; $B = 1.37$, $p = 0.01$. In sum, the results of this study lent further support for: (1) the application of structured professional judgment in the assessment of violence risk; and, additionally, (2) the use of a specific measure for assessing spousal violence risk rather than a generic measure of risk.

Rud, Skilling, and Nonemaker (2010)

This was a retrospective file-based study focused on the predictive validity of the DVSI and SARA-V2, both of which were being used at the Hennepin County Department of Community Corrections and Rehabilitation (DOCCR) Domestic Violence Unit (the DVSI as a screening tool, the SARA-V2 as a case management tool for those screened as high risk by the DVSI). The sample ($N = 1497$) was comprised primarily of male offenders referred to the specialized unit in 2001. Follow-up recidivism data were gathered from a statewide case management system.

The 8-year IPV and general recidivism rates were 41% and 56%, respectively. The majority of IPV reoffenses occurred within four years of the initial assessment. Concurrent validity was established with a highly significant correlation between the DVSI and SARA-V2 (Spearman's $rho = 0.67$, $p < 0.001$). There were also significant correlations between the SARA-V2 and IPV conviction and general conviction scores; offenders with higher-risk scores had higher rates of subsequent convictions. The SARA-V2 was identified as having a stronger correlation with first-time IPV offenders and *female* offenders. The DVSI was more highly correlated for repeat IPV offenders.

Receiver Operating Characteristic (ROC) analysis was conducted to compare the DVSI and SARA-V2 in terms of predicting IPV and general recidivism, although no AUCs were provided. A conclusory opinion was that both tools were "excellent" and could appropriately classify IPV offenders.

Belfrage, Strand, Storey, Gibas, Kropp, and Hart (2011)

This prospective study examined the utility of the SARA-V2 when used by officers from the Swedish national police. Officers who had been trained in use of the tool used it in all reported IPV cases to assess risk and develop case management plans. Recidivism data were gathered from police records during an 18-month follow-up period. In total, 429 male-to-female IPV perpetrator cases were identified.

Rather than interrater reliability, the stability of SARA-V2 ratings were investigated for 93 perpetrators with multiple police contacts. The mean SARA-V2 total score after the first police contact was 11.48 (SD = 6.08) and, subsequently, was 13.04 (SD = 6.28). The stability between first and second contacts was considered high, with an ICC_1 of 0.76. In examining summary risk ratings, there was an increase in risk judgment across the two points of contact (McNemar's $\chi 2$ = 9.77, p = 0.021). Despite this increase in risk, the stability of summary risk ratings between the initial and second contact was fair, ICC_1 = 0.45. These results suggested that police officers were able to effectively code the SARA-V2.

Consistent with previous research with the SARA-V2, the total scores and summary risk ratings were significantly correlated with the number of recommended risk management strategies (both r = 0.40, p < 0.001). In keeping with the *risk principle*, a higher number of management strategies was recommended for designated higher-risk cases. Predictive validity was assessed via determinations that higher scores on the SARA-V2 were associated with recidivism. That is, point-biserial correlations between recidivism and total SARA-V2 scores was significant, rpb = 0.18, p < 0.001. The total SARA-V2 score of recidivists was 11.45 (SD = 6.10) compared to non-recidivists at 8.86 (SD = 5.84; $t(92)$ = 3.79, p < 0.001, Cohen's d = 0.43). Lastly, ROC analyses yielded an AUC of 0.63. As such, these results suggested that the unmediated association between recidivism and SARA-V2 total scores was small-to-moderate in effect. Similar analyses supplanting the SARA-V2 total scores with summary risk ratings were less significant, with only a small magnitude of association between recidivism and summary risk. Additional analyses indicated that risk management strategies mediated the association between risk assessment (SARA total scores) and recidivism. In particular, high-risk IPV perpetrators with many recommended management strategies were less likely to have subsequent contacts with police than high-risk IPV perpetrators with few management recommendations. Alternatively, low-risk perpetrators with many management strategies were more likely to have subsequent contacts with police than low-risk perpetrators with few recommended management strategies. Both of these findings are in keeping with the Risk-Need-Responsivity principles. Overall, the authors opined that the results of the research support the use of the SARA-V2 by police officers in assessing risk for IPV and associated risk management decisions. The authors highlighted that this was the first study to demonstrate that the SARA-V2 may be useful in the prevention of violence, not just risk assessment and management.

Ryan (2016)

Using a sample of 97 IPV offenders from a forensic psychiatric setting, this was the first study to evaluate the interrater reliability (IRR) and concurrent validity of the SARA-V3. A subsample of 30 cases was used for the IRR analyses. Results showed moderate to strong interrater reliability (i.e., intraclass correlation coefficients—or ICCs—ranging from .41 to .92) for most of the individual Nature of IPV (N) and Perpetrator (P) factors. Some of the individual items had low ICCs, but the author reported that this was due to restricted range within the sample. With respect to the summary risk ratings, ICCs (averaged ratings) for Case Prioritization, Risk for Serious Physical Harm, and Risk for Imminent Violence were .57, .81, and .58 respectively. ICCs for SARA-V3 total scores were .73 for N factors, .89 for P factors, and .85 for N + P factors. Analyses for the Victim Vulnerability factors could not be conducted due to insufficient information available to code these items.

Next, the Ryan study examined the association between the SARA-V3 and other measures of IPV risk including the SARA-V2, B-SAFER, ODARA, DVRAG (Domestic Violence Risk Appraisal Guide), and DA. Importantly, the correlations between SARA-V3 and SARA-V2 domain scores were moderate to large, indicating that the two tools remain similar in content.

Further, the SARA-V3 ratings of Case Prioritization, Serious Physical Harm, and Imminent Violence all had statistically significant correlations (. 31, .30, and .28) with the SARA-V2 Summary Risk Rating. Overall, Ryan (2016) concluded there was strong concurrent validity between the SARA-V3 and SARA-V2. Further, the study found similarly strong associations between the SARA-V3 and the B-SAFER, ODARA, DVRAG, and DA.

Jung and Buro (2017)

This study investigated the predictive validity of a "modified 14-item version" of the SARA-V2, the ODARA, and a regional approach named the Family Violence Investigative Report (FVIR). Results showed a strong correlation between the ODARA and the SARA-V2 ($r = 0.72$, $p < .001$). Using the total score for the 14 items (notably not the recommended procedure), the modified SARA-V2 had large and statistically significant effect sizes in predicting convictions for any reoffending, violent reoffending, and IPV offending (AUCs were 0.76, 0.72, and 0.74 respectively). A comparison of measures showed that the ODARA and modified SARA-V2 had larger (statistically significant in the case of the ODARA but not the SARA-V2) effect sizes than the FVIR. No differences in predictive accuracy were found between the SARA-V2 and the ODARA.

Olver and Jung (2017)

In a follow up study to Jung and Buro (2017), this paper examined the incremental predictive validity of a 17-item version of the SARA-V2, the ODARA, and the FVIR. The authors reported that the 17-item and 14-item (from the Jung and Buro investigation) versions had "virtually identical" AUCs. Indeed, the reported AUCs for the 17-item SARA-V2 when predicting general, violent, and IPV recidivism were .78, .74, and .74, respectively, all statistically significant at $p < .001$. The study reported strong convergent validity amongst the three measures. Overall, the authors reported that the modified SARA-V2—again with the caveat that total scores, not summary risk ratings, were used—outperformed the ODARA and the FVIR in predicting IPV recidivism, although the incremental validity of the SARA-V2 when controlling for the other measures only approached statistical significance ($p < .063$). The authors also concluded that the ODARA added incremental validity over the other measures in predicting general recidivism, and suggested there might be some advantage in using the SARA-V2 and ODARA tools concurrently in IPV risk assessment.

Schafers (2019)

In a repeated-measures study of 88 men enrolled in a community-based IPV treatment program, risk for IPV was measured pre- and post-treatment using the SARA-V3 and ODARA. Only the N and P factors could be scored on the SARA-V3, once again due to unavailable information on victims, and summary risk ratings were not utilized. Results indicated strong correlations between the pre-treatment SARA-V3 and ODARA total scores ($r = .59$), providing further support for the convergent validity of both measures. Further, treatment attrition (dropout) was associated with higher SARA-V3 scores ($r = .45$). Importantly, the investigator found that post-treatment SARA-V3 P factor scores were reduced during the follow-up period ($d = 1.57$, $p < .001$), suggesting that the SARA-V3 is indeed dynamic in nature and able to detect changes in risk. Results also indicated that pre-treatment SARA-V3 significantly predicted recidivism; Cox regression analysis found that for every 1-point increase on the SARA-V3, the likelihood of general and violent recidivism increased by 11% and 10%, respectively. Pre-treatment SARA-V3 total scores produced AUCs of .75 ($p < .001$) for general recidivism and .68 ($p < .059$) for violent recidivism. Perhaps most interestingly, *changes* in SARA-V3 total scores and P factor scores both significantly predicted fewer new charges for violent and nonviolent reoffending. The author argued that these results support the use of the SARA-V3 as a risk management tool for tracking and affecting changes in risk that can indeed help prevent further violent behavior. Like the Belfrage et al. (2011) study, it appears to offer support for the risk principle commonly cited in correctional literature.

Conclusions

It appears that the various versions of the SARA guidelines remain popular instruments for those conducting IPV risk assessments. Feedback from participants in the hundreds of workshops conducted by the authors of the guidelines suggests that professionals appreciate the practical utility, flexibility, and discretion involved in the procedure. The authors of the SARA-V3 have also been developing administrative software and online training programs to further assist practitioners in providing reliable and time-efficient risk assessments. Practical considerations aside, it is also apparent that empirical evidence regarding the reliability and validity of SARA-V2 is well established, although we have noted in this chapter that much of the published research on the SARA has been flawed by the misapplication of the instrument. Future validation research is needed that utilizes the recommended SARA-V3 procedures, especially the steps involving risk factor relevance and scenario planning. Further, since the SARA is designed to prevent violence, the most useful research will not necessarily investigate the predictive validity of the SARA-V3, but rather the association between SARA risk assessments, risk management strategies, and violence reduction (e.g., Belfrage et al., 2011; Schafers, 2019). Finally, research and commentary on the use of the SARA-V3 (and other risk assessment tools) in assisting multi-agency (i.e., involving law enforcement, victim agencies, child protection agencies, corrections, mental health, faith-based groups, and so forth) approaches to risk management would be a welcome addition to the field.

Case Study

The following case study is presented to illustrate the use of the SARA-V3. For the purposes of this chapter, the report is condensed and briefer than what we would typically recommend in practice. However, it contains the essential elements of a SARA-V3 risk assessment.

Referral Information

Mr. K. is currently before the court on bail for one count of threatening, contrary to Section 264.1 of the Criminal Code of Canada. The victim of the threatening is his wife, Sandra K. One of the conditions of his Recognizance of Bail order is that he attend this Forensic Psychiatric Outpatient Clinic for an intimate partner violence (IPV) risk assessment. This report is based on a review of the following information: (1) Copy of the police report; (2) 90-minute interview with Mr. K.; (3) 60-minute interview with Mr. K.'s wife, the victim; and (4) criminal record information on Mr. K. At the outset of the interview the purpose of the assessment and limits of confidentiality were explained to Mr. K., who stated he understood these issues as explained to him and consented to the assessment.

Background

Personal History

Mr. K.'s description of his childhood lacked detail, but he communicated that he grew up in an environment of extreme neglect. He indicated that at age 7 his mother left him "somewhere." He could not be specific about the circumstances but recalled feeling "scared." He indicated that this pattern of being passed from caretaker to caretaker (usually relatives and "babysitters") continued throughout his childhood. Mr. K. commented that he was physically abused as a child, but he could not recall who committed the assaults. He then tearfully described an experience occurring between ages 8 and 10 that involved being sodomized on several occasions by a babysitter. He added that this was the first time that he had ever disclosed this information.

This individual reported he had difficulty in school, particularly with reading, and only completed grade 7. He believes he was diagnosed with a learning disorder, but he could not be specific. He does not admit to committing a great deal of delinquent behavior as a child, but he admitted to some shoplifting, fighting, and setting fire to outhouses. He stated that he was frequently truant, and was eventually expelled for missing too much school. Mr. K. acknowledged that he has a juvenile criminal record. He stated that he did spend some time in juvenile detention. Police records indicate that Mr. K. had five convictions as a juvenile for property offenses.

Mr. K. has been employed primarily through various labor positions, but has spent much of the past 10 years unemployed and collecting income assistance. He considers himself a reliable employee, although he admitted to having been fired on three occasions. He added that one of the dismissals was due to his alcohol use, which resulted in his arriving late. He explained that he was recently fired from work as a "mechanic's helper" because of his poor attendance. He is concerned about his financial situation and is currently in considerable debt due to a car loan, unpaid bills, and lack of employment.

Mr. K. described three long-term relationships with women (including his current relationship with Sandra), all of which involved frequent arguments and verbal abuse on his part. He admitted to past physical assaults of female partners and mentioned that, on a couple of occasions, he has forced Sandra to have sex with him. He has one previous criminal conviction for assaulting Sandra. He has a 4-year-old stepson with Sandra. According to Sandra, their son has witnessed the domestic violence.

Current Offense and Criminality

Mr. K. was advised by counsel not to discuss the circumstances around the alleged offense. According to Sandra's statement to the police, the incident occurred 5 days ago, one day after Mr. K. was fired from his job. That evening he telephoned Sandra from a pub where he was drinking with friends. He asked her to join them at the pub but she refused because it was too late to find a babysitter for her son. He began to berate Sandra for being "a drag," "a sexual bore," and "caring more for that kid than for me." He then told her that he had been fired and that she should be there to support him. When she still refused, his anger began to escalate and he began threatening her: "You're going to get it when I get home, I'm going to fucking kill you . . . I thought you learned your lesson last time." Two of Mr. K.'s associates at the bar witnessed the threat. Before Mr. K. could return home, Sandra phoned the police, who arrested Mr. K. at the bar. He refused to take full responsibility for the incident with the examiner, as he placed some of the blame on Sandra for what he described as "turning on me." Since his arrest for threatening, Mr. K. has complied with his release conditions.

According to the official criminal record, Mr. K. has three prior convictions for assault, one against Sandra and the others against a previous intimate partner. There are no other violent offenses on record. Otherwise, he has 13 convictions for property offenses (theft and fraud), and three convictions for drug possession. He has violated a conditional release on one occasion by contacting Sandra by telephone, contrary to a no-contact order following his previous assault conviction. Mr. K. has never been convicted of using a weapon or threatening to use a weapon in past offenses, but Sandra indicated that he owns two hunting rifles and that he has threatened to use them against her in the past.

Mental Health History

Mr. K. denied experiencing any significant emotional or behavioral problems in the past. He stated that he has never seen a psychologist, psychiatrist, or any other mental health professional. He admitted to an extensive history of alcohol and drug abuse. He reported that he began drinking at approximately age 11 and began using cocaine at age 15. Both alcohol and cocaine have adversely affected virtually every aspect of his life (i.e., social, occupational, and familial functioning). His last alcohol and cocaine binge was 5 days ago.

On examination, Mr. K. looked his stated age of 32. He maintained an appropriate social presentation throughout the interview. Eye contact was appropriate, and there was no evidence of unusual behavior. Mr. K. periodically wept during the interview, usually when the content focused on his childhood or his current circumstances. He expressed concern about reconciling with Sandra, and admitted that he would probably "lose it" if he was sent to jail. With respect to his mood, he conceded that he feels sad and has had frequent thoughts about suicide. He also admitted feeling anxious if he is not active, and complained that at such times thoughts will race through his head, causing discomfort. Mr. K. demonstrated little insight into his violent behavior. He attributed his past assaults to "drinking" and appeared to have some notion that he has "pent-up" feelings and anger. He indicated some interest in receiving treatment, and believes that it would help to talk to other men "like me."

There did not appear to be any distortions either in the form or content of his thinking that would indicate the presence of a major mental disorder. His memory for recent and remote events was adequate. His attention and concentration also appeared unimpaired. He denied experiencing any hallucinations or delusions. However, he does appear to have some antisocial and borderline personality traits.

Summary of Sandra K's Statement

Mrs. K. described her husband as an extremely violent man. She noted that he has assaulted her physically, verbally, and sexually. She has observed that he seems to have an attitude of "ownership" with respect to his intimate partners and is extremely jealous. She also indicated that she has witnessed him assaulting his brothers, friends, and strangers (e.g., bar fights). Mrs. K. also described her husband's behavior as impulsive and often associated with alcohol or drug intake and withdrawal. She believes that any remorse for his actions is short-lived. She also noted that the severity of her husband's violence appears to be increasing over time. She denied that weapons had ever been used in the assaults but did report that he has threatened to use weapons "a few times" to manipulate her. Sandra explained that she has reached her limit and will be seeking a separation.

Risk Assessment and Management

To assist in formulating an opinion about risk in this case, I consulted the Spousal Assault Risk Assessment Guide—Version 3 (SARA-V3), a set of structured professional guidelines for assessing risk for intimate partner violence (IPV). Based on a review of the SARA-V3, it is clear that Mr. K. has a number of risk factors associated with IPV. With respect to the *nature* of his IPV history, he has an established pattern of IPV against multiple partners that includes intimidation, threats, and physical and sexual violence. Further it appears that he has violated an IPV supervision condition on at least one occasion, and his pattern of IPV appears to be chronic and escalating. With respect to *perpetrator* risk factors, there is evidence that Mr. K. has problems with intimate relationships (that includes an imminent separation), employment, antisocial behaviors and attitudes, possible personality disorder traits, substance abuse, possible suicidality, and distorted thinking about IPV.

The most likely violent scenario will involve intimation, threats, and physical violence following real or perceived rejection or insult from an intimate partner. The conflict or triggers to his violence would likely involve jealousy, proprietary attitudes, or a motivation of power, control, or retribution. Further, based on his past pattern of violence and threats, it is plausible that the violence could be severe and involve weapons and sexual violence. The potential victims of this violence are Mrs. K. and any future intimate partners. It is also possible that Mr. K. could present a risk to any new intimate partners of Mrs. K. Overall, it is my opinion that Mr. K. represents a high priority for IPV case management due to the large amount of resources that will be needed to control his risk. Further, he is of moderate risk to engage in life-threatening violence and a high risk for imminent violence due to his difficulty in accepting his recent marital separation. The potential victims of his violence are Mrs. K. and any future intimate partners. It is also possible that Mr. K. could present a risk to any new intimate partners of Mrs. K.

Mr. K.'s risk for violence should be managed through a combination of monitoring, supervision, treatment, and victim safety planning strategies. Therefore, those supervising Mr. K. should monitor for signs of further deterioration in his relationship, employment and financial status, and mental state. It is recommended that frequent contacts be made with both Mr. and Mrs. K. to monitor his whereabouts and any attempts to contact the victim. Supervision strategies should include a no-contact order with Mrs. K., and an order not to attend her residence or workplace. He should also be prohibited from possessing weapons and consuming drugs or alcohol, and mandatory urinalysis could be considered. While on supervision in the community, electronic monitoring might also be a useful surveillance strategy. Regarding treatment, Mr. K. would benefit from attending a spousal violence treatment program and substance abuse counseling. Finally, it should be ensured that Mrs. K. has a victim safety plan in place: She should be informed of available victim services, the contact information for her local shelter, supportive counseling, and a review of security options at her home and workplace.

References

Abramsky, T., Watts, C. H., Garcia-Moreno, C., Devries, K. M., Kiss, L., Ellsberg, M., . . . Heise, L. (2011). What factors are associated with recent intimate partner violence? findings from the WHO multi-country study on women's health and domestic violence. *BMC Public Health, 11*, 109–125.

American Psychological Association. (2002). Criteria for practice guideline development and evaluation. *American Psychologist, 57*, 1048–1051.

Andrés-Pueyo, A., López, S., & Álvarez, E. (2008). Assessment of the risk of intimate partner violence and the SARA. *Papeles del Psicologo, 29*(1).

Andrews, D. A., Bonta, J., & Wormith, J. S. (1995). *Level of service inventory-Ontario revision (LSI-OR): Interview and scoring guide.* Toronto, ON: Ontario Ministry of the Solicitor General and Correctional Services.

Archer, J. (2000). Sex differences in aggression between heterosexual partners: A meta-analytic review. *Psychological Bulletin, 126*, 651–680.

Belfrage, H., & Strand, S. (2014). Measuring the outcome of structured spousal violence risk assessments using the B-SAFER: Risk in relation to recidivism and intervention. *Behavioral Sciences and the Law, 30*, 420–430.

Belfrage, H., Strand, S., Storey, J., Gibas, A., Kropp, P. R., & Hart, S. D. (2012). Assessment and management of risk for intimate partner violence by police officers using the spousal assault risk assessment guide (SARA). *Law and Human Behavior, 36*, 60–67.

Bennett Cattaneo, L., & Goodman, L. A. (2005). Risk factors for reabuse in intimate partner violence: A cross-disciplinary critical review. *Trauma, Violence and Abuse, 6*, 141–175.

Bowen, E. (2011). An overview of partner violence risk assessment and the potential role of female victim risk appraisals. *Aggression and Violent Behavior, 16*, 214–226.

Cairns, K. V. (2004). *Alberta mental health board domestic violence treatment program evaluation: Report to the partnering ministries committee.* Edmonton, AB: Alberta Mental Health Board.

Campbell, J. C. (1995). Prediction of homicide of and by battered women. In J. C. Campbell (Ed.), *Assessing dangerousness: Violence by sexual offenders, batterers, and child abusers* (pp. 96–113). Thousand Oaks, CA: Sage.

Campbell, J. C., Webster, D., & Glass, N. (2009). The danger assessment: Validation of a lethality risk assessment for intimate partner femicide. *Journal of Interpersonal Violence, 24*, 653–674.

Capaldi, D. M., Knoble, N. B., Shortt, J. W., & Kim, H. K. (2012). A systematic review of risk factors for intimate partner violence. *Partner Abuse, 3*, 231–280.

Cook, A., Hart, S. D., & Kropp, P. R. (2015). *Multi-level guidelines (MLG) for the assessment and management of group-based violence.* Vancouver, BC: Protect International Risk and Safety Services Inc.

Cooke, D., & Michie, C. (2003, April). *Content-related validity of the SARA: A psychometric evaluation.* Paper presented at the annual meeting of the International Association of Forensic Mental Health Services, Miami, FL.

Douglas, K. S., Hart, S. D., Webster, C. D., & Belfrage, H. (2013). *HCR-20-V3: Assessing risk for violence.* Burnaby, BC: Mental Health, Law, and Policy Institute, Simon Fraser University.

Dutton, D., & Kropp, P. R. (2000). A review of domestic violence risk instruments. *Trauma, Violence, & Abuse, 1*(2), 171–181.

Gelles, R., & Tolman, R. (1998). *The Kingston screening instrument for domestic violence (KSID).* Unpublished risk instrument, University of Rhode Island, Providence.

Gibas, A., Kropp, P. R., Hart, S. D., & Stewart, L. (2008, July). *Validity of the SARA in a Canadian sample of incarcerated males.* Paper presented at the Annual Conference of the International Association of Forensic Mental Health Services, Vienna, Austria.

Grann, M., & Wedin, I. (2002). Risk factors for recidivism among spousal assault and spousal homicide offenders. *Psychology, Crime, and Law, 8*, 5–23.

Guy, L. S. (2008). *Performance indicators of the structured professional judgment approach for assessing risk for violence to others: A meta-analytic survey* (Unpublished dissertation). Simon Fraser University, Burnaby, BC.

Hanson, K., Helmus, L., & Bourgon, G. (2007). *The validity of risk assessment for intimate partner violence: A meta-analysis.* Ottawa: Public Safety Canada.

Hart, S. D., Cox, D. N., & Hare, R. D. (1995). *Manual for the Hare psychopathy checklist: Screening version (PCL: SV).* Toronto, ON: Multi-Health Systems.

Hart, S. D., Douglas, K. S., & Webster, C. D. (2001). Risk management using the HCR-20: A general overview focusing on historical factors. In K. S. Douglas, C. D. Webster, S. D. Hart, D. Eaves, & J. R. P. Ogloff (Eds.), *HCR-20 violence risk management companion guide* (pp. 27–40). Burnaby, BC: Mental Health, Law, and Policy Institute, Simon Fraser University.

Hart, S. D., Kropp, P. R., Laws, D. R., Klaver, J., Logan, C., & Watt, K. A. (2003). *The risk for sexual violence protocol (RSVP): Structured professional guidelines for assessing risk of sexual violence.* Burnaby, BC: Mental Health, Law, and Policy Institute, Simon Fraser University and Pacific Psychological Assessment Corporation.

Heckert, D. A., & Gondolf, E. W. (2004). Battered women's perceptions of risk versus risk factors and instruments in predicting repeated reassault. *Journal of Interpersonal Violence, 19*, 778–800.

Helmus, L., & Bourgon, G. (2011). Taking stock of 15 years of research on the spousal assault risk assessment guide (SARA): A critical review. *International Journal of Forensic Mental Health, 10*, 64–75.

Hilton, N. Z., & Harris, G. T. (2005). Predicting wife assault: A critical review and implications for policy and practice. *Trauma, Violence, & Abuse, 6*(1), 3–23.

Hilton, N. Z., Harris, G. T., & Rice, M. E. (2010). *Risk assessment for domestically violent men.* Washington, DC: American Psychological Association.

Hilton, N. Z., Harris, G. T., Rice, M. E., Lang, C., & Cormier, C. A. (2004). A brief actuarial assessment for the prediction of wife assault recidivism: The ODARA. *Psychological Assessment, 16*(3), 267–275.

Jung, S., & Buro, K. (2017). Appraising risk for intimate partner violence in a police context. *Criminal Justice and Behavior, 44*, 240–260.

Kropp, P. R. (2008). Intimate partner violence risk assessment and management. *Violence and Victims, 23*, 202–220.

Kropp, P. R., Belfrage, H., & Hart, S. D. (2013). *Assessment of risk for honour based violence (PATRIARCH): User manual*. Vancouver, BC: Protect International Risk and Safety Services Inc.

Kropp, P. R., & Hart, S. D. (2000). The spousal assault risk assessment (SARA) guide: Reliability and validity in adult male offenders. *Law and Human Behavior, 24*, 101–118.

Kropp, P. R., Hart, S. D., & Belfrage. (2010). *Brief spousal assault form for the evaluation of risk (B-SAFER)*. Vancouver, BC: Protect International Risk and Safety Services Inc.

Kropp, P. R., Hart, S. D., & Lyon, D. R. (2008). *Guidelines for stalking assessment and management (SAM)*. Vancouver, BC: Protect International Risk and Safety Services Inc.

Kropp, P. R., Hart, S. D., Lyon, D. R., & LePard, D. (2002). Managing stalking: Coordinating, treatment and supervision. In J. Boon & L. Sheridan (Eds.), *Stalking and psychosexual obsession: Psychological perspectives for prevention, policing and treatment* (pp. 105–124). Chichester: Wiley.

Kropp, R. P., Hart, S. D., Webster, C. D., & Eaves, D. (1994). *Manual for the spousal assault risk assessment guide*. Vancouver, BC: The British Columbia Institute Against Family Violence.

Kropp, R. P., Hart, S. D., Webster, C. D., & Eaves, D. (1995). *Manual for the spousal assault risk assessment guide* (2nd ed.). Vancouver, BC: The British Columbia Institute Against Family Violence.

Kropp, P. R., Hart, S. D., Webster, C. W., & Eaves, D. (1999). *Spousal assault risk assessment: User's guide*. Toronto, ON: Multi-Health Systems.

Leen, E., Sorbring, E., Mawer, M., Holdsworth, E., Helsing, B., & Bowen, E. (2013). Prevalence, dynamic risk factors and the efficacy of primary interventions for adolescent dating violence: An international review. *Aggression and Violent Behavior, 18*, 159–174.

Loinaz, I. (2014). Typologies, risk and recidivism in partner-violent men with the B-SAFER: A pilot study. *Psychology, Crime & Law, 20*(2), 183–198.

Magdol, L., Moffitt, T. E., Caspi, A., Newman, D. L., Fagan, J., & Silva, P. A. (1997). Gender differences in partner violence in a birth cohort of 21-year-olds: Bridging the gap between clinical and epidemiological approaches. *Journal of Consulting and Clinical Psychology, 65*, 68–78.

Messing, J. T., & Thaller, J. (2013). The average predictive validity of intimate partner violence risk assessment instruments. *Journal of Interpersonal Violence, 28*, 1537–1558.

Mowat-Léger, V. (2001). *Risk factors for violence: A comparison of domestic batterers and other violent and non-violent offenders* (Unpublished doctoral dissertation). Carleton University, Ottawa.

Nicholls, T. L., Pritchard, M. M., Reeves, K. A., & Hilterman, E. (2013). Risk assessment in intimate partner violence: A systematic review of contemporary approaches. *Partner Abuse, 4*, 76–168.

Nuffield, J. (1982). *Parole decision-making in Canada: Research towards decision guidelines*. Ottawa: Ministry of Supplies and Services Canada.

Olver, M. E., & Jung, S. (2017). Incremental prediction of intimate partner violence: An examination of three risk measures. *Law and Human Behavior, 41*(5), 440–453.

Quinsey, V. L., Harris, G. T., Rice, G. T., & Cormier, C. A. (1998). *Violent offenders: Appraising and managing risk*. Washington, DC: American Psychological Association.

Richards, T. N., & Branch, K. A. (2012). The relationship between social support and adolescent dating violence: A comparison across genders. *Journal of Interpersonal Violence, 27*, 1540–1561.

Riggs, D. S., Caulfield, M. B., & Street, A. E. (2000). Risk for domestic violence: Factors associated with perpetration and victimization. *Journal of Clinical Psychology, 56*, 1289–1316.

Ringland, G. (1998). *Scenario planning: Managing for the future*. Chichester: Wiley.

Robertson, K., & Murachver, T. (2009). Attitudes and attributions associated with female and male partner violence. *Journal of Applied Social Psychology, 39*, 1481–1512.

Robinson, A. L. (2006). Reducing repeat victimization among high-risk victims of domestic violence: The benefits of a coordinated community response in Cardiff, Wales. *Violence Against Women, 12*, 761–788.

Robinson, A. L., & Tregidga, J. (2007). The perceptions of high-risk victims of domestic violence to a coordinated community response in Cardiff, Wales. *Violence Against Women, 13*, 1130–1148.

Rothman, E. F., Johnson, R. M., Azrael, D., Hall, D. M., & Weinberg, J. (2010). Perpetration of physical assault against dating partners, peers, and siblings among a locally representative sample of high school students in Boston, Massachusetts. *Archives of Pediatrics & Adolescent Medicine, 164*, 1118–1124.

Ryan, T. (2016). *An examination of the interrater reliability and concurrent validity of the spousal assault risk assessment guide: Version 3 (SARA-V3)* (Unpublished thesis). Simon Fraser University, Burnaby, BC.

Saunders, D. G., Lynch, A. B., Grayson, M., & Linz, D. (1987). The inventory of beliefs about wife beating: The construction and initial validation of a measure of beliefs and attitudes. *Violence and Victims, 2*, 39–57.

Schafers, C. L. (2019). *Risk, responsivity, and the treatment process in an intimate partner violence group program* (Unpublished dissertation). University of Saskatchewan, Saskatoon.

Schumacher, J. A., Feldbau-Kohn, S., Slep, A. M. S., & Heyman, R. E. (2001). Risk factors for male-to-female partner physical abuse. *Aggression and Violent Behavior, 6*, 281–352.

Schwartz, P. (1990). *The art of the long view.* New York: Doubleday.

Serie, C. M. B., van Tilburg, C. A., van Dam, A., & de Ruiter, C. (2017). Spousal assaulters in outpatient mental health care: The relevance of structured risk assessment. *Journal of Interpersonal Violence, 32*(11), 1658–1677.

Shepard, M. F., & Campbell, J. A. (1992). The abusive behavior inventory: A measure of psychological and physical abuse. *Journal of Interpersonal Violence, 7*, 291–305.

Singh, J. P., Grann, M., & Fazel, S. (2011). A comparative study of violence risk assessment tools: A systematic review and meta-regression analysis of 68 studies involving 25,980 participants. *Clinical Psychology Review, 31*, 499–513.

Stith, S. M., Smith, D. B., Penn, C. E., Ward, D. B., & Tritt, D. (2004). Intimate partner physical abuse perpetration and victimization risk factors: A meta-analytic review. *Aggression and Violent Behavior, 10*, 65–98.

Storey, J. E., Kropp, P. R., Hart, S. D., Belfrage, H., & Strand, S. (2014). Assessment and management of risk for intimate partner violence by police officers using the brief spousal assault form for the evaluation of risk. *Criminal Justice and Behavior, 41*(2), 256–271.

Storey, J. E., & Strand, S. (2013). Assessing violence risk among female IPV perpetrators: An examination of the B-SAFER. *Journal of Aggression, Maltreatment & Trauma, 22*(9), 964–980.

Thijssen, J., & de Ruiter, C. (2011). Identifying subtypes of spousal assaulters using the B-SAFER. *Journal of Interpersonal Violence, 26*(7), 1307–1321.

Van der Heijden, K. (1997). *Scenarios: The art of strategic conversation.* New York: Wiley.

Williams, K. R. (2012). Family violence risk assessment: A predictive cross-validation study of the domestic violence screening inventory—revised (DVSI-R). *Law and Human Behavior, 36*, 120–129.

Williams, K. R., & Houghton, A. B. (2004). Assessing the risk of domestic violence reoffending: A validation study. *Law and Human Behavior, 24*(4), 437–455.

Vest, J. R., Catlin, T. K., Chen, J. J., & Brownson, R. C. (2002). Multistate analysis of factors associated with intimate partner violence. *American Journal of Preventative Medicine, 22*, 156–164.

Wong, T., & Hisashima, M. A. (2008). *Domestic violence exploratory study on the DVSI and SARA, state of Hawaii 2003–2007.* Honolulu: Interagency Council on Intermediate Sanctions.

The Structured Assessment of Protective Factors for Violence Risk (SAPROF)

Michiel de Vries Robbé, Vivienne de Vogel, and Agnes Veldhuizen

Description of Measure

The *Structured Assessment of Protective Factors for violence risk* (SAPROF; de Vogel, de Ruiter, Bouman, & de Vries Robbé, 2009, 2012) is a structured professional judgment (SPJ) checklist for the assessment of protective factors for violence risk. It is the only SPJ risk assessment tool that focuses solely on protective factors. The tool was developed in response to the increasing desire by mental health professionals to include a focus on strengths in the violence risk assessment procedure for adults. Although the final risk judgment composed in any SPJ risk assessment inevitably implicitly incorporates the counterbalancing influence of positive factors that may compensate for the assessed risk factors, for a long time this aspect of the assessment process received little attention (de Ruiter & Nicholls, 2011; O'Shea & Dickens, 2016).

Whereas in treatment the focus on developing strengths in addition to reducing risks has been a natural two-sided approach, a shortcoming in the early days of SPJ risk assessment was the overreliance on risk factors while failing to explicitly include protective factors. Not surprisingly, the idea for including strengths in the assessment came from clinical practice. The SAPROF was developed in forensic psychiatric practice in the Netherlands in 2007. It was introduced as a strengths-based assessment tool designed to complement the structured assessment of violence risk as carried out with a wide range of commonly used risk-focused tools, such as the HCR-20 (Webster, Douglas, Eaves, & Hart, 1997). The aim of the SAPROF is to provide structure and empirical backup for the assessment of the positive side of the violence risk equation. The inclusion of protective factors is a critical component in any risk assessment. Without providing structured guidelines to assess the positive influence of empirically supported protective factors, the final risk judgment remains in part unstructured. Moreover, failing to recognize protective factors in the risk assessment process leads to imbalanced risk assessment that is inherently incomplete (Rogers, 2000).

In 2009, the English version of the SAPROF was published, which made the tool accessible for international use. The tool was received as a welcome addition to existing risk assessment practice and was quickly adopted by clinicians and researchers in various settings and countries. In the past 10 years, the tool has become a well-established component of international risk assessment practice. The SAPROF manual is now available in 17 different languages, including English, French, Spanish, and Japanese. A second edition of the manual was published in 2012, which contained an update of the introduction chapter; however, the content of the factors was not changed. The SAPROF contains 17 protective factors, organized in three scales: internal factors, motivational factors, and external factors (see Table 17.1). The first two items are historical in nature, while the remaining 15 are considered to be dynamic and thus changeable through intervention. The dynamic items are rated for the coming 6 to 12 months, similar to the R-items in the HCR-20. This implies the rating of the factors is context dependent. If a risk assessment is carried out in the light of decision-making regarding the most appropriate risk management (variations in context), different ratings could be given depending on the (hypothetical) situation the items are rated for. Thus, double rating is possible for each of the 15 dynamic factors for the different contexts proposed. For example, a patient with a history of substance abuse-related violence may demonstrate good self-control while supervised on community leaves by treatment staff; however, if this same individual is granted unsupervised leaves, his self-control may not be sufficient and thus the self-control rating will likely go down, given that the context has changed. This insight may help guide our decision regarding the feasibility of a change in risk management from supervised to unsupervised community visits for this individual.

The 17 SAPROF factors are rated as 0–1–2, with higher scores indicating the presence of protection on a certain domain. In order to be able to add nuance to the ratings and offer the potential to document smaller changes, the assessor has the opportunity to add a + or − to the numerical ratings, resulting in a 7-point rating scale (0, 0+, 1−, 1, 1+, 2−, 2). In addition to the rating of each of the 17 factors, the assessor is prompted to highlight those factors which are deemed most important to the individual who is being evaluated. Those factors which are pointed out as the strongest protective factors in place may be marked as 'Key' factors, while those factors seen as promising targets for treatment in the coming 6–12 months can be marked as 'Goal' factors (a maximum of four keys and four goals may be appointed). For one person, the Key factors may be *Self-control*, *Work* and *Social network*, while for another person they may be *Medication*, *Treatment motivation* and *Living circumstances*. Similarly, for one person it may be vital to improve *Coping* skills and *Self-control*, while for another the most promising Goal factors will be *Medication* and *Attitudes towards authority*. Through marking the most important Key and Goal factors for each individual, the risk assessment becomes more personalized. After rating the factors and highlighting Keys and Goals, the protective factors assessment concludes with a 'final protection judgment' on a 5-point scale: low-low/moderate-moderate-moderate/high-high protection for the assessed context.

The results from the protective factors assessment are then taken together with the results from the risk factors assessment as carried out by means of the preferred risk-focused tool (e.g., the HCR-20^{V3}; Douglas, Hart, Webster, & Belfrage, 2013—see Chapter 12, this volume; the VRS; Wong & Gordon, 1999–2003—see Chapter 10, this volume; or the SARA; Kropp & Hart, 2000—see Chapter 16, this volume). Based on the assessment of both the risk factors and the protective factors, the next steps in the assessment process are carried out: contemplating risk formulation narratives, consideration of possible risk scenarios, treatment and risk management planning, and finally the composition of an integrated overall final risk judgment. Similar to the final protection judgment, the final risk judgment is also recommended to be composed on a 5-point scale from low to high. The addition of the in-between categories of low/moderate and moderate/high offer the potential for more nuanced integrated final risk ratings. Although it seems most obvious to use an SPJ risk tool in conjunction with the SAPROF, it is also possible to use the SAPROF together with actuarial risk assessment tools, such as the VRAG (Quinsey, Harris, Rice, & Cormier, 1998—see Chapter 7, this volume), the LS/CMI (Andrews, Bonta, & Wormith, 2004—see Chapter 8, this volume), or the STABLE-2007 (Fernandez, Harris, Hanson, & Sparks, 2012—see Chapter 6, this volume). When using the SAPROF with an actuarial tool, the actuarial risk outcome should be viewed together with the protective factor assessment results, in order to formulate one overall integrated final risk or sexual risk judgment. Research (reviewed later in this chapter) has shown good results for risk assessment conclusions drawn from the actuarial use of the SAPROF total scores, as well as for the SPJ final judgments.

Following the successful implementation of the SAPROF in adult risk assessment practice, youth risk assessment experts increasingly requested the development of a youth version of the tool. Thus, in 2015 the SAPROF-Youth Version was published (SAPROF-YV; de Vries Robbé,

Geers, Stapel, Hilterman, & de Vogel, 2015b), which was subsequently translated into several different languages, including German, French, and Spanish. The SAPROF-YV was intended as a protective factors assessment tool to complement juvenile and young adult risk assessment (age 12–23), as carried out with well-established juvenile risk assessment tools, such as the SAVRY (Borum, Bartel, & Forth, 2006—see Chapter 18, this volume), the YLS/CMI (Hoge & Andrews, 2006—see Chapter 9, this volume), or the J-SOAP-II (Prentky & Righthand, 2003—see Chapter 13, this volume). Although the SAVRY already contains some protective factors and the YLS/CMI offers the possibility to point out a protective effect on the assessed domains, it was deemed useful by mental health professionals to add an extended list of protective factors that are empirically related to reduced violence risk.

The SAPROF-YV is not a downwards adaptation of the SAPROF but designed as an altogether new tool based on juvenile offending literature. The tool contains 16 protective factors, which show overlap with those in the SAPROF. The factors in the SAPROF-YV are organized in four domains: resilience factors, motivational factors, relational factors, and external factors. They focus more on relationships with friends and family and on future orientation and school. The use of the SAPROF-YV is identical to that of the SAPROF. For young adults (age 18–23), it is advised to carefully consider the individual's developmental stage when deciding whether the adult version (SAPROF) or youth version (SAPROF-YV) is more appropriate. If an individual still resides at home, goes to school, is dependent on his caregivers, and has a younger peer group, the youth version may be most applicable. However, if he or she lives independently, goes to work rather than school and hangs out with older individuals, the adult SAPROF is likely the better choice. Research shows that at group level, predictive validities of the adult and youth versions are similar for the group of young adults (Kleeven, de Vries Robbé, Mulder, & Popma, 2020a). Finally, since the value of protective factors is also being recognized for the risk assessment of even younger children, it was recently decided to start developing a SAPROF-Child Version, to be used together with the new version of the EARL tools—see Chapter 11, this volume.

Using the Tool in Practice

Rationale for Development and Use

As the SAPROF was developed from a treatment perspective, the aim has been to create a tool that is easy to use and is evidence based. Moreover, the tool needs to provide additional value for clinical practice and thus contains predominantly dynamic factors that are potentially changeable through intervention. When the tool is used alongside a risk-focused assessment tool, it is quick to administer (15 minutes). The tool was developed based on literature searches of protective factors that contribute to reductions in violence risk and interviews with mental health professionals regarding the usefulness of specific positive factors for treatment. A pilot version of the tool was composed and subsequently tested in a quantitative pilot study and qualitative beta-testing study (see de Vogel, de Ruiter, Bouman, & de Vries Robbé, 2007). This led to the development of the final SAPROF manual, which is intended as a guideline to inform assessment, treatment interventions, and risk management.

Although there are no specific requirements, other than general knowledge regarding violence risk and clinical experience, in regards to qualifications to be able to use the SAPROF, it is strongly recommended to attend SAPROF training by a qualified trainer before using the SAPROF in practice (for more information, please visit www.saprof.com). In the treatment context, a well-informed risk assessment should ideally be carried out by those who know the patient or client well. This is not only because they often have the most in-depth information regarding

Table 17.1 Protective Factors in the SAPROF and SAPROF-YV

SAPROF	SAPROF-Youth Version
Internal	*Resilience*
1. Intelligence	1. Social competence
2. Secure attachment in childhood	2. Coping
3. Empathy	3. Self-control
4. Coping	4. Perseverance
5. Self-control	
	Motivational
Motivational	5. Future orientation
6. Work	6. Motivation for treatment
7. Leisure activities	7. Attitude towards agreements and conditions
8. Financial management	8. Medication
9. Motivation for treatment	9. School/work
10. Attitudes towards authority	10. Leisure activities
11. Life goals	
12. Medication	*Relational*
	11. Parents/guardians
External	12. Peers
13. Social network	13. Other supportive relationships
14. Intimate relationship	
15. Professional care	*External*
16. Living circumstances	14. Pedagogical climate
17. External control	15. Professional care
	16. Court order

specific topics addressed in the assessment, but also because they are hopefully able to apply the results from the assessment in the treatment and risk management planning. Ideally, the assessment is carried out by multiple raters from different disciplines, who all know the assessed person from varying settings and can bring their own views to the assessment table in a case conference consensus meeting during which each risk and protective factor is considered carefully and risk formulation, scenarios and management strategies are discussed (see de Vogel, van den Broek, & de Vries Robbé, 2014). An assessment can only be as good as the information that is available. Thus, in-depth accurate and recent information, preferably from multiple sources, is required to be able to carry out a reliable risk assessment. This is especially true for the assessment of dynamic protective factors as input for these positive factors is not always documented well in case files. Given the fact that the SAPROF factors are to be rated for a specific context, it is vital for the quality of the assessment that dynamic information regarding each protection concept is available or can be retrieved and that the context for which the assessment is carried out is clearly defined. In case of an assessment based on file information only, the assessor should be aware of the limitation that missing information cannot be gathered and that the reliability of the assessment of the protective factors relies heavily on the quality of the file information.

Use in Different Populations

The intended use of the SAPROF was for the assessment of protective factors for violence risk, that is, general violence to others. However, given the brought perspective and general positive nature of the protective domains covered in the SAPROF factors, it is to be expected that the desistance from violence is not the only positive outcome that could be assessed with this tool. If someone demonstrates good functioning on many aspects in life, this is bound to have a positive influence on more than violence risk alone. Following the Good Lives Model (Ward, 2002), achieving protective factors increases general well-being, resulting in greater happiness and lower likelihood to offend (de Vries Robbé & Willis, 2017). In fact, many positive community outcomes could be achieved through the presence of protective factors, such as employment, stable housing, stable relationships, successful supervision, or prosocial activities (Coupland, 2015). Most of these are represented as factors in the SAPROF themselves, nevertheless they are also positively influenced by each other's presence. As an individual achieves more stable functioning and becomes better integrated in the community, the reasons for reoffending in general start to diminish. Thus, the strengthening of protective factors is also expected to have a preventive effect on general offending. Several of the SAPROF studies described later in this chapter have included general reoffending as an additional outcome and confirmed the assumed relationship between protective factors and offending reductions.

More specific types of violent behavior could also be prevented when protective factors are present, such as self-harming behavior, inpatient aggressive behavior, or sexual offending behavior. Several studies have included self-harming behavior as an outcome and found promising results for the predictive effect of the SAPROF protective factors for self-harm (e.g. Abidin et al., 2013; Judges, 2016). Not surprisingly, general well-being also helps to lower the likelihood of self-harm. Another common type of violence that could be prevented by strengthening protective factors is inpatient violence. Aggression towards staff or fellow patients is a major concern in many (forensic) psychiatric settings (Bowers et al., 2011), that could in part be prevented by developing protective factors. Indeed many studies (reviewed later in this chapter) show good predictive validity for reductions in inpatient violence. However, given the focus on community reintegration in the SAPROF, the applicability and clinical value of the general SAPROF factors appears somewhat lower in long-term inpatient settings for severely psychiatrically disordered patients (Neves, de Vries Robbé, van den Nagel, Bohle, & Veldhuizen, 2019). Therefore, an additional manual to the SAPROF has recently been developed in the Netherlands for use in long-term psychiatric care settings, both civil and forensic: the SAPROF-Long-term Care (SAPROF-LC; de Vries Robbé, van den Nagel, Bohle, & Veldhuizen, 2018). Through focusing more on diverse protective factors which are expected to be of importance to individuals in forensic as well as civil treatment settings, the SAPROF-LC aims to provide additional positive guidelines for risk management during hospitalization and assist in the prevention of inpatient violence as much as possible.

In addition, interest has grown regarding the applicability of the SAPROF for individuals with limited intellectual capabilities. For this reason, a group of experts in the United Kingdom decided to develop an additional manual specifically for use with this population called the SAPROF-Intellectual Disabilities (SAPROF-ID; de Vries Robbé, Hounsome et al., 2018). After a careful review of both the SAPROF-LC and SAPROF-ID, the additional components of both tools appeared so similar that it was proposed to merge both these new additional manuals into one SAPROF-ID/LC additional manual. This new addition to the original SAPROF is currently being tested at different sites in Europe and North America. This additional manual contains revised coding instructions for some of the existing SAPROF factors and offers seven new factors, including Social competence, Quality of life, Program participation, Treatment alliance, Self-efficacy, and Sleep.

Given the relative lack of empirical evidence for sexual offending specific protective factors at the time of development of the SAPROF, it was decided to create a general list of protective factors and test its value also for populations with a history of sexual offending. Evidence to date suggests the SAPROF factors do indeed predict non-recidivism just as well for sexual offenders, both regarding general violent reoffending and regarding new sexual offenses specifically. This being said, more research needs to be done regarding specific types of sexual offending, such as sexual violence against children and hands-off sexual offending. As new insights continue to emerge regarding the Good Lives Model (e.g., Dickson, Willis, & Mather, 2018), factors that influence desistance from sexual offending (see de Vries Robbé, Mann, Maruna, & Thornton, 2015c) and the specific influence of healthy sexual behaviors (Worling, 2013), a group of researchers in New Zealand and the United States recently initiated the development of an additional manual to the SAPROF specifically for the assessment of protective factors for sexual offending: the SAPROF-Sexual Offending (SAPROF-SO; de Vries Robbé, Willis, Thornton, & Kelley, 2018). The additional manual includes seven new SO-specific factors, including Emotional connection to adults, Sexual self-regulation, Prosocial sexual identity, Housing stability, and Prosocial sexual interests. Although the tool is still being piloted, it appears a promising addition to the original SAPROF for the risk assessment of individuals who have sexually offended. In designing the tool, it was decided to not only develop an additional SPJ SAPROF-SO manual, but to simultaneously also develop a stand-alone SAPROF-SO actuarial version. This actuarial version includes both the original SAPROF factors and the new SAPROF-SO factors in an actuarial manner, aiming to make the assessment of protective factors more applicable in actuarial risk assessment practice as well. This may be the first risk assessment tool that is being made available in an SPJ as well as an actuarial format.

Another specific population for which additional guidelines might be valuable are females. There has been considerable debate in general regarding the applicability of risk assessment tools for women, given that most tools were developed based primarily on male violent offender literature and validation studies on their use in female assessment practice have demonstrated mixed results (see de Vogel & Nicholls, 2016). Therefore, attempts have been made to provide gender-specific risk assessment guidelines which could be used to complement risk-focused assessment with the HCR-20 or its successor, the HCR-20[V3]: the Female Additional Manual (FAM and FAM[V3]; de Vogel, de Vries Robbé, van Kalmthout, & Place, 2012, 2014). Given that some scholars have expressed uncertainty about the applicability of general risk factors for both genders, the same could be argued regarding protective factors. As will be seen from the research results, the few studies to date that have included female populations have so far demonstrated mixed results. Although the literature on female-specific protective factors is limited, recently more research has emerged regarding factors that may play an important role in female desistance from offending (see Rodermond, Kruttschnitt, Slotboom, & Bijleveld, 2016; Viljoen, Viljoen, Nicholls, & de Vries Robbé, 2017). For women, protective factors such as family ties, motherhood, social network, and community participation (work, leisure activities), as well as financial situation, motivation to change, and a sense of agency, show to be of particular importance (Rodermond et al., 2016). Although a number of these factors are already represented in the SAPROF, it could be valuable to consider developing a more gender-sensitive approach to the assessment of protective factors.

In addition to these subgroup-specific SAPROF manuals, a self-assessment version of the original SAPROF factors has been developed. This semi-structured interview could be used to let patients or offenders think about their own protective factors. Pilot results with this SAPROF-Interview Self-Appraisal (de Vries Robbé & de Vogel, 2014) showed the value of the self-assessment for forensic psychiatric patients to gain insight into the importance of specific protective factors, inspired conversations between patients and treatment providers regarding the development of strengths, and offered new opportunities for treatment interventions. In general, even when only the staff SAPROF ratings were carried out, including the explicit focus on protective factors in the assessment process proved to be motivating for mental health professionals, in the sense that it created optimism regarding new treatment possibilities and a balanced approach in the assessment. Moreover, not surprisingly it was equally motivating for patients, to also hear about positive factors when discussing the assessment results, which positively impacted treatment motivation and treatment alliance. There appears to be promising value in the self-assessment specifically of positive factors. The plan is to develop a self-assessment SAPROF app which can make this self-evaluation more intuitive and easier to apply in daily practice.

Research With the SAPROF

Since the development of the SAPROF and the widespread implementation of the measure, an increasing number of validation studies have started to appear. These studies have been carried out in different settings and countries and with different patient and offender populations. In the following, we have attempted to create an overview of published studies known to the authors, which follow the general guidelines as posed in the tool's manual. Nineteen studies were found that reported on the psychometric properties of the SAPROF. It should be noted that studies which attempted to use the adult SAPROF in youth samples were not included, since the adult tool was not designed for use with juveniles. Similarly, one or two studies which applied a methodology that did not incorporate dynamic information regarding treatment changes (i.e., which related pre-trial ratings to recidivism many years later, without incorporating the effects of treatment before discharge) were not included either, since theoretically it would be unlikely pre-trial ratings of dynamic factors would provide meaningful information regarding post-treatment offending without the consideration of treatment effects. The studies described here vary in scope from large national cohort studies (e.g., all Medium secure discharge across the UK in 12 months' time; Coid et al., 2016) to studies on specific subsamples (e.g., child sexual abusers; Turner et al., 2016). In addition to the published studies presented in this chapter, many studies in different settings and populations are currently ongoing, which will likely be published in the next few years. We attempt to summarize the results from all studies on the SAPROF in an Annotated Bibliography on the SAPROF website (www.saprof.com).

Interrater Reliability

In ten different studies, most of which were published in peer-reviewed journals, the interrater reliability was analyzed. Table 17.2 shows the interrater reliability results for total SAPROF scores collected in several different countries and settings. The studies contain retrospective file studies as well as prospective clinical studies. Overall, for the studies that reported this, the average intraclass correlation coefficient (ICC_1, single measure) for the SAPROF total score was .82, which is considered excellent (Fleiss, 1986). Some studies also included ICC findings for the final protection judgment (six studies, mean ICC = .70) and integrated final risk judgment (four studies, mean ICC = .71).

Internal Consistency

Although the SAPROF aims to measure various domains of protection rather than one specific construct, several studies have attempted to measure the tool's internal consistency (e.g., Coupland, 2015; Judges, 2016; Oziel, 2016). Generally these studies find fairly good internal consistency, ranging between α = .70–.90. Nevertheless, since the protective factors in the SAPROF are not necessarily theoretically related to each other and the last three items are highly context dependent, the internal consistency findings are not particularly informative. See also the section on clinical use later in this chapter.

Convergent Validity

The convergent validity with other risk assessment tools continues to interest many researchers. What is the overlap between the SAPROF and other risk assessment tools, and in particular with risk factors assessed in commonly used risk-focused assessment tools such as the HCR-20? Most studies report correlations between SAPROF and HCR-20 total scores between r = −.50 and −.70. Whether this is unacceptably high and thus implies protective factors are for a large part

Table 17.2 Interrater Reliability of the SAPROF

Study	Design	Population	ICC_1 (unless otherwise specified)
Abidin et al., 2013 Ireland	Prospective	N = 21 inpatient secure forensic	.83 (Spearman's r)
Coid et al., 2016 United Kingdom	Prospective	N = 20 discharged Medium secure	.93
Coupland, 2015 Canada	Retrospective	N = 20 correctional violent offenders	.77
		(pre-treatment, post-treatment, release)	(.73/.79/.80)
		change scores during treatment	.82
de Vries Robbé et al., 2011 The Netherlands	Retrospective	N = 40 violent offenders discharged forensic psych patients	.88
de Vries Robbé et al., 2015a The Netherlands	Retrospective	N = 30 sexual offenders discharged forensic psych patients	.85
Kashiwagi et al., 2018 Japan	Retrospective	N = 30 inpatient secure forensic	.70
Oziel, 2016 Canada	Prospective	N = 8 in/outpatient	.86 (r)
Persson et al., 2017 Sweden	Prospective	N = 200 detainees undergoing forensic psychiatric evaluation	.86
Turner et al., 2016 Germany	Retrospective	N = 229 correctional child sexual abusers	.85
Viljoen et al., 2016 Canada	Prospective	N = 15 civil psychiatric patients	.75

Note: SAPROF total score ICCs, generally 2 raters (single measure).

the opposite of existing risk factors, or if this means we tap into the same constructs yet measure the positive side of the equation, remains up for debate. Some scholars pose protective factors are no more than the opposite of risk factors and do not exist in their own right. Others, however, proclaim that the absence of a risk factor is something essentially different from the presence of a protective factor, as the absence of a risk factor implies the risk is not further increased, while the presence of a protective factor actually counterbalances the risk factors that are present and thus lowers the overall risk (see Polaschek, 2017; Ward, 2017). How different risk and protective factors interact with each other and together influence violence risk remains largely unexplored and might very well differ between factors and individuals (for a detailed discussion of the mechanisms behind protective factors and their interaction with risk factors, see de Vries Robbé, 2014; for further reading regarding the relationship between risk factors and protective factors, see also, for example, Klepfisz, Daffern, and Day (2017), and regarding different theoretical models of interaction, see Ward, 2017).

Predictive Validity

The most important psychometric to report is the predictive validity of the SAPROF. Table 17.3 presents the predictive validity results for 19 published studies on various samples from nine different countries, which together reported over 70 different Area Under the Curve (AUC) values. However, this overview presents only the main findings regarding the SAPROF total score from each of these studies. Many studies have also reported predictive validities for risk measures, final judgments, combined risk-protection indexes, SAPROF subscale scores, and in some cases even predictive validities for individual factors (e.g., Abidin et al., 2013; Coid et al., 2016). The studied samples include diverse populations (e.g., forensic psychiatric, correctional, civil, community supervision), demographics (gender, psychopathology, offending history), and sample sizes. Moreover, the different studies vary greatly in design (retrospective, prospective), studied outcome (violence to others in general, inpatient violence, violence reconvictions, general reconvictions, sexual recidivism, treatment outcome, release decisions, self-harm, positive community outcomes, or recidivism proxies) and follow-up time (ranging from 1 month to 11 years). These differences make it virtually impossible to compare the findings from the various studies.

However, general trends can be observed. Overall, the predictive validities reported in these 19 studies show promising predictive ability of the SAPROF for a wide range of outcomes. Findings are quite consistent across countries, research designs and sample sizes. However, it can be observed from Table 17.3 that on average, studies that utilize a shorter-term follow-up timeframe for assessment predictions (1–12 months, the intended outcome of the measure) generate somewhat better predictive validities than longer-term predictions. This is not surprising, as longer-term predictions are inherently more difficult to make as dynamic factors may be subjective to changes in the years after the assessment. That being said, the AUC values for follow-up periods many years post-discharge from treatment are still surprisingly high. Both in the study by Coupland (2015) and in the studies by de Vries Robbé and colleagues (de Vries Robbé, de Vogel, & Douglas, 2013; de Vries Robbé et al., 2015a), significant predictive validities were found for violent recidivism at 10+ years after assessment. This implies that, although most factors are dynamic in nature, improvements in protective factors may have long lasting positive effects in terms of violence prevention.

Regarding the type of outcome, Table 17.3 shows that overall across the different studies, the predictive validity findings for community violent offending are equally strong to those for inpatient violence or institutional misconduct. Most inpatient studies, such as those by Abbiati et al. (2019), Abidin et al. (2013), de Vries Robbé et al. (2019), Judges (2016), Kashiwagi et al. (2018), and Persson et al. (2017), find relatively good predictive values for inpatient aggression. In the prospective clinical study by de Vries Robbé, de Vogel, Wever, Douglas, and Nijman (2016) the predictive validity of SAPROF ratings were compared for patients in the inpatient phase of treatment and for patients in the community reintegration treatment phase, which demonstrated better values for the latter. Only a few inpatient studies report less convincing predictive validities: those by Haines et al. (2018) and Viljoen et al. (2016). It should be noted that these studies concern samples that largely consist of individuals with no history of violent offending who take part in community psychiatric treatment. Another noticeable difference is that these studies concern a larger proportion of women. In addition, the findings of lower predictive validities for inpatient violence in these studies were not unique to the SAPROF; lower AUC values were generally also observed for the risk factor ratings in these studies.

A variety of other types of outcomes was studied in the various samples. Good predictive validities were reported for violent behavior after discharge (e.g., Coid et al., 2016; Coupland, 2015), for sexually violent behavior (e.g., de Vries Robbé et al., 2015), and for acquisitive or general offending behavior (e.g., Coid et al., 2016; Tozdan et al., 2016). Moreover, alternative treatment outcomes used as proxies for good inpatient functioning generated positive results: SAPROF factors showed ability to predict self-harming behavior (e.g., Abidin et al., 2013; Judges, 2016), discharge from treatment (Davoren et al., 2013; Doyle et al., 2014; de Vries Robbé et al., 2019), disruptive behavior (Neil et al., 2020), and psychiatric medication administrations and disposition breaches (Oziel, 2016). Finally, Coupland (2015) included an interesting additional outcome in his studies of discharged offenders from corrections concerning a range of positive community outcomes, including: Employment, Stable housing, Stable relationships, Successful supervision, and Prosocial activities. SAPROF ratings demonstrated good predictive validity for these measures of general well-being and positive community functioning. This approach of using positive community functioning as an alternative objective for studies on the effects of protective factors provides a valuable additional outcome measure for validation studies on the psychometric abilities of protective factor assessment instruments.

Regarding specific populations, several studies looked at the value of the SAPROF for patients with a history of sexual offending behavior. Studies by Tozdan et al. (2016) and by de Vries Robbé et al. (2015) found strong predictive validities for general recidivism, violent recidivism, and sexually violent recidivism both during and after treatment, while Turner et al. (2016) did not find the SAPROF to be predictive for sexually violent recidivism amongst discharged child sexual abusers. Similarly, mixed results have been found regarding the predictive abilities of the general protective factors represented in the SAPROF for female violent behavior. While de Vries Robbé et al. (2015) found moderate predictive value for inpatient violence by female forensic psychiatric inpatients, Viljoen et al. (2016) reported poor predictive validity for women in civil psychiatry. As posed earlier in this chapter, these mixed findings have prompted the contemplation on the possible development of additional SAPROF manuals for these specific populations.

Not reported in Table 17.3 is the general observation from the literature covered thus far that findings regarding the predictive value of the SAPROF factors show to be quite consistent across psychopathology. Although most forensic psychiatric studies include predominantly psychiatrically disordered patients, the studies by de Vries Robbé et al. (2011, 2015a) include mostly personality disordered offenders, which yielded comparably positive findings. The same was true for the studies concerning correctional samples, which generally included a wide variety of psychopathology (Abbiati et al., 2019; Coupland, 2015; Persson et al., 2017). The studies by Coid et al. (2016) and de Vries Robbé et al. (2016) made comparison between patients with a primary diagnosis of Major Mental Illness (MMI) and patients suffering primarily from a personality disorder (PD). Both studies reported good predictive validities of most SAPROF factors for samples with and without a primary diagnosis of MMI or PD psychopathology. Moreover, the latter also looked at the predictive value for patients with high psychopathy ratings as measured with the PCL-R and found similarly positive results for the effects of protective factors for this group of offenders, although in the retrospective studies for highly psychopathic patients, this positive effect did not last longer than a year after discharge. Lastly, although not reported explicitly, in the prospective inpatient study by de Vries Robbé et al. (2016) the SAPROF factors demonstrated equally good predictive validities for a subsample of patients with intellectual disabilities (ID). Nevertheless, additional protective factors of specific importance for ID populations may provide a useful complement to the SAPROF in order to make the tool more clinically applicable for this specific population which comprises a large part of the forensic patient and correctional population.

Incremental Predictive Validity

Several of the studies described in Table 17.3 also looked at incremental predictive validity over other risk assessment tools. Primarily, the incremental value compared to risk-focused tools was studied. Several studies found evidence for incremental predictive validity of the SAPROF factors over the HCR-20 or HCR-20^{V3} ratings. Although most studies did not find significant results for all of the assessed outcomes and follow-up times, different studies found evidence for incremental predictive validity for short-term (e.g., de Vries Robbé et al., 2011; Judges, 2016; Kashiwagi et al., 2018) or long-term (e.g., Coupland, 2015; de Vries Robbé et al., 2015) predictions

Table 17.3 Predictive Validity (AUC) and Incremental Validity of the SAPROF

Study	Design	Population	Outcome	Results		Incremental Predictive Validity/ Interaction With Risk Factors
				Follow-up	AUC	
Abbiati et al., 2019 Switzerland	Prospective	N = 52 ♂ Correctional Violent offenders In prison	Physically violent misconduct	12m	.80**	–
			Any misconduct	12m	.69**	
Abidin at el., 2013 Ireland	Prospective	N = 98 (94% ♂) Forensic patients secure hospital In treatment	Violent incidents	6m	.85**	Interactive effect with HCR-20
			Self-harm	6m	.77*	
Coid et al., 2016[a] United Kingdom	Prospective	N = 409 (89% ♂) Medium secure forensic psychiatric patients National cohort Community discharge	Any reported community violence	6m	.76**	Interactive effect with HCR-20
				12m	.70**	
			Acquisitive offending convictions	6m	.71**	
				12m	.73**	
			Serious offending convictions	6m	.83**	
				12m	.82**	
			Any convictions	6m	.79**	
				12m	.78**	
Coupland, 2015 Canada	Retrospective	N = 155 ♂ Correctional Incarcerated violent offenders, participated in treatment program Community discharge (release ratings)	Community recidivism Convictions:			10y(M) violence convictions (over HCR-20 pre-treatment + change)
			—all violent	10y(M)	.71**	
			—nonsexual violent	10y(M)	.72**	
			—any recidivism	10y(M)	.76**	
			Charges:			
			—all violent	10y(M)	.75**	
			—nonsexual violent	10y(M)	.76**	
			—any recidivism	10y(M)	.75**	
		N = 137 ♂ Community supervision	Positive community outcomes[b]	24m[c]	.81**	24m Positive community outcomes (over HCR-20 pre-treatment + change)
		N = 157 ♂	Major institutional misconduct	30m(M)	.58	
Davoren et al., 2013 Ireland	Prospective	N = 56 ♂ Forensic patients secure hospital In treatment	Conditional discharge	21m(M)	.81**	–

Study / Country	Design	Sample	Outcome	Time	AUC	Incremental validity
de Vries Robbé et al., 2011 The Netherlands	Retrospective	N = 105 ♂ Forensic psychiatric patients violent offending history Community discharge	Violence convictions	12m 24m 36m	.85** .80** .74**	12m + 36m violence convictions (over HCR-20)
de Vries Robbé et al., 2013[d] The Netherlands	Retrospective	N = 188 ♂ Violent/sexual offenders Forensic psychiatry Community discharge	Violence convictions	12m 36m 11y(M)	.85** .75** .73**	36m violence convictions (over HCR-20) Interactive effect with HCR-20
de Vries Robbé et al., 2015a The Netherlands	Retrospective	N = 83 ♂ Forensic psychiatric patients sexually violent offending history Community discharge	Violence convictions Sexual violence convictions	12m 36m 15y(M) 36m sex 15y(M) sex	.83** .77** .74** .76* .71**	15y(M) violence convictions (over HCR-20) 36m + 15y(M) sexual violence convictions (over SVR-20)
de Vries Robbé et al., 2016 The Netherlands	Prospective	N = 399 (78% ♂) Forensic psychiatric patients In treatment	Violent incidents —inpatient —outpatient —female —male —violent offenders —sexual offenders	12m 12m 12m 12m 12m 12m 12m	.75** .66** .78** .71** .76** .72** .84**	–
de Vries Robbé et al., 2019 Canada	Retrospective	N = 105 (91% ♂) Forensic patients (11 hospitals) In treatment	Violent incidents Review board discharge decisions	12m	.75**/.81** .80**/.82**	–
Haines et al., 2018 United Kingdom	Prospective	N = 148 (81% nonviolent, 55% ♂) Civil psychiatric patients (71% community) In treatment	Physical aggression	6m	.60	
Judges, 2016 United Kingdom	Prospective	N = 108 (86% ♂) Low and Medium secure forensic services In treatment	Violent incidents (to others or self) Violence to others Violence to self	1m 3m 6m 1m 3m 6m 1m 3m 6m	.74** .70** .75** .74** .69** .72** .83** .67 .71*	6m all violent incidents (over HCR-20[V3])

(Continued)

Table 17.3 (Continued)

Study	Design	Population	Outcome	Results Follow-up	AUC	Incremental Predictive Validity/ Interaction With Risk Factors
Kashiwagi et al., 2018 Japan	Retrospective	N = 95 ♂ Forensic patients secure hospital In treatment	Violent incidents (physical)	6m 12m	.87** .85**	6m + 12m violent incidents (over HCR-20)
Neil et al., 2020 Scotland	Retrospective	N = 75 ♂ Forensic patients secure hospital In treatment	Violent incidents —any —physical —verbal —sexual Other disruptive behavior	12m 12m 12m 12m 12m	.74** .71** .69** .70 .72**	—
Oziel, 2016 Canada	Prospective	N = 50 (86% ♂) Forensic inpatients and outpatients In treatment	Psychiatric medication adm.[e] Institutional misconduct Disposition breaches	6m 6m 6m	.71** .64[f] .79**	6m institutional misconduct (over HCR-20[V3])
Persson et al., 2017 Sweden	Prospective	N = 200 (87% ♂) Correctional Detainees undergoing forensic psychiatric evaluation In prison	Violent incidents (physical/ verbal to others)	12m	.78**	—
Tozdan et al., 2016 Germany	Prospective	N = 40 ♂ Forensic psychiatric patients sexually violent offending history Community discharge	Any recidivism	28m	.80**	—
Turner et al., 2016 Germany	Retrospective	N = 229 ♂ Correctional Incarcerated child sexual abusers Community discharge	Any recidivism Violent recidivism Sexual violent recidivism	5.7y(M) 5.7y(M) 5.7y(M)	.63* .60 .52	—

Study	Design	Sample	Outcome	Time	AUC	12m verbal aggression (over HCR-20)
Viljoen et al., 2016 Canada	Retrospective	N = 102 (61% ♂) Civil psychiatric patients In treatment	Violent incidents (inpatient/community)			
			—female	6m	.59	.51
				12m	.60	.53
			—male	6m	.67*	
				12m	.65	

Note: * p < .05; ** p < .01.

AUC values concern SAPROF total scores. All have been reversed, implying that larger AUC's reflect increased likelihood of the absence of the outcome.

In most studies, violent re-convictions also include sexually violent re-convictions.

[a] Parts of the findings from this sample were also described in several other publications: Coid, Kallis, Doyle, Shaw, & Ullrich, 2015; Doyle et al., 2014; Barnard-Croft, 2014.

[b] Positive community outcomes include: Employment, Stable housing, Stable relationships, Successful supervision, Prosocial activities; r = .53 converted into AUC.

[c] Or at the end of the supervision period, whichever came first.

[d] This study combines the violent and sexual offender samples of the studies by de Vries Robbé et al., 2011, 2015a.

[e] This study utilized recidivism proxies: Psychiatric medication administrations, Institutional misconduct, and Disposition Breaches.

[f] r = −.24 converted into AUC.

Table 17.4 Changes in SAPROF Protective Factor Ratings Over Time

Study	Design	Population	Outcome	Results	Predictive validity of change (AUC)	
Brand, 2018 The Netherlands	Prospective	N = 50 (88% ♂) forensic psychiatric	Change during inpatient treatment (3 timepoints)	Significant increase SAPROF Internal and Motivational factors	–	
Coupland, 2015 Canada	Retrospective	N = 178 ♂ violent correctional community discharge	Change during correctional treatment program (6m)	Significant increase SAPROF total score	Convictions (10y)[a] Charges (10y)[a] Positive community outcomes (24m)[a]	.65** .63** .64**
de Vries Robbé et al., 2014 The Netherlands	Retrospective	N = 108 ♂ violent/sexual forensic psychiatry community discharge	Change during inpatient treatment (5y)	Significant increase SAPROF total score	Violent reconvictions (12m) Violent reconvictions (11y)	.78* .75**
Tozdan et al., 2016 Germany	Prospective	N = 40 ♂ sexual forensic psychiatry community discharge	Change during inpatient treatment (24m)	Significant increase SAPROF Internal and Motivational factors	–	

Note: * p < .05; **p < .01

Violent re-convictions also include sexually violent re-convictions.

AUC values concern SAPROF total 'change' scores.

[a] $r = -.27/-.23/.25$ converted into AUC.

of violence. Other studies described incremental predictive validity for specific outcomes, such as verbal aggression (Viljoen et al., 2016), institutional misconduct (Oziel, 2016), and positive community outcomes (Coupland, 2015). De Vries Robbé et al. (2015) reported incremental predictive validity for medium- and long-term predictions of sexually violent offending over the use of the SVR-20. In addition to findings regarding incremental predictive validity, several studies reported interactive effects between protective factors and risk factors (e.g., Abidin et al., 2013; Coid et al., 2016; de Vries Robbé et al., 2013). It appears that the presence of protective factors is of particular importance for those individuals who are at moderate or high risk to recidivate. The observed incremental predictive validity and interaction with risk factors demonstrates that protective factors encompass more than just the reverse of risk factors; they add unique variance to the violence risk equation. Regardless of their intended clinical value, this provides empirical support for the additional value of explicitly assessing protective factors in the comprehensive assessment of violence risk.

Change

A limited number of studies have reported findings regarding change by means of repeated measures with the SAPROF protective factors during treatment (see Table 17.4). Although the treatment length varied between the studies (from 6 months to 5 years), all four studies demonstrated significant changes between pre-treatment and post-treatment ratings on SAPROF factors. Coupland (2015) and de Vries Robbé et al. (2014) also looked at predictive validity of these changes for outcome after treatment and found the improvements in SAPROF factor ratings during treatment to be predictive of offending after treatment. This was true for short-term predictions (12/24-month follow-up) as well as for longer term predictions (10+-year follow-up) and for different types of outcomes, including violent reoffending, general reoffending and positive community outcomes. These findings are promising for clinical practice as they show that improvements in protective factors accomplished during treatment have long-lasting positive effects for positive community functioning and recidivism risk reduction. Thus, successfully building protective factors in treatment contributes to safe community reintegration.

Although overall improvements in protective factors show to have a positive effect, what is considered *improvement* is not the same for internal/motivational factors as for the external contextual protection from treatment and court orders. Well-functioning individuals no longer need intensive treatment (factor 15), supervised housing (factor 16), or a court order mandating treatment and supervision (factor 17). Thus, in fact when a patient moves through treatment, these factors are actually expected to decrease, while the other dynamic factors are expected to increase. De Vries Robbé and de Vogel (2013) describe the anticipated direction of change and divide the SAPROF factors into categories of factors which are historical in nature (the *static* factors 1 and 2, Intelligence and Secure attachment in childhood; see Table 17.1), dynamic factors which are expected to increase during treatment (the *dynamic improving* factors 3–14, such as Work and Social network), and external contextual factors which are expected to be lowered when a patient's functioning changes for the better (the *dynamic decreasing* factors 15–17, such as Professional care and External control). The change study by de Vries Robbé et al. (2014) investigated this opposing effect of change during treatment for the different types of factors. Figure 17.1 shows the changes between the start and end of forensic psychiatric treatment: when factors 3–14 improve, as a result it is possible to decrease the external protection from factors 15–17. Thus, in treatment the goal will never be to accomplish a maximal total score on the SAPROF, but rather a shift in scores (transfer of protection) from external to more internal and motivational, in order to eventually be able to discharge patients safely to society with minimal external support.

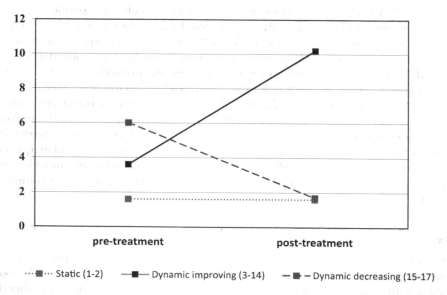

Figure 17.1 SAPROF Mean Pre- and Post-Treatment Total Scores by Category: Static Factors, Dynamic Improving Factors and Dynamic Decreasing Factors

Source: de Vries Robbé & de Vogel (2013).

Research With the SAPROF-Youth Version

Given the fact that the SAPROF-YV was published fairly recently in 2015 and the tool has only just started to become adopted widely in international juvenile risk assessment practice, the evidence base regarding the psychometric properties of the tool is still limited. Although several large-scale validation studies are currently ongoing in different countries, as of yet there are only a number of (unpublished) studies which have reported on the psychometric properties of the SAPROF-YV in juvenile treatment practice. Preliminary findings from these studies show promising results which are in line with those for the SAPROF adult version. One study on a sample of 283 juvenile and young adult boys and girls (de Vries Robbé, Veldhuizen, Helmers, Vullings, & van Hoof, 2020) reports good interrater reliability (ICC$_1$ = .85) and good predictive validity for violent recidivism within 6 months after discharge from outpatient treatment (AUC = .74, p < .01). The study differentiates in a juvenile and a young adult subsample (respective AUCs = .71 and .74). Rowe (2015) also reported predictive validities for violent (AUC = .61, p < .01) and general (AUC = .65, p < .01) reoffending for a sample of 190 court-ordered juveniles. While a study by Bhanwer (2016) regarding 69 boys and girls in an inpatient or probation setting reported predictive values for different types of inpatient aggression (minor/major verbal aggression AUC = .82, p < .01/.65, *ns*; minor/major physical aggression AUC = .64, p < .01/.69, *ns*; and sexual aggression AUC = .68, *ns*) as well as for aggressive behavior during probation (verbal AUC = .69, *ns*; physical AUC = .60, *ns*). These studies and an additional study by Schell and Rowe (2015), involving 98 predominantly male juvenile offenders and 30 inpatients, also reported on convergent validity with different juvenile risk assessment tools. Highly negative correlations were found with different risk tools (SAVRY risks, −.69; YLS/CMI risks, −.58; START:AV risks, −.70; and PCL-SV, −.66), while there was a highly positive correlation with other tools that measure strengths (SAVRY protective factors, .72; YLS/CMI strengths, .70; and START:AV strengths, .71). This implies these tools tap into similar constructs. However, the SAPROF-YV includes a range of resilience, motivational, relational, and external protective factors that offer additional guidelines for violence risk prevention and community reintegration in juveniles and young adults, which can be used in conjunction with predominantly risk-focused tools such as the SAVRY or YLS/CMI. Kleeven, de Vries Robbé, Mulder, and Popma (2020a, 2020b) recently carried out several studies including the SAPROF-YV in a sample of 353 young offenders discharged from inpatient forensic psychiatric treatment. For a subsample of 151 juveniles, they found good results in regards to SAPROF-YV interrater reliability (ICC_1 = .76) and predictive validity for general, violent, and nonviolent reoffending (respectively, 6-month AUCs = .74, p < .01; .70, p < .05; .70, p < .01). For a subsample of 202 young adult offenders, they also demonstrated good interrater reliability (ICC_1 = .81) and predictive validity (12-month AUCs = .68; .63; .67, all p < .01) for the SAPROF-YV, although these values were somewhat lower than for the juvenile subsample. Incremental predictive validity of the SAPROF-YV over the SAVRY risk factors was found for general as well as for violent recidivism. A large study by Li and colleagues (2019) in Singapore regarding risk and protective factors for 701 youth offenders on probation demonstrated that 12 out of the 13 included SAPROF-YV factors were significant indicators of probation success, with ORs ranging from 1.68 (Peers) to 13.10 (Perseverance). In a further study, among 822 young offenders under community supervision, the same research group found good interrater reliability (ICC_1 = .93) and predictive validity for the SAPROF-YV for general recidivism (24-month AUC = .80, p < .01), and incremental predictive validity over the YLS/CMI (Chu, Xu, Li, Ruby, & Chng, 2020).

Limitations and Necessary Future Research

Despite the quickly growing evidence base regarding the value of protective factors, more research is necessary to properly validate the SAPROF for a variety of different samples and settings. Validation studies are increasingly being carried out by different groups of researchers from various countries. In order to be sure to prevent bias and show true additional value for risk assessment and clinical practice in a wide range of international settings, it is of vital importance that validation studies on the SAPROF and SAPROF-YV are carried out by researchers other than the authors of these tools. Areas in need of further investigation are cross-cultural validation, validation for specific types of offending behavior (e.g., intimate partner violence, [non-contact] sexual offending, arson), and validation for specific subgroups of in- and outpatients and offenders (e.g., individuals with intellectual disabilities, with specific psychopathologies, females, young adults). Furthermore, investigation of the validity of the SAPROF and SAPROF-YV regarding alternative positive community outcomes (such as participation in school/employment, social relationships, and quality of life) would provide a valuable new approach to measure treatment effectiveness. General well-being and life success would be preferred outcomes of interventions and could serve as interesting alternative outcome variables for protective factors assessment. It would also be interesting to apply alternative risk assessment tools in future studies, to be able to evaluate the additional value of the SAPROF to other predominantly risk-focused tools, such as the VRS, the LS/CMI, and the STABLE, as well as convergent validity with the START risks and strengths.

There is a strong need for studies which assess changes in dynamic protective factors by means of repeated SAPROF evaluations over time. Taking this one step further, it would be particularly interesting to study the effects which the SAPROF assessments have on treatment planning (by means of the appointed *goal* factors) and to evaluate whether positive interventions actually result in improvements regarding protective factors, and ultimately whether the accomplished changes are related to desistance from further offending. The repeated assessment studies presented in this chapter have observed only changes in protective factors over time; they did not study what causally brought about the observed improvements in protective factors. In order to increase the value of the SAPROF as a treatment informing tool, research into the causal interference of specific factors could provide much-needed insights into the mechanisms of change. Another use of the SAPROF and other dynamic risk assessment tools which can be accomplished by means of repeated measures is routine outcome measurement, or the evaluation of treatment progress. However, high-quality dynamic information is vital for the sound evaluation of change. The demand from policy makers for treatment evaluation is an increasingly urgent matter which warrants thoughtful consideration. Evaluating changes in risk level by means of periodical assessment of dynamic risk and protective factors could provide a meaningful measure of treatment progress.

In this overview chapter, it was not possible to present in-depth descriptions of all the findings reported in the different studies. To be able to fully interpret the results from each study, it is advisable to carefully read the pertinent papers. In particular, we did not report any findings regarding subscales and individual factors for specific subgroups. Most studies do present their findings separately for subscales. Some also present psychometrics at factor level (e.g., Abidin et al., 2013; Coid et al., 2016) or demonstrate that specific factors are of particular importance for different subsamples (e.g., de Vries Robbé et al., 2013, 2016). Overall, it seems the best predicting factors for no future violence are *Self-control, Coping, Work, Motivation for treatment*, and *Attitudes towards authority*. These factors appear to be the core of the SAPROF in terms of predictive validity for desistance. Such item-level details provide further insight into the value of specific elements of the tool, for specific groups of patients or offenders.

Additionally, we did not report on any of the findings regarding the other tools used in each of the studies, most evidently the predictive validity of the applied risk-focused tools. To be able to properly interpret the findings regarding protective factors in each study, it is vital to be able to compare these with the results for other measures in the same studies and evaluate the findings in this perspective. The same goes for the overall conclusions from the SPJ assessment regarding the final protection judgment, and especially the final risk judgment. The study by de Vries Robbé et al. (2013) showed that further differentiation in risk groups based on protective factor judgments was able to meaningfully separate between those patients more or less likely to reoffend; this was especially true for the generally large 'moderate risk' group for whom it proved of vital importance to have a moderate to high level of protection in order not to recidivate.

Finally, an important variable that is increasingly being included in various studies is the actuarial calculation of the overall risk minus protection score, which is constructed by simply deducting SAPROF total scores from (for example) HCR-20 total scores in order to arrive at one final total risk score adjusted for the available protection (the *HCR-SAPROF index*). The general theoretical assumption is that risk of offending behavior is determined by a combination of risk and protective factors, which in an SPJ risk assessment are being integrated in one overall final risk judgment based on the comprehensive assessment of all risk factors and protective factors in the tools applied. Following this reasoning, the closest actuarial total score equivalent to the SPJ final judgment would in fact be the HCR-SAPROF index. Several studies have reported on this integrated index (e.g., Abbiati et al., 2019; de Vries Robbé et al., 2013; Judges, 2016; Kashiwagi et al., 2018; Persson et al., 2017), and overall they find better predictive validities for this combined risk-protection index than for either the total score of the risk factors or the total score of the protective factors alone. This finding provides additional evidence for the incremental value of explicitly attending to both risk factors and protective factors in risk assessment.

Clinical Value and Conclusions

This chapter provided an overview of the published evidence to date regarding the SAPROF. Overall, sound psychometric properties have been reported and findings are promising. For drawing conclusions from the assessment, protective factors offer additional input for risk formulation and scenario planning, as well as an evidence base for the positive counterbalance to risk factors which is implicitly taken into account when making final judgments regarding the level of risk. The real value of adding the SAPROF to any risk assessment lays not in the slight improvement in predictive accuracy, but especially in the insight that is gained regarding the importance of specific strengths for the individual. Through this, the risk assessment becomes increasingly personalized and the results from the assessment more informative for guiding treatment interventions and risk management. Assessing the protective factors for different contexts gives insight in the risk-reducing effects of the management in place in these contexts and provides argumentation regarding the necessity of prolonged intensive supervision or the possibility of increased freedom (see also the following case example). This may assist treatment phasing and risk management planning. Moreover, explicitly paying attention to protective factors may facilitate risk communication and enhance treatment motivation and treatment alliance between the assessed and the assessor (Domjancic et al., 2019; Nyman, Hofvander, Nilsson, & Wijk, 2019). In this respect, patients could also be invited more to self-assess their own protective factors, as this may motivate treatment engagement, enhance insight into problem behavior, and provide opportunities for positive change. The clinical value of the SAPROF is further illustrated in the following case example.

Case Example: Kelly

Background

Kelly is a 31-year-old woman who was sentenced to 4 years' imprisonment and mandatory inpatient treatment for murder. She grew up as an only child with an artistic, unpredictable mother and a demanding and hot-tempered father. Kelly's parents regularly cheated on each other, resulting in frequent verbal and physical fights. When Kelly was 5 years old, her parents finally separated. She stayed with her mother, who pampered her, imposed few rules, and let her drink alcohol at a young age. Both parents remarried and had more children. Kelly felt lost and no longer loved by her parents. She was a bright girl, but turned into an extremely insecure and timid child, often throwing tantrums and displaying manipulative and conning behavior. In the weekends, Kelly stayed with her father, his new wife, and their two sons. Later on, she accused her father of sexually abusing her in this period. Her father has always strongly denied the accusations and an official police investigation did not find evidence. Kelly also claimed to have been raped by a stranger, but later admits the sex was voluntary in exchange for money. As a teenager she had many short-term relationships with both men and women. After another argument with her father, she started displaying self-harming behavior by cutting her arms. When she was 16 years old, she was admitted to a psychiatric hospital because of a suicide attempt.

At age 17, Kelly got into a serious relationship with Tom, a violent man with substance abuse problems. Together, they used large amounts of alcohol and drugs while playing violent video games or watching violent movies. After Kelly told Tom about her 'bad dad,' they together decided to punish him. They went to his home and lit the house on fire. Her father was able to get away with his two sons, but his wife died in the fire. Kelly was arrested and diagnosed with a borderline personality disorder and alcohol dependency. Her PCL-R score was 13 and her total IQ score 126 (measured with the WAIS-IV).

Treatment at the Forensic Psychiatric Hospital

After her prison sentence ended, Kelly was admitted to a forensic psychiatric hospital where she was placed in a gender-mixed ward with 12 fellow patients. She presented herself as very motivated for treatment, trying hard to make a good impression and avoid criticism. Despite her apparent motivation and commitment to the treatment, she did not make much progress in the first six months. It was observed that Kelly was easily influenced by others and had trouble establishing boundaries. Kelly showed self-harming behavior, major mood swings and panic attacks when she felt stressed. Occasionally she also displayed lying and manipulative behavior. For example, she was involved in several conflicts on the ward and concealed incidents of other patients. Kelly had complex (sexual) relationships with several men and women in the hospital, sometimes simultaneously. She also offered sex in return for favors. After a year, Kelly slowly started making progress and was allowed to go on leaves outside of the hospital during which she always behaved appropriately. In the hospital she started attending classes in order to work towards a veterinary assistant degree. She also took part in individual psychotherapy, a substance abuse group, arts lessons, and sports. In addition, the regular daily program of attending her workplace, in the hospital kitchen, seemed to provide her with valuable structure.

A year later, she started with the resocialization phase of her treatment, which meant that she moved to her own apartment outside the hospital, but was still supervised closely by a specialized treatment team. Soon after she started living on her own, problems started accumulating. It became apparent this big change was not easy for Kelly. She had a hard time staying motivated for her work at the hospital, did not take good care of herself, and was involved in various sexual relationships. Also, it turned out that she had been drinking alcohol. She was readmitted to the hospital for several months to get things back on track. After taking part in a further relapse-prevention program and making new strict agreements with hospital staff regarding regular meetings with the treatment team, increased supervision, regular drug and alcohol testing, and the use of alcohol anti-craving medication (Naltrexone), she was allowed to return to her apartment. She had finished her initial veterinary assistant studies and started an internship at a veterinary clinic. Gradually, Kelly gained greater insight into her problems and risk factors. In the following months she managed to keep up her good intentions. She passed all random drug/alcohol tests and there were no incidents. During her internship at the veterinary practice, Kelly worked hard and was much appreciated by the veterinarian, who offered her a job after she finished her degree. She finalized her psychotherapy in the hospital and found a new therapist at an affiliated outpatient setting. Despite these positive developments, Kelly remained dependent on the hospital treatment staff and often visited or called them when she was stressed or found it difficult to make decisions on her own. Occasionally she made threats that things would turn out badly if the hospital would 'abandon' her. In this way, she still showed manipulative behavior.

Hospital staff was divided about their opinions regarding Kelly's progress and the need for continuation of her treatment. In order to facilitate the decision-making process regarding Kelly's discharge or extension of the resocialization phase of her court-ordered treatment for an additional year, a comprehensive risk assessment was carried out, which constitutes an in-depth evaluation of the risk factors as well as the protective factors that are present in each context. This risk assessment results in an advice to the court regarding prolongation or termination of mandatory treatment. In this advisory report the most important risk and protective factors are described in relation to each other and to the likelihood of possible violent outcome.

Risk Assessment

It was decided to conduct Kelly's risk assessment for two different contexts: (1) prolongation of the current court-ordered treatment in the resocialization phase, with intensive supervision and guarantee of readmission to the hospital in case of relapse; (2) conditional discharge from her mandatory forensic psychiatric treatment, with probation supervision and continued voluntary outpatient treatment in place. To asses Kelly's risk factors, the HCR-20^{V3} was rated. In order to complement the assessment of the risk factors with concepts of particular importance for women, the *Female Additional Manual* to the HCR-20^{V3} (FAM^{V3}; de Vogel et al., 2014) was also used, which includes eight gender-specific risk factors. Finally, to provide an in-depth assessment of Kelly's protective factors, the SAPROF was used.

Risk Factors

The most important HCR-20^{V3} historical risk factors for Kelly are problems with *Relationships*, *Substance abuse* problems, and the (borderline) *Personality disorder*. The recent past shows a more positive picture, as Kelly has made substantial progress during treatment in regards to her risk factors, such as reduced problems with *Insight*, *Instability*, and *Treatment or supervision response*. *Stress/coping* is still seen as an important dynamic risk factor, however. Loneliness is coded as an additional risk factor, as this may lead to seeking new intimate relationships and the temptation of alcohol use. In addition, the use of the FAM shows some important gender-specific additional risk factors for Kelly: *Suicidal behavior/self-harm*, *Covert/manipulative behavior*, *Low self-esteem*, and future *Problematic intimate relationships*.

Protective Factors

The SAPROF assessment provides an overview of the positive factors that are important for Kelly to keep her life on the right track. Table 17.5 presents Kelly's ratings on the SAPROF for the context of: (1) prolongation of the resocialization phase of treatment with intensive supervision by hospital staff; (2) conditional discharge from treatment with probation supervision. Her good *Intelligence* is seen as an important protective factor for Kelly, as this gives her the capacity to gain insight and facilitates her opportunities for the future (e.g., regarding work). *Secure attachment* in childhood was very limited. Kelly's *Empathy* has improved, as she now better understands the devastating impact of her violent behavior on others. Her main *Coping* skill is seeking support from her treatment team, to the point that she becomes overly dependent when she is severely stressed. For the context of discharge, seeking support from the treatment team will no longer be possible, and thus she will have to find support from the probation officer or the outpatient therapist, who are not as closely involved. The protective factors *Self-control* and *Motivation for treatment* have clearly increased during treatment but may drop somewhat again when she is no longer intensively supervised and stimulated by the treatment team. Kelly remains highly motivated to abstain from alcohol use and is willing to keep taking Naltrexone (*Medication*). She has no debts and manages her finances rather well (*Financial management*). Her *Work* in the veterinary practice is considered to be an important protective factor for Kelly, as it provides her with structure in daily life, and she loves working with animals. Her *Social network* is seen as reasonably protective. The relationship with her mother's family has improved and is quite supportive, although her mother does not recognize alcohol as a risk factor for Kelly. All contact with father is broken, and Kelly does not have many close friends, nor is she in a supportive *Intimate relationship*. She does not take part in any structured social *Leisure activities* and finds it difficult to formulate *Life goals* for the future. *Professional care* is seen as a crucial protective factor. Even in the current resocialization phase, the hospital care is highly intensive. Kelly remains open to her treatment team, but is also demanding and quickly feels neglected if she does not get the attention she needs. She sometimes tends to lie about things still, although she does not conceal important issues anymore (*Attitudes towards authority*). It is important for her to become more independent and start seeking more support from her outpatient therapist instead. Currently, the treatment team still provides supervision on the *Living circumstances* to some degree, and with the court order still in place mandating treatment, she receives intensive *External control*. In case the context changes to conditional discharge, these

Table 17.5 SAPROF Ratings for the Case of Kelly in the Context of Prolonged Treatment (Context 1) or Conditional Discharge (Context 2)

Internal Factors		Score		Key	Goal
		Context 1	**Context 2**		
1	Intelligence	2		✓	
2	Secure attachment in childhood	0		☐	
3	Empathy	1	1	☐	☐
4	Coping	1+	1−	☐	✓
5	Self-control	2	1	☐	☐
Motivational Factors		**Score**		**Key**	**Goal**
		Context 1	**Context 2**		
6	Work	2	2	✓	☐
7	Leisure activities	0	0	☐	✓
8	Financial management	2	2	☐	☐
9	Motivation for treatment	2	1	✓	☐
10	Attitudes towards authority	1	1−	☐	✓
11	Life goals	0	0	☐	☐
12	Medication	2	2	☐	☐
External factors		**Score**		**Key**	**Goal**
		Context 1	**Context 2**		
13	Social network	1	1	☐	✓
14	Intimate relationship	0	0	☐	☐
15	Professional care	2	1	✓	☐
16	Living circumstances	1	0	☐	☐
17	External control	2	1	☐	☐

Final Judgments

Final Protection Judgment		**Integrative Final Risk Judgment** (based on SAPROF + risk-focused tools)	
Context 1	**Context 2**	**Context 1**	**Context 2**
☐ Low	☐ Low	✓ Low	☐ Low
☐ Low-Moderate	☐ Low-Moderate	☐ Low-Moderate	☐ Low-Moderate
☐ Moderate	✓ Moderate	☐ Moderate	✓ Moderate
✓ Moderate-High	☐ Moderate-High	☐ Moderate-High	☐ Moderate-High
☐ High	☐ High	☐ High	☐ High

Note: Coding of the SAPROF items: 0 = not present; 1 = present to some extent; 2 = present.

Key factor: item is considered essential for the prevention of violent behavior.

Goal factor: item is considered important as a treatment target and improvement on this item is likely to have a valuable protective effect.

HCR-20[V3] and FAM[V3] ratings are not shown in the table but are included in the Integrative Final Risk Judgment.

external protective factors will be less present. Overall, her *Intelligence, Work, Motivation for treatment,* and the continued *Professional care* are seen as Key factors (i.e., factors that are deemed essential for not relapsing). Further improving her *Coping* skills, *Leisure activities,* and *Attitudes towards authority,* as well as expanding her *Social network,* are seen as Goal factors (i.e., factors that should be attended to in treatment over the coming year).

Integrating the results from both the risk-focused assessment tools HCR-20^{V3}/FAM^{V3} and the protection-focused assessment with the SAPROF, together provides an all-round view of Kelly's strengths and weaknesses. For the context of prolonged treatment in the resocialization phase of her court-ordered treatment, the final risk judgment of violent behavior in the coming year is judged as *low*. Without the context of intensive supervision/mandatory treatment, Kelly loses the valuable support and supervision from the treatment team, which may also bring down some other important protective factors, such as *Coping, Self-control,* and *Motivation for treatment.* Therefore, it is deemed more likely that Kelly would relapse into alcohol abuse and risky intimate relationships, and subsequently that her violence risk will increase (judged as *moderate*). Based on the overall risk assessment, it is advised to the court to prolong the mandatory treatment for another year, as the treatment team deems it too early for Kelly to be conditionally discharged. The major aim of treatment for the coming year would be to help Kelly become more independent and further improve the protective factors indicated as treatment goals.

The court follows the hospital's advice and extends the court order for another year. In the following 12 months, Kelly manages to expand her *Leisure activities* and *Social network,* through joining a sports club and taking part in art classes. When she feels sad or insecure, Kelly is more and more able to seek help from her outpatient therapist and from her family instead of demanding hospital staff's attention (*Coping*). One year later, a new risk assessment is carried out for Kelly, which shows a more promising expectation for the discharge context. This results in a conditional discharge from the mandatory treatment by the court, in line with the hospital's positive advice.

The additional value of coding the SAPROF in this case for two different contexts was that the in-depth evaluation of protective factors provided a more balanced risk assessment, and that the comparison of the different contexts brought further consideration regarding the necessity of intensive supervision, which could be communicated clearly with the court. Moreover, the SAPROF assessment provided additional insights into Kelly's strengths and weaknesses and offered concrete guidelines for further treatment interventions. Finally, the increased focus on positive factors made it easier to communicate the risk assessment results with Kelly and her network, and enhanced the treatment alliance between the treatment team and the patient.

References

Abbiati, M., Palix, J., Gasser, J., & Moulin, V. (2019). Predicting physically violent misconduct in prison: A comparison of four risk assessment instruments. *Behavioral Sciences & the Law, 37,* 61–77. doi:10.1002/bsl.2364

Abidin, Z., Davoren, M., Naughton, L., Gibbons, O., Nulty, A., & Kennedy, H. G. (2013). Susceptibility (risk and protective) factors for in-patient violence and self-harm: Prospective study of structured professional judgement instruments START and SAPROF, DUNDRUM-3 and DUNDRUM-4 in forensic mental health services. *BMC Psychiatry, 13,* 197. doi:10.1186/1471-244X-13-197

Andrews, D. A., Bonta, J., & Wormith, S. J. (2004). *The level of service/case management inventory (LS/CMI).* Toronto, ON: Multi-Health Systems.

Barnard-Croft, E. (2014). *A quantitative research report on the validity of the SAPROF to predict community violence, with a focus on comparisons across different diagnostic groups* (Master's thesis). University of Manchester, Manchester.

Bhanwer, A. K. (2016). *The structured assessment of protective factors for violence risk—youth version (SAPROF-YV): The association between protective factors and aggression in adolescents* (Master's thesis). Simon Fraser University, Burnaby, BC.

Borum, R., Bartel, P., & Forth, A. (2006). *Manual for the structured assessment for violence risk in youth (SAVRY)*. Odessa, FL: Psychological Assessment Resources.

Bowers, L., Stewart, D., Papadopoulos, C., Dack, C., Ross, J., Khanom, H., & Jeffery, D. (2011). *Inpatient violence and aggression: A literature review*. Report from the Conflict and Containment. London: Reduction Research Programme, Section of Mental Health Nursing, Health Service and Population Research, Institute of Psychiatry, Kings College.

Brand, J. (2018). *Effect of protective factors on outward aggression within forensic inpatients* (Master's thesis). University of Twente, Enschede, The Netherlands.

Chu, C. M., Xu, X., Li, D., Ruby, K., & Chng, G. S. (2020). The utility of SAPROF-YV ratings for predicting recidivism in male youth under community supervision in Singapore. *Criminal Justice and Behavior, 47,* 1409–1427. doi:10.1177/0093854820949595

Coid, J. W., Kallis, C., Doyle, M., Shaw, J., & Ullrich, S. (2015). Identifying causal risk factors for violence among discharged patients. *PloS One, 11,* 1–17. doi:10.1371/journal.pone.0142493

Coid, J. W., Ullrich, S., Kallis, C., Freestone, M., Gonzalez, R., Bui, L., . . . Bebbington, P. (2016). Improving risk management for violence in mental health services: A multimethods approach. *Programme grants for applied research, 4*(16). doi:10.3310/pgfar04160

Coupland, R. B. A. (2015). *An examination of dynamic risk, protective factors, and treatment-related change in violent offenders* (Doctoral thesis). University of Saskatchewan. Retrieved from https://ecommons.usask.ca/handle/10388/ETD-2015-03-1998

Davoren, M., Abidin, Z., Naughton, L., Gibbons, O., Nulty, A., Wright, B., & Kennedy, H. G. (2013). Prospective study of factors influencing conditional discharge from a forensic hospital: The DUNDRUM-3 programme completion and DUNDRUM-4 recovery structured professional judgement instruments and risk. *BMC Psychiatry, 13,* 185. doi:10.1186/1471-244X-13-185

de Ruiter, C., & Nicholls, T. L. (2011). Protective factors in forensic mental health: A new frontier. *International Journal of Forensic Mental Health, 10,* 160–170. doi:10.1080/14999013.2011.600602

de Vogel, V., & Nicholls, T. L. (2016). Gender matters: An introduction to the special issue on women and girls. *International Journal of Forensic Mental Health, 15,* 1–25. doi:10.1080/14999013.2016.1141439

de Vogel, V., de Ruiter, C., Bouman, Y., & de Vries Robbé, M. (2007). *SAPROF: Richtlijnen voor het beoordelen van beschermende factoren voor gewelddadig gedrag* (Versie 1). [*SAPROF: Guidelines for the assessment of protective factors for violence risk* (Version 1)]. Utrecht, The Netherlands: Forum Educatief.

de Vogel, V., de Ruiter, C., Bouman, Y., & de Vries Robbé, M. (2009). *SAPROF: Guidelines for the assessment of protective factors for violence risk*. Utrecht, The Netherlands: Forum Educatief.

de Vogel, V., de Ruiter, C., Bouman, Y., & de Vries Robbé, M. (2012). *SAPROF: Guidelines for the assessment of protective factors for violence risk* (2nd ed.). Utrecht, The Netherlands: Van der Hoeven Stichting.

de Vogel, V., de Vries Robbé, M., van Kalmthout, W., & Place, C. (2012). *Female additional manual (FAM). Additional guidelines to the HCR-20 for assessing risk for violence in women*. Utrecht, The Netherlands: Van der Hoeven Stichting.

de Vogel, V., de Vries Robbé, M., van Kalmthout, W., & Place, C. (2014). *FAMV3: Female additional manual. Additional guidelines to the HCR-20V3 for assessing risk for violence in women* (English version). Utrecht, The Netherlands: Van der Hoeven Kliniek.

de Vogel, V., van den Broek, E., & de Vries Robbé, M. (2014). The use of the HCR-20V3 in Dutch forensic psychiatric practice. *International Journal of Forensic Mental Health, 13,* 109–121. doi:10.1080/14999013.2014.906518

de Vries Robbé, M. (2014). *Protective factors: Validation of the structured assessment of protective factors for violence risk in forensic psychiatry*. Utrecht, The Netherlands: Van der Hoeven Kliniek. Retrieved from www.saprof.com

de Vries Robbé, M., & de Vogel, V. (2013). Protective factors for violence risk: Bringing balance to risk assessment. In C. Logan & L. Johnstone (Eds.), *Managing clinical risk: A guide to effective practice* (pp. 293–310). London: Routledge.

de Vries Robbé, M., & de Vogel, V. (2014). *SAPROF interview self-appraisal (SAPROF-ISA)*. Utrecht, The Netherlands: Van der Hoeven Kliniek.

de Vries Robbé, M., de Vogel, V., & de Spa, E. (2011). Protective factors for violence risk in forensic psychiatric patients: A retrospective validation study of the SAPROF. *International Journal of Forensic Mental Health, 10,* 178–186. doi:10.1080/14999013.2011.600232 de Vries Robbé, M., de Vogel, V., & Douglas, K. S. (2013). Risk factors and protective factors: A two-sided dynamic approach to violence risk assessment. *The Journal of Forensic Psychiatry & Psychology, 24*, 440–457. doi:10.1080/14789949.2013.818162

de Vries Robbé, M., de Vogel, V., Douglas, K. S., & Nijman, H. L. I. (2014). Changes in dynamic risk and protective factors for violence during inpatient forensic psychiatric treatment: Predicting reductions in post-discharge community recidivism. *Law and Human Behavior, 39*, 53–61. doi:10.1037/lhb0000089

de Vries Robbé, M., de Vogel, V., Koster, K., & Bogaerts, S. (2015a). Assessing protective factors for sexually violent offending with the SAPROF. *Sexual Abuse: A Journal of Research and Treatment, 27*, 51–70. doi:10.1177/1079063214550168

de Vries Robbé, M., de Vogel, V., Wever, E. C., Douglas, K. S., & Nijman, H. L. I. (2016). Risk and protective factors for inpatient aggression. *Criminal Justice and Behavior, 43*, 1364–1385. doi:10.1177/0093854816637889

de Vries Robbé, M., Geers, M. C. K., Stapel, M., Hilterman, E. L. B., & de Vogel, V. (2015b). *SAPROF— youth version: Structured assessment of protective factors for violence risk—youth version. Guidelines for the assessment of protective factors for violence risk in juveniles.* Utrecht, The Netherlands: Van der Hoeven Kliniek.

de Vries Robbé, M., Hounsome, J., Carey, J., Jones, E., Brown, A., & Whittington, R. (2018). *SAPROF— intellectual disabilities: Additional guidelines for the assessment of protective factors for violence risk in individuals with an intellectual disability. Pilot manual.* Loosdrecht: SAPROF International.

de Vries Robbé, M., Mann, R. E., Maruna, S., & Thornton, D. (2015c). An exploration of protective factors supporting desistance from sexual offending. *Sexual Abuse: A Journal of Research and Treatment, 27*, 16–33. doi:10.1177/1079063214547582

de Vries Robbé, M., Upfold, C., Rangan, M., Moulden, H., Mamak, M., & Chaimowitz, G. (2019). *Protective factors and their relation to violent incidents and release decision-making.* Paper presented at the Annual IAFMHS Conference, Montreal, Quebec.

de Vries Robbé, M., van den Nagel, A., Bohle, A., & Veldhuizen, A. (2018). *SAPROF—long-term care: Additional guidelines for the assessment of protective factors for violence risk in patients residing in long-term (forensic) psychiatric care.* Loosdrecht: SAPROF International.

de Vries Robbé, M., Veldhuizen, A., Helmers, N., Vullings, K., & van Hoof, L. (2020). *Protective factors for juvenile and young adult boys and girls.* Manuscript submitted for publication.

de Vries Robbé, M., & Willis, G. (2017). Assessment of protective factors in clinical practice. *Aggression and Violent Behavior, 32*, 55–63. doi:10.1016/j.avb.2016.12.006

de Vries Robbé, M., Willis, G., Thornton, D., & Kelley, S. (2018). *SAPROF—sexual offending. structured assessment of protective factors for violence risk sexual offending SPJ version: Pilot manual.* Loosdrecht: SAPROF International.

Dickson, S. R., Willis, G. M., & Mather, D. (2018). Protective factors and the good lives model: Combining positive approaches to assessment and treatment. In J. L. Jeglic & C. Calkins (Eds.), *New frontiers in offender treatment* (pp. 43–56). Cham, Switzerland: Springer.

Domjancic, T., Wilkie, T., Darani, S., Williams, B., Maheru, B., & Jamal, Z. (2019). Clinicians' perceptions of the implementation of the structured assessment of protective factors for violence risk (SAPROF) on an inpatient forensic unit. *International Journal of Risk and Recovery, 2*. doi:10.15173/ijrr.v2i2.3966

Douglas, K. S., Hart, S. D., Webster, C. D., & Belfrage, H. (2013). *HCR-20^{V3} assessing risk for violence: User guide.* Vancouver, BC: Mental Health, Law, and Policy Institute, Simon Fraser University.

Doyle, M., Coid, J., Archer-Power, L., Dewa, L., Hunter-Didrichsen, A., Stevenson, R., . . . Shaw, J. (2014). Discharges to prison from medium secure psychiatric units in England and Wales. *The British Journal of Psychiatry, 205*, 177–182. doi:10.1192/bjp.bp.113.136622

Fernandez, Y., Harris, A. J. R., Hanson, R. K., & Sparks, J. (2012). *STABLE-2007 coding manual: Revised 2012.* Unpublished scoring manual, Public Safety Canada, Ottawa.

Fleiss, J. L. (1986). *The design and analysis of clinical experiments.* New York: Wiley.

Haines, A., Brown, A., Javaid, S. F., Khan, F., Noblett, S., Omodunbi, O., . . . Whittington, R. (2018). Assessing protective factors for violence risk in UK general mental health services using the structured assessment of protective factors. *International Journal of Offender Therapy and Comparative Criminology, 62*, 3965–3983. doi:10.1177/0306624X17749449

Hoge, R. D., & Andrews, D. A. (2006). *Youth level of service/case management inventory (YLS/CMI): User's manual.* Toronto, ON: Multi-Health Systems.

Judges, R. C. (2016). *An exploration into the value of protective factors in violence risk assessment of psychiatric inpatients* (Doctoral dissertation). University of Nottingham. Retrieved from http://eprints.nottingham. ac.uk/32959/1/judges%20r%20research%20thesis%20amended.pdf

Kashiwagi, H., Kikuchi, A., Koyama, M., Saito, D., & Hirabayashi, N. (2018). Strength-based assessment for future violence risk: A retrospective validation study of the structured assessment of protective factors for violence risk (SAPROF) Japanese version in forensic psychiatric inpatients. *Annals of General Psychiatry, 17*, 5. doi:10.1186/s12991-018-0175-5

Kleeven, A. T. H., de Vries Robbé, M., Mulder, E. A., & Popma, A. (2020a). *Risk assessment in young adult offenders: Juvenile or adult tools?* Manuscript submitted for publication.

Kleeven, A. T. H., de Vries Robbé, M., Mulder, E. A., & Popma, A. (2020b). Risk assessment in juvenile and young adult offenders: Predictive validity of the SAVRY and SAPROF-YV. *Assessment, 1*–17, doi: 10.1177/1073191120959740

Klepfisz, G., Daffern, M., & Day, A. (2017). Understanding protective factors for violent reoffending in adults. *Aggression and Violent Behavior, 32*, 80–87. doi:10.1016/j.avb.2016.12.001

Kropp, P. R., & Hart, S. D. (2000). The spousal assault risk assessment (SARA) guide: Reliability and validity in adult male offenders. *Law and Human Behavior, 24*, 101–118. doi:10.1023/A:1005430904495

Li, D., Chu, C. M., Xu, X., Zeng, G., & Ruby, K. (2019). Risk and protective factors for probation success among youth offenders in Singapore. *Youth Violence and Juvenile Justice, 17*, 194–213. doi:10.1177/1541204018778887

Neil, C., O'Rourke, S., Ferreira, N., & Flynn, L. (2020). Protective factors in violence risk assessment: Predictive validity of the SAPROF and HCR-20V3. *International Journal of Forensic Mental Health, 19*, 84–102. doi: 10.1080/14999013.2019.1643811

Neves, A. C., de Vries Robbé, M., van den Nagel, A., Bohle, A., & Veldhuizen, A. (2019). Enhancing protective factors in the management of violence risk in long-term stay patients. In B. Völlm & P. Braun (Eds.), *Long-term forensic psychiatric care* (pp. 123–137). Cham, Switzerland: Springer Nature.

Nyman, M., Hofvander, B., Nilsson, T., & Wijk, H. (2019). Mental health nurses' experiences of risk assessments for care planning in forensic psychiatry. *International Journal of Forensic Mental Health, 1*–11. doi:10.1080/14999013.2019.1646356

O'Shea, L. E., & Dickens, G. L. (2016). Performance of protective factors assessment in risk prediction for adults: Systematic review and meta-analysis. *Clinical Psychology: Science and Practice, 23*, 126–138. doi:10.1111/cpsp.12146

Oziel, S. (2016). *The reliability and validity of the SAPROF among forensic mental health patients* (Doctoral dissertation). Ryerson University, Toronto, ON.

Persson, M., Belfrage, H., Fredriksson, B., & Kristiansson, M. (2017). Violence during imprisonment, forensic psychiatric care, and probation: Correlations and predictive validity of the risk assessment instruments COVR, LSI-R, HCR-20V3, and SAPROF. *International Journal of Forensic Mental Health, 16*, 117–129. doi:10.1080/14999013.2016.1266420

Polaschek, D. L. (2017). Protective factors, correctional treatment and desistance. *Aggression and Violent Behavior, 32*, 64–70. doi:10.1016/j.avb.2016.12.005

Prentky, R., & Righthand, S. (2003). *Juvenile sex offender assessment protocol-II (J-SOAP-II) manual.* Washington, DC: U.S. Department of Justice, Office of Justice Programs, Office of Juvenile Justice and Delinquency Prevention.

Quinsey, V. L., Harris, G. T., Rice, M. E., & Cormier, C. A. (1998). *Violent offenders: Appraising and managing risk.* Washington, DC: American Psychological Association.

Rodermond, E., Kruttschnitt, C., Slotboom, A., & Bijleveld, C. C. J. H. (2016). Female desistance: A review of the literature. *European Journal of Criminology, 13*, 3–28. doi:10.1177/1477370815597251

Rogers, R. (2000). The uncritical acceptance of risk assessment in forensic practice. *Law and Human Behavior, 24*, 595–605. doi:10.1023/A:1005575113507

Rowe, R. C. (2015, June 5). *Risks, needs, and strengths: Looking at the YLS/CMI in a different way.* Conference presentation at the CPA/N3 Conference, Ottawa.

Schell, V., & Rowe, R. C. (2015, June 5). *Assessing adolescent protective factors in both criminal justice and inpatient forensic samples.* Conference presentation at the CPA/N3 Conference, Ottawa.

Tozdan, S., Briken, P., Yoon, D., & von Franqué, F. (2016). Risk and protective factors among sexual offenders: Relapse prediction and changes during treatment. *Psychiatrische Praxis, 43*, 154–159. doi:10.1055/s-0034-1387404

Turner, D., Rettenberger, M., Yoon, D., Klein, V., Eher, R., & Briken, P. (2016). Risk assessment in child sexual abusers working with children. *Sexual Abuse: A Journal of Research and Treatment, 28*, 572–596. doi:10.1177/1079063214564390

Viljoen, S., Nicholls, T. L., Roesch, R., Gagnon, N., Douglas, K., & Brink, J. (2016). Exploring gender differences in the utility of strength-based risk assessment measures. *International Journal of Forensic Mental Health, 15*, 149–163. doi:10.1080/14999013.2016.1170739

Viljoen, S., Viljoen, J. L., Nicholls, T., & de Vries Robbé, M. (2017). The role of protective factors in forensic risk assessments. In R. Roesch & A. N. Cook (Eds.), *Handbook of forensic mental health services* (pp. 179–215). New York: Taylor & Francis.

Ward, T. (2002). Good lives and the rehabilitation of offenders: Promises and problems. *Aggression and Violent Behavior, 7*, 513–528. doi:10.1016/S1359-1789(01)00076-3

Ward, T. (2017). Prediction and agency: The role of protective factors in correctional rehabilitation and desistance. *Aggression and Violent Behavior, 32*, 19–28. doi:10.1016/j.avb.2016.11.012

Webster, C. D., Douglas, K. S., Eaves, D., & Hart, S. D. (1997). *HCR-20: Assessing the risk of violence* (Version 2). Burnaby, BC: Simon Fraser University and Forensic Psychiatric Services Commission of British Columbia.

Wong, S., & Gordon, A. (1999–2003). *Violence risk scale (VRS)*. Saskatoon: Regional Psychiatric Centre. Retrieved from www.psynergy.ca

Worling, J. R. (2013). *Desistence for adolescents who sexually harm (DASH-13)*. Unpublished scoring manual. Retrieved from www.drjamesworling.com/dash-13

The Structured Assessment of Violence Risk in Youth (SAVRY)

Randy Borum, Henny P.B. Lodewijks, Patrick A. Bartel, and Adelle E. Forth

Description of Measure

The *Structured Assessment of Violence Risk in Youth* (SAVRY) (Borum, Bartel, & Forth, 2006) is a structured professional judgment (SPJ) tool for assessing violence risk in adolescents (between the approximate ages of 12 and 18). For purposes of using the instrument, violence is defined as "an act of physical battery sufficiently severe to cause injury that would require medical attention, a threat with a weapon in hand, or any act of forcible sexual assault." Risk itself is viewed as the product of dynamic and reciprocal interplay between factors that increase, and factors that decrease, the likelihood of violent offending in the developing young person over time (Borum & Verhaagen, 2006). Although designed specifically to assess risk of violence, several studies have found the SAVRY also to be effective in estimating risk of general criminal or delinquent recidivism (Olver, Stockdale, & Wormith, 2009; Lawing, Childs, Frick, & Vincent, 2017). It has been less successful for appraising risk of sexual offending specifically, but its performance has been comparable to that of other tools designed for juvenile sex offender assessment.

As with most SPJ risk tools, the SAVRY structures professionals' inquiries so that they consider risk factors that are empirically associated with violence, determine the applicability of each risk factor for a particular examinee, and classify each factor's severity and significance (De Bortoli, Ogloff, Coles, & Dolan, 2016; Douglas, 2019; Haque & Webster, 2013). The ultimate determination of a youth's overall level of violence risk is based on the examiner's professional judgment as informed by a systematic appraisal of relevant factors. In this way, the SPJ model draws on the strengths of both the clinical and actuarial (formula-driven) approaches to decision-making and attempts to minimize their respective drawbacks (Borum & Douglas, 2003; Webster, Haque, & Hucker, 2014).

The SAVRY protocol is composed of 6 protective factors and 24 risk factors (see Table 18.1 for a list of SAVRY items). Risk factors are rationally divided into three categories: *Historical, Individual,* and *Social/Contextual.* The SAVRY risk assessment protocol also allows for listing "Additional Risk Factors" and "Additional Protective Factors" based on the assumption that SAVRY is not exhaustive in identifying all potential risk and protective factors for any given individual. In the course of conducting a risk assessment or assessing patterns in past violent episodes, additional factors or situational variables may emerge that are important in understanding a particular juvenile's potential for future violence. In such situations, the evaluator should document and consider these additional factors in the final risk decisions.

Including protective factors is essential in the risk assessment process and is an important feature of the SAVRY (Bernat, Oakes, Pettingell, & Resnick, 2012; De Bortoli et al., 2016; de Vries Robbé, & Willis, 2017; Hall et al., 2012). Protective factors are regarded differently from the simple absence of a risk factor. Indeed, protective factors are "conceptualized as variables that reflect involvement with and commitment to conventional society, that control against nonnormative

Table 18.1 Items From the Structured Assessment of Violence Risk in Youth (SAVRY)

Historical Risk Factors
- History of Violence
- History of Nonviolent Offending
- Early Initiation of Violence
- Past Supervision/Intervention Failures
- History of Self-Harm or Suicide Attempts
- Exposure to Violence in the Home
- Childhood History of Maltreatment
- Parental/Caregiver Criminality
- Early Caregiver Disruption
- Poor School Achievement

Social/Contextual Risk Factors
- Peer Delinquency
- Peer Rejection
- Stress and Poor Coping
- Poor Parental Management
- Lack of Personal/Social Support
- Community Disorganization

Individual/Clinical Risk Factors
- Negative Attitudes
- Risk Taking/Impulsivity
- Substance Use Difficulties
- Anger Management Problems
- Lack of Empathy/Remorse
- Attention Deficit/Hyperactivity Difficulties
- Poor Compliance
- Low Interest/Commitment to School

Protective Factors
- Prosocial Involvement
- Strong Social Support
- Strong Attachments and Bonds
- Positive Attitude Toward Intervention and Authority
- Strong Commitment to School
- Resilient Personality Traits

activities, and that refer to activities incompatible with normative transgression" (Jessor, van den Bos, Vanderryn, Costa, & Turbin, 1995, p. 931). Although research on protective factors is more limited than research on risk factors, a number of studies have found them to have robust effects in understanding delinquency and problem behaviors, particularly their diminution or desistance (de Vries Robbé, & Willis, 2017; Shepherd, Luebbers, & Ogloff, 2016; Ttofi, Farrington, Piquero, & DeLisi, 2016). For example, among three cohorts of adolescents, Lodewijks, de Ruiter, and Doreleijers (2010) found that protective factors added incremental utility beyond the risk factors in a regression model, that high-risk youth were much less likely to have protective factors than low-risk youth, and that that the combined effects of protective and risk factors explained desistance processes significantly better than either protective or risk factors alone.

The SAVRY is coded on the basis of reliable, available information. In most non-emergency circumstances, it is helpful to include information from an interview with the examinee, a review of relevant and available records (for example, police or probation reports, mental health and social service records), and, if possible, interviews with collateral sources in the community (for example, parents and treatment providers). The time required to gather this information will vary according to the complexity of the case. Once the information is gathered, however, it typically takes only 15 to 20 minutes to code all the SAVRY items.

Because the SAVRY does not use cutoff scores, evaluators assign a code, but not a numerical score, for each item. Risk items have a three-level coding structure for severity (High, Moderate, or Low). For example, in coding the History of Violence item, a youth would be coded as "Low" if he had committed no prior acts of violence, "Moderate" if he was known to have committed one or two violent acts, and "High" if there were three or more. Protective factors are simply coded as present or absent.

The primary objective of the SAVRY is not to "quantify" risk, but to provide operational definitions for key (empirically and professionally supported) risk factors for examiners to *apply* across different assessments and to incorporate into risk management efforts. Accordingly, when faced with uncertainty, how examiners decide to code any given risk item is less critical than how they assess that factor's association with violence in a given case. After carefully weighing the risk and protective factors relevant to a particular examinee, an evaluator must ultimately form an opinion or make a judgment about the nature and degree of the juvenile's risk for violence. As with other SPJ instruments, although the SAVRY is sufficiently flexible to accommodate varying styles of risk communication, the coding form prompts evaluators to make a final *summary risk rating* of Low, Moderate, or High. This summary risk rating is a professional judgment—not an actuarial or algorithmic one—based on the results of the entire SAVRY assessment of risk and protective factors.

Uses and Users

Fundamentally, the SAVRY is designed for use as an "aid" or a "guide" in professional risk assessments and intervention planning for violence risk management in youth. With its emphasis on dynamic factors, the SAVRY is designed also to be useful in intervention planning and monitoring of ongoing progress. This may include formulating clinical treatment plans, determining conditions of community supervision, or planning release and discharge. Those factors that contribute most strongly to increasing risk (that is, criminogenic factors) can be targeted for intervention, and protective factors may be enhanced or implemented to further the overall objective of reducing the risk of future violent behavior. The SAVRY requires a thoughtful, thorough professional assessment to ensure its effectiveness. The SAVRY's main purpose is simply to structure and guide the risk assessment process by increasing the evaluator's consistency and reliance on empirically supported factors, and to give greater transparency to the resulting risk judgment. That is, it is designed to support, rather than replace, professional judgments.

Beyond the general caveats of uses and user qualifications, one additional limitation is worth noting. The SAVRY was designed primarily to support assessments of general violence risk (potential for engaging in some violent act toward anyone during a specified time period), including assessments intended to prevent violent behavior through imposition of supervision or intervention (e.g., probation/community supervision). Assessments *of general violence risk* differ, however, from assessments of *targeted violence*, defined as circumstances where a youth comes to the official attention of a school, clinical, or juvenile justice professional because of a concern about the potential for acting violently toward an identified or identifiable person (Borum, Fein, Vossekuil, & Berglund, 1999; Borum, 2016; Vossekuil, Fein, & Berglund, 2015). If, for example, a teenage boy is referred by his school administrator because other students heard him talking about "blowing up the school," the first-line objective is typically to appraise the likelihood that the boy is on a pathway toward engaging in a violent act toward the school or particular persons at the school, not just his risk for general violence. Targeted violence cases of "threat assessments" must rely more heavily on case-specific facts rather than general nomothetic risk factors. An evaluator could not reasonably assume or dismiss concerns of a targeted attack simply because the general violence risk factors were not present (Borum, 2016).

The SAVRY may be used by professionals in a variety of disciplines who conduct assessments and/or make intervention/supervision plans concerning violence risk in youth. Professionals who engage in these activities should, of course, be aware of and comply with all relevant laws, policies and ethical standards, including only practicing within their areas of competence. At a minimum, those who use the SAVRY should have expertise (that is, knowledge, training, and experience) in child/adolescent development, youth violence and delinquency, and conducting individual assessments. In general, psychologists, psychiatrists, trained juvenile probation officers, and social workers with requisite expertise would be qualified to use the SAVRY. Professionals who meet the general user qualifications often can learn how to use the instrument by studying the manual and learning collaboratively with colleagues by comparing ratings and rationales to identify "weak spots" or rating biases.

The SAVRY Manual does not require that a specified training course be completed, though some systems have adopted their own user guidelines. The State of Connecticut, for example, created its own "Train the Trainer" program to ensure consistency when they adopted the SAVRY for use in their juvenile detention facilities. Similarly, in the Netherlands—where SAVRY assessments are required before any leave is approved for youth residing in a correctional facility or institution—examiners must complete a two-day training program which reviews the instrument's theoretical and empirical underpinnings and includes three group-reviewed case studies to facilitate consistency and appropriate coding of the instrument.

The SAVRY is designed for use primarily with adolescents between the ages of 12 and 18 years of age. It is possible to use the SAVRY when assessing people slightly younger or older than the target ages; however, because SAVRY item selection was based primarily on research with adolescents, its use outside that range requires a greater degree of caution. For young people who fall outside of the intended age range, it is recommended that evaluators also consider using one of the other age-appropriate SPJ risk protocols such as the Historical-Clinical-Risk Management-20 (HCR-20; Douglas, Hart, Webster, & Belfrage, 2013) for young adults or the Early Assessment Risk List tools (EARL; Augimeri, Keogl, Webster, & Levene, 2001; Levene et al., 2001) for children under age 12.

Questions more commonly arise about upward rather than downward extension of the SAVRY, because many juvenile detention facilities can retain jurisdiction over youth through age 21 or longer. Although the HCR-20 has been researched extensively with adults, relatively few studies have focused on the early adult period between the ages of 18 and 22. Accordingly, some have found the SAVRY to be useful in this age range, particularly in cases where the young person still (or before incarceration) lives with his or her parents and is expected to return to their care.

The SAVRY may be used for assessing both male and female adolescents, because the preponderance of existing research suggests that many risk and protective factors operate similarly for both genders, though the sensitivity and rates of exposure for each may differ (Blum, Ireland, & Blum, 2003; Connor, Steingard, Anderson, & Melloni, 2003; Geraghty & Woodhams, 2015; Hilterman Bongers, Nicholls, & Van Nieuwenhuizen, 2016; Kaltiala-Heino, Putkonen, & Eronen, 2013; Shepherd, Luebbers, & Dolan, 2013; Zahn et al., 2008). The SAVRY authors do understand and appreciate that a substantial proportion of existing research on violence risk factors has been conducted only on males. As data increasingly become available on gender-based differences on SAVRY-coded items, the authors remain open to the possibility of developing a modification for girls, but any such effort will be informed and guided by sound, convincing empirical research (Assink et al., 2015; van der Put et al., 2014).

In the current SAVRY Manual, where known research indicates a particular risk factor may apply differently to males and females, this is noted in the specific item descriptions (Geraghty & Woodhams, 2015; Hilterman et al., 2016; Penney, Lee, & Moretti, 2010). A number of studies internationally suggest, for example, that trauma—particularly from sexual abuse—may bear a stronger causal relationship to violent behavior in girls than boys (Odgers, Moretti, & Reppucci, 2005; van der Put et al., 2014). Girls in the juvenile justice system, however, are twice as likely as boys to have been physically abused and four times more likely to have been sexually abused. Also, girls' risk, more so than that of boys, may be affected by caregiver disruption—along with its consequent impact on attachments—parental delinquency, and early sexual maturation (Moretti, Obsuth, Odgers, & Reebye, 2006; van der Put et al., 2014; Wall & Barth, 2005).

Research findings from longitudinal studies such as the Gender and Aggression Project (Moretti, Odgers, & Jackson, 2004; Odgers, Moretti, & Reppucci, 2009), the Pittsburgh Girls Study (Loeber, Jennings, Ahonen, Piquero, & Farrington, 2017), and reviews by the Girls Study Group (Zahn et al., 2008) are converging around certain factors being more sensitive to gender effects including: early puberty or developmental factors, sexual abuse/assault, depression/anxiety, cross-gender peer influence, parental antisocial behavior, and attachments/bonds to school and prosocial institutions. Other lines of inquiry are identifying distinct subgroups and risk profiles of female offenders (Gammelgård, Weizmann-Henelius, Koivisto, Eronen, & Kaltiala-Heino, 2012; Henneberger, Oudekerk, Reppucci, & Odgers, 2014; Walker, Bishop, Nurius, & Logan-Greene, 2016). For example, van der Put and colleagues (2014) discerned four risk profiles among adolescent female offenders: (a) girls with delinquent parents (very high risk); (b) victims of abuse (high risk); (c) repeat offenders (high risk); and (d) first-time offenders (low risk). These kinds of emergent findings should be given special consideration when using the SAVRY with female adolescents.

The SAVRY is used throughout the world, and the instrument and manual have official translations in the following languages: Bulgarian, Catalan, Dutch, Finnish, French, German, Italian, Japanese, Norwegian, Polish, Portuguese, Russian, Slovene, Spanish, and Swedish.

Method and Rationale for Development

Adolescence is the peak developmental risk period for initiating or participating in acts of serious violence (Brame, Turner, Paternoster, & Bushway, 2012; U.S. Department of Health and Human Services, 2001; Vaughn, Salas-Wright, DeLisi, & Maynard, 2014). Consequently, risk assessments are often requested in juvenile justice settings, schools, psychiatric emergency services, civil psychiatric hospitals, outpatient clinics, and other settings. Historically, most assessments were unstructured clinical assessments conducted by mental health practitioners. Through the 1990s, however, as risk assessment research and assessment technology emerged, the need for better methods and greater reliance on empirical research became strikingly apparent.

Though some advances had been made with adult risk assessment tools, reflected by many instruments covered in this book, specialized efforts were needed for adolescent evaluations to address developmental differences in the nature of risk, relevance of risk factors, and operation of risk factors (Assink et al., 2015; Borum & Grisso, 2006; Borum & Verhaagen, 2006; Hoge, 2001, 2002; Singh & Fazel, 2010), all of which are critical determinants of youths' behavior (Mercy, & Vivolo-Kantor, 2016; van der Put et al., 2011). Violence risk in adolescents differs from adults in a variety of important ways. The base rates or normative expectations are dissimilar. While adults and adolescents share some common risk factors, the mechanism and strength of the association often varies developmentally between adolescents and adults, and even between children and adolescents (Malti & Averdijk, 2017). Deviant peer influences, for example, are more robust risk factors in teens than in younger children. Conversely, parental and family risk factors weigh more heavily into risk for younger than older youth. Moreover, in risk assessments with juveniles, many personality-related factors are less stable than is typically seen with adults, and the explicit and implicit role of the examinee's degree of psychosocial maturity is more central (Borum & Verhaagen, 2006; Cauffman, Fine, Thomas, & Monahan, 2017; Cauffman, Skeem, Dmitrieva, & Cavanagh, 2016).

In developing the SAVRY, our goal was to draw on the strengths of existing risk assessment technology and empirical findings with youth to create an instrument that would help structure and improve violence risk assessment practice—as well as risk management—with adolescents receiving services from a variety of systems (i.e., treatment, correctional, monitoring, or preventive services). Our appraisal was that a successful assessment guide would need several key features, specifically:

1. *Systematic*: covering the primary domains of known risk and protective factors, with clear operational definitions provided for each.
2. *Empirically grounded*: items need to be based on the best available research and guidelines for juvenile risk assessment practice.
3. *Developmentally informed*: risk and protective factors have to be selected on the basis of how they operate with adolescents, as opposed to children or adults.
4. *Treatment-oriented*: the risk assessment should have direct implications for treatment, which includes considering dynamic factors that can be useful targets for intervention in risk reduction.
5. *Flexible*: allowing consideration of idiographic or case-specific factors as well as those derived from research.
6. *Practical*: using the guide should not require much additional time beyond what is needed to collect information in a competent assessment. It should be inexpensive, easy to learn, and not require diagnostic judgments.

In 2000, the authors compiled items from two youth violence assessment tool prototypes, which they had been working on independently, and evaluated them for inclusion in a combined final version. Risk items were selected primarily on the size and robustness of the empirical relationship between the factor and violence as identified through prior reviews, meta-analyses, and original studies with adolescent populations (e.g., Hann & Borek, 2001; Hawkins et al., 1998, 2000; Howell, 1997; Lipsey & Derzon, 1998). The research base on protective factors for violence in adolescents was much less extensive (U.S. Department of Health & Human Services, 2001); nevertheless, the authors selected those with the greatest promise and that were measurable in a psychosocial assessment. While all included items demonstrated some empirical link to violence, a few, such as Poor Compliance, remained despite a lack of robust research because of their clinical relevance. Next, the authors constructed operational coding definitions for each SAVRY item— drawing from definitions used in prior studies where possible—and developed criteria to anchor the levels of severity. For example, the coding scheme for History of Violence item distinguishes between having no known acts of violence, as operationally defined in the SAVRY Manual (Low), having one or two acts that meet those criteria (Moderate), and having three or more (High).

A pilot version of the items and coding criteria was circulated to several risk assessment professionals for comments and applied in a few preliminary studies where researchers provided feedback about item clarity and language. The items were then revised, tightened, and integrated into a "Consultation Edition" of the SAVRY Manual released in February 2002. The SAVRY was commercially published in 2006 (Borum, Bartel, & Forth, 2006).

Between the initial "Consultation Edition" and commercial publication, the only substantive item change involved a factor first labeled as "Psychopathic Traits." In the initial coding criteria—as is true with some other SPJ instruments—the rating was linked directly to scores on the Hare Psychopathy Checklist: Youth Version (PCL:YV) (Forth, Kosson, & Hare, 2003). The authors subsequently revised the item and removed the PCL:YV from its coding for several reasons. First, the PCL:YV is a psychometric instrument designed to assess the construct of psychopathy. For applied risk assessment, however, we were mainly interested in assessing the relevant cluster of traits as a "risk marker" for violence, rather than the diagnostic construct per se in juveniles. Second, the user qualifications for the SAVRY (a risk assessment tool) are less stringent than for the PCL:YV. Third, connotations of the term *psychopathy* are uniformly negative, and the label itself is so powerful that any information about a youth as an individual may be lost once this language is applied (Boccaccini et al., 2008; Edens, Cowell, Desforges, & Fernandez, 2005; Edens & Vincent, 2008; Murrie et al., 2005, 2007). Further, given that several SAVRY items overlapped substantially with PCL:YV items, we sought to construct an item that captured only the otherwise unaccounted variance in the cluster of personality/behavioral traits. The result was the creation of a new item labeled "Low Empathy/Remorse" to substitute for the "Psychopathic Traits" factor. We examined the empirical effect of this change and found that the SAVRY including a "Psychopathic Traits" factor and one substituting a "Low Empathy/Remorse" factor correlated almost perfectly ($r = .99$) for a community and offender sample. The new "Low Empathy/Remorse" item was then included in a second printing of the SAVRY Manual, designated as "Version 1.1" and in the commercially published version.

Reliability

Internal Consistency

While the SAVRY and its component domains are not intended as formal "scales," for heuristic purposes, we analyzed the internal consistency of SAVRY Risk Total (the sum of item ratings transposed from Low, Moderate, and High to numerical values of 0, 1, and 2) in our validation sample and found it to be .82 for the offenders and .84 for the community sample (Borum, Bartel, & Forth, 2006). Subsequent investigations have found similarly high levels of internal consistency (Childs & Frick, 2016; Hilterman et al., 2016). The risk factor domains—historical, individual, social, and contextual—are aggregated conceptually and are not designed to possess the psychometric properties of a test scale; nevertheless, the domains do show good internal consistency for males and females (Childs & Frick, 2016; Chu et al., 2016; Hilterman et al., 2016; Khanna, Shaw, Dolan, & Lennox, 2014; Klein, Rettenberger, Yoon, Köhler, & Briken, 2015; Lodewijks et al., 2008c; Shepherd, Luebbers, & Ogloff, 2014).

Interrater Reliability

The primary issue of reliability for SPJ instruments, including the SAVRY, is interrater reliability, which indicates the degree of agreement between two or more different raters coding the same case based on the same information. The intraclass correlation coefficient (ICC) is a commonly used index of interrater agreement. Fleiss (1986) suggests using the following critical values for describing single measure ICCs: ICC > .75 = excellent; ICC between .60 and .75 = good; ICC between .40 and .60 = moderate; ICC < .40 = poor. Approximately 16 studies have examined the SAVRY's interrater reliability (see Table 18.2), mostly revealing good to excellent agreement between raters, with ICCs ranging from .67 to 1.0 for the SAVRY Risk Total and .72 to 1.0 for the SAVRY Summary Risk Rating. The risk factor domains—historical, individual, social, and

Table 18.2 Interrater Reliability of the SAVRY Risk Total and Summary Risk Ratings

Study	SAVRY Risk Total ICC	SAVRY Risk Judgment ICC
McEachran, 2001	.83	.72
Catchpole & Gretton, 2003	.81	.77
Dolan & Rennie, 2008	.97	.88
Lodewijks et al., 2008a	.81	.77
Meyers & Schmidt, 2008	.97	.95
Viljoen et al., 2008	.91	N/A
Vincent et al., 2012	.86	.83
Hilterman et al., 2014	.79	.76
Khanna et al., 2014	.97	.88
Shepherd, Luebbers, Ferguson et al., 2014	1.0	1.0
Chu et al., 2016	.67	.88
Gammelgard et al., 2015*	.80	.83
Klein et al., 2015	.94	N/A
Beausoleil et al., 2016	.81	.77
Childs & Frick, 2016	N/A	.79
Hilterman et al., 2016	.83	N/A

*The Gammelgård et al., 2015 study analyzed interrater reliability using point biserial correlations between raters rather than ICCs.

contextual—are aggregated conceptually and are not designed to possess the psychometric properties of a test scale; nevertheless, the domains do show good internal consistency for males and females (Childs & Frick, 2016; Chu, Goh, & Chong, 2016; Hilterman et al., 2016; Khanna et al., 2014; Klein et al., 2015; Lodewijks et al., 2008; Shepherd, Luebbers, Ferguson, Ogloff, & Dolan, 2014). Interrater reliability estimates at the domain level have also been excellent. For example, in a sample of juvenile offenders in Catalonia (Hilterman et al., 2016), the interrater reliability of the SAVRY domains were excellent (ICC: Historical = .77, Social/Contextual = .83, Individual = .84, SAVRY Risk Total = .83, Protective = .83).

Validity

Because SPJ instruments are not numerically driven, their validity is assessed somewhat differently from traditional psychological tests. SPJ tools are designed principally to improve human (professional) judgment by structuring the assessments. Traditional psychometric theory, however, conceptualizes validity as a function of classification accuracy, typically based on one or more cutoff scores. Receiver operating characteristic (ROC) analysis is commonly used in SPJ validity studies. ROC measures predictive accuracy in terms of relative improvement over chance across all possible cutting scores, not just categorical classification based on one given cut point, yielding a measure of the Area Under the Curve (AUC) with values ranging from 0 (perfect negative prediction) to 1.0 (perfect positive prediction), with .50 indicating chance prediction. Although ROC analyses have some advantages over traditional classification approaches as a measure of predictive validity—specifically, that the metric is less affected by criterion base rates—to the extent that AUCs are calculated for "scores," it is arguably an imprecise validity index for SPJ instruments as they are intended to be used in practice.

Nevertheless, validity data must be reported in metrics that users and psychometricians can understand, and that facilitate comparison of different tools or measures. To allow for more traditional validity analyses, for research (not clinical) purposes, a variable called "SAVRY Risk

Total" is sometimes used to represent the contribution of the instrument, independent of the summary risk judgment. The SAVRY Risk Total is calculated by transposing item ratings of Low, Moderate, and High to numerical values of 0, 1, and 2, respectively, and summing the values. To "quantify" the risk judgments, the summary risk ratings (of Low, Moderate, and High) may be similarly transposed. In predictive validity studies, some researchers have reported offending rates for persons in each of the relative risk categories to demonstrate the degree of calibration between judged risk and actual recidivism.

Concurrent Validity

The concurrent validity of the SAVRY has been examined in relation to past violent/delinquent behavioral criteria and to both the Youth Level of Service/Case Management Inventory (YLS/CMI; Hoge & Andrews, 2002; see Chapter 9, this volume) and the Psychopathy Checklist: Youth Version (PCL:YV; Forth et al., 2003). In offender and community samples, the SAVRY Risk Total has shown correlations between .58 and .89 with the YLS/CMI and between .66 and .78 with the PCL:YV (Borum et al., 2006; Chu et al., 2016; Hilterman, Nicholls, & van Nieuwenhuizen, 2014; Welsh, Schmidt, McKinnon, Chattha, & Meyers, 2008). The SAVRY protective domain correlates negatively with both of the other measures: −.46 and −.76 with the YLS/CMI and −.30 and −.64 with the PCL:YV. Because the YLS/CMI and PCL:YV measure only risk factors, this negative correlation is important for showing the discriminant validity of SAVRY's Protective Factors. In addition, Viljoen and colleagues (Viljoen et al., 2008) also found significant correlations between the SAVRY Risk Total and scores on the Juvenile Sex Offender Assessment Protocol-II (J-SOAP-II; Prentky & Righthand, 2003) ($r = .88$) and the Juvenile Sexual Offense Recidivism Risk Assessment Tool-II (J-SORRAT-II; Epperson, Ralston, Fowers, & DeWitt, 2005) ($r = .19$).

The summary risk rating (SRR) has also demonstrated concurrence with other violence-related tools for youth. In a study by Catchpole and Gretton (2003), the SRR correlated .64 with the YLS/CMI summary classification and .68 with the PCL:YV Total Score. Welsh et al. (2008) found a correlation of .58 between the total scores of the two instruments in a community corrections sample, while Hilterman et al. (2014) found a correlation of .74 in a Spanish adolescent sample on community probation. Shepherd, Luebbers et al. (2014) reported strong to very strong significant relationships between several SAVRY domain and YLS/CMI subscale scores, including a Total Score correlation of .87. These correlations, along with additional research referenced later in this chapter, indicate that, although the SAVRY shares variance with both these measures, it also possesses independent variance.

With regard to criterion-related concurrent validity, numerous studies using retrospective analysis and file review have revealed significant correlations between SAVRY scores and various measures of violence in juvenile justice and high-risk community-dwelling populations. In our two initial validation samples (Bartel et al., 2003), after we removed the "History of Violence" item to avoid, at a minimum, substantive criterion contamination, and hence possible validity inflation, SAVRY Total Risk scores were all significantly related to behavioral measures of institutional aggressive behavior ($r = .40$) and aggressive conduct disorder (CD) symptoms ($r = .52$), and protective factors were negatively related to both: $r = −.31$ for institutional aggression and $r = −.20$ for aggressive CD symptoms. Significant correlations have been found in other studies between SAVRY Risk Total scores and measures of violence among young male offenders in Canada ($r = .32$ in one study and $r = .25$ in another) (Catchpole & Gretton, 2003; Gretton & Abramowitz, 2002) and high-risk Native American Youth ($r = .56$ for the total sample, $r = .72$ for females, and $r = .50$ for males) (Fitch, 2002). SAVRY summary risk ratings also correlated with community violence in studies by McEachran (2001) ($r = .67$) and Gretton and Abramowitz (2002) ($r = .35$).

Incremental Validity

In our initial validation study, the SAVRY demonstrated incremental (criterion) validity (or predictive power) beyond the YLS/CMI and the PCL:YV. Hierarchical regression analyses demonstrated that adding the SAVRY improved the predictive strength of a model including the YLS/CMI and the PCL:YV in predicting both institutional aggressive behavior and serious aggressive conduct disorder symptoms. The SAVRY also accounted for a larger proportion of the explained variance than either the YLS/CMI or the PCL:YV for predicting both Aggressive CD symptoms (SAVRY β = .47 vs. .07 for the YLS/CMI and .25 for PCL:YV) and institutional aggression (SAVRY β = .26 vs. .20 for the YLS/CMI vs. .07 for PCL:YV) (Bartel et al., 2003). Welsh et al. (2008) similarly reported that the SAVRY showed strong incremental utility when added to predictive models, initially including only the YLS/CMI and the PCL:YV in predicting both general recidivism and violent recidivism. Schmidt, Campbell, and Houlding (2011), in a 10-year follow-up study also found the SAVRY total had incremental validity over YLS/CMI total. Other studies, however have not found the same result (Hilterman et al., 2014; Shepherd, Luebbers, Ferguson et al., 2014).

Predictive Validity

Using ROC analysis, which measures predictive accuracy in terms of relative improvement over chance, AUCs for the SAVRY Risk Total have shown large effects, averaging about .74 to .80 across numerous studies (see Table 18.3). A meta-analysis of youth risk assessment measures found mean-weighted correlations between SAVRY Total Scores and general recidivism of .32 and violent recidivism of .30 (Olver, Stockdale, & Wormith, 2009). Singh, Grann, and Fazel (2011) conducted a systematic review and meta-analysis of nine risk assessment tools for youth and for adults. Their total sample included 25,980 participants from 68 studies, conducted across 13 countries. The authors found that, among all nine instruments, the SAVRY produced the highest rates of predictive validity across outcome statistics.

While most predictive validity studies use the SAVRY Risk Total, many also assess the SRR. The SRR performance is consistently similar to the linear combination of the scores themselves. This trend has been evident in research on other SPJ tools as well (see Chapter 1, Heilbrun et al., this volume, for a summary), and provides some of the first empirical evidence that clinical judgments—properly structured and based on sound assessments—can achieve levels of accuracy that rival that of any other known predictors while maintaining latitude for case-specific analysis.

The SRRs are linked to actual recidivism. Catchpole and Gretton (2003), for example, reported that youth classified as Low Risk had a 6% violent recidivism rate, while those rated as Moderate Risk and High Risk had rates of 14% and 40%, respectively. Those rated as High Risk also recidivated more quickly than Moderate or Low Risk-rated youth.

Gammelgård, Weitzman-Henelius, and Kaltiala-Heino (2008) examined recidivism rates in a sample of SAVRY-assessed Finnish adolescents. Violent recidivism was reported for only 4% of those rated Low Risk, but 29% of those rated a Moderate Risk and 67% of the High Risk teens (p < .001). A corresponding logistic regression analysis, adjusting the analyses for sex, age, diagnosis, service level, and time of follow-up, showed that the odds of violent recidivism also increased for each risk level. Compared to the Low Risk group, youth rated as Moderate Risk were nearly 4 times more likely to violently offend, and youth rated as High Risk were nearly 28 times more likely. Similarly, Childs et al. (2014) similarly found that all of their juvenile probationers receiving a Low SRR successfully completed their probation, while 20% of those rated "Moderate" and 43% of those rated High were revoked.

Evidence of the superiority or incremental validity of SRRs over the Risk Total have been more mixed. For example, using ROC, McEachran (2001) reported an AUC for SAVRY Risk Total of .70, but the AUC for the SAVRY SRR was .89. Studies by Lodewijks et al. (2008a, 2008b, 2008c) also consistently found the SRRs to outperform the Risk Total scores both for institutional and community violence outcomes.

Other studies, however, particularly at the severe end of youth offending, have not found significant incremental advantages for the SRR (Hilterman et al., 2014; Schmidt et al., 2011; Shepherd, Luebbers, Ferguson et al., 2014). Viljoen and colleagues (2008) studied the validity of the SAVRY and two sexual offense-specific risk instruments for juvenile offenders (J-SOAP-II and the J-SORRAT-II) in a sample of 169 male juvenile sexual offenders. While none of the instruments showed a high degree of power in predicting sexual recidivism specifically (AUC between .51 and .54), in part due to low base rates of detected offenses), the SAVRY Risk Total performed modestly better than the others in predicting serious nonsexual violent offending (SAVRY AUC = .69 vs. .63 for J-SOAP-II and .55 for J-SORRAT-II). The SAVRY SRR (AUC = .56) did no better than the others.

Limitations and Necessary Future Research

Results from the research conducted to date generally support the use of the SAVRY as a reliable and valid tool for assessing violence risk in adolescents. Most studies so far also seem to suggest that the SAVRY predicts general offending in youth as well as it does violent offending (e.g., Welsh et al., 2008). The statistical tabulations of correlations, AUCs, and beta weights are commensurate with psychometric performance of other actuarial and SPJ risk assessment tools. Several open questions remain, however.

Future Research

First, we have not yet definitively discerned whether, and the extent to which, the examiner's summary risk rating contributes to predictive accuracy beyond what can be achieved using the SAVRY Risk Total alone. This is significant because the SAVRY is designed as an SPJ instrument, not an actuarial one. Several studies using SPJ instruments—including a couple using the SAVRY—have found higher validity indices for the summary risk rating than for the score. But at least an equal number of SAVRY studies have not found the rating to significantly outperform the total score. Furthering this line of research will offer evidence-based guidance about how the SAVRY can be most effectively used in practices.

The next generation of SAVRY research should move beyond the broad question of whether it "works" to examine how, for whom, and under what circumstances it is more and less effective. Three areas should receive particular attention: age, gender, and race/ethnicity/culture. At least one study (Viljoen et al., 2008) has found that youth risk assessment instruments performed better with older adolescents than with younger ones. Perhaps some investigators should focus on the interstitial age ranges within the different SPJ violence risk tools and compare the effectiveness between them. Regarding gender, it is clear that research on the causes and correlates of violent offending in girls is moving forward, and that some discernible differences are emerging. Researchers examining the utility of the SAVRY should include girls in their studies whenever possible, and report results for boys and girls separately, so that we can further our efforts to refine our recommendations to SAVRY users. Third, better understanding of how the SAVRY functions when assessing young people from different racial and ethnic groups will be an important issue for future investigations. Olver et al. (2009) found that effect sizes for the major youth risk

Table 18.3 Studies of the Predictive Validity of the SAVRY on Institutional or Community Violent Recidivism

Study	Design	Strength of Association with violent recidivism
Childs et al. (2013)	Probation outcome Retrospective study N = 158 (75% boys)	Prediction probation outcome Risk Rating (nonviolence), $\chi^2 (2) = 32.19$** Risk Rating (violence), $\chi^2 (2) = 23.33$***
Childs et al. (2014)	Prospective study Follow-up: 6 months after supervision N = 177 (131 boys, 46 girls)	Risk Rating, AUC = .58 (ns)
Chu et al. (2016)	Community violence Retrospective study Follow-up: average 55 months after probation N = 163 (all boys)	Total Risk violence AUC = .65* general AUC = .72** Risk Rating, AUC = .63*
Dolan and Rennie (2008)	Community violence Prospective study N = 99 (boys) Follow-up: 6 months post release	Risk Total, AUC = .64* Risk Rating, AUC = .64*
Fitch (2002)	Community violence Retrospective study N = 82 (47 boys, 35 girls) Follow-up: 18 months	Males: Risk Total, r = .50** Females: Risk Total, r = .72*** All: Risk Total, r = 56**
Gammelgård et al. (2008)	Institutional violence Retrospective study N = 147 (boys and girls)	Violent incidents: Risk Total, AUC = .71**
Gammelgård et al. (2015)	Community violence Retrospective study N= 200 (115 boys, 85 girls) Follow-up 4 years after leaving institution for psychiatry or welfare	Total Risk, AUC = .71 Risk Rating (low vs. high), OR = 6.70** Risk Rating (low vs. moderate), OR = 1.29**
Gretton and Abramowitz (2002)	Community violence Retrospective study N = 176 (94% boys) Follow-up: 12 months	Risk Total, AUC = .67* Risk Rating AUC = .74**

(Continued)

Table 18.3 (Continued)

Study	Design	Strength of Association with violent recidivism
Hilterman et al. (2014)	Self-reported community violence Prospective study N = 105 (86 boys; 19 girls) Follow-up after probation: 1 year	Risk Total, AUC = .75** Risk Rating, AUC = .68**
Lawing, Childs, Frick, and Vincent (2017)	Community violence Prospective Study Adjudicated youth on probation N = 505 (95% boys) Follow-up: 12 months	ROC Analysis not used • SAVRY predicted both violent and any reoffending over a 12-month follow-up period • Higher scores on total risk, the Historical domain, and the Individual/Clinical domain predicted shorter time to both general and violent reoffending. • Attentional problems and hyperactivity (as assessed by the ADHD risk item), poor anger control (as assessed by the anger management risk item), and low empathy/remorse also significantly predicted shorter time to both general reoffending and violent reoffending (ADHD and anger management only) • Survival analysis showed youth in the higher quartiles for composite risk indices or higher risk levels on the individual items were more likely to reoffend and to recidivate more quickly
Lodewijks et al. (2008a)	Community violence Retrospective study N = 117 (95% boys) Follow-up: 36 months	Risk Total, AUC = .65* Risk Rating, AUC = .71*
Lodewijks et al. (2008b)	Institutional violence Prospective study N = 66 (boys) Follow-up: 18 months	Violent incidents: Risk Total, AUC = .80** Risk Rating, AUC = .86*** Aggressive incidents: Risk Total, AUC = .73*
Lodewijks et al. (2008c)	Community violence Prospective study N = 82 (47 boys, 35 girls) Follow-up: 18 months post release	Risk Total, (boys) AUC = .76** (girls) AUC = .84* Risk Rating, (boys) AUC = .82*** (girls) AUC = .85***

Study	Details	Findings
McEachran (2001)	*Community violence* Retrospective study N = 108 (boys) Follow-up after release: 36 months	Risk Total: AUC = .70* Risk Rating: AUC = .89**
McGowan et al. (2011)	*Violence in a secondary special school* Retrospective study Follow-up: 12 months N = 87 (all boys)	Risk Total: AUC = .72***
Myers and Schmidt (2008)	*Community violence* Prospective study N = 121 Follow-up: 1 year and 3 years	*(Statistical significance levels not reported)* Violent recidivism: Risk Total (1 year): AUC = .66 Risk Total (3 years): AUC = .77 General recidivism: Risk Total (1 year): AUC = .75 Risk Total (3 years): AUC = .76 Nonviolent recidivism: Risk Total (1 year): AUC = .80 Risk Total (3 years): AUC = .68
Ortega-Campos, García-García, & Zaldívar-Basurto (2017)	*Community violence* Retrospective study N = 594 Spanish Youth (85% boys) Follow-up: 2 years	Risk Total: AUC = .74 Risk Rating: AUC = .75
Penney et al. (2010)	*Community violence* Prospective study Follow-up: 24 months after release N = 144 (80 boys, 64 girls)	*(Statistical significance levels not reported)* Risk Total (boys): AUC = .69 Risk Rating (boys): AUC = .64 Risk Total (girls): AUC = .72 Risk Rating (girls): AUC = .72
Perrault, Vincent, and Guy (2017)	*Community violence* Prospective study Follow-up: 18 months N = 383 (73% male)	Risk Total (nonviolent): AUC = .60 Risk Total (violent): AUC = .69 Risk Rating (nonviolent): AUC = .56 Risk Rating (violent): AUC = .63 Dynamic risk scales accounted for most of the variance in reoffending SAVRY did not differentially predict reoffending as a function of race

(Continued)

Table 18.3 (Continued)

Study	Design	Strength of Association with violent recidivism
Richard (2011)	Community violence Retrospective study Follow-up 1 year, 5 years, and 10 years after release N = 235 (all boys)	Risk Total 1 year AUC = .58* 5 years AUC = .64*** 10 years AUC = .63**
Rieger et al. (2009)	Community violence Retrospective study Follow-up mean: 5,9 years N = 83 (74 boys, 10 girls)	Risk Total (violence) AUC = .64* (serious violence) AUC = .82*** Risk Rating (violence) AUC = .64* (serious violence) AUC = .78*** (sign. levels not reported)
Schmidt et al. (2011)	Community violence Retrospective study Follow-up average 10,4 years after release N = 128 (80 boys, 40 girls)	Boys: Risk Total AUC = .78 Boys: Risk Rating AUC = .71. Girls: Risk Total AUC = .57 Girls; Risk Rating AUC = .57
Shepherd, Luebbers et al. (2014)	Community violence Prospective study N = 215 (175 boys, 38 girls) Follow-up: 6–18 months after release	Risk Total boys AUC = 66** Risk rating boys AUC = .64** Risk Total girls AUC = .65 (ns)
Shepherd, Luebbers, Ferguson et al. (2014)	Community violence Retrospective study English-Speaking Background (ESB) N = 84, Culturally and Linguistically Diverse (CALD N = 59), Indigenous and Torres Strait Islanders (IND) N = 32. Follow-up 6–18 months after release	Risk rating girls AUC = .69 (ns) Risk Total ESB AUC = .68* Risk rating ESB AUC = .66* Risk Total CALD AUC = .47 (ns) Risk rating CALD AUC = .48 (ns) Risk Total IND AUC = .76* Risk Rating IND AUC = .74*
Sijtsema (2015)	Community violence Prospective, based on a general population study Follow-up: 4–7 years N = 816 (357 boys, 429 girls)	Risk Total: Boys r = 15* Girls r = 27*
Viljoen et al. (2008)	Institutional Offending & Community Offending Prospective study N = 169 boys adjudicated for sexual offenses Follow-up: 1 year in Tx 6.5 years in community	Sexual aggression during treatment: Risk Total, AUC = .52 Risk Rating, AUC = .51 Nonsexual aggression during treatment:

Study	Sample	Results
Viljoen, Shaffer, Muir, Cochrane, and Brodersen (2019)	Community violence (probationers) Prospective study N = 166 (76% male) Average Follow-up: 2.3 years	Risk Total, AUC = .69*** Risk Rating, AUC = .59 Sexual offense in community: Risk Total, AUC = .53 Risk Rating, AUC = .51 Serious nonsexual violent offense in community: Risk Total, AUC = .69* Risk Rating, AUC = .56 Any offense in community: Risk Total, AUC = .58 Risk Rating, AUC = .50
Welsh et al. (2008)	Community violence Prospective study N = 133 (67 boys, 38 girls) Average. Follow-up: = 35.8 months	Violent: Risk Total: AUC = .66 Risk Rating: AUC = .60 Any Charge: Risk Total: AUC = .63 Risk Rating: AUC = .59 (Statistical significance levels not reported)
Woods (2013)	Community violence Prospective study Follow-up after probation: average 18 months N = 213 (all African American boys)	Risk Total AUC = .81 General recidivism: Risk Total AUC = .77 Risk Total AUC = .68*
Zhou, Witt, Cao, Chen, and Wang (2017)	Community violence (China) Prospective study Follow-up: 5 years N = 246 (all male)	Risk Total: AUC = .68

Note: Risk Total = Total of risk scores. Risk Rating = Summary risk rating (low, moderate, high) based on expert interpretation of both risk and protective scores. AUC = Area Under the Curve. OR = Odds Ratio. r = Pearson correlation coefficient.
$\chi2$ = Pearson's chi-square test*
* p < .05, ** p < .01, *** p < .001 (two-tailed).

assessment tools were somewhat attenuated when they were used in Western contexts outside Canada and suggested that "'international' differences contributed to the variability across studies" (p. 348). As was true with gender, different rates of risk factor exposure and sensitivity to protective factors also may be important here (Chapman, Desai, Falzer, & Borum, 2006).

Finally, future studies might help to understand and refine the decision-making process in forming summary risk ratings, including how evaluators incorporate protective factors into the SRR. It may be that there are clusters or "types" of high-risk cases, or that the risk rating might be made more reliably if additional structure or heuristics were provided (Falzer, 2013). The feasibility and ultimate value of adding structure to the decision process is an empirical question, but given that the risk judgment is intended to be the primary product of a SAVRY-guided assessment, it certainly merits further investigation (Seidi, Alhani, & Salsali, 2014).

Case Example

Tarik is a 16-year-old male who has been incarcerated in a juvenile justice institution for the past 18 months after being adjudicated delinquent on charges of sexual battery and misdemeanor battery. He is the youngest of three brothers and has one younger half-brother. His psychosocial history reveals significant family disruption, particularly during his childhood years. As an infant, he was placed in foster care for 2 months and, at age 2, was placed in a relative's care for 3 months. Tarik's father had a serious drug-dependence problem and regularly sold drugs as well. His father and mother had a conflict-laden relationship, characterized both by verbal and physical abuse, much of which occurred in the children's presence. His father was also physically abusive toward the boys. When Tarik was 3 years old, his mother took the children and fled to a women's shelter where they lived for a month. At age 4, Tarik had a year-long, out-of-home residential placement. He returned home to find that his mother was in a new live-in relationship with a man who physically abused all of the children and who abused her in front of them. His biological father died in a car accident (under suspicious circumstances) when Tarik was 6 years old.

When he was 8, Tarik's mother sought mental health assistance because she was unable to handle his behavior problems at home. He was defiant and oppositional toward her and dismissive of authority, in general. He stole money and cigarettes and had frequent, and sometimes serious, fights with his younger half-brother. Tarik was placed in an alternative school for children with behavioral problems, which he attended until the age of 10. At this school he repeatedly threatened to harm other children (especially girls); he touched girls inappropriately without their permission and disregarded all attempts by teachers to correct or redirect his behavior. Outside school, Tarik spent his time with other boys "hanging around" and stealing bicycles. He was caught stealing bicycles at least four times, joyriding, and walking around with a fake gun. When Tarik was 11 years old, he threatened a boy with this gun.

At the age of 13, Tarik was placed in a residential treatment facility for children with behavioral problems where he remained for nearly 2 years. According to the psychologists in the facility, Tarik had an "uncontrollable hunger for attention," which led him to tell exciting (though untrue) stories to the other boys. Tarik manipulated other residents into doing his work, and he once ran away from the institution overnight. Records revealed that Tarik twice lured two different boys into his room, where he raped one and physically assaulted the other. Tarik says, however, that he does not think of himself as a rapist and therefore does not consider himself to be guilty. He stated that the victim wanted to have sex with him, and that he only had to "persuade him a little." He reportedly feels ashamed of what happened because he does not want people (especially his Turkish family members) to think he is gay.

Within the past year at the juvenile justice institution, treatment progress has been unremarkable. He is concerned only with the logistics of his detention (e.g., leave for the weekend), rather than meeting his treatment goals. He does not believe that the treatment setting is appropriate for him, because he does not regard himself as a sex offender. Staff clinicians report that Tarik is easily offended by others and that he denies and blames others for most of his problems. He tends to anger very easily and on multiple occasions has thrown furniture. He has frequent conflicts with other residents and with group leaders and has threatened both on multiple occasions, saying things like, "I'll stab you to death." He has shown an aptitude for sports, but becomes angry and upset whenever he loses. At school, he appears to be very motivated, and his academic performance is above average.

Both in the institution and in the community, Tarik has always tried to establish a dominant (and often manipulative) position among his peers, though he has never established any friendships. Many of the other youth resent and dislike him. When he has been on leave from the institution, Tarik has sought contact with the groups of delinquent boys he associated with when

Table 18.4 Tarik's SAVRY Assessment

Historical Risk Factors

History of Violence	High
History of Nonviolent Offending	High
Early Initiation of Violence	Moderate
Past Supervision/Intervention Failures	Moderate
History of Self-Harm or Suicide Attempts	Low
Exposure to Violence in the Home	High
Childhood History of Maltreatment	High
Parental/Caregiver Criminality	High
Early Caregiver Disruption	High
Poor School Achievement	Low

Social/Contextual Risk Factors

Peer Delinquency	X (Insufficient Information)
Peer Rejection	Low
Stress and Poor Coping	High
Poor Parental Management	High
Lack of Personal/Social Support	High
Community Disorganization	X (Insufficient Information)

Individual/Clinical Risk Factors

Negative Attitudes	High
Risk Taking/Impulsivity	Moderate
Substance Use Difficulties	Low
Anger Management Problems	High
Lack of Empathy/Remorse	High
Attention Deficit/Hyperactivity Difficulties	Low
Poor Compliance	High
Low Interest/Commitment to School	Low

Protective Factors

Prosocial Involvement	Absent
Strong Social Support	Absent
Strong Attachments and Bonds	Absent
Positive Attitude Toward Intervention and Authority	Absent
Strong Commitment to School	Present
Resilient Personality Traits	Absent

he was 9 years old. Tarik's mother remains very indulgent. He manipulates her easily, and she is unable to control his behavior.

Tarik's treatment team requested a formal risk assessment to assist them in deciding whether he could be "stepped down" from a closed institution to an open institution. The critical items are marked with respect to this aim. The general conclusion is that the probability of violent risk is still high. He needs aggression replacement training and functional family therapy and needs to be more motivated for these treatment aims before being allowed to go to an open treatment facility.

The SAVRY was used as part of this assessment (see Table 18.4) to estimate the nature and degree of risk Tarik may pose, and—if necessary—to suggest ways to reduce his risk to facilitate his success in an open treatment setting. The risk assessment considered Tarik's relevant historical, social/contextual, and individual risk factors balanced against protective factors, and determined that, at the time of the examination, Tarik continued to pose a "high risk" for serious violence (i.e., physical battery) if moved to an open institutional treatment setting.

The basis for this judgment included Tarik's history of serious violence and delinquent behavior, negative early developmental events, problematic parental management, and strong cognitive and emotional skill deficiencies likely to predispose him to aggression. Six of the ten risk factors in the Historical domain—all "static" in nature—were rated as "High," with only two rated as "Low." Three of the six Social/Contextual risk factors were rated "High," predominantly indicating poor family management, lack of support, and poor coping skills. These factors, being more dynamic, led the evaluator to two recommendations: (1) that Tarik and his mother engage in functional family therapy to improve her management skills and ability to provide supervision, structure, and support, and (2) that further information be gathered about the nature of Tarik's intended community peer group and the possibility of prosocial mentoring models. Finally, Tarik was rated "High" on four of the eight Individual/Clinical risk factors, including those indicating difficulty in generating nonaggressive solutions to problems, controlling anger, feeling empathy and remorse, and engaging meaningfully in his treatment. To promote progress in these areas and diminish risk, the evaluator suggested that motivational interviewing strategies might be used to better engage Tarik in his risk reduction plan and to encourage him to set meaningful goals for himself. As his motivation shows signs of improvement, it was recommended that Tarik participate in aggression replacement therapy. Aggression replacement therapy is a skill-driven, evidence-based program that focuses on nonaggressive conflict management skills, anger control, and enhanced "moral reasoning."

References

Augimeri, L. K., Koegl, C. J., Webster, C. D., & Levene, K. S. (2001). *Early assessment risk list for boys: EARL-20B* (Version 2). Toronto, ON: Earlscourt Child and Family Centre.

Assink, M., van der Put, C. E., Hoeve, M., de Vries, S. L., Stams, G. J. J., & Oort, F. J. (2015). Risk factors for persistent delinquent behavior among juveniles: A meta-analytic review. *Clinical Psychology Review, 42*, 47–61.

Bartel, P., Forth, A., & Borum, R. (2003). *Development and concurrent validation of the structured assessment for violence risk in youth (SAVRY)*. Unpublished manuscript.

Beausoleil, V., Renner, C., Dunn, J., Hinnewaah, P., Morris, K., Hamilton, A., . . . Browne, D. T. (2016). The effect and expense of redemption reintegration services versus usual reintegration care for young African Canadians discharged from incarceration. *Health & Social Care in the Community*. doi:10.1111/hsc.12346

Bernat, D. H., Oakes, J. M., Pettingell, S. L., & Resnick, M. (2012). Risk and direct protective factors for youth violence: Results from the national longitudinal study of adolescent health. *American Journal of Preventive Medicine, 43*(2), S57–S66.

Blum, J., Ireland, M., & Blum, R. W. (2003). Gender differences in juvenile violence: A report from add health. *Journal of Adolescent Health, 32*(3), 234–240.

Boccaccini, M. T., Murrie, D. C., Clark, J., & Cornell, D. G. (2008). Describing, diagnosing, and naming psychopathy: How do youth psychopathy labels influence jurors? *Behavioral Sciences and the Law, 26*, 487–510.

Borum, R. (2016). Targeted violence in schools. In P. Kleespies (Ed.), *The Oxford handbook of behavioral emergencies and crises* (pp. 103–112). Oxford: Oxford University Press.

Borum, R., Bartel, P., & Forth, A. (2006). *Manual for the structured assessment for violence risk in youth (SAVRY)*. Odessa, FL: Psychological Assessment Resources.

Borum, R., & Douglas, K. (2003, March). New directions in violence risk assessment. *Psychiatric Times, 20*(3), 102–103.

Borum, R. Fein, R., Vossekuil, B., & Berglund, J. (1999). Threat assessment: Defining an approach for evaluating risk of targeted violence. *Behavioral Sciences and the Law, 17*, 323–337.

Borum, R., & Grisso, T. (2006). Forensic assessment from a developmental perspective. In A. Goldstein (Ed.), *Forensic psychology: Emerging topics and expanding roles* (pp. 553–570). New York: Wiley & Sons.

Borum, R., & Verhaagen, D. (2006). *Assessing and managing violence risk in juveniles*. New York: Guilford Press.

Brame, R., Turner, M. G., Paternoster, R., & Bushway, S. D. (2012). Cumulative prevalence of arrest from ages 8 to 23 in a national sample. *Pediatrics, 129*(1), 21–27.

Catchpole, R., & Gretton, H. (2003). The predictive validity of risk assessment with violent young offenders: A 1-year examination of criminal outcome. *Criminal Justice and Behavior, 30*, 688–708.

Cauffman, E., Fine, A., Thomas, A. G., & Monahan, K. C. (2017). Trajectories of violent behavior among females and males. *Child Development, 88*(1), 41–54.

Cauffman, E., Skeem, J., Dmitrieva, J., & Cavanagh, C. (2016). Comparing the stability of psychopathy scores in adolescents versus adults: How often is "fledgling psychopathy" misdiagnosed? *Psychology, Public Policy, and Law, 22*(1), 77–91.

Chapman, J. F., Desai, R. A., Falzer, P. R., & Borum, R. (2006). Violence risk and race in a sample of youth in juvenile detention: The potential to reduce disproportionate minority confinement. *Youth Violence and Juvenile Justice, 4*, 170–184.

Childs, K. K., & Frick, P. J. (2016). Age differences in the structured assessment of violence risk in youth (SAVRY). *International Journal of Forensic Mental Health, 15*, 211–221.

Childs, K., Frick, P. J., Ryals, J. S., Lingonblad, A., & Villio, M. J. (2014). A comparison of empirically based and structured professional judgment estimation of risk using the structured assessment of violence risk in youth. *Youth Violence and Juvenile Justice, 12*(1), 40–57.

Childs, K., Ryals, J., Frick, P. J., Lawing, K., Phillippi, S. W., & Deprato, D. K. (2013). Examining the validity of the structured assessment of violence risk in youth (SAVRY) for predicting probation outcomes among adjudicated juvenile offenders. *Behavioral Sciences & the Law, 31*(2), 256–270.

Chu, C. M., Goh, M. L., & Chong, D. (2016). The predictive validity of SAVRY ratings for assessing youth offenders in Singapore. A comparison with YLS/CMI ratings. *Criminal Justice and Behavior, 43*(6), 793–810.

Connor, D. F., Steingard, R. J., Anderson, J. J., & Melloni Jr, R. H. (2003). Gender differences in reactive and proactive aggression. *Child Psychiatry and Human Development, 33*(4), 279–294.

de Bortoli, L., Ogloff, J., Coles, J., & Dolan, M. (2016). Towards best practice: Combining evidence-based research, structured assessment and professional judgement. *Child & Family Social Work*. doi:10.1111/cfs.12280

de Vries Robbé, M., & Willis, G. M. (2017). Assessment of protective factors in clinical practice. *Aggression and Violent Behavior, 32*, 55–63.

Dolan, M. C., & Rennie, C. E. (2008). The structured assessment of violence risk in youth (SAVRY) as a predictor of recidivism in a U.K. cohort of adolescent offenders with conduct disorder. *Psychological Assessment, 20*, 35–46.

Douglas, K. S. (2019). Evaluating and managing risk for violence using structured professional judgment. In D. Polaschek, A. Day, & C. Hollin (Eds.) *The Wiley international handbook of correctional psychology* (pp. 427–445). New York: Wiley.

Douglas, K. S., Hart, S. D., Webster, C. D., & Belfrage, H. (2013). *HCR-20v3 assessing risk for violence—user guide*. Burnaby, BC: Mental Health, Law, and Policy Institute, Simon Fraser University.

Edens, J. F., Cowell, L. H., Desforges, D. M., & Fernandez, K. (2005). The impact of mental health evidence on support for capital punishment: Are defendants labeled psychopathic considered more deserving of death? *Behavioral Sciences and the Law, 23*, 603–623.

Edens, J., & Vincent, G. M. (2008). Juvenile psychopathy: A clinical construct in need of restraint. *Journal of Forensic Psychology Practice, 8*, 186–197.

Epperson, D. L., Ralston, C. A., Fowers, D., & DeWitt, J. (2005). *Development of a sexual offense recidivism risk assessment tool—II (JSORRAT-II)*. Unpublished manuscript, University of Iowa, Ames.

Falzer, P. R. (2013). Valuing structured professional judgment: Predictive validity, decision-making, and the clinical-actuarial conflict. *Behavioral Sciences & the Law, 31*(1), 40–54.

Fitch, D. (2002). *Analysis of common risk factors for violent behavior in native American adolescents referred for residential treatment* (Unpublished doctoral dissertation). University of Texas, Clear Lake.

Fleiss, J. L. (1986). *The design and analysis of clinical experiments*. New York: Wiley.

Forth, A. E., Kosson, D. S., & Hare, R. D. (2003). *Hare psychopathy checklist—revised: Youth version*. Toronto, ON: Multi-Health Systems.

Gammelgård, M., Koivisto, A. M., Eronen, M., & Kaltiala-Heino, R. (2015). Predictive validity of the structured assessment of violence risk in youth: A 4-year follow-up. *Criminal Behaviour and Mental Health, 25*(3), 192–206.

Gammelgård, M., Koivisto, A. M., & Eronen, M. (2015). Predictive validity of the structured assessment of violence risk in youth: A 4-year follow-up. *Criminal Behaviour and Mental Health, 25*(3),192–206.

Geraghty, K. A., & Woodhams, J. (2015). The predictive validity of risk assessment tools for female offenders: A systematic review. *Aggression and Violent Behavior, 21*, 25–38.

Gammelgård, M., Weitzman-Henelius, G., & Kaltiala-Heino, R. (2008). The predictive validity of the structured assessment of violence risk in youth (SAVRY) among institutionalized adolescents. *Journal of Forensic Psychiatry and Psychology, 19*, 352–370.

Gammelgård, M., Weizmann-Henelius, G., Koivisto, A. M., Eronen, M., & Kaltiala-Heino, R. (2012). Gender differences in violence risk profiles. *Journal of Forensic Psychiatry & Psychology, 23*(1), 76–94.

Gretton, H., & Abramowitz, C. (2002, March). *SAVRY: Contribution of items and scales to clinical risk judgments and criminal outcomes*. Paper presented at the Biennial Conference of the American Psychology and Law Society, Austin, TX.

Hall, J. E., Simon, T. R., Mercy, J. A., Loeber, R., Farrington, D. P., & Lee, R. D. (2012). Centers for disease control and prevention's expert panel on protective factors for youth violence perpetration: Background and overview. *American journal of preventive medicine, 43*(2), S1–S7.

Hann, D. A., & Borek, N. (2001). *Taking stock of risk factors for child/youth externalizing behavior problems*. Bethesda, MD: National Institute of Mental Health.

Haque, Q., & Webster, C. D. (2013). Structured professional judgement and sequential redirections. *Criminal Behaviour and Mental Health, 23*(4), 241–251.

Hawkins, J., Herrenkohl, T., Farrington, D., Brewer, D., Catalano, R., & Harachi, T. (1998). A review of predictors of youth violence. In R. Loeber & D. Farrington (Eds.), *Serious and violent juvenile offenders: Risk factors and successful interventions* (pp. 106–146). Thousand Oaks, CA: Sage.

Hawkins, J., Herrenkohl, T., Farrington, D., Brewer, D., Catalano, R., Harachi, T., & Cothern, L. (2000, April). *Predictors of youth violence: Bulletin*. Washington, DC: Office of Juvenile Justice and Delinquency Prevention.

Henneberger, A. K., Oudekerk, B. A., Reppucci, N. D., & Odgers, C. L. (2014). Differential subtypes of offending among adolescent girls predict health and criminality in adulthood. *Criminal Justice and Behavior, 41*(2), 181–195.

Hilterman, E. L. B., Bongers, I., Nicholls, T. L., & Van Nieuwenhuizen, C. (2016). Identifying gender specific risk/need areas for male and female juvenile offenders: Factor analyses with the structured assessment of violence risk in youth (SAVRY), *Law & Human Behavior, 40*(1), 82–96.

Hilterman, E. L. B., Nicholls, T. E., & van Nieuwenhuizen, C. (2014). Predictive validity of risk assessments in juvenile offenders: Comparing the SAVRY, PCL:YV and YLS/CMI with unstructured clinical assessments. *Assessment, 21*(3), 324–339.

Hoge, R. (2001). *The juvenile offender: Theory, research and applications*. Norwell, MA: Kluwer Academic, Plenum Press.

Hoge, R. (2002). Standardized instruments for assessing risk and need in youthful offenders. *Criminal Justice and Behavior, 29*, 380–396.

Hoge, R., & Andrews, D. (2002). *Youth level of service/case management inventory*. Toronto, ON: Multi-Health Systems.

Howell, J. (1997). *Juvenile justice and youth violence*. Thousand Oaks, CA: Sage.

Jessor, R., Van Den Bos, J., Vanderryn, J., Costa, F. M., & Turbin, M. S. (1995). Protective factors in adolescent problem behavior: Moderator effects and developmental change. *Developmental Psychology, 31*(6), 923–933.

Kaltiala-Heino, R., Putkonen, H., & Eronen, M. (2013). Why do girls freak out? Exploring female rage among adolescents admitted to adolescent forensic psychiatric inpatient care. *The Journal of Forensic Psychiatry & Psychology, 24*(1), 83–110.

Khanna, D., Shaw, J., Dolan, M., & Lennox, C. (2014). Does diagnosis affect the predictive accuracy of risk assessment tools for juvenile offenders: Conduct disorder and attention deficit hyperactivity disorder. *Journal of Adolescence, 37*(7), 1171–1179.

Klein, V., Rettenberger, M., Yoon, D., Köhler, N., & Briken, P. (2015). Protective factors and recidivism in accused juveniles who sexually offended. *Sexual Abuse: A Journal of Research and Treatment, 27*(1), 71–90.

Lawing, K., Childs, K. K., Frick, P. J., & Vincent, G. (2017). Use of structured professional judgment by probation officers to assess risk for recidivism in adolescent offenders. *Psychological Assessment, 29*(6), 652–663.

Levene, K. S., Augimeri, L. K., Pepler, D. J., Walsh, M. M., Webster, C. D., & Koegl, C. J. (2001). *Early assessment risk list for girls: EARL-21G* (Version 1, consultation ed.). Toronto, ON: Earlscourt Child and Family Center.

Lipsey, M., & Derzon, J. (1998). Predictors of violent or serious delinquency in adolescence and early adulthood: A synthesis of longitudinal research. In R. Loeber & D. P. Farrington (Eds.), *Serious and violent juvenile offenders: Risk factors and successful interventions* (pp. 86–105). Thousand Oaks, CA: Sage.

Lodewijks, H. P. B., Doreleijers, T. A. H., & de Ruiter, C. (2008a). SAVRY risk assessment in a Dutch sample of violent adolescents: Relation to sentencing and recidivism. *Criminal Justice and Behavior, 35*, 696–709.

Lodewijks, H. P. B., Doreleijers, T. A. H., de Ruiter, C., & Borum, R. (2008b). Predictive validity of the structured assessment of violence risk in youth (SAVRY) during residential treatment. *International Journal of Law and Psychiatry, 31*, 263–271.

Lodewijks, H. P. B., de Ruiter, C., & Doreleijers, T. A. H. (2008c). Gender differences in risk assessment and violent outcome after juvenile residential treatment. *International Journal of Forensic Mental Health, 7*, 105–117.

Lodewijks, H. P. B., de Ruiter, C., & Doreleijers, T. A. H. (2010). The impact of protective factors in desistance from violent reoffending: A comparative study in three cohorts of adolescent offenders. *Journal of Interpersonal Violence, 25*(3), 568–587.

Loeber, R., Jennings, W. G., Ahonen, L., Piquero, A. R., & Farrington, D. P. (2017). *Female delinquency from childhood to young adulthood*. Berlin: Springer International Publishing.

Malti, T., & Averdijk, M. (2017). Severe youth violence: Developmental perspectives introduction to the special section. *Child Development, 88*(1), 5–15.

McEachran, A. (2001). *The predictive validity of the PCL:YV and the SAVRY in a population of adolescent offenders* (Unpublished master's thesis). Simon Fraser University, Burnaby, BC.

McGowan, M. R., Horn, R. A., & Mellott, R. N. (2011). The predictive validity of the structured assessment of violence risk in youth in secondary educational settings. *Psychological Assessment, 23*(2), 478–486.

Mercy, J. A., & Vivolo-Kantor, A. M. (2016). The center for disease control and prevention's (CDC) youth violence prevention centers: Paving the way to prevention. *The Journal of Primary Prevention, 37*(2), 209–214.

Meyers, J., & Schmidt, F. (2008). Predictive validity of the structured assessment for violence risk in youth (SAVRY) with juvenile offenders. *Criminal Justice and Behavior, 35*, 344–355.

Moretti, M. M., Obsuth, I., Odgers, C. L., & Reebye, P. (2006). Exposure to maternal vs. paternal partner violence, PTSD, and aggression in adolescent girls and boys. *Aggressive Behavior: Official Journal of the International Society for Research on Aggression, 32*(4), 385–395.

Moretti, M. M., Odgers, C., & Jackson, M. A. (2004). *Girls and aggression: Contributing factors and intervention principles* (Vol. 19). Berlin: Springer Science & Business Media.

Murrie, D. C., Boccaccini, M. T., McCoy, W., & Cornell, D. G. (2007). Diagnostic labeling in juvenile court: How do descriptions of psychopathy and conduct disorder influence judges? *Journal of Clinical Child and Adolescent Psychology, 36*, 1–14.

Murrie, D. C., Cornell, D. G., & McCoy, W. K. (2005). Psychopathy, conduct disorder, and stigma: Does diagnostic labeling influence juvenile probation officer recommendations? *Law and Human Behavior, 29*, 323–342.

Odgers, C. L., Moretti, M. M., & Reppucci, N. D. (2005). Examining the science and practice of violence risk assessment with female adolescents. *Law and Human Behavior, 29*(1), 7–27.

Odgers, C. L., Moretti, M. M., & Reppucci, N. D. (2009). Review of findings from the gender and aggression project informing juvenile justice policy and practice through gender-sensitive research. *Court Review, 46,* 6.

Olver, M. E., Stockdale, K. C., & Wormith, J. S. (2009). Risk assessment with young offenders a meta-analysis of three assessment measures. *Criminal Justice and Behavior, 36*(4), 329–353.

Ortega-Campos, E., García-García, J., & Zaldívar-Basurto, F. (2017). The predictive validity of the structured assessment of violence risk in youth for young Spanish offenders. *Frontiers in Psychology, 8,* e577.

Penney, S. R., Lee, Z., & Moretti, M. M. (2010). Gender differences in risk factors for violence: An examination of the predictive validity of the structured assessment of violence risk in youth. *Aggressive Behavior, 36*(6), 390–404.

Perrault, R. T., Vincent, G. M., & Guy, L. S. (2017). Are risk assessments racially biased? Field study of the SAVRY and YLS/CMI in probation. *Psychological Assessment, 29*(6), 664–678.

Prentky, R. A., & Righthand, S. (2003). *Juvenile sex offender assessment protocol (J-SOAP-II): Manual.* Bridgewater, MA: Justice Research Institute.

Richard, K. M. (2011). *Predicting persistence and desistence of recidivism in youth offenders: The role of risk and protective factors in criminal offending* (Doctoral dissertation), Carleton University, Ottawa, ON.

Rieger, M., Stadtland, C., Freisleder, F. J., & Nedopil, N. (2009). Structured psychiatric assessment of risk for violent recidivism in juvenile offenders. *Der Nervenarzt, 80*(3), 295.

Schmidt, F., Campbell, M. A., & Houlding, C. (2011). Comparative analyses of the YLS/CMI, SAVRY, and PCL: YV in adolescent offenders: A 10-year follow-up into adulthood. *Youth Violence and Juvenile Justice, 9*(1), 23–42.

Seidi, J., Alhani, F., & Salsali, M. (2014). Exploration of structure of clinical judgment of nurses: A grounded theory study. *Journal of Qualitative Research in Health Sciences, 2*(4), 297–309.

Shepherd, S. M., Luebbers, S., & Dolan, M. (2013). Gender and ethnicity in juvenile risk assessment. *Criminal Justice and Behavior, 40*(4), 388–408.

Shepherd, S. M., Luebbers, S., Ferguson, M., Ogloff, J. R., & Dolan, M. (2014). The utility of the SAVRY across ethnicity in Australian young offenders. *Psychology, Public Policy, and Law, 20*(1), 31–45.

Shepherd, S. M., Luebbers, S., & Ogloff, J. R. (2014). Are youth violence risk Instruments interchangeable? Evaluating instrument convergence in a sample of incarcerated adolescent offenders. *Journal of Forensic Psychology Practice, 14*(4), 317–341.

Shepherd, S. M., Luebbers, S., & Ogloff, J. R. (2016). The role of protective factors and the relationship with recidivism for high-risk young people in detention. *Criminal Justice and Behavior, 43*(7), 863–878.

Shepherd, S. M., Luebbers, S., Ogloff, J. R., Fullam, R., & Dolan, M. (2014). The predictive validity of risk assessment approaches for young Australian offenders. *Psychiatry, Psychology and Law,* 1–17 (ahead-of-print).

Sijtsema, J. J., Kretschmer, T., & van Os, T. W. (2015). The structured assessment of violence risk in youth in a large community sample of adolescent boys and girls: The TRAILS study. *Psychological Assessment, 27*(2), 669–677.

Singh, J. P., & Fazel, S. (2010). Forensic risk assessment a metareview. *Criminal Justice and Behavior, 37*(9), 965–988.

Singh, J. P., Grann, M., & Fazel, S. (2011). A comparative study of violence risk assessment tools: A systematic review and metaregression analysis of 68 studies involving 25,980 participants. *Clinical Psychology Review, 31*(3), 499–513.

Ttofi, M. M., Farrington, D. P., Piquero, A. R., & DeLisi, M. (2016). Protective factors against offending and violence: Results from prospective longitudinal studies. *Journal of Criminal Justice, 45,* 1–3.

U.S. Department of Health and Human Services. (2001). *Youth violence: A report of the surgeon general.* Rockville, MD: U.S. Department of Health and Human Services, Substance Abuse and Mental Health Services Administration, Center for Mental Health Services, National Institutes of Health, National Institute of Mental Health.

Van der Put, C. E., Deković, M., Hoeve, M., Stams, G. J. J., van der Laan, P. H., & Langewouters, F. E. (2014). Risk assessment of girls are there any sex differences in risk factors for re-offending and in risk profiles? *Crime & Delinquency, 60*(7), 1033–1056.

Van der Put, C. E., Deković, M., Stams, G. J. J., Van Der Laan, P. H., Hoeve, M., & Van Amelsfort, L. (2011). Changes in risk factors during adolescence implications for risk assessment. *Criminal Justice and Behavior, 38*(3), 248–262.

Vaughn, M. G., Salas-Wright, C. P., DeLisi, M., & Maynard, B. R. (2014). Violence and externalizing behavior among youth in the United States is there a severe 5%? *Youth Violence and Juvenile Justice, 12*(1), 3–21.

Viljoen, J., Scalora, M., Cuadra, L., Bader, S., Chavez, V., Ullman, D., & Lawrence, L. (2008). Assessing risk for violence in adolescents who have sexually offended: A comparison of the J-SOAP-II, J-SORRAT-II, and SAVRY. *Criminal Justice and Behavior, 35*(1), 5–23.

Viljoen, J. L., Shaffer, C. S., Muir, N. M., Cochrane, D. M., & Brodersen, E. M. (2019). Improving case plans and interventions for adolescents on probation: The implementation of the SAVRY and a structured case planning form. *Criminal Justice and Behavior, 46*(1), 42–62.

Vincent, G. M., Guy, L. S., Fusco, S. L., & Gershenson, B. G. (2012). Field reliability of the SAVRY with juvenile probation officers: Implications for training. *Law and Human Behavior, 36*(3), 225.

Vossekuil, B., Fein, R. A., & Berglund, J. M. (2015). Threat assessment: Assessing the risk of targeted violence. *Journal of Threat Assessment and Management, 2*(3–4), 243–254.

Walker, S. C., Bishop, A. S., Nurius, P. S., & Logan-Greene, P. (2016). The heterogeneity of treatment needs for justice-involved girls a typology using latent class analysis. *Criminal Justice and Behavior, 43*(3), 323–342.

Wall, A. E., & Barth, R. P. (2005). Aggressive and delinquent behavior of maltreated adolescents: Risk factors and gender differences. *Stress, Trauma, and Crisis, 8*(1), 1–24.

Webster, C. D., Haque, Q., & Hucker, S. J. (2014). *Violence risk-assessment and management: Advances through structured professional judgement and sequential redirections.* New York: John Wiley & Sons.

Welsh, J., Schmidt, F., McKinnon, L., Chattha, H., & Meyers, J. (2008). A comparative study of adolescent risk assessment instruments: Predictive and incremental validity. *Assessment, 15*, 104–115.

Woods, S. P. (2013). *Predictive validity of the SAVRY within a diverse population of juvenile offenders* (MA thesis). Roger Williams University, Bristol.

Zahn, M. A., Brumbaugh, S., Steffensmeier, D., Feld, B. C., Morash, M., Chesney-Lind, M., . . . Kruttschnitt, C. (2008). *Violence by teenage girls: Trends and context.* Washington, DC: Office of Justice Programs, NCJ 218905.

Zhou, J., Witt, K., Cao, X., Chen, C., & Wang, X. (2017). Predicting reoffending using the structured assessment of violence risk in youth (SAVRY): A 5-year follow-up study of male juvenile offenders in Hunan Province, China. *PLoS One, 12*(1), e0169251.

Index

Note: **Boldface** page references indicate tables. *Italic* references indicate figures and boxed text.

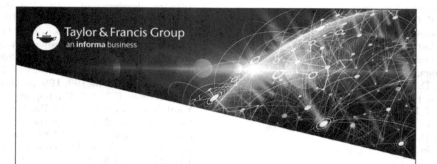